Readers are Saying...

"*LAUGHTER WASN'T RATIONED* IS...WRITTEN FROM THE HEART. Finally, I found a book that shows how the average German lived and felt. It chronicles very difficult times, sometimes with humor, but always with honesty, sincerity and courage. It is a fresh look at history, combined with a sensitive narration of life as it truly was."
— *I. Costa, Charlestown, New Hampshire*

"I WISH IT WERE REQUIRED READING for all high school students. Such a wonderful inclusion were the photos."
— *M. Moss, Medford, Oregon*

"[IT] IS A CHARMING, riveting, and horrifying book...horrifying because of the atrocities it unveils that occurred during World War II and Hitler's rule; riveting because you can't put it down since it is written by... someone who was there and experienced all she writes about; charming because it contains humor and real human vitality and grit. I am ordering five copies...to give to people I care about."
— *Katina Strauch, Editor,* Against the Grain

"I WAS A YOUNG GIRL OF FIVE LIVING IN BERLIN when the war started, and shared many of the experiences that Frau Lawson describes. I found her book fascinating, reflecting many of my own memories of this most difficult time."
— *I. Gross, Eastsound, Washington*

"I HIGHLY RECOMMEND THE BOOK! ...very easy to read, very well written. The historical background is very good and much appreciated. It gave me a much better understanding of the past. Once I started to read, I couldn't put it down till I finished!"
— *H. Hoppe, Muscatine, Iowa*

"THE GRANDEST ESSENCE of the book is its unique view of the German people's lives throughout the twentieth century. [It] is not one which most Americans have been privy to in my experience, and therefore it is an amazing educational resource in that regard... The book reads like a novel and engages the reader entertainingly with its author's human spirit."
— *C. Grubb, Charlestown, West Virginia*

"SO MANY AMERICANS HAVE SUCH A DISTORTED PICTURE of Germany, and the Germans, during the war years. I do hope that the book will help to change some opinions."
— *B.M. Simpson, Arlington, Virginia*

"DOROTHEA SKILLFULLY WEAVES TWO STORIES into one book, with a captivating autobiography of her life growing up in Germany between the two world wars — so different from the structured American system — plus a cognitive documentary on how insidiously Hitler ingratiated himself into Germany's burgeoning economy of brilliant minds before unleashing his true motives."
— *K. Dye, Port Clinton, Ohio*

"HAVING HEARD STORIES ALL MY LIFE from family and friends about Germany during the war as well as post-war time, *Laughter Wasn't Rationed* only confirms these tales. It was a pleasure to read Mrs. Lawson's well written personal account with a rather witty style although portraying a very serious and uneasy time of history for us Germans."
— *Christiane Mandukich, Publisher, Gutenberg II, Inc.*

"THIS BOOK IS AN IMPORTANT ACCOUNT of Germany's darkest period of the last century. It reads so well as the author shows great personal strength and wonderful humor in describing those fateful years. Excellent memories for the German reader and very informative for the American."
— *C. O'Brien, Bellevue, Washington*

LAUGHTER WASN'T RATIONED

Laughter
Wasn't Rationed

A Personal Journey Through Germany's
World Wars and Postwar Years

by
Dorothea von Schwanenflügel Lawson

TRICOR PRESS

Copyright © 1999 Sylvia D. Cole
Previously published with the subtitle *Remembering the War Years in Germany*.

Published by Tricor Press
P.O. Box 4372, Alexandria, VA 22303-4372
E-mail: info@tricorpress.com
Web site: http://www.tricorpress.com

Second Edition

Design and layout by Barbara Shaw
Cover by Jeanne Krohn / Krohn Design

Publisher's Cataloging-in-Publication

Lawson, Dorothea von Schwanenflügel, 1916-
    Laughter wasn't rationed : a personal journey through
Germany's world wars and postwar years / by Dorothea von
Schwanenflügel Lawson.--2nd ed.
    p. cm.
    LCCN 00-107988
    ISBN 0-9673830-4-8

    1. Lawson, Dorothea von Schwanenflügel, 1916-
2. World War, 1939-1945--Personal narratives, German.
3. Women--Germany--Biography. 4. German American women--
Biography. I. Title.

D811.5.L356 2001   940.53'161'092
                      QBI00-901480

To Mutti, Papa and Günter
Who didn't know the word "impossible."

Acknowledgements

Thoughts alone do not make a book. I was very fortunate to have the help of family and friends who believed in me.

I am especially grateful to:

Sylvia, my youngest daughter. What would I have done without your endless typing, re-typing and editing over the years? Thank you for listening to all my frustrations and getting this book to print.

Roswitha, my oldest. Your support from far away meant a lot to me and your constructive criticism was most welcome.

Many friends contributed their time as a favor to me, and were never too busy when I called with yet another question. I would particularly like to thank:

Bob Maust for his editing, condensing (though I wouldn't always let him!), and his enthusiasm.

Gudrun Watson for her attention to detail, infinite patience and tireless book promotion.

Fred Altman for his help in the beginning and his impromptu editing.

Jim Schneider for his advice, suggestions and willingness to help me along the way.

Helen Sehrt for her review, translations and just being my listening ear.

Marjorie Shelley for helping with the early drafts.

Contents

Preface to The Second Edition

This book has been a long time in the making—more than ten years. Actually I never gave much thought to writing my memoirs until my American friends strongly urged me to do so. They were amazed at my insider's account of the World Wars and the difficult times that followed.

You will read here about my eventful life and that of my family and friends. At times it was hard to relive the past with some of its ever so vivid occurrences. My story is real. Of course it is strongly intertwined with politics because there is no way to separate one from the other.

While I have happy childhood memories, I grew up in Germany during the 1920s when the country was still reeling from the aftermath of World War I. Then came the twelve years of the dictator-type rule under Hitler, the end of free speech and World War II. Life was never the same again, yet nothing could kill our positive attitude and healthy sense of humor.

Many who have already read *Laughter Wasn't Rationed* told me that I introduced them to a totally different side of Germany's turbulent years. You will see how the average citizen coped on a day-to-day basis, a different picture than that promulgated by the press.

At the request of readers, I have added a few more photos in this second edition. Unfortunately many things were lost or damaged during the war years, including family pictures, so my choice was limited.

An ever guiding force has been helping me throughout my entire life and nature has blessed me with a strong will and constitution. We have entered the new millennium and my generation is coming to an end. However, I am fortunate to be here still, and it is a pleasure to share my first-hand account with you.

Dorothea von Schwanenflügel Lawson
November 2000

Westward Ho

I guess the reason I am still here today to tell my story is because I come from a long line of survivors. Being strong-willed seems to run in my family.

Take my grandmother, for instance. We called her Grandma or *Omi*. She was born in 1863 in Russia, at the time when Russia and Germany shared the same border because there was no independent Poland from 1772 to 1918. Omi grew up in a typical upper-class household with servants. She had her own horse and carried a gun in her long pants. She was the last child of a large family, a kind of "post-script" with a will of her own. (Did I inherit that?) Her mother had died when she was a child, and her father, as a widower, could not handle her, and neither could any of the staff in the house. But Omi herself could handle the wildest horses, the ones nobody even dared to touch. She would ride them, and they became obedient under her lead, and tame as lambs.

With no schools around, she had a private tutor. However, as soon as he would come through the front door, she would make a dash for a back window, grabbing gun and belt, and off she rode into the woods. She would be gone for hours, leaving everyone frantically searching for her—father, as well as servants. To tame her wild ways, she was finally sent to a boarding school for girls in Germany. This resulted in her constantly crossing the border between Russia and Germany for many years. During her frequent journeys back and forth, she fell in love with one of the border officials. He was from a middle-class family and he was considered beneath her socially. With her determination for independence she broke the convention of her time and insisted on marrying him. You can imagine the uproar this news caused in her family when she carried out her plan. Her older brothers never forgave her for fighting the upper class etiquette. They themselves were in prominent positions in Russia and Germany, and strongly felt that such a marriage had disgraced the entire family. They stopped any and all contact with her. My dear Omi didn't know anything about women's lib, but practiced it far ahead of her time.

Her widowed father, my wealthy great-grandfather, quite suddenly remarried, a beautiful young lady from Russia, who wasted no time in persuading him to invest most of his money in a bank in Moscow. At her suggestion they took a trip there—a trip from which they never returned. They disappeared and so did the fortune. At once his sons investigated the mysterious disappearance of their aged father and his money. However, all inquiries were unsuccessful. It seemed they were powerless, facing a plot cleverly arranged by a young lady, leaving no trace behind. This was Russia around 1900.

All of these tragedies were of no concern to my grandmother. She was the outcast anyway! While the others were having their problems, she loved and enjoyed her married life. She could have lived happily ever after if fate hadn't intervened. While out riding one day, Omi's husband had a fatal accident and died unexpectedly. By now it was 1897 and Omi found herself being a widow with four children, three girls and one boy, at the young age of thirty-four. The oldest of the children, a girl who was only ten at the time, was my mother, born in Siemianice, a district of Kempen (now Poland or Russia?). Although Omi's brothers originally wanted to have nothing to do with her, one of them suddenly had a change of heart and offered to take her in. This brother held at that time a high rank in the forestry service of the *Fürst* (Prince) of Pless in Silesia. This prince was a close friend of the last German emperor, who visited there frequently.

Omi knew of her big brother's large family, his active life style and social entertainments. She detested the thought of facing a future dependent on an arrogant sister-in-law and living with her four children on their charity. Giving it a lot of thought, she finally made the most impossible decision for that time—to go her own way and to provide for her children herself.

Over the years, Omi put to use her excellent education and knowledge of Russian, French cooking, and elegant housekeeping, this at a time when it was totally unheard of for a young lady to manage her own affairs. The feminists of today would adore her and use her as a role model. At first Omi worked in an officer's club in Gleiwitz, Upper

Silesia, taking over the management of the daily meals and big receptions for visiting dignitaries. These VIP's often showed up in the kitchen to meet her and thank her for her efforts, which made her very proud. Working hard, Omi's salary increased steadily, and it was not long before she used her profits to buy a *Hotel-Pension* (inn) in Krummhübel in the *Riesengebirge* (since 1945 part of Poland), the highest elevation of the Sudeten mountain range. She named it *Villa Marie*, and was her own boss from then on. Word of mouth brought her many wealthy guests who came to relax and absorb the fresh air in the midst of picture book mountains and lakes.

Omi's great talent to master her own life so well was all ignored by her brothers and their snobbish families. Of course her swanky relatives could not acknowledge such success since it was almost unheard of that a lady of her upbringing and class would work for a living.

I still cherish the many keepsakes, postcards and photographs of that time, which show Omi's *Villa Marie*, a four-story half-timbered house with enclosed sun rooms and a big shiny red tile roof. It sat in a park-like garden, surrounded by woods and mountains. Though my prints are yellowed by now, on some of them, Omi gently smiles at me, standing in her flower garden, tall, slender and very much a refined lady, looking proud and distinguished in her elegant, high-collared long dress. Her business must have been very prosperous under her skillful management, because shortly thereafter, she sold it and bought an even bigger estate nearby, the *Villa Daheim*, in a similar style but even more elegant, as other postcards reveal. *Daheim* means at home, and that was the way everybody felt there in an especially warm atmosphere.

My mother, I called her *Mutti*, told me often of her good times there with my Aunts Frieda and Grete, and how exceptionally Omi organized everything. Without radio or TV, she arranged games in the evenings in the big gathering room, with cards or dice, and led discussions of current affairs. She also encouraged the guests to play the piano. Often they sang folk songs while snuggled around the huge tile stove, which was especially cozy on cold winter evenings when everyone returned from tobogganing and skiing.

At Christmas a tall tree reached from the floor all the way to the high ceiling. Everyone, including the guests, participated in going out to the woods to cut it and later to decorate it. By that time the whole

Villa Daheim

house smelled enticingly from Omi's honey cookies. The recipe has been handed down for generations, and just like Omi and Mutti, I make them every year for my family.

Mutti got married in 1911. She moved with my father, a businessman, to their own place in Gleiwitz and lived there happily after—but not for too long. Life never goes as planned. Meanwhile my brother Günter was born in 1913. A son and heir, what a joy—until the outbreak of World War I in 1914. He was just one year old, Papa was at the front, when Mutti had to flee with him from Gleiwitz to Omi in Krummhübel. Unexpectedly the Russian Narew-army under General Samsonow had invaded East Prussia, endangering the entire East German border, since there was no Poland as a buffer state. At that threatening moment, General Paul von Hindenburg, already retired since 1911, was called back to duty. It was due to his strategy that Russian troops were defeated August 26-30, 1914, at Tannenberg and also later at the Masuren Lakes. When all signs of danger were gone, Mutti returned home to Gleiwitz.

In March 1916 I became another addition to the family, a true war product. Was that an omen? Because stormy periods, good and bad, never left me all my life. Overjoyed about my arrival Mutti named me Dorothea, which is Greek and means "gift of God." She always chose our names. When later in life I asked her what gave her that idea, she told me that she picked my name from Goethe's poetry "Hermann and Dorothea." Unfortunately I never met a Hermann in my life. Besides some reddish blond hair, I inherited the family's sense of humor and a positive outlook on life. My own weakness is a love for history and sagas, which the reader can easily detect in the pages following me through my life.

So I was born in the middle of World War I, while my father, whom I called Papa (emphasis on the second syllable, as in Pa-PAH) was in Rumania with the German army. The following year, in 1917, during the Bolshevist October revolution, Russia once again threatened with its hostile attacks across the German border. Mutti fled once more, this time with both of us children. She had me as a toddler on her arm, and my little brother Günter clinging to her skirts, while Aunt Frieda took care of most of the luggage. Omi had sent her over from Krummhübel to assist us. While we were waiting in an overcrowded train station, a strange woman suddenly took Günter by the hand and tried to walk away with him. "Frieda, get the boy!" Mutti cried out alarmed, all her attention focused on her little son. Aunt Frieda was able to retrieve the child just as the train was approaching. People were rushing and pushing, and we were shoved inside the train lugging our cumbersome baggage.

But Mutti's handbag had disappeared, cleverly cut off, with only the handles remaining looped over her arm. Since she was holding me on that same arm, and carrying a suitcase in the other hand, she did not discover the stolen purse until after boarding the train. Mutti had lost all her documents, her money, and our train tickets. She was devastated. But this was a small disaster compared to all those which would follow later. At least the train conductor was sympathetic toward our unfortunate situation and let us continue the train ride to Krummhübel without any tickets. Our place of refuge was once again with Omi. Mutti's younger sisters, Frieda and Grete, also lived there permanently. Here we were a big, harmonious group, whether guests or family.

In the meantime Aunt Frieda had gotten married. Her husband, Uncle Konstantin, called Conny for short, gave me a new ball, an extraordinary present in those days. I got so excited, expecting to bounce it all over. But this ball wasn't made of rubber, which was scarce during the war, but instead, was sewn together with colored cloth—beautiful to look at, but I couldn't do much with it, except to roll it on the floor. What a disappointment.

In November 1918 the war was over, and lost for Germany. Its outcome had been decided by the American involvement in April 1917. When all belligerent states were exhausted and broke, the U.S. assisted Great Britain and France with fresh troops and materiel as a new powerful fighting ally, preventing the collapse of the Entente Powers. (This later enabled them to dictate the Versailles Treaty.)

In Russia, a bloody civil war raged and the Communist ideology engulfed the rest of Europe. To the bitter end, our troops still remained undefeated deep in enemy territory, far from our own borders. Field Marshal Paul von Hindenburg led them back home to find a state of civil unrest, with street battles flaring up all over. In order to prevent a civil war, he persuaded our Emperor William II to temporarily take refuge in the Netherlands until calm could be restored. Unfortunately, he never returned.

It was the emperor's privileged unit, his treasured navy, that was responsible for the overthrow of the German monarchy. His naval expansion had turned the German navy into a respected sea power, and a threat to the mighty British navy. On November 3, 1918, revolting sailors rioted in Kiel. In Berlin, they marched with the red flags of Marxism through the Brandenburg Gate, a popular and historic crossing point in the center of the city.

It was the traumatic shock of this revolution and the resulting abdication of our last Emperor Wilhelm II that later emerged into the first German democracy, the Weimar Republic, which started under heavy handicaps. Founded far from Berlin in the quiet city of Weimar, in the atmosphere of Goethe and Schiller, it was to be a symbolic reminder that Germany was a nation of poets and thinkers, not rowdy Communists. In 1920, the Dutch government refused to surrender the former German Emperor Wilhelm II to the Entente Powers as requested.

Papa was still in Rumania when the war ended, and came home with painful rheumatism which stayed with him for the rest of his life. He was emaciated, down to 108 pounds, and had to be hospitalized for quite a while before he could join us in Krummhübel.

Times were desperate. For us in Germany the war was superseded by political turmoil, shortage of housing, rising poverty and hunger. Food was rationed and in even shorter supply than in the hungry turnip winters of 1916/17. We were starving. Aunt Frieda and Aunt Grete had to go on weekly food hoarding trips. Luckily they knew the area well and were good skiers.

They started their secret mission by nightfall. Following secluded passes over the mountains, they sneaked across the Bohemian border into Austria where they knew of a worthwhile food source. (This took place before the break-up of the multi-national Austrian-Hungarian Empire and before Czechoslovakia was created.) Being familiar with the frontier guards, they knew where and when they would be patrolling, and how to carefully avoid them on their return trip before day-

Aunt Grete (left) and Aunt Frieda on their food hoarding trip.

break with their knapsacks filled with butter, cheese, meat and bacon. Luckily we didn't know at the time that these dangerous food adventures would repeatedly become a vital necessity in the course of our lives.

Meanwhile, the last troops of the German armed forces were slowly returning home from all fronts. Mutti's brother (my Uncle Alfred) and Omi's pride and joy, was not among them. Uncle Alfred was the only one for whom Omi could afford the expensive tuition for a higher education. Prior to the war, he had been offered a promising position in a well known bank in India. His sponsor was a family friend who had arranged what appeared to be a very lucrative career for him. Omi already had big plans to present her son as a successful business man to her snobbish relatives who had always been ashamed of her. For a long time, Omi hoped that he might be a prisoner of war and would return since she had never received any official death notification, or found him on any death register. He must have been killed at the West Front somewhere in France. We never knew his actual fate.

Omi had faced many upheavals in her life, but she never got over the loss of her only son—a fate that would repeat itself in our family and other families all over the world. Each war has its own particular tragedies and sufferings, as Omi had experienced already.

World War I wasn't even started by Germany. It was unleashed on June 28, 1914, in Sarajevo, by a fanatic Serbian student who assassinated Crown-prince Franz Ferdinand of Habsburg, the heir to the Austro-Hungarian throne. It was the igniting spark that triggered the chain of events which brought about the outbreak of a world conflagration. Austria declared war on its Serbian province. Thereafter Germany, as an ally of Austria, was forced to assist the brother country. Russia was tied to the Serbs, France and Britain to Russia.

Nevertheless, Germany was blamed for the war. In 1919, the Entente Powers imposed the Versailles Treaty on Germany. The German delegation was even excluded from the "Peace Conference" until the terms were ready for submission. In vain they protested vigorously that such harsh and unjust conditions were not at all in keeping with the prerequisites on which Germany had laid down its arms. *Vae victis*, woe to the vanquished.

The Versailles Treaty was a disaster for Germany. It resulted in losses of large parts of our old ethnic territories. Because of Germany's geographic position in the heart of northern Europe, it shared now and then frontiers with as many as eight or nine other nations. It had hardly any natural borders, but many greedy neighbors. Its open borders and their vulnerability were a problem for centuries. The course of history reveals that in all the wars of European states against one another, Germany, in fact, was more often the victim of aggression and invasion from its neighbors than the other way around—as with the French Louis XIV, or Napoleon, or the repeated French grip after the German Saar, just to mention a few.

This time parts of our empire were grabbed by France, Denmark, and Belgium. The Memel territory of East Prussia went to Lithuania. New countries were created partly on German soil like Czechoslovakia and Poland. England took some islands. Germany was stripped of all colonial possessions seized by the Entente Powers.

Reparations of undetermined but astronomical figures were imposed, which would have been impossible for any country to pay. Nonetheless, they were to continue for an indefinite time. The enormous sum of 5 billion dollars was due immediately. It was a mystery to Papa where such an amount was to come from. (At that time, one dollar was equivalent to more than four German marks.) All private and government possessions abroad were confiscated. Even almost all our merchant marine was seized and German rivers declared international territory, open to all. There were many more endless and unfair incriminations to bleed Germany, like the French occupation of the German Rhineland for fifteen years in the peacetime 1930s. All of these unrealistic conditions caused vehement criticism even among other nations.

Until this day I ask myself how Americans might have responded if such severe and unfair treatment and excessive concessions had been imposed on them. The U.S. did not ratify the Versailles Treaty in 1919, but concluded a separate peace treaty in 1921 in Berlin. (Years later Papa repeatedly said that if the U.S. would have stayed out of the First World War, Germany and Europe would have been better off. We still would have had our emperor and a more reasonable peace treaty between the warring nations, no Versailles Treaty, no Hitler and no Second World War.)

The Versailles Treaty had many flaws and, therefore, was poorly suited for world peace and resolving problems. Instead, it gave rise to economic chaos, starvation and deprivations. It was pre-programmed with a direct route from the First to the Second World War, barely twenty years later. In Germany many new political parties were conjured up, one of them the forerunner of the Nazi Party.

Our new government was very unpopular among Germans from the beginning because of its acceptance of the humiliating terms and overburdened conditions of the Versailles Treaty. East Prussia was completely cut off from Germany by the newly established Polish corridor, created from chunks of the German provinces of Posen, and West Prussia. The German city of Danzig became an isolated free town within new Poland (similarly problematic as was later Berlin in the Soviet zone of East Germany after World War II).

In addition, France, Belgium and Italy demanded enormous quantities of coal for the next ten years. We needed this coal very badly for ourselves. Gas and electricity were already rationed, and so was coal for private consumption. I remember that often we could only burn a few briquettes in our iron stove, which barely took the chill off a room.

It was only after Papa had halfway recovered at Omi's house that our family of four was ready to return home to Gleiwitz in Upper Silesia. Mutti packed our old-fashioned wicker basket with sturdy handles, to be carried by two people, which consumed an amazing amount of our belongings. Omi, with loving care, added all kinds of edibles like home-made bread and other nutritious items from my aunts' last hoarding trip. In a town like Gleiwitz, food became a rare commodity and was restricted by ration cards. Even Günter got his own little knapsack filled to the brim.

A well-known coachman from downtown arrived with his horse and carriage and took us to the train station. We were fortunate to catch one of the rare trains. Life was far from normal, including transportation. Our homeward journey took several hours. How happy we were to be able to pick up our lives again. The place was still there, untouched. Fortunately we did not know yet that it would be for a very short interlude only. In our happy homecoming we just forgot to count on the oncoming drastic political changes which made any pleasant plans short-lived.

And Omi's women's lib had not ended yet by any means, just the opposite. So far successful, the battle started anew. Suddenly, after a lost war, she faced a changed and completely uncertain future, under surely worse circumstances than before. She must have asked herself a hundred times, "Do I have to struggle again after twenty years, and fight anew for an unsure future survival? Who of my regular guests can still afford long vacations in my big villa? I have to pay taxes, but from what income?" From now on, critical times started for almost everyone.

Glück und Glas, wie leicht bricht das. Fortune and glass, how easily they can break. How true. In 1919, Papa didn't understand the world any more. For him the old order had collapsed and was replaced by chaos. In Russia the bloody Bolshevist revolution raged under Lenin. England's colonial empire was crumbling. The Austro-Hungarian empire broke up into independent states. The Versailles Treaty re-drew the whole map of Europe. Old states vanished and new ones were created, but without any logical concern for cultural, political and ethnical compatibility, the cause of later conflicts. (See the newly created Czechoslovakia of 1918, which split up again in 1993 into two states, or even worse the new Yugoslavia where century-old animosities smoldered as predictable, political fireworks with never-ending bloodshed.) The future of our own native soil was in jeopardy.

Papa couldn't believe that our homeland, Upper Silesia, my birthplace, was even assigned to the newly established Republic of Poland. This area of Silesia had been part of Germany already in 1163 under the German Emperor Frederick I, called Barbarossa. For the past centuries it had belonged to either Austria or Prussia. Papa's land was German, not Polish. The new political map revealed that a large part of the newly established republic of Poland consisted now of different nationalities with their own languages, not only Germans, but also Lithuanians, Russians and others. For that reason the new Polish government was bound to respect the national minority rights, to maintain their national and cultural identities, and to retain their language, all under the guidelines of the recently created League of Nations in Geneva. Papa called it wishful thinking.

Polish hatred, especially against Germans, was not new to him. In the near future, only Polish would be allowed as the official language. Papa rebelled and compared New Poland with seven hundred-year old Switzerland, an open-minded, multi-lingual country of different peoples and cultures where four official languages (German, French, Italian and Romansch, each equally recognized) peacefully coexisted. The people lived in harmony with each other.

Papa questioned Polish tolerance, and had no faith in a similar peaceful coexistence. But he insisted on speaking German, our mother tongue. Extremely worried, Mutti foresaw that this alone would bring us into serious conflicts sooner or later, especially us children while playing outside. Besides, Papa feared that the ethnic German population faced a dubious future. Therefore he felt forced to move us, to live anywhere other than the newly established Poland.

Such a drastic change meant we had to leave everything behind. What we could not foresee then was that our hometown, Gleiwitz, would remain German after all, following an overwhelming plebiscite in 1922, with over 90 percent against union with Poland.

After careful consideration and lengthy discussions with Mutti, Papa packed up his family and all of our worldly possessions to move to Münster in Westphalia, close to the Dutch border. This meant a trip from southeast to northwest, across the entire country. What a traumatic decision for my parents, what a risky experience and profound upheaval for all of us. I don't remember why Papa picked Münster, but that's where we headed when I was three years old and my brother Günter just six. Later, looking back, it proved to be the right move and worth all the frustration and anxiety before and after our arrival.

As was to be expected, the move was long and tedious, and was done by horse-drawn wagon. But horse-drawn wagons were not easily obtained either, and Papa had to accomplish this through whatever means possible. Approaching the Westphalian plain around Münster, lush farmland with livestock and prosperous-looking farmhouses stretched as far as we could see. We were fascinated by the rural beauty. Wide, fertile and well-tended fields alternated with wooded areas and heather land, here and there dotted with numerous moated castles where the local lords still resided. Mutti and Papa praised it as a rich agricultural region, suitable for our hungry stomachs, since Germany was still starving. Here we felt as if we were entering the promised land, which stretched wide toward the Netherlands and the lower Rhine valley. Already from afar, Münster's gothic skyline of church steeples beckoned to us.

Münster, since 1815 the capital of Westphalia, was a beautiful medieval metropolis. Our Germanic ancestors had arrived here as early as four thousand years ago, coming down from the North and settling the area of present Germany. Around 800 A.D., Emperor Charles the Great (Charlemagne) had gathered the different German tribes into one large realm that included what is now France, Germany and North Italy. He laid the foundation of the Holy Roman Empire of German nation. As early as 805 A.D. he founded here a monastery for missionary work, around which the town grew. The word "monastery," gradually evolved into Münster, and the city developed into a stronghold of Catholicism. We could easily see that. The monumental cathedral with its towering steeples and the many multi-spired churches seemed to leap majestically high into the sky, each a jewel of Roman and Gothic architecture. Münster put its best foot forward with clean streets, impeccably maintained gardens, parks, notable edifices, and numerous small and large family-owned shops, as well as spacious squares and market places. We passed several elegant manors of the local lords, and an abundance of clerical buildings and cloisters, stamping Münster's image.

The area had emerged into the light of history already in the third century as an ancient pre-Christian Saxon settlement, a farming community originally called Mimigernaford, favored by its location on an old trade route at the river Aa. Now we crossed that little but important river that found its way right through the middle of town with its clear waters bouncing along in its stone bed. Only now Papa hardly glanced at what he had praised so highly earlier. All his attention was centered first and foremost on a new place for us to move into. But that was easier said than done.

Because our country was so badly reduced, in 1919 many Germans were left homeless in their ancestral land and streamed into what was left of German territory, causing an enormous need for housing. Residents of large land masses like the United States have no way of experiencing the intimacy of a cramped living space in a country like ours. Following World War I, after adjoining countries had grabbed a slice of our native territory, what was left for us was less than the size of California but with a population of 80 million.

Housing was so scarce that when we arrived, it was even rationed by law. Many bigger buildings had been confiscated as military hospitals. What were our chances going to be? Papa had a heated argument with the housing office, his first of many. His initial experience was that not everything that glitters is gold. At present, there was no alternative but to put new arrivals temporarily into empty military barracks. To Papa's horror, that's what we were assigned as living quarters, too, at least for a transition period. Most of our furniture had to be stored.

While Mutti and Papa despaired and tried intensively to solve the unexpected housing problem, a most joyous time started for Günter and me. In the large yard of the barracks some water was left in long stone troughs where the horses used to drink. Günter helped me climb into them while he followed, and we splashed in there happily with little boats Günter had created out of newspaper. What Mutti thought about it when we came home dripping wet, I don't remember. Our lodging was temporary anyway.

After Papa vehemently fought over the restrictive housing rules, the mayor's office assigned us to a very old villa on Gral Strasse. The owners, an elderly couple, were compelled to make room for us on the first floor. All this did not make sense to Papa since shortly after we arrived, he had bought an apartment house with eight units in Hittordorf Strasse, but we were not allowed to occupy any of the apartments for ourselves as he was entitled to under the owner's right, a German law still in effect today.

Meanwhile Omi had sold her property in Krummhübel right after she had married off her last daughter, my Aunt Grete, and also arrived one day in Münster on Gral Strasse, with a horse-drawn moving truck. It was loaded with treasures, such as bags of flour and sugar, and big sacks of potatoes and coal. All these rated highly, since Germany lacked natural resources, unlike the United States. We had a shortage of everything. Every little bit was rationed.

She also brought me a special present—a ripe banana. I had never seen or tasted one before and I noticed it had an unusual odor. My enthusiasm was gone immediately. So I hid that strange yellow object between my toys. Mutti wondered where it had gone so quickly, and I was forced to bring it out of hiding. She peeled it and I was urged to taste it. But I couldn't bring myself to eat one little bite of that odd-smelling squishy object. Even today I still remember my screams, and their trying to make me swallow at least one tiny bite of this rare, precious fruit. Although I love bananas now, as soon as I detect the smell of an overripe banana, I right away associate it with my first experience. My stomach remembers it, too.

The next event involved the old chimney of our new homestead, which did not want to stay on the age-worn roof any longer. Without any warning, it fell down during a storm like a ton of bricks, crashing through the glass ceiling of our enclosed porch (like a greenhouse), which connected the kitchen with the living room. A thunder-like bang shook the whole house, at the exact moment when Mutti had passed through there with a tray. We all were appalled.

That frightening incident overcame Papa's last scruples about violating housing regulations. To tell the truth, he had already worked out a plan. In order to get more rights to a better living space, he bought a second, bigger apartment house on Lignerstrasse, with Omi's financial help from the sale of her inn. This time one of the apartments was reserved for us by the public rental office. Again it would have been too small for all of us, but the former owner, Mr. Obst, a widower, happened to live nearby in a spacious four-bedroom apartment on Ludgeriplatz number six (Saint Ludgerus Square), next to the promenade, a green avenue of lime trees. His home had become much too large for him, but was just the right size for us. He gladly wanted to move into the smaller apartment assigned to us in the house he used to own, and let Papa have his large one.

So the two men pushed ahead to cook up a scheme. Without asking anyone's permission, two horse-drawn moving trucks appeared very early one morning for an apartment swap. One in front of each place, changing all the furniture around as in a merry-go-round, both at the same time, as quickly as possible, with horses no less. They often passed each other during this hasty move. What a wonderful commotion! Günter and I kept jumping on the wagons during this exchange and were thrown off many times. To my surprise, after all the wagon confusion I slept that night in a new place, but still in my old bed on the third floor of a four-story house, which was to be my home for the next fifteen years of my life. Contrary to all rules and regulations of a long-winded housing democracy, Papa, on his own, had quickly and successfully settled his family of five in a very spacious place. Even though this move was not officially authorized by the lodging office, they gave their approval later anyway—happy to have one fault-finder less among their many disgruntled citizens.

We lived now on Ludgeriplatz, in the middle of lots of landscaped greenery. Its name was derived from Münster's first bishop, Ludgerus. In this very Catholic town, we were, of course, close to Ludgeristrasse with the nearby Ludgeri Church on Marienplatz (Mary's Square) and the statue of Saint Mary, all dedicated to the patron saint of the town.

We were also due our personal confrontation with the holy Ludgerus. Above our balcony was his sculpture in stone. In his outstretched hand, right above our heads, he held a weather-beaten, rusty iron hoop. During a heavy storm he dropped it on our balcony, but at night, which was very thoughtful of him. We didn't know the significance of the hoop. He may have dropped it on us as a warning because we were one of the few Lutherans in his stronghold of Catholicism. During the time of the Reformation, for a short period only, Luther's new gospel was preached from all pulpits. But Catholicism won back the rebelling town. Now we Lutherans showed up again. Saint Ludgerus above us must not have been in favor of our new intrusion and bombarded us with his iron hoop as a prelude to more animosities to come.

Finally we were settled—quite comfortably as it seemed. But our new life would not have been complete without some additional misery. Papa's father lived in Ostrowo in the old Prussian province of Posen at the Warthe River, which had been colonized by Germans as far back as 1253 but then annexed to new Poland in 1919. People were deeply affected. The German population lived there suddenly on Polish territory and under increasing Polish pressure. They could opt in favor of Germany and leave, but only if (and that was a very big and troublesome IF) the new immigrants either had relatives in Germany to live with, or if they could prove a job existed for them or an employer expected them—similar to the present U.S. immigration policy. Back in 1920, we lived already in a time of widespread unemployment.

By now it was public knowledge that the old ethnic German population in new Poland had been abused from the beginning. Their legal rights were violated, even in areas inhabited predominantly by Germans, despite the agreement with the League of Nations in Geneva. But no one seemed to care.

Grandfather was an old man, and Papa was determined to look after his well-being, and to make any decisions about his future right on the spot, which meant in Ostrowo. Papa's plan was that we would all take a trip to visit grandfather in new Poland, except for Omi. She preferred to continue setting up housekeeping in our new home in Münster.

So early one morning, the four of us left by train, although such a trip was much easier said than done in 1921. It proved to be a long and traumatic ride, a kind of guilt trip. I recall very vividly our crossing the newly-erected German-Polish border into the new "Polish Corridor," known also as the Danzig Corridor, which was created to give the new Poland, established in 1918, additional land, and an outlet to the Baltic sea.

At the crossing of the border from Germany into former Germany, we were locked into our train compartment by Polish officials with big badges and bleak faces. It was already dark outside and the inside was only scarcely lit by a feeble bulb. Günter and I had to sit still from then on and were not allowed to talk, as we would have spoken German. Only Mutti and Papa knew Polish. Then men in strange uniforms unlocked our compartment and entered. They were the Polish border police. With grim faces they started to inspect everything—first our passports and other papers, then all our luggage, and finally they even conducted body searches.

I had to hold still and was very frightened. No wonder. At that time I was not even five years old! Why did Papa tolerate that rude activity and let them do all those things to us? At home, nobody dared to even talk back to him. What would come next? When they finally left, after one last inspection, they locked us in again, and the train took off on its way into the Polish Corridor, leaving us quite shaken.

Somehow we arrived much later in Ostrowo in grandfather's

Omi
(Picture taken in 1898)

home. He lay sick in bed and was being taken care of by his two widowed daughters, Papa's stepsisters, who lived with their father. All of them looked to me much older than we were. No wonder, Papa had been the youngest of thirteen children. During our ten-day stay with them we had to run many errands to decide the future of our relatives. Günter and I always had to tag along but were instructed to keep our mouths shut, because German was not tolerated any more. At grandfather's place, long discussions were held, and it was finally decided that none of these

Mutti with Günter (standing)
and me on her lap.

three would, or wanted to, leave the land of their birth. Papa himself was born there in 1879. Much later, I came to understand that this particular trip was also a sort of a good-bye to Papa's place where he grew up, and a farewell to grandfather who wanted to see us all once more before he died.

We returned to Münster without them and by a similar troublesome journey as on the way out. How happy we were to be finally home again, and so glad to see Omi in our new spacious domicile. Once again we were able to pick up our own lives the best way possible. Papa sent money regularly to Ostrowo, until grandfather's death some years later. He sent it even though we often did not have much left for ourselves during the approaching inflation. Many years later the step-sisters were able to emigrate and move to Hamburg in North Germany, a port at the Elbe River. There we met them again under more peaceful circumstances.

Back then I was not aware of how tough our everyday life had become after World War I, and how the adults had to cope and adjust to an unending procession of new problems in a time called peace—but without peace.

$\mathcal{P}$overty or Plenty

$\mathcal{W}\!e$ enjoyed our new and comfortable home. The entrance hall alone was room-sized with a large bright window where fresh flowers always bloomed on the window sill. Omi had her eye on the party-sized dining room and wanted to put her cooking talents to practical use by opening a small, family-style restaurant here to help support our family. But Papa, old fashioned patriarch that he was, decided he would be the only bread-winner in his family. Women took care of the three "K's"—*Kinder, Kirche, und Küche* (children, church and kitchen).

Omi baked the best smelling bread. All cooking was done on a huge coal stove in a very large Westphalian country kitchen with two big windows. Tiles covered the floor and half of the walls. Though we had a modern gas stove, it could rarely be used. Gas was sharply rationed for household consumption and mainly reserved for industry use. But Omi knew a way out. In the morning when I got out of bed, she would quickly slip the bread dough dish under my warm feather-bed to make it rise faster. We had only coal-fired stoves, no central heating, and besides, coal was also being rationed.

But that wasn't our only use of coal. We also needed it for ironing, which was done without electricity. That was rationed, too! The irons of those days consisted of two parts. There was a little door at the back, and the inner iron bolt was removed and inserted into the coals of the cooking stove. When it glowed red hot, one had to grasp the bolt with a metal hook and return it to the inner part of the iron. Then the little hinged door was closed. Hopefully it was hot enough, but not too hot, for that boring ironing job. Meanwhile a second iron bolt was put into the fire. These inserts had to be exchanged constantly—and in those days, before permanent press clothes, everything had to be ironed, especially the starched, stiff, white detachable men's collars. I was fascinated by the way Omi and Mutti handled these glowing, red pieces dangling on a long hook, always worried that they might drop one, but they never did. What a hard life that must have been for them. It is still puzzling to me how my family managed to survive during the hard postwar years.

However, for me, there were good times also. Right in the beginning, I found a copper pfennig (penny) just in front of our house. A German pfennig is considered to be a good luck charm. I gladly picked it up according to our proverb: he who doesn't honor the pfennig isn't worth the *Taler*, an old silver coin worth three marks, first minted in 1518 in Joachimsthal, Bohemia. It was the forerunner of the dollar, which derived its name from the German *Taler*.

I liked to play on the front balcony off the living room, overlooking the city promenade. It was built on the site of the ancient city wall and deep moats that had encircled the old city in the twelfth century, and was redesigned as a park-like ring stretching around as a green belt for three and a half miles. Linden trees, blooming bushes and colorful flower beds created the attractive promenade of my youth.

I enjoyed using the balcony because it afforded me a front row view of the passing scene below. With fascination I watched the frequent funeral processions passing through the promenade on their way to the nearby cemetery. They were led by brass bands playing sad tunes, which went right through my bones. Then followed a horse-drawn hearse, the coffin covered with beautiful wreaths and a big flag. Many people slowly walked behind, the men with top hats, all dressed in black. Mutti explained, "These are the veterans." I thought that was their family name and often wondered how she knew all these dead people. But I was sure they were all in heaven now.

Directly in front of the house was a large green lawn with a monument in the center commemorating the dead of the 7th Westphalian Train Battalion of World War I. It was encircled by a gravel path and benches. What an ideal place for me and my dolls! Beyond that was a small market place with a few shops.

Every morning Mutti sent me to one of these shops with our old aluminum can to get the meager allowance of fresh milk for Günter and me that we were entitled to, according to our ration card. One morning something terrible happened. As I was hopping along on my way home and swinging the can in the process, milk dripped out of the bottom. I ran home frantically as the drops changed into a thin white stream, marking my way—like in Hänsel and Gretel. What a loss! Was it my fault because I had swung the can? To my surprise Mutti didn't even scold me. Instead, she quickly poured what was left into a jar and then sadly examined the hole to see if it could be soldered again, for containers could not be replaced so easily after World War I.

My daily walk to the dairy was not at all dull. I always passed two big bronze statues in front of that little market place, mounted high up on stone bases, facing each other from opposite sides of the main street. On one side stood a man, a farm hand with his horse, and on the other, a maid with a bull, both looking down on the traffic beneath them. They stood so straight and appeared to me so regal and proud, that I always said hello to them first on my milk trip.

These statues marked the former Ludgeri gate, when it was one of the eleven gates to the inner city. Beyond the town walls it once was surrounded by rich farm land. In the Middle Ages such a city gate was locked at night, and on the ramparts, watchmen stood guard over the town's people until early next morning when the gates were opened again. Now the statues stood in the middle of a park-like ground through which the tracks of the street cars traveled. Farmers were still coming to town, only now from a much greater distance, providing us with their fresh agricultural products twice a week. Mutti and I went marketing there when Günter was in school.

Looking back, my childhood was constantly full of traps. One afternoon, Mutti sent me to get fresh rolls from the bakery at our little market place. The store was owned by two ladies I knew very well. They were widows from World War I who now struggled alone to continue their husbands' business. Friendly as usual they gave me my rolls as well as a handful of small change. My counting ability was limited but when I looked at the coins on my way home, I was sure I had been given too many. My first reaction was to return to the store and tell them about this mistake. But while I was mulling this over, I had already approached the corner of the promenade, close to the spot where every day a man stood with his ice cream cart. Though I always looked longingly at his tempting cones, I had never been allowed to buy one, as much as I would have yearned for it. In my imagination this must have been like a gift from heaven.

I had no sooner gotten there when the man asked me what flavor I wanted, vanilla or strawberry? He already had a cone in his hand and opened the lids of his containers with that tempting cold delicacy. Reluctantly I gave him a 5-pfennig coin, and he handed me my richly filled cone. What a stroke of luck! However, now that I had the ice cream in my hand, I was no longer all that thrilled about my secret acquisition. First I had to gulp it down rather quickly so I would be home on time, and then, with my bad conscience, it didn't even taste as exceptional as I had expected.

Quickly wiping my fingers and mouth on my dress as I entered the kitchen, I hastily put the rolls and small change on the table, hoping to make a speedy exit. But unfortunately Mutti was just brewing fresh coffee. She cast a glance at my purchase and called me back right away. "Dorothea, the change is short five pfennigs!" Horrified I looked at the pile of coins on the table. She chastised me for being so scatter-brained and said I had to go back to the bakery and have this mistake corrected. I was dumbfounded, but didn't even have much time for that, since Mutti put everything back in my hands right away and sent me out the door, with the rolls and the left-over money.

There I was on the street again with a big guilty conscience and no money of my own with which to replace the loss. How could I ever confess what a terrible thing I had done? So, very reluctantly, I returned to the bakery and first milled around outside. Finally I entered with shaking knees. The two friendly ladies were there as before, and I put everything on the counter and muttered, "There is something wrong with the change," which was the truth. I told them through my tears that five pfennigs were missing, which was also true, and that I didn't have any money to replace them. I didn't have to say much more. They laughed. I shouldn't cry because of that, and proceeded to replace the missing coin. Deeply relieved, I packed everything into my little basket and quickly ran out of the store.

In Sunday school I had learned about a guardian angel and on my way home I thanked mine for helping me in this dilemma, even though it was assistance at cheating, and that he was not away on vacation when I needed him. I quickly promised him also not to do anything like that ever again, a promise I have always kept. Confessing my escapade later to Günter he asked, "Why did you only get ice cream for five pfennigs?

Why not for ten, when everything was going so well!"

But that wouldn't have worked much longer anyway. Times became even tougher, although everyone thought they were already hard enough with higher taxes and raised prices sparked by the outrageous reparation payments imposed on the Weimar Republic.

Another daily task was an early morning visit to a bakery at the Marienplatz, to get fresh rolls for my parents' breakfast. I was a well-known customer and sometimes was given a cookie, which made the trip more interesting. Each morning Mutti gave me a 10-pfennig coin and I bought four crunchy rolls with it, still warm from the oven—until one morning when the baker gave me only three rolls, and one pfennig back. I refused to leave and told the baker, "My mother wants me to bring home four rolls." But the baker said, "Listen little girl, the price has changed. One roll costs 3 pfennigs now. Do you understand?" But I didn't understand how things can change overnight and I was unsure of Mutti's reaction. It was even a greater surprise when Mutti and Papa did understand. There was a new word I now learned—"inflation." Papa shrugged, and every morning thereafter, Mutti gave me 12 pfennigs for the same four rolls.

I kept thinking to myself, "when you ask for more money you get it. It is that easy." So I tried to do the same as the baker had done and asked Mutti for a little pocket money, for I never was given any money just for my own use as some of my older playmates were. Strangely enough the system did not work for me. Instead I was told, "You don't need any money. You have everything you need right here at home." That was my first experience with inflation. Soon the time would come when every morning one had to realize that prices had risen again and the German money was declining in value daily.

Meanwhile our extra supplies from Omi were close to extinction. The speed of their decrease rapidly increased our food problem—five people solely with the meager amounts from the food ration cards. To add to our alarming situation, we knew food was available in Münster's fertile countryside, if you happened to know a farmer. Suddenly everyone around us remembered a long-lost country cousin. Only we were without any food-supplying relatives. What were we going to do?

Wonder of wonders, not before long, the vital answer walked directly into our house. In the 1920s, it was customary for tenants to pay the monthly rent in cash, in person. That's what our dear Mr. Obst did. After Papa had bought his apartment house and they both had swapped apartments, he had become our tenant and visited us regularly. His name Obst means fruit, and fruitful were our relationships. He and Papa depended on each other for solutions to our endless postwar problems. Recently the government had passed an emergency decree that increased taxes on real estate, because of the outrageous billions of reparation payments Germany had to pay in *Goldmark*. The exact amount hadn't even been decided yet, which hung over us as an indeterminate factor. (At that time 4 *Goldmark* were about one dollar.)

Mr. Obst was retired, but previously had owned a well-established delicatessen. As a native Westphalian he knew practically everybody in town as well as in the country. He promised to take charge of our dilemma, and it didn't take long before he provided us with our "own" special farmer—Mrs. Schonebeck. She lived only a two-hour walk away from us. Mutti didn't waste any time to venture out to her with a basket on her arm, and me in tow. It was easy to find her farm. We just walked along the promenade and then followed Mecklinburger Chaussee out of town through meadows and fields dotted with cows and horses. The bubbling Aa River ran alongside now and then with its waters tumbling crystal clear over pebbles. If Mutti had let me splash in there, that would have made my day.

Finally we arrived. With great expectations we entered an expansive green courtyard. Under widely spaced old trees we saw at the left Mrs. Schonebeck's home. It was one of those typical Westphalian farm houses where people and livestock lived under the same wide, low-pitched, roof. The stables were simply an extension of the house. At the right side the land was open, an attractive variegated quilt of different shapes of crops. The Aa River flowed peacefully behind the house, a soothing picture of rural peace and tranquility.

Coming closer, Mutti pointed out two crossed horses' heads at the gable carved out of wood. She said this was in accordance with an ancient heathen belief that the horse was considered to be sacred to the Teutons (like the cow in India), and would ward off evil. I spotted something else on the roof and exclaimed, "Look, Mutti, there is a stork's nest!" I remembered that storks deliver babies, but as hard as I looked, there were no babies.

Now we knocked at the main entrance, but there was no answer. Mutti carefully tried the latch and the door sprang open. We entered a huge hall with an enormous beamed ceiling and a stone floor of big blocks, some with the centers worn down through centuries of use. Heavy oak tables and benches with straight backs lined the front wall to both sides of the entrance door. On the wall, on wooden shelves, china cups and plates were arranged in an orderly fashion. Heavy logs crackled cozily in an enormous fireplace, which was the focal point. Above it, on wooden beams, as was the Westphalian custom, savory-smelling hams were suspended from hooks high up in the massive chimney for natural smoking. We knew these hams were a world-renowned, Westphalian delicacy and their delightful odor now filled the entire room. We watched how the smoke, after having done its work, escaped through an opening in the roof, with the wood permanently stained from smoke accumulating over the years.

Our fascination was interrupted by Mrs. Schonebeck's appearance from the rear, where she had been busy. She was middle-aged with rosy cheeks and the typical skin of country people who are out in the fresh air a lot. Now she wiped her right hand on her big blue apron and with the other she smoothed her hair that formed a knot at the back of her head. She approached us with a friendly smile and shook hands even with me. Her warm welcome lifted our spirits. We all sat down at one of the wooden tables close by the windows, and while the adults started talking business, I watched the chickens in the courtyard. Mrs. Schonebeck already knew about our needy circumstances from dear Mr. Obst, and Mutti seemed very relieved that we came. Now I had to sit perfectly still and wait while the two adults went to the back of the house. When they returned, Mutti's basket looked very heavy and was covered with a towel to keep out unwanted snoopers during our walk home. As we left we were encouraged to return the following week. That was more than we had hoped for.

From then on, once a week, Mutti and I hiked out to that farm to upgrade our modest menus with fresh produce from the country. Hopefully this would also include eggs, butter or milk, all bought without ration cards. Very proudly I got my own little knapsack to help carry the supplies. This was already our second food hoarding trip since 1918. Mrs. Schonebeck was a remarkable help and saved us from what others had to do—smuggle food at night from the nearby Dutch border. Hoarding was strictly forbidden and punished with high fines. It was also dangerous, with a big risk of being caught by the police along both sides of the border, and everything being confiscated.

En route on our regular trips to the farm, all I could think of was, "will the farm lady give me an extra apple like the last time?" On the rare occasion that we had one at home, I only got half of it, sharing it equally with Günter. When we arrived, Mrs. Schonebeck would take me across the cozy hall to the back, passing a large barn with the cattle. Their stables warmed the whole house comfortably. The cows were big and scary though. They all looked at me with their enormous goggle-eyes. Even though they were behind some wooden barriers, I was always quite relieved when I had passed by them.

Finally we reached the storage area. Shelves were stocked with the produce from her big garden behind the house. A delightful aroma of fresh fruit permeated the air. There I got my apple. Since I had asked Mutti once, loud and clear, the way children do, "why only one apple when there are so many?" Mutti told me to hush and instructed me to say nothing but *Guten Tag, Danke,* and *Auf Wiedersehen* (hello, thank you, good-bye) on all future visits.

In town, the Aa River formed a lake at the promenade just between us and the cemetery. The rather small lake of my time has nowadays been transformed into one of over 108 acres. World War II, with its terrible destructiveness, created a thing of beauty by scooping out the Aa meadows with wide-spread bombing raids. Today it is a paradise for all kinds of water sports and regattas, surrounded by a pleasant three-mile path for landlubbers, with benches, rest areas, coffee houses and restaurants.

When I again visited the area after World War II, while living in Berlin, Mrs. Schonebeck had disappeared and her old farm house had been turned into a modern country-style café. But at least it had retained its old rustic appearance and atmosphere. Once more I walked across the huge hall with the worn stone pavement, only now the warm smell of cows and smoked ham had been replaced with the fine aroma of fresh, hot coffee, and with cozy indoor and outdoor seating. On my second visit there years later, in the 1980s, to my big disappointment the old familiar Schonebeck place was gone completely. What a mistake to expect the Münster of my childhood not to have changed.

Back in the 1920s I stayed undernourished despite all the good care I got from my family—as "good" as was possible at the time. The whole population was poorly fed and the main topic of conversation was food. Back then the magic cure was cod-liver oil and I got my share of it one day, when a big case of these bottles showed up in our home. It was prepared like a soft drink, not in a concentrated form, and tasted really terrible. The bottles had to be kept cool. We had no electric refrigerators and our ice box worked only with a big block of ice that was delivered every other morning. The cooling space was not large enough to store my numerous bottles, so Mutti kept some of them in cold water for several hours. When the drink became lukewarm it was really unpalatable. My crying was useless. That health cure was horrible.

Despite all the untiring efforts, I stayed gaunt and pale, and our family doctor, Dr. Lewis on Bahnhofstrasse, recommended a few weeks stay by the ocean, on one of the Frisian islands that fringe the North Sea coast like a string of pearls. We chose the resort island of Borkum, the closest to the Dutch islands with an ocean climate and exceptionally healthy air. Two weeks were all we could afford, but that didn't stop us from being excited about the unexpected vacation.

On one summer day, during Günter's school break, we left by train early in the morning, provided with food in brown bags, and reached the little harbor town Norden before noon. From there we had to continue by ship at high tide. After a two-hour crossing we were greeted by the enormous lighthouse of Borkum. Now we landed on a very large resort island. As soon as Mutti had settled us in our rented accommodations, we took off to explore the beach. In the middle were big cabanas on wheels for changing our clothes, of course with men and women strictly separated. We wasted no time and immediately built a sand castle. All that was much more fun than drinking cod-liver oil at home. The restful two weeks there were good for all of us. Some photographs survived over the years and later added to our family amusement. How funny we all looked in our outfits. Mutti with a dress-like bathing suit in the water, and I with the addition of a big bow on top of my head. For swimming, we were more dressed than undressed, according to the fashion of that time. Günter presented himself in a full bathing suit, striped like a zebra, and Papa in something similar, only a couple of sizes larger. Swimming trunks, bikinis, or even nudism were as far away as a trip to the moon. For me everything was a new adventure.

The following year, in the spring of 1922, I had to enroll in school. There was no kindergarten. The school year customarily started right after Easter. Mutti accompanied me on my first day, on foot, a walk of thirty minutes. We went together to my assigned classroom where the teacher, a woman, provided us with a lot of basic information, like the school hours and lesson plans. Quiet and very shy, I kept watching the many other girls timidly instead of paying attention to what was being stated in detail. So when Mutti asked me later what was said in class, I had no idea. She got very angry and instructed me to stop daydreaming and pay better attention. This immediately gave me the impression that paying attention must be something extremely difficult and that Günter was right, since he had already warned me about school.

Previously he had entered *Sexta*, the fifth grade of the *Schiller Gymnasium* (high school), and at the age of nine, the poor boy had seven classes of Latin per week. Later French was added, but he hated Latin the most and taught me the following rhyme:

Aqua — das Wasser	Aqua means water
Vinum — der Wein	Vinum means wine
Scher dich zum Teufel	Go to hell
Verflixtes Latein	Damned Latin

Our school system was very strict right from the start. The average German was an educated person. School was compulsory until the age of fifteen or more, and provided the fundamentals for basic knowledge, and had done so for hundreds of years. As was customary, classes were held six days a week. Right away there was homework for the different subjects, like reading, writing, and arithmetic. Writing was especially difficult. I had to learn four different methods, one right after the other. We started with German script (Gothic type), then Sütterlin, a new way of writing invented by Mr. Sütterlin, a graphologist, which was abolished right after I mastered it, and later Latin script and printing as it is known in the U.S.

At least my way to school was very simple. I just walked along the promenade for half an hour to the schoolhouse, in rain, wind, snow and ice. So here I was at the age of six, early in the morning, walking along with my primer and slate in the satchel on my back, a wet sponge and dry cloth for the slate hanging outside on a string, and a breakfast pouch, containing a very modest sandwich, dangling from my neck in front of me. I must have looked like a live Hummel figure! The sandwich was for the "big" fifteen-minute break around 10 a.m. Unlike American schools, cafeterias did not exist.

School doctors frequently inspected all the children and found that they were anemic and undernourished. This included me, pale and frail. My teeth also lacked calcium, in spite of Mutti's best possible care. The bad teeth couldn't have been caused by candies, which were a rarity, and chocolate was a magic word.

One morning, Mutti gave me a cup to take to school along with my simple sandwich. She talked about a newspaper article that had something to do with my cup. At school, we children were gathered in endless lines in front of our gymnasium, our cups in hand. Slowly we made our way inside. On an elevated platform stood an enormous kettle and next to it another huge container. Standing behind it were two strange ladies dressed in what looked to me like a uniform. In an orderly single file we approached the platform, full of curiosity as to what would be given to us.

Now finally it was my turn. As instructed, I held up my little cup to the nice lady and she filled it up to the brim with milk from a big ladle she had dipped down into that enormous kettle. The second lady reached into the other container and broke off a large piece of delicious smelling, sweet tasting white bread, and put it into my other hand. I was then pushed forward to make room for the next child. What a treasure I was holding in both of my hands, and it was all for me. Those nice ladies must be angels I thought, and they had also told me to come back every day. In no time I had eaten all of it, even before leaving the gymnasium. It was just heavenly.

My cup was little, and because it was filled to the brim, I repeatedly spilled some of the wonderful milk. Mutti solved that problem by giving me a much bigger container with a sturdy handle. This regular school feeding went on day after day, week after week, all for free. I eventually learned the magic word for that miracle—our angels were called Quakers, a religious, charitable organization from the U.S. In the early 1920s, the generous action of the Quakers to undernourished children like myself brought great relief and added much to the restoration of our health and survival. This was at a time when the entire population suffered from starvation as a result of the British blockade, which still remained in effect long after the armistice. One day, much, much later, the Quakers vanished again, as quietly as they had appeared. By that time food had become more plentiful and we could buy milk in school.

Now, as a senior citizen, living in the U.S. myself, I still recall the Quakers quite vividly. After more than fifty years I found them in the Washington, D.C. area under the name of "Friends Meeting of Washington," and could finally repay them for their love and care. I also learned that their name "Quakers" is a nickname, but not for me and my generation in Germany. For us they were the personified salvation in a desperate time of hand-to-mouth existence.

Meanwhile great economic chaos resulted from the extreme reparation payments amounting to billions of marks and goods to the victors. Bankruptcy and unemployment flourished. Impoverishment and hunger were daily guests in nearly every home. Nevertheless, the French Reparation Commission was incensed about Germany's incomplete delivery of its goods under the Versailles Treaty, even though many clauses were impossible to fulfill. There was still a minor outstanding amount of wood and coal deliveries. We lacked them daily for ourselves and could heat only one room at a time. Gas and electricity were available only at certain hours.

But France insisted on immediate compliance of the outstanding dues. On January 11, 1923, as a reprisal against the minor deficiencies of reparation deliveries, an army of sixty thousand French and Belgian troops marched high-handed into the Rhine-Ruhr area, Germany's principal industrial region. That arbitrary military occupation touched off an acute domestic crisis. Lawlessness began. Papa raged, "Does this mean we have neither war nor peace now? This is a resumption of the war with different means and against the Versailles Treaty."

Immediately our own government protested vehemently, but to no avail. In self-defense, the 10 million panic-stricken Ruhr population started a desperate passive resistance overnight through non-cooperation. Water, gas and electricity were shut off in all confiscated buildings. The seized mines stopped mining coal. Newspapers, forced to print the invaders' announcements, stopped publishing. Streetcars stood still when French soldiers got on, and the stores would not sell them anything. No

wonder, all our goods were rationed and already in extremely short supply in this large industrial region. The invaders were confronted by the
entire population who were united, dogged and silently represented a
wave of indignation throughout all of Germany. Papa furiously commented, "We lived for five years in a time called 'peace' in the history
books and the world press, and now we have such an illegal war-like
occupation!" But it got even worse. France inflicted a state of martial
law and an intensified stage of siege, including a curfew.

Friends arriving from the occupied Rhineland told us that mine
owners were arrested and German citizens were pushed off the sidewalks by the occupying French military forces. Many were black troops
from French African colonies. Germans were treated as second and third-
class citizens in their own country. The enforced French blockade prohibited any delivery of coal and iron products outside the Ruhr area.
We in Münster, like all of Germany, depended on it. On February 15,
1923, the French even barricaded their invaded part with a customs requirement, which separated it totally from the rest of Germany.

Regardless of the catastrophic results, on March 2, 1923, the French
invaders also seized the entire railroad system. By now it had reached
the state of an undeclared war between France and the German
Rhineland. Tension heightened, evoking new Communist strife and an-
archy. Violent outbursts brought us close to a civil war.

The height of the new crisis touched off more bankruptcies and
more unemployment, plunging us into a greater disaster. The German
Goldmark was adjusted to one U.S. dollar. Overnight it steadily deteriorated in value with the result that a galloping inflation was well underway with its millions of paper money. At the beginning of June 1923,
one dollar amounted to 7,260 marks, by the end of the month to 49,000
marks, and at the end of July to 10,300,000 marks. Only the paper mills
benefitted, working day and night to print the worthless currency. Despair, hunger and panic seized the population.

New bills couldn't be printed quickly enough. Towns like Münster
were responsible for issuing their own scrip. Salaries were paid with
millions and billions. Money was picked up and delivered in huge laundry baskets. I remember Mutti telling me that a friend of Papa's who
worked in the revenue office did not get paid monthly any more, but
weekly, then daily, then four times a day, and finally every hour. His

wife waited in his office to collect the money the moment he was paid, so she could take it to the baker right away before it lost the value of even one loaf of bread. As an ironic consequence, counterfeiters were put out of business, too.

Papa used to say in grim humor, "One should have a private ducat mannequin!" referring to the legendary figure of a tiny seated man who was grinning because every time he relieved himself, ducats (gold coins) dropped out continuously. To this day it represents the town of Goslar's ancient rights to mint coins. Our coins were made of aluminum with the fantastic denominations of 500, and 1,000, worth only a pfennig.

Finally, one dollar rose from four marks to 4 trillion marks. I remember when Papa had to pay 80 million marks postage for a letter. The envelope looked like a picture puzzle with so many stamps on it and hardly any room for the address. Inflation had reached such grotesque proportions that money was virtually worthless. The heaviest losers were the middle class and the pensioners. They saw their savings being completely wiped out, and faced poverty overnight.

To complicate the monetary problems, the tribute had to be paid in *Goldmark*. Mutti told me that before the war one *Goldmark* equalled one mark and that she had real shiny gold coins in her purse just to go marketing, and that she spent less than 3 marks for her purchases, which included a roast with all the trimmings. By 1923, one *Goldmark* alone had the value of 1 billion paper marks. I don't know how the many nations of the Reparations Commission could keep up with all these irrational numbers of an undetermined size and duration of tribute payments. Believe me, they didn't!

Just at the height of my family's struggle with inflation, our private miracle emerged called "*Tante Wanda aus Amerika.*" She was Papa's stepsister and was only twelve years old when she went to America at the invitation of an uncle who had immigrated earlier. (We must have that in our genes. I went on the same adventure in 1962, living in Berlin when the Wall went up.)

Aunt Wanda suddenly arrived from the U.S. and her spontaneous assistance performed miracles. The first one was a new pair of bright blue house slippers for me which she had crocheted herself coming over by boat. Her enormous luggage contained surprises for everybody. Suddenly money of "stable value" was in the house. Günter explained to me that the new miracle was called a "dollar." We children had had a very happy time without any money. Now Aunt Wanda would take care of all our needs with remarkable ease. Since she was childless we were kissed and hugged all the time. She also supplied us with chewing gum, a novelty to us that Papa hated, thinking it vulgar. So we chewed it secretly with great pleasure.

Dear Aunt Wanda was a constant super Santa Claus. For a handful of her powerful dollars she bought two big pieces of land, one for each of her two sisters in Hohen-Neuendorf, a suburb of Berlin. All three women were war-widows. Their husbands had fought on opposite sides. Aunt Wanda's generous assistance was enormous. After many beneficial weeks she returned to the U.S., leaving us behind in better shape than we had been in for a long time.

During Germany's trying time I felt I had a normal childhood. The problems of the 1920s were unknown to me. My life was occupied with new school work which, at the age of seven, was my main concern. It was normal for us to stretch old clothing to make it last. The saving ethic helped us. Mutti would make me a new dress out of her old one, and I wore it proudly. We were raised very modestly and didn't have the abundance of things that children take for granted these days—like sweets. They were reserved for special occasions. No between-meal snacks, but I didn't know any differently. We were all in the same boat. A small piece of chocolate on Sundays, shared with Günter, was something to look forward to the entire week. We ate it very slowly to make it last longer. Even today I cannot bring myself to waste anything, especially food.

By now the arbitrary French occupation of the Ruhr area endangered the stability of all of Germany. It was impossible to support the cut-off area with goods from unoccupied Germany, where people didn't have enough for themselves. Germany was even more hard pressed, for it lacked all the natural resources of the U.S. The growing shortage of almost all basic daily necessities, especially food, caused looting and sacking. Frequent Communistic revolts recurred.

To make life's agony complete, in November 1923, a small group of radicals attempted a revolt in Bavaria. Papa read to us a newspaper article about an unknown man, an ex-soldier of the war, named Adolf Hitler, a member of the newly-founded, but insignificant, "Workers'

Party," who had provoked a riot in Munich. The article further said that he was joined by General Erich Ludendorff, a man well-known from World War I. (Hitler knew even then how to use notable people for his purposes.) Together they had proclaimed a national revolution and called for action.

On November 9, the rioters had set out for a march to Munich's town hall, to seize control of the Bavarian government. But before they reached their target the revolt collapsed, scattered under police fire, and ended with bloodshed on the street, leaving nineteen people dead. Hitler himself had scrambled to safety. Papa put the newspaper down, "What will be next?" he groaned. "What we don't need are more crazy people."

After the failure of the attempted coup, General Ludendorff walked off free and was not heard of much later. The new Workers' Party was outlawed. Hitler, as the ringleader, was convicted of treason and sentenced to prison for five years in a fortress at Landsberg on the Lech River in Bavaria, together with some fellow combatants like Himmler, Hess, Röhm and others. Unfortunately they all were freed prematurely in December 1924, after roughly one year.

The Munich riot went down in history as the Beer Hall Revolt, only this time Hitler had picked the wrong moment. Just one week later our devastating inflation period came to a sudden halt. On November 15, 1923, our money was adjusted to the new *Rentenmark*. For 1,000 billion old paper marks, one *Rentenmark* was issued. The stabilization was painful, but there was new hope that economic and political conditions would start to improve slowly. An obscure man like Hitler, not even a German but an Austrian vagabond, was easily forgotten and written off as a crackpot.

I have my own vivid remembrances about the money stabilization. Mutti and Papa came into my room with a big bucket and just dumped it out. Bundles and bundles of worthless bank notes with gigantic numbers, flew all over the room. "Here are your latest toys," they laughed in grim humor. "Play with them because they are not good for anything else any more." With all their long lines of zeroes, I thought my family was loaded. Too bad it was only a paper dream.

My other recollection of a raging inflation was at school, when our beloved math teacher, Miss Zimmermann, told us one of her own experiences from years ago. As soon as she received her salary, she rushed to the store to buy a badly needed pair of shoes. When she got there she was told that she hadn't brought enough money for the entire pair. What she had would only pay for one shoe. She had the choice of the left or the right one, so she took the right one. She returned soon with another salary in hand hoping to be able to afford the other shoe now. She was wrong again. Even her increased salary was not enough any more for the second shoe. Prices had gone up by leaps and bounds. So she waited for the next pay raise. She told us that this was the time when the price for a pair of trousers was 10,000 marks in the morning, 20,000 marks at midday, and 30,000 marks in the evening. Too bad I do not remember if she ever got her left shoe!

In the meager years of the early 1920s, the highlight of every Saturday was when Mutti baked a modest cake. Günter and I hung around the kitchen, not to miss the moment when she emptied the dough out of the bowl. We were eager to clean it with our fingers, licking off every little bit appreciatively. That was really a treat.

Otherwise we often chased each other and played tag, which didn't cost anything. I was usually the only girl among boys of all ages. Often the games grew rough, and Günter had to come to my rescue. If our parents would have known this I would have had to stay home. This had to be avoided at all costs. Grown-ups couldn't be expected to appreciate all of our activities, and there was ample opportunity for innocent mischief. We also played many board games at home like checkers. We children couldn't miss what we never had.

On Sunday afternoons we frequently went with friends to some of the coffee houses in the countryside. One was named *Tannenhof* because it was surrounded by fir trees. The area was called Saint Mauritz, the name of another patron saint. We started out with the streetcar, then continued on foot for about an hour. Günter carefully carried the package with Mutti's baked goods. This was less expensive than buying pastry there. Unwatched, we acted silly and sometimes he accidentally dropped that troublesome cake bundle. But we all ate every crumb of it later, irrespective of its condition. When we arrived at the restaurant we only ordered coffee as most people did, to economize. I would glance wistfully at the displayed pastry tarts, but I never got one. Maybe that's one reason why they still fascinate me to this day.

The wheel of time continued to spin. We luckily had survived the raging inflation and hopefully picked up our normal lives again. In August 1924, Germany accepted the American Dawes Plan. Because no attempt had been made to determine the total amount of reparations nor a final date, Germany was supposed to pay one billion *Goldmark* the first five years, then raise it to about 2.5 billion each following year for an indefinite time, or until doomsday!

Papa was appalled at such unrealistic assessments of our war debt payments. Mr. Charles G. Dawes meant business by advancing more foreign loans. He had American exports in mind and one must feed the cow before one can milk it. Papa shook his head, "That means debts are paid off with greater debts instead of freeing us from the necessity of foreign aid. We are driving out one devil with another. How shall that end?" The answer was higher taxes and utility rates, along with pay cuts and growing billions of reparation debts. The original terms escalated and what was bad got worse. What would be next?

*A*dvent Adventures

*Y*es, we had problems during the hard postwar period, but Mutti and Papa always seemed to have a solution. We didn't know we were poor since all of us were poor together. This way Günter and I assumed we had a normal and happy childhood.

Take Christmas for instance. In the States, the holiday season begins with Thanksgiving. However, in Germany, Thanksgiving is unknown. We had no Indians to start the custom and celebrate it with. Instead, our Christmas season begins with the first of the four Sundays of Advent and the old custom of the Advent wreath with its four candles. The first one is lit on the first Sunday of Advent. An additional one would be lit each following week until all four are lit together on the last Sunday before Christmas.

In Münster these wreaths were displayed in every flower shop richly decorated, and hung in churches and schools. Günter and I badly wanted such a wreath at home, too, but his pocket money couldn't swing it. It didn't dawn on us to just ask our parents to buy one in a time without special wishes. So we thought it would be fun to make one on our own and to surprise them with it.

Across from our house was a big green bush that would do nicely for our purpose. We often had played hide-and-seek under its low, widespread branches. Armed with knife and scissors we sneaked out one afternoon and cut an armful of these precious branches. Then we staggered upstairs, dragged them into the bathroom and locked ourselves in. With wire and string we created an enormous wreath and decorated it with walnuts which Günter painted gold, some of Mutti's ribbons, and four candles bought with Günter's precious sacrificed savings. The final product weighed a ton. In the evening we fastened it with heavy string to our fragile dining room chandelier—our parents' most cherished possession—right above the dining room table. We both had to stand on chairs on the table to reach up high to make our heavy creation dangle from the old-fashioned, lofty ceiling.

Now our parents were invited to see our surprise. They were surprised all right, but not the way we had expected. The moment Papa saw it he screamed, "Take that monster down before the chandelier falls!" So down came our creation, this time with Papa's help, and much faster than we had managed to put it up by ourselves. Oh, how disappointed we were, and close to tears. Now lying on the big dining room table, it was so enormous that it hung over on both sides.

That was only the first shock. The second one followed when Mutti took a closer look at the strange greenery. "Where did you collect all that splendor?" The answer was easy. We only had to point out the window to the badly-plucked shrub at the corner. As luck would have it, that particular bush happened to be under the protection of the Nature Preserve. If the park police had caught us, the fine would have been so high that we could have bought the most expensive wreath in any store, including all the Christmas presents.

Finally, Mutti and Papa came to the point of praising our efforts, and the lovely idea. After all, it was the thought that counted. Now we sat around it and Mutti lit the first candle. Papa got out his violin and played some pre-Christmas songs. Needless to say, from then on, Mutti bought our Advent wreath well ahead every year to prevent us from repeating such a prank a second time.

In keeping with another old German custom, we got an Advent calendar to hang on the wall. It had twenty-four little "doors," each hiding a Christmas symbol. Starting on December 1 and continuing each day through Christmas Eve, Günter and I alternatingly opened one of the little doors each morning, eager to see what surprise was behind it. It might be a picture of nuts, a red apple, an angel, a cute lamb, a bright star or a Christmas tree. Nowadays the calendars must contain chocolates to satisfy today's youngsters. The final door, a big double one, would be opened on December 24 and revealed the Christ child in a manger. That last door we opened together. What joy. Christmas would be that night.

However, before Holy Eve, for us children the next Advent adventure started on December 6, the birthday of Saint *Nikolaus* as we call Santa Claus. He comes stomping out of a snow-capped winter forest.

The evening before we put a shoe at the door or on the window sill so that he could leave something in it for us when he passed by at night, such as the first orange of the season, a chocolate star, and some nuts.

But how did our *Nikolaus* get to America? His image was imported as Santa Claus by Thomas Nast who immigrated in 1846 from the Pfalz, Germany, at the Rhine River. In tender remembrance of his childhood he gave to all the children in America the historical *Nikolaus* a home at the North Pole, coming down from there in a sled with his eight reindeer and his promising sack filled with presents. As a gifted graphic artist he also fathered the political symbols of the donkey and the elephant. What would America do without them? In addition, he created the figure of Uncle Sam and the symbol of the dollar sign. Theodore Roosevelt honored him in the name of the nation by naming a mountain after him, "Mount Nast" in Colorado.

But the historical Saint Nicholas came from Turkey. He was born in 270 A.D. in Patara and died in 342 A.D. in Asia Minor as the Bishop of Myra. Of course we know him best for his love of children and who has presents for everyone, some materialistic, some spiritual. Günter and I were more in favor of the material part. We could hardly wait to set out our shoes on the fifth of December before bedtime, so we could collect next morning all the goodies Saint Nicholas had left while passing by during the night. Of course he would only leave something if we had cleaned and polished our shoes.

We would stuff newspaper in the toes so that the few items he left for us would overflow. That made it look like so much more. Somehow, in December we always behaved our best. We also stuck a long list of our Christmas wishes into the shoe, which hopefully was picked up by Santa. For naughty children he would leave a rod. Papa warned us that if our Christmas lists were too long, they might be torn up by Santa. But Mutti usually took care of shortening them. We believed that nothing was impossible for Santa.

Several times during our early childhood, Santa showed up in person with his big sack and his long snow-white beard, hardly showing his face under his long red cap. All of a sudden he appeared, right after we were tucked into our beds, escorted by both of our parents. We were terribly frightened to have him unexpectedly so close by. Would he tell our parents what he knew about us? (You see, Santa keeps a big notebook in heaven in which he records all the children's good and bad deeds. That is why he is so well informed.) To be on the safe side, we quickly crawled deeper under our down comforters. Santa gave us a detailed lecture. It was amazing how much he knew about us, especially since Günter and I were often in hot water. At times, he threatened us with his rod. Once he even smacked it on Günter's comforter as a warning. His voice somehow sounded strange to us for an old man. We eagerly waited for the end, when he would throw nuts and Christmas sweets on our beds before leaving.

It really was too bad that Omi never got to see him. For some inexplicable reason she never felt well on the nights that Santa appeared and always retired to her room early. But the next day, when we told her everything that had happened, she always seemed very interested and listened to every detail.

At the beginning of December the towns of Germany start their historical Christmas markets and keep them open continuously until Christmas Eve. Church squares and public market places turn into glamorous fairy-tale stages. In rows of illuminated closely-spaced stalls, vendors extol everything from toys to hand-carved nativity scenes, a manifold selection of all kinds of arts and crafts, not to forget the colorful wooden nutcrackers, a holiday favorite. We walked through a Christmas wonderland with magic in the air, an enchanting atmosphere, accompanied by the chimes of a glockenspiel, the tempting aroma of Christmas stollen, and the scent of pine cones and fir needles.

Some Christmas fairs go back to the crusades as do those of Munich, Stuttgart and Augsburg. But the best known of all is the *Christkindlmarkt* in Nuremberg. The famous Nuremberger *Pfefferkuchen*, gingerbread cookies, are exported all over the world. I get mine sent to the States regularly every year.

To roam leisurely through such an open-air Christmas market is a delight for young and old, the children's eyes open wide with wonder. It's a boom for merchants and a temptation for people. They are in the mood to spend their money and browse for hand-crafted articles and tree decorations. As darkness falls, all the festive illuminations sparkle and the warm glow of candles gets everybody into an especially joyous mood. There are so many sights and smells to take in, that one does not know where to begin. Soon we came to the booths with the mouthwatering, sizzling *Bratwursts* and freshly fried potato pancakes. This is accompanied by sipping *Glühwein*, a special hot drink of the season, a clove-spiced red wine served steaming in dainty glasses with handles. It keeps the soul and body simultaneously warm and vigorous, and the relaxed atmosphere encourages vivid conversation with friends as well as strangers.

Clinging to local tradition, in some places the *Sternsinger* (star singers) go caroling from house to house carrying a big lantern shaped as a star. They are rewarded with sweets and fruit for their enthusiastic performances. This is similar to the custom of caroling in the U.S., which was brought over by German settlers, together with the Christmas tree, as late as 1850.

At no other time of the year is so much baking done. We had our own recipes like most families do and our specialty is a poppy seed cake, a recipe handed down from Omi to Mutti to me. It is a sweet yeast loaf with a rolled-in thick filling of poppy seeds, a half pound per small loaf, finely ground, soaked in hot milk and enriched generously with ground almonds, eggs, butter, sugar, and a dash of rum.

In my childhood, however, December 24 always started with tears. This was due to my family's favorite annual holiday meal—a carp in the evening, which I detested. In vain I would beg Mutti to change that traditional menu. The carp was always bought alive in a fish store downtown and wrapped in thick layers of wet newspaper for the transport home. Since our shopping was done on foot, it was a difficult twenty-minute walk with a marketing bag that was constantly flopping around with a most active carp, revolting against his captivity.

When we finally arrived at home, the carp was set free in our bathtub. What a relief! Günter and I loved to play with the now happily swimming fish, feeding it and giving it a name—until it was time to say "goodbye," and Omi's skilled hands took over to end its life, quickly and painlessly, as she assured us. We were never present for this. But our carp-friend, though dead by now, still tried to jump out of the spicy water in the big fish pot. Omi would hold the lid tightly, but the poor carp would bang its tail loudly against it several times before surrendering. She assured us that our carp was really dead and did not know that he was being cooked.

Later, at dinner, Günter and I could hardly eat, since each bite reminded us of the happy moments we shared with our new friend from the bathtub. But, we were forced to finish what was served on our plates. Only after I threw up successfully, did I not have to eat any more fish that night. Unfortunately this performance did not prevent my having to eat carp the following year. The adults always complimented Omi on how delicious the meal was, and called it *carp au bleu*. I hated it, and even today I do not like fish or going fishing.

Then finally the part of the evening arrived which we had impatiently awaited all day. While church bells were ringing outside as we all helped clean up in the kitchen, mysterious things were going on inside around the Christmas tree, behind closed doors in the living room. We clearly heard talking and rumbling. Could it be that the Christ Child had arrived? (It was imagined as a big angel and numerous Christmas carols gave evidence of its glorification.) Then we heard Papa say, "Goodbye dear Christ Child, until next year!" That was the moment when he opened the big folding door between the living and dining rooms, and we saw the sparkling Christmas tree for the first time. The warm glow of the lighted candles filled the darkened room. The tree was a live one, of course, and its fresh scent filled the air. Papa had told us that Martin Luther had cut down and decorated the first Christmas tree in 1535 to dramatize for his children the inspiring glory of Christmas. The green color symbolized eternal hope. Our tree stretched from floor to ceiling and was covered with silver tinsel, sweets, and a big gold star at the top. In keeping with German tradition, the flickering wax candles were real. To be on the safe side, Papa always kept a bucket of water and a big wet cloth behind the door, just in case the tree caught on fire. The happy holiday dream finally became true.

If we thought we could storm in now to see what the Christ Child had left for us, we were wrong. Papa would take out his violin and we all sat down and had to sing Christmas songs first, which of course included Silent Night. Next followed a recitation of poems we children had to learn by heart for that occasion. All of this seemed to take an awfully long time, but, that was the ritual. Finally we were allowed to race to our presents, which were never wrapped. Mutti always arranged them nicely on a table which Günter and I shared. We thought our modest gifts were fabulous and never knew where to look first, or what to touch next. For instance, my old doll got a lovely new outfit, which had been sewed and knitted by Mutti. I believed the Christ child had made it. Günter would find another car for his train. There might also be a red rubber ball, picture books, and of course a new pair of warm house shoes which we put on right away. Times were tough in the early 1920s. I vividly remember once getting a warm muff made out of rabbit fur, with a matching collar for my coat. I certainly was proud of that outfit for our cold winter days and wore it for years.

And then it was time to compare our traditional Christmas plates. These were made of sturdy cardboard, shaped like stars in a beautiful, scalloped design, with lovely Christmas scenes and decorations in vivid colors. We would keep them year after year; mine with angels and stars, and Günter's with fir trees and animals. We would have been very disappointed if Mutti had bought new ones. These were our old, well-known friends, always filled with fruit, nuts, chocolates and *marzipan*, a soft candy made out of almond paste. The Christ Child must have been for equality because both of us always had exactly the same items on our plates. It never failed.

Every year Mutti made a gingerbread house, even in our adult years. The cardboard on the outside was decorated with sweets, and the windows were made of red gelatin sheets. A candle burning inside gave it a warm glow. Cotton served as a waving steam cloud coming out of the chimney. In front were Hänsel and Gretel with the witch and her black hunch-backed cat with its tail straight up, all beautiful porcelain figurines. A touch of powdered sugar dusted as snow over everything gave the little scene the festive look of a wintry splendor, a trace of magic fairyland for us.

December 24, Holy Eve, is our highest holiday in the year. All shops and offices close at noon and remain closed for the next two days as legal holidays. People spend the afternoon with last-minute preparations for the evening celebration and everybody tries to join their families for that event. It is a great honor for an outsider to be invited. Bells call people to church all evening, especially to the midnight service. December 25 is the day for inviting and being invited, and for eating the traditional Christmas goose. Then the 26th is the time to joyfully celebrate with a theater performance or a ball. In my teenage years, this was a wonderful occasion to show off our new Christmas dresses. (Europeans may have a hard time getting used to only one Christmas holiday in the States.) Time was taken for everything. It cannot be compared to today where, in our very materialistic world, it seems that when the wrapping paper comes off the presents, everything is over. But customs are different throughout the world, and we all love the one we are used to the best.

According to tradition, the Christmas tree was lit every evening until January 6, the Holy Three Kings day (Epiphany). Then all decorations were taken down and we all helped. First the silver tinsel-strands were carefully wrapped in tissue paper for future years, I still do that today, then the candles were taken down, and last all the sweets since we were forbidden to pick goodies from the tree. There were always two of the same kind to fill our Christmas plates again. With the ornaments put away for another year, the magic of "Silent Night, Holy Night" was put asleep, to become alive again next year at the first of Advent.

Unfortunately, the holidays of 1924 were the last ones we got to spend with our dear Omi. She became sick and I could rarely visit with her any more. Instead, two nuns came alternately every evening from a close-by convent, even though we were Protestants. It was very fortunate that they assisted us night after night for quite a long time. I understood Omi was very well taken care of through such loving care, and she could stay at home with us. She must have suffered great pains. I learned a new word, "morphine," as a means to ease severe agony. One morning Omi had died of cancer. She was only in her sixties. I could not believe it; she had always been an important part of my world.

I remember the moment when I asked Mutti why Omi had to die. She turned away, and tears ran down her cheeks. That was my second shock in one day, because Mutti always had an answer. For the first time I saw her cry and didn't dare ask any more questions. Through all our hard times and shared burdens we had become a very close-knit family. Now, unbelievably, Omi would be taken away from us and brought to the cemetery in the same way I had watched the funerals of the veterans from our balcony, with everybody following on foot. This time the walk would start from our house. She was an irreplaceable loss for all of us.

But there was another event later that shook me. I often had played with Willi Hasse, a neighbor's boy much younger than I. His father had been out of work for some time. To earn some extra money he carried our coal buckets from the basement up to the third floor. For a while I didn't see little Willi. Going marketing with Mutti one day we stood next to his mother, and she was crying bitterly. Now I watched Mutti shifting our paid for groceries from our shopping basket into hers. I understood little of what was said, but I learned that Willi had died of starvation. What a shock! Now I cried, too. He had been too weak to fight a small cold. What a loss. Two deaths in one year, that was hard for me to cope with.

And so was for my parents a political adventure. In April 1925, a new presidential election was held with a rather frightening selection of candidates. Our supreme Field Marshal Paul von Hindenburg, who had retired for the second time since 1919, was brought forward by the conservatives, and so was Wilhelm Marx from the Catholic Center Party, against the radical Communist leader Ernst Thälmann. Papa called it an incredible and contrasting range of choices. People's emotions were stirred. We were alarmed that a fanatic Communist like Thälmann had even been considered. In addition, he got a shocking 2 million votes. Papa did not understand the German people any more. To our relief, loyal and dependable Paul von Hindenburg was elected President.

August 1925 brought a new ray of hope for us. The French finally evacuated the Ruhr district, which they had unlawfully occupied for two and a half years. Papa viewed their withdrawal as a great relief of our hard-hit economy. Indeed, living conditions began to improve modestly. We had learned to appreciate the slightest change for the better. We children suffered only with the diversity of our schoolwork.

Günter and I (1925)

Nevertheless, misfortune was only temporarily dormant since Hitler was released prematurely from prison. Now thirty-five years old, he didn't waste any time re-establishing the Workers' Party in 1925, but this time as its undisputed leader. Even though the Party had been outlawed two years earlier, nobody seemed to care any more. Hitler renamed his movement the National Socialist German Workers' Party, abbreviated in German to NSDAP or NAZI, this time with the aim to attain political power legally. He made the swastika the symbol of his Nazi Party.

It was during his time in prison that he dictated his book *Mein Kampf* to Rudolf Hess. However, this book, which outlined all of Hitler's plans in detail, was regarded only as the sick fantasy of a fanatic, created by political, economic and personal failure. Nobody bothered to read it. Papa said from the beginning that his generation had its emperor, Wilhelm II, with law and order, and that there was no chance for a radical like Hitler. So he regarded *Mein Kampf* as a waste of time.

The new *Rentenmark*, in effect since two years, took all our attention and effort to finally build a more stable life. Our bleeding German economy eventually seemed to revive to some extent, with even a boom in art and literature, known as the roaring twenties. Also my family managed to have a few prosperous, normal years, as the following chapters will illustrate. What we did not know then was that the new prosperity was an illusion. Germany lived on borrowed Allied money all these years. We were only enjoying the government's dance on the edge of a volcano as the war debts grew into a greedy monster forever craving foreign aid.

*I*ntegration—Sooner or Later

I needed my own aid at home because integration became a problem in many ways. Surprisingly, as a schoolgirl, it became a question of religion. Münster had 120,000 residents and more than thirty Catholic churches and chapels, but only three for us Lutherans. They were supported by church taxes collected by the state. Church and government were closely linked. Ministers and priests, were paid the same as government officials and not as in the U.S., by the congregation. My school offered religious instruction twice a week as a regular part of the curriculum, believing that moral training, such as the ten Commandments, was as important as academic subjects.

Münster was a primarily Catholic town, an Episcopal seat. Günter and I grew up with a group of mostly Catholic children in our neighborhood, but both of us attended predominantly Lutheran schools. The German calendar contains many dates to remind us to celebrate religious events. But in Münster, Good Friday created a conflict between Protestants and Catholics.

For a long time it was only a Protestant holiday. For the Catholics it was mainly a fasting day, and they would pound their rugs in the garden and make other racket, just to demonstrate their Catholicism. All these provocations did not make any sense since Good Friday is highly acknowledged in every Christian religion.

In the early 1920s, I got my share of the religious skirmishes every Good Friday. The entire school would meet in the morning in the Lutheran Apostles' Church, a hall church of the twelfth century which once belonged to a Franciscan order. But it was forced out during secularization in 1804 under Napoleon I when he conquered Europe. He abolished all religious activities and stabled his horses in the Apostles' Church. When Europe was freed in 1813 of French occupation after Napoleon's defeat at Leipzig, Prussian authorities gave the deserted church to the Lutherans. This way it became ours, but not to everyone's taste. Some Catholic fanatics never forgot nor forgave that switch, and it seemed I had to suffer for it.

Each Good Friday I would walk alone from home to the Apostles' Church for the service on that holy day. It was a thirty-minute walk which led me through the Prinzipalmarkt, a main shopping street and Münster's pride and joy. Visualize an open wide street a block long, with the fourteenth century town hall at one end and the contemporary church of Saint Lambert at the other. Both sides were framed by colonnades of high-gabled medieval town houses, an expression of the growing civic pride of the twelfth century burghers. Münster had prospered as a member of the powerful Hanseatic League of seafaring merchants of northern Europe, a mighty protective federation of free cities along the Baltic Sea that had joined together for mutual commercial benefit. Artistically ornamented townhouses were built on narrow plots, four stories high. To gain more living space, their top floors projected far out over the street and were supported by an arcade of ornamented stone pillars, forming a sheltered path for shops and coffee houses.

Hidden behind these pillars, groups of Catholic children waited to harass me. For them it was no holiday. About half a dozen of them would follow me, taunting me, and screaming that the devil was going to get me. Frightened I started running and they chased after me until we came to my church. There the Lutheran boys standing outside came to my rescue, and the chase started in the opposite direction, this time with the Lutherans in hot pursuit. Thus the Reformation was still alive among those of my generation. We didn't know why, only on that particular day sharp dissents divided Catholics and Lutherans.

Afterwards I gave Mutti a dramatic account of my frightening morning, hoping for sympathy. But she called it exaggeration since most of our neighbors and friends were Catholic and no hostilities ever arose. Despite my sufferings I had to concede she was right, since I had been chased by strangers.

Günter and I had many Catholic playmates. As a matter of fact, every Saturday we would help them make up their weekly list of sins which was required regularly by their school. For them it was a pain in the neck, but we had great fun suggesting offenses for their list:

"Did you steal some sugar from your mother?"

"Sorry, we already used that 'sin' last week."

"Did you swipe some pfennigs?"

"We couldn't write *that* down!"

"O.k., so put down you lied twice."

"Great! We haven't used that for a while." Since each lie counted as one sin, the number of small lies we made up together depended on the number of sins they were still short of on their list. We dutifully did our part to fill the required quota. But often we all ran out of ideas. We must have been really good kids! After all, we couldn't write everything down. Consequently we chose their sins carefully.

On their school report card, the first item was always church attendance. If it said "not regularly," that was very bad and could also reflect on all the other grades, not to mention the trouble which would follow at home. After we completed their list of sins, we all went to the nearby church of Saint Ludger to play our favorite game. Our Catholic friends would go inside, rush through their visit as gracefully as possible, and hasten to the exit at the opposite end. Meanwhile Günter and I would run around the church outside, the longer route. Whoever was first at the exit was the big winner. So our friends actually didn't lie when they wrote down "yes" they had been regular church-goers.

Every year, Münster faithfully observed several traditional church processions. In 1382 there had been the devastating plague, followed in 1383 by a catastrophic fire, when house after house was gutted by flames spreading from one narrow street to another. It was so disastrous, with so many lives lost, that on November 23, 1383, Münster's first Great Procession was started. It was headed by the bishop himself, repenting in sack-cloth and ashes, to humbly ask God to be more merciful to the town. This Great Procession and others, like the very solemn one of Corpus Christi, are still tradition today.

The whole town participated. Families would erect altars in their house entrances and place pictures or statues of saints in their windows, lavishly decorated with flowers and flickering candles. An immense and picturesque procession wound through the streets. Priests, dressed up in splendid gold brocade vestments, walked under gorgeous baldachins, borne by four men. Another priest carried the holy monstrance, followed by altar boys and the children who would partake of their first communion that year, the girls dressed all in white. Singing alternated with short recitations of sacred Latin sermons and tiny bells ringing. There were stops at the family altars for prayers and blessings, and a lot of walking, singing and public worship. Children strewed carpets of flowers on the way. I found all of this fascinating. Even though I did not understand any of the Latin or the actions, it was fun to wind through the city in the crowd, alongside my Catholic friends, and kneeling when they did. Mutti was shocked about my behavior. This was a solemn occasion and not a public show. She tried to stop me, but this was too interesting to miss. More than once I was blessed with holy water since the priest did not know that I was Lutheran.

These annual old church traditions were interrupted later by Nazi orders. First, the children were forbidden to participate and had to attend school instead. Then other Nazi interference followed. For example, church banners were forbidden to be carried so that they might not be more prominent than Hitler's swastika.

We girls were always separated in Catholic and Lutheran high schools. Mine was the *Freiherr vom Stein Schule* named after the great Prussian reformer in the cabinet of Queen Luise, early in the nineteenth century. The other school was run by nuns. Since these two schools were in constant rivalry with each other as the one leading in academics, we girls got an excellent education in each one.

The European educational system varies from the American one considerably. All subjects are not studied each day in the week. Our curriculum was crammed with at least a dozen different compulsory subjects at a time, dictated to us by a strict lesson plan at the beginning of every school year, with no chance to pick and choose. The classes started each morning at 8 a.m. and lasted until 1:30 p.m., Monday through Saturday, with five or six different subjects of approximately fifty minutes each.

Our first foreign language was introduced at the age of ten. For me it was a struggle to learn French. English was added three years later. We were also taught academic subjects such as geometry and algebra, either physics or chemistry, history, geography, biology, religion (bible study), and later religious philosophy and the faith of other creeds. Additional subjects were non-academic classes like drawing, art, gymnastics, chorus, needlework or sewing, each twice a week. In most subjects, homework was constantly due, both written and oral.

There were only a few minutes between classes and one big break of fifteen minutes when we ate our brown bag lunch. Dinner at home, our main meal, was around 2 p.m. This hectic schedule only worked smoothly because we all had our assigned seats in the classroom, which we kept the entire year. Rather than running from room to room, like here in the U.S., we stayed in place, and the teachers were the ones who changed. Thus, everyone was taught the same subjects at the same time. This program led, after thirteen years, to the *Abitur*, a high school graduation examination, which was a prerequisite for entering the university. We had time off from school only ten days at Easter, Pentecost and Christmas. Our big summer vacation lasted merely five or six weeks.

During one of our art classes we went to Saint Paul's Cathedral to see Münster's pride and joy, the elaborate astronomical clock. It is a mathematical marvel of the late Middle Ages, a masterpiece of science and art. About three stories tall, it stands in a large colonnade. The clockwork is designed to tell the time, date and the accurate positions of the stars known back then, until the year 2071.

Daily at noon, as the clock struck twelve, we watched it come to life, starting with a charming Glockenspiel and then many ornate figures would act out religious scenes. All day long a giant figure of a carved, wooden man, marked with a long stick the present day on a calendar along with pertinent details for the day, such as the stars and Catholic saints. I had a hard time comprehending that this mathematical miracle, with its intricate wheelwork, was activated only by hidden, massive weights.

On April 8, 1932, Hitler showed up in Münster. Joseph Goebbels, a high-ranking Nazi, had drummed up a massive election campaign in our enormous Münsterland Hall. Normally it was used for all kinds of large-scale events such as exhibitions, or horse and bicycle races. Since we were not Hitler's favorite city, being predominantly Catholic, it was his only visit. I can't remember anything spectacular about it, or if Goebbels was even able to fill that huge hall. A Westphalian is not easily deflected from his chosen path, which was opposite to Nazism.

The sensation of the year, undoubtedly, was not Hitler with his detested Nazi Party, but rather the extensive preparations for an enormous folk festival in June. We awaited the visit of the historic *Pankgrafen*, founded by knights and templers centuries ago in Berlin-Wedding at the river Panke. They supported many acts of public welfare. But from time to time they went out on their journeys of chivalry, dressed in medieval costumes, to serve their knight's duties in private warfare. In 1932, it was the 550-year celebration of their founding. They would venture to Westphalia to "conquer" Münster, taking it by storm. Our Senate accepted the challenge.

We definitely had no time for the Nazis. The "enemy" showed up as expected to storm our city. They appeared in their historical mercenary costumes of the Wallenstein era of 350 years ago—gorgeous to look at, but impractical for storming old ramparts. It was a long and wonderful spectacle to see the fight about a small piece of old city wall, all under our applause, a jovial and hilarious battle. When the evening came, the quarrelsome *Pankgrafen* marched peacefully in a beautiful procession into the brightly decorated city center. Münster was in a very historical mood, also celebrating the anniversary of the Peace of Westphalia, which took place approximately three hundred years earlier. A commemorative coin had even been minted as a replica of the original one. Today it is a collector's item.

The fun part lasted for two days, with eating, drinking and dancing in restaurants and wood-panelled, cozy beer pubs, which could be found on almost every corner of Münster. For our visiting "enemy," each evening was brought to a close, as in old days, by the tower-watchman of Saint Lambert who tooted his horn to the four winds every half hour during the night. How could we even imagine at the time that our fun-filled war play would be followed in just a few years by the real thing.

In school, a must in German literature, even after 1933, was the novella *Die Judenbuche*, The Jews' beech tree, a true event which was in great contrast to Nazi ideology. It is a somber life story based on real occurrences dealing with crime and guilt, where destiny in the long run avenges the mysterious murder of a Jew, by doing him justice. It was written by our famous Westphalian poetess, Annette von Droste-Hülshoff, also Germany's greatest female poet of the nineteenth century. She had set the scene in the eighteenth century using Münster's landscape of moor-land, heather, and fog-laced forests, often gloomy and misty. On school outings we visited her family estate, the moated Hülshoff castle, and also her manor *Rüschhaus* where she created famous works of world literature. Today Münster is especially proud that her picture appears on the new 20 mark bills printed in the 1980s. For me it is a friendly reminder of my school time there—until the new Euro!

Another vivid memory of my last school year in Münster, when I was eighteen, was *Karneval*, a long-standing local tradition. It goes back to an ancient heathen custom to exorcise evil demons and bad spirits of winter with ugly masks and loud noises. Today it is a fun-filled festivity that is celebrated with parades and masquerade balls, similar to the Mardi Gras in New Orleans at the same time of the year.

Whether young or old, from farmer to professor, they participated whole-heartedly. One evening I accompanied my parents and friends to a fancy carnival ball in the restaurant *Schnellmann*, a family gathering place in town. We all sat around a large table. When the rousing carnival songs were played—a new one was added to the repertoire each year—everybody loosened up and we started singing and swaying to the music with arms linked together, called *schunkeln*. Though during the dancing Papa got suspicious when the same man would ask me repeatedly for a dance.

One of the evening's highlights was a contest to conduct the big orchestra, for ladies only. The best performer got a prize. The catch was that the lady had to do the directing while standing on top of a tall table, with as much temperamental gesticulation as possible, and with her skirt hiked up so her footwork could be seen. Quite naturally, all the men became cavaliers and were most anxious to help the different ladies get up there.

The fun and frolic went on until Rose Monday and Shrove Tuesday, or Mardi Gras, the highlights of the pre-Lenten carnival. Nobody wanted to miss either day. My recollection of Rose Monday is that after school I met my parents in a local restaurant. They had picked out a window table for lunch on the second floor far in advance, an ideal spot for watching the yearly Rose Monday carnival parade afterwards as a highlight of the crazy season. The day was also called Mad Monday, meaning to live it up before Lent. And live it up we did!

It was a colorful parade. The entire local theater company took part in it with floats and all of the theatrical posturing and satire on politics, fairy tales, jokes about the town, the Anabaptists, and the town's dignitaries. There were marching bands, and Prince Carnival and his princess reigned on the throne with crown and scepter. He proudly swung the key of the town hall that had been turned over to him for the day to emphasize Prince Carnival's rule. (A new couple was proclaimed every year.) They graciously threw candies to the cheering spectators along the route.

We went home at 4 p.m. and then to bed right away. Because we would join the fun again later. We got up again at 8 p.m. for an extensive crazy night visiting different restaurants, again together with friends. What fun we had making the tour and listening to the witty *Büttenreden* (satirical portrayals of the time). Again, Papa watched me closely while I danced. Besides all the devils and witches, many people put on a beautiful display of exquisite and expensive historical costumes. Some were more undressed than dressed. It was early morning when we came home tired but convinced that we had not missed a thing. Unfortunately I had to be in school in a few hours.

Next day, Shrove Tuesday, the last day of the carnival, a delegation of university students came to our lyceum for girls, asking the director to close the school at 10 a.m. because it would be impossible to hold the reserved seats for their dates at the restaurants any longer, particularly at the *Ratskeller*. Since all the faculty badly wanted to go, too, the school closed for the rest of the day.

We all stormed into town to the Prinzipalmarkt where a band provided non-stop fiery carnival music out in the open. All traffic was completely blocked and anyone foolish enough to drive along the Prinzipalmarkt got hopelessly stuck in the dancing crowd. It amused us girls to see some of our austere male teachers in the wine taverns, closely engaged with some women who were not their wives. They certainly did not welcome our attention, but being in the center of action, it was easy to be spotted. The *Fasching Krapfen*, especially rich and delicious doughnuts, were in heavy demand. We munched on them right in the street. After coming home exhausted I had to stay there. That was the end of my carnival, because it became too wild later on.

All restaurants closed their front doors dutifully at midnight, because Lent had started, but the back doors were kept open for popular traffic in and out. On Ash Wednesday morning, some of the revelers were scattered around the benches at the many Catholic churches, their harlequin trousers barely concealed by their overcoats. But they had performed their religious duty by showing up at church and getting ashes placed on their foreheads. Some slept there peacefully, lacking the ability to get home without more rest. It is next to impossible to duplicate the atmosphere of carnival just anywhere. One can only copy the custom, but not the spirit.

On Saturdays, Münster was full of the pealing of church bells, the traditionally festive ringing in of the weekends. Often several bells could be heard at the same time from our numerous churches. Their sounds never clashed. They were melodious and beautifully harmonized with each other. I believe church bells don't take sides. They ring for the Catholics, the Protestants, or whoever likes to listen to their sound.

The Nazis knew the power of the festive peal of the church bells very well, which was a thorn in their sides. They were frustrated anyway with the great undiminished power of the Christian churches and the continual, often daring, speeches from their pulpits here in Münster. The most powerful figures were the Bishop, Count of Galen, and for us Lutherans, Karl Koch, leader of the Protestant church. On October 9, 1939, shortly after World War II had started, the ringing of the church bells was forbidden altogether in Münster by the Nazi government. Only triumphal bell ringing was allowed, or ordered, at war victory celebrations. Many church bells throughout Germany were even confiscated. This served a dual purpose: they could not be rung anymore at church services against Nazi order, and the war industry was provided with badly needed basic material. Sadly, in that process many beautiful, century-old pieces of art were melted down to their original substance, just plain metal.

At the end of the Prinzipalmarkt stood the church of Saint Lambert, the parish church of Count of Galen who was ordained bishop of Münster on October 28, 1933. Over the years his church was the place of several very famous and historical speeches castigating the regime's euthanasia program and other injustices, particularly his speeches on July 13 and August 14, 1941. He received distinct warnings from the Nazi Party because of these most daring proclamations in opposition to all Nazi guidelines, and he risked imprisonment and death. At first his beautiful old church bells dating from 1494 to 1619 were saved from confiscation. But the intrepid bishop continued his courageous sermons and stood like a rock in his congregation. After his third, especially fiery sermon on March 22, 1942, which took immense bravery, he was ordered to deliver Saint Lambert's ancient bells for the war industry, as a punishment for disobeying Nazi orders. More than a million copies of these three famous protest sermons, as well as his pastoral letters, were distributed beyond his diocese, and went out into the whole world. The Nazis feared him, knowing that the pen can be mightier than the sword. Münster was called "The Rome of the North."

Saint Lambert's Church was always overcrowded, but not only with believers. Also present were the secret Nazi informers of the Gestapo, the secret state police, who carefully jotted down every word of these fiery sermons. After the bishop's last fearless speech there was no mercy any more. A delegation of Nazi police appeared in his episcopal palace with the order to arrest him. The bishop made them wait until he had changed into his complete episcopal vestments. Then he presented himself in his austere dignity. Standing in front of the bailiffs with his crozier and high miter made this over six-foot tall man look even more majestic and intimidating. Nobody dared to lay a hand on him, and so the delegation left without its prey. Undoubtedly they had also learned why this bishop was called the "Lion of Münster," a figure of historic greatness fighting for the church and the rights of men.

The defeat was relayed to the propaganda minister Joseph Goebbels in Berlin, a former Catholic himself. Once his father, a bookkeeper and devoted church-goer, had enabled him to pursue Germanistic studies (literature, linguistics, philosophy) with the financial support of the Albertus Magnus Society, a Dominican order. So Goebbels knew a lot about the enormous power and popularity of that bishop and his church. In fear of public outcry and undying support for their bishop, he ordered the postponement of Galen's execution until the "final victory." He did not dare risk a revolt. The Nazi government was well aware of the hostile undercurrent against Hitler right from the beginning of his seizure of power, and that it was steadily increasing as the war progressed.

Goebbels persecuted the church with the murderous hatred of an apostate and the biting tongue of a fanatic. He arrested priests and monks. That he did not dare to hang, or at least imprison, the bishop, as was done with many affirmed church members and political opponents, shows how strong the power of popular resistance had grown. There had already been one early failed attempt on Hitler's life on November 9, 1939, in Munich in the Hofbräuhaus, and the Party had tried to suppress this news. Now fearing the public reaction, the Nazis were careful not to let matters come to a head. Martyrs were undesired.

From 1943-1945, during World War II, Münster suffered from particularly heavy air raids. I never understood why Münster was struck to the ground. It was one of the oldest and most beautiful medieval towns in Germany such as Rothenburg in Bavaria. Both cities were irreplaceable jewels of the Middle Ages. In the course of its long history, Münster had endured and survived many storms, but not the Allied bombing. It had the oldest school of any kind in Germany, the *Schula Paulina*, the Cathedral School of the time of Charlemagne when education was the domain of the clergy. Today it is called the Paulinum, by now over a thousand years old. On October 10, 1943, during a severe air raid, the Saint Clemens Cloister was hit and unfortunately all fifty nuns living there perished, buried under the ruins. What Hitler couldn't bring about, the Allied bombs now did.

On the afternoon of October 28, 1944, the fatal moment for the Gothic town hall of the fourteenth century had come. It stood engulfed in flames. Hours later, at 6:25 p.m., it collapsed in a storm of exploding bombs during an Allied, day air raid. The world-famous, magnificent, Gothic step-like gable facade crashed onto the pavement of the Prinzipalmarkt. In one moment it had been reduced to rubble along with nearly all the other patrician gable-fronted houses in the Prinzipalmarkt. A period of over six hundred years had fallen victim to bombs. Only some eerie, hollow-eyed windows were left here and there.

In another Allied bombardment on Palm Sunday, March 25, 1945, Münster's foundations were shaken up again and the nave of Saint Lambert collapsed, the famous church of Bishop Count of Galen's powerful seat of Nazi resistance. It was now among Münster's lost treasures. All the surrounding houses were flattened. My old Apostles' Church was badly damaged and my school was gone, too. Meanwhile the bombs fell into already existing shell holes. There was no water left for extinguishing fires. Over 90 percent of the architectural heritage in the historic center was destroyed by a barrage of bombs. On *Karsamstag*, the day before Easter, March 31, 1945, at 2 p.m., the first American tanks entered devastated Münster, shooting into the remaining ruins, all that was left of the inner historic city.

The bombing caused the total destruction of old residential districts and also of one of my parents' apartment houses. All tenants who hadn't fled to the countryside were dead. By then I was in Berlin and stayed there right up to the bitter end. Now the war had ended for Münster, but not for all of Germany. The devastated city was occupied by the Allied Forces, and the Bishop Count of Galen fought with the same fearless courage shown earlier against Hitler, this time against the arbitrariness of the conquerors.

Since historic Münster was almost destroyed people vegetated in the ruins. The city council planned to abandon the old grounds completely and construct a new Münster somewhere else, possibly near the town of Roxel. But they had not "reckoned with the host," and the initiative of the returning citizens who had fled to the country. They had never thought of abandoning their historic foundation, and the townsfolk took the initiative into their own hands. There was no time for self-pity, but only for immediate action. With love, devotion, an astonishing vitality and hard work, they cleared the colossal chaos of rubble with shovels, hammers, cement mixers, and the strong will to rebuild. This time the Catholics and Protestants worked together.

After endless months of mostly unpaid hard labor, seven days a week, the wartime destruction gave way to postwar faithful reconstruction. Fresh life appeared in the ruins. People took pains to preserve the former character of the old city with a touch of modernization to fulfill the needs of a present day community pulsating in harmony with tradition and progress. In spite of the immense destruction, Münster arose again like a phoenix out of the ashes, recapturing some of its past glory and history. But much still remains to be done. The reconstruction is far from finished and the city still bears the scars of the war.

Münster's Gothic town hall, once the most beautiful in Germany, was now faithfully reconstructed down to the last detail according to its original appearance. This was done at a breathtaking speed so it would be ready for the three hundred-year anniversary on October 24, 1948, which was attended by a great number of European dignitaries and heads of State. In 1648, it had been the site of the signing of the famous Westphalian Peace Treaty in the town hall's Peace Chamber, which finally ended the Thirty-Years War, one of the most disastrous European wars. It had first started in 1618 in Prague, known in history as the

Defenestration, which triggered a religious war throughout Europe for thirty years. Its course transformed German territory, located in the center of Europe, into a major battle ground for other nations' armed conflicts, which almost destroyed our country. Their repeated attacks, famine and the plague took a high toll, about half of the German population. The war ended in a European political-state rivalry and altered the map of Europe.

Germany lay in ruins and had become a puppet of foreign powers. Important provinces were seized by neighboring countries but Strassburg remained with Germany. The old first German Empire was doomed and the emperor became a nominal ruler only. It left Germany a fragmented patchwork of four kingdoms and a multitude of principalities and city-states. Austria and Prussia rose to power. Switzerland, then only a confederation of cantons, obtained its national independence from the German Empire, and so did the Protestant Netherlands. In 1648 Münster had emerged as the city of peace, even religious peace, with equal rights for both faiths, Catholicism and Protestantism, in peaceful co-existence in Germany—at least for a while.

To Your Health!

In 1926, Germany was admitted to the League of Nations, which was established after World War I in Geneva. That appeared to Papa as being important for future international cooperation. Since our economic stability had improved somehow, he had less politics and more private plans in mind for this summer, primarily his health. Papa suffered severely from rheumatism, which he had brought home from World War I as an undesirable lifelong "souvenir."

Seeking a cure at a spa has always been very common in Europe, and Papa intended to take his at Wildbad, a resort located in the Black Forest, known as part of the spa route, which runs through wooded hills and mountains bordering on the Rhine valley, famous for its healing mineral springs.

Taking a cure in Germany can actually be a lot of fun, and not only for the well-to-do. It is like taking a paid vacation since referrals to these spas are made by the public health insurance, which all lower income people are required to be a part of and pay monthly premiums. It also covers routine dental care. All members may apply for several weeks of therapy in state-subsidized spas, which is cheerfully funded by the social welfare system for public health and fitness. So naturally everyone suffers from some symptoms at one time or another, even if the ailment may be imaginary in order to enjoy a "sick" vacation. One can apply for these cures every few years and the public insurance pays all or part of the expenses. No one is excluded. Whoever desires a more luxurious cure catering to the rich and famous, like people who pay for the higher private insurance, has an unlimited selection of spas to choose from. For many people the spa "flirtation," with a so-called *Kurschatten* (cure-shadow) is a standard component of the cure, just like the massages and mud packs.

The Wildbad spa was advertised as an ideal climatic health resort to those suffering from rheumatism, with strong curative powers where salutary mineral springs gush hot out of the earth. The facilities ranged from drinking the waters to taking full therapeutic baths and treatments. Papa enthusiastically read the brochure to us, noting that Charlemagne had sought relief there around the year 800 A.D., and there was some indication that the Romans had known of the resort long before Charlemagne's visit. Papa seemed to feel better already with all this good news and he was desperate enough to try it out for himself. He decided that the whole family would make the journey to Wildbad together so that he would have some company during the experimental four-week treatment.

The trip was scheduled during our summer school vacation, and Günter and I eagerly looked forward to a new adventure, even though we were only allowed to pack one very small toy in our knapsacks. Early one morning a taxi took us to the train station with our heavy luggage. Excitedly we climbed aboard the train to begin our nine-hour ride. We were fortunate to find a compartment where we could all be together and even more fortunate that Günter and I had window seats. Our train rolled out of Münster's flat countryside and gradually the scenery changed from the northern lowlands into the rolling hills and mountains of the South. Mutti had prepared sandwiches to eat along the way, and during station stops Papa bought drinks from the platform vendors to go with the food. Everything was new and exciting for us. As we rode along we wondered why the cows were in the Prussian colors of black and white in the North, but brown and white in the South. It is still that way today. We also passed pretty little onion-topped church steeples that are so typical of Bavaria.

By evening we finally reached Wildbad. The trees were indeed very tall here and the air cool and refreshing. Papa took a taxi to our hotel, which sat slightly above the village, and we passed rustic country houses with wooden carved balconies. The hotel stood in the middle of a manicured lawn, an impressive looking four-story building, with tall multicolored wooden shutters and flower-laden balconies. A soft fragrance of blooming bushes filled the quiet evening air. What a perfect setting for an adventurous vacation, and we entered with high hopes.

Papa ordered a light supper, which was soon served in the large dining room where we already were assigned a table for our four-week stay, luckily next to a big window so Günter and I wouldn't miss any outside activities while eating. From our rooms on the second floor we had a great view of the spa park, which was illuminated at night. How exciting all of this was.

So far Günter and I were completely unaware that the entire style of gracious living at a spa was geared toward adults, and taking children into this type of hotel could also be torture for them as well as their parents. Breakfast on the first morning was exceptional—a soft boiled egg and crisp croissants with butter and jam, plus much to our delight, small pastries. As children we were supposed to be quiet, according to the old rule that children should be seen but not heard. That was no problem for Günter and me. Our eyes were bigger than our stomachs and it would be difficult to make any noise when your mouth was full of sweets.

After breakfast we took a stroll through the village because Papa had to set up his therapeutic program with the medical staff. Wildbad was nestled in a narrow valley hugged by woods and mountains, with many pastel-colored half-timbered houses, so typical of that area. Our parents called it an enchanting health resort. In the center of an old market place was a big basin with water-spewing stone animals. As tempting as this gushing water was, we weren't allowed to splash our hands in it, only admire it from afar.

Back at the hotel for lunch Günter and I expected a fun meal like breakfast. Instead, a warm, three-course meal was served. We hated it on sight. It was too much adult food, and besides that, we were still full from breakfast a few hours ago. But we had to eat everything that was served and learned the hard way that more food, forced into an already full stomach, could be sheer torture.

After lunch we walked through the wide, lush spa park with well-groomed flower beds and promenades where guests could stroll leisurely under the trees and rest on shady benches. There was no romping around for us children. We had to be well-behaved, holding hands, while walking in front of our parents along the little river Enz. What fun was that? The bubbling creek beckoned to us and we longingly kept eyeing some pebbles we would have loved to throw in.

The worst part of the day, though, was the evening meal, a four-course dinner. Obviously the menu paid no attention to calories or cholesterol. It began with a soup, which we children found unnecessary, followed by a warm fish dish. That sight alone turned my stomach. Then came the main course, which was rich and sickening, and finally dessert. Günter and I would have had enough with just the dessert, and that probably twice. But we had to eat everything else first. Our stomachs were not used to such an amount of food and eating habits. Instead, we had to stuff it all in or we wouldn't have gotten any dessert, the only attractive part of the entire meal. After dinner, instead of running through the garden, we had to sit still in an elegant parlor while the men smoked thick cigars, which made me cough. Fifty percent of this ordeal was true suffering, but the other half was exaggerated in protest against our boredom. What kind of vacation was that for us children?

All the lavish courses were meant to make up for the past lean years. The menu did not spare any adult the pleasure of his palate. We children, however, with our limited stomach capacity, were unable to consume such an abundance of rich food. So it did not take long at dinner the next evening before I whispered terrified to Mutti that I felt sick to my stomach. It earned me a stern look from Papa which meant behave! But I couldn't any longer. I ran away from the table during the fish dish, and raced across the elegant dining room filled with distinguished dinner guests consuming their excellent meals, and out the door. There I couldn't hold the food down any more, and the management of the fine hotel could identify the evening courses once more on the exquisite, red carpeting of the elegant entrance hall. This time I did not even fake it like with Omi's wonderful blue carp years earlier. This time it was for real.

Strangely enough, my whole family was suddenly around me and I was taken upstairs. Obviously they must have lost their own appetites. Even the manager of the hotel appeared in our rooms, followed by a waiter who brought me a delicious omelet. "That poor child," by that they meant me, "had to get at least something to eat." What an unexpected success. After that incident we were served children's meals and portions, and Günter profited from my endured suffering.

We quickly settled into a daily routine. Papa loved everything to be organized, even our vacations. Every morning started with his scheduled special treatments. This procedure took hours with therapeutic baths, mud packs and massages, all in the customary style and routine of a German cure that all spa guests believe in. Meanwhile, Mutti took Günter and me to the huge indoor swimming pool filled with thermal spring water for the fitness and indoor activities of the visitors.

Günter knew how to swim and took off right away. I stayed at the shallow end, more afraid than amused. Mutti was also a good swimmer and wanted to teach me. She put an enormous cork belt around my waist, the fashionable but clumsy life preserver back in 1926 which is now outdated. Then she showed me the breast stroke and kept her face above the water all the time. I liked that part, but when I tried it, my big cork girdle insisted on slipping backwards. In no time my behind was lifted high out of the water and my head hopelessly dipped under. I didn't see any fun in that at all.

After many unsuccessful attempts I had to try it on my own. To get rid of that cumbersome belt one day I pulled on one end of the loose slip knot on my back, and right away it sailed away on its own. Bye-bye belt! Now I was free to jump around again and discovered to my own amazement that I could suddenly swim, and proudly followed Mutti into the deep end of the pool.

Papa needed to rest after his morning treatments, but that was not to be for us children. He had planned a daily schedule for our entire vacation. It is very wrong to assume that such a trip was the incarnation of freedom and fun. We had to bring along some school books, especially the vocabularies, Günter's in Latin and mine in French. When Papa rested, Mutti would hear our lessons in our adjacent room. If I didn't know the correct answer, I sometimes tried to get away with just mumbling something with a lot of nasal sounds to make it sound like French. But Mutti made me spell out the word, and I got caught. We never could find enough reasons to get out of that boring study period.

Looking back on those episodes much later, I had the hunch that Mutti did not like those lessons any more than we did, but they were Papa's order. At that time the man, as the sole bread-winner, dominated the entire family life with strict supervision. He was the head of the household and controlled all activities, social, educational or whatever else.

Dear marvelous Mutti was not disturbed by pontifical decrees and handled our everyday life her own way without ruffling any feathers.

Calling it defending her rights would be a big understatement. Often she would just do the opposite, according to the German saying: "*Er ist der Herr im Haus. Sie macht trotzdem was sie will.*" He is the master of the house. She does what she wants anyway. And in the end it appeared to be what Papa had wanted all along.

Since our meal problem was solved, the swimming accomplished and our vocabulary lessons occasionally forgotten, the fun could begin. We would stroll along the gently murmuring Enz through the richly colored spa park, fringed with numerous exotic botanical rarities, tulip trees, cypresses and many more wonders of Mother Nature that I had never seen. The only exotic plant I was familiar with was a lovely palm tree at home in our living room. It thrived beautifully since Mutti had a green thumb. The park also offered all kinds of amenities. Admission was free because it was included in the pre-paid "cure tax."

Amidst the cultivated green surroundings and flowers was a large outdoor pavilion where daily concerts were given, which was surrounded by a seating area for about two hundred people. Children had to be quiet so they wouldn't disturb the adults while they were listening or dozing off during the music. In bad weather, the concerts were held under the roof of an enormous open-air recreation hall where there was also a pump room with a well of mineral water and drinking facilities. That special area was covered with glazed tiles and was spotless. Behind the bar, which was shaped like a half moon, pleasant young employees dressed in native costumes served mineral water to the guests. From time to time they went down a spiral staircase to the well, where we could see the spring water gushing out of the earth like a fountain, before it was collected in pitchers. That valuable liquid was served in tall glass mugs with a sturdy handle. It was even bottled for export.

But that healthy and famous mineral water was another one of Mother Nature's tricks, created in one of her bad moments. Things which are supposed to be beneficial for one's health often taste and even smell bad, like sulphur. Since drinking the water was included in the cure-tax, everyone consumed a large quantity of it several times a day. Günter and I also got our glasses, and we had fun watching the newcomers make faces with their first taste of the precious liquid. We must have looked like a drinking bunch, all walking around with our tall mugs or sitting on benches in the park.

For me it was much more interesting to walk up and down the section that was flanked by souvenir and toy stands. I had my eye on a special kind of doll from the very beginning, one in a traditional Black Forest costume. Her hat, called a *Bollenhut*, (*Boll* means ball) was covered with fourteen large colorful pompons, representing the fourteen Catholic saints. The pompons are black for married women, and red for those who are unmarried. I kept pointing out the dolls with the red pompons and my parents found them "nice." That was all. Getting more to the point, I was unaware that the price for one was several hundred marks, my wish was out of the question, and my spirits were crushed. Down the drain went my longing for something to hold in my arms.

It was boredom more than anything else that made me covet that particular doll. These typical Black Forest dolls were more for looks than play and Mutti soon found something else to lift my spirits, and also to keep me busy. In one of the booths snakes were sold—not live ones, but made out of many interlocking wood segments, about a foot long, which flip-flopped in such a way that they looked real. They were brightly colored and not at all as ugly as in nature. Oh yes, I wanted such a fascinating snake.

Mutti bought me one, and I was overjoyed. Holding it in my hand exactly as the salesman had done, I easily brought it to life with carefully applied pressure. Then my snake would swing its tail or reach for something we wanted to point at. Günter and I really perfected maneuvering it. From then on I never went anywhere without my snake. While promenading in the crowd I made my harmless snake pop out now and then to startle the unsuspecting recipients of this "treat," who were resting on their benches. The game worked, accompanied by their horrified shrieks. Mutti had not anticipated this outcome with the snake, and she told me that one does not frighten old people.

In the evenings we again strolled along the river Enz, here but a small mountain stream, babbling along with soft ripples. We watched the trouts leaping between the small rocks. At the edge of the woods stood the gigantic statue of a stag that long ago had supposedly led wounded people to the healing spring. In gratitude, special festive days were dedicated to the stag. During this time of summer the large white statue could be seen after dark illuminated by shafts of lights. It seemed as if the stag were just coming out onto the meadow, standing there in full light and beauty. The statue looked so proud and real to me that I wondered why it never moved. There were great celebrations around the white deer later in the evening by candlelight. But we only saw the preparations, since we children had to go to bed early every night.

Before our stay in Wildbad came to an end, our parents planned a surprise for Günter and me. Papa announced, "What would a trip to the Black Forest be without a visit to a genuine watchmaker's cuckoo clock shop?" We children were not aware of the high reputation of the local fine-art craftsmanship as something no tourist passes up, and wondered about Papa's excitement. He had already mapped out a route and we took off the next morning on foot for a day's excursion, an incidental benefit also "for doing something for our health," as Papa called it. His painful rheumatism seemed cured to us. Now we hiked miles outside Wildbad on winding roads through forests and glades. Sometimes a little waterfall tumbled noisily to the bottom of a narrow gap between rocks, too deep for us to touch. Finally after several hours, breaking out of the woods, our road dropped towards the bottom of a green wooded valley with a storybook scenery.

We had arrived at a quaint little village far off the beaten track in the middle of a blooming meadow. It was dotted with typical half-timbered houses beneath immense deep roofs that made the buildings look like chickens protected by a mother hen. When we entered one of these cozy, flower-laden places, we were suddenly surrounded by cuckoo clocks everywhere. They cuckooed like crazy from all the walls. What a display! This sure was a spectacle! "Choose one," Papa encouraged us. Totally fascinated, we were unable to make any choices from among such an overwhelming selection. Fortunately Mutti solved our problem and picked one out for us that was not too big and not too small. Every half hour and on the hour, a replica of a little colorful bird would pop its head out of a tiny door and chirp "cuckoo," up to twelve times at noon and midnight. With every cuckoo he would nod forward, making him look as if he were alive. The watchmaker's shop was like a fairyland, and we were the proud owners of a new "toy" that even talked to us.

Happily we carried our carefully wrapped new acquisition back to the hotel. Without it we would have missed the most enjoyable event of the entire trip. Now we weren't so disappointed anymore about what the adults called a marvelous spa experience. Since we were to return home two days later, we didn't unwrap the package until we were back in Münster. There our cuckoo clock got a privileged place on the wall. It had to be wound up every night by pulling the two pine cone-shaped weights that hung on brass chains, which looked like gold to me. Günter and I took turns in winding up our cuckoo clock. From then on, it was highly treasured and cuckooed throughout our entire life, which wasn't always appreciated by our house guests. After their first night's stay, they usually asked if the cuckooing couldn't be stopped, particularly during the night! It was just too much for them, especially the twelve times at midnight. Our family was so used to it that something was missing in the house when we forgot to wind the clock and we couldn't sleep without that familiar cuckoo.

The yearly cures seemed to have been beneficial to Papa and he continued to take them regularly, but without us for it was too boring. Ten years later when we lived in Berlin, Papa would go in the company of his friend Mr. Behrmann. His wife, Mutti and I would drive the men down to their destination in our car, and we women would take off on our own trip afterwards. I always drove since I was the only one in the family with a license. Although Günter had one, he was seldom home.

On one of these trips out to Wildbad, we decided to take a scenic mountain route and promptly got lost. The winding road narrowed increasingly. Luckily a priest happened to be passing by and Papa immediately asked him for directions. He pleasantly told us the correct way and then asked who would take over the driving now. There were two couples in the car besides me at the steering wheel. He got truly upset that none of the men would continue the drive over such a dangerous, winding mountain route. We didn't enlighten him about the fact that Papa, sitting next to me, didn't even know how to drive. The worried priest put his hand on my arm through the open window to hold us back, and he was obviously disturbed when we continued on, with me behind the wheel. Since it runs in the family that we tend to look much younger than our birth certificate states, he must have taken me for merely a teenager. We were sure that this nice and caring man would say a prayer for all of us, which can never hurt. So our drive continued carefully through small twisting curves and along steep slopes until we hit the main road again, and arrived safely in Wildbad. After unloading the men, we would return after four weeks to pick them up again.

I especially remember one return trip when we three women stopped first in a different resort, probably the famous Bad-Pyrmont, where the spring water tasted even worse than in Wildbad. We obtained an empty wine bottle from a store owner and filled it with that nasty spring water. Then we asked him to cork it for us, to make it look like a genuine bottle of wine. It was not the first time he had been asked to do that trick, and his work was perfect.

When we arrived home, we uncorked the "fine wine" in front of the men and presented our drink very elegantly in wine glasses on a tray, toasting them formally with good wishes for their restored health. The men liked all that attention and took a big swallow of the precious liquid, but only for a fraction of a second, because they immediately spit it back into the glass, not at all in a gentleman-like manner. We tried to assure them of the healthy properties of that drink, but to no avail. At least it was not poison. It only tasted like it. Later we appeased their anger with a fine bottle of good wine from Papa's wine cellar. Skal!

Love Thy Neighbor, But Not Too Much

Totensonntag, Germany's Memorial Day, is celebrated every year at the end of November. In Münster, we would go to the cemetery to visit Omi's grave in the early afternoon. As always, it was a cold and miserable day, typical of our gloomy November weather. But in spite of this, we would all go on that special day to show our respect. Günter and I walked in front of our parents, together carrying a large wreath, while Mutti held a bouquet of flowers. Omi was buried in the separate section for Lutherans. In Münster, the Catholics and Lutherans were kept neatly apart even in death. It went so far that when a couple died, and both were of different faiths (mixed marriages were a sin anyway) they were buried each in their respective section which was separated by a high stone wall that kept the deceased divided. A tall iron gate connected the two graveyards.

To add to the sadness of the occasion, a brass band played somber tunes at the military graves to honor the dead veterans. It could be heard from afar and gave me goose bumps, leaving us in a very depressed mood. Our ritual always ended with hot coffee and cake to warm up our bodies and souls after these cold excursions. Each year we repeated this ceremony. After World War II, we could no longer visit Omi's grave because severe bombings had turned the large cemetery into a field of huge craters. Later, all of the remains were collected and reburied in a common grave, regardless of their religion.

I liked open air events more, and one Easter Monday, the well-known Gerhardt Fieseler and Ernst Udet gave a big aviation show at our airport. Fieseler was internationally famous as a stunt flyer and the builder of the Fieseler-Storch airplane which was renowned for its reliability of operation. Udet, then only known as a fighter pilot of World War I, was also a famous stunt flyer. Later, as a high ranking General in World

War II, he was murdered in 1941 because he was under suspicion of being involved in a secret plot against Hitler.

To brighten our daily life, Papa bought a piano one day, one of the old upright black instruments in fashion then. Actually that kind is still popular today, but rather than calling it plain black, the color has been elevated to "ebony" and the price now matches the color. Papa played the violin and it was his ambition to make good musicians out of us as pianists. I loved to sing but could never carry a tune, which did not discourage Papa at all. Günter and I started with private lessons. Once a week we went to Mrs. Altmann, dragging the sheet music along. She was a warm-hearted war widow who loved children, and I got away with just about everything—like sitting under the keyboard and asking her to play for me, just to pass the time. Since I was very young, my hands were too small to reach the eighth key of the octave, and with only seven of them, the tunes often did not sound like music. In addition to our weekly lesson, we were supposed to practice one hour daily, and that was my longest sixty minutes of the entire day. I often tried to skip this ordeal, but Papa usually managed to catch me. Günter's resistance to piano playing was much more successful as he frequently just disappeared when it was time to practice.

My true love was dancing, and I was thrilled to become a member of a children's dance group that was started by our gymnastics teacher. Because of my enthusiastic dancing, I was selected for the leading role in a pantomime of several acts of the Cinderella fairy tale which we performed for a housewives' club. Mutti made my costumes consisting of an outer ugly dark dress and a golden one worn underneath. On stage, kneeling alone in tears, as the good fairy would touch me, I secretly opened the snaps of the ugly dark dress and it fell off as I stood up, revealing the beautiful golden one, bringing "aahs" from the audience. Then followed one of my solo dances as I prepared to meet the prince. Since the programmed dance steps were too unimaginative for me, I would make up my own dances according to my feeling for the music, which was agreeable to the teacher because it eliminated lengthy rehearsals. Although we received great applause and invitations from other clubs, Mutti was not so thrilled, even though she had her hairdresser create cute Shirley Temple-like curls out of my straight hair in order to enhance my looks. However, she became more alarmed than impressed as she watched me dancing with such great enthusiasm and obvious talent. Her plans for me involved things other than dancing. As a result this was the end of it, under Mutti's clever pretense that I needed to devote my attention full time to my schoolwork to improve my "C" in French. But I have retained my love for dancing to this day.

When Günter was confirmed at the age of fifteen in the Apostles' Church on Easter 1928, the most common presents were books, and he received quite a number of them. In vogue at that time was Hans Grimm's *Volk ohne Raum* (People without Living Space), which took place in Africa. That book title later became the slogan for the Nazis. On this occasion, at the age of twelve, I too received a present, my first bicycle. However, it came with conditions attached, including having to clean it regularly. I promised everything, hoping that Günter, of course, would help me.

During the Easter vacation our family went to Saint Goar in the Rhine valley, where the river makes a sharp bend around the steep rock of the Lorelei. Papa explained that the Rhine had been a major route for commercial ships and pleasure crafts for two thousand years and that even the Romans had used this route to Germany. This is a fairy tale region with many medieval castles and cathedrals and we could see in the distance the two old fortresses, "Cat" and "Mouse." They have faced each other across the Rhine for more than five centuries, and according to legend, fought each other over the right to collect river tolls— two neighbors in animosity.

Burg Rheinfels, built high above the Rhine gorge over seven hundred years ago, was once one of the strongest castles in the area. Today, it has been partially restored and as we entered the courtyard, it seemed as if we had stepped back into the Middle Ages. A guided walking tour led us through its many subterranean gloomy vaults and spooky tunnels, some being so low we had to stoop to move through them. After that strenuous experience we all relaxed in the castle's newly opened beer garden.

The next day we crossed the Rhine River to the small town of Saint Goarshausen, clinging to the narrow bank between the river and the legendary Lorelei rock which rises four hundred fifty feet almost vertically out of the swirling waters. According to an old saga, the bewitching Lorelei sat high on the cliff grooming her long blond hair with a golden comb while her siren-singing lured boatmen to their death on the reefs beneath her. The saga continues that the evil spell was broken when she threw herself from the cliff and vanished forever into the reefs below. Here the narrowest part of the river creates dangerous rapids and visibility around the sharp bend is zero. Today, a tower with a signal system provides safety for the river traffic.

Upon arriving home after our exciting trip, Günter and I had a hard time getting used to our heavy load of homework. And for the first time in my life, I got sick. Dr. Lewis, our Jewish family doctor, diagnosed my illness to be a frontal cavity catarrh and light meningitis. I felt miserable and had a high fever. He came daily for two weeks, sometimes as late as midnight. He was a very busy, well-liked doctor who still made house calls. With his help I survived, and though weak, went back to school after three weeks. Günter said I "jumped from death's shovel again." The English equivalent is that you had one foot in the grave and the other on a banana peel.

I had to work extra hard to catch up on all the classwork I had missed. Günter and I would do our homework together on a large table in his room, but too often we did everything but study. He would write notes to his girl friends in my school which he wanted me to deliver the next day, and I was proud to play Cupid for him. While Günter was writing notes, I would be busy embroidering colorful tablecloths for Mutti's birthday or for Christmas. But, we often did actual homework, and Günter would solve my math problems while I looked up his long list of Latin vocabulary in the dictionary. He used to keep his Latin book under his pillow at night, hoping the knowledge would enter his head through osmosis, as with the magic *Nürnberger Trichter* (Nueremberg funnel). According to an old folk tale, it was put on top of one's head, and wisdom just penetrated into the brain without effort.

After my illness, the slow return of my health and strength concerned Dr. Lewis, and to speed up my full recovery he advised that I be taken to the seashore, specifically the Frisian Islands. They stretch miles off shore parallel to the North Sea coastline, and have an ocean climate that is well known for its healthy cures. So, during summer vacation we all took off for several weeks to the island of Langeoog which was noted for its eight-mile long fine sandy beaches. Everything was fine at first. Günter and I were enjoying swimming in a sheltered area of the ocean, building a big sand castle on the beach, and playing hide and seek among the sand dunes or hundreds of beautiful colored beach chairs with rounded hoods shaped like baskets. At low tide it was fun to collect sea shells in the mud flats. But my pleasure was short-lived. One night a powerful spring tide hit the island and the next morning, after the storm finally subsided, to my amazement a huge section of the beach was partly engulfed by the sea. Our beautiful large sand castle was gone. Now a crew cleaned up the debris tossed around by the rough tide during the night. Our peaceful beach had changed into a wild and frightening area.

I felt uneasy about how different the beach suddenly looked. Because of the rough water, we had been warned not to swim out beyond the first of three flags which marked our swimming area. I did not want to go swimming at all, but Günter started teasing me about being afraid of a little rough water and would not stop until I lost my temper. Shouting, "Just watch what I dare to do!" I ran into the stormy ocean. I would show him! But I immediately lost my footing in the shifting sandy bottom, and as I tried to swim back, the waves battered me under. In no time I was being pulled farther out past the first and second flag, I could hear the watch tower's horn signalling that a swimmer had gone out too far into the ocean.

I panicked. Terrified, I started screaming for help while being pushed under water constantly by powerful waves. Suddenly, Günter was at my side and shouted into my ear to hold onto him. Being much taller and stronger than I, he grabbed my hair and arms and began pulling me toward the shore. Somehow, we made it and I landed breathlessly in Mutti's arms. Even though the whole incident took only a few minutes, I was totally exhausted. A lifeboat had been sent out after Günter and me already. My enthusiasm for the ocean was gone. No love for Neptune anymore. The next day I turned down Günter's invitation to go swimming with him even though the water was calm. I should have taken him up on his suggestion because my frightening experience made me shun the water for years. Shortly thereafter we returned home.

As autumn approached, Münster's most popular festival, the feast of Saint Lambert, would start. It probably dates back to the heathen Germanic festival of sun worship, in Münster christianized in honor of Saint Lambert. According to a medieval custom, guild workers were given candles to illuminate their work because twilight fell early. This was a major event. Light was not usually provided since candles were expensive. (Nowadays candles have become cheaper, labor more expensive.)

For three days the festival is celebrated with fervor by the whole town, starting on the sixteenth of September. Children sing traditional songs while dancing around a three-legged pyramid that is wrapped with asparagus greens and richly illuminated by Chinese lanterns. The center of this activity takes place at the Saint Lambert fountain in front of the Saint Lambert Church. Everybody joins in. The traditional songs and dances were also acted out in separate neighborhoods and we performed ours in our courtyard. We all would play the farmer's game, sung in a low German dialect that is closely related to English, which is like the American "The Farmer in the Dell." (That song is still sung to the same melody as the original German one.)

Prior to the festival date, we would ride our bicycles out into the country and gather bundles of heather, now in glorious full bloom, and use it for a lavender mantle around our home-made pyramid instead of the expensive asparagus greens. The final step was to decorate it with Chinese lanterns. Then we would solicit our parents, neighbors and friends for contributions for fireworks so our own private festival would have a spectacular finale. Each year we looked forward to this public festival the same way children in the U.S. anticipate Halloween, which is unknown in Germany. In the medieval times Halloween was a holy day, the night before All Saints' Day. Today it is mainly a night for costume fun.

For us in Germany, October 31 is associated with the day in 1517 when Martin Luther nailed his ninety-five theses to the door of the Castle Church in Wittenberg on the eve of All Saints' Day. As a monk in a late medieval monastery, a preacher and professor of theology, he was challenging some practices of the Pope, such as granting indulgences for money. Luther, on the other hand, preached that salvation is a free gift of God. He wrote his theses in Latin so as to provoke discussion only among the clergy. However, they translated them into German and Gutenberg's newly invented printing technology allowed the message to spread rapidly throughout the land. He intended with his theses to reform the church, not split it, but the result was the founding of Protestantism.

We in Münster always found a good excuse to celebrate another festival, like the baker's "Good Monday." It dates back to 1683 when the Turks laid siege to Vienna, which was then part of the German empire, the first German Reich. So it happened that two young bakers from Münster were in Vienna, according to the custom of the time that young journeymen traveled around the country. At the crack of dawn, when they were preparing their bread, they heard digging underneath them, and soon, part of their bakery floor collapsed into a secret underground passage. A small band of Turks stormed out of this tunnel to invade Vienna, but Münster's bakers gave alarm and the invasion of Vienna had failed.

The two brave bakers were immediately called before the emperor and were granted one free wish for saving the city from the Turks, but all they wanted was that all bakers in their home town of Münster be given one free enjoyable holiday each year. The emperor gladly agreed to their *Guten Montag* (Good Monday), as it came to be known. In 1683, this was their only free day during the year, and ever since, it is celebrated in June all day long and we admired their magnificent parades in medieval costumes to relive the historic event. Croissants or crescents were served in town, symbolizing the curved shape of the Turkish moon.

Papa had more of a love for our present time and all the latest gadgetry in the world, and was particularly intrigued with the early pioneer days of radio. In Germany, radio began as a state institution, and not as private enterprise as in the U.S. with numerous competing radio stations. Münster acquired its own broadcast transmitter in the 1920s, the first one of its kind in all of Westphalia. One afternoon, Papa sent Mutti and Günter downtown on a very time-consuming errand while I had to stay home and practice my piano lesson. Shortly after they left, the door bell rang and a strange man came in whom Papa led into the adjoining living room. He closed the door into the dining room in which I was practicing, leaving it ajar just enough that he could supervise me hammering away at my Czerny exercises. I could hear the opening of cardboard boxes and other strange noises in addition to quiet conversation, but was unable to see anything that was happening in the room. No matter how often I tried, I had no luck in satisfying my curiosity.

In the meantime, Mutti and Günter had come home, and Papa would not allow them to go into the living room either. Mutti freed me from the piano stool, and Günter was angry with me because I was unable to provide any information on what had happened before they arrived, and as usual, he called me a stupid little girl again. He never failed to remind me he was three years older than I, and since his birthday was March 8 and mine March 15, he took special delight in taunting me about being four years older during that one week between our birthdays. But at mine he always bought me a hyacinth with his pocket money because I loved this flower, even though I had no money to buy him anything.

Before I could think of a good rebuttal to Günter's hurtful remark, we heard the strange man finally leaving. Now we were all allowed to enter the living room where, with a big gesture, Papa pointed to a small apparatus sitting on a side table. He explained that this was our first radio, ready to listen to, only I couldn't hear anything. It was one of the first crystal detector sets that used headphones because it had no speakers. It operated from a type of big storage battery sitting on the floor, which I was forbidden to ever touch because its acid was highly poisonous, but which Günter and I later often had to take downtown to be recharged.

There were two sets of headphones, each of which could be separated into two individual earphones. In this manner Günter and I shared one set and Mutti and Papa shared the other since everybody wanted to be first to listen to this new invention. Papa fumbled with the needle on the crystal detector as he had been instructed by the installer, but did not have much success. Günter, with no instruction, took one look at it and had it working in no time. Suddenly I heard music and a lady singing, followed by a group of people in discussion. How fantastic! Papa was the best anyone could have. I don't remember what those early radio programs consisted of because Günter and I had to go to bed at 8 p.m. so we didn't hear any evening broadcasts. They must have been poor compared to those of today. There didn't seem to be anything geared towards children, and I remember that the programs were never interrupted by commercials.

A few years later Günter announced he would build his own radio and asked for a raise in his allowance. Papa first wanted more details, but soon gave up and provided the extra money when he could not understand all of the technical terms Günter heaped on him. We didn't know how he did it, but using shellac records, he built a set that worked beautifully. And, although we didn't know it at that time, it would be our only link to the outside world in the upcoming years. Now Günter and I had our own radio set, and like Papa's, it only had head phones. A fee of several marks had to be paid monthly at the post office for each radio set owned and Papa, as usual, paid for everything. Today everything is deregularized and and the later practice of having all commercials first and then the program with no interruptions has been discontinued. This upset many Germans because the commercials break the flow and enjoyment of the performance. Now, German radio and TV programs have the commercials spaced throughout the program as in the U.S.

We could not imagine then that only a few years later, the Nazi government would take over the entire broadcasting system because they well recognized its potential value as a single nationwide means of communicating their propaganda and manipulating the masses. In March 1933, Goebbels declared in a meeting with all program producers, "The radio belongs to us and nobody else. It will render services for our ideas exclusively, and no other voice shall be heard." And, that is how it remained until April of 1945.

To love your neighbor is not always easy, particularly in different times such as periods of great political differences. It wasn't easy in the early 1930s either as the following chapter will illustrate.

Who Fools Whom

By 1929, the ten years of exorbitant reparation demands far exceeded Germany's financial ability and had brought the country to the brink of disaster. The new American Young Plan of 1929, a revision of the Dawes Plan of 1924, greatly reduced the annual payments, although still excessive, and spread them out over fifty-nine additional years to 1988.

Papa shook his head. "That means seventy years after the last war. Again a figment of the imagination. Hopefully we will all live that long. I would be 109 years old by then." He was right again, as the near future proved. The United States advanced the money to meet the payments, so Germany continued to sink deeper into debt as we lived on borrowed dollars, and eventually could no longer even make the interest payments on the U.S. loans.

Around that time I was having my very own problems. Shortly after Easter, at age thirteen, I enrolled in the first year of high school, the eighth grade, or *Untertertia*. This meant I had to take English as my second compulsory foreign language. What a load! (Ours was the King's English, not the American version.) Now, in addition to eight academic and non-academic subjects, I had to handle three languages each four times a week: German, French and English, with literature and grammar alternating. There were some mornings when I had them in such rapid sequence that I had difficulty arranging my mouth quickly enough for the next foreign pronunciation exercise. In French we had to stress a nasal sound, in English to slur the language—the more the better, while German calls for distinct vowels and clear sounds.

The relationship between teachers and students was much more formal than in the United States, and our English teacher, Miss Koss, typified that distance. The class was afraid of her because she was severe and seldom smiled, although there wasn't much to smile about in 1929. Her first instruction in learning English was: "Always capitalize yourself with a big I." This was strange to us because in German we always capitalize the addressed person, the "you," to give them the honor, and not ourselves. She also insisted that our English pronunciation would be better if we spoke as if we had a hot potato in our mouth, and the more we mumbled, the more like English it would sound. We agreed and persevered, but otherwise we found her very dull and as unpredictable as the English spelling.

Looking back years later, I have thought more tolerantly about our poor middle-aged Miss Koss. She had a right to be bitter. First, her generation had lost many of its loved ones during the war years 1914-1918, followed by dashed hopes in post-war times. And, secondly, in a period of so-called peace, she had to struggle alone through one crisis after another, and the worst was yet to come.

Suddenly, a gigantic world-wide economic catastrophe resulted from the crash of the New York stock market in October 1929. You will remember it as Black Friday, with the veterans' march on Washington, when the Great Depression made Americans poor overnight. Immediately the U.S. recalled all short-term loans and Germany's house of cards of borrowed prosperity collapsed. For the second time in the 1920s, another rampant inflation wiped out all savings and well-to-do citizens became welfare recipients overnight. Life savings could not buy a loaf of bread, and mass unemployment skyrocketed. Political radicalism flared up.

During this period of national unrest, the Nazis made their appearance on our political scene. For the previous ten years, Germany had been governed by emergency decrees and the parliament was constantly being dissolved as one chancellor followed another, some lasting only several months. Our daily life became intolerable, and even common people were changed into impoverished, hungry, embittered fanatics, willing to grasp at any straw of hope. These chaotic conditions offered great advantages to Hitler, although the Nazis thus far were merely tolerated along with the Communists and more than thirty other political parties. The Weimar Republic never had a true chance to make democracy work because the victorious powers of World War I had undermined it with excessive demands and reprisals. Thus, the growing millions of unemployed were receptive to the Nazi slogans that Hitler was a man of the common people who would be their savior in this time of despair.

In 1929, the Nazis easily multiplied their delegates in the government, and political opinions were deeply divided, even among friends. Most of us were haunted by the dread of Communism, which aided Hitler in gaining more power. For many people, something radical was welcomed, though with hesitation, because they were fed up with the Weimar government and longed for a fresh political start.

The depression was at its worst, and revolts between Communist and Nazi gangs resulted in open street fighting and bloody riots, bringing the country to the brink of civil war. Both parties favored the elimination of our moderate Weimar Republic, but which successor, Nazis or Communists, would present the greater threat? Public disorder became the norm and made it difficult for authorities to maintain peace and order. My family wanted me home before dark.

In 1931, President Hoover declared a one-year moratorium on German reparation payments to the U.S., and in 1932, at a conference in Lausanne, Switzerland, the European powers established the total national debt of 3 billion *Reichsmark*. These endless reprisals of war debts with borrowed money provided Hitler with all the ammunition he needed. In his demagogic propaganda he accused all nations of plundering Germany incessantly. He easily inflamed the masses. The 6 million jobless people living on the edge of poverty were his most willing followers, and as a result, in future government elections, the Nazis gained more seats. They were masters in organizing people and arousing national enthusiasm and hope. Hitler preached that the thirteen years of war-debt payments was "debt slavery" and blamed the current government as the cause of all evil.

The political crisis came to a peak with the presidential election of March 13, 1932. Although our President von Hindenburg was re-elected for a second term at age eighty-five with 18 million votes, we were increasingly alarmed that the Communists received 5 million votes, twice as many as in 1925, and Hitler 11 million. Papa could not picture Hitler in power either and feared that the general disillusion with our major political parties in this crisis-ridden atmosphere was leading us straight into his clutches and the violent Nazi storm troops. He called them "rabble rousers" and a "collection of weirdos heading for trouble," and he no longer understood the German people for falling into Hitler's trap.

Searching for more peaceful events, Papa attended a meeting of a non-political World War I veterans organization called *Stahlhelm* (Steel Helmet). The women's counterpart was a cultural and charitable society called *Luisenbund*, named after Queen Luise of Prussia (1776–1810). Papa wanted both Mutti and me to join, if only to develop some outside non-radical interests distant from Nazi propaganda. Mutti did not want to get involved, but in 1932, at age sixteen, I became a member. Papa was pleased since he was always in favor of supporting beneficial organizations.

My joining the *Luisenbund* was an interesting experience. I learned that after World War I the last Crown Princess of Germany, Cecilie of Mecklenburg-Schwerin (1886-1954) had founded the *Luisenbund* together with her maid, as a social, conservative women's organization which functioned under her patronage and leadership. I had already met her earlier, when she spoke in public at a large meeting in Münster, and she immediately impressed me as being a warmhearted and caring person.

The membership came from various social backgrounds, but we all wore the same graceful dresses made of royal blue linen with high bodices, short puffed sleeves, and wide skirts. It was the popular style during Queen Luise's lifetime, which even she wore. It's known today as the princess style. Our meetings involved music, literature and history, and it was a relief to engage in cultural discussions away from the politics and emotional turmoil that cluttered our daily lives. Queen Luise, the most loved and popular Prussian queen ever, was our role model and the mother of our first German emperor in 1871, William I. Young, beautiful, intelligent and broad-minded, she supported the liberal ideas of Baron vom Stein, the great Prussian reformer of the early nineteenth century. We were required in school to have a broad knowledge of famous people in our history, so I was familiar with all this and since my school, *Freiherr vom Stein Schule*, was named after him, I felt like an insider.

We especially admired Queen Luise for her humane act in liberating farmers from slavery in 1807 and allowing them to become independent land owners. For three hundred years, farmers had been treated as serfs, stripped of all their rights after they lost the Peasant War of 1524-25, a bloody revolt provoked by the forced labor system of feudal masters. Farmers now proudly wore their beautiful old native costumes, known today as the dirndl look, which, to my delight, is frequently copied world-wide in modern fashions.

We lived at the height of a crisis, and radicalism rocked the country. Hitler saw and seized his chance. As a fiery orator who was passionate and hypnotic, he knew how to sway the masses to his side. The Nazi propaganda machine demonstrated fanatical patriotism, with swastika banners, against the red flags of international Communism. Papa commented that to him they both looked very red. Giant Nazi posters, and uniformed marching troops were to convince the public of his strength and power. He used the appealing slogans of, "Order, work, peace and prosperity"; "All things for all men"; "Restore national dignity"; and "Our dismembered country will no longer be the doormat of other nations." It was nearly impossible for us to escape the turmoil, even when only going shopping downtown. Since the old system seemed to have failed, anyone who offered to rebuild Germany was at least offering hope where there was none, so quite a few voters were willing to try anything new. Their new piper would lead them to the "promised land," and many liked his tune. Hitler was well aware that in politics, psychology is more important than facts and he brilliantly painted an illusion that with him, peace and prosperity were just around the corner.

I also vividly recall how confusing the voting was. At the Reichstag election in July 1932, the parliament was split up into thirty-six political parties, and trying to select only one added to the confusion and irritation of the voters. They didn't know which party to believe. As a result, many were undecided and just abstained from voting altogether.

Papa was furious with those who merely discussed their politics amongst themselves at their beer tables. This was an ineffective substitute for casting their vote. "Do something! Get off your tushes and vote!" Such a demand didn't make Papa very popular among our friends, but it would have made him a good politician. Unfortunately his opinion was not asked for. He always felt strongly that voting was not only a citizen's privilege, but also a civic duty and that the worst thing is for good people to do nothing because a silent majority gets you nowhere and will just smooth the way for the evil.

Meanwhile, the Nazi and Communist party leaders staged wild and impressive demonstrations to urge their followers to vote. As a result both radical parties easily gained seats in parliament at the expense of the split-up moderate parties that diminished in significance. Papa was ready to climb the walls about the outcome. The Nazi party, with 230 seats, was now the strongest in parliament, but still a minority. Most Germans feared Communism, which threatened to gain power.

Nevertheless, Hitler still failed to seize power in the July 1932 election. Without these crisis-stricken years of the early 1930s, a violent extremist like Hitler would never even have had a chance. Now mass unemployment and increasing poverty caused public despair that paved the way for his success. Then events went head over heels:

August 23, 1932:
Hindenburg offered Hitler the position of vice-chancellor under Chancellor von Papen. Hitler refused. "All or nothing."

September 12, 1932:
The parliament was dissolved again.

November 6, 1932:
In a new election the Communists gained remarkably.

November 17, 1932:
Von Papen resigned as chancellor.

November 24, 1932:
Hitler was offered the chancellorship, but only under certain conditions. Hitler refused again. "All or nothing." Hindenburg declined to offer full power.

December 2, 1932:
General Kurt von Schleicher formed a new cabinet.

At that time, the Allies finally had considered terminating all of our war debt payments for the near future. Papa stated triumphantly, "This means the fatal reparation burden will finally be lifted from the shoulders of our government. Who needs Hitler's promises any more for a new course?" Papa was convinced that everybody could see such a fabulous turning point. But for our poorly informed public, Hitler's loud-mouthed propaganda completely stifled the forthcoming financial impetus. He didn't let people have time to think while striving for full power.

On January 28, 1933, General Kurt von Schleicher, chancellor since only one month, resigned after failing to gain cooperation of the numerous parties. In the parliament there was a clear majority of moderate middle of the road thinkers, but they refused to give up their special interests and join together to form a new order, and halt the march of Hitlerism during the twilight period of the Weimar Republic. Two days later, despite all of Papa's hopes, the unthinkable for him now became reality.

On January 30, 1933, Adolf Hitler, a forty-four year old native of Austria, an unknown private of World War I who had only been a German citizen for a short time and was a leader of a minority party, was appointed Chancellor of Germany. He was swept into power by catastrophic circumstances, not by a popular election. The Third Reich came into being.

In celebration of Hitler's appointment, Joseph Goebbels, a corrupt propagandist whom people mockingly called the "lame little fanatic" because he was born with a clubfoot, staged a huge spectacle of torchlight parades with endless rows of uniformed brown storm troopers (the SA) and black-coated Party elite forces (the SS) who were carrying Nazi banners. They stomped with marching music through the Brandenburg Gate to the State Chancery on Wilhelmstrasse 77. With these massed Nazi troops, Goebbels had boldly ignored the ban against any political demonstrations in the government quarters of Berlin.

The tumult lasted for hours and Radio Berlin passionately described how Hitler, from a high window, enthusiastically took the salute from the followers massed in the square below. He presented himself with the stiff-arm Nazi Party salute—right arm stretched in front at eye level, palm down—which from that day, would become the official German greeting along with *Heil* (hail) *Hitler*. In a mammoth long-winded declaration, Hitler promised "a new course," a "bulwark against Communism," and "a resurrection of Germany." He further promised to give the country a new future, bring it out of political ties, and renew all our hopes that we were robbed of since 1918.

We listened to the endless tumult on the radio with mixed feelings and the foreboding of some radical and dramatic changes. What Hitler did not let the citizens know was that the Allies were at that time considering terminating all of Germany's war debt payments in the near future. This would have automatically resolved much of the present economic crisis and would have greatly diminished the effect of the Nazi propaganda. Now, if the war debt payments were actually terminated by the Allies, Hitler could take credit for it.

Günter was no longer at home, since he had joined the Merchant Marine, the only possibility at that time for someone who wanted to go to sea. According to the Versailles Treaty, the German navy could consist of no more than fifteen thousand men. This small quota was quickly filled up with volunteers on long waiting lists. The entire German army was to consist of not more than a hundred thousand men. That limited number would just about fill up a football field.

Papa took a dim view of Hitler's official entrance into the government, even though it was only under the supreme auspices of President Hindenburg. Hitler had come to power by the choice of the working class between either Communism or the Nazis, and under the charisma of Hindenburg who symbolized honesty, loyalty, justice, peace and order. The public hope was still focused on our president. The new government was presented to the German people as a coalition in which everyone would work together for the benefit of the people and state. That set us at ease again. Maybe we were on the brink of a fresh start.

The Nazis held only three of the eleven seats in the new cabinet, with most of the key positions assigned to non-Nazi men. What a relief! That looked like a balanced choice. We were assured that our democracy would be continued within the terms of the constitution. The Vice Chancellor was Franz von Papen.

We felt that Hitler might go the way of many previous chancellors who were replaced or resigned after a short term in office. The common feeling was: Let's see how long Hitler will last. (He was degradingly called the "loud drummer of Braunau," his birthplace in Austria.) Perhaps he would be here today and gone tomorrow like so many of the chancellors who preceded him, particularly when faced with the tough issues.

The Nazis were the strongest party at the time, but still in the minority. They entered the government with less than one-third of the votes. The thirty-five moderate political parties, although individually significant, each believed they could manipulate Hitler for their own purpose and eventually push him aside. But Hitler was a master at using those who sought to use him, as would be proven in future events.

On February 27, 1933, less than one month after Hitler was appointed Chancellor, the Reichstag building, the German House of Parliament, was mysteriously set on fire. Built in the 1880s, it had been the government meeting place since the days of the monarchy. Suddenly, with flames shooting high in the air over Berlin, the interior was almost totally destroyed.

We all were stunned. How could that happen? The Nazis immediately accused the Communists. It was reported they had evidence that a revolutionist from the Netherlands named Marcus van der Lubbe had set the fire as the Communist signal for a nationwide rebellion like the 1917 Bolshevik revolution in Russia. Goebbels, the master of propaganda, managed to provoke a storm of public outrage against the Communists with his untrue press releases. This gave Hitler the long awaited chance for prompt emergency decrees, and to immediately suspend constitutional rights. With one stroke of the pen, he had eliminated many of his opponents. The Communist Party was immediately outlawed and an extensive wave of mass arrests swept over the country. Whoever was against Hitler was now labeled a Communist and liquidated, such as Social Democrats, union leaders, intellectuals, workers and private people. With swift-moving brutality, a murderous campaign started. There were no trials and Goebbels' propaganda justified it as being essential to prevent a breakdown in security.

The public was shocked and powerless to act against the reign of terror backed by Hitler and the Nazis after only a month in power. There was a general skepticism about the mysterious circumstances of the Reichstag fire. Rumors persisted that the Nazis had set the blaze themselves to have a legal excuse for a ruthless elimination of political enemies. There were two facts concerning the fire which pointed the finger of suspicion at the Nazis. First, the building was saturated from top to bottom with gasoline, which was available in quantity only to the Nazis, and it broke out in several stories simultaneously, so it could not have been the work of one person. Secondly, large quantities of gasoline could have been transported through a well-known underground tunnel that connected one of Hermann Göring's palatial headquarters with the cellars of the Parliament building. He held high positions in the Nazi government and was reported as being present at the scene of the so-called arson right from the time it started. This was enough for people to simply put two and two together.

To disguise the truth, and to deceive the public about the so-called arson, a big, showy four-month trial was staged that same year against the young van der Lubbe. As expected, he was found guilty and sentenced to death. For us, he was obviously a victim, but not the instigator of the fire.

This was the beginning of a number of significant outbreaks of fire by a power-hungry maniac—first the Parliament building, then the books, later the synagogues, and finally the whole world at war. In the end, the German cities and Hitler himself in his Reichs chancery were burned up. He provoked his fate himself, as expressed by Goethe in his poetic language in the ballad *Der Zauberlehrling* (The Sorcerer's Apprentice) which we all learned in school:

> *Herr, die Not ist gross*
> *die ich rief die Geister*
> *werd' ich nun nicht los!*

"Master! The spirits that I invoked, I can no longer rid myself of."

From the beginning, the promised new government cooperation didn't seem to work at all, nor did it turn out as peaceful and profitable as hoped for. The Parliament entered a tumultuous stage where parties refused to work with each other or with the Nazis. This all ended in a clash of political conflicts and on March 5, 1933, just six days after the burning of the Reichstag, a new, and our last free, election was held. Goebbels beat the propaganda drums with might and main. Spectacular rallies and massive campaigns were staged everywhere, and giant election posters with well-known slogans for bread, work and peace were plastered on every wall, and goodness knows the people yearned for all of them. Fiery radio speeches by Hitler and Goebbels were broadcast over the now state-controlled radio, while loudspeakers in public squares blared with nationalist enthusiasm. Nazi propaganda pamphlets read, "Leader, command us. We follow you!" It was impossible to listen to the radio or walk in the streets without being assailed by march music and Nazi Party songs.

In spite of all that vehement campaigning, which was a true masterpiece of Goebbels' skilled and powerful propaganda machine, it did not bring a Nazi majority. They received only 43.7 percent of the votes, which was really a distorted figure, since less than 70 percent of those eligible actually voted. The Nazis were given a favorable nod from roughly one-third of the voting population. This meant most still opposed Hitler.

We in Münster faced our own upheaval when a group of SA "Brown-Shirts" appeared at the city council and demanded that the town hall hoist the swastika flag. When the city council refused, they demanded that Chief Mayor, Dr. Karl Zuhorn, give that command, but he also refused. The delegation then threatened to report the Chief Mayor to Berlin and have him replaced by a State Commissioner. Rather than have this happen, the swastika flag was hoisted over the town hall on Monday, March 6, 1933. What a strange sight in this Catholic town.

A few days later another Nazi order came to lower the swastika in a special ceremonial performance. Our Chief Mayor refused to be present, and on May 19, 1933, he was dismissed from his position by Nazi order, effective immediately, and he left Münster. The Nazis even tried to institute a disciplinary action against him, which was rejected by our town's magistrate. We all were shocked by such despotic events. Ever since, our churches and the university were spied upon for subversive remarks. (In 1945, Dr. Zuhorn reappeared and was called back by the British to his old position as Chief Mayor of the town, on July 14, 1945.)

By now, everyone was deeply disturbed by Hitler being in power and was afraid that this "house painter of Austria" with his "silver tongue" would overturn the centuries-old German tradition and its conservative government. Hitler recognized the public alarm and to appear more reliable, orchestrated a brilliant show under the sly supervision of Joseph Goebbels to keep alive the illusion of a national uprising against the Communist threat. His goal was to suppress the people's growing suspicion that to a great extent, it all might be nothing but a Nazi exaggeration.

So, very quickly, on March 21, 1933, Goebbels staged an impressive scene for public view in the historic Garrison Church in Potsdam, in front of the sarcophagi of Frederick II, the most beloved Prussian king, and his father William I. This theatrical and sentimental gathering in the presence of Germany's high society was recorded as the "Day of Potsdam." Goebbels did everything to feed the illusion of an appeasement between new and conservative Germany. It was staged under the theme which linked "Hindenburg, the old patriarch" with "Hitler the new man," as a reconciliation of conservative Germany with the young up-start Nazi government. It was cleverly designed to affirm full cooperation and harmony between them, and Hitler, theatrically and successfully, stirred everyone's emotions when he promised, over the tomb of Frederick the Great, to continue the constitutional state. He even invoked God to help him rescue Christianity from Bolshevism, and promised to place the church under his firm protection. We could not believe how he represented himself as a heaven-sent leader.

The next day, all the newspapers showed a touching picture of the historic handshake between Hindenburg and Hitler. Hitler, for the first time appearing in civilian clothes rather than his Nazi uniform, was posed in the photograph respectfully bending over Hindenburg's hand, like a good school boy before his teacher. Now he modestly called himself a "soldier from World War I" and a "Chancellor of the people." How dignified he looked, as if he were tamed already. To the public it appeared that here was a true opportunity to jointly master a promising future. The Goebbels propaganda was again successful, completely lulling the people into a false sense of security, as they were totally assured that he would certainly continue our democratic form of government. Papa was not fooled and called it rubbish; just another trick to blind the undecided people.

Alas, we were soon to learn that Papa was right; nothing had changed. It all was a clever bluff with only lip service, and Hitler continued his quest as before for absolute dictatorship. People were driven to despair with the massive unemployment, and Hitler did not waste any time in exploiting the emergency situation. He keenly understood how to mobilize fear and to proclaim that only through his plan a better future could be hoped for. As such, only two days later, on March 23, 1933, while still under the spell of the "Day of Potsdam," he emphatically declared in the Parliament that his Four-Year Plan was the only means of overcoming the grave economic crisis, relieve the suffering of the people and strengthen the state. "Give me four years time," he shouted incessantly over the radio and hammered that phrase into everybody's brain. He demanded passage of the Enabling Act which would give him more authority to accomplish some badly needed reforms that were necessary for the economic recovery and to produce a high standard at a low cost. His fiery demands stated that it was either his recovery plan or complete capitulation to Bolshevism. He never spelled out his program; it was enough that we should trust him.

Hindenburg was the only one who envisaged drastic results from the Enabling Act and he vehemently opposed its passage. But, the more short-sighted politicians surrounding him could not read the handwriting on the wall, and feverish for reforms, they accepted Hitler's request for liberty of action, limited to four years, to work his plan. Papa said, "that's like giving the devil a little finger and he takes the whole body." How right he was! Within two months, with relative ease, Hitler had gained absolute dictatorial powers and completely eliminated the Parliament's power. No veto was possible. Soon nothing would be left of the modest man of Potsdam who humbly bowed his head when shaking hands with President Hindenburg. All his promises seemed forgotten, and unlikely ever to be remembered in the foreseeable future.

Hitler's snow-balling power was beyond us. The extent of the radical changes couldn't even be predicted and that Hitler would turn out the same as putting a fox in a chicken coop. To prevent such a disaster from recurring, in the German government of today an Enabling Act is outlawed and cannot ever be proposed again.

The present crisis blew over and we felt foolishly assured everything would go on within the terms of the constitution. The adults attended to their professions and I to my schoolwork. I looked forward to my first ballroom dancing class with all my classmates. Mutti sewed my pretty dresses as all the other mothers did.

Everyday life went on as though nothing was wrong in our world. President Hindenburg was our trust in the future, and the slow descent of democracy into dictatorship went unnoticed, although more and more Nazi elements dominated all life. Gradually, even our school came under the grip of the Nazis. According to the latest school rule, we were required to stand at the beginning of each class and greet the teacher with a *Heil Hitler* salute and the teacher had to return it.

Only two among us eighteen students had been members of the Nazi Party before 1933. One was Elfriede. We were surprised to learn that she was a Party member. A year ago she had transferred into our class from another town, and we never really knew much about her except that she was very sensitive with an idealistic and calm nature. She rarely ever spoke about politics, and was well-liked. Sports were never her favorite activities either. Years later she suffered from severe depression. It was assumed that what she had eventually learned about the Nazis had embittered her and shattered her idealism and confidence in their pro-claimed goals.

The other Nazi Party member who was part of our class all those years, Rosemarie, suddenly felt herself to be an authority on everything and even challenged our beloved Dr. Heller during his history class. He of all people! We all were devoted to him and fondly called him "Papa Heller." Since Rosemarie took philosophy as an elective, she felt very superior and in need of showering us with her unsolicited opinions so many times, that it created a very tense situation not only for Papa Heller, but also for the entire class.

With Hitler's takeover, the Nazi Party had been closed immediately to new membership. In May 1933, it was reopened and was "graciously" accepting new members. These new ones rushing in were jokingly called *Maikäfer*, May bugs, which appear in abundance in Germany every May. As children we loved to play with them since these bugs were quite easy to catch in the bushes. We kept them as pets in a shoe box, after we punched a few air holes in the lid, and fed them beech leaves. These insects are brown and about an inch long, with a hard shell, and as thick as your small finger. For them brown is their true and natural color. The new members were named after these bugs because of the matching Party brown, but this label was a degradation and the new Nazis hated to be branded as such.

Nazi Party membership became compulsory for those depending on a government salary and pension such as teachers, and we were not surprised to see Papa Heller appear in class one morning with his new Nazi Party badge in his lapel, clearly visible to all of us, including Rosemarie. Now these two were on the same level. It didn't matter any more if she agreed or disagreed and, stripped of her importance, she kept quiet. Peace had returned to our class and Papa Heller could present his history material as in former years, out of the old textbook from before the Nazi time.

People were flocking to join the Nazi Party since the Party effectively controlled who worked and where. It was like the old adage, "if you can't beat them, join them." If you didn't, you risked more than your job. Several, the "hangers-on," the Nazi Party opportunists, just wanted to be one of the first on the winning team. Others, "the me-too-ers," simply drifted with the political tide according to the saying: the hand that feeds me calls the tune.

As a result, the Party grew enormously at a rapid pace. The official name was NSDAP which stood for the "National Socialist German Labor Party," but the socialist part of the name was misleading since its totalitarian system demanded complete subordination. Since people's wit is always on the alert, the meaning of the initials was transformed at once into "_Na Suchst Du Auch Pöstchen_?" Well, are you also seeking positions?

The Nazi storm troops, or S.A., also changed in structure as many Communists, fearing for their own and their families' safety, defected to the Nazis and even joined the S.A. This infiltration was so strong that it served as material for new jokes right away. I especially remember this one:

> The S.A. is marching along the street in one of their frequent demonstrations. Some men approach from the opposite direction, loudly cursing the Nazis. The S.A. leader whispers to them hastily, "For heavens sake, shut up. A real Nazi is marching in the last row!"

With the influx of new members, the Party neatly separated the new and old ones into distinct classes for evaluation and privileges. Those who were members prior to 1933 wore the golden Party badge and were the favored ones, and their loyalty was rewarded with all kinds of perquisites and rights, like appointments to principal positions of government. With their new air of importance, they considered themselves more important than their responsibilities, making themselves feared through arrogance and violence. These Party bullies commanded by terror as a poor substitute for intelligence and experience as they extended Nazi control down into the local administration levels. This behavior led to friction with the population, but the Nazis were in command and these aggressive new little Hitlers appeared abruptly from everywhere. The riff-raff came into power.

It didn't take long before the youth leader of Germany, Baldur von Schirach, would make his presence known by wanting to greet Germany's youth in visits to selected cities, and Münster was one of them. All school children had to line up along the street where he was supposed to drive through in his car. We were ordered to appear in Salzstrasse, a lively main avenue not far from school. It was the teacher's responsibility to assure that everyone showed up at the designated spot and time. Those who didn't had to be reported, and any "no-shows" reflected the teacher's inability to teach us effectively enough about the Nazi doctrines. To protect ourselves and our teachers, we were all there, even my half-Jewish classmate, Hertha Simon, out of loyalty to the rest of us. Her mother was Jewish and her father had abandoned his wife and three teen-aged children so he wouldn't ruin his career as a chief engineer. Thus far, nobody in class paid any attention as to any Jewish or non-Jewish descent.

All of the school children in Münster were lined up at the specified time and place waiting for the arrival of the youth leader. We waited one hour, then a second hour, and the only "no show" was the man from Berlin. We were not allowed to leave, so we sat on the curb, but this was not acceptable to the patrolling brown-shirted authorities, so we were made to stand up again—and then sat down as soon as they were out of sight. Finally, after more than three hours, the German youth leader's car arrived and whizzed by in about three seconds. We had to greet him with the customary *Heil*, and then he was gone, like a ghost, now you see him, now you don't, and we could all go home. A friend of mine who stood in front of the townhall told me later that when the leader arrived, he jumped out of the car, didn't say a word to the waiting children, and rushed inside to his welcome banquet which was only for the Party top brass. Our statistical role was over. The next day our pictures appeared in all the newspapers with the caption in bold print telling how joyfully Münster's youth had greeted its leader and what a show of enthusiasm there had been. This was only the beginning of such routine nonsense and arranged mass gatherings that would be repeated on many other, and often far-fetched, occasions.

We were constantly besieged with new orders, and one of these was the selection of a second national anthem. After World War I, the German national hymn, "Hail to the Emperor" with the black-white-red flag had to be replaced. President von Hindenburg took the lyrics from the 1841 poem of Hoffman von Fallersleben, *Deutschlandlied*, and made it the national anthem of the first German republic, along with reinstating the historic black-red-gold flag of 1848. But, one national anthem was now insufficient and the *Horst-Wessel Lied*, the long-standing Nazi Party song, was forcibly added and the swastika had to be displayed at all times as the national flag of Germany.

Horst Wessel was a good-looking, intelligent university dropout who had been a member of the Nazi Party since 1926. He was a talented writer who got a lot of public attention by composing both the lyrics and music of the *Horst-Wessel Lied*. Hitler's background was just the opposite. Only half educated, he had spent vagabond years in Vienna as a billboard painter, often living in homeless shelters. In 1913, Hitler came to Munich; in 1914 he enlisted in a Bavarian regiment, and just made it to the rank of corporal. After World War I he was often jobless and regarded as an outsider without friends. Around 1919/20 he joined the German Workers Party as its seventh member. It didn't take him long to oust the original founder, to incorporate the organization into his own party, the NSDAP, and to make himself the undisputed leader. His constant fear of a possible challenger who would push him aside, the same way he had usurped his leader's place, dated from those early years and resulted later in his overzealousness in persecuting other rivals.

However, in 1930, at age twenty-three, the popular Horst Wessel died a sudden death which the Nazis claimed occurred in a Communist raid in Berlin. Hitler needed a martyr and it was convenient to blame the Communists for what was strongly assumed to be Hitler's own doing. The Nazis shed some crocodile tears in the glorification of the popular writer, who fitted much better in their plans as a dead martyr than as a living author with growing recognition, who could gain too much fame and power. In 1934, in one of Goebbels' masterfully staged propaganda shows, the grave of Horst Wessel in Berlin was assigned a Nazi guard of honor. Hitler made martyrdom out of murder. The outcome of all this was that from 1933 on, we had to sing both anthems, first the three verses of our *Deutschlandlied* and then the entire *Horst-Wessel Lied*, giving the obligatory new Nazi salute throughout both songs. The only benefit we gained from all of this was development of strong muscles in our right arm.

The Song of Germany, the *Deutschlandlied*, is misinterpreted by other nations as meaning that Germany wants to govern the whole world. The lyrics were already written around 1841 when the tidal wave of the industrial revolution swept across Europe. Jobs had disappeared as each machine replaced many workers who felt left behind in a struggle for survival. This sparked the need for far-reaching reforms and democratic rights. The old feudal regimes were alarmed and feared a serious threat to conventional society, and violently rejected arising liberal demands of the emerging bourgeoisie. The democratic intellectual leaders were in the universities. People demanded reforms and a monarchy on a democratic and constitutional basis. When denied, all over Europe revolutionary upheavals broke out and barricades went up, inspired by the bloody French revolution in Paris in February 1848. In March rebellions spread to Berlin. The military was called in to crush all progressive demands for a free press and greater independence, which were exceptionally reactionary for that time. Today this is a normal part of the constitution. Political parties in the modern sense did not yet exist. To escape persecution, and in search of freedom, the biggest emigration wave of the German bourgeois intellectuals started. Ten thousand fled to Switzerland; one of them was the composer Richard Wagner. The poet Heinrich Heine had escaped to Paris.

Many more thousands left for America. Americans may not be aware that among the "Forty-Eighters" were most valuable immigrants, such as: Karl Schurz, Secretary of the Interior under President Hayes; Emmanuel Gottlieb Leutze, who in 1851 painted "Washington crossing the Delaware;" and John A. Sutter, who discovered gold in the Sacramento Valley in California. This started the Gold Rush of 1849 so that California's population and cities grew. Later his family started its wine business, and today you still see Sutter wines sold in the stores.

One who was banished was Hoffmann von Fallersleben, poet, historian and professor of the University of Breslau in Silesia. From his exile on the island of Helgoland he pined for his homeland and wrote his *Deutschlandlied*, expressing his great homesickness for his country, which he loved above everything in the world. His song had no other meaning. At that time Germany was a multitude of thirty-nine principalities, bishoprics and free cities, unified thirty years later under Chancellor Otto von Bismarck with a nationalist policy. The melody is Joseph Haydn's old Austrian Emperor's Hymn. Americans are familiar with it since it is the same as the Anglican hymn "Glorious Things of Thee Are Spoken," and the alma mater song "Hail Columbia" of Columbia University in New York.

Since 1952, only the third and most lyric verse of the *Deutschlandlied* had been adopted as the official words of our national anthem today. It begins with "unity and justice and freedom" for the German fatherland.

If you reflect, other anthems are much more belligerent, such as the Marseillaise, the French national anthem in which they sing about the bloody flags everyone should raise on the day of victory, and march on, march on. Imagine if the Germans would sing something like that! The French anthem today also cannot be interpreted literally.

A humorous variation of the first line of the *Deutschlandlied* was created when the U.S. Secretary of State John Foster Dulles (1888-1959) prevented Communism from expanding and kept the Communists away from the doorstep of Berlin during the crisis when Stalin tried to oust the Western Allies. On the spur of the moment we now sang *Deutschland, Deutschland über Dulles*, identifying the city of Berlin with the western world. In great gratitude to the Dulles-Adenaur era and western steadfastness against Soviet aggression, Berlin has a John Foster Dulles Allee (avenue) that leads to the Congress Hall, which was a gift to Berlin from the Benjamin Franklin Society.

$\mathscr{T}$he Chameleon,
Master of Camouflage

$\mathscr{O}$n April 1, 1933, our Nazi government appealed to us for a nation-wide "non-Aryan" boycott. Hitler misused the word "Aryan." For him it was a Germanic race of blond and blue-eyed people. "Aryan" actually referred to an Indo-European language spoken as well by darker-skinned nations. To try to make it more palatable to the population, Nazi propaganda proclaimed that the German middle class had been ruined by inflation and mass unemployment. Therefore they needed to be freed of the excessive Jewish competition in business, in civil service jobs and as lawyers, teachers, and doctors. My interest in newspapers was not too great at that time as I was thoroughly occupied with various academic school pursuits. So I experienced the "proposed" boycott the hard way.

One day I needed something for our sewing class in school. As I had done for years, I went to our haberdashery on Ludgeristrasse, a Jewish firm with the name of Lapp. They were always stocked for our special needs. As I approached the store, I saw that overnight, one of these new eye-catching anti-Jewish pamphlets had appeared in the window: "Germans, defend yourself! Buy only at Aryan stores." An SA-man was planted in front with his feet wide apart, partly blocking the entrance, and I had to squeeze past him on my way inside, like many others did. When I came out with my purchase he gave me a dirty look and grunted, "Can't you read?"

Obviously people were not very enthusiastic about avoiding the old established Jewish stores. When the "proposed" boycott in Münster did not have the desired effect, on April 7, 1933, all Jewish businesses were ordered boycotted "to defend us against Jewish rivalry." On my next visit to Lapp's store, I found the SA guard posted there in a more menacing posture. This time he filled the entire doorway and gave me a very rude and sharp-tongued warning never to dare to set foot in this store again before it was "Aryanized," as it was called. I was shocked and had to turn away empty-handed. After that, my parents warned me to stay out of any dangerous Nazi crossfire.

Shortly thereafter, I accompanied Mutti to our Jewish family doctor of many years, Dr. Lewis, on Bahnhofstrasse. We all were fond of him, especially I; as a child, to my great joy, he had sent me twice to the seashore for recuperation when I was sick. His practice was upstairs on the second floor, adjacent to his private apartment, a very common arrangement at that time. But on this particular day the stairwell was filled with lingering and whispering patients. What were they doing out there? Was the waiting room so crowded today?

Upstairs we didn't have to ring the doorbell either as usual. Strangely enough the door to his practice was already wide open. We were received in the entrance hall by his long-time assistant, who had tears in her eyes. Oh, the doctor is sick himself, I thought. But Mutti, sensing an uncommon situation, sent me back out into the stairwell immediately. I wondered why and from outside I watched them whispering very excitedly. After a while Mutti came out, too. She said that Dr. Lewis would no longer be taking care of us and that his practice was closed. She was very upset, and so were all the other patients we passed while leaving. They still stayed and insisted on being treated. Mutti never told me what was discussed inside. She always followed the rule that what I didn't know, I couldn't talk about, and it couldn't be held against me—a common rule at that time. Luckily we were a healthy family and never returned to the practice of his Aryan replacement. Shortly thereafter, Dr. Lewis left Germany.

At home, at the dinner table, Papa told us what went on downtown in the very well-known textile store owned by a Mr. Wolf. The name Wolf could be a Jewish or an Aryan name, so the store remained open. But a relative with the Jewish name Oswald was rumored to have been arrested because he had an Aryan fiancée and was accused of miscegenation. All intermarriages with Jews were frowned upon and both parties threatened with severe punishment.

Meanwhile nobody and no area of life was excluded from harsh Nazi control. The same month it was announced that all student fraternities would be dissolved and merged into one new Nazi student union. And we had so many of these traditional student associations, such as the

Borussen, the *Germanen*, the *Alemannen*, the *Wingolf* and many more. Most of them were founded in 1815 in Jena, initiated by the Wars of Independence against Napoleon's conquest over Europe under the motto: freedom, honor, fatherland. The colors of their banners, black, red and gold, later became the colors of the Weimar Republic as well as of Germany today. Student fraternities had been often combined with gymnastics and glee clubs. Friedrich Ludwig Jahn, known as the father of gymnastics, promoted physical fitness for people of all ages in the nineteenth century. To my delight, he had made gymnastics popular as a matter of health, strength, and mental well-being, with walking as the most common exercise.

It had been Münster's tradition that on Sundays and holidays, after the 11 a.m. mass in Saint Lambert, the Prinzipalmarkt belonged to the citizens, especially the students. There we socialized, strolling under the arcades. The high school boys, like Günter, would wear their various colored caps, indicating their schools and classes, while we girls were identified by our different multicolored school ribbons which we wore proudly on the lapels of our coats and jackets, in a stylish, slanted way. At noon, the whole crowd moved over to the Cathedral Square for the free one-hour military band concert. The entire place turned into a colorful picture when the various student fraternities arrived in their different gala outfits with gold braid and buttons, and with their shakos and caps. After their traditional parade they scattered and we all mingled. It was always a splendid occasion for us to display our new outfits and while promenading, to see and be seen.

Now, suddenly, we were going to be robbed of all our harmless glamour because it was next to go on Hitler's list. Especially, the various colorful fraternity outfits were an eyesore for him, since he never finished school himself. He dissolved the traditional fraternities and consolidated all students, whether they liked it or not, into one Nazi student body, submissive to Nazi Party doctrine. In this and in other areas Hitler gradually exercised his control. From now on, we were to live in a brown monotony that stereotyped a mass of people. (These old fraternities were reestablished after World War II and restored to their former traditions.)

The newly-appointed student union leaders in brown shirts started a surprising and strange activity. They combed through public and even private libraries to confiscate a long list of books. Since they appeared with legal authorization, nobody dared to hinder them. Differences of opinion were not allowed. Political dissidents who refused to conform to Nazi policies were persecuted with an emphatic "invitation" to correction classes. Our lives did not belong to us anymore.

Orders for these book confiscations were backed by Goebbels' Central Office for Information and Propaganda in Berlin. They published a list of over a hundred authors and their banned books. In a mass propaganda effort, the German people were "promised" to be "protected" from now on against all "un-German" writings, left-wing decadence and Jewish influence. Now we would finally overcome all evil symptoms in German intellectual life, accomplishing a radical cleansing and elimination of destructive elements in German literature, and that from abroad published in Germany.

What were all these long-winded announcements supposed to mean? The list of outlawed books read like a catalog of the greatest German and foreign authors of different time periods, such as Heinrich Heine, Heinrich and Thomas Mann, Erich Kästner, Stephan Zweig, Marcel Proust, Sigmund Freud, Émile Zola, Theodor Heuss, even the scientist Albert Einstein. (Thanks to Hitler's ignorance the Nazis didn't get the atom bomb.) The list of famous names grew constantly, and I was not the only one in class who had read some of their books and never felt "un-German."

But circumstances became more critical. Our class, like all others of Münster's schools, was instructed to participate in a program called a "patriotic meeting." It was going to take place on May 10, 1933 on Hindenburgplatz, the biggest square in Münster, in front of the former Prince-Bishop's castle. From this we surmised right away that a mass demonstration was planned.

My class, following orders, met on the designated afternoon and at the assigned location. We had a very convenient meeting place on the edge of the promenade and the Hindenburgplatz. I don't remember if that was due to the thoughtful arrangement of Papa Heller for us girls, away from the crowd, or if we even had a choice. But that location, far away from the full action, suited our lack of interest just fine. It was known by now that the patriotic meeting would be nothing more than a mass book-burning rally. All day long the books had been hauled in trucks and wagons by Party functionaries and piled up in the center of the square. The books were counted by weight, actual kilos, and not by number. The SA was also present to give more importance to the whole occasion.

My entire class was required to show up in the afternoon. As usual, the teachers' attendance list had to be handed in the following day to a supervisor. The whole population was called upon to participate, but my parents stayed home. So far they were not registered on any list of employers or employees, such as government or public workers, and had escaped orders to attend. Papa was self-employed. Mutti, "only" a housewife, was against any mass gatherings and wanted me to come home as quickly as possible.

The entire proceeding was led by the SA, the SS, and student activists in brown shirts, leaders of the new German Student Union. A band played marches and patriotic songs, alternating with speaking choruses. All we could hear was deafening screaming, something about "un-German" literature. Screaming was the chief method of getting messages effectively across. We did not mind not hearing well, especially when the boys from the Schiller Gymnasium were assembled not far from us. They got all of our attention.

During this whole episode, the books were supposed to burn in a glorious bonfire. Various efforts were made, but the "un-German" literature wouldn't cooperate and refused to go up in flames. The books smoldered but stayed intact. No wonder they wouldn't burn, piled up much too tightly in a big heap. To Papa Heller's dismay, we thought the whole fiasco was hilarious, and started to giggle. He urged us to stand around him and put on serious faces, at least to stop laughing. Obviously he understood more about our dangerous, amused behavior than we teenagers did. Also the Brown-shirts were patrolling.

If I remember correctly, when all efforts failed, they poured gasoline over the books. The fuel burned brilliantly, throwing ghostly shadows in the twilight, but the books still resisted being consumed, and left behind only an acrid smell. We were not very enthusiastic anyway, but tired, lingering there for more than three hours. It had started to rain and we wanted to go home. When we left, the Brown-shirts were still trying to rekindle the fire.

At home that evening, we learned from the radio that mass rallies were held in all university towns throughout Germany. What shocking news! In Berlin, the demonstration took place in the square in front of the opera house, directly opposite the university. It was announced that over twenty thousand books were burned there. What a disgrace for that historic place founded by Frederick II around 1740. Over the radio it was touted as being an exciting and successful event. It was hard to outperform the Nazis when it came to stagecraft—now and later. The demonstration was portrayed by Goebbels as a glorious and symbolic act supported by the German people. What a big lie, with many more to follow. This one in reality was a cultural and political fiasco.

The nationwide book burning shocked not only us but also the entire world as barbaric. It was one of the blackest days in recent German history and only a prelude to what would follow. As an immediate result, it prompted the emigration of many of our best minds and gifted intellectuals, well-known scientists, famous artists and writers, who were scattered to the four winds. The Nazis were destroying ideas, not only people. No secret was made of their determination to discriminate against the Jews and to drive them all out of the country. Fortunately many Jews left while they could. (Henry Kissinger, the later Secretary of State under President Richard Nixon, emigrated to America with his Jewish family under Nazi pressure from the town of Fürth in Bavaria in 1938.) We, the people, were catapulted, unprotected and powerless, into one crisis after another by the rapidly occurring events during the first months of 1933.

The way the public really felt was unmistakably demonstrated by the new political jokes that sprang up, such as this one:

A housewife goes to the public library. "I would like to check out some books for my husband. He is at home, sick in bed." "Well," says the librarian, "May I suggest something from the very new, highly interesting literature recommended by our present government?" "No, thank you," says the housewife. "My husband isn't *that* sick!"

There was always something new. Earlier that month, all independent labor unions were abolished and replaced by one Nazi labor organization, *Die Deutsche Arbeitsfront*, covering all workers. Membership was compulsory. As a result, control was centralized and striking impossible. This new rule, however, did not affect us. Papa was self-employed, Günter had been transferred from the merchant marine into the navy, and I was just a school girl. By now, hardly any organization was left outside the Nazi Party.

Meanwhile our daily problems became more complicated and depressing with every "wonderful" improvement the Nazi government proclaimed. Their powerful propaganda was endless. "All for one and one for all" was heard over and over again on the radio, in endless public speeches and in mass meetings. Party uniforms and marching boots were indispensable symbolic rituals. Hitler, with his great oratorical talent, mobilized the people like a hypnotist. The louder the propaganda became, the more Papa had his doubts about the hasty promises of a paradise gained by just following Hitler's Four-Year Plan.

Papa was very outspoken, much to Mutti's dismay. What happened soon was a rapid series of monumental changes that more than justified Papa's distrust. The youth of the country were urged to be "organized" immediately with one of the inside groups of the Nazi Party as a means of mass political indoctrination. How lucky for me that I was already organized last year, thanks to Papa, in the *Luisenbund*. So I felt safe from Nazi pressure to join any of their political youth organization. I felt free to travel my own path.

The second big change that shook Papa was the sudden "reorganization" of the *Stahlhelm*, the harmless World War I veterans' association he was familiar with. On June 21, 1933, it was summarily incorporated into the Nazi Party. All men up to the age of thirty-three were recruited into the SA. From then on they were forced to wear brown Nazi shirts, which generated right away the "brown pest" Nazi jokes— like the following one:

> The block warden, a snooping watchdog himself, is spying
> again on all tenants and he asks, without waiting for an an-
> swer, "Do you own a dog? If you do, why isn't it brown?"

The older members of the *Stahlhelm*, above the age of thirty-three, were forcefully merged with the Nazi veterans. Thereafter, the *Stahlhelm's* name completely vanished.

The third and most upsetting change of all followed hot on the heels, this time concerning me. The Nazis robbed me of my security of being a member of the *Luisenbund*. One day they made a public announcement that they would generously "comply" with our "longstanding wish" to join the Nazi women organizations. It was a lightening stroke that left us without power to reject this much-feared compulsory move. Forcefully, I was turned into a member of Hitler's youth movement. All younger members, up to the age of eighteen, like myself, were mandatorily incorporated into the BDM which stood for *Bund Deutscher Mädchen* (League of German Maidens), the female equivalent of the Hitler Youth for boys. All others, over eighteen, were transferred into the *NS-Frauenschaft* (Nazi Women's League). My *Luisenbund* was dissolved overnight, like the *Stahlhelm*, and all simply through the power of the Enabling Act. Everyone was on the same uniformed level now, which also meant that we were nonexistent. In fact, we were so equal— Nazi equal, of course—that no other organization could function anymore, thereby eliminating all organized foundation for any opponents.

Papa was furious but powerless against such Nazi order. The idea was simple and crude. They used us to fill up the still scanty BDM membership. Externally, our feminine blue dresses were changed into the brown Nazi uniforms, but internally our feelings stayed the same. Though I couldn't wear my nice princess-style dress anymore, it turned out that I never wore their outfit either during my short stay as a compulsory member, as time would tell.

My squad of about twenty girls met on designated evenings at 8 p.m. sharp, in a spacious room especially set aside for us in one of the historic houses on Prinzipalmarkt. The walls were plastered with a huge Hitler portrait and Nazi pamphlets. My group leader, who was around twenty years old, turned out to be a rough and energetic woman with a total lack of charm. Every meeting was prefaced and concluded with performing the *Heil* salute. We would sit down at both sides of a long table. A typical evening's program was a lecture on seemingly endless repetitions of Nazi ideology and would end with: "Never doubt the Führer, the Führer is always right."

She hated me on sight, which she made quite obvious from the start. To begin with, there was my former membership in something as reactionary as the *Luisenbund*, an organization not worth existing any more. Now I sat there in civilian clothing. In addition, I didn't seem to follow her Nazi Party line enthusiastically enough, but rather passively, being too reserved during her long-winded discussions. Mutti had instructed me, "Keep your mouth shut. Don't trigger a confrontation."

The disgust was mutual. I couldn't stand her or her crude language, and her silly commands, which she shouted incessantly. Her lectures were as dull as she was. I could never remember what she preached, or the topic being discussed, except that Nazi ideology was our only salvation. With the many hours we had to put into our meetings, it seemed to me that something better and more useful could have been done with that time. However, I was in no position to show my hostility as candidly as she did, if I wanted to avoid a backfire with nasty consequences for me. I was in a no-win situation.

Another topic of intense discussion was men, and the encouragement of childbirth. The mandatory feminine ideal was a healthy mother. We were duty-bound to bear all the children Hitler wanted and we were indebted to the fatherland to produce them, whether legitimately or illegitimately. It made no difference as long as plenty of babies were "produced," especially those of his adored Nordic racial purity. Just as the farmer breeds cattle eugenically, Hitler wanted to breed people from healthy stock to create a new race of supermen. We had to be physically strong for childbirth. Intellectual education was a prerogative only for men in a society ruled entirely by men.

The BDM guideline for an ideal family or single woman was: donate a child to the Führer. One has to consider all of this at a time when families would kick their daughters out if they came home pregnant and unwed. If this had happened to me, I am sure Papa would have shut me up in a convent, even though we were Protestants. Sexual liberation didn't come about until thirty years later.

Since all of this teaching was a well-known fact, it did not take long before the vernacular changed the meaning of the letters BDM into several sarcastic modifications like _Bubi Drück Mich!_ (honey hug me) and _Bedarfsartikel Deutscher Männer_ (necessities of German men—for their fun and babies). It was dangerous to be caught making these descriptive and degrading remarks.

The Nazis dedicated the second Sunday in May as the official Mothers Day. That sounds the same as in the rest of the world. But oh no! It was to be observed as a special national holiday. The mother was idolized as a heroine of the home-front. With every childbirth, the more the better, she won a battle for her fatherland. Hitler made childbirth a popular duty in our male-dominated society.

Later Hitler even created a reward, an honor pin, the _Mutterkreuz_, a special cross awarded on three levels to all mothers "of favorable standing," which meant from healthy stock with preference for blond and blue eyed females, (No black hair please!) who fulfilled the baby quota. The competition was to show who had the most babies. A bronze medal was bestowed on mothers with four or five children, a silver one for six or seven children, and finally a gold one for outstanding achievement of eight or more children. These crosses were supposed to be worn openly around the neck on a bright blue ribbon (what? not a brown one?) with the inscription: *Das Kind adelt die Mutter,* the child ennobles the mother. People sarcastically called this prestigious award *Kaninchenorden,* or rabbit award. For Hitler we were guinea pigs for his colossal genetic experiment to produce a master race.

After each BDM meeting we were lined up to march through the town accompanied by loud singing, preferably Nazi songs. This took place after 10 p.m. when other people wanted to sleep. I am, and always have been, a good walker but those man-like giant strides, stomping through the streets in a pseudo-military fashion, made it hard even for me to keep up. It all struck me as being the beginning of the end of people's individuality.

Our everyday life was now dictated by politics and we had no say in it. Since the Nazis were in power, the daily diet was "coordination," with the official title of *Genosse,* which is comparable to the Soviet comrade. We were all at the mercy of the government's arbitrary actions, and it was not long before a new "brilliant idea" came from Berlin with a most incisive new regulation. From now on, all athletic associations, like local gymnastics and sports clubs, were placed under the authority of the government's athletic leader in Berlin. This meant we were deprived of our last freedom—sport. This extended Nazi domination to all nonpolitical areas. Suddenly everybody who belonged to a sports club was transformed into a member of the *Deutscher Reichsbund für Leibesübungen,* the German government organization for all physical exercise, a strongly centralized system.

That was a very hard blow for us in Münster. We had long-standing sporting traditions for all types of activities, even riding clubs, Westphalia being horse breeding country. Traditionally we had a large physical education program in school, and particularly *Turnen* (gymnastics) was practiced twice a week in the morning and once in the afternoon. Outdoor activities were so popular in school that one hiking day was scheduled every month, which included a class cookout.

At Münster's periphery was the airport *Loddenheide* for balloon and flying sports, including glider flying. It was traditional on Easter morning for Papa to take Günter and me to watch their many performances. We Münsteraner liked outdoor activities. For as long as I can remember, not only Münster but all of Germany had well-organized athletic activities long before Hitler. To force us into a new form of sports club was like carrying coals to Newcastle. This was to make us comply blindly with their "follow the leader" ideology. A joke was again an escape from out of the Nazi sport strait-jacket:

> Hitler sits on the bank of the Spree River in Berlin and tries
> to fish, but with no success. No fish will bite, not even with
> the biggest worms as bait. He loudly complains about it to a
> Berliner passing by. "What do you expect?" the man says to
> Hitler. "Here even the fish don't dare to open their mouths
> any more!"

Our Christian churches were increasingly exposed to great pressure. All Christian youth organizations, such as in America the YMCA and the CYO, first came under severe criticism, then were finally strictly forbidden by 1935. Hitler completely ignored his promise, of just some months ago at the "Day of Potsdam," to take the church under his protection. Instead, doctrines violating Christian principles were freely taught. Our parents looked mistrustfully at these new practices which were rocking old fundamentals. Young ones were incited to oppose their "old-fashioned" parents to destroy family ties and force a new Nazi identity on them. It became very clear that Hitler, as a demagogue, who brilliantly understood how to arouse enthusiasm, strived for a controlled, supervised Nazi youth. He deliberately took advantage of the enthusiastic impressionability of young people. The youth had to hail him with the slogan "Führer command us, we follow you."

Meanwhile, for the adults, the constant suppression and persecution of all their own political parties reached its peak on July 14, 1933, when the Nazis abolished each of them overnight, and the Nazi Party was declared the only legal one. It was called "the path of political union for a new foundation." It was the mold of a totalitarian one-party police state. Any opposition was killed with one coup. Doubts about the government's orders, under an extremely wide interpretation, were treated the same as active opposition and we were punished accordingly with no appeal to any court. The door was open for persecution of everyone—Germans, German Jews, private citizens, as well as the church. Even the monarchistic fraternal organizations were forbidden and dissolved, as well as the freemasons.

Only four months after the book burning rally, on September 10, 1933, Joseph Goebbels, as new Propaganda Minister, established a new Chamber of Arts and Culture, which he used to dictate his personal guiding principles as the only acceptable view of German culture, the new Nazi cultural strait-jacket. All modern art was condemned as decadent. Jazz, called an invention of the devil, was forbidden. The Nazi government cleverly integrated all radio, press, theater, music activities and film into their system as most important tools of propaganda and to manipulate the masses. Goebbels knew very well the potential of film as an unparalleled propaganda weapon and took over the UFA (*Universum Film AG*) a motion picture industry in Berlin-Babelsberg, for years the German equivalent of Hollywood, with its films of international fame. He cleverly used the power of entertainment as an escape from reality and as a beautiful illusion to cover up the bitter pills to come. The movies he controlled in his "personal" way to such an extent that the route to stardom was via one of his bedrooms, the "casting couch."

There was constantly something new. In our history class Papa Heller had just explained to us the importance of the League of Nations, founded in Geneva in 1919. Its value was the safeguarding of world peace. How fortunate Germany was to have been admitted in 1926. But on October 14, 1933, Goebbels declared, also in Geneva, that Germany was withdrawing from the League of Nations. We, the people, were totally unaware and were not even asked for our opinion, much less considered to have one. We only heard the results.

Papa worried about that unexpected news and discussed it at our dinner table. Why was our membership so suddenly withdrawn after only seven years, since it had successfully led us out of our foreign policy isolation after 1918? Of course the U.S. was never a member of the League of Nations, but that was another continent, across the ocean, far away from Europe's centuries of wars and its regional conflicts.

So it happened that we were topsy-turvy in public and private life within only nine months. We were painfully aware by now that all this had only been possible by the passing of the Enabling Act which had been enacted even against Hindenburg's strong warning. Only some months earlier Hitler had reached power merely as leader of a minority party. In that brief time, he had quickly brought about suppression of all differently-minded people. Blind obedience was demanded from everybody, friend or foe. From now on freedom of speech would exist only behind closed doors. We were still not fully aware of the changes and went on attending to our everyday life. Much more would happen than we ever thought possible.

The popular anti-Nazi jokes, whispered from ear to ear, continued to be an outlet for the people's desperation. The Berliners had, and still have, a special sharp-tongued and witty side. For example, I remember two of the German jokes that seemed to symbolize Hitler's stunningly rapid ascent to power: *Heil Hitler* was from now on the obligatory and official greeting. In one joke a fellow Nazi asks Hitler if it would not be advisable to continue the customary German greeting of *Guten Tag,* good day. Hitler furiously shouts, "No way! As long as I am in power, we will not have any 'good day' here any more!"

Another joke was based on the ironic double meaning of the words *aufgehoben* and *Rechte. Aufgehoben* can mean raised as well as canceled. *Rechte* means right hand and also rights, or justice, just as in English, permitting different interpretations. So when asked: "What does the Hitler salute mean?" There were two different meanings for the same answer. The answer of the Nazis was: *Aufgehobene Rechte*—raised right hand. That of the people was *Aufgehobene Rechte*—canceled rights.

First Flight Out of the Nest

The summer of 1933 promised to be exciting for me. I would go to Neuchâtel, Switzerland, for two months, to improve my school French. A couple was recommended to us who took in students to teach them the language. Since our summer vacation lasted only six weeks, my parents had to submit written requests and battle endless regulations to get approval for an additional two weeks absence from school. Mutti and I had planned this whole project far in advance. Papa always wanted the best for his family, and gladly paid generously for everything.

The required permission was reluctantly granted. I got my first passport and a big new suitcase filled with all kinds of unexpected purchases as a prelude to my adventure. Students from other classes came to see me and wanted to hear every detail about my trip. I really felt important. Today one would call this "to be in," though usually I was more "out" than "in." The others visited places that I was not allowed to go to. They also whispered about their boyfriends, but I, with my strict parents, had none to show off. I received numerous requests to help other students with their French homework upon my return. I promised everything, not realizing how limited my improvement would be after only two months in Switzerland.

Early in July I took off on my dream trip. My parents and I traveled together by train until we had to separate in Southern Germany. From there they went on to the Wildbad spa in the Black Forest. Now they were worried about letting me continue on to Switzerland alone—alone not only on a trip, but also to a foreign country and to people they had never actually met. They gave me so much advice that in the end I was unable to remember a single one. Besides, I could not wait to be on my own for the first time in my life.

I crossed the border at Basel, at the Rhine River where three countries meet, Switzerland, France and Germany. Now all alone, I felt surrounded by confusion. My large suitcase, checked all the way through, showed up at the border for inspection. I felt uncomfortable when I was stopped by a stern German customs official who brusquely asked for my passport, all my luggage, and the exact purpose of my trip. He then gave me a long and searching look. The Nazi government didn't like us to travel outside of the country. The Swiss checkpoint was just a formality. German was spoken here. When I continued on I regained my spirit of adventure. I was awed by the beauty of the new country. The landscape became more and more breathtaking with every turn the train took through green valleys, along picturesque lakes and houses with bloom-laden flower boxes, and the constantly spectacular view of the towering silhouette of the Swiss Alps. In Biel, a town where mostly German was used, I had to change trains. From there I was off to Neuchâtel, where the best French was said to be spoken.

I had eaten in the diner, and it was evening when I reached my destination with the pleasant surprise of a pink and gold sunset. With high hopes I waited at the station to be picked up by my host family, as had been agreed upon by mail. After a while, not too many people were left. Just then a strange man approached me. He was of medium build, about Papa's age, and had an enormous walrus moustache. He quickly detected that I was the person he had come to collect, introduced himself as my host, and picked up my luggage, which he loaded onto a cart. Then we took off on foot to his house across town. En route he kept up a constant chatter about the town with its historical thirteenth century castle, and its famous university and schools. He pointed to the shimmering Lac Neuchâtel with its charming surroundings, lakeside resorts and steep slopes covered with vineyards.

While all of this poured over me in French, I guessed more than I understood and stole a glance at his strange drooping moustache, which I didn't find particularly attractive. What did he do with those funny-looking long strings at night—leave them above or under the covers? He also must have forgotten that I came here to improve my French and that I was not conversant in his native language.

When we arrived at his house it was dark and I couldn't see much, except that it seemed to be a pleasant residential area. I was greeted by his wife, a friendly middle-aged lady, who showed me around. It was a very old place, not unusual for Neuchâtel, where many respectable houses date back to the fifteenth and sixteenth centuries. My own room was up a short flight of steps, like in a modern split-level. It had a large window framed by thick, heavy, dark red velvet drapes caught with a braided tassel on each side, which I was told never to touch. "There is no need to close them since nobody can see you getting undressed," she explained. But there were no other curtains either, only a large, gleaming window pane. To top it off, my window was facing the street. She wished me good night, and we would meet again the next morning for breakfast. I felt uncomfortable and switched the light off as soon as I was alone. It was after 10 p.m. already and I got acquainted with my room with only the light of a bright street lantern outside.

The wardrobe I was to use was outside in a little hall, close to the steps leading downstairs. Like everything else it was very old and I would not have minded admiring it in a museum. Its door hinges squeaked loudly with every move and gave me goosebumps in the dark because I found no lightswitch to turn on. Feeling helpless, I soon gave up trying to hang my clothes in there and decided against any further unpacking. Deeply disappointed, I crawled into bed, dead tired, and somehow disillusioned about my great adventure. During the night I heard all kinds of strange crackling and rustling, both indoors and out, or did I imagine that? I was sure the noises were real.

Next morning before breakfast the lady showed me her garden behind the house and explained the many flowers to me, in French, of course, which I understood poorly. I noticed right away that there was no fence around the yard. On two sides the garden ended in a sudden steep, rocky slope. I was never fond of heights and saw with alarm that the deck chairs were close to the edge. When I voiced my concern, the lady just laughed, "you will get used to it." But I already saw myself tumbling down that slope.

Breakfast was served in an alcove of the living room. Only French was spoken. Every one of my mistakes was corrected severely by the master of the house, especially if I made the same mistake twice due to my nervousness. So I kept quiet for the rest of the meal. In between, the long strings of his strange moustache indulged in the morning coffee, too, like in the old song "they always droop in Papa's soup, they're always in the way." I tried not to look in his direction, which was almost impossible since we all sat close together around a small table.

Maybe it wasn't so bad, only very different from home, but I had expected glamour and beauty. Instead, I got regulations and very strict corrections. They also didn't hear the odd noises at night, and just looked at me strangely when I mentioned them. Then they started to line up my schedule for the day. Whatever it was, I did not listen, being preoccupied with my disappointment and lost in my own thoughts and strange new surroundings. As soon as I could, I withdrew into my room before starting with their dull, detailed program.

So there I stood, very confused in the midst of my barely unpacked suitcase, the red drapes which I was not supposed to touch, and many other strange old things besides that squeaking wardrobe across from my room and the precipice of a garden outside. I was desperate. All this for two long months to come? Impossible! My only thought was to get out of there. I hastily grabbed my handbag, and leaving everything behind, tiptoed out of the house, unnoticed by the couple who was busy elsewhere.

I just ran down the street I had come up the evening before. Everything looked quite pleasant in daylight. The fresh morning air cooled me off and I thought to myself, "What now?" and continued walking slowly, always straight ahead. Suddenly there was a side street on my right. Where should I go? I was scared.

On my left was a garden, elevated by four or five feet and supported by a strong stone wall. Above, on the lawn, was a tall wooden pole with a sign, *Pensionat Mistral*, and a hand pointing into the side street to my right. What luck! What a relief! There must be a boarding school, young people, and warmth. I took a second good look at the sign and entered that side street at once.

I was all alone in the early morning, with nobody to ask for directions. Right and left I passed well-cared-for villas with flower gardens. In one of them a boy was playing. In my best French I tried to ask him where the Mistral was. But the more I asked him the more he withdrew. Before he could vanish completely, I screamed in despair, in German, "Wait! Please! Don't run away!" That he understood and returned immediately. He told me he had escaped with his family from Germany only a few days ago and didn't know any French, but he knew where the boarding school was located, just around the corner at the end of the short street.

In only three more minutes I was there, in front of a large attractive residence on broad, well-maintained grounds. There in big golden letters above the cast-iron gate was written *Pensionat Mistral*, the name of the boarding school. There I stood, less than fifteen minutes after escaping from the other place, where I had left behind my suitcase with all my belongings, including the money which I had handed over to the couple the previous night for my two-month stay. To return there was now out of the question. With mixed feelings I rang the doorbell. This first step was the hardest. A friendly lady opened the gate and bid me good morning, which immediately strengthened my rather dwindling courage, and asked me to come in. We then sat down in the parlor.

I told her my story, half in French and half in German, and how I found her place. "How did you find us?" she asked me again. I once more told her about the sign. She wanted to know exactly which sign because she didn't know of any. "Oh yes," I explained to her again. "The name of this place is written on a big wooden panel with a hand pointing in your direction." She just shook her head. My description didn't seem to make any sense to her, but my French couldn't have been that

Pensionat Mistral

bad. A long silence followed. After another very appraising look, which seemed endless to me, at least runaways were not that common at that time, she decided to take me in as a student. She also promised to straighten everything out with the other couple whom she seemed to know, including the money I had left with them, and to explain somehow why I had rushed off early this morning.

Right away I was introduced to about twenty girls from all over the world with different languages and backgrounds. We soon all went out for a walk. One teacher was in front and another in back of the "herd," the protected boarding school way. The teachers wanted to see my sign, too, and of course it was no problem for me to lead the whole group back to the place where I had found it this morning.

Coming closer now, I found the elevated garden with its four to five-foot high stone wall, and up there, behind the fence above it... where was the sign? There was no sign any more. Even I could not see it now. "They must have taken it away," I explained. But who were "they?" I got up on my tiptoes to look for the hole in the very well-groomed lawn which the big pole must have left when it was removed. There was no hole either. Now I was the one who didn't understand, or did I? I remember that sign even today. *Pensionat Mistral*, a name I had never heard of before. For me it was no mystery but a realistic event that repeated itself throughout my life, where a mysterious force guided me. Maybe the sign's purpose was fulfilled. As Shakespeare said, "There are more things between heaven and earth, Horatio, than are dreamt of in your philosophy."

I found myself surrounded by puzzled schoolmates and a head-shaking teacher. But she changed the subject quickly by suggesting we call my parents soon at their hotel in Wildbad. When they had phoned the old couple earlier that morning, they were shocked to hear that I could not be found anywhere, and that nobody knew why or where I had vanished to after breakfast.

When we returned from our walk, my luggage was already in my new room. It was a comfortable, charming and bright place on the third floor. From a very large window I could look out over our garden and the shimmering Lac de Neuchâtel, an incredible panorama of water and mountains. We were situated high above the lake. A long flight of steps led down to the lakeside promenade that was lined with trees and flowers, very pleasant for evening strolls. There was even a special swimming area in the lake and boats for our use. I shared my new room with a Swiss girl from Lucerne, and we liked each other on sight. Here I did not need any window curtains. Only Mother Nature and the moon could peer into my room. But I could look out into a new world of great beauty.

Needless to say, my phone call to my parents did not calm them down when they heard I had impulsively changed my place of residence in less than twenty-four hours. This from a daughter who was never allowed to do much on her own!

A French-speaking couple ran and owned the boarding school, and two female teachers were with us all the time. There were house rules and schedules. We could not just leave as we pleased. We were an international group from various European countries, some from Switzerland and a few from Germany, like myself. For our meals we all sat around a long table, and our hosts presided at the foot and the head. He would cut the bread at his end, and as it was passed around we had to say, "*Ayez la bonté de me passer le pain, s'il vous plaît.*" Have the kindness to pass me the bread, if you please. We would repeat this phrase for whatever item happened to be passed around the table. This stilted phrase would be laughed at today as being super-polite and outdated, but I was so proud of it at the time.

Meanwhile I should have been deliriously happy in world-famous Neuchâtel, but instead, I was terribly homesick. My generation was in no rush to grow up. I was a teenager and for the first time I was not only away from home, but also in a foreign country with a different currency and language. I had trouble understanding French, especially at the speed with which it was spoken. Papa Heller at home talked much slower and explained everything also in German.

We were located close to the heart of town. I was the only one who was allowed to leave the house by herself to walk early each morning downtown to the school called the *École de Commerce pour Jeunes Gens*, in order to attend my French *cours de vacances* (summer session language course) there. It was a very strict learning program planned in advance by my parents. The student body, comprised of numerous nationalities, was allowed to speak only French, even during rest periods. One day I was caught speaking German on the stairway with another student, and was rudely reprimanded by one of the female instructors that only French would be "tolerated." Her public scolding was so severe for this small disobedience that we later asked ourselves if perhaps Germans were not welcome there.

I got a similar feeling shortly thereafter when I was exploring with a classmate a street lined with interesting shops. We entered one of them to buy material for a needlepoint handbag I had in mind to make for Mutti during my stay. This shop specialized in fine embroidery, famous Swiss lace and needlework. The saleslady ignored me completely no matter how often I tried to tell her, in my best French, that it was my turn now. She treated me like thin air. My classmate whispered, "Let's get out of here." We finally left and went to another store she knew very well. There I could even speak German, and she told me that in the first store I would never have been served. I had no idea then that every German was taken for one of those new Nazis.

I didn't expect that hostile reaction since Switzerland is over 74 percent German in culture and language. French is used only by about 20 percent of the population. The rest use Italian and Romansch, a disappearing language derived from Latin. My parents preferred to send me to French Switzerland rather than to France for my language study. Of course they had no idea that I would run into dislike in such an open-minded country. I certainly never wrote home about that experience. They worried enough already and would never have guessed that discrimination would occur, especially in Neuchâtel, an old city with the German name of Neuenburg. For ages it had belonged to the kings of Prussia as personal property.

Walking in a park one day, I found a tall statue of a Prussian king. I forgot which one it was, but I remember writing home about this discovery right away. Papa thought this was so interesting that he kept that letter for quite a while. My parents were fond of conservative Switzerland—so conservative that Geneva was the first canton to introduce the right to vote for women as late as 1960. For my parents, here was a country known as an international and broad-minded center, a safe place for their teen-aged daughter.

All German-speaking girls were in the *Mistral* for the same reason as I, to learn French. And if we would have talked less German amongst ourselves, we would have learned a lot more. My parents blamed me for this later, too. One of our fellow students was a striking-looking, black-haired Spanish girl, just fifteen. She was not only beautiful, but she also acted so grown-up. We all envied her. She came from an old aristocratic family, and her parents had left her in the security of a boarding school in Switzerland, far away from a threatened revolution. (The Spanish Civil War broke out on July 18, 1936.)

After studying each other secretly for a while one afternoon, she confessed in tears that she envied all of us. We, being older, stayed younger much longer. Spanish girls aged more rapidly and if she wasn't married by the time she was twenty, there would not be much hope left for her. We all had much more freedom and could wait for the big love of our life to come along. We also could go home after the summer, but she had to stay. This admission came so unexpectedly for us that our admiration and envy changed into pity. Suddenly we saw our own world through her eyes. Now I looked at my home and the strict but loving rules more appreciatively.

There was a Jewish girl, Sara, from Vienna, who was only thirteen. She shared with her mother the most beautiful room with a big balcony on the second floor. We thought it was unusual for a girl to live with one of her parents at a boarding school. The mother was so pleasant everybody loved her, and we forgot that this was a place for young girls only. She played the piano beautifully and would often entertain us in the evenings in the big living room. I loved to hear her play Auguste Durand's Première Valse. She encouraged me to buy the sheet music for myself, which I did, and she helped me play it. I still have this particular waltz and can't help but think of her whenever I come across it.

One day her husband arrived, too, from Vienna and also stayed at the *Mistral*. He was like a father to all of us. We all used to go down to the lake together to swim or to row in our own boat. In the afternoon around five, we often watched the Zeppelin passing over the lake to the north, slowly and majestically. It looked like a big silver cigar, glittering in the sunlight high in the sky, before arriving at its base in Friedrichshafen in the evening.

Once, during our regular afternoon break in the garden with juice and sweet rolls, the French-Swiss lady who owned the boarding school asked me very unexpectedly, "How is your *Monsieur* E'etlair?" (That was the way she pronounced Hitler, but it sounded to me like "eclair.") It took me a moment to figure out what she meant. Why had she asked me that? I didn't know what to say. The lady knew, I was sure, more about our brand new chancellor and the Nazis, than we German students did. Before I could think about some kind of an answer, Sara's father thoughtfully came to my rescue. "How is she supposed to know?" After a small pause he added, "It is not her fault." I wasn't fully aware at the time what he meant. We students were involved mostly with our studies and interesting social activities, not with politics. So the subject was dropped. Later he patted me on the head saying, "*Armes Kind*," poor child, because that's what we still were in 1933.

Sara's father also affectionately stroked my head one afternoon before we all left for our swim in the lake, but this time without Sara and only with the two governesses. I didn't know then that this was his gentle and personal way of saying good-bye to me. That day we stayed unusually long at the lake. Upon our return, the Jewish family had gone—no good-bye, no trace of them. We were very hurt and disappointed and missed them right away. They had become a part of the house as well as our lives, and left an empty spot. All our questions as to when and why were very clearly dropped and the subject abruptly changed to something else. We gathered that the family had left for somewhere unknown. Much later I realized they may have anticipated that soon Austria would follow Hitler's path. But I never forgot them, especially when I played the Première Valse in the evening. Perhaps Sara may read these lines some day, too.

At the time I did not know that many intelligent and highly educated Jews, like Einstein, were leaving Germany, and in the case of Sara's family, also Austria, and had to disappear into thin air. It took me years to realize that people outside of Germany, like Sara's family, were much better informed and alert about Germany at that time than we were ourselves. It was as if we were on stage, involved only in our little role, but they were the spectators in the audience with a much better general view and understanding, and were provided with foreign newspapers.

August 1 is a big national holiday in Switzerland like the Fourth of July in the United States. Both countries' celebrations go back to their founding days. Only in Switzerland, their past goes back to the year 1291. The CH on the Swiss license plates stands for the Confederation Helvetae. We learned that in their more than five hundred-year old tradition, only a native-born Swiss can be a member of the Pope's guard.

Their colorful uniforms, designed by Michelangelo, can still be seen today in the Vatican.

The city was going to hold its annual festival with a huge fire on Mount Chaumont, overlooking the town. All day long people started walking up the 3,838 feet to be close to the planned bonfire and torchlight celebration with fireworks. We all wanted very badly to be part of that, too. To our disappointment we were divided into two groups. Only the non-Germans could go with the teachers. The others, including me, would take a boat ride on the lake with the couple that owned the boarding school. The simple explanation was that we would have a great view of the fireworks from the water. But we already knew better from experience; they wanted to keep us away from the crowds, not knowing how the Germans would be accepted. The *Mistral* felt responsible for our safety, being aware of fanatics who turned up everywhere.

From the lake we had a terrific view of the many bonfires on the surrounding mountains, as well as the spectacular fireworks. We had to stay close to our escorts at all times and were also instructed not to talk so much—so we would "see and hear better," as it was put. It was a memorable evening.

Later in August, the time approached for being graded in my French summer course. During that period we had to hand in many written compositions and make little speeches standing in front of the entire class. That was very hard for me to do under the critical eye of different teachers. I was advised just to look over their heads, and it worked.

Finally the last day of school arrived and we all got our report cards. I looked at mine and was shocked. Every grade was a six from top to bottom. One of my classmates had the same grades and was very happy about them. Seeing my startled face, she looked at my report card and congratulated me. It took me a while to understand that six was the best mark one could get. This was exactly opposite from Münster where a one would have been the highest grade and a five the worst. A six didn't even exist. I wondered how I was ever going to explain that to my parents.

It was time for us classmates to say good-bye to each other. We would all return to our different parts of the world and to our separate lives. In the *Mistral*, everyone was very proud of me and my good grades. I had learned all of my lessons but still could not speak French. If foreign languages were so easily mastered, Esperanto would never have been invented in Europe back in 1887.

Even though we endured some moments of hostility, we German students didn't feel persecuted in any way. Adolf Hitler had been the chancellor since January 1933, and a number of very disturbing events had taken place in the previous seven months which must surely have accounted for the reactions we experienced in Neuchâtel. Except for these isolated displays and the safeguarding of our supervisors, the summer had been exceptional.

When my two months were up, I was very anxious to get home again. As a matter of fact, I was so excited, that when I changed trains and countries in Basel, I expected my suitcase to do the same. However, when I arrived in Münster, there was no suitcase. Fortunately Günter happened to be on leave from the navy and came to help me at the checkout. One of the officials at the train station was very understanding and promised to take matters into his own hands. But that wouldn't make my suitcase appear right now. Papa's comment was, "One cannot let that girl do anything on her own!" That wasn't my opinion at all, but why argue.

In any case, they all wanted to know everything about my trip, and I had a lot to tell. Several days later my suitcase showed up in Münster. Günter and I went together to the train station, and sure enough there was the same helpful official whom we had met the first time and who had been so understanding. He smiled about my inexperience, but didn't inspect my suitcase either. Instead, he wanted to know more about Switzerland. He asked me many specific questions, and was very eager for details. I told him precisely all I knew, very flattered by his attention. Years later, recalling our conversation about Switzerland, I wondered about the true reason for his great interest. Today, since I understand a lot more about politics myself, I see his questions back in September 1933 in a very different light, and I hope he got to Switzerland himself, for whatever reason.

$\mathscr{P}$lays and Plots

$\mathscr{B}$y 1934, people were finally starting to build a more stable life. Hitler's appearance on our political scene was so swift that by the time we found out who he really was, he was already firmly entrenched with absolute power over the government, and, it seemed, over every phase of our private lives.

There had been rumors as to the methods by which Hitler had gained his powerful hold on the government, and even though there was strong evidence of their truth, you would never find any hint of his wrongdoing in the German press. We had just gone through his brutal liquidation of Ernst Röhm, founding father of the Nazi Party and well known as a crony of Hitler. Since 1931 he had been chief of the entire SA (the feared brown shirts) which he had initially organized, and had developed into the strongest Nazi force. In recognition of his long and faithful service, he was promoted in 1933 as a minister without portfolio in Hitler's cabinet.

It was said that Röhm had planned to develop his SA into kind of a people's army as a parallel force to our regular army, and this ambition alarmed Hitler, who even as chancellor was afraid of plots against him by his own circle of friends. He immediately became suspicious of his closest confidant Röhm and proceeded with a plan to eliminate him.

On June 30, 1934, Röhm had assembled his staff of high ranking SA leaders for a routine meeting in the Hotel Hanslbauer in the Upper Bavaria town of Wiessee, by the lake Tegernsee. That night, as the meeting turned into the usual drinking orgy, the SS surrounded the place and then stormed in, arresting all persons present and shooting many of them to death on the spot. This murderous assault against his old accomplice became known as the *Röhm-Putsch* in Nazi history. The people called it the "German Bartholomew Night" because it was similar to the deceitful 1572 slaughter of the Protestant Huguenots in Paris.

The newspaper headlines had proclaimed a dangerous plot against Hitler, but it was never proven that Ernst Röhm had planned any plot. In Hitler's speech to the Reichstag, he played it down as allegedly having been done to maintain order, assure national security, and to protect the German people.

The result of all this deeply concerned us because the SA, without Röhm, lost its importance and was degraded to a kind of pre-military training. The SS (*Schutzstaffel*) or Hitler's safeguard escort, which formerly was nothing but a subdivision of the SA, now ascended to a frightful level of power within Germany. It became a state within a state, and the hated and unscrupulous Heinrich Himmler, chief of the black-coated SS, rose to a power only second to Hitler's—a few men controlling all others. This went to such an extreme that the SS, with its arrogant behavior, even grew into rivalry with the German general staff of the armed forces, which would have fatal consequences later in World War II.

Arbitrary mass arrests of political undesirables followed, with one of the most notable being Hitler's bloody revenge on Gregor Strasser, who often dared to oppose Hitler, and whose less aggressive tactics had made him too popular even among non-Nazis. Also eliminated was General Kurt von Schleicher who had been our last chancellor for just two months before Hitler took over. It was he who warned President Hindenburg to never allow Hitler, that rude Bohemian corporal, to ever attain any power in the government. Hitler never forgot that humiliation, and in cold revenge, had the SS murder the general and his wife in their Berlin home.

The murder was presented as the result of a burglary, but everybody knew the truth. The Nazi cover-up of the atrocity was too evident, no matter how hard a cynical Goebbels tried to suppress it. Papa was incensed about such a wave of political violence in which Hitler would dare to liquidate everyone who was only a potential political opponent. It was cold-blooded murder of thousands, the exact number was never known, and no one was safe from the terrorism. We were deprived of our most basic civil rights, which was the way Hitler knew how to assure his position. Also, to make himself look more civilized, he wanted to rid himself of the roughnecks who had brought him into power.

Political occurrences like these affected me, too. We had planned that I would go to England for the summer to improve my English, as I had done the previous summer in Switzerland with French, and I was very excited about taking my second trip to a foreign country. However, we had read in the newspapers about some hostile acts against Germans in England, and even against newsstands which carried German newspapers. In view of this, my trip was canceled because my parents feared it would not be safe for me to go there by myself. We later realized that these alarming reports had been greatly exaggerated in the German press to discourage us from taking trips out of the country. The government did not want us to exchange money or ideas with foreign nations.

Also, around this same time, the long-time principal of our school retired due to illness and was replaced by a different one, who immediately changed school policies. Before the summer vacation of 1934, according to new rules, we had to participate in a new mandatory program in which some of the upper classes had to take part in a two-week educational Nazi summer camp program instead of attending school.

In this particular year, a nationwide Goethe-Schiller festival was celebrated in the very romantic eight hundred-year old town of Weimar at the river Ilm, in Thuringia, which was once known as the German Athens. Weimar grew into a cultural center under Karl-Auguste, Duke of Weimar, when our famous classical poet Johann Wolfgang von Goethe (1749-1832) was the leading figure at his court. Goethe means to Germans what Shakespeare means to English speaking people.

Weimar gained fame because of intellectual leaders such as Schiller, Wieland, Herder, Franz Liszt and others who had great influence in Europe, and gave Germany the reputation of being a nation of poets and thinkers. For a German, visiting Weimar is like a pilgrimage to Mecca, and thousands of visitors were expected for the festival that year. Our beloved teacher, Papa Heller, took advantage of these cultural events, and somehow managed to arrange an academic trip there for at least two of the upper classes, which included mine. We were to participate for one week in a large cultural and educational program, and since this would take care of the first week of the two weeks we were supposed to be in the Nazi summer camp, no other valuable school time would be lost.

All eighteen students in our class wanted to go but not all could afford the extra expense since some students had widowed mothers from

World War I and others had unemployed fathers. And then there was our half-Jewish classmate, Hertha Simon, the most gifted student in our class. Our class decided that we would go only if everyone was included, and to raise the extra money to cover the expenses for the needy ones, we put on a play, Schiller's classical drama The Bride from Messina, and charged admission.

By producing the performances as a total class effort, we all raised the money together and no one felt as if she were receiving charity. After several performances, our small admission charge collected not only enough to cover needed travel expenses, but also some pocket money. We all eagerly packed our suitcases.

Departing by train in July, we arrived at the remote small town of Weimar and were assigned lodging in private homes, all close to each other. Two girls shared a room, my roommate being Gertrud. We were very lucky to be staying with a widow who enjoyed mothering us. The whole class would meet for all meals at a local restaurant.

Each morning during breakfast, that day's excursion was discussed, and, of course our first stop was a guided tour of the home where Johann Wolfgang von Goethe had lived for more than fifty years, an impressive three-story structure. The residence was given to him by the reigning prince and close friend Duke Karl August of Saxe-Weimar. Goethe was the greatest German classical poet of the nineteenth century and greatly influenced European literature.

In the afternoon we walked out to Goethe's small two-story summer house which was half hidden by a hedge on the edge of a large park, and looked very peaceful with blooming espalier roses winding over the entire front. The scene was very familiar to me since I had a framed picture of it at home, which had been given to me as one of my confirmation presents three years ago, and I still have it today.

This small house and all of its furnishings had also been a gift from his royal friend, and Goethe had worked here for many years before moving to the larger house in town. But he always returned to this peaceful spot. No wonder, the house radiated a special atmosphere. We were touched and passed through it with deep admiration. In one room was the high desk at which he wrote his poetry standing up, mostly at night. Everything was left the way the great poet had lived; how simple, how modest in many ways. With the daylight fading, we finally left when the late evening sun cast a warm glow through the windows and turned the modest furnishings into a golden color. For us it was breathtaking, a great moment of sharing the past.

Each following day we explored something new. The homes of Goethe and Schiller were now museums and contained the valuable collections of their handwritten works, which were kept under glass for preservation and safekeeping. Then we walked over to the princely vault where both poets are buried next to each other and stood there for a moment of silent respect. During our exciting week, we saw so many of the objects of cultural and historical interest in Weimar that, in the end, they all seemed to run together.

Every evening we went to the theater to view a classical play. Following the performance on our last night, we all joined in a torchlight parade through Weimar, which ended back at the monument of Goethe and Schiller in front of the National Theater. It was now past midnight, and we were all exhausted from the week's activities. We also had to meet at the theater again early next morning since Papa Heller had arranged for us and other classes to get a tour backstage, to permit us an interesting glimpse of all the activities behind the scenes. How fascinating that sounded at night—as the finale to our cultural week.

But next morning, when the alarm went off much too early for Gertrud and me, we just turned over in bed. We figured we wouldn't be missed in the crowd of so many students. Unfortunately everyone in our class had the same idea, and only Rosemarie showed up. But breakfast we all attended punctually. Did we get scolded! We never saw Papa Heller so mad. His was the only class which did not appear. Since the blame was evenly distributed among all of us, we did not take it too personally, just looked appropriately guilty. Only Rosemarie smiled, beaming with her Nazi sense of duty. We also had to be packed and ready to leave right after breakfast for the train ride to nearby Eisenach in Thuringia.

When we arrived there, we were crammed into a bus for a hasty visit to the legendary Wartburg castle, built in 1067. It stands on a small rocky cliff overlooking the town. There we peeked into the historic chamber of Saint Elizabeth whose entire life was devoted to charity, a sort of Mother Theresa of her time, and, following her death in 1231, she was canonized in 1235.

We next entered the room where Martin Luther had accomplished the monumental task of translating the New Testament from Greek into vernacular German in less than a year (1521-1522). Papa Heller explained that his bible translation had also standardized our German language as the first literary work to be written in modern High German. But we had to rush through every phase of our fascinating visit since it was mandatory that we report to the Nazi camp that evening.

Upon arrival late that night, we couldn't imagine what would be in store for us. Of course we would be sleeping in bunk beds in a large dormitory, but totally unexpected was how we would be transformed overnight from free-spirited individuals into pliable masses of nobodies. We immediately learned that for the next week our lives would be controlled through a strict regimentation. It was clear that the primary purpose of the camp was mass political indoctrination. The drum beaters were young leaders in uniform. Every move from 6 a.m. reveille to taps at 10 p.m. was in accordance with a strict schedule. Each day started with raising the swastika flag outside, and a shouted *Heil* and homage to Hitler, with us standing in straight lines in rain or shine.

Following breakfast, and continuing throughout the day, there was a boring, repetitive cycle of political brainwashing, such as: any disastrous situation was the fault of Hitler's predecessors. And, that Hitler was the only one who could correct the mess resulting from mismanagement of the past fourteen years, and the new freeway projects he initiated had already reduced unemployment. Two lanes in each direction seemed enormous in the 1930s and were supposed to be extended from year to year for traffic to zip along at 120 miles per hour. They raved that again it took Hitler to do it for the benefit of the people and that we were to be proud of him every single day. Although these new freeways were supposed to improve ease of long distance driving, their true purpose was for the rapid movement of troops and supplies in time of war. Our loyal Nazi camp leaders may have never even imagined the purely strategic reasons. Nothing could shake their faith in Hitler. The average person in Germany had no car to be interested in speed, and the Volkswagen had not yet been invented.

The *Heil Hitler* salute prefaced and concluded all meetings, and on our frequent marches, we sang Nazi songs. That sort of enthusiasm unnerved us. We had lost our pleasant, easy-going lifestyle and now faced a grim, strict future of regimented daily routine, with no chance for free will or independent thinking. No wonder that the classes which had already spent one week in the camp were envious of us for the days we had managed to avoid the new camp routine.

In the evenings, Papa Heller was able to organize some sociable games for us to help break up the monotonous schedule. We thought that these seven days would never end, but they did and we were able to pack up and return to Münster. That week in the Nazi summer camp gave me a vivid idea of what the Nazi's highly advertised *Arbeitsdienst*, the six months of volunteer national labor service, would be like, which all girls were constantly urged to sign up for and to take part in. We all returned home with memories for a lifetime. The mark left on me was: never again if I can avoid it!

A picture from my school days. Papa Heller is standing on the far right.
I am third from right (same row).

I was looking forward to being home again for the six weeks of summer vacation which would soon be starting, and traveling with my family to Berlin where Papa frequently had to go on business. We always stayed at the same hotel because we knew the owners, Mr. and Mrs. Wischmann, quite well. On such visits, we frequently had our afternoon coffee hour with them at their family table. Mrs. Wischmann was a marvelous pastry cook. I was always instructed never to ask for a second helping, but Mrs.

Wischmann was quite aware of this admonition and of my craving for pastry. She automatically served me a second piece as a matter of course. I pretended to be astounded, but devoured it with gusto. Then I would catch the little wink she gave me in an unguarded moment.

While we were there, Mutti and I would go sightseeing for the entire day, and because of our mutual love for museums, would visit as many as time permitted. Usually we started with the ones on Museum Island in the heart of old Berlin. We always went first to the Pergamon Museum, a large three-winged building, with the world-famous Pergamon Altar, part of an ancient Hellenic temple, and the monumental Market Gate of Miletus as well as other architectural wonders of Asia Minor (now Turkey), all on the original gigantic scale. We had learned that these acquisitions were discovered through the German archaeologist Heinrich Schliemann's large excavations of ancient Troy in the late nineteenth century in Turkey, and were transported stone by stone to Berlin and reassembled there in 1902 in enormous buildings especially designed for their display.

With the Soviets' arrival in Berlin in 1945, the Trojan gold, a vast collection of several thousand precious and ornate jewelry pieces (also called the treasures of Priam, the King of Troy), vanished to Moscow into the basements of the Puschkin museum. They are still there, as Russian President Boris Yeltsin admitted in 1993, and the debates about their return are severe. Later, in the Egyptian museum, we viewed the bust of the most famous Egyptian queen, Nefertiti, created more than 3,300 years ago.

Papa and Mr. Wischmann, being both friends and businessmen, decided to enter into a joint business venture, which Mutti viewed as an unnecessary new headache. Papa would purchase a lodge with a café in Birkenwerder, a lovely suburb of Berlin, and Mr. Wischmann would operate it as the manager, with a profit for both of them. Papa named it "Café and Restaurant Hindenburg."

The property was located in a big garden with a shaded dance floor under old trees. A widow who had run the café for years and took care of the house lived upstairs in a separate apartment. There was a large dining room and corner bar downstairs, and an L-shaped veranda ran around the front where one could sit at tables with a beautiful view of the gardens. The extra bedrooms upstairs could easily be rented to guests since there was a nearby lake. Papa planned to dedicate his new business venture by holding a family reunion there. There was plenty of room for everyone and since we owned it, there would be no charge. We were our best guests.

The family gathering was scheduled on August 2, 1934, and my two aunts and uncles with their children arrived, and also my girlfriend Elsa with her parents from Schweidnitz. (Elsa's and my father had been old friends and so were we girls.) Papa had planned a joyful family celebration with swimming in the lake and dancing to a live band on the garden dance floor, a perfect fun-filled family gathering. But a news report suddenly changed all that.

On that special day, Mutti, Papa and I rode from Berlin to Birkenwerder by S-Bahn, an electrified inner city railway like in Chicago. Suddenly our fellow passengers started whispering, pointing to the half-mast flags outside. At 9 a.m. that morning, President Hindenburg had died at his estate Neudeck in East Prussia, now Russia. That sudden news hit us like a bombshell. He was an old man, eighty-seven, but many people lived a lot longer than that. Mutti and Papa were shocked and exchanged that special look I knew from the past. Their eyes met, and there was that silent "Oh, my God" in their expression.

Hindenburg's death put a sudden damper on the happily planned family reunion. Instead of Papa cheerily greeting his guests, we all sat in the café like a flock of startled chickens, listening to the radio for more details. Among the other guests in the dining room were some brown Party uniforms, sitting at a separate table. As soon as they had left, a worried conversation started. Mr. Wischmann had already warned Papa to be more careful with his political opinions in public. Quite regularly some Nazis came around in civilian clothing so they would look like harmless guests, but their true purpose was to spy on people's attitudes. The meshes of the spider's web thrown over us were already that tight.

The Nazi government immediately turned the President's death into a public showcase for a big national event of mourning. Although Hindenburg had previously requested only a small private funeral with burial on his estate in the family vault in Neudeck, Hitler planned a gigantic state funeral inside the famous memorial erected in Tannenberg, East Prussia, where in August 1914, Field Marshal Hindenburg, the German hero, had defeated the invading Russian army.

The Nazi government lost no time in taking advantage of Hindenburg's death, and the very next day, the cabinet hastily met and arbitrarily merged the chancellorship with the presidency, thereby abolishing the title of president and terminating the constitutional state. Within twenty-four hours, Hitler had achieved full power over Germany, as the head of state, including supreme command over all the military forces—before Hindenburg was even in his grave.

But all this behind the scenes activity did not reach the attention of the public, and the news was filled only with the funeral preparations to honor our beloved Hindenburg. Two weeks of national mourning were declared. Hitler's image had been enhanced by having a man like Hindenburg at the head of the government. Now he was gone, a terrible loss. We were left with Nazi propaganda, creating a vast structure of ignorance and misinformation.

We couldn't imagine yet how all this would concern us to a disastrous degree in the future. To select for Hitler the very title of *Führer* for his newly established position, which in the German language has multiple meanings, was a masterpiece of skillful Goebbel propaganda. It can mean commandant, manager, leader, guide, driver or pilot, depending on the context of use. For example, a museum guide would be a *Museum-Führer* and a street-car conductor a *Strassenbahn-Führer*.

I must add here an example of how the rise and fall of the title *Führer* was a cause of considerable embarrassment to me after the war, in the 1960s, during a visit to the Versailles palace near Paris. I had become separated from my French group, and was suddenly surrounded by Spanish and English-speaking tourists. I raised my voice to my German girlfriend, "*Wo ist mein Führer? Ich kann meinen Führer nicht sehen!*" Where is my "guide?" I can't see my guide! This brought complete silence and everyone glared at me. Fortunately our French guide located us and quickly pulled me out of sight whispering, "Stop shouting for your *Führer*. Are you crazy?"

Since Hitler had eliminated any political opposition through the Enabling Act a year and a half before, the death of Hindenburg made him the unrestricted totalitarian ruler of Germany. He could legally and irrevocably liquidate those considered to be political dissidents or undesirable to Nazi principals. As in the past, now, and in the future— friend or enemy, German or German Jew, could be eliminated without asking any other authority. We were force-fed obedience. A "state within the state" was created. Every election in the future, and there were many to come, was nothing but a farce, because there were no other political parties anymore which could have fought for peoples' votes. Hitler's will alone would become the bible of his new Germany.

In August 1934, we still had been totally unsuspecting of what was brewing behind our backs. We just picked up our lives, one day at a time, and somehow continued our family reunion. Elsa and I were one year away from the *Abitur* and studied together in the veranda. This way we also kept an eye on everything that was going on inside and out, especially watching the young men who would be available later for dancing in the garden. They were not in overabundance after World War I (but not as decimated as after World War II). However, their availability was of little benefit to me because I could seldom escape Papa's strict supervision, which lasted into my twenties. Papa, who foresaw everything, wanted us at the big family table and not sitting somewhere else, let alone at the bar. That was absolutely forbidden. Elsa's father was much more liberal, but Papa was stronger and we all wanted to live in peace. This also meant that we had to go to bed at 10 p.m.

All in all it was a very happy time, one of the last comparatively carefree family meetings. But Hindenburg's death was a forerunner of unfortunate events to come. Mr. Wischmann was a man of refreshing humor. He had always joked about death, and that he wanted his coffin equipped with a cold buffet and a secret exit, so he would not miss anything after he was gone. Well, life goes on without consulting us. Shortly thereafter he died of a heart attack while he was driving from the Café in Birkenwerder to his hotel in the city. He was found in his stalled car on the wrong side of the road. It must have rolled into the opposite lane when he lost control, which brought it to the attention of the police. It was a shock to all of us.

The Wischmanns had no children of their own to carry on the business. Our lodge and café in Birkenwerder had to be sold again. Now Mutti easily could have said, "I told you so." But she didn't have to. We all knew she was right, including Papa. All this was disastrous for Mrs. Wischmann. A nephew was to inherit and take over the hotel in Berlin. He moved in under her guidance, and everything seemed to have a pleasant ending after all.

When my family moved to Berlin in 1935, Mrs. Wischmann was often our guest, and so were all our relatives and friends. As fate would have it, in just a few years it would serve as a refuge for many of them who would become homeless because of the war. How could we be aware of such a future when Hitler only talked peace on every occasion, until his war in 1939.

To conclude this example of the best laid plans of man, Mrs. Wischmann died a few years after her husband. Hitler took care of the future again. Her death spared her the sight and agony of the complete loss of her life's work. The nephew, being a young man, was soon drafted into the army, went off to war, and never returned. And, finally, the hotel itself was blasted into ruins after a night bombing raid.

To cap the story, in an ironic twist, the site of that hotel, Friedrichstrasse 44, was located on what was to be the border between East and West Berlin. The property was appropriated for a guard point which was to become known worldwide as "Checkpoint Charlie," the key American crossing point into the Soviet sector. Germany fell victim to the disagreement among the victorious Powers and so did Berlin. What a blessing that we could not foresee the future, even though we sometimes were tempted to try to unveil it impatiently.

".Finished" at Last

In 1935 my schooling was nearing its end, but the year first produced political fireworks. The German Saar Basin, a center of our important coal and steel industry that bordered on France and Luxemburg, was placed forcibly under the auspices of the League of Nations for fifteen years (1920-1935) by the Versailles Treaty. The Saar had been German territory for ages, but the French had always wanted it. Now it was ready for a free plebiscite to determine if it would be reunited with Germany or France.

Hertha Simon's Jewish mother was born in the Saar, so she took a trip there to exercise her voting rights on January 13, together with her three children, to show them her homeland. The plebiscite resulted in the overwhelming vote of 90 percent for the return to Germany. Hitler boasted of it as a peaceful defiance of the Versailles Treaty.

Before the *Abitur*, each of us had to turn in a handwritten autobiography, of course using old German script. The Roman script, the same writing as in the U.S., could only be used for our foreign languages, English, French, and Latin. Since under Hitler men were dominant beings and women were relegated to be homemakers, I carefully wrote down something like, "I will devote my future to home economics," in order to be inconspicuous for whoever looked at my statement.

Hertha returned just in time for the week of written examinations, which took place each day from 8 a.m. until noon. Monday started with German literature, of course in German script. English, French and mathematics followed on succeeding days. In March the week for oral exams was scheduled. We were examined individually in our large art room in front of an imposing panel of teachers and important school officials.

At first every student was tested on her knowledge of the two new compulsory subjects added to our curriculum by the Nazis since 1933—

Rassenkunde, racial issues, and *Vererbungslehre,* genetics. Both taught the classifications of different races, their inequality, and the claim to leadership of the "superior" ones like the Nordic races. They dealt with dominant and recessive hereditary characteristics and the doctrine of racial purity as an important factor in marriage for pure-blooded Germans. Hitler's biological point of view was supposed to be drilled into every student. Luckily our teachers had given us the questions and answers beforehand, so we made no mistakes.

Then followed the elective, in which we were expected to be especially knowledgeable. Mine was religion. I had to talk about Schleiermacher, a theologian and philosopher, and his relation to the Greek philosopher Plato. Today I wonder what I said. The audience was impressed, but I can't remember one word. So far so good. My next subject was French, literature and grammar. Later I was called in again for mathematics, integral and differential calculus.

We were especially afraid of history for one good reason: as a mandatory requirement we had to read Alfred Rosenberg's book *The Myth of the Twentieth Century,* a bulky volume, burdened with his bewildering sophisticated speculations. Rosenberg, an anti-Jewish propagandist, was looked upon as the Nazi philosopher. I didn't understand any of his book. Mutti, bless her heart, offered to read it with me, but though we tried our darndest, we just couldn't plow through it. We found it totally confusing, crammed with new but aimless verbiage, everything far-fetched. We gave up together and so did the entire class. Papa Heller was obliged to recommend the book to us students, but he never checked if we read it. Though it was the most printed book on the market, together with Hitler's *Mein Kampf* (10 million were published), they were the least read. Both books afforded Hitler an enormous income. Luckily, they were not even mentioned during our history exam. (Rosenberg was later sentenced to death at the Nuremberg Trials in 1946.)

At the end of the week, we had all passed. Hertha Simon was the only one who graduated with an "A." A few other students, including me, were awarded a "B," the rest of the class a "C," but most important, we all were now eligible to attend the university. At that time, Papa was already in Berlin and I sent him a telegram that I had passed successfully. He was so proud that he showed it to everyone.

I don't believe in numerology, but the way the important days of the *Abitur* coincided with our family birthdays, and later events in life, was most amazing. All my oral exams were on March 8, Günter's birthday. As a celebration, there was no prom or formal dance. Instead we met our teachers in an elegant restaurant on March 15, my birthday. For this occasion we had prepared our own amusing class newspaper with jokes and poems about everybody, students as well as teachers. That created an unforgettable birthday party for me.

Apparently we could not live any more without some political surprises. The next day, March 16, 1935, encouraged by the return of the Saar Basin, Hitler announced that the clause of the Versailles Treaty which limited Germany's army to one hundred thousand men was invalid. Overnight, compulsory military service was restored, "for a peacetime army." All this happened without any serious objection from the Entente Powers. Since Hitler got away with his gamble so well, our newspapers were full of Goebbels' propaganda praising the success of the Führer. Many men were drafted, and the unemployed taken off the street by the thousands. But all that did not concern me. We girls were in the middle of our *Abitur* celebration.

Our solemn graduation ceremony followed on March 19 in the big auditorium. This was Mutti's birthday. We all appeared in formal dresses, not with the caps and gowns traditionally worn for graduation ceremonies in the U.S., sometimes even for graduation from kindergarten, as with my grandson in California. In Germany caps and gowns are limited to university graduates only. In our joy we didn't realize that this was our good-bye. I would leave for Berlin. Hertha Simon's mother would go to England with her three "partly non-Aryan" children (as half Jews were labeled) and leave Germany for good. We would never meet again.

With Papa in Berlin, only Mutti was present at the ceremony. Afterwards, we two topped off my special day and her birthday in a glamorous café on the Prinzipalmarkt. Next day we would also leave for Berlin.

After such an exciting day, we nearly forgot about our most pressing problem: how to handle my rather short compulsory membership in the BDM, the League of German Maidens. A strict Nazi law required that as soon as one's address changed, one had to inform the BDM leader. Mutti and I deliberated what to do since they might have found me in

Berlin anyway, because every change of address had to be registered with the police. This is still the custom in Germany today, similar to the registration for social security in the United States. Not notifying the BDM could have caused very serious and unforeseen consequences.

So I went to my BDM leader with a heavy heart. She lived near our promenade. Now I had to meet her again after a year's excused absence for *Abitur* preparations. When I arrived at her house, to my surprise I did not have to ring the bell or knock on the door. The entrance was already wide open, very unusual in Germany. The place was crowded with people in Party uniforms rushing in and out. I was pushed aside as being unimportant since I was wearing only civilian clothes.

I didn't spot my leader anywhere. How could I discreetly find out more about that strange activity here without drawing unwanted attention to myself? Just then everybody was silenced and an announcement was made. Keeping myself hidden near the entrance, I could not believe my ears. My leader had died, apparently very suddenly, but it wasn't clear to me how or when. It seemed to be a strange and mysterious death. What a shock! Had she created too many enemies? What should I do now? On the one hand I was sure I had to notify someone about my leaving Münster. On the other, why disturb this rather busy assembly? Undecided as I was, I retreated as inconspicuously as I had appeared, sure that no one would miss me.

At home I was far less sure of what to do now. Mutti and I debated this unexpected and tricky dilemma from all angles, until we finally came up with a solution. The law said that one had to go to the BDM leader when a change of address occurred. I had been there. That my leader had died unexpectedly was not covered by any order. With a sense of relief we decided there were no further laws that would apply to such a case. So we did nothing. In case my transient membership became known later, I could always say that I did go to see my leader, without stating precisely when. Being nineteen by now, I would have been automatically transferred in Münster from the BDM into the *NS Frauenschaft*, the Nazi Women's League. Since I would be new in Berlin, I would be on no local BDM list from which they could transfer me. What a lucky break! My whole future looked like it would be free of Nazi ties.

Prior to our move, Papa had been in Berlin already for several weeks to make arrangements for a new home in one of the western suburbs called Zehlendorf-West. It was a recently developed, elegant area. In 1920, Berlin had merged with urban suburbs and rural estates to form Greater Berlin, the size of Munich, Frankfurt and Stuttgart together. With 4 million inhabitants, Berlin was the third largest city in the world after New York and London, and also a giant financial and industrial center.

Our train from Münster arrived in Berlin the afternoon of March 20, 1935. I pictured myself entering an exciting new life, but it started more in a vagabond style, living out of a suitcase in a hotel room in the city, on lively Friedrichstrasse, until the furniture arrived. The owners, the Wischmanns, were old business friends.

Early next morning Papa took us to see our new home. We went by S-Bahn, meaning *Stadt-Bahn*, which was like an above-ground subway. It had opened in 1882 and ran at short intervals around the clock. Within half an hour we were out of the heart of Berlin and amongst greenery and fresh air, leaving behind the sounds of a bustling city.

From the S-Bahn station we walked three minutes to our new house. From now on I would live on Margarethen Strasse 1a, a short, private tree-lined street. We were the second house from the corner of Lindenthaler Allee (avenue). Behind a white wooden fence stood elevated a red brick villa, three stories high, in the middle of a garden. The gardener was busy planting flowers on three terraces of field stones.

Mr. Behrmann, the architect, greeted us and we went around the house together to the back, and he showed us the large beautiful stone terrace for outdoor living. From there we entered the house and its first floor of three spacious rooms with parquet floors, a Florida room, tiled kitchen with two windows and a pantry, a half-bath and hall with the main entrance to the street. A curved staircase led us upstairs to three bedrooms. Mine was a corner room with windows on two sides and a tiled balcony, the size of a deck, which was above the Florida room. It looked just beautiful, even though it was still empty. Mutti surprised me with the news that we would shop for furniture the next day. I was overjoyed. Here was definitely the place for the new start I had in mind. I was going to attend the university.

On the third floor, next to a spacious attic for hanging the laundry, was a comfortable room with running warm and cold water for a maid. Like the other houses we had a stone, walk-out daylight basement with a furnace for the central heating. From there, doors opened to a big storeroom, the laundry, and a coal bin. An iron door led to the outside in front of the garage whose entrance was sheltered by the house above. The garage was still empty, but large enough for my future dream, a big car.

Mr. Behrmann commented on the magnificent surroundings of Berlin with the many square miles of lakes, rivers and woodlands covering one third of the city. "You can take boat rides on the Havel and Spree rivers and will forget completely that you are living in a cosmopolitan capital," he said. "Berlin can claim to be the greenest metropolis of Europe." We could see he was a proud Berliner.

We would also live here on historical ground, he continued. Zehlendorf had existed already in 1242. Flattered by my interest in history he added that five minutes from here was the Potsdamer Chaussee (highway), an old arterial road with the historical resting place where King Frederick II paused on his coach ride from Potsdam to Berlin, his royal residence. I was fascinated, but had no chance for further questions. Mr. Behrmann surprised us with his wife's invitation to lunch. His house was only five minutes away on foot and I was eager to see more of my new surroundings. Mrs. Behrmann was pleasant and warmhearted. We were also joined by Mr. Thiemer, the other architect of the team. The Behrmanns had three children around my age, two boys and a girl. This was a wonderful welcome and the beginning of a close friendship.

Two days later our furniture arrived and we got settled. Finally I could explore more of Berlin. The transportation facilities were excellent, consisting of the S-Bahn, busses and the subway, with convenient transfer points that took me almost anywhere. In no time I was strolling along the two-mile long Kurfürstendamm, the heartbeat of Berlin, called *Ku'Damm* for short, a boulevard as famous as Fifth Avenue in New York. It was a paradise for shoppers, lined with stores offering the finest of products, theaters, movie houses, hotels, gourmet restaurants and sidewalk cafés where people could watch the world go by.

Berlin had many faces. It was a cultural center with two great opera houses and the world-renowned Berlin Philharmonic Orchestra, as well as many museums and art galleries. Fostering my love of history, tradition was waiting around every corner, with royal palaces, impressive monuments and the famous Brandenburg Gate with its four-horsed Quadriga, driven by the Goddess Victoria, since 1788 the symbol of Berlin.

I walked through the central passageway and on the other side began Berlin's main promenade, the historic three-quarter mile long and two hundred feet wide grand boulevard *Unter Den Linden* (beneath the lime trees). It goes back to Frederick the Great, and was lined with historic buildings, the famous Hotel Adlon, restaurants and cafés, embassies, the arsenal, the State Opera House, and the cathedral. (After 1945 it became part of East Berlin, and under the Soviets it was stripped of its soul, beauty and history and turned into the most lifeless and saddest dead-end street in the world, reflecting the drabness of a ghost town à la Soviet tristesse, with the Brandenburg Gate as the divider between East and West.) I strolled along for a while admiring everything, but aiming for an imposing building on the left farther down, the Friedrich Wilhelm University (now Humboldt University). Here I stopped at a palatial building, originally built for a prince in the eighteenth century.

Berlin's university was one of our younger ones, but with the reputation of being one of the best. It was founded in 1810 by Wilhelm von Humboldt, the philosopher, scientist, statesman, and diplomat, and his brother Alexander, an explorer and one of the founders of modern geography. Both were honored by statues to the right and left of the entrance. There I stood with deep admiration. What an exciting experience it would be to attend classes where the philosopher Hegel, the physicists Max Planck and Albert Einstein, and the physician Robert Koch taught at various times, just to name a few, and where Karl Marx and Friedrich Engels, the founder of the theory of Communism, had been students. My secret plan was to study medicine. My hopes were high, and I couldn't wait to tell my parents about my future plans.

When I returned, Mutti first had her own family surprise. That morning she had hired a maid. Though my parents planned to get one eventually, Mrs. Behrmann had speeded up the decision, by sending someone over. Her name was Alma and she did not look like a maid at all. She wasn't one either, but rather a sales person from the elegant department store Wertheim at Potsdamer Platz, one of the liveliest areas of pre-war Berlin.

This was the period when jobs were parcelled out by government regulations to keep unemployment down. Even young sales girls in stores, Alma was just twenty-five, were forced to leave their positions and perform domestic duty in a household for a whole year, as a so-called *Haustochter*, house daughter, a maid with a fancier title. Mutti described her as well-mannered, willing, and also very desperate. Mrs. Behrmann had known Alma for years from shopping at Wertheim. She wanted to save her from ending up in unpleasant surroundings. Good-hearted as Mutti was, she was willing to try her. If it did not work out, one year would not last forever. Alma would move in next week. She had also told Mutti that wives of well-paid husbands were urged to do only volunteer work and give up their paid positions to people in reduced circumstances, preferably men.

Now it was my turn with the news, and I depicted my university plans with great enthusiasm. For a change Papa agreed and gladly offered to take over the tuition, which was much less than in the States. (Today, students pay hardly any tuition at all in Germany.) My academic future looked bright and exciting. However, we had completely forgotten to consider Nazi ordinances, which we should have been used to by now. We knew that since the Enabling Act, Hitler could interfere freely with as many new laws as he wished, like meddling with Alma's life. Only this time it would concern me. Suddenly, from early 1935 on, there was a state requirement for all students, male and female, to complete six months of compulsory service in a Nazi labor camp before attending the university.

So far, serving in a labor camp had been more or less a free choice, but not any more. My way to any German university was blocked without this Nazi camp service, which was extended to twelve months some years later. What a dilemma.

The new state requirement for labor camps, officially lauded as volunteer work for public benefit, was to be fulfilled in various fields. Men worked either in the swamps, or in the construction of our first freeways, similar to President Roosevelt's CCC, the Civilian Conservation Corps. Women worked mainly on farms, while living in camps. That may not sound so bad, but the true purpose was to instill Nazi ideology on the youth and their still plastic minds, with Nazi lectures as its central discipline, to remake the nation. Every evening, called club night, was dominated by lessons from their single-minded point of view.

That reminded me very vividly of my one week in a Nazi summer camp the previous year with all its ugly political pressure, and with the charm of a prison. The boys' sports looked more like pre-military training with spades on their shoulders instead of guns. Women were also sent as maids to poor laborer families who had more children than they could afford or handle. Hitler wanted numerous offspring, very useful as future cannon fodder. Food and clothing were supplied. So far I was not on any list in Berlin to be drafted from, and Mutti warned me to stay out of further political crossfire. Registering for *Arbeitsdienst* could immediately reopen my incomplete BDM membership. Neither my parents nor I wanted any exposure to such an investigation and consequences.

My dreams were so near and yet so far. I was dropped from cloud nine to Nazi reality, with all my ambitions shattered. For Papa it didn't matter so much. In his opinion my life was carefree, pleasant, and I would get married anyway. How I hated that often-repeated statement. Married to whom? I was hardly allowed to look at a man when Papa was around. In Münster I had felt overprotected during my teenage years, particularly on social occasions such as our school dances. The custom was for parents to attend, and mine invariably did. Papa was very definite in his stand that only parents could take the girls home afterwards, on foot. His ways were successful in keeping all young men away from me, at least at a safe distance.

There was never a dispute about preparing me for a profession and making my own money. My family wanted me to continue my education. But where would we find a place or organization that had still escaped the binding Nazi government regulations? Mutti, always successful in resolving my problems, suggested I go to Bad Godesberg on the Rhine River for a while, to the "House of Flora Frenzel," a well-known boarding school for young ladies. It had the European finishing school character, similar to the *Mistral* in Neuchâtel I attended in the summer of 1933. I liked the idea of getting away from home, since Berlin had too many disappointing limitations for me.

This school was recommended to us by a former student who was in a similar predicament. Bypassing all controversial Nazi questions she had escaped any interference. We also ran quickly through the school's apolitical formalities. I was gladly accepted and would start with their educational program on May 1, 1935, only a few weeks after our arrival in Berlin.

All travel plans were soon completed. I was hustled off to the train station early in the morning on May 1. Berlin was an exceptionally busy place with people rushing and gathering everywhere. Waiting for my train, we easily drew stares from passers-by who gave us undisguised critical looks, and that for two good reasons. First, there I stood with a tennis racket in my hand in the midst of an unexpected snowfall, and secondly, with my big suitcase, I looked too much like having no interest or time for the Nazi's special May Day Parade, or in the brand new national holiday for all working people.

For outsiders the May 1 celebration may look similar to Labor Day in the U.S., but in the States, the workers can relax and enjoy the day; not so with Hitler. He introduced a holiday more strenuous than work with compulsory marches and meetings, which lasted all day. May 1 was and still is a major Communist holiday with workers having to march and parade like in the former Soviet Union. Hitler copied it as a welcome occasion for his mass rallies, replete with marching music, insignia, and emotional Nazi slogans over loudspeakers. Everybody's presence was checked by somebody, and all the somebodies again controlled by their superiors, straight up the ladder of a strict hierarchy. It was thoroughly organized as to who and where to meet, at what designated location and appointed time, to guarantee that every unit (offices, schools, factories, and other organizations) followed the party line. Masses of people were required to stand and wait for hours in rain or shine, similar to my own former Nazi school meetings in Münster.

Obviously my family did not have time for a Nazi May-Day parade or Hitler's fiery and long-winded speeches prefaced by stirring music from Beethoven. He repeatedly recycled the same sermon: he was but a simple soldier in 1918, then dramatized his founding of the Nazi Party, the 1923 Beer-hall revolution, which then led into long harangues against the Weimar Republic, and finally he boasted highly of his loyalty to his old cronies. But he conveniently ignored his purging of several of them, eliminating rigorously any opposition in his own party.

That carried through the first hour at least. Finally he would come to the point of the day. He would not make idle promises blah, blah, blah. The word "speech" was an understatement for his fanatic, hysterically screamed sentences, "One for all, and all for one," and then destroying everyone's will with, "A person is nothing, the Reich is all!" All this was pounded into people's ears in his bombastic oratorical flight in his one-man shows.

No wonder people stared at us. Obviously, rather than celebrating, I was leaving Berlin. Also it had been common knowledge that whoever escaped the marching should at least be smart enough to keep out of sight and stay home. As soon as my train entered the station, after a quick good-bye kiss, I rushed aboard. Within minutes I was on my way to Bad Godesberg for a new cultural adventure. Mutti and Papa went straight home to avoid the crowds, parades, and Hitler speeches.

Beautiful weather with the moderate climate of the Rhine valley greeted me in Bad Godesberg, a garden town and spa on the west bank of the river. There was no parading here as in Berlin. What a relief. A teacher was to meet me at the train station and escort me to the school—most likely on foot. Getting off the train, I spotted a nervous and spindly-looking lady and thought to myself, "If that is my teacher, I don't need her help." There is an aspect of my nature which delights in circumventing authority and exercising independence. On a sudden impulse I successfully sneaked my luggage piecemeal out of the train station, all unnoticed by her.

Outside I hailed a taxi waiting in front of the station and gave the driver directions, just as I had seen Papa do all the time. He invariably preferred taxis, for he thought a car was too much trouble. After only a ten-minute ride among affluent villas and well-kept parks, we stopped in front of an impressive looking four-story building surrounded by a park-like garden, not exactly with the appearance of a school. I paid the driver, and as Papa always did, gave him a generous tip, and let him carry my luggage through the garden gate up the stairs to the front door. It was already wide open, since everyone was expecting us—the teacher and me. I entered with big hopes, but alone.

My unconventional arrival caused quite a scene. Here I was, a young girl in a conservative town, arriving in a taxi like royalty. This just wasn't done! Nearly everyone was on foot, occasionally on a bicycle. Not only did I arrive by taxi, but also unescorted. The school authorities, Mrs. Frenzel and her husband, a lawyer, were quite annoyed by this event, including the fact that I had "missed" my teacher. By no means was this the first or even the last time that my impulsive actions would get me into trouble, since I always could be counted on inadvertently doing or saying the wrong thing. But all the girls thought it great that I had made my entry in such a style—something they had never dared to try themselves.

The poor teacher arrived much later, on foot, extremely distressed over missing me. She was indeed the one I had spotted at the train station, already in her thirties, practically a senior citizen! Everybody liked her, and so would I, with plenty of time to realize how inconsiderate I had been. But I would probably succumb to the same temptation given the same opportunity.

Soon everybody met for the evening meal in the dining room, sitting around a long table, presided over by Mrs. Frenzel. I was introduced to everybody, the other teacher, and Mrs. Frenzel's mother, a warm-hearted little lady whom everybody tenderly called *Muttchen*, meaning Granny. Our student body ranged in age from seventeen to nineteen. Some young ladies came from England and the Netherlands, as well as from Germany. I also learned about the many house rules and that we should never leave unescorted. On that one, I had already offended them with my unorthodox arrival, and this before even starting their educational program. The boarding school's emphasis was on etiquette, music, literature, English as a foreign language, social studies and perfect housekeeping.

From morning to night our schedule was planned and organized. Breakfast at 7:30 a.m. was followed by two hours of theory such as world literature, English, or music appreciation. At 10 a.m. we were divided into two groups. One went into the school's large well-equipped kitchen to learn gourmet cooking. The other group was given highly detailed instructions on supervising the housekeeping, and final touches such as flower arrangements, table setting, and all the necessities of gracious living with *Gemütlichkeit* (cozy atmosphere). The main cleaning and most dishes were done by two hired maids.

The control over our "outside" contacts was rigid. All our mail and telephone calls were censored. I expected to have a problem with that restriction, for Günter would be sure to call me. And so he did soon, just for fun since he knew it would be frowned upon. I was summoned into the office because of his call from the Naval Academy in Flensburg.

Nobody believed that it was only my brother calling. To make matters worse, he also sent a picture postcard of himself on his new motorcycle, looking very handsome. The girls wanted to write to him secretly by general delivery. As if I didn't get into enough trouble on my own without Günter's outside help.

Günter on his motorcycle

Soon after, he wrote me that a party with friends was coming up and he would be willing to be the victim of my new culinary art. So, on my own I baked him a wonderful cake that looked very promising in the oven. Unfortunately it collapsed hopelessly when I took it out. I had baked a huge crater with a high rim. What a dirty trick of a cake. There was no time to bake a new one. Without any hesitation I filled my crater with a thick apple paste. After wrapping my masterpiece extra carefully, I mailed it to Flensburg. Günter assured me later that the cake was delicious, and that he and his friends ate it right out of the carton with the aid of some spoons.

The "gourmet cooks." I am on the left.

After the noon meal, we were sent regularly for a rest period to our bedrooms which were directly above the teachers' floor. They were sure to be aware of every sound overhead, but we slipped away noiselessly through a back staircase. Behind the tennis courts, a small creek marked the boundary line at the back of the property. We called this area the *Bosporous*—our open gate between two worlds. Here was also our outdoor "smoking salon." Smoking was considered unladylike. Hitler's recent decree that "the German woman does not smoke," was one more reason to try it out. Just as in the old story of the forbidden fruit. I was eager to do it, too. The sooner the better.

Some girls already smoked very elegantly with long fancy cigarette holders. The Dutch girls preferred longer-lasting cigarillos, but that looked too masculine to me. My attempts ended up in a lot of coughing. Plain logic told me: one cigarette doesn't last long. One would need several all the time; they also were expensive and I would only burn up my money. Did I really want to turn into a chain smoker, staining my fingers? So that was the end of my cigarette adventure. Besides, I knew a far better way for spending my allowance—on strawberry tarts loaded with whipped cream.

There was a second importance to our *Bosporous*. The small creek was easy to cross and so was the wire fence leading to a remote corner of the adjoining public school yard, our escape route to the nearby café, which we called "Café Five." "Five" was its house number. That was our private heaven where we left our pocket money and hearts, meeting some students of the close-by college.

Soon misfortune lurked around the corner. A teacher from the public school watched us "trespassing through their property" as she called it, and promptly phoned the House Flora Frenzel. Our school was in an uproar. Meanwhile we were blissfully enjoying ourselves in Café Five, until we returned to face the music. That put an end to our escapades— at least for a while. For some time, the atmosphere in the house was very gloomy.

However, the school had to face much bigger, and more political problems since its mere existence was contrary to the Nazi plan. Mrs. Frenzel avoided a conflict between Social Studies and the required message of Nazi socialism by having a student, a member of the BDM, occasionally give an orientation lecture to the class. Nobody liked it, including the speaker, but it kept the Nazi snoopers at bay.

In June, government propaganda raved interminably about Hitler's peaceful intentions and international good will. Since British wealth depended on the sea, he had just signed on June 18, 1935, an Anglo-German Naval Agreement with England, in which Germany's sea forces would not exceed 35 percent of Great Britain's. "Didn't our beloved Führer provide again the security of world peace in the future?" Goebbels exuberantly blasted over the radio. I could vividly picture Papa's critical face at home, mumbling something about *Goebbels-Schnauze* (Goebbels' big trap). But, duty bound, we at school acknowledged this new "peaceful political event" in our social studies.

Nevertheless, we were not safe from being heckled occasionally by some ardent members of the Nazi Women's League. They would pay us surprise visits with the intent to enlighten us with one of their educational harangues on any facet of Nazi doctrine. After all, they were not about to let us forget that a school like ours existed only because of their gracious mercy. At their arrival we were assembled in our classroom to listen. They started the same old brain-washing, always ending with the usual ultimatum to be a true Party-liner, or else! How familiar all that sounded to me from my BDM meetings in Münster.

These dry Nazi lectures passed over our heads like water over a duck's back. We were bored stiff. The Nazi speakers on the other hand were favorably impressed by our quiet attention, so they thought, unaware that we were half asleep and forced to listen. We carefully avoided any controversial discussions afterwards. The four foreign girls with only a limited knowledge of German just played along with us, completely missing what we were lectured about.

Our music teacher was Anne Borchers, who we lovingly called Ännchen. She was a soft-voiced, charming lady, the perfect person to guide us into the world of music and who also wanted us to develop a basic appreciation of opera. She told us how the old Siegfried saga inspired Richard Wagner to compose his Ring of the Nibelungs, a series of four operas, and that we would soon be going to see the Valkyrie, which was playing in the opera-house in Cologne. Even though I was used to going to the theater in Münster with my parents, this was an unforgettable event, and I am still thrilled by opera.

One afternoon Ännchen took us by streetcar to the nearby provincial town of Bonn, the birthplace of Beethoven. Bonn had a two thousand year-old history, founded as a Roman fortress, called Bonna. (In 1949 Bonn was amazingly promoted to be the temporary capital of the young German Federal Republic, ironically called "Mini Capital" or "Federal Village" by the Berliners.)

Ännchen told us that Ludwig van Beethoven, Bonn's greatest son, had an unhappy childhood. His father squandered away all his earnings on drink. Nevertheless, he tried to turn his talented son into a child prodigy like Mozart. She led us to his birthplace, an old house in the Bonn-Gasse, now a museum. It was modestly set back in a garden-like courtyard in the ancient part of town, now rather humble looking between modern and larger buildings. There we stood at Beethoven's piano where at the age of eleven, he created his first composition. The sheet music was displayed under glass. Respectfully we walked around the rooms filled with manuscripts, letters and many of his personal belongings.

Then we were off to his monument on the market place and we looked up at his statue in awe. As we knew, Hitler, the would-be artist, now took advantage of Beethoven's powerful music to introduce his numerous bloated speeches, usually a mixture of arrogance and distorted history. What presumption! Hitler grabbed the coattail of this giant genius for his own personal advantage.

Ännchen was also my private piano teacher. I loved her soft voice and the consideration she gave me. We sometimes talked more than we played during my piano lesson since I felt my playing was indifferent. But she encouraged me to play in the living room where we would gather in the evenings. "None of the other girls play" she said, "so you are better than all of them. Practice, play and enjoy it." I had never thought of it that way, and followed her advice. My parents' silver wedding anniversary was coming up in January 1936, and of course Papa expected me to exhibit my accomplishments. I detested that. But Ännchen overcame my phobia and trained me in the "Rustle of Spring" by Sinding, an impressive piece of music.

Since we all could swim, we frequently took boat rides up and down the Rhine where romantic castle ruins crowned the vineyard covered hills. It was incredible that two thousand years ago the Roman legionnaires introduced wine growing here on green hillsides. One day a wine grower guided us through his vineyard very carefully on narrow paths in a single file. Amazed, I observed that the cultivation, including grape gathering, had to be done exclusively by hand, an incredible task. I started to wonder that the price of the wine, produced through such a laborious process, was not much higher.

One early morning we took off on a day trip by bus to the picturesque Ahr valley, Germany's northernmost wine region. Here vineyards were nestled among steep hills. We were guests of a wine-grower, an old friend of the Frenzels. In their dimly lit stone cellars wine slumbered in heavy oak casks to become clear and pure gold.

Mrs. Frenzel left us to make arrangements for our lunch in a nearby garden restaurant. That meant we had our extensive wine tastings on an empty stomach. Slowly walking from barrel to barrel, we sipped samples from small test glasses, and listened to the explanations that accompanied each wine. The later the grapes were picked, the sweeter the wine. We eagerly mixed them all. It was just new and marvelous, until we emerged from the cool cellar into the warm sun outside. Suddenly the whole world was rolling like a ship, and we bumped into each other. Dizzy, with arms linked for support, we staggered along the country road, blocking its entire width. At the garden restaurant lunch was already waiting, and Mr. Frenzel made us quickly sit down around the long table under the disapproving eye of his wife. Totally tipsy, we collapsed, holding our pounding heads. Soon the food worked wonders in sobering us up, and we enjoyed every single bite. Also, we discovered how wonderful plain fresh water can taste. What I learned right then and there was: no alcohol on an empty stomach, and I still adhere to that today.

Mr. and Mrs. Frenzel with our tipsy group. (I'm on the far left, second row.)

On our side of the Rhine River bank, in an elaborate setting, was the mysterious Hotel Dreesen. Though we always wanted to visit their elegant café where lovely music was enticing, we never were taken there. A secret lingered around that place. One day, Aunt Frieda's surprise visit shed some light on it. She invited me out one afternoon, of course with Mrs. Frenzel's permission, and I was eager to visit that mysterious hotel. Sitting there in the elegant café, I looked around curiously, trying to discover the secret. Aunt Frieda laughed and told me what everybody knew in Gleiwitz. Only we, close by, were in the dark.

Dreesen was the name of the hotel's owner, who was also an intimate friend of Hitler. Special meetings of Party wheels were going on in here, often with Hitler's secret presence. So it was a hidden Nazi stronghold. I suddenly had the feeling that one of the waiters was always watching. Maybe newcomers were not welcome here. So Mrs. Frenzel had a very good reason for keeping her students away from Nazi establishments like this one.

While leisurely sipping our coffee, we couldn't even imagine that this mysterious hotel would be used, only three years later, as the place for a preliminary conference with British Prime Minister Neville Chamberlain during his second visit to Adolf Hitler to discuss the Munich Pact (April 29, 1938). We could imagine even less that nine years later, the Hotel Dreesen would arouse international attention. At the end of the war, the Nazis had changed it into a barricaded prison for members of the Vichy regime, captured by the German troops in their hasty retreat from France, and held here captive, surrounded by barbed wire and guarded by the SS.

Across the river from us, rose the *Siebengebirge* (seven-mountain range), a fairy tale region with the legendary *Drachenfels*, rock of the dragon. Its wine is called dragon blood and its name goes back to the ancient tale of a dreaded dragon who haunted the Rhine valley while guarding a cursed treasure, the "Rhine Gold." He was slain by brave Siegfried, a knight of King Gunter of Burgund. This was part of the *Nibelungenlied*, the great German epic that was passed down for generations by word of mouth until it was written down around 800 A.D. We climbed uphill over the rocky slopes for several hours to the place where, according to the saga, the dragon was slain fifteen hundred years ago.

There was an exchange of social affairs between House Flora Frenzel and the Bonn University fraternities. Even though they had been officially dissolved by Hitler two years ago, some still managed to keep up a few social activities in their privately owned club houses. These fraternities, like the *Wingolf* or the *Germanen*, invited us to their stylish balls. We, in turn, invited them to our formal dinner dances. The main purpose was to practice social graces.

Before each social affair Frau Frenzel scrupulously inspected our attire, and we had to parade in front of her in the living room. Particular attention was given to the upper exposure to make sure it was never too revealing. Many tears were shed in silent protest over being denied low-cut dresses, which looked as if they stayed up by magic, what we considered sophisticated embellishment.

After the lecture on how to sit as a lady, her instructions on "table etiquette" followed. Wine was always drunk on social occasions, and there were rigid rules. In Germany it is customary to propose a toast with the first sip and others usually follow with polite compliments. For the first toast the young lady would raise her glass and sip, the second time a lady would only raise her glass, the third time she would merely nod and smile, but not too inviting a smile—the young gentleman may misunderstand! The instruction did not go beyond three toasts, but the young men frequently extended that number. The rules were often bent a little by us girls.

However, soon our dancing program was in serious danger of being terminated. The explosion came when a Bonn student had the temerity to telephone the school at night, and a "Mister Germany" wanted to speak to "Miss England." This caused an uproar. It became obvious that private contacts had been made at the dances with some of the escorts. Of course both English girls protested their innocence in a charming broken German, "We nix know Mr. Germany." We marshalled all the support available in defense of dancing. Charming Muttchen and Mr. Frenzel were on our side. After the favorable decision on dancing, even our weekly group trips to the hairdresser were more closely supervised and we had to forego the secret visits to the post office to get general delivery letters.

On one of our group tours, which extended over several days, we toured the Rhine area by a privately rented bus, chaperoned by the Frenzels and one of the teachers. Happily singing old folk songs, we forgot all about Hitler and the Nazis. Instead, we enjoyed cultural treasures like old cloisters, mighty cathedrals and storybook towns where colorful geraniums bloomed in window boxes and hanging baskets. Germany has churches nestled into the smallest hillside. In one village the river bank was so narrow that the church could only be entered through the restaurant in front. As a result, the women usually ended up in church, while the men inadvertently got lost in the restaurant.

One day we arrived at the bustling wine village of Rüdesheim on the Rhine with its half-timbered houses and narrow cobblestone streets, a romantic, busy tourist center at the foot of the Niederwald mountain. It was the time of the vibrant wine festivals, with tables and benches in the street, music and dancing, like a public fun-fair. But before we could pay our tribute to Bacchus, the god of wine, we drove up to the Niederwald monument. It represents the founding of the second German Reich in 1871. We were impressed by the massive landmark with the huge Germania statue on top (similar to the Statue of Liberty in New York). It could be seen from afar. We had a breathtaking view down on the big bend of the Rhine River below.

By now we had seen enough and were eager to return to Rüdesheim for our evening meals in one of the popular *Weinstuben* (taverns) in the famous Drosselgasse. Old artistic wrought iron inn signs dangled decoratively above tavern entrances, an invitation to try their locally grown products.

Our inn was filled with lively international tourist traffic. We sat at our reserved long table and right away spotted many university students touring here. Of course we tried to make eye contact with them. Before long, some came over to ask for a dance. But we were not allowed to dance for Mrs. Frenzel's rule was if everyone was not asked to dance, no one could. Consequently, we didn't, at least not that evening.

Overnight we girls were housed in a youth hostel, a travel bargain in Germany since 1909, and after 1925 in other countries. It supplied young people like us with inexpensive, comfortable and clean accommodations. We girls slept in a dormitory while our teacher had a private room. The Frenzels stayed more elegantly in a hotel. We all would meet next morning, right after breakfast, at the market square.

That night we girls were particularly noisy, which was against the rules after 10 p.m. We were talking about how to escape the teacher's watchful eye the next morning so we could take an early, quick stroll through town, to experience the social contacts we had missed that evening when a complaining innkeeper stepped in. As we went on whispering we debated what would happen if we were caught tomorrow. The strongest threat had always been expulsion from school. But if we all were involved, it would be deserted. Over this clever conclusion we finally went to sleep peacefully.

Next morning, right after breakfast, instead of meeting at the market place, we dodged into the Drosselgasse. We left the startled teacher no choice but to appear there alone with an empty bus, hoping that we might have walked over already. Mrs. Frenzel did not know whether to be more enraged or alarmed. But her husband assured her he would find us and headed straight for the Drosselgasse. There we were in one of the taverns, dancing and sampling wine in the company of some early-bird students, enjoying our newly-found freedom.

What a shock to suddenly see Mr. Frenzel show up! To our relief he somehow sympathized with our need to break loose for a good time. We ended up in fraternal conspiracy. His advice was to look guilty and stay silent during his wife's expected lecture, and he would present our case. Unfortunately we had to return with him immediately, leaving behind the disappointed students. He must have been a very good lawyer because his defense worked. One "chewing out" ended the episode and was never referred to again. We peacefully continued our trip and Mr. Frenzel, quite amused, enjoyed the grateful admiration of twenty young girls. We must have been out of our minds taking off like that in a strange town, but times were not as dangerous as today.

Our last sightseeing highlight was the old Roman city of Trier on the Moselle River, founded at the time of Christ. We were anxious to climb up to the ancient Porta Nigra (Black Gate) and were amazed over how well the Romans had built it so that it was still standing there.

It was autumn when we returned from our trip. The grapevine leaves had turned into a glowing golden and dark red. The last grapes were harvested. November became a very important month for me. I wanted to fulfill the last two gymnastic feats in five athletic areas, which had to be completed within one year, to earn the bronze athletic badge of the German Sports Federation for girls over eighteen. The silver and gold awards were bestowed on older people. I had passed the long jump, high jump and swimming already in Münster, but further training was prohibited because of preparations for the *Abitur*. Study took precedence over sports.

I was determined to get my sports badge now, and not let the deadline date slip by, and had trained in our garden for the last two tests, the shot-put and running. So November 26 was the big day. Just as I rushed out of the house in nervous excitement, one of the teachers slipped me a piece of paper to hand in at the bakery on my way to the stadium. That certainly was a strange message, written in big letters running into each other—*1OBERLÄNDER.* To the baker I said, "10 *Berländer*, please," whatever that might be—perhaps one of those local rolls. The baker looked at the paper with a long "hmmmm" and added, "I see." I had no time to find out what he "saw." Since he always delivered his products to the school, I rushed off to the athletic field.

The judges were all men, what luck, for they would be more benevolent. I quickly changed into my gym clothes and we started with the shot-putting, using an iron ball weighing 4 kilos (8.81 lbs). On my first try I reached twenty-four and a half feet—more than required. Their praise was a welcome lift for the last test, running one and a half miles around the athletic field in less than twelve minutes. I made it in only 10:21 minutes, totally exhausted. Formal congratulations followed. They entered my brand new test scores immediately in my old book that listed the three first events. The other was a big oval medal, three inches wide, of course decorated with the swastika, though it was not on the cover of the book. It was an old blue book with the wreath instead of the Nazi emblem.

After 1945 some Americans offered to buy both from me as souvenir for a substantial amount, but I did not sell them even though I needed the dollars badly. I had worked too hard for those decorations and could not part with them. I still have them today—lying useless and forgotten in a drawer.

But back to 1935. Returning to school dead tired from my glorious afternoon, I was greeted with a big hello, but unfortunately it had absolutely nothing to do with my victory. Instead, I was steered into the kitchen, where everybody was in an uproar. In my absence, ten enormous loaves of bread had arrived from the bakery, every one of them several pounds of solid, sturdy local country-style bread. They were piled up in an enormous heap on our kitchen table. Apparently my slip of paper had not read 10 *Berländer*, but rather 1 *Oberländer*. Just one was enough to feed us all for a while. But since I had mentioned ten, which the baker acknowledged with his long "hmmm," all of them were delivered. But why did the O of *Oberländer* look like a zero stuck next to the one? Why was I the only one taking the blame, and why wasn't the order placed by phone rather than by messenger?

Since Mrs. Frenzel did not know what to do with all these giant loaves, nine were offered to the Nazi Women's League. They wasted no time in picking up this generous donation for the "Nazi Party and the poor," and followed me hard on my heels into the kitchen. The Nazi women praised our unselfish good will to no end. Loaded with nine loaves they left, feeling especially benevolent towards us. Unfortunately I was told that the surplus expenses had to come out of my own pocket money so I would learn to pay better attention. How I hated that comment since I had heard it often enough in my life.

Since my mistake had brought our school into an unforeseen, elevated position of esteem with the Nazi Women's League, we could count on being exempted from their further visits in the foreseeable future. In the end I was even released from the penalty since the extra loaves turned out to be a blessing and solved a political problem for all of us. Our un-Nazi school was suddenly on friendly terms with the Nazi Party. That assured our existence—at least for a while. (Four years later the government confiscated the school, and converted the building into a rest home for wounded soldiers.)

Meanwhile the Christmas season was approaching, and we all would go home for the holidays. I wouldn't return afterwards. 1936 was the year of the Olympics in Berlin and I wanted to be back for that worldwide event. My parents also felt that enough water had passed over the dam concerning my transient BDM membership. Berlin was busy with extensive preparations for the XI Olympic Games. Who would be interested in my lack of participation in Nazi organizations?

My education was considered "finished at last," not to mention that I could have learned most of what was taught right at home—but who listens to one's own parents? It had added a new dimension to my life, though.

$\mathcal{F}$un and Games
Before Armageddon

$\mathcal{H}$ere I was back in Berlin so that I would not miss Hitler's ambitious 1936 Olympics. The capital, and largest city in Germany, was totally absorbed with enormous preparations for the summer games, so I had little concern that anyone would be interested in my sketchy BDM background.

Long before Hitler, Germany had been designated to host the 1936 winter Olympics in Garmisch, Bavaria, while the summer Olympics were to be held in Barcelona, Spain. However, due to the growing threat of a civil war in that country, their Olympic games had to be canceled, and Hitler immediately took this opportunity to have them scheduled to be held in Berlin. This provided him with an excellent year-long opportunity to lay aside political and other differences and present to the whole world a new recovered and peace-loving country, which stressed athletic contests and international fellowship. His propaganda was amazingly effective. Advance ticket sales were snatched up at home and abroad, and all the nations would come to be impressed by Hitler's new Germany.

My arrival in Berlin was in the midst of the building turmoil in preparation for the summer games. Existing sports facilities were being enlarged, and a huge new oval Olympic stadium to seat over one hundred thousand spectators was under construction. Two gigantic statues of nude discus throwers symbolized the strong, male dominated country, and they are still standing there today. The entire structure was surrounded by old trees that had been transplanted to the area, and to the amazement of many, adapted and grew in their new environment. Germany's largest amphitheater, modeled after the Hollywood Bowl, was being built to accommodate twenty-five thousand spectators. Located in a natural wooded ravine, it would offer entertainment under the stars, such as operas, concerts and stage plays.

In the midst of all the Olympic excitement, our family had an equally important event to celebrate, the silver wedding anniversary of my parents on January 17. All of our relatives and many close friends came for the family celebration. Some were our house guests and others were lodged in a nearby hotel. There was a festive dinner accompanied by Papa's good wine and vivacious conversation about practically every subject on earth. As was customary, the guests helped entertain with amusing self-composed songs and humorous scrapbooks recalling events of the last twenty-five years. Aunt Frieda was the one with the wittiest stories. She was forever my favorite aunt.

One subject that was most vehemently discussed was not Hitler, but whether Edward, Prince of Wales and future king of England, would marry the twice-divorced American born Mrs. Wallis Warfield-Simpson. Since her second divorce was not even final, the British press called it the scandal of the century. Papa's outspoken opinion was that to allow her to become a future queen of England would offend all royal dignity and decency. However, we young ones playfully stated that such a marriage would also bring a fresh breeze to the stuffy English court. Papa was shocked and immediately changed the subject. Later, to prove his modern thinking, to the surprise of everyone, he offered us cigarettes, which I declined. He got cross with me, because he was convinced I smoked behind his back anyway. This time I did not justify his suspicions, since I felt it was not the right moment to let him in on my secret smoking experience in Bad Godesberg. Papa himself smoked good cigars with a fine aroma.

Another topic of discussion was the winter Olympic games in Garmisch, Bavaria, which is a typical alpine town whose beauty attracts tourists all year round. "Why don't we go to see the games since they are taking place right here in Germany?" Papa declared. We all happily agreed and were excited to be going.

A few days after all the guests had departed from the anniversary celebration, we left for Munich by night train. When we arrived at the hotel, we obviously were directed to the wrong floor, because the rooms assigned to us were already occupied. Papa asked Mutti and me to wait while he would go back downstairs and clear up the mistake. It was customary in German hotels to leave your shoes outside your door at night for hotel service to pick them up and return them freshly polished the next morning. Mutti and I noticed something very humorous—a dainty pair of elegant women's shoes sitting outside one door, and next door, a sturdy pair of men's boots. We couldn't resist the temptation to change things around, so we placed one dainty women's shoe fastened to one boot in front of each door without being seen.

A moment later, one door opened a crack, and a naked, hairy masculine arm fished for the boots and pulled them inside. From behind the closed door, to our great amusement, came a colorful explosion of Bavarian swearing, followed by the dainty shoe flying back out into the hall just as Papa was returning from downstairs, barely escaping that furious shot. He demanded to know what was going on here. How could we know? We had just arrived ourselves. With pious looks, we followed him to our proper rooms on the floor above.

Papa's hotel reservation always consisted of a single room for him and a room for Mutti and myself together so I could be properly chaperoned. But, with all these precautions, I immediately managed to get involved in an amusing episode. Mutti sent me to Papa's room with something that he needed immediately, so I hurried down the hall and knocked on the door of what I thought was his room, and then rushed in. To my surprise, I was in a strange man's bedroom and he was standing there dressed only in long johns with one foot up on the shoe rack fixing his boot. For a moment, we were both startled and I stammered something about a wrong room. He just laughed and said, "I don't think so," and added as I was rushing out the door, "Come back any time!" Mutti was amused by the incident, but I never told Papa because he would have been climbing the walls if he knew I was in the bedroom of a strange man who was dressed only in his underwear.

There was no problem in getting from Munich to Garmisch because a continuous train shuttle transported the huge crowds from all over the world to and from the Olympic areas. We had not expected such a world-wide interest in the German Olympics and were surprised about the multitude of international visitors. En route to Garmisch, we saw numerous freight trains transporting snow for the games in case the weather did not cooperate.

Patiently like everybody else, we stood for hours watching the athletes compete and finally decided it was time for some refreshments. It was impossible to obtain any information because everyone was a foreigner and spoke a different language. Every restaurant and coffee house in the area was crowded with long lines outside in the cold. We decided to break away from the main thoroughfare to avoid the crowds and followed some locals who turned into a small side street which was a shortcut back to the train station. We wanted to get something to eat in Munich, hoping for a special treat. Unexpectedly we got a different one right then and there.

Suddenly we were squeezed against the wall of the narrow passage by oncoming heavy traffic of government vehicles, and there, with no warning, was Adolf Hitler zooming by in his open Mercedes-Benz with his uniformed body guards. We were flabbergasted. Everybody was carefully scrutinized by the secret service and automatically raised their arms in the familiar Hitler salute. What kind of spook had just rushed by here? What were Hitler and his entourage doing on this small hidden side street? He wore his hat deep down on his forehead. It was rumored to be bullet-proof, especially the shield half over his eyes. Was he afraid of the masses? For a while we had dismissed the Nazi regime from our minds, but now it had suddenly caught up with us again.

Back in Munich our life seemed to return to a state of normalcy. In our hotel there was dinner and dancing in a carefree, pre-carnival atmosphere with the usual partying. Did we live in two different and opposing worlds parallel to each other?

During our absence our home in Berlin was well taken care of by our new sixteen-year-old maid, Lotte. The first one, Alma, had gotten married to escape further Nazi orders. Lotte was pleasant, honest, and very eager to learn Mutti's excellent way of cooking. She was to stay with us until Hitler interfered in 1943 (but that's another story). Her father, a streetcar conductor, stopped by shortly after she began working for us to ask how she was doing. However, his real reason was to inconspicuously check on her living and working conditions since she had to quit a previous job because the people took unfair advantage of her. Papa invited him for a glass of beer on the terrace, and they began a friendship that lasted for many years through good times and times of unimaginable hardship.

Everything was calm following the ambitious winter Olympics when suddenly, on March 7, 1936, Hitler boldly violated the Versailles Treaty by sending at dawn a German battalion over the Rhine River into the demilitarized area of the Rhineland. This 19-mile strip of German soil had been off-limits to the German military since 1918. We held our breath. Did that provocation mean war? But wonder of wonders, nobody stopped Hitler in his surprise move of a speedy re-occupation of

Lotte, our new maid

our demilitarized Rhineland. The far superior French army could have easily repulsed the invasion of the small, inexperienced German force, but took no action.

The mighty Entente Powers, who were obviously preoccupied at that time with their own world problems, and who before had denied everything to the Weimar Republic, backed off now and accepted what Hitler called a correction of an unjust decree of the Treaty of Versailles. Hitler, the master of timing in accomplishing his bloodless coup, pledged to the Reichstag that, "Germany makes no territorial claims in Europe and will never break the peace." Germany and the whole world believed him, and within our country, he gained increased admiration and popularity. After all, it had been eighteen years since the last war. Even Papa agreed that finally we should be able to move freely within our own German borders. Hitler's Rhineland coup was accepted world-wide as a "fait accompli." In hindsight, we now know that if the French army had resisted Hitler's speedy re-occupation of the demilitarized Rhineland, the coup attempt would have been a fiasco and his fate would have been sealed. What an opportunity had slipped by to turn world history around.

Life returned to normal, and in my case, very exciting. Although we did not own a car, I had taken driving lessons in the midst of Berlin's traffic, and in May 1936, when I was twenty, I received my license. There is no preliminary learner's permit first as in the United States, and your license is issued for life. I still have it today. Some days later Papa bought our first car, a four-door black *Wanderer* that easily seated five people comfortably, and was fully equipped with everything what could be called an "extra," including a big yellow fog light, a windshield defroster, and matching suitcases. In those days there was no radio, heater or automatic transmission. Papa had debated between a Mercedes, Audi, BMW, and the Wanderer, a company that no longer exists. Since I was the only one in the family with a driver's license, besides Günter who was seldom home, I became very possessive of the car and watched carefully that everyone wiped off their feet thoroughly on the long running boards on each side before entering "my" car. I always wondered why they went out of style.

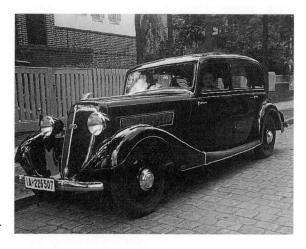

My new Wanderer

Alone in the car as I carefully cruised the streets of Berlin, I was not as sure of my driving skills as when accompanied by my instructor. Of course I never admitted this at home and always showed great confidence in my driving ability.

When Papa came along, which, thank God, was seldom, we were forced to adhere to a special seating arrangement as if we were in a taxi. I sat alone in the front while Mutti sat behind me in the rear seat and Papa next to her so he could have an unobstructed view of the traffic, and incessantly gave me driving instructions from the back, regardless of our entirely different views and judgments. As was bound to happen, I once followed Papa's obviously wrong instructions to the letter and deliberately, but slowly, ran into a pillar. My hope was that from then on, he would leave the driving up to me. But Papa said that when a car hits something, it is always the driver's fault, with no excuses. Fortunately Papa's preference for taxis all his life minimized my "back-seat driver" problem.

The traffic policemen in Berlin were very popular public figures. They reflected dignity, were diplomatic, and had the remarkable ability to gain public cooperation. They stood on wooden platforms in the middle of the busiest intersections, and were responsible for keeping traffic running smoothly and swiftly with their white gloved hand signals. They developed a nodding relationship with hundreds, and speaking acquaintance with dozens of motorists who regularly passed through their intersection. Their degree of popularity was attested by the wide circle of presents around their platform at Christmas time.

My first experience as a traffic violator came when I was picking up my friend Elsa at the railroad station, and proudly showed off my car and driving skills. Naturally we were in high spirits and chattered away as we headed home across a large, busy square in Steglitz, where several main streets intersect. As I approached the officer he raised his hand, which I took as a signal to cross, but he meant for me to stop. So I drove right into the middle of the busy intersection. The officer's whistle brought all oncoming traffic to a sudden halt.

To my embarrassment he left his stand, walked over to my car and said, "Miss, what are you doing here? Is your license still warm?" (His phrase for brand new.) Thoroughly irritated I told him, "I thought you waved for me to proceed!" He muttered, "Naturally, I should take the time to stop all attractive women and arrange a date. But right now I am busy." He accepted my confused apology with a twinkle in his eyes, and much to my relief, did not give me a ticket. Returning to his stand, he waved me on as the only car through the intersection while laughter came from the waiting vehicles.

We agreed not to breathe a word of this incident at home. In my years of driving that car, I never had an accident, not even a single repair. These old cars must have been built for life. Even a flat tire was no problem as this was before women's lib. I soon learned that standing beside my car in feminine helplessness with a jack dangling awkwardly from my hand would soon result in some gallant gentleman coming to my rescue to change the flat tire.

By now Hitler had indoctrinated the people with the idea of a rejuvenated Germany and the average citizen could not help being impressed by the unexpected boom and remarkable progress that had been made toward that promised glorious future. Under the eternal slogan of "Work and Peace," an enormous work program had been developed that was rapidly eliminating the unemployment of 7 million people that had been rampant throughout Germany a mere three years ago. It was no wonder that the fast-growing industrial workers' class was greatly impressed by the new public programs that provided full-time employment, and they stuck to the Party. They didn't realize that progress was being achieved partly by compulsory service in labor camps, the military forces, and construction of the *Reichsautobahn*, a high speed freeway intended for moving the military rapidly across Germany in the future.

There was also a new program called KDF, short for *Kraft durch Freude*, or strength through joy. Government propaganda announced inexpensive leisure time activities for the working class, which would add greatly to the quality of their lives. An entire fleet of new cruise ships was constructed for pleasure trips and new convalescent homes were built. What the public was not told was that these convalescent homes were intended to serve as future military hospitals, and the ships for fast transport of the troops.

Hitler was a master in manipulating public opinion. KDF provided marvelous vacation excursions to the working class for very little money, which was something they could have never even dreamed of before. Pleasure trips were at that time exceptional and sensational, and not at all common-place like today. Only a few could afford them. Working people now had the opportunity to take their entire family on cruises on luxury liners to far away places such as the Norwegian fjords or the island of Madeira in the Atlantic ocean. These extravagant journeys were invented and presided over by Robert Ley who arranged them to suit his own pleasure, which meant he was always stone drunk, and became known as the Reichs-drunkard. (Accused in the Nuremberg trial, he committed suicide in 1945.)

Hitler had restored national pride after the humiliation of the Versailles Treaty. He gave the illusion of peace while at the same time, hidden from public view, his war machine was already running at full speed and workers were desperately needed everywhere. Unfortunately, the foreign politicians willingly conceded to him the many bloodless victories in foreign policy, when before they had constantly denied the smallest relief to the young, peaceful Weimar Republic of the 1920s in their crisis-haunted years and desperate efforts to make the new democracy work.

Hitler opened the Berlin summer Olympics on August 1, 1936, as a giant propaganda campaign of the Nazi state, stating, "I called the youth of the world and they all came!" The Nazi government had spared no efforts to portray a peaceful and rejuvenated Germany with the best organized Olympic games possible. The whole world came to admire Hitler's showcase of the Third Reich. Berlin took delight in being the center of benevolent international attention where the visitors could watch Germany's brilliant achievement. And, the colorful Olympics served as an excellent opportunity to screen the obscure, true image and goals of the Nazi regime.

Most of the Olympic tickets were made available only to people outside of Germany in order to attract as many foreign visitors as possible. As such, it was almost impossible for a Berliner to get some for any of the main events. We got stuck with some tickets that were left over for a boxing match and Papa immediately decided he wanted no part of that. So only our house guests, Aunt Frieda and Cousin Edith, came along with Mutti and me.

On the way, Aunt Frieda suggested that we go have coffee at Hitler's, which we took as one of her usual practical jokes. But she was serious. "We don't go to Adolf Hitler," she explained, "but to Alois Hitler, his stepbrother. He runs a restaurant at the *Wittenbergplatz* near the famous department store *Kaufhaus des Westens*, known as Ka De We." Coming from Upper Silesia, she knew more than we Berliners did. So off we went to Alois Hitler.

According to Aunt Frieda's hometown newspaper, Hitler had established his stepbrother in a restaurant so people could see and associate with a Hitler relative. And there was Alois, passing our table and looking surprisingly like his brother Adolf. The place was crowded with tourists. They all wanted to witness the spectacle. More propaganda to make Adolf appear as a good family man. It was also said that Alois was not so fond of his role. The restaurant was bombed out later with the entire area, and he was never heard of again.

We finally arrived at the Olympics site where we had ringside seats for the boxing match. This was the first one I had ever seen, and would also be my last. We were so close to the ring that we not only clearly saw every punch, but could also hear them. Cousin Edith and I held hands in fright. One of the boxers was much shorter than the other, and to us, it looked like a fight between "David and Goliath," only with the opposite result. It was a bloody event and although we mainly closed our eyes or looked away from the ring, we were surrounded by an eager crowd cheering the participants on.

Directly behind us sat some enthusiastic Polish gentlemen. They bent over, pressing their binoculars into our hands, so we could see even more clearly. But we kept our eyes closed most of the time. The much smaller athlete started to bleed, but that didn't hinder them from whispering in broken German, "See wonderful box better now." Every further connection to them was soon cut off by our mothers and the binoculars returned to them, to their disappointment—and ours. Of course, the smaller boxer lost, but he was the favorite of the crowd for his courageous fight against such a larger opponent.

One morning, we four females decided to drive out to the newly constructed Olympic village which was about ten miles from the stadium. It hosted the more than three thousand athletes who were participating in the games and since it had been so highly praised, we were curious to see it for ourselves. About half way there, we passed a young Chinese athlete walking toward the village on this rather warm day. He had obviously missed the shuttle bus and he looked so forlorn that we offered him a ride, which he gladly accepted, bowing politely before entering the car. Upon arrival at the Olympic village, he guided us to his quarters and then offered to give us a tour if we could wait until he freshened up.

We learned that his name was Sze-To Kwong and he was a well-educated university student with a limited knowledge of both German and English. After our tour, he invited us to stay for lunch which featured cuisines from around the world, and he wanted us to try his. Mutti declined politely since Papa expected us home for our meal. Kwong bowed again, politely but so very disappointed, that Aunt Frieda impulsively invited him to dine with us on his next free day. He graciously accepted. Mutti was shocked at Aunt Frieda's invitation and his spontaneous acceptance, but she disguised it very well. She envisioned Papa's negative reaction to such a surprise, and, hence, that visit was discussed rather doubtfully on the way home. Aunt Frieda had watched with amusement the way Kwong looked at me constantly. She obviously enjoyed bringing a Chinese experience into our pleasant but regimented home life.

Shortly thereafter, he arrived for a German meal at our house. He was used to European cuisine and proved to be most charming and intelligent. Even Papa had to admit that he was enjoyable and interesting company, and showed a genuine liking for him until he violated proper German etiquette by calling me Dorothea instead of Miss Schmidt. To Papa's even greater dislike, Kwong stood close behind me while I was playing folk songs on the piano and placed his hand on my shoulder in a friendly gesture. For Papa that was just too much intimacy from a man I had just met. What he proceeded to say in German, Kwong luckily could not understand. Aunt Frieda was more amused by the minute.

Later, our guest invited me to a theater performance for the next evening, but Papa made an excuse for me, citing a previous engagement. Before leaving, Kwong suggested that we meet some of his fellow Chinese student friends who lived in Berlin so that we could keep in touch. But, Papa again declined politely, already envisioning his only daughter eloping off to China. Fortunately he did not know that Kwong had whispered he would write to me from home.

By now the festive Olympics were coming to an end, and we were lucky to have seats for the spectacular closing ceremonies directly across the stadium from the Hitler box. The entire evening performance was staged as an impressive publicity campaign for the Third Reich, a demonstration of serenity. Germany had been awarded a total of eighty-nine medals, a surprise win even over the United States. Hitler's objective to show the superiority of his "master race," and the inferiority of the black people was upset by the black U.S. athlete, Jesse Owens, who won four gold medals in defeating Hitler's finest, and the masses cheered him as the hero of Berlin.

With ceremonial fanfares, the parade of athletes entered carrying their flags of all nations. As a token of fraternization, the youth of the world were called to the 1940 Olympics to be held in Tokyo. The ceremonies ended with a huge firework display. Rockets shot up from around the stadium, forming a bright huge dome of light over us, and illuminating the night sky as clear as day. Everyone marvelled at such a gigantic finale, and it was praised highly the next day in the newspapers, but no one knew at that time that this 1936 Olympics would be the last for twelve years.

The colorful Berlin Olympics received international acclaim from the excellent movies produced by Leni Riefenstahl, who was an artist with the camera and without peer in her field. She was exactly what Hitler needed for his propaganda to cover his hidden goals with art. Her movies were shown over and over in Germany. This magnificent show window of the glorious 1936 games was carefully designed to conceal the true character of the Nazi regime and the world blindly fell for it. This prompted many foreigners to overlook what was really going on behind this brown curtain. Fun and games were combined with secret political murders. Brutal retaliations were never far away, which was well-known outside Germany and to a greater extent than at home. But the international misgivings were accompanied with only a shrug of the shoulders. Hitler's ambitious Olympics were favorably admired world-wide, bringing him global prestige.

The Olympic flame died, and with it any illusion of peace. Nobody could anticipate that these games were the last before the world would become inflamed in war just three years later. Japan had to wait until 1964 to host them in Tokyo in a completely changed environment.

Some days later I received a postcard from Sze-To Kwong from Italy in the form of a photo where he was standing at the coliseum in Rome. Two weeks later a voluminous letter arrived from China and Papa made me open it in front of him. It contained several photographs of Kwong's whole family, at least a dozen adults and children, male and female, posed in a garden. Also enclosed was a postcard written in Chinese and Papa wanted to know what it said, but how was I supposed to know. I didn't know Chinese either! I never replied to Kwong's letter as Papa had strictly forbidden it, and I never heard from him again. I don't know if he never wrote, or if Papa intercepted the mail and never gave me his letters. But I kept everything for many years and never found out what was written on that card.

I've often wondered how he may have fared during the Chinese revolution between Chiang-Kai-Shek and Mao Tse Tung. I certainly appreciated his attentions but not enough to pack my bags and run off to China, as Papa had feared, for an unpredictable future. I didn't have to go away to China for that. I had it right here at home.

As far as any trip abroad was concerned, traveling outside Germany was restricted. Only limited funds were allowed to be taken out of the country. In a nationwide effort, the citizens were called upon to stay

Sze-To Kwong

home. Foreign newspapers became rare and then extinct in order to "protect" us from outside opinions. Our situation became not unlike circumstances later behind the Iron Curtain. Slowly but continuously, we were drawn into political and intellectual isolation, without being aware of it at first.

Nevertheless, Leni Riefenstahl's movie "Olympia" was the greatest sports documentary ever made. Her film is available even today, though the Nazi regime is long gone. It can be seen on television and obtained on video tape in the U.S. But a rumor would not die that her fame and place in the spotlight could not protect her own brother when he incurred Hitler's displeasure, for whatever reason, and the die was cast. He was trans-

ferred to a death battalion at the East front with no return. He died soon thereafter—it was said, in combat. We never found out if this was true or not. But everything was possible. The Nazis were masters in concealing their malicious crimes.

Kwong in China

The Calm Before the Storm

Our life returned to the normal routine after the exciting Olympics summer came to an end. Although our pleasant maid, Lotte, did most of the housework, Mutti, insisted that I help her, if for no other reason than to know at some future date how much to expect from my own maid. Thanks to Hitler, I never had one, but at the time, we had no idea how much I would profit in life from her foresight and wise, down-to-earth attitude.

For the time being, my life was pleasant and free of important responsibilities which provided ample opportunities to enjoy leisure activities such as tennis at the local sports club and visiting the white beaches of Lake Wannsee, Berlin's bathing paradise called the Lido of Berlin. Elsa and I often drove out there during her frequent visits, and as we saw the huge crowds enjoying the beach it was hard to believe that only about twenty-five years prior, bathing outdoors was prohibited. It was my heart's desire that my brother, Günter, would marry Elsa so that I would get to keep them both. However, they did not cooperate with my matchmaking. Elsa wanted to be a librarian and had thus far successfully avoided the BDM since she had never been a member of an organization from which she could be transferred, like my mandatory transfer from the *Luisenbund*. Her circumstances for avoiding the BDM in her home town of Schweidnitz, Silesia, were quite tragic, as she now told me.

In the spring of 1935, she and her seven classmates in the Friedrich Lyceum, were eager to learn higher mathematics, not because they loved the subject, just the opposite, they detested it, but they looked up to their beloved teacher, Dr. Oppenheimer. She had been the highly-respected and admired director of the school long before Hitler, and her class would have done anything for her, even pay attention to trigonometry. That's what they all were trying to do when one morning the classroom door burst open and in the middle of Dr. Oppenheimer's lesson, four husky SA men barged in. Dr. Oppenheimer rose quietly, took a moment to smooth down her skirt, and followed them wordlessly out of the room, and the door slammed shut again.

All this occurred so unexpectedly, that the class was not really aware of what had happened. It was over in a flash. Now they broke out in revolt and rushed to the principal's office, where they found a brand new director, a man in a brown uniform, who refused to provide any information on the whereabouts of their beloved teacher. There had been a wild rumor in school about an expulsion of Jews and it just so happened that their adored teacher and director was Jewish. The new principal immediately ordered that the entire class enter the BDM. They all stubbornly rejected this command unless their questions about the whereabouts of their cherished teacher were answered. Deeply shocked they returned to their classrooms.

Dr. Oppenheimer was never heard from again, so none of the class entered the BDM. Because of their refusal, all the parents were immediately ordered to appear in school and were informed that they had to make their daughters enter the BDM. But the parents "regretted having no influence" since they were adults. "Later we wondered," Elsa said, "that we got away with that bold refusal." But it was also the time when happenings like these were hushed-up as much as possible. The Nazis were careful to implement their anti-Jewish measures with discretion so they would not arouse any wide-spread public attention, being well aware that the people would strongly oppose them. I was deeply shocked to hear all that now.

On November 1, 1935, Elsa was drafted for her compulsory "voluntary" six months service in a Nazi labor camp, where she was assigned to the little town of Neugabel in Silesia to help with the harvesting of the sugar beet crop. Her group consisted of thirty girls under the command of two young leaders. The clothing that they furnished was practical and unfeminine, but suitable for hard work in muddy fields. The weather was cold and rainy, and each day started with flag raising in frosty temperatures with chattering teeth, followed by breakfast at 6 a.m. Every day was spent in the cold, muddy fields, kneeling with a long knife in her bare hands, which were soon bloody and calloused. All these "labor maidens" spent the winter months working in the stables of the small farms around the camp where the farmers could not afford outside help. There they also had to do kitchen work and the laundry, of course without washing machines. Elsa managed to endure the six months and was finally discharged on April 1, 1936. The clothing she had been given was left in the camp to be cleaned and then passed on to the next group, like in the military service.

Elsa then started to pursue her ambition to be a librarian and began looking for a place to train as an apprentice. She was fortunate to be accepted by a well-respected publishing house, Rütten and Loenig, in Potsdam. The firm was located in an enchanting little castle in the middle of the public park of Charlottenhof.

Her starting salary was 30 *Reichsmark* per month. Today, this would be considered chicken feed, but half a pound of butter or a hot dog was only 80 pfennigs (20 cents) at that time. Her parents paid the rent for a comfortable private room in a villa nearby, and she spent the weekends with us, since Potsdam was only a half-hour drive from Berlin. I always picked her up from work by car, though the first time I caused quite a commotion. Back then the horn was allowed to be blown only in a rare emergency. But to let Elsa know that I had arrived, I not only blew the horn, but signaled to her in an alarming SOS code—three short, three long, and three more short toots. Everybody in the castle stormed to the windows to see what was disturbing their quiet world. But it was only the new and youngest apprentice who was being picked up for the weekend. I could put on such a show since there never was a policeman around. After a while, everyone got used to my regular, noisy weekend arrival. Though later I shortened my SOS signal to less than nine toots.

Other than the weekends, my life had become rather boring. It seemed to lack any meaning or usefulness compared with Elsa's and it did not fulfill my rather active nature. And, I became disenchanted with living at home, restricted beyond my willingness, and declared I would seek work, earn my own living, and move out—a questionable threat since there were many handicaps. A major one was my lack of any background in a field that would be useful in business, as my parents pointed out. I reluctantly agreed with them, and decided I had no choice but to continue my boring life at home, and, as I was told, being ungrateful for my sheltered and carefree existence.

My brother, Günter, who had joined the Merchant Marine some

years before, had been transferred involuntarily to the German navy and fortunately just happened to be home from the naval academy in Flensburg for a visit. Being familiar with this family clash of wills, he came into my room waving a newspaper. "Here's your solution," he whispered triumphantly, and showed me an article on the Lessing College in downtown Berlin. It outlined the benefits of taking a course on advanced cosmetics and skin care, and fortunately, no political commitment was required. "This is a knowledge you can use all your life for yourself. This would get you out of the house into the real world," he pointed out. Both excited, we made a pact.

Next morning after breakfast, Günter found a reason for us to drive downtown together, and he took me straight to the school. He waited outside while I was interviewed by the director, Mrs. Hanna Völker, a lovely lady who explained the extent of the program and how it dealt with anatomy, dermatology, chemistry, massage and facials, which were all closely aligned to a medical background. (This type of schooling is not found in the United States.) I was ready to enroll, but unfortunately the present class that started the next morning was already filled. Overwhelmed by the loss of such an opportunity, I broke out in tears and apparently convinced her that my future depended upon being admitted to the program. Warm-hearted as she was, she looked through her files again and decided that she could fit me into the current class after all, but I had to be there punctually at 8 a.m. the next morning with the tuition, as all the other students had paid in advance. I agreed to everything, even though I had no idea how my parents would react to my latest intentions, nor how I would obtain the necessary tuition fee by the next morning.

As usual, I turned to Mutti for support. She was not exactly enthusiastic about my surprise, but agreed to casually bring up the subject at our midday meal. As expected, Papa became furious, not only because I had not first discussed this with him, but he abhorred the use of lipstick and the whole cosmetic gamut. He refused to discuss the matter, and that was final. I realized the futility of further argument, but my mind was made up, too, to pursue the schooling.

Early the next morning, it was a beautiful day in October, before the others were up, I left for the school, but without the tuition. That was my biggest problem. Günter did not have enough money with him to help me out. I cannot remember the excuse I gave Mrs. Völker, but it must have been convincing because she let me start the classes. Anatomy and dermatology were taught by Professor Rost, chemistry by Dr. Unger, and practical application by other staff members. During the evening meal at home I talked about the interesting subjects I was studying, but Papa was still angry and played deaf, though he never said one word about my leaving this morning against his will.

Günter told me later the first thing Papa had done that morning was to check the garage to see if I had taken the car. But, I had been smart enough not to pour oil on the fire and had used public transportation. Mutti gave me the money for the tuition, with Papa's approval, so he was still the undisputed boss and I got what I wanted. Classes were taught Monday through Saturday from morning into the afternoon, and I continued to talk about my studies each day at the evening meal. Papa slowly became reconciled to my latest interest as he had always done in the past, and began paying my expenses without further objection. He eventually became so impressed by my schooling that he suggested that I take the family car since it would make it much more convenient to get to and from school each day.

Around this same time, on October 27, 1936, the family interest turned to more important political events. Hitler and Mussolini united in the "Berlin-Rome Axis," which the newspapers praised as another success following the July German-Austrian agreement, to respect each other's sovereignty. This was all glorified by the press as a guarantee for peace in the future, and we gladly believed it. On November 14, we received the good news that the German government had denounced the international control of all German rivers, which had been one of the restraints of the Versailles Treaty. For once, Papa agreed with Hitler, because every German felt that seventeen years were long enough for such an unfair burden. The action received no protest from England or the United States and little or no concern from other nations. It seemed that everyone was eager to grant Hitler those concessions which they had constantly denied to the Weimar Republic.

Our family peace ran the risk of an internal storm one fateful day when I had a mishap with our elegant black Wanderer auto. I took the narrow turn through the open, wooden garden gate at too high a speed, executing a most elegant curve. The gate was framed by two white, wooden pillars, with both its panels opening to the inside, and I misjudged the space available for the car to pass through. Günter came running as he heard the crash, and arrived to find the splintered right gate hanging at a sharp angle, as if someone had tried out his ax on it. The car survived the encounter quite well though, thanks to its sturdy bumpers. Papa was due home at any time, and since he was not tolerant of my mistakes, Günter promised to handle the matter better with me out of sight. I rushed inside and nervously watched from behind the curtain at the window above the garage.

Soon Papa could be seen crossing the street with his quick steps, which I must have inherited. Totally absorbed in his thoughts, he passed the mangled garage gate, and aimed for the small garden door—but wait! Suddenly he paused. Wasn't there something different? He turned around and walked back to the scene of disaster. Before Papa could utter one angry word, Günter immediately went into a lengthy explanation of sharp angles, and the difficulties of maneuvering into an entrance designed for smaller cars, not such a big one as Papa had bought. It was a pure miracle that something like this had not happened much earlier, and indeed the entrance needed widening—which was done some years later through the courtesy of a bomb.

Papa was never very enthusiastic about Günter's lengthy theories, but could not admit it. He mumbled something in anger while checking the broken gate and found that it could still be locked, much to Günter's and my relief. Especially tired of more of Günter's explanations, he went inside. Mutti, well aware of what was happening outside, had already served dinner to distract Papa from wood and hinges. Since he insisted on meals being served piping hot, there was no time for further delay or discussion of the gate. We forever wondered how he could stand everything so hot. In spite of his "unhealthy" style of living, he lived into his nineties. Later, he never said one word to me about the gate incident, and I remained the driver for the family since neither of my parents ever had any desire to learn to drive.

On weekends we sometimes visited with Elsa the nearby rococo castle of Frederick II in Potsdam called *Sans Souci*, which meant "without worry." It was built in 1745-1748 as his summer residence and contained a wealth of art treasures. We spent happy hours admiring old Flemish and Italian masterpieces in the picture gallery there.

Sunday mornings were always special when Günter was home. He would drive us out to one of Berlin's most famous *Weinstuben, Habel unter den Linden,* where he and Papa would spend the morning indulging in good wine. At the same time, Mutti and I would be dropped off at the corner of Friedrichstrasse at the equally famous *Café Kranzler,* which was connected with Berlin's history and noted for serving delicious tarts by waitresses dressed in old fashioned costumes.

Café Kranzler as it looks today.

Around noon, Günter would hand me the car keys and state that since I liked to drive so much, I could drive them all home. I knew the reason for his generosity was that he had consumed too much wine. He would sit in the front seat next to me, while Papa and Mutti sat in the rear. And, since Günter blocked Papa's view, there were no back-seat driving instructions, which made for a very pleasant and quiet drive home.

In December, though, Papa's peace of mind was disturbed again by a political event. Edward VIII, since January 1936 King of England, insisted on marrying Wallis Warfield-Simpson, a twice-divorced American, and was forced to abdicate the throne in favor of his brother George VI, the father of Queen Elizabeth II. Papa did not understand British royalty.

Similarly, I did not understand my brother Günter when he was home on Christmas leave. Though he was an excellent driver, he loved cruising around in the car at too high a speed, while stating that the ships in the navy were much swifter. He didn't want to hear from me the difference between the streets of Berlin and the ocean.

The morning of New Year's Eve was one of those times when we were racing around with last minute preparations. Although he usually ran the yellow lights, on this day he decided against it and slammed on his brakes which the car behind us hadn't expected. Bang, there went our tail lights, but the damage to both cars was minimal. We were all insured so there was no argument. Since Günter was leaving in two days, I had to arrange for the repairs. I could already envision the smirk on the repair shop attendant's face when I appeared with a dented car—typical woman driver! Günter did not feel sorry for me at all. He thought I owed him that for helping me out on the smashed garage gate incident. When he left again he just smiled, "Until next time sis, and keep the car in shape!" In Flensburg he had a motorbike.

1937 turned out nicely for Elsa. At the weekend parties at my tennis club, she started a romance with her future husband. Returning to Potsdam on Sunday night, she was always well provided with goodies from Mutti, to brighten up her modest but happy life. She was Mutti's godchild and was like a member of the family and a sister to me.

I completed my course at Lessing College in March 1937 and passed the final examination with a grade of superior. Very proudly I accepted my certificate and State diploma. However, once again I was not to use my acquired knowledge professionally because in order to start working, I would need a work permit. The newly founded Nazi Labor Front required that all employers and employees be members of the organization. Every worker had to keep an employment book, which contained an entry of every position held, and it was impossible to obtain any work without this "workmen's passport."

Since trying to get a work permit might reveal my uncooperative political past, the subject of leading my own life was dropped again. My parents kept telling me to just enjoy my freedom and life style because I would soon be getting married anyway. It seemed that marriage was the main topic of everyone's conversation since Edward VIII had finally married his great love, Mrs. Wallis Warfield-Simpson. Following their March 1937 marriage in Paris, he had to live abroad in exile as the Duke of Windsor because his wife was not welcome in England and never allowed to set her foot on that sacred soil.

For the time being, I returned to my private "exile" at home. Elsa kept me informed about her very interesting work at the publishing house. She was meeting noted authors of that time such as Rudolf Binding, and especially Wilhelm von Simpson, whose dictation she took in his home for his two famous books *The Barrings* and *The Grandson*. Sometimes, on weekends, we would take a three-hour drive to see Aunt Grete in Zerbst. Papa had bought a large property there in the early 1920s with a multi-family house and a business selling farming equipment, which was run by my uncle.

It was Elsa who told us of the new ghastly rumor concerning "book burning." None of us had forgotten the upsetting rally of 1933. The Nazis apparently thought they had overlooked too many writings. This time their strategies were more secretive. The director of the publishing house, Dr. Gerz, at great personal risk, made it known that everybody should quickly remove from the premises as many of the banned books as they wanted. (That brilliant man and two others of his staff did not survive the coming war.) Elsa was very happy with her cherished new possessions, although her joy was subdued by the method by which they were obtained—sneaking them out of the building in suitcases. I also received my share of these secret presents. But this episode had changed the atmosphere at work. From then on, everybody was more careful with his or her opinions, critical remarks and jokes.

The Berliners were constantly kept busy with festivities where they had to display the flag on their homes because of some Nazi Party events. Papa followed the flag hoisting orders his own way by displaying a flag in our old imperial colors of black, white and red. The brown patrol soon informed him that he was displaying the wrong flag, and only the swastika was to be hoisted. Papa hated that hooked cross borrowed from old runes, and we did not own one, but he finally was forced into obtaining it like everybody else. However, when he next had to hoist it, he did it at a side window, and our old imperial flag still flew out front. Again the brown patrol came by to inform us that the swastika had to go in front of the house. Papa complied, but flew our imperial flag from the side window. Finally, Mutti convinced him that he would only endanger all of us if he continued to defy the Nazis.

Papa finally got it right; the swastika flag out front.

This order for "flags out" on the numerous Nazi celebration days reminds me of a joke that went around at that time:

> In history class the teacher asks, "Why do we put out all the flags today?" No one in the class seems to know the reason. "Think about it," the teacher encourages the boys. "You there, Hans, in the first row. Tell me." Hans shrugs his shoulders and finally stammers hesitatingly, "Because we have to!"

Our daily lives were conditioned by Nazi protocol, rules and regulations, and, slowly but forcefully, we had a calendar year of national holidays. January 30 celebrated the day in 1933 when Hitler seized power, Hitler's birthday in April, May 1 as "All Workers Day," the farmers harvest ritual in autumn, and the Nueremberg party rallies in September with mass marching in clicking boots and all the pomp of the Third Reich. There was a different and impressive title every year:

1933 — Party Rally of the Day of Victory
1934 — Party Rally of the Triumph of Willpower
1935 — Party Rally of Freedom
1936 — Party Rally of Honor
1937 — Party Rally of Work
1938 — Party Rally of Greater Germany
1939 — Party Rally of Peace

The last one, scheduled for September 1939, ironically had to be cancéled ahead of time because of Hitler's not so peaceful war plans. Instead, more men were called up to the military service.

The Nazi calendar relegated Christmas and Easter to minor importance. Each major event was celebrated with mass meetings, decorated with huge flags and banners, and to convey a picture of faithful support, all business enterprises and government employees were forced to participate. To assure that everyone was present at each exaggerated event, attendance was easily checked through the chain of command. Hitler was the man of the masses, and he knew how to influence people with theatrical demonstrations.

Our entire life was supposed to be standardized, preferably in Party uniforms. So far, we had managed to avoid uniforms, except Günter, a young naval officer. He had to supply proof of his pure Aryan lineage. We attempted to locate long-lost relatives (Omi's brothers) through church files and townhall records, but were unsuccessful. Finally, because of incomplete documents, the navy had to accept Günter's blond hair as sufficient proof of his Aryan descent. Young men were in demand by the Nazis.

Goebbels, the devious advocate of the Nazi ideology, created the Hitler myth by planting Hitler in everyone's mind as the glorified leader, the undoubted Führer. His photograph was displayed in every classroom, office, public building, organization, and preferably, in every home, because visual images are remembered better than words. Hitler's picture never appeared in our home or in the homes of our friends.

Throughout all this, our private lives went on. On November 28, 1937, we attended a big ball in the famous *Hotel Adlon*, close to the Brandenburg Gate, celebrating Elsa's engagement and her resignation from her treasured position with the publishing firm in preparation for her marriage early in 1938. But, before Elsa's wedding, another audacious political event was the center of everyone's interest.

On March 13, 1938, Austria was annexed into a "Greater Germany," with "no resistance." Hitler's swift military action was called the long-awaited reunion with our 6 million blood brothers, which was fortunate and prosperous for both sides. The radio and press carried long, cleverly devised statements about the enthusiastic reception that Hitler had received in Vienna. Austria had broken off from the German Empire with the Westphalian Peace Treaty of 1648, which ended the Thirty-

*Elsa's engagement celebration. (L to R: Mutti, Papa, Mr. Behrmann,
Elsa, Heinz, me and Mrs. Behrmann)*

Year-War, and this was hailed as the peaceful and willing re-joining of
these two "Brother States." Hitler proudly proclaimed it as the union of
Germany with "his" homeland, since he had been born in Austria. Later
we learned that it was a more forceful annexation, and not at all as peaceful as proclaimed. But Hitler's bold long-range plans were served.

Again, France, Great Britain and the Soviet Union didn't object either when their superior force could have easily crushed the Nazi regime. Instead, they actually supported Hitler, which helped him to more
easily achieve his goal. His method was that after every concession he
followed with a new demand.

Around the same time, Papa became involved in a real estate trans-
action on Limastrasse (pronounced lee-ma). A Mr. Dreyfus, a Jew, owned
nearby a big home, located on a huge lot of many acres of front yard.
He had been trying since before 1933 to sell but the price per square
meter was too high. Our two architect friends, Franz Behrmann and
Paul Thiemer, suggested Papa buy one of the lots. Papa loved the idea
and the lot's location, and bought it from Mr. Dreyfus in private negotiations. Papa paid the asking price and arranged payment with Mr.
Dreyfus personally. They celebrated their deal over a bottle of wine, and
Mr. Dreyfus left Germany soon thereafter. The well-known movie star
Gustav Fröhlich bought a lot next to our's from Mr. Dreyfus at the same
time and in the same manner. This way we became neighbors for many
years.

Papa started to have a beautiful apartment house built on his lot, surrounded by a huge yard. The groundbreaking ceremony was on Mutti's birthday on March 19, 1938. But building materials were scarce or rationed and construction crept along at a slow pace. We were not aware that the shortages were caused by a war industry running at full speed. It was not long before Papa came up with a frustrated saying: *Wer sich mal so richtig ärgern will, der soll sich ein Haus bauen!* He who wants to be really annoyed, should try to build a house. Nothing but one aggravation after the other. But Papa wanted everything in the old solid style. That took a lot of maneuvering and "detours," called black market years later. As usual in life he was successful, and the architects also knew that many roads lead to Rome. Luckily we escaped soon to a family festivity.

On April 9, 1938, Elsa got married to Heinz in her hometown of Schweidnitz in Silesia. We came from Berlin by car. The same morning we were all required to vote, which was a farce, as if we would ever be truly asked for our own opinion in our one-party state. Voting served only propaganda purposes. Everything was again Goebbels' skillful indoctrination and the slogan of the election was: *Dem Führer Dein Ja* (your Yes for the Führer), referring to the reunion with Austria the previous month. The ballot instructed the voters what to do by the printing—a very big "YES" and a very, very small "no."

Voting was mandatory and proclaimed as a secret ballot. The booths were generally only a formality. However, we voted openly at the desk of supervising Nazi officials, and to vote anything but YES would have been suicide. The slits in the voting boxes were very wide and provided a clear view of how the ballot was marked. I can't remember any envelopes either.

After the polls had closed, the official announcements proclaimed Hitler had received 98 percent of the votes cast. Who dared to doubt such an outcome? We were free to keep our mouths shut and follow orders, the same as years later behind the Iron Curtain, an easy way to enforce political conformity.

For Elsa's wedding, our black Wanderer was beautifully decorated as the bridal car to drive the couple to the church. I was riding with my escort in another car, and just as the procession was about to leave, we had an unexpected snow fall. I had previously tried to explain to the driver of my car, one of the guests, that there was a safety device on the ignition that had to be released before you could start the motor, but being a man, he did not need instructions from a female on how to start a car. Now what was bound to happen, happened.

So there we were, all lined up to leave for the church ceremony, with the bridal car the first one in line, but it would not start. After several futile attempts, and hearing nothing but a click of the engine, the driver of my car, who was by now slightly irritated since the whole procession was stuck, had no choice but to ask me to come up and start the vehicle. Since I was three cars back, I had to wade through the snow to the lead car, where I released the safety device and the engine roared into action with everybody applauding my engineering talent.

Following a solemn church service, we all met in the private room of an elegant restaurant for a festive wedding banquet. Everyone was enjoying themselves with the usual appropriate speeches and toasts. I had made an amusing wedding newspaper in witty rhymes for Elsa and Heinz, as well as several funny songs for everyone to sing along from their own copy. The festivity was in full swing when the groom's distant cousin, who attended the celebration in his brown uniform, insisted that we stop the festivities to listen to Hitler's speech on the radio about the successful voting. Papa loudly proclaimed that this was a private party, but even though we were thirty and the brown uniform was only one, it was not safe to not listen to the speech. It also was not clear if this cousin was even invited or if he came on his own to "brighten up" our celebration. Only Heinz knew him and he had merely sent a formal wedding announcement, as his only but distant relative, and not an invitation at all.

That incident evoked the following old joke being whispered around the table:

> At school a teacher asks the class, "How high do you esteem the Party?" "About five feet," replies little Johann eagerly. "How did you come up with that number?" the puzzled teacher wonders. "That's easy," explains little Johann. "My father is six feet tall, and he always holds his hand under his chin saying he has the Party up to here!"

That gesture was perfect for our own party, too. Heinz had even arranged a honeymoon in Italy. Because of his talent for making impossible things go so well, Elsa called him tenderly her *Heinzelmann*, after the little gnomes of the holy town of Cologne on the Rhine.

Another miracle happened the same month. In May of 1938, Hitler introduced us to the first Volkswagen. Every newspaper had pictures of him sitting in the car which he proclaimed as the "affordable people's car for the average German." Although Hitler did not design the car, he did specify certain requirements as to maximum weight, average gas mileage and maximum cost which had to be considered in the design and manufacturing of the automobile, which was actually built by Ferdinand Porsche. It was rumored that Hitler also authorized many patented devices to be installed in the car, disregarding the rights of the inventors. These forced agreements of the patent owners was phrased as "free donation for the welfare of the people." Again, Hitler had a devious plan in the introduction of his "people's car." The Volkswagen was not designed for peaceful use by the masses as advertised, but in reality, was the basic plan for the construction of the German Jeep to be used in the planned war that was soon to begin.

The Storm Clouds Gather

Our building project on Limastrasse was a brilliantly planned three-story duplex, built in a U shape with five luxurious apartments on each side. Both ends were to have a large balcony on the third floor sitting above the Florida rooms on the second floor which would provide a marvelous view of the nearby Lake Waldsee. However, either our architect, Mr. Behrmann, got tired of the constant battle to obtain necessary building materials through other than normal channels, or he was trying to save money when he suggested doing away with the balconies and just putting roofs over the Florida rooms. But the contract called for balconies and Mutti wanted them for their added living convenience and Mr. Thiemer, the other architect, agreed with her. Thus, this deviation from the original contract as proposed by Mr. Behrmann caused some serious disagreements. The workers had already started to erect the wooden roof beams and Mutti knew she had to act quickly, so she and I concocted a plot to solve the problem in a peaceful manner over good food and wine. Elsa and Heinz had returned from their honeymoon in Italy, and we had a lot of news to catch up on. They lived close by in a garden apartment, and we brought them in on our little scheme to provide neutral conversation that was not related to building a house.

Shortly thereafter, our family, along with the Behrmanns, Elsa and Heinz, set out on an evening of entertainment. We had selected Berlin's popular *Haus Vaterland* at Potsdamer Platz, a colossal building of several stories which contained many different restaurants under one roof. Each specialized in the atmosphere of a different part of Germany, and also the ambience of other countries.

We started on the first floor in "Bavaria" where we sat at long wooden tables, as in the *Hofbräuhaus* in Munich, drinking beer and being served by men in *Lederhosen*, while a cheery female band dressed in low-cut dirndls played and yodeled. A life-like Bavarian alpine scene covered one entire wall of the hall. There, every hour on the hour, lighting and sound effects produced a violent thunderstorm with a heavy downpour, followed by a typical alpine glow as the storm, passed.

Our second stop was the Rhine terraces which featured formal dining with soft violin music and dancing. This restaurant had a large three-dimensional scene with a wide Rhine landscape with romantic castles on the hillsides and busy boat traffic on the river. Here also a thunderstorm was simulated with appropriate sound effects, followed by the reappearance of sunshine. The band played suitable music about the Rhine, wine and women.

The next stop was for a special wine sampling in the *Grinzig* where you looked down from cozy arcades on a scene of the Danube and Vienna with the famous Stephan's cathedral. Here the *Heurige*, a wine made from recently pressed grapes, was served in special decanters and had the characteristic of going to the stomach and the head at the same time. Everyone was in a good mood and all the troubles with the building project were happily washed away by the wine. Now seemed the ideal time to put Mutti's plan in action. While looking down on the scene of the waters of the Danube, Mutti compared it to the rejuvenating waters of the Wildbad spa and suggested to Papa and Mr. Behrmann that the two overworked men desperately needed to take some time off and relax there together. Everyone, including Papa, enthusiastically approved of the idea, and on the spur of the moment, an early departure date was set for the trip. We were eager to get home and get packed, and Mutti would gladly assist with that. But Papa insisted on making one more stop at the Turkish café. Here, in dim light, we relaxed in low, soft seats, sipping mocha out of tiny cups while watching changing scenes of the Bosporous that gave the illusion you were in Istanbul with ships passing back and forth as lighting changed the scene from daylight to dark.

Two days later, Papa and Mr. Behrmann left for a month's visit to the rejuvenating waters of the Wildbad spa, totally unaware of our sudden concern for their health. As soon as they had departed, our dependable accomplice and lifelong friend, architect Paul Thiemer, took over and put Mutti's plan into operation. Although the workers cursed in anger, all of the roof beams came down again and the large balconies were constructed. The result was sensational. All this was hastily accomplished in just four weeks, and proved to add tremendously to the beauty and style of the apartment buildings. Even Papa and Mr. Behrmann agreed peacefully when they viewed the finished product upon their return.

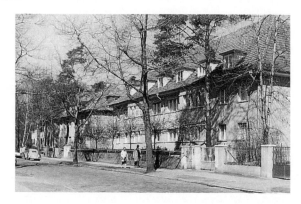

The apartment duplex on Lima-strasse.

While we were happily building our apartment house, the Czechoslovakian crisis had deepened. We were now informed that, as a result of the Munich agreement of September 29, 1938, between Germany, Italy, France and Great Britain, Hitler had taken back the German Sudetenland, which had been given to the newly-founded Czechoslovakia by the Versailles Treaty. Although Czechoslovakia was not even present at the conference, abandoned by the western powers to appease Hitler, we all applauded the peaceful return of old ethnic German land that was the home of over 3 million of our people. We felt that the world seemed to have a guilty conscience because of the harsh terms of the Versailles Treaty and was willing to please Hitler. He had stated that with the German Sudetenland his territorial demands would be satisfied, and we, and the world, believed him. However, the Polish and Hungarian governments also renewed their claims against Czechoslovakia to regain the land they lost to that new country in 1919.

Shortly thereafter, while visiting my Aunt Frieda in Gleiwitz, Upper Silesia, we drove to the nearby Sudetenland where we were greeted very warmly by the people as soon as they recognized our German license plate. Our destination was the little spa town of Lindewiese. The Czechs had changed its name to Dolny Lipowna (my spelling may be incorrect). The spa had been visited frequently by my relatives prior to World War I. The people working at our run-down but spotlessly clean German hotel told us that since 1919, life had grown from bad to worse under the Czech regime and they were hoping that unification with Germany would bring prosperity and equality of rights in their German homeland. We spent some wonderful days there while my relatives looked up old familiar places.

Upon returning home from my visit to Aunt Frieda, my life returned to the same old routine of tennis at the club, short driving trips and being a good daughter at home who had to wait for the right husband to come along. I felt that I was missing a meaningful purpose and fulfillment in my life. Elsa understood my situation with great sympathy. Then, in October, I accidently found a tempting ad in the newspaper about an institute in Leipzig called Bach's Foreign Language and Business School. Without delay I took my discovery to her. It sounded very tempting to both of us, my opportunity to acquire some skills that might enhance my qualifications for professional work. Elsa agreed eagerly and I immediately made a long distance phone call from her place to the school to get more information.

I was connected with a Dr. Peters, the director of the school who told me that there were no Nazi restrictions and that the next course, scheduled to start in November, was almost filled. Remembering my frantic last minute experience at the Lessing College, I asked him to register me at once, which meant I had to be there in two weeks with 1,000 marks due upon enrollment. "My father will take care of that," I promised. All this happened in only a few minutes. Again, I had made a decision on impulse without discussing it first with my parents. Elsa and I were absolutely convinced that regardless of some immediate thunderstorms at home, the plan to attend that school was a capital idea and would be rewarded by future opportunities.

Experience had taught me to work through Mutti. As usual, we chose the dinner table as the ideal time and place to bring up the matter. Papa was a music lover and we brought into the conversation about Johann Sebastian Bach having spent his creative years in Leipzig and how he was closely identified with the Thomas Choir, a famous boys' choir that Papa was familiar with. Thus far, the conversation appealed to him. Then we mentioned that there was a wonderful language institute in Leipzig called the Bach School which I would like to attend, though this Bach had nothing to do with the composer Bach. This way we had arrived at the subject at last. Papa promised to think about it, though we couldn't give him much time for that. When he realized I was not really asking his permission, but merely for him to write a check for the tuition, he became very angry and shouted, "I'm tired of your head-over-heels surprises!" Now we went through the usual procedure of him saying "no" at first, but later cooling off and writing the check, but he stayed upset until I left two weeks later with a big suitcase, generous pocket money, and my heart full of hopes.

On a beautiful November morning, a one-hour express train ride brought me from Berlin to the monumental thirty-track Leipzig railway station which compared in grandeur to Victoria Station in London and Grand Central Station in New York. I took a taxi to the school's dormitory on Wächterstrasse, a multi-storied villa surrounded by a large garden, next to the Polish consulate. Mrs. Bach had assigned me to a second floor room with a roommate named Gerda Schmidt, thus putting the two Schmidts together. I considered myself fashionably dressed in my elegant knee-length coat, silver fox cape, a new black velvet hat, black leather boots almost to the knee and restrained make-up, and hoped I would make a favorable impression on my new roommate. I wondered how she would look.

With pleasant expectation, I knocked on the door and was greeted by a tall, serious looking, plainly dressed but striking Nordic beauty with beautiful big blue eyes. I could see the surprise and displeasure in her face as she greeted me. As she confessed later, her first thought was, "Oh my God, one of those swanky, extravagant Berliners, and I am stuck with her in the same room for the whole semester!" We were both startled. The contrast could not have been greater. Finally we introduced ourselves and decided on who would have which bed and which dresser, always trying to let the other have the more convenient place. Maybe the other wasn't that bad after all, we reasoned and went over to the school together for registration where we took some tests, and received our schedules and homework assignments for the next day.

There were very strict rules concerning attending every single class and being punctual for all of them. It was evident that there would be no wasted time in the daily lesson plan. Although placed in different groups, we both were assigned the same subjects such as English language and culture, commerce, business correspondence, shorthand in both English and German, plus various academic subjects. The school was determined to give us our money's worth—actually more than we had counted on. Before returning to our dormitory, we met some of our male and female classmates and took a short stroll through the town, an interesting mixture of trade, art and history, which we would explore some other time. Then, Gerda and I headed for home.

After changing into our nightgowns, we found out rather quickly that we were very much alike beneath our very different shells, and had a great deal in common, so much in fact, that we started a friendship that exists to this day. We both came from strict homes and wanted to get out into the big world on our own. Gerda, who was two years younger than I, came from the small town Domjüch in Mecklenburg, North Germany, where everybody knew each other. She also was unable to escape the BDM. However, her association was more like the Girl Scouts with sports, folk dancing and singing old German songs around the campfire at night. Quite a difference from my experience with the BDM in Münster. Her father was a doctor there and headed the clinic for the retarded and those with mental disorders. Her younger brother studied medicine, her older sister wanted to be a librarian, and Gerda was interested in foreign languages. (The truth was that there was not enough money to pay the university tuition for all three children as she told me in bitterness one day.) I later discovered that she also had a marvelous talent for drawing and painting.

Next morning, November 4, 1938, we showed up at school for breakfast at 7:30 a.m. and classes started full speed at 8 a.m., including a lot of homework. After lunch there were more classes and later an afternoon coffee with rolls and some free time for studies. Dinner was served at 6 p.m., and then it was back to our rooms to study until lights out at 10 p.m. We took our study seriously, and bribed the porter out of an extra key so we could go out to a nearby café to continue our studies. This left little time for sleep, but we always managed to be on time for breakfast and classes the next morning, thanks to our very noisy alarm clock which we placed out of reach on a porcelain plate. It made an unbelievable racket. We took turns jumping out of bed to turn it off and waking each other. Our system worked quite successfully. Once, we were awakened during the night by the building shaking, and we both jumped out of bed and ran to the window, but there was nothing unusual outside. In the morning we were told that the area had experienced a slight earthquake. That was our first experience with Mother Nature's unfriendly way to shake people up.

The government announced that on Wednesday, November 9, a commemoration service would be held for those Nazi Party members who died on the march to the Munich town hall during the rebellion of 1923. Instead of classes, it was mandatory that everybody in the school be present to listen to one of Hitler's tiresome radio speeches, an idiotic repetition of his old catch phrases, culminating in hysterical ovations by his buddies in the Reichstag. So we all sat there in a big hall with serious faces, pretending to be interested, since no one knew who may have snuck in to report those not properly attentive.

In the middle of that same night after Hitler's speech, an earth-shaking commotion occurred outside. Assuming it was another earthquake, we rushed to the window and saw fires blazing at different places beyond the trees of our yard. Then we heard repeated explosions and shouting and screaming coming from all directions. The entire city seemed to be on fire, but except for the glow in the sky, we couldn't see a thing. It was obvious that there was some sort of disaster, as we could hear police sirens and fire engines continuously racing through town. Still bewildered as to the cause, we crawled back to bed. It was not until the next morning that we learned the full extent of what had happened during the night.

The morning headline of the government-controlled newspaper was "Revenge" and proclaimed that what had happened the previous night was in retaliation against the Jews for the assassination of Ernst von Rath, an attaché in the German Embassy in Paris, by a young Polish Jew whose parents had been expelled from Germany. This was the excuse that Hitler had been waiting for to launch his evil Nazi-organized anti-Jewish rioting, as he knew there would be little, if any, complaint from the rest of the world nations. President Roosevelt had organized a world conference in the town of Evian, France, from July 6-14, to help the Jews in Germany under the motto "we are our brother's keeper," but none of the thirty-two countries attending offered sanctuary to the Jewish refugees. The Nazi government had even permitted German Jewish representatives to participate. This gave Hitler the green light for Nazi persecution of the Jews, since they had obviously been abandoned by the rest of the world at a time when they could still leave Germany if they had an asylum to turn to. That is a tragic but true, historical fact. Whoever is interested in more details can read them in the N.Y. Herald Tribune of July 8, 1938. A similar article also appeared in the New York Post on August 8, 1988.

The world's outcry later about the Jewish fate in Europe was too little and too late after they had bolted their own doors. Now Goebbels, in a fanatical inflammatory radio speech misrepresented that racing inferno as though it had been the result of spontaneous outrage of the population. What a lie! We were stunned. As always we were confronted with the complete facts without even being asked or allowed to have an opinion.

After school on November 10, Gerda and I went downtown and saw the results of the previous night's terror. The streets were littered with broken glass from the windows of vandalized and looted Jewish shops, and the synagogue was still burning. Police and firemen had blocked off some areas. Everything turned out to be a well organized storm of hate of the Nazi Party squads who, camouflaged in civilian clothing, had struck Jewish property and synagogues throughout the night not only in Leipzig, but nationwide in Germany and Austria. This infamous act on November 9, 1938, became known worldwide as the "Crystal Night" or the "Night Of The Broken Glass."

Deeply depressed, we returned to the dormitory and found the yard of the adjacent Polish consulate jammed with fugitives seeking protection. As we looked at each other while passing along our common wire-mesh fence that separated us, no one knew what the other was thinking, and not a word was spoken. How could we let them know that this was a Nazi-organized plot we were powerless against and had no part in, and which we abhorred as a violation of human dignity. In a dictatorship one does not even dare criticize government actions because Hitler not only persecuted the Jews, but also anyone who spoke out against him, and that to the full extent of his destructive power. Suddenly civilization seemed to be over and such inhuman event would stigmatize us, the German people.

We had danced with some of the employees of the Polish consulate at tea dances in the Hotel Astoria, which was popular with business people. And now this! Did fire and fanaticism of one group have to intrude upon and destroy the private lives of all the others? The atmosphere in the dormitory was very subdued. We were shocked, disgusted, and absolutely helpless.

After early classes on Saturday morning I caught the express train to Berlin to spend the weekend at home since Papa's birthday was on November 13, and Mutti always arranged a family get-together with friends to celebrate the occasion. She especially wanted me home to re-store domestic harmony since Papa was still angry that I left so sud-denly for Leipzig, and she felt that the birthday surrounded by all of us would help to improve his disposition.

Günter's train was due at 3:30 p.m. and I was going to pick him up in my car at the station as usual. I was in the process of getting dressed when I noticed I was running late, so I quickly slipped on a long coat over my underwear and rushed out to the garage. Feeling secure that no one would see me in my own car, I jumped into the driver's seat and pressed the starter button, but nothing happened. After frantically try-ing again and again to start the car with no success, I gave up in disgust and ran to the nearby taxi stand. As I jumped into the taxi, my coat flew open and I suddenly realized with horror that I had on neither a dress nor a slip, and the taxi driver saw that, too. Hastily pulling my coat tight around me under his doubtful looks, we took off for the railway sta-tion. It was then that I realized that the only thing I had in my hand was my car keys—no purse and no money. Oh, Günter was going to pay for this ride!

When we arrived at the station, he was waiting for me out front. How handsome he looked in his navy blue uniform. Seeing me waving from the taxi, he got in. When I explained my problem he said he had no intention of paying for the ride either, and the taxi driver listened to our conversation. When Günter came home he never spent any money, just the opposite. Being a young officer was more of an honor than a source of income, and Papa sent him a check regularly. When we ar-rived home, Papa was standing out front to find out why the car was still there but the daughter was gone. I quickly vanished into the house while Papa paid for the cab and Günter, as usual, took care of my trouble.

Everybody was in good spirits as long as I stayed out of Papa's sight. He acted as if he was still angry about the Leipzig incident and didn't like to have his position as head of the household challenged. But, he was always an exemplary host with an excellent supply of good wines and spirits. When Papa refilled a guest's glass and the guest asked modestly for only half of one, he would ask with a twinkle in his eye, "The upper or the lower half?" and while saying so, had already refilled it. We always had a marvelous atmosphere in our home, something we call *Gemütlichkeit*. We frequently had company because Papa hated to go out. I have inherited this penchant for hospitality and to this day I do not feel comfortable until I have served something to my guests.

There were many topics at the dinner table that evening. The Volkswagen plant in Wolfsburg, North Germany, was to produce Hitler's new affordable people's car and he wanted every German to have one. Advance orders were being taken for the VW (the later legendary Beetle) which required pre-delivery installment payments of 5 marks a week, (approximately 5 dollars a month) toward the final delivery of 1,000 marks when the cars came off the production line. Everyone, including Günter, who wanted the new VW made the advance payments into a special fund, but this turned out to be just another clever trick of Hitler to collect money. Needless to say, no one ever got their car or had their money refunded because it had already gone into financing Hitler's massive war preparations. The promised VW was only on the drawing board, and all of the advance payments collected went into financing the construction of the German army jeep.

Another heated discussion was the continuous civil war in Spain (1936-1939), and the impact it was having on the political atmosphere in Europe. Had it divided Europe politically into right and left factions? Hitler and Mussolini were supporting General Francisco Franco against the Spanish Communists supported by Russia and the leftist Abraham Lincoln Brigade of the United States. Papa commented how lucky we were that all of these hostilities were taking place on Spanish soil so far away from our own country. My own thoughts went back to Switzerland and the *Pensionat Mistral*. What had happened to that nice Spanish girl whose parents had sent her there five years ago for security reasons? We were totally unaware that in less than a year we would be involved in a war ourselves.

Finally, at peace with Papa, I returned to school in Leipzig for a few short weeks until it was Christmas recess, and then I found myself back home again. During the short holiday vacation, I was kept busy with the study material assigned, and was back in Leipzig again on January 3, 1939,

for the start of classes. As so often in the past, our private lives continued, the same way as happened later to others throughout the world, in
spite of wars in Korea, Vietnam, Afghanistan, Yugoslavia and other countries. Forgetfulness must be a wide-spread, human survival attribute.
Nevertheless, the Crystal Night of a few months ago threw its shadow
over everything and hung in the air like a bad omen.

Although we students had all returned punctually, our foreign language teachers had not. They were native to the country whose language
they taught, such as England, France and Spain, and we wondered why
they had not come back from vacation to their homeland.

One of the English language teachers, Mr. Neads, everybody took
for an agent. Mine was Miss Taylor. She was friendly and helpful but
somehow inaccessible, even during our frequent social gatherings in the
evening when we would sing English songs. All the native foreign language teachers stuck together. They must have thought everyone of us
to be a Nazi. We never discussed politics so they had no way of knowing that we were there to avoid government-ruled institutions.

Now many classes had to be canceled so Gerda and I used these
unexpected free days to visit the historical monument of the "Battle of
Nations" that commemorated Napoleon's defeat in October 1813, which
freed Europe from French rule. After more than a week's delay, our foreign language teachers gradually started to return. Mr. Neads was the
last one to show up on Monday, January 16 and we students had to
make up for all of the canceled classes. But, being young, we survived
the added workload.

More and more often Gerda and I would leave before the dormitory
lights were turned off at 10 p.m. and go to the little nearby café to continue
our studies. We would sit at a rear table sipping coffee to keep awake and
would usually return to the locked dormitory around midnight, using our
extra key to get in. Studying until late on weeknights and dancing until 2
a.m. on Saturdays created a busy, but very satisfying life.

On several weekends, I went home to accompany my parents and
friends to various balls, such as the film ball, where I had the thrill of
dancing close to the famous Swedish movie star Zarah Leander. At one
of these balls I met a nice gentleman who asked if he could visit me at
the school in Leipzig. I said "yes," since I figured that plans made at a
ball are usually forgotten by the next day.

On January 30, 1939, the entire school had to listen to celebrations and speeches of the Nazi assumption of power six years previous. It was another one of these endless, obligatory shows in which we had to participate, duty-bound, in order to keep the school in good standing. We all sat quietly listening to Hitler's endless self-glorification for hours, as he was a master in saying nothing new with great emphasis. Then he stressed his gratitude to his old faithful combatants, many of whom he had already executed in cold calculation, but this must have just slipped his mind, the mind of a charlatan with a Charley Chaplin moustache. We badly wanted to leave, but we had to sit with fake attention throughout because we never knew who may be watching and reporting on our every action.

Gerda's older sister also lived in Leipzig and sometimes would visit us. She was a secluded and studious type who was only interested in her books and never wanted to come dancing with us. By now, some time had passed since the Crystal Night and we again met members of the Polish consulate at dances. We had a wonderful time with complete disregard of the strained relationship between our governments, never thinking that war would break out within a few months that would turn us into enemies. I often wondered how many of our nice dance partners survived the war.

In one of my stylish outfits

On Sunday, February 12, a large convertible with two gentlemen blew its horn in front of our dormitory and all the girls rushed to the windows. There he was, the dance partner from the ball in Berlin wanting to go sightseeing with me. He asked me to bring along a girlfriend for his friend, so Gerda came along, too. The four of us spent a great day touring the Leipzig vicinity, but that was it. Somehow people appear differently in daylight than during an evening at a ball. When I think back today how Gerda and I just took off with two strangers, it was something I would never want my daughters to do. But, times were different then and so were the people. We had very strict laws and few major crimes. The death penalty was imposed for murder, and the sentence was carried out immediately.

On Wednesday, February 15, the Bach School held a carnival dance in the huge *Friedrichshallen*. Gerda and I didn't get home until 6 a.m. In wise forethought, there was no school the next day. Soon though, final examinations started, and we had tests in the daytime and danced at night at "The Three Kings." Today, as I recall those times, I do not know how we had the stamina for the pace we maintained. It must have been the energy you have in your early twenties that drives you to live each day to the fullest. Both Gerda and I passed the English course "with distinction," and after graduation parties at the end of February, 1939, I returned home. Gerda stayed on in Leipzig for the French course, but we kept in close touch in a friendship that has now endured for more than sixty years through political crisis and war.

Hitler had promised to be the rock of the country. How he rocked not only us, but the entire world, would soon be fully known.

All Hell Breaks Loose

In early 1939, Papa became concerned that drastic changes would occur because the highly experienced leaders in areas of finance, military and diplomatic establishments, were replaced with Hitler's submissive henchmen. This enabled Hitler to have unrestricted control through his handpicked puppets of the monetary, military and foreign service elements of the governments. General Wilhelm Keitel was appointed General Fieldmarshal of the army, who soon was called in the vernacular *Lakeitel,* with his dog-like lackey devotion to Hitler's commands. Joachim von Ribbentrop (a former champagne salesman), appointed as the Minister of Foreign Affairs, was mockingly named *Rippentroppen,* meaning rib drops, because he was the strong medicine Hitler needed to impose his will upon the foreign service. (The character and actions of both men in their assigned duties is best shown by the fact that both were found guilty of war crimes and sentenced to death at the Nuremberg Trials in 1945.)

These new appointments were a further intrusion and regimentation of almost every aspect of our private lives as we were being Nazified from the government down to the personal level, and this made us very uneasy. In the previous year, our first ration cards for butter had been issued. At first, the changes were not so noticeable since the Nazi regime had gained growing acceptability among the working class due to the rapid elimination of the mass unemployment that had existed for years. Living standards had risen and Hitler's rhetoric of "Everything for every man!" was the slogan constantly pounded into workers' heads. But, working conditions gradually usurped their personal freedom and killed their initial enthusiasm. The ever increasing overtime work had drastically reduced their free time, and they often had to work far from home, being with their families only on weekends. Further, the overtime pay was expected to be donated to the Fatherland.

The farmers did not fare much better than the workers. Over the years they had barely eked out a living, but now a generous government subsidy was granted to enhance their income. But, they paid for this by being forced into a government-controlled monopoly called the National Nutrition Producing Department, which was given the mission of assuring Germany's future food supply. The farmer was now required to do everything in accordance with the government's instructions. A new hereditary farmstead law with the slogan "blood and soil" restricted the sale or subdivision of any farm of less than 125 hectares (309 acres). And, a new nationwide holiday was created to honor the German farmer which was observed annually as a harvest celebration in October, not at all comparable to the American Thanksgiving. Throughout the day, there were rousing radio reports, mass rallies with fiery speeches to evoke the farmers' pride, and, parades this time with farmers marching, preferably in brown uniforms.

The free and independent farmer had been turned into a gigantic agricultural government-controlled cartel. But, the country folk were not easily dazzled and were well aware of their restrictions in the shift of state emphasis from production to control. The Nazis seemed to have a law that was for and against the same things, and regardless of what you did, it was impossible to please them—an endless wrangle with authorities. However, with their inborn natural shrewdness, they were able to outwit the government's attempt to control as illustrated by this lengthy amusing farmers' joke, an ironic parody:

> In a rural community it was time for the farmers to be routinely inspected by an agriculture commission. The inspectors arrive at the first farmer in the village and ask, "What do you feed your chickens? They look splendid!"
>
> "Grain," answers the farmer proudly.
>
> "Grain!" shout the inspectors. "You are wasting the valuable food of our people. What a crime. Never do that again or you will go to jail."
>
> The farmer quickly sends his little boy to the next neighbor to warn him not to say "grain."
>
> The inspectors arrive at the neighbor's farm and ask: "What do you feed your chickens? They look splendid."
>
> "Potatoes," answers the farmer proudly.

"Potatoes!" shout the inspectors. "You are wasting the valuable food of our people. What a crime. Never do that again or you will go to jail."

Quickly, that farmer sends his little boy to the next neighbor to warn him not to say "grain" or "potatoes."

The inspectors arrive at the next farm and ask: "What are you feeding your chickens? They look splendid!"

"Leftovers," says the farmer proudly.

"Leftovers!" shout the inspectors. "What a careless household are you running here? You are wasting the valuable food of our people. What a crime. Never do that again or you will go to jail."

The farmer quickly sends his little boy to the next neighbor to warn him not to say "grain," "potatoes," or "leftovers." The inspectors arrive. "What are you feeding your chickens? They look splendid!"

"I don't feed them anything," says the farmer grinning. "At noon I give the rooster 5 marks and he takes them all out to lunch!"

Another catch was the *Volksempfänger*, the first new mass produced utility radio set which was so inexpensive that everyone could afford one "for people's leisure." Even every little country inn had one, and Goebbels knew how to use the potential of this media for his propaganda. His incessant fanatical rhetoric was being beamed into almost every home constantly, since his theory was that if a lie is repeated often enough, it will eventually be accepted as truth. Immediately a new joke made the rounds:

An old woman takes her new little radio to church and the priest wonders why. "Oh," she explains, "It has to go to confession. It lies too much!"

The new radio was called Goebbels' big trap, and he the Reich's ballyhoo minister. No matter how cynically and unscrupulously Goebbels dominated the new media, he still had forgotten to reckon with the free wit of the people against his endless false propaganda. That made him the target of many caustic jokes like this one:

Goebbels, the Minister of Public Instruction and Propaganda, wants to know how life is in Heaven so he can decide where

he wants to be for eternity. Saint Peter shows him many splendid rooms. Goebbels likes the one with music, go-go girls and
other amusements the best. That's where he wants to be after
death. Eventually he dies and finds himself in a terrible place
with hard work, bad food and intense heat. Right away he
complains to Saint Peter. "It's like hell here." "That's where
you are," confirms Saint Peter. Goebbels flares up in anger,
"But this is not at all like what you previously showed me!"
Saint Peter smiles amusedly, "What I showed you before was
only our propaganda department."

Good humor is born in bad times to help live through them. Laughter is a powerful weapon. The constant political jokes which shot up
like mushrooms, were much hated by the Nazis, which made them all
the more appreciated by the people. The Berliners, with their sharp
senses and quick tongues, made their humor especially effective, and
these jokes spread throughout all of Germany.

Cabarets were a tradition in Berlin. The comedians often took great
risks in their stinging political satires and were repeatedly picked up by
the Gestapo, the Nazi Secret State Police. Well known for these risqué
comments was a cabaret in the city where the first-row seats were mostly
occupied by Gestapo members, appearing of course in civilian clothes,
who were jotting down notes of everything that was said. One night, a
comedian noticed the Gestapo in the front row writing rapidly, so he
stopped his act and stepped to the edge of the stage. Addressing them
he asked, "Can you follow me, or do I have to follow you?" And often
the comedians had to follow, and the cabaret was closed temporarily.

A thorn in the Nazis' side was Grete Weiser, a famous Berlin screen
comedienne and character actress. She told the most daring jokes and
hilarious parodies of the Nazi leaders, using Berlin slang to make them
even funnier and more degrading. Once she told her audience she had
asked her maid what she thought about "that new boss" (referring to
Hitler). The maid's answer was short, clear and dangerous: "*Wat ick
brauch is an Kaiser. Prolet bin ick selber.*" What I need is an emperor.
Proletarian I am myself (like Hitler).

She often made fun of the very pompous lifestyle of the top Party
wheels compared with the modest life demanded of the population. So
she ended one particular performance by informing the audience in her

humorous way that after a Nazi meeting concerning "public welfare," all the luxurious limousines parked outside were exclusively for the Nazi Party brass, and the rest of us were supposed to walk to save gasoline. She was immediately seized by the Gestapo because she had defamed the Nazi government. Returning after her release, she told the audience in her dry wit, "The Nazis had every right to imprison me that last time, because I lied. For once, one of those limousines did not belong to the big wheels." Thereupon she was arrested again.

She was also the one who created the degrading song about Hermann Göring, a general and leader of the air forces, dressed flamboyantly with a passion for wearing clinking medals. This didn't escape ridicule. Unfortunately I only remember the refrain in Berlin slang:

Links Lametta, rechts Lametta	Tinsel on this and that side
Und der Bauch wird imma fetta	With his belly swelling wide
Im fliegen is er Meester	Flying is his fame
Hermann heest er.	Hermann is his name.

Göring was also known for his vanity and delight in wearing decorations, as reflected in this popular joke:

One morning Göring had a very important reception to attend, and the whole house was in a frenzy because nobody could find his medals. His valet was finally summoned. When he was told what the problem was, he just smiled and left. In two minutes he was back with the whole cluster. Everybody breathed a sigh of relief; "Where were they?" "Still on his pajamas of course!"

Hitler's fiftieth birthday on April 20, 1939, was celebrated with great fanfare, Hitler as a new Bismarck, with all of the symbolic rituals of a great military display and mass civilian rallies. As usual, attendance was mandatory. The Condor League, which had returned with honors from their participation in the Spanish Civil War, marched proudly in the parade. It was rumored that Hitler had sent his elite force to Spain to test his advanced military equipment in actual combat. Mutti and I were shopping downtown, so we were caught up in the turmoil and the noisy clicking of hobnailed boots, a sound we had long since tired of. The day would end with Hitler's speech, declaring himself as a man of peace and emphasizing his slogan of "Work and Peace" that was leading the nation to prosperity and a new national pride. Many Germans were delighted with our miraculous recovery. Hitler had gambled often and won, and all peacefully. The general hope was that it might continue that way. A month ago we had just gone through his "peaceful" annexation of Czechoslovakia. Now Hitler led us to believe that the terrible times following World War I were all behind us and that prosperity would soon reign.

The mania of the German Aryan race still remained, but we were not fully aware of it because it was masterfully disguised from the public eye, as testified by General Jodl in the Nuremberg Trials. Gerda had recently told me that she had heard about the open persecutions of Germans in Poland. Her information came from a classmate at Bach's School, Maruschka. We had called her that since it is a German idiom for "girl" in Polish. She was the daughter of a German dentist living in Poland. Her family had stayed in their native land when their part of Germany had become Polish territory in 1919. She always had called her life at home a martyrdom. Polish children would not even speak to German children. Every Polish schoolchild was required to learn and sing the "Rota," composed by Maria Konopnicka, an inflammatory song of hatred against the Germans. After twenty years of conflict and violence, Germans were systematically deprived of their rights and subjected to unspeakable humiliations, all with disregard of their assured rights of self-determination under the Geneva conference. But nobody in the world seemed to care about these incessant violations.

Maruschka also talked about a law introduced on June 22, 1937, which prohibited the right of inheritance for German children, based on the concept that Polish territory is only for Poles. That led to a great extent to liquidation of private possessions. When parents died, young farmers were driven from their centuries-old ancestors' land, without any compensation. Anti-German fliers stated: "Away with the Germans! They have eaten our bread long enough," and even the Catholic church preached against the Protestant Germans. The Anglo-French pact of mutual assistance of March 31, 1939 gave Poland false courage for bolder and more unrealistic boasts. On that same day, the Polish military newspaper *Polska Zbrojna* carried a statement by the Deputy Minister of War, Gluchowski, that Poland could easily crush the Germans because the entire German army was a bluff, their soldiers were pushovers and their tanks were made of cardboard. "We are ready!" was his boldest statement. Were they ready for victory in a war that hadn't even broken out yet?

On May 23, 1939, a partial mobilization of the Polish army, which included the drafting of German men living in Poland, created serious tension between the Poles and the ethnic Germans. The Polish military newspaper continued to publish inflammatory speeches of Captain Polenski, which stressed the "old traditional inherited hatred" against the Germans as the "arch enemy" of Poland. The propaganda climaxed with the cry, "Next week we invade Berlin! Let's march into East Prussia and Danzig." Since all mail to Germany was censored, Maruschka's parents wrote her in code not to come home because no German was safe and thousands of ethnic Germans had begun in panic a secret exodus from the Polish corridor into Germany and East Prussia. That flood of German escapees was even persecuted by the Poles. Now we knew that the reported cruelties against Germans in Poland were the truth, and not just more of Goebbels' propaganda. Maruschka, the now homeless German-Polish girl who had just turned twenty-one on May 21, 1939, was given a position by Mrs. Bach as an assistant instructor in the school.

On June 1, 1939, the Polish military newspaper announced Captain Polenski's battle cry, and that a war against Germany, Poland's mortal enemy, would be like a holy crusade because Protestant Germans are enemies of Catholic Poland. Protestant clergymen were forced on long inhuman marches to unknown destinations and many were slain during these brutal deportations, like Superintendent Reisel and Dr. Blau from the Protestant church of Posen. Even Protestant graveyards were vandalized. German schools had to be closed because the children were stoned and beaten on their way to school. Thousands of Poles took to the streets shouting, "Death to the Germans!" After this, Maruschka no longer received any letters from home since any message to Germany was stopped completely by the Polish government, and she was unable to obtain any information as to the whereabouts of her parents. And this was many months before the war broke out.

Since 1919, there had always been a serious problem regarding the free German city of Danzig which was 95 percent German. It was one of the busiest harbors on the Baltic Sea and situated next to Gdingen, Polish Gydnia, which was the Polish harbor constructed after 1920 to give Poland its own access to the Baltic Sea. The Versailles Treaty made

Danzig a German city state within the newly founded Polish territory. It became a territorial island (similar to later the city of Berlin), and Poland immediately changed its German name of Danzig to the Polish Gdansk.

German Danzig was a port of great strategic value to Germany, although it had to adhere to Polish customs regulations. For twenty years, Poland had denied the Weimar Republic's request for at least one railroad as an unobstructed entry into Danzig and an access to isolated East Prussia. No air traffic existed. Even if it did, it would have needed to obtain permission from the Polish government to cross the Polish Corridor. This free access problem over the land-locked German territories was a source of constant friction between the two countries since 1919. The hostility grew over the years as oppressive measures were taken against the ethnic German population, and culminated in the prohibition of the German language. This had intensified in the spring of 1939, and the ethnic German population in Poland was under constant attack, with windows of German houses, shops and churches being smashed and people being attacked and killed. We hoped that some solution could be found for these almost unbearable circumstances before the situation got completely out of hand.

As the summer of 1939 progressed, the German-Polish situation became worse. Each country blamed the other for being uncooperative and for escalating the hostile atmosphere that was now on the edge of open conflict. The tone of newspapers in both countries became more aggressive and the Polish Vice Minister of War again called the German army a big bluff and that his own war machine was far superior. Poland began calling up reservists and Germany started drafting young men and alerted the people to be prepared for an "inevitable" hardship, a dreadful feeling for us.

Since the death of Hindenburg, Hitler became the self-appointed high commander of all armed forces and all military men had to swear a personal oath of loyalty to the Führer, not to the country. However, he was still stating that his ultimate goal was peace because as a common soldier, he had experienced the horrors of war. Despite this, our life was full of puzzling surprises. On August 23, 1939, the Ribbentrop-Molotov Pact was signed as a non-aggression pact between Germany and Russia for the next ten years. Since Hitler called himself the last anti-Communist force and Stalin was his mortal enemy, we wondered what kind of a shady political deal this was that Stalin was suddenly his friend. The pact was presented to the German people as the new path to lasting peace. What could we really believe anymore?

People at once came up with a simple sarcastic joke as a witty riddle:

"What is the difference between Berlin and Moscow?"

"The climate. In Moscow it is much colder."

There was a similarity between the two countries in that both proclaimed themselves as a "workers' paradise" but ruled with an iron hand whether under the Soviet star or the swastika.

Gerda had been offered a Foreign Office position at the German Embassy in Moscow to replace a young lady who would be leaving soon. But, she was advised to first learn Russian because it would come in handy with the new German-Soviet friendship pact. She began her studies with the Russian language teacher for foreign diplomats in the Foreign Office, a very fine, well-educated gentleman. She told us that there was alarming news from home where a sudden mobilization of labor had taken place. On August 25, numerous men, women, and even young girls were called to Fürstenwalde for work in an armament industry, and her father's clinic suddenly lost many of its personnel. Also, a big Nazi labor camp for men located near Domjüch had vanished overnight and nobody knew where it had gone, or why. What were all these drastic changes supposed to mean?

In the latter part of August, I was visiting the resort town of Swinemünde on the Baltic Sea with Mrs. Behrmann and her daughter Sophie. We had driven down together for a weekend at the beach, and had barely arrived when we noticed an air of uncertainty and tension. People were whispering about hasty departures for home, and the very next day, an official order was issued for everybody to leave within twenty-four hours. No reason was given, but that evening as we were walking on the beach, we saw on the far horizon ghostly silhouettes of big ships passing in the distance. We thought, God in heaven, these look like cruisers and other warships. Everybody seemed suddenly possessed by unrest. Our suitcases were already packed and we departed for Berlin early next morning as the radio already was announcing new demands to save fuel. And more food ration cards were being introduced.

The press informed us that in trying to find a peaceful solution, renewed demands had been made lately on Poland with regard to a land route to German Danzig (Gdansk) and isolated East Prussia. Thus far, the Poles had refused to discuss the matter and now, a long anticipated crisis was breaking out. Border shooting incidents were occurring more frequently and these were not limited to the Danzig-Polish frontier. When reading about these occurrences repeatedly in the newspaper, Mutti and Papa exchanged serious looks constantly. By the end of August, the question of German access to Danzig and East Prussia was coming to a head, and a crisis seemed unavoidable. President Roosevelt appealed to all parties involved to seek a peaceful solution, but each side refused to give ground. We were frightened at the thought of another war.

On August 28, England proposed that Polish-German negotiators meet in Berlin the next day, but no Polish negotiator was sent. Instead, on August 30, Poland ordered mobilization of its entire country, and concentrated troops on the German frontiers, and German newspapers reported this action as a negative response to the mediation proposal. Whoever is interested in history can find books about Poland's complicity in the outbreak of the war, because of its twenty-year refusal to compromise on an access road through the Polish corridor to the isolated German town of Danzig and East Prussia.

On Friday morning, September 1, 1939, Hitler gave his rousing speech from the Kroll Opera House in Berlin, the council hall for the so-called parliament of the Nazi regime. From there he shouted over the radio, addressing the German Reichstag: "Since 5:45 this morning we have been shooting back! By now the German troops are crossing the Polish frontier. We will not take it any longer...." His fiery speech went on endlessly and enthusiastically while my parents and I listened in shock. For six years we had heard nothing but peace. We had hoped for last desperate efforts, but now all that peace-loving propaganda proved to have just one flaw—another means of giving rise to false hopes.

The war dominated the press, and the morning news was an extensive and frantic propaganda effort by Hitler to make the war look popular, like a kettle of boiling water that finally lets off steam. However, there was little, if any, response from the population. Mutti and Papa sat on the couch (I can still see them as if it were today), looked at each other with terrified expressions and said, "*Krieg!*" War! That word suddenly hung over our house like the sword of Damocles. They were horrified.

During the previous days, Mutti and Papa had frequently talked about the terrifying experiences of the last war and how happy they were to have survived the way they did. "My God, what would this new war bring? Wasn't one war enough in our lifetime?" Exactly twenty-one years after the end of the last one, total mobilization was now ordered for another war caused merely by a dispute over free land entry to German Danzig and East Prussia. Papa groaned, "There can be no joy and wars can never be won, by anybody, since they take the youngest and the best of us all."

We were in low spirits and so were our friends and neighbors. The heroic and noisy behavior was only shouted over the radio. We were numb with fear. An American friend who was in Berlin at that time told me later that she was the only pedestrian walking on the city's main boulevard *Unter den Linden*, at 11:30 in the morning. All the streets were totally empty except for new draftees standing in open trucks, crammed tightly together, as they were driven demonstratively through the Brandenburg Gate. There were no cheering crowds as they rode off to a grim future, their life plans shattered overnight. Their faces looked shocked. Later she was the only guest in *Café Kranzler* where the two waiters were whispering to each other about the bleak tomorrow.

Every newspaper published the same slogans to manipulate public opinion. Since we were completely shut off from the outside world, it was difficult to judge to what extent we could truly believe what we heard or read. We knew that Hitler was at the peak of his power and free to do whatever he desired, and Goebbels assisted him effectively in muzzling the press that he ruled alone. Only his censored news was published and any anti-war criticism would invite the death penalty. But despite Goebbels' war readiness, we were burdened with all kinds of new demands. A total blackout was ordered at night for all houses, street lights and vehicles, and air raid wardens were assigned to make sure that all orders were adhered to. It was pitch dark at night and flashlights quickly sold out in all stores. We suddenly lived in the dark in more ways than one because it was forbidden, at the risk of going to jail, to listen to foreign broadcasts or to spread any foreign information.

To add to our despair, two days later, France and Great Britain declared war on Germany on September 3, 1939, honoring their Anglo-Polish treaty with the guaranty of mutual assistance. Europe stumbled into World War II. However, they never declared war on the Soviet Union despite the fact that the pact signed by Hitler and Stalin only ten days prior, clearly opened the way for both pact-partners to invade Poland. Stalin took advantage of this, allowing Hitler to strike first, then, as expected, he overran Poland from the East to grab his share from the late non-aggression pact with Germany. In doing so, Stalin defaulted on his ten-year Polish-Russian non-aggression pact of July 25, 1932, after only seven years. In addition to Poland, Stalin also invaded neutral Finland and the Baltic states from which he deported thousands of Estonians to Siberia, and he grabbed part of Rumania and Bessarabia. All his unleashed wars proceeded without any serious international opposition or outcry for justice from the Western Allies.

Poland, contrary to all its former arrogant bragging, was poorly equipped with outdated military material, and tried to attack tanks on horseback. Due to the lack of promised assistance from England and France, Hitler's *Blitzkrieg,* or lightening war, with modern ground forces and supported by massive aircraft, overran Poland in just eighteen days. Hitler could never have done this without the strategic backing of Stalin, even though Germany seemed to have the most powerful army in the world at that time. Being invaded simultaneously from the West by Germany and from the East by the Soviets, Poland had no chance whatsoever and was split between Hitler and Stalin, with Stalin getting the more valuable half with the important mineral resources.

Hitler's revenge for the Versailles Treaty was now complete as he had taken back the German city of Danzig and obtained a land connection to isolated East Prussia. But he paid the high price of unleashing a new war. Stalin had taken two hundred thousand Polish prisoners during the Soviet invasion, of which fifteen thousand were officers. These fifteen thousand Polish officers were all executed by a cruel order of Stalin. The slaughter took place in the Katyn forest, near Smolensk, each officer killed with the typical gunshot in the back of the head. Later, when the mass graves were discovered, the Soviets tried to blame the massacre on the Germans, but research and history proved otherwise.

According to an article in the "Washington Journal," published on April 14, 1989, a monument had been erected in Warsaw in the Powazki Cemetery after World War II, to honor those thousands of Polish officers murdered in 1939. The article states that Stalin had falsely accused the German army of this massacre, but it was later proven that this was just one of the many massacres ordered by Stalin during his reign of terror. The inscription on the Warsaw monument was subsequently changed to reflect the truth, and, in 1990, the Soviets admitted their guilt.

For us at home, the privacy of bank accounts, telephones, and letters was already abolished and invalidated, justified by the statement that only bad people have secrets. This way every move we made was easily controlled by the government. We lived in a Nazi strait-jacket. Nevertheless, the latest shocking news leaked out, even though the government had tried very hard to suppress it to keep from embarrassing the Party.

Lady Unity Mitford, a close friend of Hitler and a niece of Winston Churchill, had committed suicide in the English Garden, a beautiful public park in Munich, on September 1, the day war broke out. This was the same place where her notorious romance with Hitler had taken place some years before when she had come to Munich because of her infatuation with him, his pretentious ideals and peace policy. Her passion for him was so well known that Hitler was asked if he would marry her, and it is said that he replied he would never marry a non-German. She must have spoken German very well, since Hitler hardly knew any foreign language. When Hitler invaded Poland, her idealistic picture of him was shattered and she took her life.

Lady Mitford was not the only one disillusioned. Hitler was a master at deceiving people at home and abroad. To portray himself as a peaceful, nature-loving family man, he had his picture taken with children or his German shepherd, portraying love with a big benevolent smile. However, research has proven that the word "love" evidently did not exist in his vocabulary since it was never once used by him.

The Nazis were masters of concealment and brainwashing, as evidenced by the fact that the outside world knew more about the terrible occurrences that took place under Hitler's command than we did. People never knew what kind of person he really was. On different occasions, he defied the Versailles Treaty, which was overlooked by the Allies. They realized that the unjust terms of the Versailles Treaty was the cause of Germany's economic chaos, and were impressed how rapidly Hitler had reduced the massive unemployment in his first few years of power. Millions, and not only Germans, had been under his spell, and in later years his personal magnetism was often discussed, but never understood.

The German submarines scored major victories in the first weeks of war. On October 14, 1939, Lieutenant Commander Günther Prien and his crew of the U-47 succeeded in entering the supposedly safe English naval base of Scapa Flow on the Orkney Islands in the North Atlantic, and torpedoed the battleship Royal Oak. This was a devastating blow to the British, but made Commander Prien our first war hero. Upon his safe return from sea, he was rewarded with a reception by Hitler in the Chancellery in Berlin. Mutti and I were downtown running some errands when people started shouting and saluting along Leipzigerstrasse, a main shopping avenue. Then we saw Günther Prien passing by on his way to the reception, standing triumphantly in an open car and happily waving to the cheering crowd. Although the people were impressed, Hitler was not. He was enraged at Prien's triumphal entry since only he, Hitler, should drive through town with such fanfare. In 1941 it was reported that Commander Prien did not return from a submarine mission, but after the war it was rumored that in reality he had died in a concentration camp. Just another example of Hitler's dangerous mania and jealousy.

The war was only six weeks old when Goebbels introduced our first national Socialist welfare war relief action which was a compulsory charity for helping the poor during the cold winter. At a huge rally in Berlin on October 10, 1939, in the Sports Palace, the gathering place for famous Nazi Party conventions, he screamed over the loudspeakers, "Nobody should starve or freeze!" which the people immediately turned into a joke: "Nobody should starve without freezing." We knew that the Nazis were not concerned about the public welfare, despite their empty clichés, but rather, how much money they could collect.

Goebbels announced that street collections would begin using boxes with the slogan "a dime for the poor." What poor? We did not understand who these poor people were because the Nazis had continually told us that everybody had employment with a good income. The next action was to declare the first Sunday of every month as *Eintopfsonntag*, a simple soup Sunday. On that day we were supposed to eat sparingly and make generous monetary contributions instead. The same applied for restaurants where you were supposed to eat sparingly but pay for a full price meal as a supplemental donation. This in no time led to the next joke:

"If you fix a roast goose, it has to be brown like Hitler, fat like
Göring, and completely plucked like the German people."
There were numerous ruthless fund raising schemes for obscure purposes. The workers' true wages were continually shrinking because pay
raises on paper were immediately consumed by drastically increased
deductions of pay for "voluntary" contributions, while their pressure of
work had increased, toiling for the Fatherland. As usual, the people re-
ciprocated immediately with a new cynical joke:

Hitler, Göring and Goebbels request a typical German meal
in a country inn. They are served a simple soup, which they
eat reluctantly. Upon leaving the inn, they notice a common
worker enjoying his sumptuous meal. Amazed, they inquire
curiously how he could afford something as splendid as that.
The man smiles cunningly, "Somebody in payroll made a
mistake and paid me my deductions instead of my net pay!"

It seemed the Nazis always needed more money. People were harassed to subscribe "voluntarily" to government loans, which were similar to the U.S. municipal bonds. Our long-time bank director discreetly
reminded Papa as soon as a new Nazi loan had been issued for railways,
freeways, and other public improvements. (In Germany, investments
were generally handled through banks rather than brokers.) This was
always meant as a friendly warning for us to stay inconspicuously on
good terms with the government.

We were not only required to economize in every way, but to contribute ad nauseam as a normal patriotic duty. Of course no one ever
received a penny back from all those compulsory government loans. In
addition to all the "voluntary" contributions, we were also heavily taxed,
especially on so-called luxury items such as furs, jewelry, tobacco and
liquor. However, prices for every day food items on ration cards such as
milk, butter, eggs and bread never changed in all those years of other
price fluctuations. This helped to offset the other undesirable impacts
on the modest budgets of most people.

During those hectic first weeks of war, the head of the black-coated
SS, the hated Heinrich Himmler, came up with his propagating command, a plan to replenish the men anticipated to be lost in battle. He
issued a call for all single women of "good blood and race" to become
mothers and bear the children of soldiers going into war. The soldiers

were not only to fight and possibly give their lives for the Fatherland, but also to augment the German race by leaving behind as many pregnant women as possible. The "Fountain of Life" was Himmler's most famous breeding place for producing the finest bloodlines. Brides of SS men had to furnish Aryan proof as far back as even 1648, the Westphalian Peace Treaty following the Thirty-Year-War. Wives of functionaries, SS-men and also unwed mothers gave birth to their children in a relaxed environment with generous government support. We lived in a society that glorified race, size, and strength, while the disadvantaged ones were oppressed.

Germany was male dominated under the Nazi regime, and the function of women was considered that of child bearing. As early as 1933, Hitler had ruled that males would be given preference over females in employment applications, and in 1936, women were no longer permitted to be lawyers, judges or doctors, only supporting medical personnel. One year later, women were excluded from the higher civil service positions. And, beginning in 1938, couples who had been married for five years and still had no children were forced to pay considerably higher taxes as punishment for their *Eheträgheit*, marriage laziness. Marriage was no longer considered a union of love, but a sole purpose to produce children, as was already programmed in his book *Mein Kampf.* We would have been better forewarned if only we had read it.

November 9, 1939, brought a startling event—an assassination attempt made on Hitler's life in the *Hofbräuhaus*, the famous and popular Bavarian beer parlor in Munich, the city now considered the capital of the Nazi movement. This hall was hallowed as a sanctuary and the first meeting place of the then unknown young Nazi Party. What a convenient occasion for one of Hitler's favorite pompous assemblies, naturally accompanied by one of his endless speeches. The prelude for this was often the popular *Badenweiler* March. The whole spectacle was staged in memory of his failed attempt to seize power in Munich in November of 1923 and to honor the deaths of his faithful comrades in that rebellion. It has been since learned that during that 1923 incident, Hitler himself did not act very bravely, as he threw himself on the floor and then quickly vanished when the opportunity arose, deserting the others.

This current assassination attempt had been carefully planned with a deadly bomb planted to explode during Hitler's speech. But something unexpected happened. For some unknown reason, he shortened his speech and had moved away from his usual position when the bomb exploded. Hitler was unhurt, although it killed some of his close friends and caused considerable structural damage to the building. When the failed attempt became known, Papa sarcastically remarked, "What a pity for the damaged *Hofbräuhaus!*" Mutti was extremely worried that he might utter this dangerous wisecrack with a double meaning in public. However, people were already whispering a new sarcastic joke which expressed their dashed hopes about Hitler's escape from death:

An old woman tries to read a new poster on the walls. Since she is nearsighted, she asks a man to tell her what it says. He gladly helps out. "Germany is finally free again," he reads aloud. "Oh," the old woman wonders. "Is Hitler dead? And nobody even told me!"

The press initially tried to downplay the attempt on Hitler's life. If it had succeeded, it might have stopped the war after less than three months, and it is impossible to imagine how different world history would have been from then on. But now, the tragic failure only enhanced Hitler's ego and he called it his "divine calling" and this miraculous escape was proof that providence had chosen him as the nation's Führer to lead us to the final victory. From then on, his favorite and often repeated expression relative to his leadership was "supernatural guidance," and that from a man whose party attacked the churches and squashed the practicing of religion as the human Antichrist with the mark of Cain. He was now the undisputed almighty Führer with the aura of "His Majesty," if not of God himself.

Goebbels now started an insane personality cult around Hitler as a counterpart of the Stalin myth in the Soviet Union. The people viewed this action with another sarcastic joke:

There is a great turmoil in heaven and Saint Peter, very upset, runs to God and complains, "A man arrived here in heaven with a very long beard and he has the insolence to pretend he is me!" God smiles amusedly and calms down Saint Peter. "Don't take that too seriously, my friend. Down on earth there is a man with a very little moustache running around who is pretending to be me!"

These political jokes were sand thrown into the gears of the Nazi propaganda machinery and also greatly feared. Goebbels threatened to persecute anyone who told jokes that ridiculed the Party. However, his threat remained virtually ineffective and the jokes continued, only now carefully whispered, like this one:

> A man once overheard Goebbels, a habitual liar, say, "If I ever told a lie in my life, for every one, I will turn over in my grave." When the man arrives in heaven he curiously inquires where Goebbels is. Saint Peter tells him, "Not here. He is being used as a ventilator in Hell."

This type of sharp, political satire was not only a source of humor for us, but also a means of silent resistance. I only wish I could remember more of it. As an inexhaustible source of daring humor, Berlin was a hot-bed of these jokes.

From the beginning, Hitler led people astray, first by claiming that he did not demand any salary for himself and worked only for the love and benefit of his people. Of course, no mention was made of his enormous income since 1933 for his book *Mein Kampf.* It was on the obligatory gift list for every celebration, replacing all the fine gold watches and other precious souvenirs that had previously been awarded. Every school library and household was required to have it, and by 1939, it was in its 41st printing. It was Germany's most printed, but least read book.

Hitler may not have taken a direct salary, but in various ways, he used vast sums of the people's money. First, as was customary, he received free benefits as the head of the state such as chauffeured limousines, body guards, servants and free living and lodging, which amounted to a luxurious lifestyle. Secondly, the old existing State Chancery in Berlin, Wilhelmstrasse was not impressive enough for his public use and he had his architect, Albert Speer, remodel it extensively with an extravagant marble in the pseudo-classic style. Before it had been good enough all these years for our frugal *Reichspräsident* von Hindenburg, who used taxpayers' money always wisely, and never for himself. But nothing was monumental enough for Hitler—the "modest" man of the people.

And finally, Hitler acquired the chalet *Berghof* above Berchtesgaden on the mountain Obersalzberg for his personal use as a private and carefree retreat. He had this once modest chalet enlarged into a luxurious mansion, which could be reached only by his private lift built through solid rock. From his "eagle's nest" he ruled as the lord almighty in a Nazi sanctuary, and played the cunningly staged role of the lonely man on the mountain who is absorbed with the fate of his people. In reality, he lived a life of luxury, even with a mistress who had remained invisible, which was not known until after their suicide in 1945, while the common people paid for it through steadily increasing taxes and highly enforced donations.

The people first admired Hitler's "unselfish" waiver of a claim to his salary, but gradually realized they were again a victim of stereotyped concepts through Nazi propaganda. They were kept deliberately ignorant and led by their noses year in and year out, until many could not see the forest for the trees. As the order of the day, every individual had to be subordinate to the welfare of the Fatherland, which meant to Hitler's dictatorship, or was considered an enemy of the people and treated accordingly. We were a population reduced to silence and obeying commands. It was our responsibility to live up to the Nazi's expectations—or else!

Hermann Hunsinger

A typical scene from the Hitler days

*W*icked Cerberus of War!

*O*h Cerberus, you three-headed monster hound of Hell, you have invited us in with a smile and there is no return now. We got into your clutches and you will not release us until the bitter end. So Hitler lured us into war, a hell on earth. There is no glory in war itself, and no reward for coming in second like in sports. And, it is we, the people, who endure the deepest wounds in any war.

We observed a very quiet Christmas, and as all the church bells rang on New Year's Eve, we greeted 1940 with foreboding, wondering what kind of year we could expect. Our family gathered at home with friends that night and Papa and I played a Dutch folk song, "We gather together to ask the Lord's blessing," which ends with the cry: "Lord make us free!" On that evening, it was a blessing that we could not foresee what we were in for, and how many more times we would repeat that ceremony, always with the false hope that the new year would bring peace.

1940 started rather quietly on the West front, a deceptive period of martial stalemate. The French sat behind their Maginot Line, considered to be the strongest fortification in Europe and regarded as impregnable. The Germans were lined up behind their West Wall, the Siegfried Line, a gigantic fortification, with a similar reputation. Nothing had happened so far and that stand-off was called a *Sitz-Krieg,* Sit-Down War. Not a single shot had been fired, and we hoped that perhaps it would never happen. France remained inactive and it seemed all might turn into a "Go Home War." How wrong we were in our naive optimism.

For us at home, the war was distant and remote. January and February brought the usual snow and slush, and Berlin had a strict snow emergency removal program. Home owners were liable to clear their sidewalks by 6 a.m., wide enough for two people to pass comfortably, and to sprinkle sand, ashes, grit or salt. But, these strict laws did not dampen our spirits, and everyone, young and old alike, was out having fun. Our family took turns clearing the sidewalk, and my shift was on weekends.

One cold morning in February 1940, I was faced by a blanket of deep new snow when I walked outside, armed with my shovel and broom. The snowplow had been through the night before and thrown more snow on our sidewalk, so my job was going to be twice as hard. As I was getting ready to start, I noticed a young man shoveling diagonally across the street in front of house number four, where a female servant usually cleared the sidewalk. I had never seen him before, and as I was staring at him, he looked over at me. Flustered, I started shoveling and he also continued. Before long, he stopped and looked over again, and although I knew he was glancing at me, I pretended not to notice. From time to time though, I stole a quick peek across the street, wondering if his repeated glances were deliberate or just casual. We were shoveling toward each other, and as we got closer, I noticed that he was tall and slender, and really quite good looking.

After an hour's work, we were finally right across the street from each other and I was somewhat embarrassed, wondering what kind of impression I made standing there in my work clothes with my hair blowing in all directions. The handsome stranger bid me "Good morning" and just as we started a casual conversation about the weather, Papa unfortunately chose that moment to appear on the scene to tell me I had a telephone call. Talk about wrong timing! It seemed that every day after that, whenever I came out to shovel, the young man also appeared on the opposite side of the street with his shovel and a nice smile. He meanwhile introduced himself as Sieghardt von Schwanenflügel, and told me that he and his older two sisters lived with their parents and several little spitzes in the large house number four, along with a cook and a maid. I now realized he was the only son of an old aristocratic family from Göttingen.

As the winter passed and the snow melted, we were robbed of our opportunity to meet casually on the street. However, with spring, it was time to get my car out of the garage and on Saturday mornings I would wash it in our driveway. Well, what do you know? There was that nice neighbor again coming over to offer me some advice on driving. I listened attentively, even though I was familiar with the instructions he was giving, but to prolong the conversation, I kept asking questions, which he gladly answered. It seemed that each time we met, one of us would always be called away. I was not aware at the time that Sieghardt's father had already selected a bride for him, but he obviously wanted to make his own choice. Although we were attracted to each other, neither one of us was the aggressive type and never had a chance to arrange a date during any of our short meetings. Sieghardt was not drafted during the early part of the war because the position he held in the family's firm was considered essential to the war effort, although I never learned the particulars of his important position.

On April 9, 1940, we were astonished to hear a radio report that the French and British governments had violated Norwegian neutrality by mining Norwegian territorial waters. Also, without regard to strong protests from Norway, they had landed troops in various Norwegian ports, which had led to serious military confrontations with the Western intruders. This had a serious impact on Germany because badly needed oil from Russia and metals from Sweden were shipped through several Norwegian ports and this endangered our supply line. To prevent the loss of resources essential to the military effort, German forces had made a surprise appearance in Norway by land, sea and air. Early that morning our troops had passed through Denmark meeting hardly any local resistance.

Events now happened more quickly than we could follow in the newspapers, and by the end of April, after intense combat, the British and French had been driven out and the Germans were there to stay. The Norwegian resistance had turned against Germany and was also quickly defeated. King Haakon VII escaped with his cabinet to London, although he had fought the British and French during their initial invasion. Norway was now firmly under German control, a second Blitzkrieg? Another success story! This time Mutti and Papa hardly had time to exchange their alarmed glances. Joseph Terboven was appointed as German commissioner, who turned out to be a very despicable person who governed Norway ruthlessly. We had not heard from Günter for some time and were concerned about where he had been during the naval operations in Norwegian waters.

Heinz, the husband of my friend Elsa, also was not drafted because his current employment was considered essential to the war effort. He was working in the government Forest Office in Berlin and in May, had just received orders transferring him to Oslo, Norway, as a contractor for lumber to be used in construction of some mysterious airports at unknown locations. Even though he was under the command of the German occupation forces, he was free to stay in the home of old Norwegian friends who lived just outside of Oslo in Holmenkollen. Elsa planned to visit Heinz during the Christmas season, and being able to see him again in seven months softened the blow of separation.

Shocking news continued daily, and on May 10, 1940, we were informed that Hitler had started his western offensive against France. The German army had marched into neutral Holland and Belgium, who surrendered after a severe struggle. What a horrid report. That was the end of the peaceful confrontation. France had felt secure behind its Maginot Line, but Hitler bypassed the fortification at the North, entering via the low countries and then attacking France from behind the Maginot Line. England had sent troops across the Channel to support France, but they were quickly surrounded at Dunkirk, a harbor town on the north coast of France. Goebbels boasted that the German troops had executed a great coup and were not to be stopped.

Cousin Hans, who was at Dunkirk as a young officer, told us later about the violent controversy our generals had with Hitler. The entire British army could have been taken prisoners, a master stroke, and the war with Great Britain would have been over. But Hitler, obsessed by his blind love-hate relationship with England, held back the army in the unrealistic hope that he could reach an alliance with England, the other "Nordic race." This delay, for illogical reasons, allowed the British army, from May 27 to June 4, to accomplish a desperate retreat by sea in hundreds of boats of all kinds which took them safely back to England, leaving all their military equipment on the French shore. Had Hitler permitted decisive action at Dunkirk, the war with England could have been over before it really started.

After the fall of Dunkirk, Italy entered the war, too, as a German Ally. Hans also told us about a planned invasion and occupation of England known as "Operation Sea Lion." Every available German vessel stood by ready to transport the troops across the Channel, but the operation was called off when Göring could not guarantee the air superiority necessary to support a German army in England.

Winston Churchill, who became British Prime Minister on May 10, was stunned by the massive loss of war equipment at Dunkirk which left the British virtually unarmed, and he immediately appealed to the United States for new military supplies. It was reported that the U.S. population wanted to remain neutral, but President Roosevelt clandestinely agreed to assist. Large shipments of weapons crossed the ocean to Great Britain, and this involvement in the European war through support of the British constantly increased in violation of neutrality laws. Germany answered this action by a total naval blockade of Great Britain to cut off the supply route from the U.S., and our fleet of U-boats was brought into action and ruled the Atlantic Ocean during 1940/41.

France fell in forty days with us unexpectedly attacking them from behind the Maginot Line, and it collapsed. Goebbels triumphantly announced that the swastika was flying from the most famous landmark in Paris, the Eiffel Tower. The Blitzkrieg in western Europe was over. Marshal Petain formed a new French government in Vichy, known as the Vichy Government, which functioned as a puppet of the German occupation force. Hitler avenged the humiliation of twenty-two years ago by requiring that the French capitulation take place in the same railroad car in Compiegne, north of Paris, where the Germans had to sign their surrender to France after World War I. Goebbels praised and glorified the reversal of fate. Many Germans felt that a wrong was righted. French General Charles De Gaulle would not accept the terms of surrender and fled to London to organize a French resistance against the German occupation and Vichy Government. About this same time, in July 1940, Hitler made an open peace offer to England in an unusually civilized address to the Reichstag. But England, well aware of the many broken promises previously made by Hitler, refused the offer. Thus ended our hopes for a quick end of the war.

The French government was not prepared for the rapid advance of the Germans into Paris, and tried to move their highly classified strategic material by freight train to the still unconquered south of France. However, German troops arrived in the small town of La Charité, several miles south of Paris, just as such a train tried too late to make a hasty getaway to the South. But a sharpshooter disabled the engine with a bullet into the boiler. The Germans captured carloads of the most highly classified documents of the joint French and British war planning. It took several large German airplanes to transport the top secret strategic war material to the German Army High Command in Fontainebleu, parts of which were published in our German newspapers. The most astonishing was the headline which read: "The Planned Attack on the Soviet Union by France and England," and for once, this was the incredible truth and not another of Goebbels' monstrous lies.

The captured documents outlined the long-range joint French and British war plans. After the German Blitzkrieg in Poland, England and France were determined to keep the French borders safe with a North Plan and a South Plan. The North Plan was to expand the war into neutral countries such as Norway and Sweden, followed by the South Plan into the Balkans. An Allied expeditionary corps was to land in Scandinavia in the winter of 1939/40 during the Soviet invasion of Finland. After their anticipated North Plan success in Scandinavia, they planned to follow through on June 30, 1940, with their South Plan to attack the Russian oil centers in the Caucasus. It was planned to accomplish this through air attacks from British Iraq and French Syria.

On February 22, 1940, French General Gamelin informed Prime Minister Daladier that these plans would render the Soviet Union powerless. In March 1940, London pressured France to deploy bomber squadrons to Syria to provide air strikes on the more than one hundred oil refineries between Baku and Batum. Following the strikes, it was planned that the Levant army of 150,000 well trained, mechanized French troops already in Syria would then invade, and it was estimated that they could crush the hated Soviets within two weeks. They would then encourage the anti-Soviet Caucasian people to rebel against Moscow. But these plans burst like soap bubbles. However, the North Plan failed as soon as it started when the Germans immediately drove the British out of Norway. And, the South Plan never had a chance to get started after Dunkirk and the fall of Paris in June of 1940.

Not only were the highlights of the secret British and French plans published in German newspapers, but Germany even provided some of the conspiracy information to Russia for publication in "TASS," the official government newspaper of the Soviets. It was rumored that Stalin, in return, delivered oil for the German aircraft. The strange twist to the unsuccessful British/French plan was that instead of attacking the Soviets in June 1940 as spelled out in their South Plan, they became their allies in 1941, the Communists and Anti-Communists aligned together in a war against Nazi Germany—strange bedfellows! Later, in the 1980s, a respected German magazine, "*Bunte*," published a very detailed account of the captured secret plans under the title "The War That Never Took Place." The article stated that the original documents were transported from France to Germany, to Ebersdorf in Thuringia, where they were later seized by the Americans at the end of World War II.

Now Paris acted quickly and the sensitive material was sent back to French army headquarters on the Seine where it remains today under classified storage. However, Germany retained copies of the plan and a book is to be published by the German author, Dr. Günter Drescher, that will make this secret information available as true history. Unfortunately for France and England, it will reveal that they planned to violate the neutrality laws of other countries and that they were not the peace-loving nations as represented by history.

I joined the Red Cross as a volunteer in 1940 which required that I buy a uniform and have my picture taken for the official identification card. They rejected my picture twice because too much hair showed under my cap and we often had to appear for special inspections to have the length of our dress checked to make sure that we were not showing too much leg. We were supposed to look clean and simple, not sexy. As my first faux pas, I naively mentioned that I had no experience in hospital work but was willing to learn. I was told in no uncertain terms

In my Red Cross uniform. (This picture they didn't reject!)

that I would not be working in hospitals. "Newcomers do not get the 'best' assignments where all the men are." However, if I did my work well, whatever that might be, I would receive blue stars to wear on my white collar to identify the different grade of helpers. Helper was the title for the lowest grade, mine. I made my second faux pas when I mentioned that I joined to help, not to earn blue stars. Needless to say, my collar was never adorned by any. Mutti told me to relax; these were just the Nazi regulations.

I finally did get my first call to duty. Hitler had established a special program called "Mother and Child," to encourage women to have more children, even if they could not afford them, and they were enticed by receiving special treatment in free day-care centers. Young Red Cross helpers like myself were called to assist with this project. One day, I was assigned to such a center located in Schlachtensee, within walking distance of my home. About twenty mothers arrived with their offspring in the early morning and we four helpers took care of the babies while the mothers spent a pleasant day being entertained in the house and garden and served special meals in comfort. Meanwhile, we volunteers were struggling with over twenty screaming babies who refused to sleep.

I also had my first experience changing diapers, and this was before the days of disposables. Our Nazi supervisor ordered us to dump the soiled ones with their contents into a four-foot high container of cold water which stood outside. The heavy linen cloth sank to the bottom and all kinds of "diaper fillings," produced numerously by these sweet little ones, began to rise to the surface, where they swam around in circles. We had to give the diapers their first rinse by hand, and without rubber gloves. I was not too enthusiastic about this and closed my eyes as I fished deep down in the brown liquid that used to be called water. The second rinse was more pleasant, if one could call it that. This continual changing and washing of diapers went from 8 a.m. to 6 p.m., and I thought that the day would never end.

At the conclusion of this first assignment, I had already lost my initial enthusiasm for the volunteer work and I was terribly disappointed, this time with the entire world, including babies. However, I found a way not to repeat the day-care center experience by signing up immediately for a Red Cross course in first aid. I had also learned to keep my mouth shut and did not tell anyone about my former education in anatomy. This time I let them be impressed by my quick understanding due to their excellent teaching. Upon completing the course I was occasionally called to work under the supervision of a trained nurse in a Red Cross station at the bicycle race track in Wannsee. The young cyclists liked to speed and fell more than they pedaled, and I became accustomed to seeing blood. The young boys would scream as I poured a strong disinfectant into their open wounds and it seemed to me we gave rather cruel treatments. I also became skilled in putting all kinds of different bandages around their arms, legs and heads for relief.

Meanwhile Gerda had successfully finished her Russian language course for the promised assignment in the German Embassy in Moscow, but nobody seemed willing to discuss the new position. What she didn't know was that a war against the Soviet Union was imminent. Cerberus was about to raise another ugly head; luckily, she never received the assignment in Moscow. But, by mere accident, she heard about a job requiring language skills in the Propaganda Ministry in the Press Archives. The lady who currently held the position was leaving to be married. Gerda could start immediately and learn the job by working with her before she departed. Her office was on the first floor of the public relations department on Mauerstrasse, in the government quarter, and whenever I happened to be downtown, we only could talk through her open, but barred window.

One day on my ride home on the S-Bahn (I was not permitted to drive my car anymore in order to save gasoline) I noticed a good-looking gentleman watching me. I was irritated because I could not escape his looks. He changed trains in Nikolassee like I did, and then entered my compartment, sitting down across from me. Two stations later when I exited the train, he also got off and followed me on the three-minute walk to my house. Our maid Lotte was standing at the kitchen window and after a while she whispered to me, "He is still out there, across the street." I thought nobody would have noticed.

Now I acted quickly, being curious what would happen next. So, I found an excuse to quickly visit the Behrmanns, and left the house again. He followed me on the short five-minute walk to our friend's home, where I tried not to stay too long. When I came out, he was waiting across the street, and this time, he came over and politely approached me. "I have never used this way before to approach a lady, but…" I was impressed, not knowing that men usually use this opening line. He wanted to meet me and talk some more. I found it more practical to talk right now, so we walked for a while through the streets, of course avoiding my own neighborhood.

He told me that he had just returned from Spain where he was employed as an engineer on a special project. He was to go back in two months and wanted to be married by then so he could take a wife with him. I thought that was awfully quick and thinking of my strict father's reaction, I had to smile—a response the gentleman did not exactly take for a "no" in his plans. Since it was Saturday and I had Red Cross duty at the Wannsee bicycle track the next day, I agreed to meet him there. I did not want to be picked up at home, what he had in mind.

He was a very nice and well-educated gentleman in his late thirties—ancient as far as I was concerned! He told me that in Spain, everything was so different. When a lady is invited out, just about the whole family comes along, of course at the expense of the man. After such a date, it happened to a friend of his that he was invited to the family's house. There, during an unwatched moment alone with the girl, he kissed her. Suddenly he was surrounded by the whole family who congratulated him on his engagement. But his friend had nothing like that in mind, just a kiss. Now secretly and quickly he had to leave Spain if he wanted to get out of this situation unharmed because he had no intention to marry.

My date definitely wanted a German wife and he promised a carefree and interesting life in Spain within a respectable social group, returning each year to Germany during the two hottest months. It sounded so nice, like a fairy tale, but to get married next month and leave with him for Spain was another story. He wanted to meet my family. No way! I already envisioned how Papa would explode—a man I had met on the street, he would call it. I must not have fallen in love with him either because I suggested that he look for someone else…too bad he could not stay longer…no time to get to know each other better. Neutral Spain sounded like a better place to be than Berlin in these war-torn years, but hardly reason enough for a hasty marriage. Adios Spain! I wondered later what German engineers did over there during the war and what might have happened to him.

All was quiet on the home front as our troops were far away in other nations' territory. Nevertheless, there were calls for Red Cross helpers to assist in feeding the German soldiers who were routed through Berlin and passed through the Grunewald train station. We cooked soup in huge kettles right there on the station platform and passed it and a coffee-substitute through the train windows. Because of the scarcity of ingredients, our allotted daily Red Cross cooking ration was skimpy and the soup was mainly water. But, we made the best of it, often improving the meager contents with something we brought from home at the sacrifice of our own rations. Sometimes I thought the soldiers appreciated our company more than the food.

Trains with prisoners of war would also pass through, mostly young men who looked depressed and afraid of what an uncertain future held for them. I tried to converse with them in their native language of either English or French, and their reactions would differ depending upon their own former experience with Germans. Some disgustingly even refused our simple hot servings and that really hurt me, because they did not know that it was the best we had to offer. How could they! For them, we were the terrible Nazis and they couldn't imagine that someone even cared about them.

Once in a while, one of them would show a flicker of gratitude in his face as he accepted the soup from me, and I was repeatedly warned by an over-zealous Nazi Red Cross leader about my friendly manner, which was considered "fraternizing" with the enemy. It seemed I never could do anything right! I couldn't understand this attitude since they themselves had taught us that the mission of the Red Cross was to alleviate the misery of all soldiers, our own as well as the prisoners of war. Many of the POWs were Günter's age and I didn't feel any hostility toward them because they had not started the war either. They were just following orders like everyone else, including me as I volunteered at the train station. Since I was not professionally employed, I was asked to take over the night shift. I didn't mind, since it looked to me like meaningful help in the war.

Everyone has their own ideas about offering human assistance and I remember my first lesson while riding the train downtown in my brand new Red Cross uniform. A mother with three small children asked me to assist her while leaving the terminal at Potsdamer Platz and to take her children through the station gate, which I gladly did, proud to have been asked for my services. What I did not know, but she did, was that Red Cross helpers could take children through the gate for free. As soon as we passed through, she collected her offspring and laughed at how cleverly she had used me to avoid paying the fare for them, leaving me standing there with a perplexed look on my face.

Günter came home for an unexpected leave from the navy and we noticed that he had undergone a personality change. He had been on convoy duty during the Norway occupation and his experience in the battles was quite different from what was reported in the newspaper. Although he did not talk much about it, he told us that there were huge losses on both sides and that they had fished friend and foe out of the sea. They were mostly young men of different nationalities, many who were dead, but all were laid out on deck in long rows, the dead among the living. In his short report, more was left unspoken than said. This was a prime example of how the actual truth was distorted by the glamorous versions of the war news in the Nazi-controlled newspapers. Although fairy tales used to begin with, "Once upon a time," now they started with, "The communique of the High Command reports..." while triumphant victory fanfares drowned out our own losses and wicked Cerberus kept us in hell.

Despite the war, the theaters and movies continued their regular programs as an important morale factor and to influence the public, as if there were no war. The government had made it a point to pay considerable attention to outstanding personalities, so they showed excellent movies about Frederick the Great, Robert Koch, the founder of bacteriology, and Wilhelm Röntgen, the discoverer of x-rays. However, they always glorified one single person such as a leader in history or science, and used that person to focus our attention on the one "great" leader of our time, Hitler, the Führer. Unfortunately, we failed to notice this and the entire deception was wasted on us.

Nothing Ventured, Nothing Gained!

We had little personal involvement with the war during the early years, and most of our knowledge of it came from the newspapers. Our closest exposure to warfare was the blackouts every night and the issuance of many additional ration cards since practically everything was rationed by now, such as food, clothing, tobacco, gasoline and even a bar of soap. The textile card was worth one hundred points and had to last for a whole year. Points were deducted for each item purchased, from clothing to the smallest need such as a spool of thread. Once the one hundred points were used up, we couldn't even buy hosiery, and I never mended so many stockings and runs in all my life.

We had periodic air raid drills in Berlin in which we had to go down into our personal shelters. Ours was in the basement with a heavy metal door leading out into the yard in front of the garage. On nice, warm evenings, we would turn these occasional drills into a casual outdoor meeting with our neighbors and Papa would serve a glass of wine. We often were joined by our next door neighbor, Mrs. Vogel, a widow and a real Berliner with a heart of gold, generous and outspoken with a sense of humor. Since she lived alone in her big house, she had recently taken in a young woman from Belgium as a guest. Maria was a petite, black haired, bundle of energy who had come to Berlin seeking a better paying job than she had back home, and, to get away from her husband. She had left her two young daughters in Belgium, but sent money to them regularly and hoped they could join her in Berlin when she was settled.

Well, nothing ventured, nothing gained. It so happened that after several attempts, Maria finally obtained a suitable job in an old established retail carpet store in downtown Berlin which was owned by Mrs. Vogel and managed by her son. One day, while visiting the store, she met Maria and was so impressed by this new employee that when she learned that she did not have a suitable place to live, she spontaneously invited Maria to come and stay with her. These two became good friends in spite of a considerable age difference. Maria quickly learned German and spoke it with a lovely soft French accent and we all liked her very much.

One evening while we were all outside in the yard at "alarm time" enjoying some of Papa's good wine, we suddenly heard practice shooting from some nearby anti-aircraft artillery and Maria was very shocked by the gunfire. Quite upset, she turned to Papa and said in broken German, "*Oh, Herr Schmi-i-ied, Sie haben geschi-s-sssen!*" What she had tried to say was, Mr. Schmidt, they have "shot" (*geschossen*), but with her wrong pronunciation, the word came out as "shit" (*geschissen*). In German, the word for "you" (formal) and "they" is the same, so she actually told Papa that he had shit! Suppressing his laughter, Papa replied with a straight face, "No, I did not," but Maria excitingly insisted, "but we all could hear it!" not realizing her faux pas. Papa replied that he did not hear anything of the kind, and poor Maria was beside herself because as he spoke, the anti-aircraft artillery was test firing again. She repeated her statement, which Papa immediately denied, and we finally all broke out laughing at this hilarious dialogue of misunderstanding. Maria was puzzled and irritated, until we finally took mercy on her and explained the small difference between two very tricky words. She was very embarrassed but also most thankful that her faux pas did not occur among strangers, and we toasted our friendship and the flak shooting with a sip of wine.

Our fun and games with the war did not last forever. In Berlin the government organized street collections of money for all sorts of dubious causes. They were called "charity for the poor," but no one ever knew who these "poor" were or where all the money really went. People from public and private offices, and even students from schools were signed up on alternate weekends to take to the streets with their collection cans. My turn came as a Red Cross volunteer and I was checked against a list when I picked up an empty can, and again checked off when I returned with the filled one. I hated standing on the street and asking people for money as many people either said they had given already or just pushed my can aside as I held it out to them. In order to shame every one into giving, a paper flower was handed out to be worn on the lapel as proof of having made a donation. Of course no one wanted to be seen in public without a lapel flower. Naturally everyone tried to disappear as rapidly as possible when they saw someone with a collection can. This resulted in a new joke:

> An enormous crowd of people was causing a terrible traffic congestion and the police was helpless because requests and even threats could not disperse them. Finally, one policeman said to another, "Run quickly and get some collection cans and you will see how fast they will all vanish."

My appearance on the street with a collection can was just long enough to satisfy my supervisor. Meanwhile Mutti and Papa had been saving all of the small value coins at home that they could gather and these made my can appear heavy and full when I returned to the Red Cross office that evening. That little manipulation made me look like I had worked really hard on the street. Even worse than the street collections were the door-to-door solicitations which used an open pre-printed list of names of people living on the street of the collection list. People were required to certify in writing, for everyone to see, the amount of their "voluntary" contribution. Consequently, everyone on our street gave because if one did not sign for an appropriate sum there would be a blank space next to their name, and no one could risk that. This was like an inescapable new tax.

We were still able to have good times with our friends which made us temporarily forget all of the compulsory duties. Our architect friends, Franz Behrmann and Paul Thiemer, had built many beautiful modern villas in our rather new suburb. Mrs. Behrmann kept up social connections with the numerous home owners and everyone got together now and then for a private party in one of the homes. I really enjoyed it when Günter would come home for a weekend and bring along some of his navy buddies to be my dance partners. I also particularly remember Mrs. Schmock, who had been married twice and had two daughters from her first marriage, Nora and Ilse, who were both older than I. Nora had been engaged to a young lawyer, but it had to be dissolved under one of Hitler's many laws because she was half-Jewish, or partly non-Aryan. The girls' retained the name of their natural Jewish father, Rosenthal, and Mr. Schmock wanted to adopt both girls and change their obviously Jewish name, but the girls refused in honor of their father who had fought and died for Germany in World War I.

One evening, I went downtown with the two girls to see a movie, and when they gave the name of Rosenthal to pick up our reserved tickets, the girl in the ticket booth gave us all a dirty look and practically threw the tickets at them. Nora and Ilse were red-faced with anger and I was shocked, never having experienced anything like that in my sheltered world. Now I understood why Mutti strongly felt that the girls should accept their stepfather's name since their natural father would not want them to suffer. Later, in 1942, they suddenly disappeared into hiding in the country, and three years later, were fleeing again to escape from the fast approaching Soviets. They safely arrived back in Berlin and survived Hitler's downfall.

Here I am in 1940.

The war continued throughout 1940, and we could see no end to it, although the government led us to believe the opposite, thanks to Goebbels' viciously misleading propaganda. If peace was imminent, why was I called more frequently to work at the Red Cross making bandages for wounded soldiers from our private supplies? (The hospital supplies had to be used more sparingly because there were so many wounded.) We were assigned to collect old, thin window curtains from private households, which were then washed and cut into thin strips. The strips were then tightly rolled, wrapped individually and stacked in boxes to be picked up by one of the many trains carrying wounded soldiers. These trains usually traveled through Berlin at night to avoid detection by the public, and often their need for bandages far exceeded our ability to supply them. During my volunteer service, I met Sieghardt's sister Ilse, and we often worked together.

Another urgent request was for "knee rolls" which were used to elevate the stumps of soldiers whose leg(s) had just been amputated so that the train ride would be more comfortable for them. Again, we went out and collected all kinds of material from family, friends, neighbors and dressmakers to sew outside covers which were then stuffed very tightly with cut-up sewing scraps. There was no foam rubber available or even known to us. As with bandages, the requests for rolls from the doctors on the trains were often greater than we could provide with our limited resources, and that hurt us to be so helpless in the face of such a large demand. The train loads of wounded soldiers was a shocking experience for us who were living secure and unharmed at home, and it gave us a real insight into how terrible war actually is on the battlefield.

The victorious slogans on the radio got continuously louder while the discussions about the war between friends and neighbors got continuously softer, because expressing the truth became dangerous. Any voiced personal opinion that did not glorify the war effort was considered demoralizing and was treated as treason. The same applied to listening to any foreign radio broadcasts and my parents instructed me not to speak to anyone on the outside concerning what I saw, knew or heard. The press and radio had moved away from reality and hoped that their printed or broadcasted glorious accomplishments would be believed by the public.

On days when I was not making bandages or knee-rolls, I was sent to a temporary military hospital which had been set up in vacant houses of the nearby suburb of Nikolassee where we helped with the wounded military men. I will never forget entering a room filled with amputees and seeing one who had lost both legs trying to hurry into his bed by swinging himself over various pieces of furniture on his hands and arms like a monkey. Reaching his bed, he quickly covered himself with a blanket and lay there beaming with joy at having someone to come to visit and talk to. This was our purpose for being there, radiating cheerfulness, and although I always tried to maintain a friendly smile to cheer up the soldiers, I often felt like I needed some cheering up myself facing such grim scenes.

There was another temporary hospital for the pilots of the new high speed dive bomber, the Stuka, a new ace-unit. In combat, they would dive at high speed toward the ground targets and then swing up rapidly to avoid crashing. These acrobatics with the airplane were so abrupt and severe that they sometimes damaged the pilots' brain, and we were counseled before our visit as to what to expect. Nevertheless, I was shocked to see these handsome, daring young men, with childlike smiles on their faces whose future had already been destroyed. This was something else that the public was not permitted to learn about. Thinking of Sieghardt, I was relieved that he still was not drafted, after seeing the fate of so many others. Thanks to Goebbels' unending propaganda, everything was wonderful, nothing but joyful victories, but they continued to keep drafting more men.

Our sheltered home life changed abruptly in August of 1940 when the British retaliated for the German air force bombing of England, by having the Royal Air Force bomb German cities, and Berlin experienced the first real taste of war. We couldn't believe when the air raid sirens began to howl during the night and the radio announced that a British bomber wing was approaching. We were thunder-struck, hastily grabbed our emergency baggage and rushed down into our air raid shelter.

Shortly thereafter, we could hear the bombers roaring overhead and our anti-aircraft artillery firing briskly. This was real! Everything was trembling as bombs were exploding around the city, but fortunately, none dropped in our immediate area. Greater Berlin was protected by an outer and inner circle of anti-aircraft artillery. What about Göring's arrogant statement that if there was ever a foreign air power over Berlin his name would be "Meyer!" There was minimal damage to the city from the first bombing, but the shock to the people's morale was significant. With their usual grim humor, Berliners now referred to the vain Göring as "Mr. Meyer."

Thereafter, the dreaded air raid sirens howled more often and the Royal Air Force in greater numbers continued their nightly attacks, inflicting severe damage in some parts of the city and there were reports of civilian casualties. From September on, the air raids were intensified by both Germany and England, and the increasingly frequent sound of roaring bombers and exploding bombs caused growing terror on both sides of the Channel. By now we had already one year of war and what we wanted most was peace before the dark cold winter would set in.

By the end of 1940, we were all approaching our second gloomy wartime Christmas, and as a special holiday present from the government, we were informed that women would now be drafted for labor in factories manufacturing ammunition or military uniforms. The future looked as dark as ever. Elsa had left to visit her husband Heinz in Oslo for Christmas, but the new year of 1941 had a sudden surprise for her also. Terboven, the German Commissioner of Oslo, announced that no wives of German civilian workers would be allowed in Norway any longer, and resident permits for them were discontinued. The true reason for this new self-serving rule was that Terboven did not want his own wife up there because he was having ongoing affairs with the beautiful Norwegian women.

Many German soldiers had followed his example of fooling around and numerous babies were sired by German soldiers while the Norwegian husbands had fled to England to escape German capture, another ironic phenomenon of the war. All of these illegitimate and unwanted babies of Nordic blood were recruited for the NS "fountain of youth" in Nazi nurseries and kindergartens in Oslo, and were available for immediate adoption. The mothers wanted them gone before the husbands returned so they would not be confronted with a hard to explain new family addition. King Haakon VII and his cabinet had formed a new government in London.

When the new rule about German wives was published, Elsa had already been in Oslo for several weeks with the intention of remaining there with Heinz and their friends. Earlier she had obtained a position in Oslo as a secretary with the newly formed "German Newspaper In Norway" which was published for the German military. The director of this paper, Mr. Kurtz, was very understanding of her new awkward situation because his wife was also there with him and he intended to keep it that way. He proposed to Elsa that she go back to Berlin temporarily to start working with the recently formed Berlin branch office, and when everything had calmed down, he would transfer her back to Oslo. However, they finally decided against this because of the danger to Heinz for violating the law. He had been spared thus far from military duty, and Elsa was afraid the punishment, if caught, could be a draft order, at a time when more and more of those filled the mailboxes.

She returned to Berlin at the end of January 1941 and immediately came and offered me her promised position as she was going to live with her parents in Silesia. She locked up her beautiful apartment in Berlin and as fate would have it, she would never see it again. It was later completely destroyed in the bombing and she lost everything except what she had carried to Silesia in her suitcase. By leaving she had saved her life.

I was apprehensive about applying for the job since I had no administrative skills and no office experience, but Elsa had urged me to go for the interview anyway because the job would save me from soon being called up for compulsory labor in heavy industry as a replacement for thousands of workers who were being drafted for military service. What a frightening prospect! Nothing ventured, nothing gained. So, the very next day, February 1, I went downtown for what had been scheduled as Elsa's interview. The whole idea seemed kind of crazy and heavy hearted I went right into the lion's den to apply for the job.

The editor, Mr. Link, greeted me very kindly, addressing me as Mrs. Werner. I had no choice but to immediately inform him that I was not her, but Dorothea Schmidt, her replacement, and had come to apply for her position, and I explained the circumstances about the swap. "Oh?" He looked puzzled as he asked if I was familiar with her work and if I knew how to operate a teleprinter. What a question. I had never even seen one, let alone knew how to work it. Since honesty seemed to be the best policy under the circumstances, I naively replied "no."

At first, Mr. Link seemed to be rather astonished, then amused by my openness. I felt I had no chance to get the job, so we continued chatting for a while about other subjects as well as the duties of the Berlin office. As usual, I was outspoken about my opinions since I felt I was completely unqualified for the position. Suddenly, Mr. Link changed the subject abruptly with, "you are hired. You can start to work right away—today." I was speechless, and could not believe it when he told me that the starting salary would be 250 marks a month which was a handsome salary for that time. And, there would be a raise after three months and another after six months. I would be his first employee, and he was going to hire a messenger, and that would make three of us. Then he showed me how he had already divided the large office space into three rooms so we each had a private working space. I was immediately fascinated by the entire business world and I was determined to make a success of my first professional employment.

One of my jobs would be to handle the incoming mail, which was to be placed on the right side of his desk, always with the letter from his wife in Frankfurt on top as the most important message. On that first day, I was constantly retyping the same letter since Mr. Link kept returning it to me for correction again and again. Also, at that time, I could not compose a very good business letter, and since my typing was far below standard, I realized that I sure had a lot to learn. But, the starting salary of 250 marks was unbelievable at a time when a good pair of leather shoes cost only eight to twelve marks, and all other items a tiny fraction of what prices were later. My family was astonished when I told them that evening that I had been hired at such a lucrative salary. By now, during the war, no interfering Nazi questions were asked anymore. Mr. Link next hired a messenger by the name of Paul, a dependable man in his fifties and an invalid from the First World War. It did not take long before we had the office work organized among us and we developed into a discreet, diligent, hard working team, with each of us proud of our individual roles.

When I glanced out of my office window, I saw Charlotttenstrasse 16, the downtown office of the company owned by Sieghardt's family which was diagonally across the street, and he worked there every day. What a coincidence; we not only lived across the street from each other, but now we also worked across the street, an unlikely situation that might have been arranged in a soap opera. More or less accidently, we both rode the same S-Bahn to work since gasoline was strictly rationed, and on weekends, he started inviting me out for dinner. That was easier said than done because there was a problem with food ration coupons. All food was rationed, including what we ate in restaurants and every single ingredient in the meal was deducted from our ration allowance. The only exception was in places like the exclusive restaurant Hotel Kaiserhof, or the famous Hotel Adlon, where one could be served lobster and other delicacies without ration cards, but at a very expensive price. We became regular customers at such places because money was no problem with Sieghardt who was a very generous person, but food stamps were. In so many ways it was a crazy world we were living in.

I had been assuming more and more responsibilities in the office, and after only a few weeks, I was given signatory authority for checks to pay all office expenses including the salaries for Paul and me. The German newspaper in Oslo had been in existence for about a year, and the function of our new office was to feed news and pictures from Germany. To illustrate different literary articles for Oslo, I often went to various picture archives and chose a selection for possible publication. I was really proud of myself when not only one, but several of my selections would cover many pages in the next edition. Since my choice of pictures had no political significance, I was spared any contact with Heinrich Hoffmann, Hitler's official photographer, who became rich and famous even after the war and was one of only three persons found not guilty at the Nuremberg Trials.

Another of my duties was to take all of the delicate phone calls from complaining authors when Oslo started printing installments of their works without their consent. This went beyond my own life experience, so I always talked to them in my normal conversational way, understanding their position and trying to make them see our side as well. To my astonishment, we always came to a mutual agreement and continued with the publication with the author's permission. One day, Sieghardt was waiting for me at work and overheard such a telephone conversation and just shook his head in amazement at how easily and successfully the matter was resolved. I have always had my own style of negotiating, even until today, with or without the consent of others. Experience was my best teacher.

My biggest headache at work was the Oslo teleprinter which was located with about ten other noisy ones in the basement hall in another part of the press building across the inner courtyard. This place was used jointly by all of the numerous newspapers that were located in our large complex. Messages typed directly into the Oslo telex machine had to be kept short in order to keep the line open for incoming transmissions from Oslo. So, my work required two separate processes. First, in another room, I had to type all articles into a tricky typewriter that never showed on a piece of paper what had been typed. Instead, it punched only code holes in a long narrow paper strip which came out of one side and piled up on the floor. All of the other secretaries had years of experience with that mysterious "hole language" and had no problem in reading it, but which I was never able to master. Then I had to go into the adjacent hall and feed the endless code tape into the Oslo telex. I had no idea how many errors there were in the text I had typed until it now appeared simultaneously on our machine and Oslo's in printed form, and I could readily see all of my mistakes.

Sometimes Oslo stopped the machine and transmitted back, "What do you mean?" when my typing errors or omissions had screwed up the text because I had been constantly interrupted by other girls questioning me while I worked on the mysterious code tape. Thank goodness, I could type the correction directly into our machine and it was received in Oslo at the same time. I was embarrassed about holding up the process and often wondered why they did not hire a more skilled secretary. But they didn't even complain and I was proud of my very first job and wanted to keep it. The other girls were very curious about what was going on in our office and there was also a touch of envy of my independent position, because I was so new in the field. My trials and tribulations are hard to comprehend in today's world where the good old teletype machine has been replaced by the computer and fax machine.

In the spring of 1941, there were continuous war reports from the Balkans which I had to forward to Oslo. It seemed that every country in that area was involved in fighting and invading each other, and I had to be especially careful to keep the names of countries and leaders correct or otherwise cause my own war in the office. Much to my relief, I was responsible for only a small portion of the political aspects of transmission, and the highly secret material was transmitted into the Oslo machine personally by Mr. Link.

I learned that on October 28 the previous year, much to Hitler's chagrin, Mussolini had started a surprise assault on Greece in an effort to make the Mediterranean his *Mare nostre*. But, his private war with Greece did not fare well, and a furious Hitler had to send German forces to Greece to save his Italian ally from an embarrassing defeat. So, in April of 1941, Greece surrendered to Germany and the swastika flew over Athens. At the same time, our newspaper carried the news item that the Italian army in Libya was also in jeopardy, and to prevent another Italian disaster similar to Greece, German troops were sent to North Africa under Fieldmarshal Rommel, who commanded both German and Italian forces. Again, Hitler had to get Mussolini off the hook, and we later learned that these Italian disasters caused Hitler to postpone his planned attack on the Soviet Union, thus losing the valuable summer months.

These Italian fiascos were the basis for another sarcastic joke about the Italian war partner:

"These losses are not the fault of the poor Italians. Their engines are built the wrong way. They have only one forward gear, but three in reverse!"

In spite of my secretarial shortcomings, I got along well with everyone at work and was soon given the nickname, *Schmidtchen* (Little Schmidt). Mr. Link was especially concerned that I not become involved in the teletype room gossip, and since I was naturally reserved, this was no problem for me. I was frequently called personally to the Oslo machine concerning "confidential" matters, and this involved a question and answer type conversation typed directly into the telex machine. I always took the paper record with me when I left the hall, and I knew that the other girls were very curious as to what was transpiring on that Oslo telex machine. They could not understand why these very private and confidential calls from the Oslo director's office were made to me and not to my boss, Mr. Link. What they did not know was that the typical text of one of those highly confidential messages would go like this:

"Hello Schmidtchen, are you there?" I would respond and enter my password. "Greetings from Director Kurtz! We hardly ever get any fresh lettuce or other vegetables here. Can you get us some? In return, do you want some cans of sardines, fish or nylons?" This swapping of our private shopping needs was a wonderful deal for both of us and I answered nosy questions about the transmissions with, "It was just routine information," which was true as far as Mr. Kurtz and I were concerned.

I would immediately go marketing during office hours for all of the fresh vegetables that I could buy, from cucumbers to radishes, parsley, lettuce and much, much more, and through a lot of finagling, was usually able to obtain everything without food coupons. For quite a while I was able to regularly buy cigarettes at a nearby store without any ration card, just with money and a smile, until the overly charming store owner realized that I was only interested in his merchandise. These cigarettes could easily be swapped for coupon-free purchases of vegetables at other stores. When I ran out of cigarettes, I just offered higher prices and that also worked.

After I returned from my shopping spree, dependable and loyal Paul would pack my purchases very carefully with the mail into our locked, custom-exempt, courier sack and take it by bike directly to Tempelhof airport for a flight to Oslo. Since these courier sacks were locked and opened only in the privacy of our offices in Berlin and Oslo, it was very simple to exchange our shopping needs. Oslo usually received our pouch within twenty-four hours and when it was returned to us, it was not unusual to find nylons or socks, chocolates, canned fish and soap intermingled with the routine correspondence. These items were easily obtainable in Oslo, but unavailable in Berlin, and our office shared equally in these delectables. I then surprised my parents with the share I took home. The purchases were paid for with office funds without having to pay black market prices. Shopping in a time of war wasn't so bad after all, if one knew how!

A few months after I had started at the Berlin branch, the office in Oslo planned a first anniversary celebration and I was also invited to attend. Mr. Link did not really need my services on the visit, but since the newspaper had rented a room for me, and Elsa's husband Heinz was in Oslo, he thought I would enjoy to spend a few days there on my own. I immediately bought a Norwegian dictionary which had common use phrases because I remembered from my previous visit to French-speaking Switzerland how the people appreciated a friendly "please" or "thank you" in their native language. I experienced my first airplane flight on the trip to Oslo, which was a real thrill. The plane was not one of those modern jets but a Junkers machine, a small propeller plane that specialized in bumpy rides. Somehow I was able not to get air sick. Most surprising was how mild the weather was in this spring of 1941 for a country that was so far north.

Director Kurtz and his wife met me at the airport. She greeted me, laughing, "It's a good thing you didn't bring a coat along. Here the stores are full of merchandise. You can buy freely what you want without any restrictions." A great idea, but I didn't have much Norwegian money. She solved that problem, too. "Since you are working for us in Berlin you can get an advance on your salary." What a generous offer and what a temptation to buy everything in sight!

When the ceremony for the newspaper had concluded, I was on my own and the first thing I wanted to do was to meet Director Kurtz' secretary with whom I had so many telex machine conversations. Together, we fixed a big surprise package for Paul, who had to stay behind in Berlin to keep the home-fires burning. Since he was a quiet man and afraid of flying, he was content and looking forward to the promised package. The courier pouch, stuffed with rarities no longer available in Berlin, was sent off immediately, and this time, Paul could have the contents all to himself.

Oslo had a shortage of hotel rooms, so I stayed in the private apartment of a widow. This suited me fine since I was anxious to meet Norwegian people. However, things did not work out as I had hoped. The landlady didn't share my naive enthusiasm, and although she was civil, she was very reserved and made me feel like I was one of those "unwanted" guests in her country. The ice was not broken even a little bit until the end of my stay in her very homey place. As I reflect on the situation, her attitude should not have surprised me because I was one of the enemy that was so much in evidence in Norway during the war and I was sure that even if I had worn a sign around my neck which said, "I am a German, but not a Nazi", she would not have believed me.

Since Heinz was working during the day, I explored the ancient city of Oslo on my own. Although founded by the Vikings, this capital of Norway was quite modern by today's standards. Built in a semi-circle around the bay of the Oslo Fjord, the city contained many beautiful structures such as the Storting, the Norwegian Parliament, the royal palace, an imposing cathedral, and many other interesting sights I had read about but would not have time to explore. But a major attraction for me was the streets lined with small and large stores which were all full of merchandise that was available for sale to anyone without ration coupons. I started with the delicatessen. At the sight of all that food, I thought I was in Utopia. The Norwegian cuisine consists of a lot of fish, from fresh herring to delicious smoked salmon, due to their long coast line along the North Sea and the Atlantic ocean. I found the staggering variety of different foods in every store just overwhelming. Being used to ration cards for every little item, I wanted to use my opportunities wisely.

Upon entering the stores, I found the salespeople varied in their attitude toward me. Some were friendly and helpful while others were completely indifferent and ignored you completely even when I politely asked for assistance in their own language. There was no self-service. I was hungry and intended to start with some of their delicious Norwegian cheese and sausage displayed in abundance. I meant to eat my purchase right away on a park bench. After all, I could not start a conversation with the store clerks with, "Hey, I am not a Nazi!" They believed all Germans were terrible Nazis and gave no one the benefit of the doubt. Many hastily judged us to be the same as their own fascist leader Vidkun Quisling. In 1933 he had founded the "Nasjonal Samling," a kind of Norwegian Nazi Party. While collaborating with the Germans during the occupation he created in 1942 a new "National Government." (For this he was later tried for treason and was shot in 1945. The name "Quisling" became world-wide a synonym for a traitor.)

Each day after Heinz finished work, he would take me on a tour of the Oslo area in his Volkswagen even though the car was to be used for official business only. On our first trip out to Holmenkollen to meet Heinz's friends, we unexpectedly passed Terboven, the hated German Commissioner, and his entourage. What bad luck! I held my breath but he was so busy with his own "enchanting female company" that we passed unnoticed and unharmed. This man was incalculable and we were on a prohibited private trip, and so was Terboven himself.

Heinz told me many special episodes of Terboven's personal, weird kind of humor. At one of his big parties, he suddenly approached the male guests with an enormous pair of scissors and cut off every man's tie, one by one, just below the knot, while roaring with laughter. But it was not funny at all, at a time of severe shortages of all kinds of material, when in Germany every item was rationed. It was just one of his crude war-time jokes that was totally out of place. By now Terboven was the most feared and hated man in Oslo, dreaded not only by the Norwegians, but by many Germans as well.

Heinz's Norwegian friends gave me a warm welcome, and it was such a change not to be judged solely on my nationality. They knew that in any dictatorship the man in the street was not responsible for the actions of his government. Together, we went out to see the ski slopes on which the most famous skiers in the world have competed. It was so peaceful and quiet here without any air raid alarms and to be able to relax in good company without the constant war news. Heinz had planned another surprise for me. One evening we left a movie theater around midnight and stepped outside into daylight, the midnight sun, a night when the sun does not sink below the horizon. Everything gave the impression of a strange, but somehow dimmed glow and I stood there enthralled at this spectacle. I had read about this phenomenon in books, but now I had personally witnessed this unparalleled miracle of nature.

My last shopping spree was spent in one of Oslo's elegant and well-stocked department stores, and I went overboard with the availability of all that unrationed high quality merchandise. All the sales girls looked to me like beauty queens, stunningly blond and very tastefully dressed. I bought as much underwear and clothes as I could carry, as well as cigars for Papa, and in no time had spent my total salary advance from the newspaper office. With my suitcase filled with many delicacies, wearing a new light blue coat and new shoes, and carrying a new black coat for Mutti over my arm (we both wore them for years, long after the war), I was ready for the Kurtzes to drive me to the airport. It was a warm day, and the black tar on the airport runway was melting under my feet and unto my new white shoes as I walked to the plane. I was never able to completely remove the dark stains, but happily wore them anyway since it was such a treat to finally have a new pair of shoes.

There was a very friendly atmosphere on the plane to Berlin, again one of the small propeller machines. The windows were much bigger than today and the roar of the engines much louder. Before take-off, the two pilots mingled with the passengers and answered any questions. As soon as we were in the air, one of the pilots came back and asked me to join them in the cockpit. Sitting between them, I could see everything underneath since I was surrounded by glass. It was a beautiful day, and the countryside below looked like a chest of toys. The controls of the airplane did not look much different than those on my car, and as soon as I commented on this, the pilots wanted me try it out for myself. They showed me how easy it was to control the plane by tipping it from side to side and dipping it up and down. However, this scared me more than impressed me and I decided not to accept their offer to try to fly the plane, a decision which I have always regretted.

We soon passed over the clear blue waters of the sea and you could see all the way to the bottom. But what was that, buried deep down there? "A sunken war ship," the pilots explained. It was still clearly visible, the ruin of a former marine pride lost forever in the ocean depths. But how many men had lost their lives there—fathers, husbands, brothers and sons of whatever nationality and whose families would be waiting forever in vain for them to come home. What I had just seen was the true and ugly face of the real war, and this put a sudden damper on my joyful plane ride. Dampers came more often as the years of war passed. Depressed, I returned to my seat. One can read about sunken ships every day in the newspaper, but actually seeing one down there on the bottom of the ocean leaves a lasting and disturbing feeling that one can never forget.

Since my brother Günter was a naval officer and constantly at sea, I decided not to say anything at home about the sunken war ship that I had seen. I put on a joyful front by showing everything that I had brought home for us from Oslo and telling Mutti and Papa about my exciting days in beautiful Norway. It looked to them as if I had returned from a treasure hunt.

*H*ow I Became a Swan

*W*ithin a few days after my return from Oslo, Mr. Link also arrived and our usual office routine resumed, although it didn't last very long. On May 10, 1941, we received the unbelievable news of the mysterious and abrupt flight to England of Rudolph Hess, Hitler's deputy. We all were wondering if this was some type of a political mission, and if so, was it with Hitler's consent. It was only about a year ago that Hitler himself had made a peace offer to England which had been rejected. We in the office soon learned more details about this bizarre episode, but Mr. Link received strict orders from Goebbels to hold back all public announcements to await the world's reaction. Hess had taken off alone from the town of Augsburg for a night flight to Scotland to establish contact with the Duke of Hamilton, whom he considered to be a personal friend, and had left a letter behind explaining his actions as favorable for peace negotiations. However, since Hess was acting ostensibly solely on his own without Hitler's consent, his mission resulted in confused reactions in England as to what to do besides imprisoning him.

There were rumors that Hess, unarmed and defenseless, had been killed by an irate farmer as he landed in a field. Hitler was furious and acted as though Hess had taken it upon himself to negotiate a peace without his knowledge, and, except for a short bulletin with bare facts, all other news reports on the matter to foreign press or Oslo were strictly forbidden. The whole humiliating affair was suppressed in silence as if it had never occurred, and all former pictures of Hess in daily newsreels were eliminated immediately. Martin Bohrmann, a sinister hard-line Party member, succeeded to the position previously held by the now disgraced Rudolph Hess. Mr. Link told me how jubilant Goebbels was that the world press did not make a big issue of this Nazi humiliation, as he would have done if the situation was reversed. However, the Berliners' sharp-tongued sarcasm didn't let it rest, and soon came up with this joke:

After Hess arrived in England, he was introduced to Churchill who greeted him with, "So, you are the madman, that lunatic from Berlin." "Not at all Mr. Churchill," Hess replied. "I am only his deputy."

The entire German press was strictly controlled by Goebbels, and Mr. Link had to appear at the mandatory daily briefings as to what could and could not be printed. During these absences, sometimes for half a day, he would put me in charge of the whole office. Occasionally, he would return with confidential "blue papers," named after the color of paper on which they were printed, which were released from a special department. Every editor received these blue sheets, which were never used for publication, and from time to time, were burned in the inner courtyard under strict supervision. Mr. Link always kept our blue papers locked in the big bookcase and I could always see them through the glass door. However, one day the key was left in the lock during one of Mr. Link's absences, and my curiosity got the best of me. I did not feel that I was overstepping my bounds since I was temporarily in charge of the office, so I opened the case and started to read the material.

I wish I had never done that because those papers were reports of Polish and Czech brutalities committed against German citizens and soldiers, horrible crimes such as being blinded, having their tongues cut out, arms and legs broken, and other dreadful tortures. I was so stunned as I read page after page with names, dates and places that I did not hear Mr. Link return and got caught red-handed. For the first, and the last time, he was outraged and shouted, "This is not reading material for a young lady!" He forbade me to ever touch the blue pages again or to talk to anyone about what I had read. I promised, but wanted to know more and asked him if this information was really true. He said, "Yes, unfortunately yes, but it will never be published to avoid terrifying families who have their men at the front." The bookcase was never left unlocked again as long as there were blue papers inside, but I was unable to keep this frightening information to myself, so I confided in Mutti and Papa. They were also shocked and, for my own protection, urged me to discuss only with them what I heard or read in the office. Books were published after the war which validated the horror stories contained in those blue papers.

Apart from this serious incident, Mr. Link and I got along famously and there were times when he needed my discreet protection while he was out of the office searching for an apartment for his wife and little son who were still living in Frankfurt. When Oslo would call, I would tell them that Mr. Link was at the Propaganda Ministry, and when the Propaganda Ministry called, Mr. Link would just happen to be out on an important mission for Oslo. He never found a suitable available apartment even though he asked me to come along to provide a female's viewpoint. As it turned out, it was fortunate that his family never moved because they were spared the terrible end of World War II in Berlin.

There was a mysterious place close by to which Mr. Link would occasionally send Paul and he would return shortly with hot coffee and cookies or rolls for all three of us, veritable treasures and without ration cards. I never discovered where these treats originated, but whenever I would find my boss sound asleep on the office sofa in the morning after a mandatory night air raid and fire watch, I would give Paul some of my own money and no food stamps and send him to that mysterious place. While sipping the hot coffee, Mr. Link would say, "You are a wonderful secretary, even though your typing leaves much to be desired."

We had barely recuperated from the news of Rudolph Hess' mysterious flight to England five weeks earlier, when we were shocked by another radio news flash on Sunday morning, June 22, 1941. Goebbels read a proclamation of the Führer: "Since three o'clock this morning, our troops have marched into the Soviet Union in a mass attack along a two thousand mile front." We held our breath as this was followed by a memorandum from Foreign Minister von Ribbentrop which stated, "Four thousand aircraft and tanks have already been destroyed on the ground or have been captured and four thousand prisoners have been taken." Papa was stunned and exclaimed, "But this is Hitler's attack on his recent ally and now that he has expanded the war into Russia, the nightmare of a two-front war zone is exactly what Hitler branded as a mistake by our generals in World War I." At that moment, the phone rang and I was asked to report to the newspaper office immediately, while Mutti and Papa waited frantically to hear what news I would bring home that night that would be more reliable than Goebbels' carefully diluted reports to the public.

Hitler had boldly announced that we should have faith because no one was capable of running our country better than he, and that he would crush the Soviet Union in a rapid campaign. He believed his power was boundless, but the murderous Russian winter of about 40 degrees below zero centigrade was sufficient to defeat Napoleon, so how did Hitler believe that our soldiers could defeat Russia on an endless front from the Baltic to the Black Sea before winter set in? I asked Mr. Link what would happen now that the badly needed Russian oil supply would no longer be available. He pointed to a large wall map where he had marked all of the conquered countries which might be able to provide some oil. I had to type nothing but morale building-type reports of new victories from North to South and how German troops had reached the outskirts of Minsk, Moscow and Stalingrad.

Although only a layman, it appeared to me that this enormous rapid gain of territory was too extensive and would overly strain our line of combat. And, then it happened. No Blitzkrieg anymore. The German army, outfitted only in light summer uniforms, was halted in the early onset of heavy frost and a blinding snow storm with savage freezing temperatures. "General Winter" became a merciless Russian ally, and frostbite became more lethal than the Soviet army. The ill-equipped troops had to endure and die in the freezing cold because Hitler rejected the warning of his generals and had forbidden the issue of winter clothing because his summer Blitzkrieg would crush the Russians long before winter would start.

Now Goebbels besought the public in a vehement radio campaign for a country-wide sacrifice which he called a Winter War Relief Action in which the public was to donate warm, winter clothing from their households. Because of a military blunder, thousands of German soldiers suffered and died in the icy cold snow storms on the Russian front, or returned home as amputees, while the Soviet soldiers were protected by their fur caps and heavy sheepskin coats. We were furious, but it was not the proper time to raise the question of guilt. The war must be hell out there. So we sacrificed again, not for the government, but for the suffering men who had been ordered into the murderous winter campaign. We hastily donated our warm sweaters, woolen caps and scarfs, gloves and winter boots. Sieghardt even took his brand new skis and skiing outfit to the collection depot because he felt it was more urgently needed right now on the Eastern Front. However, a lot of the sacrificial donations never reached the freezing soldiers because they were "short-stopped" by greedy people in some rear army bases.

As a part of Goebbels' Winter War Relief Action, a radio musical request program, called *Wunschkonzert*, was introduced every Sunday as a link between home and the soldiers at the front. In addition to musical requests from the home front and war front, there were frequent personal announcements for front line soldiers of childbirth and even very touching brief conversations between the soldier and his wife. The program was a morale builder as it cleverly diverted the public attention from the grimness of war and softened the burden of separation as everyone would anxiously listen to see if their message with name and address had been announced.

Movie houses, theaters and the Berlin Philharmonic Orchestra continued with their regular performances, each trying to give the illusion of a normal life. The prior summer Sieghardt had purchased winter season tickets for Friday nights in the Charlottenburg Opera House, one of the two famous ones in Berlin, the other being the State Opera House. Now, under the Nazis, a rivalry had developed among the "faithful" around Hitler that had even affected the theater. Goebbels had control in the State Opera and Göring controlled the other, and since these two could not stand each other, they constantly competed to have their opera provide the best performances and we entered the battle of the muses. As a result of their hatred and envy of each other, we were treated to outstanding performances and for a short while each Friday at the opera, Sieghardt and I escaped from the reality of war.

While we sought good fortune, misfortune sought us. In the early days of December, 1941, Germany was dealt two blows. First, an unexpected Soviet counterattack made it crystal clear that there was no more Blitzkrieg on the Eastern Front. And, on December 7, Japan bombed the American naval base at Pearl Harbor, Hawaii, and the United States declared war on Japan the next day, realizing Roosevelt's long-time dream of a military union with Great Britain. Great Britain declared war on Japan, and on December 11, Germany and Italy declared war on the United States to support their ally, Japan. The war now took on a global expansion.

While typing all this at the office, it seemed to me that hardly any country was left that had not declared war on someone, except neutral

Spain, and I had to be very careful not to confuse the names of countries who were at war with each other. Now even the United States was mobilized against us, and with a power that kept Britain afloat and Russia fighting. Germany was now completely isolated between Russia on the east and Great Britain and United States on the west, and we spent our third war-time Christmas wondering how this would all end.

Berlin had many pillars on which advertisements were displayed, but now comic picture posters of fictitious symbolic figures were added for government propaganda to enforce reduction of private consumption of energy. One showed a gruesome face of a one-eyed pirate called *Kohlenklau* (coal snatcher), a thief who stole valuable coal by recklessly wasting it, thereby stealing from the economy. The other was, *Groschengrab* (dime death), an equally wicked character who thoughtlessly wasted energy, thereby throwing money away, and again stealing from the economy.

Whenever we ran out of something, or some plans failed, it was always the fault of the people, never the government, which of course, was always blameless. We were supposed to tighten our belts even more and sacrifice for our country and these slogans were underlined with the widespread motto, "*Räder rollen für den Sieg*" (wheels roll for victory). Another slogan was "*Feind hört mit*" (the enemy is listening), which is similar to the American "big brother is watching you." These posters were warning us against giving information to the enemy. What enemy? We were cut off from the outside world and surrounded by snooping Nazi spies. We were also continually threatened for spreading rumors, especially those which contradicted official government news.

It was forbidden to listen to foreign radio broadcasts and was subject to punishment for high treason. Goebbels was ready to find the enemy at home. A gradual inner resistance grew against the regime and the latest political joke was always a good barometer of the mood of the people who were well aware of Goebbels' twisted truths and muzzled press:

> A journalist in Berlin learned that he is on Goebbels' black list. In panic, he rushes to the Propaganda Ministry to beg a big wheel there to immediately remove his name from the list. The important Nazi quietly tells him, "As a true Nazi I must reject this criminal demand, but as a human being, I ask how much is it worth to you?"

Things gradually got worse, but life always goes on no matter what is happening around us. Pearl Harbor was far away and one only read about it in the newspapers, just as years later we would read about Korea and Vietnam. My private life was here and real, and even with the current circumstances, was pleasant. Sieghardt and I were dating more frequently and we enjoyed each others' company. The weather on one particular opera Friday, March 6, 1942, was especially miserable with cold rain storms and both of us had gotten drenched after work. Instead of heading for the bus to the opera, Sieghardt aimed for a nearby telephone booth into which we both crammed. I wondered why and he just laughed and said, "Let's just go home because it's time that we told your family and…," and I suddenly realized that this was the old fashioned way of a proposal to get the approval of the bride's father. Carried away by emotion, we had our engagement kiss right there in the phone booth. Why head for the opera and watch someone else's romantic love story when we had our own realistic blissful one right here, although less glamorous as we stood there drenched and tired.

Once we got home, Papa invited Sieghardt into his study and a serious discussion began behind closed doors. All of the females in the house knew what was going on in there, and that Papa would be asking the same old-fashioned questions like: "Do you think you can support my daughter?" This was particularly amusing, and we knew it was only a formality, since Sieghardt was the son of an old, established and wealthy aristocratic family. They finally came out, and Papa announced, "We now have a new member in the family, my son-in-law!" Everyone's happiness was obvious, although, so far, no one had bothered to ask me. This called for a bottle of champagne, which Lotte had already brought up from the basement and put on ice. Sieghardt told his family that same evening, which was no surprise to his mother since he had asked her a long time ago for old gold pieces, even broken ones. The only way to get a real gold wedding ring was to turn in your own gold or otherwise put up with a fake one. Two days later, on Sunday, March 8, which was Günter's birthday, we all got together for a family celebration. The official announcement was made the following Sunday, March 15, which by coincidence was also my birthday.

My life had another abrupt change when Mr. Link was unexpectedly drafted into the military service. It was a sudden last handshake as he said, "Goodbye Schmidtchen, take care and keep the flag flying until I get back." Paul and I knew right away that he would probably never be back, and now I had the responsibility of running the office. It was a completely new situation and I had a lot to learn. Fortunately, the political functions were turned over to another editor in the house which freed me from my duties of typing political subjects. Paul was loyal to me and grateful for his job in our very small office. Neither of us were Party members or ever intended to be, but as head of an office in the Nazi press building, I was occasionally requested to join a Nazi women's organization. I told them that I would as soon as the workload in our office became more manageable, hoping I could avoid taking any action until I would be leaving to get married.

Our official engagement picture

One day, Paul told me that the other messengers had started to tease him about how it felt to be "ordered around" by a female half his age, and he jokingly told them that it was tolerable. There was constant gossip being circulated among the many offices, and the messengers were the primary source of true and fictitious stories. It annoyed them that Paul did not contribute his share by revealing what went on in our office, and they were all suspicious about our quiet bureau and those occasional bulky courier sacks because they couldn't imagine official correspondence taking up that much space. No, it couldn't, but our private and very secretive method of exchanging goodies with our office in Oslo was none of their business.

As the war progressed, circumstances became worse for all of us. The air raid alarms were becoming ever more frightening and those social gatherings with our neighbors over wine which we had two years earlier were now a thing of the past. The long tones of the sirens, which howled up and down from a low to high pitch, ground their sinister and grueling air raid alerts more frequently. They never failed to set our teeth on edge. As soon as we heard our anti-aircraft artillery in action we knew that the enemy bombers were directly over us, and there was nothing to do but take shelter and wait, hope and pray to be spared one more time. After a terrible shelling, the long high pitch tone of the "all-clear" signal finally sounded through the night, telling us that we had survived one more attack—until the next aerial bombardment.

The frequent air raids had left ruins even in our quiet residential suburb, and prayers were offered during Sunday church services for those who had not survived. The bomb detonations made the whole area tremble like an earthquake and it seemed strange that it was the houses on the corner that were hit first. Fortunately, our house was the second one from the end. Our emergency suitcases and food remained in the bomb shelter for hasty evacuation in case the house was hit and we had survived with only the basement remaining intact. The building code had long required that extra reinforcements be installed in basements so that they could carry the weight of a collapsing house in a direct hit. When our house was built in 1938 on Limastrasse, the true purpose of this law was not mentioned. It was then simply stated as "for safety and support."

Early in the war, air raid wardens had been assigned to each block, group of houses or to a single large building. In our suburb, the wardens were primarily fellow citizens like ourselves, but elsewhere they were dangerous Nazi watch dogs. Those wardens would come unannounced to people's doors and pretend they had to check if everyone had obeyed the black-out orders or other restrictions. They would snoop around inside for any evidence that you had been listening to foreign broadcasts, and any reported violation was dealt with harshly. Hitler's iron hand reached everywhere and you couldn't escape it, not even in your own home. Bit by bit, we became trapped physically and emotionally.

At the office, there were mandatory night watches, with the male and female supervisors alike taking turns. It was a frightening experience for me because I had to take the S-Bahn to get to the office. The lights in the compartments were so dim that I could barely see my fellow passengers. Then when I reached Potsdamer Platz, it was a twenty-minute walk through pitch black streets to my office building. There had been murders reported repeatedly on the S-Bahn, and although the murderer was eventually caught and executed on the spot, it provided fuel for Papa to take matters into his own hands. He vigorously pursued every one of his contacts and finally freed me from the night watches downtown.

As the summer of 1942 approached, I had to find a replacement to break in for my rather unusual position. This proved to be difficult because most people wanted routine office duties and were reluctant to assume the responsibilities of office manager. I finally found someone who became interested when I mentioned the prospect of goodies from Oslo, and eventually was able to say goodbye to Norway and my faithful friend Paul. I was grieved to learn that shortly thereafter, dear Paul had not survived one of Berlin's severe night bombing attacks. He lived in a small apartment in an old multi-family building in the center of town, and just vanished as a direct hit turned the building into a flaming pile of rubble impossible to search through or to identify anyone later. And, soon thereafter, I was informed that Mr. Link, while home on leave, was instantly killed by a train when he either fell or was accidently pushed between the cars in one of the overcrowded and pitch dark train stations.

My foreboding at our last goodbye had come true. So now I was the only survivor of our office trio, and the thought crossed my mind, for how long? Would my time run out also? But I had plans right now and a strong will to survive. The front lines were far from the German borders and my world looked rosy as my marriage to the man I loved was approaching.

I was to be married on September 17, 1942, and my cousin Edith and Hans in Gleiwitz were to be married one month sooner, on August 22. Mutti, Papa, Sieghardt and I went there modestly by train because travel by car was prohibited. Everything was ready for the wedding when we arrived because the family had been busy for weeks making all of the preparations, including providing the food. This was not an easy task when everything was controlled by purchase permits or ration cards. But as usual, people find a way. And, one could arrange "friendly favors", which is a modern adaptation of the old barter system. You have what I want and I have what you want, so we exchanged without the necessity of a ration card. The same applied to wedding presents. The method of obtaining gifts was called "to organize" which had taken on the meaning similar to the English phrase "to rustle up." Through this method of organizing, we performed miracles. Articles ranging from luxury items to kitchen utensils, which had been unavailable for so long that the average German knew of them only by hearsay, suddenly and miraculously reappeared. When one was asked how they ever obtained these rare genuine items, the answer would always be, "We organized!"

As was customary, I had brought my self-composed wedding newspaper and the traditional *Tischgesang* (table song), which was sung during the wedding dinner and was filled with humorous allusions to past funny events of the wedding party and guests. The melody of a catchy, well-known tune was easy for poor singers to follow, and everybody got their own copy. The *Tischgesang* contained all of the hidden ways that one could organize and advice on what to do with unwanted wedding gifts. They could easily be passed on to the next unsuspecting bride and groom, which in this case, happened to be Sieghardt and me.

Back in Berlin, Mutti and I continued our own wedding plans. Our friend, Mrs. Behrmann, had been taking us to the country beyond Potsdam to meet her farmer friends in Beelitz, in order to augment our supply of ration card meals. This reminded us of the barter trips we used to make in the early 1920s back in Münster and even before that in 1918 in Krummhübel. What a recurrence of life, now for the third time. We also went together to gather mushrooms in the large forests around Berlin, where, thanks to Mrs. Behrmann's experience in this field, we never picked any of the poisonous "look-alikes." I always favored the very tasty yellow, chanterelle mushrooms which emerge in great abundance after a rainy day and can easily make a delicious meal, even replacing meat.

Sieghardt's membership in the Wannsee rowing and social club came in handy when we needed a boat to row to a farmer's village in the country called Fahrland, far beyond Potsdam. It took us an entire day navigating the lakes and rivers to complete our food excursion, returning with a boat laden with fruits, vegetables and potatoes from the farmers. However, getting supplemental food from the country was considered "hoarding" and strictly forbidden. If caught, the food was confiscated and a heavy fine imposed, and police were always looking for boats that were sitting low in the water, an indication of heavy cargo on board. We kept our rural acquisitions covered with a raincoat, and whenever we saw a police boat approaching, I would be stretched out on top of our loot, smiling and waving even though it was nerve-wracking. Fortunately, we were never stopped.

After these "hoarding" trips, Mutti and I would can part of the goodies for my future married household. But right now, we had to supply our wedding needs first, and our farmer friends took part in our romance with extra supplies of eggs, butter, milk and their special homemade potato pound cakes. They tasted great, especially for our not too fastidious tastes in the third year of the war. In our neighborhood where we all knew each other, all of the stores were old family establishments and they also helped out with extra food supplies. To show our appreciation, we in return gave them many of our potato cakes. For a while, the war had been forgotten as we looked forward to our wedding, even ignoring the hardships we had to put up with to arrange it.

On the eve before the wedding, family and close friends gathered at the home of my parents to celebrate *Polterabend*, a German tradition meaning Crockery Eve. Presents were brought that night, or to the wedding, since there was no bridal shower and a bachelor's party was unknown. Crockery Eve is a very noisy and joyful affair and for the neighbors a chance to get rid of all of their chipped and broken china pieces, but never glass. According to custom, pottery smashed in front of the house door is supposed to bring the couple good luck. This ritual is probably a holdover of a heathen Germanic rite to drive evil spirits away with the shattering noises. It was then the duty of Sieghardt and me to go out front with a dust pan and broom and clean up the mess. The guests watched this very carefully because, by old tradition, the one who works the hardest will be the one who is burdened with the work in the upcoming marriage. But, we were so busy cleaning up together that we had no time to pay attention to tradition. Our evening was interrupted several times by the shattering of crockery outside, and each time we had to go out and clean it up. We hoped they would run out of old china by midnight because we needed to get our rest for the long and tiring day that was ahead of us.

The following morning after a gathering for breakfast at my parents' house and Lotte's untiring help, Sieghardt and I had to rush off with our witnesses for the civil ceremony in the town hall. (A German wedding has both a civil and a church ceremony.) After lunch, I changed into my wedding gown, a long and nervous procedure, with the help of Mutti, Elsa and a hairdresser. We had somehow "organized" (without textile ration cards) the beautiful lace and embroidery dress material which our dressmaker made into a white dream with a long train and a matching veil. I had received a tiny myrtle tree in a pot at my confirmation in 1931. The myrtle is a wedding plant whose evergreen leaves symbolize blessing and vitality, and according to an old custom, I had carefully nurtured it all these years to be used for my bridal wreath. The local flower shop made a beautiful creation out of it to be worn on my head.

Our church wedding was scheduled for three o'clock in the nearby Johannis Church in Schlachtensee, and Sieghardt and I drove up in a beautiful horse-drawn carriage with a little page to hold the long train of my wedding gown. Papa had arranged everything including taxis for all the guests. The church was crowded with people from our suburb that we had known for years, including the baker who donated a fancy cake and the butcher who provided a roast, and those parishioners who just love to shed tears at wedding ceremonies. Sieghardt looked very handsome and elegant, and so did all the young officers. Günter was there in his navy uniform and my

My wedding day
(Our arrival with horse and carriage)

cousins in their blue air force and green army uniforms. All the women had managed to look lovely in spite of the textile ration cards.

We lined up in the church's vestibule for the procession in accordance with proper etiquette: first Mutti and my father-in-law, then Papa with my mother-in-law, and so on. There is no wedding rehearsal the night before, and as the organ prelude began, they all proceeded down the aisle to their reserved seats. Now it was Sieghardt's and my turn. The bride is not given away as in the United States, and we walked down the aisle together preceded by a little boy and girl, cute children of one of the guests, dropping flowers from a small basket, and followed by a page holding up the long train. Our wedding ceremony was solemn and ended with the exchange of rings.

Many pictures were taken outside of the church afterwards while our friends and neighbors congratulated us. A light rain had begun to fall and one old lady said, "Oh this means tears in the marriage." "Not at all," her friend contradicted. "Those raindrops are pearls." They were both right because in the future, bitter and sweet times often followed close together. The people slowly dispersed, along with the rain and we finally departed for our private wedding celebration at the home of my in-laws.

It was after four o'clock when our horse drawn carriage pulled up in front of the house, and everyone else was already there and waiting for the start of the reception. Papa had hired a live band and we learned later that he had requested them to play the wedding march by Felix Mendelssohn-Bartholdy as we entered the house. However, the band leader politely declined and after a heated discussion, he finally whispered to Papa, "We are not permitted to play Mendelssohn's music because he was a Jewish composer." Papa immediately reacted with, "What's that got to do with the music? At my daughter's wedding I select the music that is played and I want Mendelssohn's wedding march—right now! The bride and groom are already coming through the garden gate!" But the conductor warned, "Mr. Schmidt, you endanger all of us here."

So we entered the house to the wedding march of Lohengrin by Wagner, being happily congratulated by the guests, unaware of the vehement musical struggle. The band turned out to be excellent and was most likely as unpolitical as Papa, but it was strictly forbidden to perform non-Aryan compositions. They played soft background music during our sit-down dinner for twenty-four people, which was a grandiose event for 1942. It was customary for the groom to provide the beverages and the bride's family to take care of the menu. We had seven people working in the kitchen and Lotte and her girlfriend acted as waitresses, wearing their cute outfits proudly.

When the party was in full swing, everyone, including the band, had mellowed from the good wine. The musical dispute with Papa was forgotten. This was good for all of us because one radical Nazi in the crowd would have been enough to report Papa, which would have had unpredictable consequences. Along with the numerous toasts and humorous poems, songs and wedding newspaper, the latest Hitler joke was told:

Two friends meet on the Kurfüstendamm and one says to the other, "Have you heard that 98 percent of the people voted for Hitler's concepts?" "That's really strange," says the friend, "Since I only run into the other 2 percent all the time."

What we had to go through to start a married life supplied the dinner guests with a never-ending source of entertainment. We needed everything from scratch, including a place to live. Our only hope was our apartment house on Limastrasse but all apartments were occupied with long leases. However, there were two nice unoccupied rooms in the attic with big windows and a bathroom. Our architect friend, Paul Thiemer, was working on a floor plan to convert the attic into a comfortable apartment that included a kitchen and small foyer. However, apartments were not permitted on the third floor, so he started without a permit, as soon as he had "organized" all of the necessary material and hired a reliable, retired carpenter. But, the construction office in the town hall found out about it and he had to appear there with an appropriately guilty face, but with the help of his old friends in different offices, he succeeded so that Papa ended up having to pay only a small fine and no questions were asked as to where the building materials had come from. So we toasted architect Thiemer.

Papa had never really intended for us to live in that attic apartment. There was an old lady, Mrs. Birkholz, living alone in a large one-bedroom apartment on the first floor which had a big entrance hall, glass enclosed veranda like a Florida room, a porch and a private yard. Her married son lived in one of the spacious three bedroom apartments on the second floor where she spent most of her time. Papa convinced her that she didn't need all that space in her present place and that she would be happier in the new smaller one which was directly above her son. She would also be paying much lower rent. The papers for the change of residence were in the process of being signed and everything was to be completed by the time we returned from our honeymoon. This called for another toast, this time for Papa.

Obtaining furniture was almost as difficult as finding housing. Since the war industry was using all of the raw material, everything needed not only a purchase permit but also a source of supply. It so happened that after Mutti and I had purchased a bedroom set in one of the stores and stored it in the basement, we discovered another more suitable one from a private source, which was also stored down there. Lotte, newly engaged, became very interested in our double success and asked what we intended to do with the first purchase. When Mutti told her it would be her Christmas present she was overwhelmed. Then, Uncle Conny announced that kitchen furniture for me was also on its way. This was reason for another happy toast.

Later in the evening, everything got into full swing as the band changed over to dance music. After our first dance, Sieghardt and I vanished unnoticed around midnight and were driven to the famous Hotel Adlon next to the Pariser Platz and the Brandenburg Gate. It is the most distinguished hotel in Berlin and a society gathering place. Here Sieghardt had reserved an elegant suite for two days. What a wonderful way to start a married life. From there, we departed on our honeymoon to the romantic and historic town of Eisenach, located at the foot of the Thuringer mountain range with the legendary Wartburg castle, where we planned to stay for two weeks at a hotel named Kaiserhof (Emperor's court). When Mutti sent us a welcome telegram addressed to Sieghardt and Dorothea von Schwanenflügel in Eisenach in the Kaiserhof, the telephone operator exclaimed, "Oh, that sounds just like in a fairy tale!" We felt like it and had already learned to enjoy things as long as they lasted, knowing that even fairy tales do not last forever. And ours was soon cut short.

We had just returned from tracing the footsteps of Saint Elizabeth, Martin Luther and Johann Sebastian Bach, thrilled to have walked on the same streets they had centuries before, when Mutti called with an urgent message. We were to return home immediately because

Sieghardt's draft notification for military service was expected any day. We had to cancel all remaining plans for our honeymoon and that evening, tried to enjoy our last candlelight dinner in front of the fireplace pretending to be so happy to go home again, but carefully avoiding the reason for our hasty departure.

We left by train early the next morning for our return to an uncertain future. Since we had come back so hastily, the old lady had not moved upstairs into her new apartment so we had to temporarily stay with my parents. Another surprise awaited us when I looked into our garage and found the car was missing. Papa told us that several Nazi leaders had shown up one day with a paper indicating that our car was confiscated based on the slogan, "wheels are rolling for victory." Obviously our wheels were urgently needed. Our car would be used only temporarily for the armed forces, of course without compensation. That would not be necessary because after final victory, our German government would present us with a brand new vehicle. So, Papa had no choice but to turn over the keys, and the men in brown uniforms drove off in our car, never to be seen again.

Then came the next surprise. Much to my relief, Sieghardt's draft notification had been postponed because his firm had orders to produce metal plaques with a special engraving for military aircraft. Sieghardt's party membership also worked to his advantage because it made him superior to those Nazi fellow workers who used every occasion to complain about others. Usually, their targets were long-standing employees who were of mixed blood, part Jewish, or related to someone who was partly non-Aryan. Sieghardt would patiently listen to their complaints, thank them for their information and would end each meeting with, "I'll look into it." Later, he would warn the accused ones to be more careful, particularly with any remarks that could prove to be dangerous when overheard by the troublemakers. Those the others complained about were people who were also excluded by law from any assistance normally given to those who had suffered bomb damage. Sieghardt would allow them to secretly take home from the factory whatever they needed so that they could make the necessary repairs. Some never forgot the badly needed assistance that he gave at his own risk, and came forward after the war when Party members were the "criminal ones."

Sieghardt was constantly under pressure to enter one of the three Nazi formations, either the SA, the SS or the NSKK (National Socialist Motor Corps). He chose the NSKK, the least political, but had to show cause for his selection. Since the NSKK was mainly for pre-military training in either motorized units or cavalry, he was granted the cavalry because of his former horseback riding experience. And, to his further advantage, all military horseback riding training was held in Düppel, a suburb close to us where he had ridden for pleasure long before the war. Now he had to appear periodically in the NSKK uniform for horseback riding exercises, but he never pursued any rank. We considered this far better than assignment to an SA or SS unit.

We were finally able to move into our apartment on December 18, and were wonderfully surprised to find a beautiful Chippendale dining room set waiting for us, plus the kitchen furniture from Uncle Conny. Mutti and I had been searching for a long time throughout Berlin for the many every day items and other useful occasional "what nots" to fill up the cupboards and drawers. Available china was of a poor quality, but a large "Rosenthal" store at Potsdamer Platz still carried their famous high quality porcelain, and we went there hoping to find a blue set, my favorite color. No blue was available, but Mutti bought me a table setting for twelve with a green and gold pattern that was rather modern for the time. (I always admired how up-to-date Mutti was with everything.) Although I was very happy with my new china, Mutti promised that I would receive an even more beautiful blue set after the war. (We had no way of knowing that in just a few years we would be lucky just to have saved part of what we had. I never got the blue china set, but still highly treasure the green and gold one).

We celebrated our fourth war-time Christmas, and our first one together, in our new home. The main topic of conversation among my in-laws revolved around: "Is she pregnant or isn't she?" (Yes, she was!) This was an important subject for them because Sieghardt had two older unmarried sisters and my father-in-law had already whispered into my ear at the wedding dinner that he expected three male heirs, a doctor, a lawyer and one to take over his firm. But, life went on no matter how much we tried to deny the nightmare of war in that winter of 1942.

No Blitzkrieg anymore, but our troops were tragically surrounded at Stalingrad in freezing temperatures, and the city was hell on earth, with great losses on both sides. Marshall Paulus had planned a potential escape in December 1942, but Hitler ordered that under no circumstances the army would retreat. Meanwhile Field Marshall Rommel, the Desert Fox, was fighting joint British and American armies in North Africa and we at home were living under constant intensified bombardment. After especially heavy air raids, we would be rewarded with rations of *Bohnenkaffee*, coffee made from real coffee beans, to celebrate our survival. This extra allowance, awarded as disaster relief, was ironically nicknamed *Zitter-Zulage* (shiver and shake bonus), which was a very appropriate name under the circumstances.

The *Bohnenkaffee* had been upgraded to a special reward and was one of those rarities from a time long ago. The coffee substitute that we got with our ration card, called *Muckefuck* (a murky drink) produced a black brew whose only feature in common with real coffee was its color. It was a dishwater-colored morning beverage whose taste defied description and provided a new widely-spread cynical coffee klatsch joke:

At a lady's coffee klatsch, all the women are complaining that they had no real coffee anymore. Two weeks later the hostess runs into one of her former guests in a distant Berlin suburb and the guest wonders, "What are you doing in this god-forsaken area?" Quite upset, the hostess replies, "A spy reported to the Gestapo that at our coffee klatsch we were complaining about not having any real coffee anymore. As my punishment I have to come out here to the Nazi headquarters every day for two weeks and say, 'Heil Hitler, we can do without *Bohnenkaffee*,' but tomorrow is my last time." Two weeks later the same two ladies happen to meet again at that same spot. The surprised guest asks, "What are you still doing here?" The hostess, very upset, replies, "Oh, something very unforseen happened on what should have been my last day. I mixed up everything and blurted out, 'Heil *Bohnenkaffee*, we can do without Hitler,' which made them very angry and I now have to come for two more weeks to recite the version they want to hear."

For the German people there was hidden sarcasm. Everyone would have gone to jail or worse for blurting out such a "mistake"—a mistake which really revealed people's true feelings.

The Dream Child

After four years of marriage, when it appeared that Elsa and Heinz would never have any children of their own, they finally decided on adoption. But, in Nazi Germany, the word "adoption" did not exist. Rather, the SS was available upon request to father Nordic babies, alias Hitler's so-called "fountain of life." This alternative was absolutely out of the question for them. They were aware of all the illegitimate and unwanted babies in Norway that had been fathered by German soldiers, and who could be easily adopted for a very practical reason. Their Norwegian mothers, whose husbands were in England to escape the German army, absolutely did not want them since it would be difficult to explain this sudden addition to the family. So, the adoptions were mutually beneficial as it served to eliminate conflicts in Norwegian homes and the German army. Heinz's Norwegian friends had just adopted their second boy from this seemingly inexhaustible source, and were in the process of taking in two more children, cute little twin girls.

So it happened that in the autumn of 1942, Elsa returned to Oslo and visited with Heinz one of the orphanages. They were warmly received and given complete freedom to observe the children at play, and both soon had their eye on a special little boy who even bore a resemblance to Elsa. He would be the one. There was a personal record on each child which provided the background on both parents. In their case, the mother was a married Norwegian farm girl and the father a German soldier whose own marriage was childless. In all probability, the wife would have been happy to take his son as their own if he had had the courage to tell her about him.

Ironically, the child's father came from Silesia, the same area of Germany as Elsa, and his wife could easily run into the child without knowing it was his. The Norwegian mother was told that her baby had been adopted by a German couple and would be well cared for in a loving home. Elsa and Heinz named him Tor-Kristian, because he was born in the Norwegian harbor town of Kristiansand, and had him baptized and entered into the parish register there. But, they were frustrated by the seemingly endless red tape in having the adoption finalized, and it was early January 1943 when Elsa finally could pick up her little boy in Germany in a kindergarten near Leipzig. By now Kristian was seven months old and afflicted with a severe whooping cough. Being totally inexperienced in her new maternal role, she felt helpless with that suffering bundle in her arms and immediately went home to her mother in Schweidnitz for assistance. The only thing that mattered now was that she finally had her dream child, whether sick or healthy. I was still expecting ours sometime in July.

We had just experienced the fourth wartime Christmas and our German troops were suffering through their second savage Russian winter. Rumors were spreading that we were losing the battle of Stalingrad, a strong concentration of forces on both sides, Soviet and German. The days of January 1943 drifted by somehow frightfully for us. Then came January 30, the tenth anniversary of our Nazi regime. The long years under their brutal dictatorship looked like a somber eternity to us, anything but a blessing. On this day, Hitler's inevitable and repetitive speech was broadcast as usual, but there was something new added this time: "We must exert all our strength and effort to save our culture and Christianity from the hordes in the East!" We were dumbfounded by such a statement from a deceitful man who had personally and forcibly crushed the church, dissolved convents, and imprisoned and killed priests and pastors, as I knew from Münster. Hitler was safe, sheltered in his deep bomb-proof bunker, while the German people were being killed like flies, but we could do nothing but vent our rage in the latest riddle:

Hitler, Himmler and other accomplices hide in a bunker. The bunker gets a direct hit. QUESTION: "Who is saved?" ANSWER: "The German people!"

On February 2 we received the catastrophic radio news broadcast that the German Sixth Army had surrendered at Stalingrad. We knew that General Paulus had previously urgently recommended a promising break-through to the West which would have saved them from the trap of encirclement. But Hitler ordered him to hold his ground at all costs without regard to the fact that the entire army could be annihilated. And, that is exactly what happened. The word "defeat" was never used, but rather, this military disaster was referred to as the "heroic last days" when the swastika had been hoisted over the ruins until the very last moment. Who cared?

We received this news with horror, a mixed feeling of despair and futile rage against the government and Hitler's blundering misjudgment. What had happened to the hundreds of thousands of German soldiers who had vanished in the snow of the vast expanse of Russia? We were told that General Paulus had finally surrendered the small rest that remained from the original quarter million men without consent of Hitler in order to save them from freezing to death in temperatures reaching minus 28 degrees Fahrenheit. Approximately ninety thousand men, which is all that remained of the entire Sixth Army, marched into Soviet captivity, and only about five thousand of them ever returned from the Russian prison camps.

On February 3, 1943, Goebbels announced that the battle of Stalingrad was over and there would be three days of national mourning. For the first time during the war, all amusement places remained closed during this period. We were shocked when our friends, the Behrmanns, were notified that their youngest son "had died a heroic death as a defender of Germany…and in this time of mourning, we all should be inspired by his sacrifice to defend the German Reich more vigorously. He died so that Germany may live." Later, we learned that a grenade had torn off his legs and he bled to death on the battlefield. We were shocked. He was younger than I and had just finished high school when he was drafted.

No longer did we hear routine reports of triumphs as the offensive war had now turned into a defensive one, and Stalingrad was the turning point in favor of the Allies. Goebbels proclaimed that we had to make necessary sacrifices for the Fatherland and to hold out. We immediately knew that when the government finally admitted something negative, the situation must be ten times worse than they were telling us.

On February 18, Goebbels gave an extremely fanatical speech in which he called for "total war" as the shortest route to victory. What did that demagogue demand? For us the war was very "total" already. An elite German army had just been annihilated, sacrificed by Hitler, and we civilians were being bombed with greater force and frequency than ever before.

On March 2, we experienced a massive air attack in Berlin, the worst ever, with heavy losses of buildings and people. There were rumors that school children and pregnant mothers may now be evacuated into the country. After one of these air raids, Mutti spotted me in a water bucket brigade of neighbors fighting a fire in an adjacent house. Oh, how furious she was! This was no place for me, being five months pregnant, but who thought of that at the sight of fire and people screaming for water. Terrible times brought all of us closer together.

Long ago we had anticipated the probability of losing everything in an air raid, so we had sent emergency packages for safekeeping to Aunt Frieda in Gleiwitz and Aunt Grete in Zerbst. Their homes seemed relatively safe from bombing. These packages contained the bare essentials, such as clothing, eating utensils and combs, knowing that we would have to be self-sufficient if disaster struck.

We heard another rumor that the government was going to remove all maids from homes in which there were no children and draft them into heavy military industry. Lotte, our long-time maid, was alarmed and we decided that she should immediately look for a safe position. Being intelligent and dependable, she quickly found work in our nearby post office just a five-minute walk from our house, so of course, she could keep her room with us. About the same time, her fiancé suddenly arrived home on a short convalescent leave after being wounded at the Eastern Front. A bullet had hit him in the chest, but was deflected by the sturdy pocket watch that Lotte had given him which he wore over his heart at all times. While home, he and Lotte moved all of her new furniture and other presents to his parent's three-story home in the country not far from Berlin. They ran a well established butcher shop in their large house and also had reserved a private apartment for the young couple after the war. When her fiancé returned to the front, Lotte would often spend the weekend with his parents who loved her dearly and she always returned well provided with little extras for everybody. But her bright future was soon darkened. With the advancing Soviets also came the shadow of death. Her fiancé never returned and the home and business of her prospective in-laws were destroyed and everyone killed by the invading Red Army. Only Lotte survived in Berlin.

With so many young men away at the front, the government arranged for marriage by proxy in ceremonies in which the bride sat at home next to an empty chair on which a helmet was placed to represent the absent groom. Far away at the front, the groom sat next to an empty chair on which flowers were placed to represent the bride, and they said their "I do's" over a special telephone hook-up. Such proxy wedding arrangements were glorified in both the newspapers and newsreels, and also relieved the concern of many a young woman who found herself pregnant after her boyfriend's home leave. What would the government think of next? The Nazi Party strongly encouraged childbirth with special privileges and tax exemptions, which greatly favored my present situation since I was already pregnant.

I was exempt from being drafted into heavy defense industry and was allowed to stay at home as an ordinary housewife before and after the birth of my child. However, it didn't take long for the Nazi Women's League to spot me walking around the neighborhood and, being suspicious, they wanted to know why I was not on their membership list. I innocently replied, "Oh, I am registered in Münster," although I never had registered there either. I knew that they would have a hard time verifying this because Münster had been mostly destroyed by now and it seemed quite unlikely that my records would have survived the bombing.

In the meantime towns were burning and almost every major city in Germany had been hit. The front lines were collapsing, and the war was moving closer to German soil. Because of the heavy loss of industrial manpower and capability, prisoners of war and even some Jews were put to work to keep the badly crippled industrial production running. It was about this time that I saw my first *Judenstern* (Star of David). I remember it as a palm-size yellow star on a black piece of cloth. It had to be worn by every Jew above the age of six. This Nazi law was humiliating for them and embarrassing for us. Any opposition from the Jewish people or us was considered a crime. There were rumors that some Jews had been "relocated" to other areas and to labor camps, which sounded like our familiar labor service where we had to work on farms somewhere in the East. Of course, we were kept ignorant of the real truth, and every rumor was treated as plotting high treason and disgracing the government, punishable by death.

In Berlin, we were subjected to bombing almost every night. Mr. Birkholz, our tenant on Limastrasse, was a member of *Organization Todt,* which was responsible for government road construction and engineering projects. With his assistance we built an underground bunker in our spacious backyard. Equipped with only shovels, we dug a shallow trench about twenty-five feet long, five feet wide, and less than six feet high. We secured the inside walls with wooden planks and covered the top with metal sheets and sand we had dug up earlier. As a result, the final product looked like a giant mole-hill. It was our plan that some tenants would take cover in the bunker while others stayed in the house. This way, if the house was hit, those in the bunker could help dig out the others who were buried alive, and vice versa.

Shortly after the bunker was finished, Mutti happened to be visiting me one afternoon when the sirens started howling unexpectedly and there was no time for her to run home. We decided to be the first ones to use our new bunker because all of the other women were afraid to go in. This was one of the worst day attacks we had ever had. The roaring airplanes, the firing of our anti-aircraft guns, the whistling of the falling bombs followed by ear-splitting detonations, the endless screams for help of people whose houses were hit, and the trembling earth was more frightening than we had ever experienced in the basement of our house. It was pure hell. We were terrified as we clung together while crouching on the ground in the bunker. The attack seemed endless. When the ordeal was over we emerged still trembling, and found several houses close by in flames. A very shaken Mutti urged me to never go anywhere but in the basement during any future air raids.

Life was getting harder and the war outlook was grim, but to express any negative opinion in public was to invite the death penalty. Some people just seemed to vanish, as did our long-time dentist in our neighborhood. His home and practice was in a nearby apartment building and one day when I arrived for my appointment, there was a sign on the door which said his practice was closed and that he had moved away. I could not understand why he had not notified his long-time patients, but when I tried to question other tenants in the building, they just looked frightened and quickly closed their doors without answering me. It was not until after the war, and people dared to talk freely again, that the truth finally came out. My dentist had been suspected of being involved in some secret underground conspiracy against Hitler that had begun long before the 1944 assassination attempt. One night, the Gestapo picked him up along with his wife and children, and they were never seen again. This was like a practice of the dark Middle Ages, involving the arrest and annihilation of the entire family.

A new dentist named Reichelt, who appeared to be in his forties, moved into the vacant corner villa next to my parents. He called himself a "dentist artist." It quickly became known that his clientele consisted of high ranking members of the Nazi Party which made him very unpopular on our rather conservative street and no one sought his company or dental work.

Not long after he moved in, his maid, Klara, began piling flammable trash against our common chain link fence. The heap became larger each day, and besides being ugly, was unlawful because it would be a fire hazard during an air raid. Papa politely asked Klara to move the trash pile further back in her yard away from our side, but this was to no avail. It kept getting larger and finally began spilling over the fence and into Papa's garden. This time, he demanded that the piling of flammable trash be stopped, but Klara just replied that she only did what Mr. Reichelt ordered her to do.

Papa accidently met Mr. Reichelt one morning and brought up the subject, but the dentist arrogantly replied that what he did on his premises was nobody's business. Papa pointed out to him that it was definitely his business because the accumulation of trash between their properties was illegal and a dangerous fire hazard. Again, the dentist reacted very rudely so Papa finally told him that if they could not come to a neighborly understanding, he was going to turn the matter over to the local authorities. Thereupon Reichelt became furious and screamed that he would once and for all settle this as he stormed into the house. The very next morning, Papa received a threatening letter from the dentist, way out of line, referring to his high level contacts in the Party, some he even mentioned by name, and Papa would suffer serious consequences if he dared to criticize him, a respected member of the Party, or his actions any further. Mutti was terrified and begged Papa to control his justified rage and just avoid the next door neighbor. For now, there was also hope that in case of fire caused by fire bombs, the solid stone walls of my parents' house might protect them from that precarious side of the fence.

By this time, trying to prepare for the arrival of our own dream child was a nerve wracking experience because I needed so many items that were unavailable. The government issued expectant mothers special purchase permits which entitled us to a specific number of designated baby items, but these permits were not valid until the seventh month of pregnancy. (The "child loving" government waited that long in case there was a miscarriage.) Fortunately, Uncle Conny had already sent us a large baby bed ration card-free from his huge furniture store in Gleiwitz.

Elsa was in a more fortunate position since she had already something to show off, a live baby. Nevertheless, all the purchase permit allowances were scanty. She had also been lucky enough to get hold of a used stroller, even though it constantly lost one of its wheels. Just to be able to have this luxury was the most important thing. Her mother also did what Mutti did—cut old linen into pieces and use the outer parts as sheets for a baby bed, and the thinner, worn out center part as diapers, which were needed profusely. Disposable ones did not exist. The meager two sheets and two pillowcases granted on ration cards were insufficient when babies wet them constantly. Soap was also rationed. On the other hand, the government was very generous in supplying pregnant women with an extra quota of dairy products and grains, and my allowance far exceeded what I needed, so Mutti's household also benefitted.

Our ration card system was a puzzle in itself and an aggravation to both the customer and the shopkeepers. They were not really cards, but sheets of paper in different colors and shades, at least ten different ones for food alone, and the items were classified into the smallest quantity such as grams (not pounds), for example, 100 grams of butter. We guarded these sheets as if they were pure gold because they were irreplaceable. The month was divided into three ten-day segments. Too bad if the month had thirty-one days, because then you had to stretch the last segment to last eleven days.

There were separate cards for soap, cleaning materials and tobacco, plus a clothing card with a hundred points that had to last one year and also included sewing materials. The shopkeepers had their own share of problems. They had to cut off each individual little coupon with the designated weight from the appropriate card, and if you purchased several different types of items such as butter, flour and sugar, this required coupons from different cards. They collected them separately in individual little boxes behind the counter, carefully out of reach of the customers, to avoid any temptation on their part to reuse these precious coupons again. After closing, the shopkeeper had to start with his odious and lengthy "homework," having to paste the multitude of collected little coupons on large sheets of paper according to color, quantity and value, page after page, to then turn in that big bundle to the official distribution office, in order to receive credit to replenish his stock.

It was always to our disadvantage when our scanty grams of margarine or fat were spread on heavy, triple strength wax paper before being weighed. The thicker the paper, the stronger the dispute between customer and shopkeeper, because a few valuable grams were lost. Every store used the same method, and we wondered about their source of the identical heavy paper! The grocers also developed a special technique for weighing our rationed potatoes and vegetables. Before placing them on the scale, they put them first into huge paper cones they made out of several sheets of old newspapers, since this added a few more grams on the scales. Whoever wanted to live in peace with the grocers had better learn to accept this.

Meanwhile the whole family was eagerly looking forward to the arrival of our baby, and Papa even planned to provide us with an extra room. There was a spacious six-room apartment next to ours which was occupied only by Mrs. Kage, a widow for some time. She was willing to give up an adjacent room in return for lower rent. So Papa contracted with a handyman to have a door cut through the solid brick wall from our entrance hall. Dust and grime were everywhere, but we didn't mind the cleaning up process afterwards because we had gained one more spacious room and were ready for the baby's arrival.

Unfortunately the Allies continued their bombing of German towns with greater intensity and they usually arrived over Berlin after 9 p.m. The radio would warn us that they were on their way. The howling of our sirens soon followed and we would rush to our bomb shelter in the basement. About twenty tenants flocked together down there, waiting and hoping to be spared again as we heard the bombers roaring overhead and our anti-aircraft firing at them. There was no such thing as getting a good night's sleep.

With mounting defeats on the Eastern Front, times became even tougher. By now, the Soviets continuously swelled their ranks with an apparently inexhaustible supply of manpower and war materials from the U.S. and was steadily moving westward, following the retreating German forces toward our frontier. This had a drastic effect on the German people, and especially on my girlfriend Gerda, whose sister, Irmtraut, was working as a librarian in Insterburg, East Prussia. She had always been the studious type who lived quietly in her own world with her beloved books, although she had lately been very depressed from the loss of a dear friend on the Eastern Front.

On April 4, 1943, Gerda received an alarming phone call from her father in Domjüch concerning a telegram with the tragic news of Irmtraut's suicide. He had no further details, only the urgent request that he come to arrange for the funeral and take care of her belongings. Gerda's mother was too sick to go and her brother was with the army somewhere at the front. So it was up to her to accompany her father on that heartbreaking trip. All travel was restricted so he had to use the telegram to prove the urgency of their trip in order to obtain his and Gerda's train ticket to East Prussia.

After a strenuous half-day trip, they arrived in Insterburg, which is very near the eastern border of Germany. Here, they learned the sad details of how Gerda's sister died. She had been rooming with a family, and one evening had gone into the bathroom and the landlord wondered what took her so long, until he saw blood running out from under the door. Panic-stricken, he rushed in and found her dead on the floor in a pool of blood. She had used a kitchen knife to slash her wrists and neck arteries. He carried her to her bed, which also was soon soaked with blood, and that is how her father found her.

How desperate and lonely must a young woman be to take her life that way? During her last vacation at home she had repeatedly begged her father, a doctor, for poison in case of a crisis, which he had denied her. How should a father react? If he had consented to her request and she had taken the poison, he would have felt great guilt about her death. But now this. In November of that year she would have been twenty-three years old. The body was removed to the nearest crematorium in Tilsit. Though it was impossible to arrange a hasty funeral, they promised to send the urn with the ashes to their home as soon as possible. Gerda and her father were fortunate to find a room in a private home to stay overnight, and deeply depressed they departed for home the next morning to await the arrival of the urn and to have a proper burial.

Life and death were so close together. Weeks later, in July, my family was impatiently looking forward to the birth of my baby. Most excited was my mother-in-law whose birthday was July 11, and she had told everyone that I would give her a marvelous birthday present, her first grandchild. Sieghardt's two sisters were both single and there was no indication that they had any intentions to change their status. Everyone talked of a grandson only and my in-laws had even decided on the name of Heiso, which was an old name in Sieghardt's eight hundred-year old family tree. That our baby might be a girl wasn't even considered. Sieghardt and I were not prejudiced and I was prepared for any eventuality, and if it was a girl, I had secretly planned to give her the beautiful old name of Roswitha (pronounced Ross-Veeta) or white rose. This was a famous name in German literature dating back to the Middle Ages to Roswitha von Gandersheim, the first German female poet.

The nearby Hubertus Hospital had escaped bomb damage, so my child could be delivered there, and promptly on the evening of July 10, I went into heavy labor and was rushed to the hospital. I had a beautiful private room with bath and a balcony overlooking a large garden. Most of the experienced nurses were in the military and the current head nurse at the hospital was on leave.

But nothing happened that night besides heavy labor pains, and the next day the doctor determined that the baby had turned into a breech delivery which would require some surgery. So on my mother-in-law's birthday, everybody was alarmed instead of overjoyed. Sieghardt remained the entire day with me despite the protests of the nurses, until he was ordered to leave in the evening. Now Mutti appeared and intended to stay regardless of what the nurses said. She had a good personal reason because her first child, a boy, was also a breech delivery who died soon after birth and she always felt his death was due to the negligence of her doctor. My doctor could not be found either and Mutti insisted on staying until late that evening. Then a nurse got rid of her by taking me to the delivery room where she could not follow. Very upset, she was forced to go home.

During the day I had been given injections every three hours to increase the labor pains and this routine continued into my second night at the hospital. Now an assistant nurse sat at my bedside crocheting a delicate lace pattern and showed her displeasure at my groaning which had apparently made her lose some loops.

Early next morning, she said the doctor had called in and would soon be here, and finally after thirty-six hours of labor, at eight o'clock on the morning of July 12, 1943, a healthy and lovely baby girl saw the light of day. When they asked me for her name, my answer was promptly "Roswitha." Everybody in the family wondered about that afterwards. Like any proud parent, to me, she was the most beautiful baby I had ever seen.

When I awoke from a refreshing sleep in my room, though the surgery still pained me greatly, I couldn't resist the urge to admire my new slender figure. As an added temptation, there was a long mirror between the two windows and I very carefully slipped off my bed and started to walk slowly in that direction. But I didn't get very far before I noticed traces of blood on the floor and started screaming for help. My crocheting nurse from the previous night immediately burst in to straighten out the "hell raiser," and upon seeing the puddle of blood at my feet, it was she who now screamed, "Don't move! I will get the doctor." Suddenly, I was surrounded by a doctor and nurses, all in an uproar, and they gently picked me up and carried me back to my bed. My doctor again could not be found, but his replacement was skilled, friendly and available, and I liked him even better than my own doctor. He was very concerned and instructed me never to try to get out of bed on my own again.

After the excitement had died down, I was alone in my room when the air raid sirens began howling, announcing a daytime air raid on Berlin. Immediately, all babies, including my little girl, were taken into the bomb shelter underneath the hospital. Suddenly, my door flew open and a nurse burst in, grabbed some clothes from my closet and threw them at me with the abrupt order to get dressed at once. "I can't do that without assistance," I called out, but she was already hastily leaving and shouted, "When the bombs are falling, believe me, you can!" and away she ran. What was I supposed to do now? Since one can only follow one order at a time, I stayed right where I was and crawled deeper down under the covers. (How was that supposed to protect me?) Alone and terrified, I waited for the bombing, but luckily, the Allied aircraft did not reach Berlin and I breathed a sigh of relief when the sirens blared the "all clear" signal.

When the head nurse returned two days later, there was a significant change in the discipline and atmosphere. She must have heard about the lax and indifferent attitude that had been afforded the patients in her absence, and things changed for the better abruptly. There had been open hostility against Sieghardt and me because he was not in uniform when most of the other men his age had been drafted, and that I was in a private room and had my own doctor. The nurses had been objecting to Sieghardt's evening visits, but this changed now, too. Also, I had been advised to stay in the hospital longer than usual, but Sieghardt had already hired a retired private nurse who could care for me at home so that the baby and I could leave sooner. Finally, the three of us were at home together.

Living under constant air attacks became a way of life for us, and our routine started with the first warning howl of the air raid sirens. All windows had to be opened so that the glass wouldn't shatter from the concussions of the explosions because window glass had become scarce. Doors to homes had to remain unlocked during the night alarms, in order to provide shelter for people caught in the streets. Although unlocked doors would appear to be an open invitation for stealing, it was not a problem because there was the death penalty for anyone caught stealing during an alarm. Then we rushed with our daily necessities into our bomb shelter. We even had our fur coats in the cellar year round, which may have looked foolish in the summer, but they could serve as a bed if need be.

The baby carriage was outfitted at all times with an emergency supply of diapers and baby food, and as the most important item, a big wet cloth. If the house was bombed, the cloth was to be thrown over the baby carriage with the hood up to provide breathing space under there so that the baby would not suffocate from the blinding dust of collapsing walls. We adults also made damp cloth masks for our own use. It was always nerve wracking to hear the radio announce that an attack on Berlin was imminent. Often the lights would go out and the walls would shake like an earthquake from the detonating bombs. The heavy iron sheets leaning against the outside of the building to protect the low basement windows would be lifted up and blown away in all directions with a big clatter by the sucking pressure of an exploding aerial mine—the kind that would tear your lungs apart even at a far distance if you were caught outside. But as long as we could hear all that and feel the vibration without the solid walls collapsing, we knew we were not hit—this time—but somebody else close by.

Many times, day or night, little Roswitha would be carried from her bed to the baby carriage, taken into the cellar, and then back upstairs again when the air raid was over. Of course, she reacted with crying at such repeated confusion, while we felt like we were sleepwalking. In no time our beloved dream child had turned into a non-stop "scream child." No wonder!

Our nerve-wracking life also took its toll on my system and my natural milk supply for the baby was barely adequate. Mutti was concerned about this and insisted on supplementing my diet with *Mehlsuppe* (gruel), a mixture of water, milk and flour seasoned with a pinch of salt, in that order. I hated it. She made it as thin as possible so that I could drink it. I dutifully followed her orders and forced the vile mixture down several times a day, always holding my breath. It may have helped to increase my milk supply for the baby, but my own girth became more noticeable. This was the wrong kind of success and there was no way that I could get larger clothes.

Meanwhile, the British had started dropping phosphorus incendiary bombs, illegal weapons that ignited in open air. There was no way of fighting them with the regular fire hoses because water only activated another explosion of the firebrand into many more unmanageable fragments. They had to be quickly covered by hand with sand to cut off any oxygen before it ate its way through everything, burning any material and people in its path. Furniture and other moveable belongings would be rescued out of burning houses and deposited in the street, and if the owners were unable to immediately claim them, they were picked up by government trucks and held at public storage until people could prove ownership. Everyone was advised to label their belongings with a permanent identification mark such as name, telephone number or address, which was usually done with an engraving tool or permanent ink. I still have some items that have this engraved information on the back.

During the war, there was an agreement among relatives and friends to leave a second and third address where we could be found if we had to flee our primary residence or were bombed out. Since we in Berlin were still so far from the front lines, our home seemed to be safe enough to serve as the central point for such information, and this proved to be very valuable in the future.

It seemed we never received any good news. The next bad one came from the Southern Front that the German-Italian fighting in North Africa had ended in May with a breakdown of the Axis forces and surrender to the British. In July, we learned that the Allies were even landing on Italian soil on the island of Sicily. Fascism had collapsed and Mussolini had been stripped of all of his power by order of the Italian King Victor Emmanuel III, and was being held prisoner high on the desolate Abruzzi mountains northeast of Rome. Papa commented, "Too bad we Germans no longer have an emperor to do the same with Hitler." Unfortunately, he was his majesty himself, with no higher authority. Nevertheless, it was rumored that a bomb had been planted in his airplane. Since nothing had happened so far, it either must have been found, did not explode, or the rumor was only wishful thinking.

Our next shock concerned Elsa and Heinz. Heinz had been expecting draft orders, but was not prepared for what he received. Being tall and impressively Nordic, he was called to the *Waffen-SS*, a feared and hated SS-unit that had recently been incorporated into the German armed forces as a kind of elite troop. Many men were forcibly drafted into the SS by now, and were no longer volunteers. Now he was one of the victims. Heinz knew that trying to escape assignment to such a dubious and frightening Nazi "honor" seemed hopeless, but was determined to at least try. He sent a humble but diplomatic petition to his

Elsa, Kristian and Heinz

draft board requesting assignment to the infantry since his father and father-in-law served as infantry officers in World War I, as did other members of his family, and he would like to have the honor to follow in the family tradition and proudly wear the field-gray of the German army. He sent the petition off in haste in order not to miss the deadline to appear. Everything was considerably exaggerated, but who was to judge?

After nervous days of waiting, between hope and despair, a new draft notice appeared in the mailbox, this time for assignment to the infantry. They never thought they could be so happy about receiving a draft notice they had dreaded for years. Soon afterward, Heinz was assigned to an installation near Berlin to undergo a short infantry training course, and upon completion, was quickly promoted to an officer cadet and rushed to the Italian front, right into the massacre of Monte Cassino about seventy-five miles south of Rome.

The tide of the war had definitely turned in favor of the Allies and Hitler's once very successful offensive war had deteriorated into a hopeless defensive, one with constant retreat occurring on all frontiers. Nevertheless, Goebbels proclaimed, "He who doubts our victory is a traitor!" and any opinion expressed to the contrary was punished accordingly. Germany's arms industry was severely crippled by the incessant air raids.

My brother Günter was commanding a torpedo boat that was fighting the U.S. convoys in the Atlantic to hinder their constant delivery of new war materials to the British and Soviets. We rarely heard from him, and that one time that he came home for a surprise short leave he didn't tell us very much concerning his duties, only some personal experiences. Once he unexpectedly had to share his cabin on the torpedo boat for several days and nights with a high ranking commander. I asked him if it didn't make him nervous as a young officer to be sharing such a confined space with an officer of such high rank. He just laughed, "No problem. Once you have seen your high commander in long johns it becomes very easy to talk with him."

Life in Berlin became more and more catastrophic as some parts of the city were constantly in flames, and we lived with uncertainty and fear from hour to hour. Goebbels indirectly admitted the desperate situation for us in the capital when he ordered most of the school children to be evacuated from the city. My girlfriend Lucie, who I met in the U.S.

years later, personally experienced this evacuation order and told me how it had been carried out. She was about eleven years old in July 1943 when her entire school was forcefully relocated without notification to the parents. All of the children were transported by freight train to an undisclosed location and parents were not told of the children's where-abouts. Her mother searched for her throughout Germany for five days until she finally located her in Ziegenhals, Upper Silesia, and demanded her child back. Her arrival was kept a secret because all the children were crying for their mothers. Lucie was quietly whisked away and they both returned to Berlin where her mother kept her hidden. Many of her less fortunate classmates later fell victim to the Soviets.

Goebbels also ordered the immediate evacuation of all pre-school children from Berlin. Where could you go that was safe? I tried to ig-nore the order and our families had constant discussions, one day fa-voring the evacuation and the next day being against it. It was a heart-rendering decision. No one wanted to be separated from their family in these trying times. If we had to perish, why not all together? However, after more devastating air raids shook the buildings, not only Goebbels, but my whole family, insisted on my evacuation with the baby. Hasty consideration was given to the little town of Zerbst about fifty miles southwest of Berlin which had never experienced an air raid and where Mutti and Papa had owned considerable property since 1924. It included a multi-family house and a farm machinery business run by my Uncle Bodo who lived there with my Aunt Grete, two daughters, a son, and lately a tiny grandson. We had always kept two furnished rooms in the house, which had a private entrance for our own use, and Günter and I had spent many carefree summer vacations there during our school days. However, both of these rooms had been requisitioned by the authori-ties the previous year to house bombed-out people from one of the big cities.

After a telephone call to Aunt Grete, she promised to accommodate me and the baby in her own apartment. Heavy-hearted I packed up for immediate evacuation while being interrupted in the process by the howling of air raid sirens. It was on August 7, Roswitha was not even four weeks old and by now we lovingly called her Vita (Vee-ta), when Sieghardt bundled us up in great haste to depart for Zerbst in his firm's delivery truck. To use any kind of car for private purposes like ours was strictly forbidden and risky, but so was our entire life. Necessity knows no laws, and we took the risk. Our small emergency baggage had quickly escalated to a pretty sizeable bundle, realizing that everything could be lost in Berlin in one single air raid. In our suburb there had been attacks already on purely civilian targets with considerable losses.

Short goodbyes are the least painful, but ours still was tearful and heart-breaking. Everyone was terribly depressed to watch me leave with my baby clasped in my arms. Our drive took only a few hours and Sieghardt had to return home that same day. I kissed him goodbye with a heavy heart. Would we ever see each other again? Though this thought was on both of our minds, neither one of us uttered a word. We smiled bravely, postponing tears for later. He departed immediately, lovingly provided with one of Aunt Grete's ducks and other country products which were not available in Berlin. In my absence, he would eat all of his meals with my family and I knew he would be in good hands with Mutti. Thus came the abrupt end of a dream. What unexpected disasters would next be looming over the horizon?

No Rest for the Weary

Living with my relatives in Zerbst was a pleasant relief from the continual air raids we experienced in Berlin, but the baby and I increased the household to eight and I realized the inconvenience we caused. I gave Aunt Grete my food ration card, and some household money, but I could not contribute any additional food. This created a problem because my relatives now had to share with me the extra food supply they got from the farmers, who were their long-time business customers. Fortunately, there were fruit trees and berry bushes in the garden that Papa had planted many years ago, and, Aunt Grete had a small flock of chickens and ducks running around in an enclosure. All of the household tasks were divided, and I tried to fit in.

Aunt Grete would often send me with the baby carriage for a stroll in the nearby public park. She said the fresh air there was good for the baby, but it was mostly because a crying Vita was setting a bad example for her own little grandson who joined her in a not very melodious duet at the top of his lungs. So, I spent many happy afternoons strolling with my baby carriage through the park that I knew so well from many carefree summer vacations. In the 1920s, I had even ridden here in town in the last horse-drawn street cars.

Zerbst, with its medieval relics of walls, old battlements and mighty ghostly towers reminded me vividly of Münster. On our way to the park, we would pass under a massive stone gate of an ancient former fortress, and I always felt that I was entering into another world. It was a rambling park with many old trees, blooming bushes and benches in shady promenades. I cherished my hours there alone with no alarms, no bombing and no relatives, only peaceful co-existence with Mother Nature. The weather cooperated, too. Little Vita thoroughly enjoyed watching the leaves blowing in the trees. Looking at her I thought, "Oh, you little devil with an angel's face. Why couldn't you be this peaceful at home?"

With my enthusiasm for history, I loved to stroll by the summer castle of the Princes of Anhalt/Zerbst, whose most famous ancestor was Catherine the Great, Empress of Russia.

Occasionally, Sieghardt would pop in for a brief visit, and he always felt like he was depriving us of our food when he stayed for a meal. But, he never left without being lovingly provided with farm products like eggs, bacon and a duck to take back to Mutti since these were rationed back home.

In Berlin, the most recent satirical saying was, "Enjoy the war because peace will be worse!" an ironic attitude which gave way to grim sarcastic humor and fear of the unknown future, and was indicative of the constant widening rift between the government and the people. By September 8, Italy had surrendered to the Allies. Nevertheless, on September 13, Goebbels fed us another so-called huge success story. He heralded in gigantic headlines how, on Hitler's order, paratroopers in a bold surprise stroke had freed Mussolini from his captivity on the Gran Sasso in the inaccessible Abruzzi mountains near Rome where the new Italian government had held Mussolini prisoner since July 25, 1943. It was indeed an heroic act on the part of our German paratroopers, but we asked ourselves WHY? Were these efforts worth it to risk the lives of our soldiers with high losses when Italy had surrendered unconditionally just a few days earlier? The Fascist regime had been dissolved months ago. Now Mussolini was Hitler's guest of honor, two hot-headed dictators together. Of what benefit could that be to us?

By now one of my cousins was expecting her second baby and she would soon need more space for her expanding family. (As fate would have it, she became a widow before the baby was ever born). So I thought to myself, "Why upset my relatives with a new space problem?" It was time for Vita and me to return home. On our first wedding anniversary, I was here alone and Sieghardt was in Berlin and I wanted us to be together as a family for whatever little time we may have left. On October 13, 1943, Italy had declared war on Germany. What was I doing here in Zerbst? So, without further ado, one day in the latter part of October, Sieghardt showed up with his family's delivery truck to fetch us home again. A quick farewell and thank you, and we were on our way back to Berlin.

Our house was still there, undamaged, and our apartment was just the way I had left it before my three-month sojourn into the country. One of the first things I noticed was that the garbage collection had changed. Only the driver of the truck was a German, but all of the other workers were prisoners of war. That told me we had a growing shortage of our own men. The POWs often opened the lids from the cans to search for anything that might be edible or wearable, although this rummaging was strictly forbidden as was our leaving something in there for them. Orders here, orders there, orders everywhere. As soon as I heard the garbage truck arriving next door, I dashed out to the full can in the rear of our yard and pretended to put something in it while leaving a brown paper bag on top containing oat flakes and an apple. This had to be done with the greatest caution because you never knew who might be spying on you.

I had just returned to our glass enclosed Florida room when I saw the POW coming, and as I watched, he noticed the paper bag and, looking around furtively, hastily slipped it under his bulky jacket. Then, he slowly rolled the full can from the back of the yard to the street, and as he passed close to the Florida room with its clear visibility in all directions, he risked a glance towards me. As our eyes met for a split second, I smiled and his cheerless face lit up for a moment as if he knew that the bag was from me. That short scene made me determine to continue my modest contributions, and as the garbage truck made its weekly visit, there was always a little package of something to eat where it could be found without being obvious. I was not the only one who was doing this, but no one ever admitted it or would even talk about it because POWs were only a statistic to the Nazi government.

By now little Vita was four months old and we arranged to have her baptized on Papa's birthday, November 13. Our pastor would hold the ceremony in the early afternoon in the nearby Johannes Church in Schlachtensee where we had been married. We all went there together, pushing the baby carriage along for the thirty-minute walk. There were no church bells to ring because all three had been confiscated and melted down for production of war material. The only bell that had escaped this fate was sitting in the belfry, our thirteenth century *Zuckerhut*, a sugar-loaf shaped bell that had been given to the church at its founding in 1912. It was the oldest one in Berlin and did not swing or have a clapper, but rather, was struck from the outside seven times during the

Lord's prayer, one time for each of the seven requests. Therefore, it was called the Lord's Prayer bell, and was the only one heard during the baptism ceremony. Vita was surprisingly quiet during the holy rite, which had to be brief so that we would not get caught on the streets during the next air raid. Afterwards, she was entered in the parish register as Roswitha Elisabeth Linda, named after the two proud grandmothers.

Here we are with our bundle of joy—Roswitha. (1944)

It was fortunate that we had not postponed Vita's baptism because shortly thereafter our church was heavily bombed with even the organ destroyed. There was no way to make repairs, so the rain and snow caused further damage. Though out of destruction can come restoration as it happened following the war. With the generous financial assistance of the American Episcopal Church in Westfield, Massachusetts, under Reverend Hall and Bishop Lawrenz, the church was restored. The Westfield congregation even sent food packages which were gratefully received in those post-war days. In 1950, the vicar, Mary Heilner, helped for two years to rebuild the "House of Youth" right on the ruin of the old one on Ilsensteinweg number 19, and it is named the Mary-Heilner Home to this day, and parish members visit each other in friendship across the ocean.

About two weeks after our church had been bombed, the Berlin zoo was blasted to bits in a massive attack. Some of the wild animals raged frantically through the streets and had to be shot. The Kaiser Wilhelm Memorial Church went up in flames as well, and everything around it, including the Kurfürstendamm, the famous central boulevard.

Due to the increasing horror of Allied bombings, Papa and our neighbor, Mrs. Vogel, decided to jointly construct an underground bunker in the back yard as an emergency shelter in addition to our basements. They took down the common fence and drew a horseshoe shaped outline in the soil with entrances on both ends. It had to be curved because the middle afforded the most protection against bomb splinters. We realized it would be a task far beyond the capabilities of our few family members, even though Maria stood there already, armed with an enormous coal shovel to start the project. But fortunately, Mrs. Vogel had some connections. Although her business in the city had been completely destroyed, she still had contact with many of her long-time loyal workers.

A few days later, at the end of November, about a half-dozen men arrived with far better equipment than our simple garden tools. With the required skill, they started to dig a trench about seven feet deep, securing the walls with whatever planking could be found to prevent a cave in. Additional material was needed to support the one hundred-foot curved roof, but our work team overcame all obstacles surprisingly well. Some would leave for a while and return with what was needed. We didn't ask where it came from since we knew that nearby building ruins were abandoned with their owners gone or dead. This way, long, heavy metal sheets appeared that could be used as a roof strong enough to support a thick layer of the soil that had been excavated from the trench. It took five days of hard labor and we did our part to feed them and to pay generously. Strangely enough, the workers never requested any money for the material, and it was definitely not the time to wonder about it afterwards.

In the end, our home-made shelter was nothing more than a covered slit trench that rose about five feet above the ground and looked like a giant worm bent in pain. Our primitive bunker could not compare to the professionally built one of our Nazi neighbor, Mr. Reichelt. A detachment of a dozen soldiers from an engineering unit arrived and constructed a concrete bunker in his back yard at a time when every soldier and all material was critically needed in the war effort. In addition to providing a bunker to protect their friend, the Nazis supplied him with food that was no longer available on the market. Our entire street was in silent revolt, but we had no choice but to be concerned about our own survival and that became our major goal in life.

Meanwhile I had reached the point where I was only able to breast feed Vita once a day and had to supplement her diet with a baby food called *Alete*. This was a white powder in a can bought at a pharmacy and diluted with water at home. According to the label, it was delicious and nutritious, enriched with vitamins and minerals vital for a healthy baby. Fortunately, Vita liked the taste, and I believed the label and bought it regularly. Our long-time pharmacist had his drug store just around the corner which made it very convenient for me.

While buying the *Alete*, I always took a small bottle along and asked him for "baby oil." He had children of his own, including a little daughter also named Roswitha, so he was very understanding of my needs, and always graciously filled the bottle without question as to its true use. This oil was a wonderful supplement to my cooking and it came without a ration card. Since my little scheme worked so well, I eventually increased the size of the bottle, hoping it wouldn't matter, until one day he paused, looked at me and winked, "This goes on the baby's bottom." We both knew what the oil was being used for and that the law was being bent. I just smiled, while he gave me a freshly filled bottle, indicating that the subject needed no further discussion. However, from that point on, I never increased the size of the "baby oil" bottle and always made sure I did my shopping when there were no other customers in the pharmacy.

Sieghardt had recently been suffering from tormenting headaches and a high fever. The doctor soon diagnosed it as meningitis. We had a sad Christmas in 1943 as hundreds of Royal Air Force bombers carried out a devastating early morning raid on the city. Fortunately, our suburb was not severely hit this time. Sieghardt was too ill to go church and I decorated a little Christmas tree in our bedroom, and the baby and I spent Holy Eve at his bedside. It was not easy trying to be cheerful as we spent our second Christmas in our young marriage. Finally the doctor recommended that Sieghardt leave Berlin to convalesce at a quieter place, but where? Most hotels had been confiscated for military rest centers. We wrote to every hotel for which I could find an address, at least twenty, and requested a room for a young family of three, whose little baby was very quiet and seldom cried. In fact, Vita cried day and night, and I optimistically hoped that this would promptly cease in quiet surroundings as it did in the peaceful park in Zerbst. But nobody wanted us.

But then suddenly a miracle occurred. The Hotel Post in Neustadt, a small village in the Black Forest, accepted our reservation for a stay of four weeks, effective February 1, 1944. We could not believe our luck and I told little Vita the good news right away, and urged her to be well behaved from now on, but she couldn't care less and went on crying. Everyone was happy for us and relieved to see the three of us to be leaving soon because during these war times, it was important for families to spread out so that the lucky survivors could assist those who had not been so fortunate. We would have to depart by the end of January, in less than two weeks. There was much planning and packing to be done to get out of Berlin again, away from the increasing alarms, fire, bombs and destruction.

One day before our departure, the mailman delivered a postcard from the hotel regretfully canceling our reservation with no reason given. But we were supposed to leave tomorrow! Although Sieghardt was still sick, he had gone to the office that morning to take care of some final arrangements at work and I stood there numbly looking at that distressing postcard when a devilish thought crossed my mind. What if the message never reached us? It was not uncommon for mail to be lost in the midst of bomb fires. In desperation, I called Mutti and asked her to come over right away so that we could discuss this dilemma alone with our female intuition. The one thing we did not need right now was the male logic of, "It's been canceled so we can't go."

Mutti and I debated the issue from all angles and we decided that when Goebbels ordered the women with small children out of Berlin, he didn't tell them where to go or even care if they had a place to turn to. So, why should we be concerned about a canceled reservation when there was no other alternative for us? Traveling across the country in war time was a risky venture by itself, but how could we stand by and let this trip elude us? Hitler's "mother and child" centers would be available for us to use along the way. Blessed be that Nazi idea now. It even looked brilliant at the moment, and it seemed very unlikely that we could end up as homeless people. Why not go straight to Neustadt to claim our promised reservations and then see what would happen at our unexpected arrival?

Sieghardt came home shortly thereafter and went about final preparations for the trip, totally unaware of what had happened in his ab-

NO REST FOR THE WEARY   291

sence. I watched him work, free of worry. Why disturb his peace of mind? So I brushed off any second thoughts about the risk we would be taking, thinking that we would cross that bridge when we came to it.

We had just accomplished the nearly impossible by successfully obtaining train tickets at a time when every kind of transportation was subject to priorities for war interests. Our ration cards had been exchanged for travel coupons. How could we be stopped now? I was much more eager than Sieghardt to make this trip and get away from that hellish city where we lived in fear day and night. We probably would never see our home again because sooner or later it was bound to be hit during an air raid and if it happened, dear God, let it be during our absence.

The next day proceeded as planned. Vita was with Mutti and the two grandmothers took care of getting her ready with all of her paraphernalia, such as a bag with baby food, her blanket, clean diapers and a separate bag for dirty ones to be washed later. They would really accumulate on a train trip of over twenty-four hours. We packed more than we normally would since that might be our only possessions in the future. The train left in the evening. There were no reservations possible for seats, so it was imperative that we arrive early with our luggage and hopefully get it aboard and find a seat for each of us. We took one last sad look at our beloved home, locked the door and left with our voluminous luggage for the train station. It was amazing what we could carry.

Luckily, it was only a short walk to the S-Bahn station and we arrived safely downtown on the platform, by now in total blackout. It seemed like everyone else had the same idea as we did about arriving early because it was crowded already. Soon our train arrived and stopped with an ear-splitting shriek of the wheels. Now there was pandemonium as everyone was pushing and shoving, trying to exit and board at the same time, hopelessly jamming the doors. Some people even tried to get on by climbing through the windows.

Suddenly above the din of the crowd, I heard Mutti's voice shouting my name, and I shouted back until finally we found each other in the dark. Now we all huddled around our luggage with the baby on Mutti's arm while Sieghardt fought his way onto the train with a suitcase and was lost right away in the throng of people. We soon heard him calling us from a window nearby. He had claimed a seat for me in

the compartment next to his. (He rode in a separate compartment reserved for the disabled.) What luck! Now I had the seemingly impossible task to make my way inside with a suitcase.

It appeared hopeless to reach him since we all bumped and stepped
on each other. He stood in the passageway and dragged in the baggage
which both of our mothers heaved up to him. Everything finally seemed
to be inside, although I had lost count of all the pieces in the darkness.
The aisles were only scantily lit by dim lamps. The last thing handed to
me was the baby, my most precious bundle. I put her on my seat in the
darkened compartment and went back to the window while Sieghardt
went outside to say goodbye to our brave mothers. As he turned around
in the darkness, he stumbled over an object left sitting on the platform,
exclaiming in pain, "What damn idiot left his suitcase standing here?"
He briefly turned on his flashlight and immediately recognized his own
suitcase which, up to this point, had not even been missed. I couldn't
help chuckling at the situation.

By then it was high time for our mothers to return home for fear of
being caught downtown by an early alarm. We called a last good-bye to
each other, while Sieghardt dragged his heavy suitcase on board and
tried to find a place for it because there was luggage everywhere, and
the aisles were jammed with people who had not found a seat. We had
brought a small hammock for the baby to sleep in, with all her own
bedding and we fastened it now between my luggage rack and the one
across from me, to create a comfortable bed for Vita. In theory this had
been great, but in reality, it looked more like torture. The distance between the luggage racks was much too short and the hammock didn't
stretch out very far. We heaved Vita in anyway but she looked as if she
had been dumped into a sack and must have felt like it because she immediately started to cry loud and bitterly. So the hammock came down
again. Luckily we recognized faint contours by now as our eyes adjusted
to the darkness. There was no alternative left but for me to hold my
voluminous bundle on my lap, staying awake most of the night for fear
she might slip to the floor if I dozed off.

During the night we stopped several times in the open country in
total darkness to avoid being seen by Allied bombers who were attacking the town we were approaching. As early morning arrived, Vita awakened and before she could remember that it was time to cry, I quickly

put something in her mouth to pacify her. And then, I began to search for the bag with baby food which luckily was within reach in the luggage rack above my seat. Next came the unpleasant task of changing the diaper in a crowded compartment with other people sitting around you. Fortunately, another woman came to my rescue and held the bedding while I fished out a clean diaper from one bag and carefully deposited the dirty one in another. Everyone was watching and I was expecting some complaints from other passengers, my companions in misery, but they were obviously too tired even for that.

Meanwhile they also had their own difficulties. The restrooms became a problem for everyone because some people who could not find seats had taken them over as their traveling compartment, using the commode as a seat they shared, taking turns to sit down, and refusing to give it up. This meant that every time the train stopped, people had to rush off to the public restrooms on the station platform. In no time long waiting lines formed and they had to make sure that the train did not leave without them.

It would take us the entire day to reach our destination so I started thinking about feeding my husband who hadn't eaten since early in the afternoon of the previous day. We had to bring along our own food tucked inside the baby's food bag. I left Vita on my seat and took some of the sandwiches and squeezed through the crowded aisle to him in the next compartment, and was just handing him the food when I heard someone shouting, "There is a seat occupied only by a baby!" I barely got back in time to grab my child and hold her on my lap again, and then proceeded to munch on my sandwich.

On February 1, 1944, we reached the major railroad junction at Frankfurt around 10 a.m. and as we slowly entered the city it was shocking to see the widespread air raid destruction just as in Berlin. We had to change trains here for one that went to the South, and getting all of our luggage off without the help of our mothers looked like an impossible task. At least it was daylight and strangers lent us a hand. The first thing we immediately saw were big signs for the "mother and child" facilities close by on the platform and we decided to take advantage of them. We ended up in clean, well-equipped accommodations staffed with nurses to help you with the baby. They also provided us with a simple, but tasty hot soup without asking for money or food stamps, although we left a donation at each facility we visited on our trip south throughout the day. I had been on this train before. First in 1926 as a child en route to the Wildbad spa, and then later as a teenager on my way to Switzerland. What a change of circumstances with this ride.

Finally, in the evening, we made our last troublesome transfer, this time to a little old fashioned choo-choo train that chugged along slowly puffing up the mountains to our final destination. It was a peaceful and beautiful ride through a winter wonderland that made me forget all about the calamity of a canceled hotel reservation. The rail route twisted and turned as it climbed the mountain and the scenery became more breathtaking with every turn. No wonder that the fairy tale of Hansel and Gretel originated in these dark pine forests. The ugly war was left behind like a bad nightmare. As Sieghardt looked at the peaceful countryside, he said with a sigh of relief, "Now the worst is over," which brought me back to the harsh reality of what might await us at the hotel.

Suddenly our little train stopped with a jerk and we had arrived in the remote, peaceful and snowbound village of Neustadt. We were the only passengers getting off, and found no porters or taxi, only deep snow and moonlight. Being so close to the dilemma, I didn't have an overdose of courage left, but if I allowed myself now to get weak and confess, we were in deep trouble. So be it. I said to myself, if there is no turning back, one has to go forward.

A small office on the station platform was still open. Sieghardt persuaded the official on duty to loan us one of the largest baggage carts so we could move our luggage to the hotel, with the baby on top. We promised to return it in the morning. "Just keep going straight ahead," the man advised. We were obviously on the main street, only moderately lit at night with the town already asleep. It was too dark to get a good glimpse. Caught in a new snowfall, we began pushing and pulling the heavily loaded cart through the deep snow and got stuck alternately on the path that seemed endless to us, but which the man had described as short. It was exhausting. Finally we found ourselves in front of our hotel whose entrance was lit by an ornamental hanging lamp. What a nice looking place from the outside, I thought. Let's see how friendly it will be from the inside.

Sieghardt knocked on the locked door and a disabled old man

limped out who seemed quite friendly and, without asking any questions, assisted us to the best of his ability in moving our luggage inside. I was particularly interested in getting everything inside as quickly as possible, this hopefully being the first step to success. We were shown into a large entrance hall in which the lights had already been dimmed at that late hour. A man, obviously the hotel owner, was busy with paper work behind the large reception desk, working under a hanging lamp which provided some extra light. I noticed the place was arranged with comfortable seating areas. Now the man raised his head and demanded to know what was going on so unexpectedly at this late hour, and upon seeing us, asked what we were doing here at this time of night.

Sieghardt dropped the last of the luggage and approached the desk, announcing in his most polite and charming manner, that we had finally arrived. He presented the hotel's reservation card, and I heard him say, "You have a lovely place here in a wonderful region. Here is our hotel confirmation and we are looking forward to some very restful weeks." Watching the owner's puzzled face, I quickly settled myself on a bench in the back of the entrance hall and pretended to be very busy with the baby while I strained to hear the conversation.

Pointing to Sieghardt's reservation card, the owner said in disbelief," But this reservation was canceled days ago!" and immediately the two got into a heated discussion, but I could not hear clearly what was being said. Too bad because the dispute seemed to intensify. I saw Sieghardt pointing again and again to the written confirmation with today's date and the owner shaking his head with a negative gesture. Now I began to get worried. Was no room available for us? Oh my God, had I gone too far this time with my forever positive attitude? It looked like my little scheme may have backfired. I watched Sieghardt shake his head in desperation and then heard him state loudly and firmly, "I don't know anything about a cancellation of our reservation." How true. "How can my family be stranded here now?" That was exactly what I had been afraid of, too.

Suddenly it became very quiet at the desk. Why? I risked another glance at them. Now both men were looking at me and the baby, who, in our favor, was cooperating by being a little angel and not crying for a change. I tried to appear as helpless and desperate as possible, which was not very hard to do after an exhausting journey of more than thirty hours. A long thoughtful silence followed and hung threateningly over us. Suddenly, between my hope and desperation, I noticed the owner reluctantly push something toward Sieghardt and saw him pick it up. That must have been a room key. I felt like jumping for joy, but a maid was already approaching me to go give us a hand with our belongings. What a relief. As I followed her, the thought crossed my mind that if I had known how difficult and risky travel had become, especially with a baby, would I still have....? I discarded that thought immediately because we were here now and fortune favors the brave.

The hotel promised to return our borrowed cart to the train station and we were escorted to the second floor where our room was located on the far end of a pleasant looking carpeted hallway that was decorated with fresh green plants on small tables. The maid opened the last door and switched on the lights to reveal a very spacious and cozy room which was tastefully furnished with twin beds and a reading corner with a table, armchairs and a lamp. Two more maids followed us into the room with a crib for the baby which the hotel had thoughtfully supplied. What more could we ask for?

I put little Vita down and as soon as we were alone I began to laugh to no end as I danced around the room. Sieghardt looked at me as if I had lost my mind. What was so funny after all his trouble to get us in here? He wanted to give me a detailed description of the unforeseen problems he had faced downstairs to obtain the room, but I was no longer interested in the details I had missed earlier. Ignoring his disappointment in my lack of interest in his troubles, I stopped dancing and began rummaging in my handbag and finally fished out the corpus delicti. "Take a look." He stopped his success story in mid-sentence as I handed him the postcard. Puzzled, he read the short message, and then read it again, and became very irritated. "But this is…" "No, it was. You know how easily mail gets lost these days or delayed. Well, this time, it got lost in my handbag, since this was our only chance." He was completely speechless and didn't know whether to be happy or hurt that he didn't know earlier about the room cancellation. I assured him that he would not have been able to act so innocently if he had known, and that was logic even a man could accept.

At that moment there was a knock at the door and I quickly hid the damaging evidence back in my handbag. It was the maid and she had returned to make up our beds and ask for our sheets. "What sheets?" I asked. "The ones you brought with you," she replied. But of course we had not brought any since we were not aware that this was now common practice in hotels in this fourth year of the war. The maid had no choice but to notify the hotel proprietor's wife that the unexpected guests had not even brought any sheets. The wife appeared shortly thereafter with a frown on her face, but also carrying a set of the hotel's bed linen, and the maid proceeded to make up the beds. We were finally settled in, comfy and cozy, but that was a delusion. Vita's span of good will was used up and she started to cry again in a healthy voice, and there seemed to be nothing that would calm her down. Finally she could only be stopped by putting a bottle with *Alete* into her wide, open mouth. Thank goodness it worked. We were very eager to reserve what was left of our good impression. The baby's feeding schedule had been violated for a long time anyway.

When Vita finally fell asleep again we ventured downstairs. Although the hour was late, we were invited into the dining room. It was a friendly place with several windows. Most tables, and there were many, were set already for breakfast the next morning. All the other guests had already retired to their rooms to enjoy an alarm-free night. We were served and hungrily ate a tasty meal of hot soup and sandwiches, which was both good and plentiful. It was so different here than in Berlin with no pressure and everyone being so pleasant. They didn't even ask us for our ration cards. Usually if you didn't present them first you were not served. Here, they merely asked that we turn them in the next day, week by week for the duration of our stay. Sieghardt and I couldn't believe how fortunate we were to have found this wonderful place. He reached across the table and squeezed my hand. "Blessed be your handbag." No one would ever have known what that meant—except us.

When we returned to the room, we found the baby still sound asleep and were eager to do the same. We were looking forward optimistically to the luxury of an undisturbed night's sleep without any air raids, a pleasure that we had missed for years. Outside a silent snow fell, lulling us to sleep. But Vita had plans of her own. Shortly after midnight, we had just closed our eyes, she opened hers and started to cry, which was her usual schedule at home, accurate like an alarm clock. First she whimpered softly but my usual humming this time was to no avail. Instead, she began to try out all different scales of her healthy vocal cords. We had neighbors in the adjoining room, separated only by a locked, wooden door, so I had to get up to quiet her down. Throughout the night, she would follow her usual routine, crying regularly every two to three hours according to the different alarms she was used to from home. I shuttled her between her crib and my bed for the rest of the night. Finally, at daybreak, I fell into an exhausted sleep, aching all over, but still unaware that that was only the prelude for the next disaster.

I soon awoke with a mysterious pain and found I was lying in a puddle of blood. Why? There was no logical reason for it. Terrified, I jumped out of bed, at once wide awake and in despair—not about me, but about the hotel's fresh bed linen which had to last for one week. I hastily stripped my bed of the soiled sheet and tried to wash out the fatal red puddle with our gooey grey soap, but to no avail. Fortunately, we were sleeping in twin beds. By now we were all awake, Vita peacefully singing and Sieghardt highly alarmed about what to do. He peeked out the door trying desperately to catch our maid in the corridor. Miraculously she appeared and Sieghardt offered her a good sum of money for a clean sheet. But no luck. Even though she needed the money badly, it was impossible because only the hotel owner's wife had the key to the linen closet.

For a good tip the maid at least broke the bad news to her and took the soiled sheet off our hands. We got dressed quickly, and shortly thereafter, they both appeared at our door. To our great relief, the owner's wife was very understanding about the sheet, but what she did not tolerate so much was that our neighbors had already complained about the baby's crying all night long. They had demanded to be moved immediately to a room as far away from us as possible. There went the rest of our good impression. Vita, our sweet darling, was here in her second exile and not even seven months old. The room next to us would now be occupied by a mother who also had a baby, and the two could cry in unison. We couldn't foresee any other trouble right now, or at least, that was what we thought.

Babes in the Woods and on the Road

It was marvelous at this simple little hotel in an area where there were no air raids and less food shortage. However, our days would be full of other surprises. After breakfast, while Sieghardt went into town to rent a baby carriage, I discovered in our room that Vita's bed was sprinkled with little black dots. How strange, everything had been so clean when we left her sound asleep to go down for breakfast. Now she was wide awake and playing with her hands as though she was pushing something away. I brushed the spots off, still wondering about them.

Meanwhile Sieghardt returned with a very sturdy vehicle and we bundled Vita up like a little Eskimo because it was bitter cold outside even though the sun was peeking through the morning clouds. Sieghardt fastened some sled runners under the carriage wheels and we were off to explore the little snow-bound town, easily sliding Vita along with us. It was a clear winter day and we got a much better impression of Neustadt than we had the night before. It was a snow-frosted small town with half-timbered houses with red tiled roofs and carved wooden balconies, and looked just like a tourist brochure for a winter resort. There were large and small footpaths that wound around through the wooded uplands, and we followed a steep road that zigzagged through snow-clung tall firs up to the higher peaks. The view from the top was breathtaking with visibility for miles into the surrounding Black Forest countryside.

We returned to the hotel for the noon meal, tired but happy, and I took Vita upstairs for her nap. But what was that in her crib? I noticed more of those strange black droppings, this time slightly larger than those in the morning. No, that couldn't be. They looked like mouse turds. When Sieghardt arrived, I greeted him with, "We had visitors in our room," and showed him the black droppings which unquestionably indicated there were mice on the loose. What now? We decided to say nothing for the time being, but we knew that we could never again leave Vita alone in the room while she was sleeping.

Thus far, we had only met the other guests on a formal basis at breakfast so it didn't seem proper to question them on our first day about the apparent mouse problem. That night, we heard a rustling sound under our beds, and Sieghardt took his flashlight to investigate while I peeked underneath from my side. There was a cute little mouse, surprised by the bright light, standing on its hind legs and looking at us with enormous black eyes. Then it ran out to my side and before I could react, it vanished into the wall.

The next day, while talking guardedly to other long-time guests, we found that our little visitor from the night before was just one of a large rodent family living in the hotel. But, nobody complained because they had all been bombed out at home and were grateful to have a roof over their heads, even if it meant sharing their space with a family of mice. We determined that they made their headquarters in the bakery next door, but many guests kept extra food hidden in their rooms which had been accumulated without ration cards, so the mice were interested in that supply also and paid regular visits all over the house.

We learned that the other hotel guests were either from Hamburg or the Rhineland where devastating air raids had left them homeless and they had been quartered here by the government. We now realized that the cancellation of our reservation had been beyond the hotel owner's control, and we were all the more grateful for our accommodations. After hearing about the ill fortune of the other guests, we were not overly concerned about the mice anymore. The people from the Rhineland told us grimly the latest jokes of Tünnes and Schäl, two comical figures from the city of Cologne:

> Tünnes proudly shows his friend Schäl his new motorbike. Schäl wonders why he bought it since all gasoline is strictly rationed. Tünnes laughs, "I don't need gasoline because here everything goes down hill anyway."

Another sarcastic one was:

> Tünnes returns from a trip to Switzerland and tells his friend Schäl the latest news: "In Switzerland they now have a Minister of the Navy." Schäl wonders why. "But they have no ocean."

Tünnes explains, "See, we also have a Minister of Justice!"

The hotel guests from Hamburg were equally bitter over the destruction of their historic old city at the Elbe River that had been founded by Charlemagne as a missionary base to spread Christianity. It had once been one of Europe's largest seaports. Now the city and harbor had been leveled to the ground by massive Allied bombardments. The underground railway served as a public bomb shelter, but more than fifty thousand people, mostly women and children, had been killed in one night. Their corpses floated along the Elbe River and some were even washed into the open sea sixty-eight miles away. These hotel guests were part of the eight hundred thousand people who had lost everything but their lives, and this hotel room was now the only home that they had.

I told them that I was familiar with the elegantly terraced café-restaurant in Wedel outside of Hamburg, a place called *Willkommen-Höft* (Welcome Host) overlooking the Elbe River's international shipping lane. It was famous for welcoming all incoming ocean liners, and as each ship passed by on its way to the harbor, it was greeted by having its name and background announced over a loudspeaker. Then the ship's flag was raised while its national anthem was played, and the captain would acknowledge this greeting by blowing the ship's horn. Since more than twenty thousand international vessels passed by each year, this was a world famous tourist attraction. This reminiscence started a lively conversation.

Neustadt was less of a commercial tourist attraction than the better known winter resorts, but it was the perfect place for Sieghardt to relax in comfort and peace to absorb the fresh, healing mountain air with its pine scent. On one exceptionally clear and beautiful day, we explored the rural area at the edge of town. As we were roaming through the peaceful countryside with its farm houses blanketed with snow and framed by spectacular white mountains, we became aware of a large formation of high flying Allied bombers approaching very rapidly. Spontaneously, we looked for cover, reacting to our ever present fear of air raids. We fled under some trees, the only shelter available. At that moment, we saw some farmers casually passing by, and panic-stricken, we shouted to them, "Take cover! We are about to be attacked!" But they only laughed, "Don't worry. Those bombers are not interested in us. They only pass over here when aiming for the large cities." And untroubled, they continued on their way. This was a new and disturbing experience for us to stand there in safety as a spectator to the forthcoming devastation of some distant city and being helpless to do nothing about it.

At the end of our first week at the hotel, there was a marked improvement in Sieghardt's health, but at the end of the second restful one, we received an alarming phone call from home that shattered our fairy tale world. Sieghardt was about to be drafted and was to immediately return home alone, while the baby and I were to go to Uncle Conny and Aunt Frieda in Gleiwitz, Upper Silesia, near the East German border. The family had decided that the baby and I should not return to Berlin because of the increased intensity of the air raids. I was to stay with the baby in the hotel for the remaining two weeks of our reservation. But I did not want to be left alone there and immediately decided to depart with Sieghardt the next morning as far as Frankfurt. There, he would help me catch a train east while he continued on to Berlin. We abruptly terminated our vacation and had to repack our suitcases for separate return trips, and my luggage by far was the bulkier with all of the baby paraphernalia. While we regretted having to leave in haste, the other hotel guests envied us for having a home to return to. How different we looked at life.

Very early on the cold morning of February 16, with heavy hearts, we again climbed on the little old fashioned choo choo train for the first leg of our journey. This time we had no eye for all the beauty. Hours later when we arrived in Frankfurt and saw all of the air raid devastation, we felt as if we had just left paradise. Sieghardt helped me with the luggage and we both struggled through the crowded station to make my train connection to the East. With his help, I even got a seat. There was little time to talk before he had to leave to catch his own train to Berlin, both knowing that we were facing a possible long separation and a very uncertain future. "Let me know as soon as you have arrived," he urged me. But when would I arrive and where could I reach him while he was off to the military? "I'll call you," I promised, having no idea when that might be. We both tried to smile and be cheerful, but weren't very successful, and with a last kiss, I departed on my train traveling in the opposite direction from his.

It looked like an impossible trip this time from west to east, traveling alone with the baby in a chilly compartment with every seat taken and no room for changing diapers. Poor little Vita had spent these first seven months of her life being shuttled from one safe haven to another. My mind drifted back to the many events since her birth last July. It had been a tough life. Now, all alone, we felt abandoned on our way to industrial Upper Silesia after the fresh mountain air of the Black Forest.

Several hours later we reached our first transfer point, and the other passengers helped me unload my luggage onto the station platform. I placed my largest suitcase flat on the concrete ground and put the baby on top of it and sat beside her with all of the other bundles arranged around us. We must have been a picture of despair because as soon as my train entered the station, military personnel of all ranks came to my assistance. Nobody wanted to carry a crying baby and I had both of my hands full with her all bundled up. They helped load my luggage into the overcrowded train for the next leg of the journey, which was to take all day.

By the time we reached Dresden it was dark, and the transfer looked so hopeless that I approached a high-ranking officer who looked to me like a general. Since I had spotted a reserved, but empty first-class compartment, I asked him to help me get into it, which he did without asking any questions. When you are desperate, everything seems to work out if you just act confidently enough and off we went in unexpected luxury—until the conductor came by and questioned my presence there. I can't remember what kind of story I told him, but after I paid a small fine with a smile, he ignored me for the rest of the trip, until my last transfer point in Breslau, Silesia, at three o'clock in the morning. There he was again to help me off the train. The station platform was almost deserted at that early hour and those few people who were there looked as tired as we were. However, when the train arrived for the last part of the journey, some of them helped me to get aboard. People who were sleeping moved closer together to make room for me with the baby on my lap. After a ride of more than twenty-four hours, hungry and exhausted, we finally pulled into Gleiwitz at dawn.

Fellow passengers helped me get off the train, and this time it was for good. Thank heaven! Here we would stay. I laid Vita on top of a suitcase and immediately looked for a nearby telephone booth on the station platform. Fortunately even she was too tired to cry. It was February 17, 1944, when I dialed my relative's telephone number and a very sleepy Aunt Frieda answered. "Dorothea, you sure are an early bird. What is so urgent?" I told her that Sieghardt had been suddenly called back to Berlin during our vacation in Neustadt and that I had been traveling since yesterday morning. She impulsively interrupted me with, "You must be out of your mind. Where are you now?"

"I am here," I replied.

"Where here?"

"Here in Gleiwitz."

She came back with, "You are where?"

A long pause followed. And then it finally dawned on me that I had arrived totally unannounced. "Oh, you don't know. Mutti didn't tell you?" But how could she. She believed me to be staying in Neustadt for another two weeks. There it was again. Another one of my hasty decisions was causing trouble. Practical Aunt Frieda caught on quickly, confirming calmly, "You are at the train station? Then just stay there. Uncle Conny will come to get you and we can fill in the details later." That was my Aunt Frieda, no fuss and immediate help.

I was so happy to see Uncle Conny when he came to rescue us. His spacious car easily held the two of us and all of our luggage. Our new temporary home was well known to me because I had spent many enjoyable visits there in the past. We arrived to a big welcome. Everyone was up by now and we sat down to a big family breakfast. I had not realized that they already had a full house because Cousin Edith with her baby boy and mother-in-law had come from Berlin where they had been bombed out. Now, they had to make room for Vita and me, but this did not faze Aunt Frieda, and in no time, she had rearranged the sleeping facilities. Fortunately it was a spacious apartment over their large furniture store. She moved Vita and myself into the room that had been occupied by Edith's baby boy, and put him in with his mother. Vita and I were now settled in our third exile from Berlin.

People here lived in a different world, as air raids were just something that they read about in the newspapers, and alarm tests were looked upon as an annoyance. Uncle Conny, as a business man, could drive his private car whenever he wanted, food was more plentiful and their social life consisted of sold-out matinees at the theater, all unheard of in Berlin. I was anxious to listen to the radio for the latest news of Berlin to see which part of town had been hit this time. Aunt Frieda smiled quoting the slogan, "Let's enjoy the war, peace will be worse." She knew that today's good times in Gleiwitz were just an illusion, but she masked her smoldering fear by a seemingly nonchalant attitude. One could not help notice that our front lines in the East, even though they were still thousands of miles away, were slowly being driven back closer and closer to Germany. I finally received some good news—Sieghardt's imminent draft notice had turned out to be another false alarm. We never knew what the next day would bring, so we quickly learned to adjust to our ever changing life.

We were experiencing an early spring, and I had no seasonal clothing with me, and it was impossible to buy anything here without extra clothing points. The only solution was to obtain my wardrobe from home, but it was too risky to have it mailed because it may never arrive. So, it was decided that I would journey to Berlin and leave Vita in Aunt Frieda's care, the first time I had ever been parted from my baby. Since we all knew of the risks involved, I prepared a hastily handwritten last will appointing Vita as my sole heir and left it in Aunt Frieda's bank deposit box along with all the valuables I had with me. This trip to Berlin would serve two purposes. Gleiwitz had plenty of butter, meat and other extra food supplies that were available without ration cards through Uncle Conny's business connections, and I could carry a suitcase full of these to Mutti. In return, Aunt Frieda asked that I bring back fresh fruits and vegetables which for some strange reason, were in short supply here. My emergency trip would turn into a barter exchange between Gleiwitz and Berlin.

The only ticket available to Berlin was on a night train, and as usual, it was overcrowded so I had to stand the entire long night. When I arrived the next morning I was horrified at the extent of damage that had occurred since I left, but was overjoyed to find Papa and Mutti alive and well. Sleep was looked upon as needless luxury. Mutti and I immediately set out to obtain the requested fruits and vegetables for Aunt Frieda. We took the S-Bahn to Potsdam and then continued hiking for several hours to our farmer friends in Beelitz. There was no problem getting the produce we needed without any food ration cards, but at the usual higher price. On the way back we managed to hitch a ride with a farmer who was headed for Potsdam which certainly helped with our loaded knapsacks and bags that also contained asparagus. Of course, there was a good fee involved and cigarettes from our ration cards. Luckily neither of us smoked.

All too soon my hasty two-day visit and one night's sleep was over and I had to return to Gleiwitz and Vita. We kept our heart-breaking goodbyes simple and short, and played our roles well... "See you soon"..."Have a safe trip." But there was always that thought in our minds—will we ever see each other again? I arrived in Gleiwitz safe and sound, but dead tired, and this same short trip to Berlin would be repeated several times in the future for one urgent reason or another.

Sieghardt's sister Linda with a friend.
(Picture taken at my wedding.)

On a sunny Saturday morning on April 29, 1944, the birthday of Sieghardt's sister Linda, disaster struck our home in Berlin. Fortunately, the telephones kept working because the cables were underground, and that evening Mutti was able to tell me what had happened. Around noon she was in the kitchen picking up a small present to take across the street for an informal birthday visit when the air raid sirens started howling. Papa was downtown and she heard Maria calling her from the garden, "Let's get into our bunker. Hurry!" With sudden intuition, instead of rushing to the bomb shelter in the basement as Mutti usually did, she ran out into the yard and almost collided with Mrs. Vogel. Together they rushed into the new bunker for the first time, and all three of them clung together as they heard the roaring approach of the bomber formation thundering above.

This time, our residential suburb Zehlendorf-West was under attack and bombs were detonating everywhere with earsplitting blasts as if all the houses were going to be leveled. People outside were screaming, "Fire, fire!" but no one dared to leave their shelter to help. The whole area was trembling violently like an earthquake under the intensity of the repeated bombing, until finally there was a deafening quietness, and then the "all clear" signal sounded. The three women, still scared stiff, sat in the bunker as if paralyzed, well aware that once more they had escaped death.

At that moment, they heard a man's voice shouting in desperation, "Else, Else, where are you?" It was Papa looking for Mutti. Leaving our S-Bahn station, he had been stopped by police and forcefully pushed into a nearby public shelter. Now he rushed home within a matter of minutes, past burning houses, stumbling in panic over all the debris, only to see our devastated street. To his great relief, however, all three women emerged from the bunker—but to what sight!

Mrs. Vogel's house had taken a direct hit and stood in flames spreading an infernal heat. The women rushed for garden hoses, but the front of our lawn was gone. A monstrous crater took its place, but worse than that was that somehow the water had been cut off to Mrs. Vogel's house. Of course the fire department only responded to fires in public buildings and we were left to our own resources. Quick-thinking Maria rushed from the back yard into the basement of the burning house, a life-threatening venture, and pulled out packed luggage and bedding that had been stored there for emergency. She and Mrs. Vogel sat on the lawn among their rescued belongings, looking rather forlorn. Numb and in total shock, they helplessly watched the flames devouring their home with all of its beautiful antique furniture, paintings and memories, until it finally collapsed with an ear-splitting crash. All was lost except for their few possessions in the suitcases, which looked like a treasure to them.

Our house was also extensively damaged, but the full extent was not immediately noticeable. While Mutti and Papa were fighting a fire that had broken out on the first floor, the people across the street yelled, "It's burning on the second floor, too!" Right away they all rushed over and found the curtains and bed in Günter's room upstairs in flames. Luckily our water was still running so the fire for the most part was extinguished. The rest, still smoldering, Mutti threw out of the window.

The house was still habitable, even though long, gaping vertical cracks went through two solid brick walls on the side, and part of the front wall had caved in. Nevertheless, Mutti rushed over to our neighbors and offered to take them in. The tougher the times, the more bonded we felt to each other. Right away, their few rescued belongings were moved into our house. Furniture was rearranged, and a room prepared upstairs for the two homeless neighbors. They broke out in tears and tried to make themselves at home.

Public soup kitchens were set up in our suburb and since there was no gas, electricity or hot water, everyone went there for a free hot meal. Papa immediately inspected the house from top to bottom and found that our bomb shelter in the basement must have gone through a drastic upheaval because an exploded aerial mine nearby had rearranged everything. A heavy trunk packed with china and crystal was now sitting on the opposite side of the cellar, and all the luggage had changed places. The massive iron cover of the coal stove that belonged to the central heating system had been lifted off by the air suction and tossed clear across the basement. If Mutti had gone there as usual, she would have been killed. Maria's call to come to the bunker had saved her. Ironically she and Mrs. Vogel got a new home with Mutti and Papa. Heaven spares us if it's not time for us to go.

They did not check the glass and china in the big trunk. What for? If everything was broken, they would see it soon enough later. If not, who had the time to repack it again? Years later, when we finally unpacked it, we were surprised that almost nothing was broken. The suction of the aerial mine must have set it down very gently, even though it tore people's lungs apart immediately. With water splashed all over to fight the fire, my sheet music took an unwanted bath. Some of it I still have today, with burnt holes, like my beautiful Premiere Waltz by Auguste Durand. I never bought a new copy. My damaged one is full of memories of Switzerland.

Another surprise was found in the dining room facing the back yard. The large buffet's top section must have been sucked into the air and taken flight because it was sitting now upright on the floor in front of the bottom section. The glasses inside were not even broken, but stood straight up as if they had just been placed there. Even the glass doors were intact. The big brass front door knob was blasted away and had landed diagonally across the street on the second-floor balcony of Sieghardt's home. Some of the massive rocks from our rock garden were catapulted into the upstairs bedroom of a neighbor's house across the street and actually landed on their beds, creating a snowstorm of down feathers. Other rocks from the garden were hurled through our kitchen window and flew across the kitchen and through the buffet, where they smashed the tile of the wall behind it. Except for some pieces in their direct flight path, the other china in the kitchen buffet was hardly chipped. Mutti's birthday present for Linda was still on the kitchen table, just pushed to another corner. That is a birthday she has never forgotten.

Almost every house around Papa received severe damage, including the one of the Nazi dentist who lived next door. Nobody helped him, the Nazi protegé. His pile of trash, which had been a fire hazard and the cause of disputes, went up in flames and fortunately, the wind was very cooperative and blew the burning trash away from Papa's property and against the dentist's house.

Back in Gleiwitz, May passed with the German army on a long retreat from Russia toward the German border. Although heavy losses were occurring on all fronts, Goebbels was shouting over the radio, "He who doubts our victory is a traitor! He who listens to the word of the enemies' radio is a criminal!" With the war approaching Gleiwitz, my family feared for my safety and it was time for me to pack up again and leave. Although they were still far from the front lines, my relatives felt increasingly uneasy, but finally decided to stay for the time being. They had never experienced packing up and leaving with only a suitcase in one's hand. Nobody knew that better than I.

For me, it was "on the road again." That evening, after a last tearful hug, Uncle Conny drove us to the same railroad station where we had arrived three months earlier, and helped Vita and me into another all night train back to Berlin. Would we ever meet again, and if yes, where and under what circumstances? On June 3, I was back in Berlin, for good I hoped, but again it was to be only a visit on the run. The very next day, the Allies entered Rome and my family again feared for the safety of Vita and me. Sieghardt's mother knew of a lovely older couple with a comfortable home in the small village of Joachimsthal, about sixty miles north of Berlin. So I unpacked, repacked, and on June 5, I was on the move again!

Sieghardt took us by train to our new asylum in the Schorfheide, a 145-square mile area of wilderness, rich in deer, forests, creeks and lakes. Upon our arrival we were met by our new host, Mr. Böhmke, a friendly man in his sixties. He loaded our luggage on a handcart and we walked together through a little clean village with red-tiled roofs, which had been untouched by the war. His house stood in a large garden on the outskirts of the village, and the huge wooded preservation began right behind his property. I was both amazed and relieved at the sight of my new and fourth exile in less than one year.

Mrs. Böhmke was well known to Sieghardt because for years she occasionally came to his mother's house to take care of the mending and sewing. She was well liked by everybody. There was also her un-married sister, both refined people in their fifties, and they all loved little Vita at first sight. One of the three bedrooms upstairs had already been prepared for us, complete with a rented baby crib and freshly picked flowers from their garden on the table. There was a big kitchen down-stairs with a cozy breakfast corner, and a large living room. Their for-mal dining room had been requisitioned by the housing office for a couple from Berlin who had been left homeless after an air raid. They had a separate entrance and I was told that they stayed pretty much to themselves. Sieghardt was relieved to see us both settled in such a safe place and took care of the financial part before he had to rush back to Berlin. He kissed Vita goodbye and was deeply disappointed that she hardly recognized him, but how could she, since in her eleven months she had seen so many people, but seldom her own father.

The next day was June 6, 1944 and we heard that the Allied troops had landed along the Normandy coast of France. The German radio practically ignored this news item, playing it down as usual, but we were shocked. Normandy, though, was far away and our own problems were very real right here. I had settled in with Vita despite of all my reluc-tance to move again, and we seemed more at home each day. My new hosts were warm-hearted, industrious people and with their many fruit trees, berry bushes and a vegetable garden, there was plenty of food with-out any ration restrictions.

On June 12, Goebbels blasted over the radio that we would achieve final victory with a new weapon called the V-1, a long-range flying bomb, and exclaimed, "London will now feel what Berlin had to suffer." He bragged of how many V-1s and even V-2s we had, attempting to psy-chologically instill in us a sense of revenge and superiority. But, no one believed that this new miracle weapon would save us from a lost war. Our cities had been reduced to rubble. The enemy was fast approaching our borders from the east and west, and all this flying bomb would do is create more war-torn cities and more killing of mostly civilians like us.

On many nice summer days, I frequently went with Mr. Böhmke into the nearby woods to gather all kinds of berries and many mushrooms. He was an authority on every type of plant and flower that grew in the area, so we could safely eat what we picked. I also learned that all of the beautiful oil paintings in the house, primarily biblical scenes, were done by him. He also had the rare gift of diagnosing people's illnesses by just touching them, and occasionally he had corrected a doctor's diagnosis. Although he did not want this ability to be common knowledge, people heard about it by word of mouth and sought his help, which was always free as an act of charity. He told me that one day a journalist came to write a story about him, but he sent him away because he didn't want that kind of publicity. This man amazed me the more I got to know him, and we often talked about life, and life after death, two frequently discussed topics since everyone knew somebody who had been killed during the war. In his strong Christian belief, he naturally detested the ungodly Nazis.

July 12, 1944 was Vita's first birthday and Mrs. Böhmke had made a cake. Sieghardt and his mother came over by train because she didn't want to miss the first birthday of her only grandchild. My parents did not make it because this was their third grandchild. (Günter had two lovely daughters already.) I was happy to see them both and was very anxious for news of my family in Berlin. It was a beautiful day and we spent nearly all of it in the garden. We took pictures of Vita as she tried her first few wobbly steps holding on to Sieghardt's hand, and she was more interested in trying on his hat than in her modest little presents. She was kissed and hugged all day, especially by her grandmother, and the day flew by so fast that it was soon time for them to return to Berlin. They took along some fresh jam I had made for Mutti from the wild berries as well as fresh fruits and mushrooms for everyone, and the Böhmkes added food from their house and garden.

On July 20, we were hit by the next Nazi news. A time bomb had detonated during a high level military meeting in Hitler's heavily guarded headquarters in East Prussia, called *Wolfsschanze*, wolf's lair. Goebbels announced in his cynical way that the enemies of the nation had failed in their attempts and that "our beloved Führer" had only minor injuries. For us, the good news was that someone finally had the courage to try to eliminate Hitler and his lawless regime, because without him, the Nazi terror would have been broken. We all knew how Goebbels and Göring plotted against each other and that the entire group around Hitler was torn by hatred in an endless power struggle. The ice cold Himmler, the former chicken farmer, had created enough enemies, so people would have killed him.

Unfortunately, the assault failed and we heard Hitler on the radio exclaiming, "Fate has saved me for my missionary calling. Providence elected me to rule until full victory." We thought that these phrases, heard too often, were more his pact with the devil. What arrogant self-deceit since it was his refusal to allow qualified generals to plot the military strategy while his bad command decisions and blunders had resulted in nothing but military failures.

We carefully discussed this latest news behind closed doors, and even the couple who always kept to themselves participated. They seemed better informed than we were, and we wondered if they were hiding from the Gestapo for some reason, but this was not the time to ask questions. Subsequent radio reports gave more details. Hitler had only slight injuries because the briefcase that contained a time bomb, which stood next to his feet under the table, had been pushed away by someone who was trying to get closer to him as he was explaining a map spread out on the conference table. Through the force of the explosion parts of the house came crashing down killing many around him. Why not Hitler?

A killing frenzy began as people were accused of being part of the conspiracy. One officer, Colonel Claus Schenk, Count of Stauffenberg, was shot to death, and in addition, his entire family was to be eliminated down to the last heir. Hitler swore a violent revenge on anyone involved in the assassination plot and the retaliation court was in session instantly, issuing death penalties to all who showed the slightest suspicion of having plotted against him. Systematically, Hitler was executing many of his most qualified officers. Mr. Böhmke cautioned us to keep our opinions to ourselves since it could prove deadly to say things out loud.

Meanwhile the Allies continued to strike our major cities, and we watched, shivering, from our garden as countless bomber squadrons roared overhead and soon were dropping their deadly cargo over Berlin. Shortly thereafter, the sky on the horizon would turn red and huge columns of smoke rose up into the clouds, visible to us over sixty miles away. We watched them setting their dreaded "Christmas Trees," so called because of the sparkling signal rockets which fell from the sky like glittering stars to mark a special area to be wiped out by precision bombing. Each time I watched these descending firestorms from my safe haven, I asked myself in fear, "Will my loved ones survive that inferno this time? When I call later, will they still answer the phone?" Oddly enough, through all of that bombing, the phone connections still worked. We carefully went along with our everyday lives in this remote hamlet, still hearing radio reports of continued purges of military officers accused of being part of the assassination plot. Thousands were sentenced to death and we asked ourselves who will be left to lead our armies at the front, with the best men now killed at home?

Among the good friends of the Böhmkes was an attractive young mother with a beautiful teenage daughter. The mother had not heard from her husband at the Eastern Front for a long time and naturally was very worried about it. To cheer her up we debated that Goebbels had probably stopped the mail service between the front and home to keep both sides from knowing what was really going on. We learned later, that as soon as the dreaded Soviets approached and were frighteningly close, tragedy hit. She panicked, took poison, and forced her daughter to take it, too. Neighbors heard the poor girl screaming and begging not to have to die, but her mother chose death for both of them rather than to fall into the hands of the approaching Soviets. Later, the husband, who was believed dead, found his way back home, only two find two graves in the cemetery. His grief was beyond description and he was very bitter towards the neighbors for not assisting his loved ones to survive safely as they had themselves.

The Allies entered Paris on August 25, 1944, closely followed by de Gaulle, who had returned with the exile government from London. Yet the purge of German officers was still in full force, and it was rumored that the Nazi political leaders were now supervising all military headquarters to better control them and reduce their independence. Hitler issued a new decree on August 31, which required everyone to work a sixty-four hour week as a sacrifice for victory. This was just another government trick to offset the scarcity of labor because of increased drafting of personnel into the military, which now involved even workers in the defense industry.

We entered our fifth year of war on September 1 and it was indeed a sad anniversary. All theaters were closed now but movies continued to be shown. The British took Brussels on September 3, and one week later they entered the Netherlands. With enormous sacrifices on both sides, the Allies were to cross the German border in the West and we could hear the artillery rumbling in the East. The Soviet troops had rolled over Poland on their way to Germany. Could it be that they might have advanced far enough for us to hear their big guns, now sounding closer and closer, or was it an incessant German battalion? No matter what, the collapse in the East and West was only a matter of time and the war would soon be fought within the German borders.

What was I still doing here? Why didn't I just end our restless search for sanctuary throughout Germany, now going on for more than one year, and go back home to be with my family? How much more time had we left before the enemy would be at our front door? If we were going to die, why not die together? My family must have felt the same because early one morning Sieghardt appeared to finally take us home. It was a sad good-bye to my last asylum as we had all become such good friends and did not know if we would ever see each other again. The Böhmkes gave us large provisions of food from the house and garden to take back to our families in Berlin, and Vita started to cry when we began to depart. She had learned to know and love these people, and was not sure who this strange man was who was carrying her away in his arms.

We reached Berlin that same day and it was appalling to see the widespread destruction with entire streets lying in ruins. We enjoyed a big family reunion with no one mentioning why I was back home, although we all were probably thinking that this was the beginning of the end for all of us. My own place was miraculously in the same condition as when I left it in July, 1943, fourteen months ago. It seemed to me that I could have safely stayed right here all along rather than wander from place to place seeking safety. But, that had not been allowed, typical of our unpredictable life that we did not control anymore. So, now we waited to see what tomorrow would bring, but come what may, this is where I would stay.

Don't Play With the Shark

Upon returning from my endless wanderings through Germany with Vita, I noticed several major changes at home. The fear of the approaching Soviets had caused many of our long-time tenants to flee to the West with nothing but their suitcases, and bombed-out strangers had temporarily moved in. Mrs. Kage from across the hall introduced me to her new boarders, a homeless couple by the name of Huber. They were pleasant, both handicapped, but very self-sufficient, and he came to my aid when I was alone during an air raid and needed assistance quickly to get the loaded baby carriage down into the basement shelter.

We were horrified to hear of Hitler's continued actions against those being implicated in the assassination plot. The worst address in Berlin was Prinz Albrecht Strasse, the Gestapo headquarters. The People's Supreme Court, presided over by the infamous Roland Freisler who was secretly called the "Beast of Berlin," was handing down death sentences to be carried out in the most horrible manner. The accused were hung alive from metal meat hooks mounted to the ceiling of the Plötzensee prison execution chamber, and then slowly died an agonizing death from slow strangulation. It was rumored that more than twenty generals were executed in this inhuman manner, along with several thousand other persons under suspicion. In the Nazi police state, the Gestapo held the power of life and death with its tyranny and terror, and there was no right of appeal. Hell must have been empty because all the devils were here. The Berliners' sardonic sense of humor provided a vivid picture of the people's true feeling:

Two friends meet on the street. The first one asks, "What's new?" "There are two things new," the second one responds. "One is good and one is bad." "Oh, let's hear the good news first!" "Hitler is dead." "And the bad news?" "It's not true!"

Soon another shock followed. Field Marshall Erwin Rommel died all of a sudden from his injuries. This was one of those moments when Mutti and Papa exchanged their doubtful looks. The grapevine whispered that Erwin Rommel, suspected for being involved in the assassination plot, as revenge, had been given two choices— either being condemned, executed and his entire family wiped out, or, being pardoned and required to take poison under supervision of the SS. Rommel chose the latter to save his wife and eight-year old son Manfred (who later became the Lord Mayor of Stuttgart). The government was fearful of a strong reaction from a suspicious public, so in order to squelch rumors about his death, "the famous desert fox, admired by friend and foe" was given a hero's funeral in Ulm with full military honors.

Goebbels continued to scream over the radio, "Our fervent oath is total victory. Hold out!" His magical solution was to mobilize, on September 25, 1944, all males between the ages of sixteen and sixty as the new "Fatherland Front." That meant boys had to leave school and the retired had to march. The newly created unit was called *Volkssturm* (folk's storm). They had no uniforms, were poorly equipped, untrained, and were under the command of petty Party functionaries. We watched them marching through the streets, more desperate than enthusiastic, looking like a pitiful mobilization of the last reserve. At their sight people shook their heads and made bitter remarks about their true effectiveness: "Those with last names from A-K pretend to shoot and yell 'bang, bang,' while those from L-Z shout 'boom.' That's Goebbels' rescue for us."

It did not take a military genius to realize that our overall military power was collapsing. In the fifth year of the war, our air force had been almost driven from the sky and our navy from the sea. The German army was retreating on all fronts and constant Allied bombing had crippled the defense industry. New posters read, "One struggle, one victory," and this was supposed to be accomplished by Goebbels' propaganda of retaliation with legendary secret weapons. This spawned another sarcastic riddle:

What is the difference between lightning, thunder and retaliation?

Lightning can be seen but not heard; thunder can be heard but not seen; but retaliation can neither be seen nor heard.

By now my parents had their own problems. The wind whistled

through several gaping cracks in the walls of their air raid-damaged house. Papa repeatedly checked everything and worried, "Is it safe enough to continue to live here?" Finally, he decided to move the family and the entire household furnishings to Zerbst where he owned property with a big exhibition hall for displaying farm machinery, which now stood empty. There was plenty of room for all of us to set up temporary housekeeping and he even talked it over with some of the neighbors. Many wanted to get out of Berlin. Mrs. Vogel, and Maria were undecided about leaving since Mrs. Vogel had family here.

Word spread mysteriously. One morning, three uniformed Nazis suddenly showed up, and strangely enough, they had somehow learned of our plans for moving. One was an architect who discussed with Papa the condition of the house, and recommended that it be vacated so that necessary repairs could be made immediately. He further stated, "We will move you and your furniture to Zerbst at no cost and the Building and Repair Committee will take care of all of the necessary repair work, and then we will use the house temporarily for an urgently needed district office."

Now the cat was out of the bag, but Papa secretly wondered how they had learned about his plans to move to Zerbst. While listening to the offer, he watched the other two men who were marching around, and picked up bits of their private conversation about moving some walls and windows. That was too much for Papa, and he interrupted, "Nothing is going to be changed around here. This is my house!" "We know that," said the leader, "but it will make it much more suitable for us when we move in, only temporarily of course."

Just then, Mutti called Papa aside and whispered to him to get ahold of his temper because it was obvious that a fight with the Nazi official would be lost before it even began. Only a sound argument with a superior attitude could be effective, and Papa was very good at this. The architect arrogantly continued that since Papa had already agreed to their generous offer, the only thing that needed to be finalized was the date that he would be leaving. Papa acted astonished and talked of some misunderstanding because he had never planned to so hastily abandon his duties here. He went on: "I have full confidence in our government and I also took in two boarders who had lost their business and home, and I wouldn't want the Party to be burdened with finding them a new place."

Papa knew this argument was in his favor, because every air raid was creating more homeless survivors which further burdened the government in providing shelter for them. "Anyway," he added, "I feel perfectly safe here in Berlin and believe it is my duty to hold out right here until final victory." If the Nazi officer had said that the house was going to be used to shelter homeless people, Papa would have had no argument, but he had outwitted them, and since no contract had been signed, the three men left as quickly as they had appeared. Finally alone again, Papa could contain himself no longer and burst out with, "The final victory will be getting rid of all of the arrogant Brown Shirts and returning to peace, law and order!"

We had just survived the crude attempt of the Nazis to grab our house when we experienced our next calamity. Sieghardt was drafted. It was a real shock for me. Why couldn't the lost war be ended? Immediately, on October 20, 1944, he was sent for brief artillery training to Frankfurt on the Oder River, east of Berlin (now Poland).

Then Gerda called and told us she had to give up her desk in the archives and report for war-service duty as an unskilled worker in the Carl Flohr factory, which manufactured elevators, escalators, cranes and electric motors. The firm was located on the opposite side of the city from where she lived so she had to get up at 4:30 a.m. six days a week in order to be at work by 7 a.m. The firm was now repairing electrical motors needed for war production and, on her first morning, she was assigned as an assistant mechanic. A long-retired foreman was called back to work and had to break her in without any previous training in a profession that usually took a three-year apprenticeship.

She had to learn how to operate many different dangerous tools, standing at a metal bench working with high voltage appliances. With each accidental mistake, the entire working crew got an electric shock. This didn't make her co-workers very happy. The motors were dirty. A special potent soap cleaned off all the greasy oil but left her hands badly bruised and hurting. In addition to her female co-workers, there were also Russian, Polish and French prisoners of war which created an amusing system of communication with a gibberish of languages and hand signals. She joked about a new and very practical sideline that she had started, and invited me to participate in it. The women would bring in their pots to be soldered and their flatirons for repair, which she and her boss would secretly take care of between their regular duties. They were a good team without any hostility towards each other, probably because no Nazi trouble-shooters were left.

My friend Gerda

Due to the constant air raids, it was impossible to visit each other, so we kept in touch by telephone. She told me about Robert, a French POW, who volunteered to teach French to everyone while learning German in return. After work, Germans and POWs together would often continue their language studies in a nearby little coffee house, and exchange ideas and experiences. Afterwards, everybody returned home and the POWs would walk back to the factory without any guards. Gerda said that this experience had taught her that if people could just meet without government and political intervention, there would be no more wars.

Meanwhile we were receiving numerous telephone calls from our friends in Schweidnitz, telling us of the worsening situation in Silesia. The household of Elsa's parents had swelled from four people to fourteen, as relatives with their children fled from East Prussia. Every available space in the house from the basement to the attic was occupied, and budgeting the food ration cards to figure out the daily provisions had turned into a mathematical nightmare. While standing in line at the market there was the ever present fear of spies who would denounce mercilessly everyone who could be suspected of subversive remarks.

Schweidnitz was now experiencing air raid warnings, but thus far there had been no actual attacks. An endless stream of homeless refugees, primarily women and children, were passing through in the dead of winter. According to Elsa's parents, they were fugitives from East Prussia, and even Latvia and Lithuania, who were trying to escape the ravages of the rapidly advancing Soviet army. More and more were arriving thirsty and exhausted each day. Our friends spent many hours handing out hot tea to them and they were grateful for anything, even if it was only a drink of warm water. Some no longer had the strength to go on, and were happy just to lay inside on a bare floor. The feared Red Army, with their reported rapes and massacres, had already approached Poland, and Elsa was horrified by the thought that they themselves might share the same fate before too long as those refugees now passing their home.

We had not heard from Günter for a long time, but mail was very slow and unreliable these days. Likewise, Elsa had not heard from her husband, Heinz, either. Strangely enough, movies still played every day, mostly light old amusing pictures. We asked ourselves if this was to divert us from our misery. Just as when the roman Republic declined and the people were given "bread and circuses."

Then, if by magic, Günter unexpectedly dropped in one evening. He had come straight from Bremerhaven after visiting his young wife, Johanna, and their two little girls, Dagmar and Helke. Now he was on his way to Greece to assume command of a torpedo boat on the Aegean Sea. Papa looked doubtfully over Günter's shoulder as he was writing out his new mailing address: Torpedo boat TA 18, 9th Flotilla, M 530 70, boat M54290. "How will you get from Berlin to Greece in the war?" he asked. But Günter assured us that he would manage it somehow since it had to be done, though he gave us no details. Now with a trembling voice, Papa said, "Don't go back. This war is lost and over. You may never even arrive in Greece. Anything can happen between here and there!" — a desperate plea from a loving father.

His advice to Günter caught us by surprise because he had always taught us to have a strong sense of duty and honor. But, Papa had gone through all the misery of the lost First World War and well remembered its bitter end, and this war obviously was going to end the same way. But Günter would not even consider not returning to his command. "I cannot desert my crew. They are counting on me." So the delicate subject was dropped and our conversation returned to present family matters, although we felt a strange premonition.

The next day, Günter stopped by my place for a quick goodbye, looking so handsome in his blue uniform. I was always proud of him, the confidante of my childhood. At the end of his short visit, as we walked together to the front door, he suddenly mentioned that all of his friends whose second child had just been born had never returned. Then, he looked at me gravely, "You know, I now also have two children." I felt a tug at my heart and tried to brush it off with forced cheerfulness, and laughed, "Oh, you know that the devil doesn't want you!" What a stupid thing to say, and I was shocked when he reacted so seriously with, "Don't be so sure." With a last embrace, he stepped outside, quickly closing the house door behind him. Watching him through the glass, I saw him hesitate, turn back to me, and with a very sad face he lifted his hand for a last goodbye. With that, he hurriedly turned and was gone.

There I stood with my last impression of him and all I could think was, "Oh God, be merciful. Don't let this be our last good-bye." I knew it had been an emotional farewell for both of us and decided not to say anything to Mutti and Papa about this last talk with Günter. It would only add to their worries about him.

Some days later, Gerda called to tell me about her new position. Since November 20, she had been assigned to help out with the payroll at the factory's office and was very nervous about making mistakes with the money, numbers and the many different deductions. So far her home address was still with her mother in Domjüch, even though she lived in a furnished room in Berlin. Train travel was severely restricted, but she was able to obtain a worker's roundtrip commuter ticket which allowed her to make an occasional quick visit home on a Sunday.

Long before Hitler, her father was the medical superintendent of an institute for the mentally retarded in Domjüch, but now he was suddenly transferred to a hospital in Schwerin, and the institute was closed by the Nazis and renamed the "Tuberculosis Sanatorium." Since Gerda's father had only a small room allocated to him in the new hospital, Gerda's mother was permitted to stay in their house in Domjüch until a new home could be found for them. There was no information as to what happened to the former inmates of the mental institute, other than they had been "relocated", and no one dared to say what they thought and feared. In prior years, some Nazi authority would arrive from time to time and demand to see the files of all of the patients. They then decided which patients could stay and which had to be prepared for immediate transfer. Nobody ever knew the destination of those transferred. Disabled Germans were expendable and not worth the documentation involved. Since the Domjüch establishment was self-supporting, with its own farm, there was extra food for Gerda to take back to Berlin.

In Berlin, we observed the third Christmas since my marriage but we made no holiday preparations and had very little Christmas spirit, only taking precautions for our survival, facing the harsh winter that lay ahead. Mutti had a small tree, so I took little Vita over to my parents' home. We were still scared stiff that the Allied bombers would drop an extra Christmas present on us, this time their target was the Rhineland to destroy German resistance against the approaching Allied forces which, by the end of 1944, had already reached the German border. We heard that Hitler had moved his headquarters back into the Berlin Reichs Chancery.

He began 1945 with his usual New Year's proclamation, ignoring his fading glory and all of the obvious disastrous facts, acting optimistic about the outcome of the war, and even thanked God for all his help, particularly for his rescue from many dangers. We thought it was a little late for him to be remembering the Lord after his unholy and cruel persecution of the churches, their institutions and the martyrdom of the priesthood, as I remembered very well from Münster. It was confirmed that Hitler refused to look at any city in ruins, even once, and the government suddenly became very invisible to the public, with only Goebbels occasionally making an official appearance. Survival became the primary objective of every citizen while the government officials played ostrich and hid their heads in the sand. Our food supply on ration cards hadn't changed much in the past year, but power was being shut off longer during the designated black-out periods. And to add to our struggle with less power and heat, Mother Nature presented us with deep snow.

Sieghardt was transferred to Küstrin on the Oder River and on January 2, after a short oral examination, was promoted to a reserve officer candidate. He was declared fit for active duty and assigned to the cavalry because of his civilian horseback riding experience. More than a year had passed since his serious illness and he never regained his full health. But right now any crawling creature that could still walk and breathe was drafted. About a week later, he was again transferred to a military training area in Brandenburg. Goebbels' carefully worded communiques could not hide the fact that everything was collapsing on all fronts, with the Allies already on German soil to the West, and the Red Army would soon be pouring in from the East. What would be our next fate?

For me it was a surprise visitor. One morning, Elsa's husband, Heinz, knocked on my door, looking haggard and very upset. Exhausted he sat down and breathlessly told me that his unit had been transferred out of Italy a long time ago and that he had been assigned to one new unit after another since then. Now, he had managed a quick detour through Berlin on his way to his next assignment in the East where the Soviets had started their major offensive. He told me that Hitler was following the scorched earth principle and had ordered a complete destruction of any territory that could not be held any longer. He desperately wanted to talk to his family in Schweidnitz, and strangely enough the phone lines were still open when I tried to put the call through. The conversation was rather garbled. "Women and children out of Silesia now," I heard him say, "on foot if necessary, and make your way westward. Silesia will soon be overrun by the Red Army. Take whatever you can carry and leave right now!" Elsa was shocked and reacted with indecision. "We all have to be on the run, too? And that immediately?" Here the phone connection was broken.

Relieved that his message had gone through, he put down the receiver. Heinz looked weary. He and his clothing sorely needed cleaning. Luckily he had some underwear in his backpack, so I urged him to freshen up while I fixed a simple soup. He enjoyed it as if it was a sumptuous meal. He gladly took a nap on the couch while I washed his belongings, which had to be done by hand in cold water with a very clayey soap. As soon as I had hung his underwear and socks out on the clothesline, the air raid sirens began to howl. Heinz instinctively jumped up from a sound sleep, and I called out to him to help me get Vita downstairs into the shelter. My neighbors looked at me strangely arriving with a man, but I introduced him to everyone and we did what we always did, wait and hope to be spared once more.

The first attack was over and the second had not yet started when I suddenly remembered the damp wash upstairs. Since the electricity was on during alarms, I called to Heinz, "Now I can quickly dry your underwear with a hot iron!" and to the horror of the others, rushed upstairs. During the next attack, I was back downstairs, and in this manner I was able to finish the ironing between the bombings. Shortly after the all-clear signal, a refreshed Heinz packed his belongings and left with the luxury of clean underwear. His apartment, which had recently been hit by a bomb, was not far away and he was going to make a quick side trip to it to see what was left. We promised to keep each other posted as we did before, since we in Berlin were kind of a central clearinghouse for family information.

This episode with Heinz in the air raid shelter reminded me vividly of another time when my scramble to get into the shelter did not go quite so smoothly. We women had protected our valuables by hiding them in pockets we had created between the inner and outer material layers of our corsets. In these spaces, we sewed in emergency money, jewelry, and important personal documents. Without a birth certificate you could not exist, even after surviving a bombing raid. This corset hideaway was very practical for me because it left my hands free for the baby. Since air raids could occur at any time of the day or night, we always left our apartment doors open so people could easily help each other in emergencies.

One night I was so dead tired that I didn't hear the air raid sirens until suddenly Mr. Huber from across the hall was standing at my bed shaking me awake. "Don't you hear the sirens?" Naturally, I hadn't, and in my sheer panic, my reflexes took over. I leaped out of bed and yanked my nightgown over my head and standing there stark naked, I yelled, "My baby, my corset!" Mr. Huber threw me my corset with all of its valuables in it, while he fetched the baby, who by now was loudly crying, and put her in the baby carriage in the hall. He took off with her to join the other tenants who were rushing into the shelter downstairs while I finished dressing. I was the last to arrive, loaded with my big handbag, and was scolded by the others for being so late. They had no idea as to why and Mr. Huber tactfully didn't mention the episode in my birthday suit, or offer any explanation.

Next we received an alarming phone call from Aunt Frieda who was not calling from Gleiwitz, but from Aunt Grete's home in Zerbst. In fear of the swiftly advancing Red Army, she had abandoned her home, and with her teenage son, her daughter with her two boys and some suitcases, had caught a train to the West. Her husband, Uncle Conny, refused to abandon his business that had been his life's work, and insisted on staying. Once she had everyone safely at Aunt Grete's home, she immediately returned to Gleiwitz to get some of her personal belongings (so far the suitcases were filled with baby things), and to try once more to convince Uncle Conny to leave. But, half way there, at Breslau, the train stopped as all service further east had been discontinued because of the approaching Red Army. She was lucky to catch one of the last overcrowded westbound trains back to Zerbst. Those who did not make it had to flee on foot. That was very different from Goebbels' propaganda, and we didn't know whether Upper Silesia, my birthplace, was in front of or behind our front lines.

We immediately invited Aunt Frieda with her children and grandchildren to join us in Berlin. They arrived shortly thereafter, hoping we may have some news of Uncle Conny and friends from Gleiwitz. There were no messages from there and our relatives stayed only a few days, and then decided to head further west to the town of Hannover in north Germany, once a cultural center with a thousand-year old history, which now lay in ruins. We didn't understand why they wanted to go there, but helped them out with necessities.

Aunt Frieda needed her good humor more than ever. She had lost everything except the clothing on her back, and didn't know where Uncle Conny was. As was so typical of her, despite of that, she had the latest sarcastic Hitler joke that made the rounds in Gleiwitz:

A man appears at the registrar's office. "I want my name changed." "Oh, but what is your name?" asks the official. "My name is Adolf Stinktier (skunk)." "I understand," says the official. "How embarrassing. Would you prefer to be a Mr. Miller or Meyer or ...?" "No, no," interrupts the man. "You misunderstand completely. I do not mind the 'Stinktier' at all, but I do not want to be an 'Adolf' any more!"

Right after they left, a message from Cousin Hans got through that he had dared to return to Gleiwitz again to look for his family and found Uncle Conny thrown out of his house by the Soviets, empty-handed, but still alive. Hans got him out of town and headed him westward, and the last we heard was that he wandered aimlessly on foot together with thousands of refugees from the East, if he had survived at all. Years later, we learned that he eventually ended up in Münster which by then was mostly destroyed, and he had no idea what had happened to his family.

After the war, a radio program called "Daily Announcements of Lost People" broadcasted the names of individuals and their current address who were looking for family members. Aunt Frieda heard her name called. She responded and this way Uncle Conny was united again with his family in Hannover. They had nothing to call their own and were living primitively in a demolished house that had been declared uninhabitable. One day, Hans knocked on the door and their reunion was full of tears and laughter. Now there were six of them, with no money and no income, just the clothes on their back. Fighting for survival was the name of the game.

I found this radio program still on the air in 1988. In addition, the magazine *Das Goldene Blatt* (The Golden Paper) published weekly articles under the heading "Attention we try to help you," and even included pictures of missing loved ones. Many readers are still searching for family members. *Das Goldene Blatt* can be bought in western Europe, from Greece to Spain.

In late January 1945, some days after Papa had received the message from Cousin Hans, he also received a call from his friend Paul, Elsa's father, who had a leading position with the railroad. He had received orders to run refugee trains in the direction of Berlin to provide a means of escape for the population. Since the trains started from his area, he had been able to get seats on the first one for his family, especially for his sick wife who had been bedridden with pneumonia and a high fever. She had managed to struggle out of bed and onto the train, but they had to leave without him two nights ago in complete darkness to avoid detection during air raids. They didn't even get a chance to take a last look at their hometown. At every stop along the way, frantic people climbed aboard until there was no more room left for the luggage they carried and they were forced to leave it behind to make room for more refugees. Elsa's father would leave on the last train, whenever that would be.

After such a shocking message we prepared for their arrival. But the old locomotive broke down in Oschatz, a town near Leipzig and the passengers were stranded now in a place already overflowing with refugees. Luckily Elsa's family found shelter in the basement of a villa, consisting of two little rooms, and only because the landlady took pity on them. She had an old table down there, some chairs, and two straw mattresses. She even added a pot and some dishes and cups. The biggest luxury was their own lavatory and a worn-out faucet that still produced a trickle of cold water. Here they would have to exist until the arrival of Elsa's father. Two days later he came on the last train with loaded suitcases that looked like they were full of treasures. He also brought the good news that Heinz had called at the last minute and was told where to find them. Elsa was elated that he had survived so far. Her father had to escort a train with refugees to Landshut in lower Bavaria and could take them at the same time, but Elsa wanted to stay where she was because this was the only address that Heinz knew to look for her and Kristian after the war was over—which surely must be soon. Elsa's parents promised to leave a message at the train station at Landshut as soon as they found a place somehow, somewhere, sometime, and they also would notify us in Berlin. With a last kiss, their ways split and no one knew when or where, or if ever, they would meet again.

At the same time a mass exodus of panic-stricken people from East Prussia and other neighboring areas started as the Red Army came closer. Fleeing had previously been forbidden by harsh Nazi orders because inhabited villages would be defended more vigorously by our soldiers than deserted ones. By the end of January, access to East Prussia had been cut off and no trains or trucks could get through. The Navy mobilized all types of available vessels in an attempt to rescue those refugees trapped at Baltic seaports. Seized with panic, people even dared to escape over the frozen bay, but only at night, because low-flying Soviet planes fired on them during the day.

Sieghardt was still in military training close to home at Wandern, so I took off on January 19 to his base to take him some badly needed items and to bring back any excess belongings. Leaving little Vita with Mutti, and after a complicated trip with innumerable transfers on slow, local trains, I reached Zielenzig, a town near Wandern, late in the evening and found a room in a private home for the night. The landlady even invited me to stay as long as I wanted because her husband and sons were in the military and she could use the extra money. Such an unexpected offer I could not refuse, so my planned one night stay turned into three. It was common practice for wives from Berlin to meet their husbands in the barracks, so I was with Sieghardt as often as possible. He looked pale and thin and had lost more weight, but appeared to have recovered somehow from his earlier serious illness. I brought him up-to-date on all of the family news and we enjoyed every moment together, and I cherished those alarm-free nights. I returned home on January 22, and I was lucky I did, because all of the express and local trains stopped running the very next day. By now the Soviets were in Warsaw, Poland.

On January 30, 1945, exactly twelve years to the day after Hitler's assumption of power, the former Nazi vacation liner, Wilhelm Gustloff, departed from the Gotenhafen (Gdingen) harbor on the Baltic sea with over six thousand refugees on board, primarily women and children. They were protected by only one German torpedo boat against the many Soviet submarines lying in wait. Shortly after leaving the harbor, the ship was torpedoed and sank within sixty minutes, sending over five thousand people to a watery grave in the ice cold water. That unimaginable and tragic catastrophe involving innocent civilians triggered a bitter joke:

> Hitler is standing in front of his picture hanging on the wall
> and asks, "What will happen to the two of us?" The picture
> answers, "We will exchange places. People will take me down
> and hang you instead!"

Sieghardt's unit was relocated to Paretz on the Havel River, and I will never forget that date, February 2, because the very next day I had to go downtown by S-Bahn to pick up an important item that he needed from the family firm. Early that Saturday morning I took Vita over to Mutti who told me that I was out of my mind to venture downtown, but as determined as I was, I thought that all it took was some guts. Now and then we had days with fewer "surprises" from the sky. So I left and promised to be back in a few hours. The morning non-stop S-Bahn took me to Potsdamer Platz in just ten minutes, from where I had a twenty-minute walk to the firm which was located in the heart of the city. I quickly picked up the item Sieghardt wanted and left immediately, figuring I would be back home within the hour.

Unbeknown to me, as I left the building, an early air raid warning was announced for Berlin on the radio. How could I have known that? In those days, there were no portable radios that are so common today, so I proceeded without knowing of the impending danger. I had only gone about a block when the air raid sirens started wailing and, panic-stricken, I started running toward the S-Bahn station at Potsdamer Platz. But, right away I was stopped by the police and forced into the nearest public air raid shelter along with other people who had been caught on the street.

I ended up in the basement in one of the old solid stone buildings with reinforced ceilings and sturdy pillars to support the structure in case it collapsed. Benches framed the walls. There was an air raid warden in command, and we had just sat down when we felt a frightening attack. The building began to tremble and shake like I had never experienced before. All the people huddled together and some started to cry. We winced with every whiz of a dropping bomb, and they exploded one after the other. I sat there numb with fear, cowering against a wall with my arms in front of my face. I wanted to die rather than be mutilated with a distorted face, without arms or legs ... but there was my baby at home.

I knew I had to survive because of her. With all of these thoughts flashing through my mind, I looked up terrified—right into the face of an old neighbor who was approaching me. It was Dr. Hecht, the principal of a high school in Zehlendorf, who addressed me calmly with, "What are you doing here?" I was as surprised to see him as he was to see me. We shook hands, a warm, firm handshake. Thank goodness I was not alone anymore. We were crowded together with at least thirty other people. He suggested we should stay in opposite corners, yet keep an eye on each other, so if one of us was killed the other could notify the family. So we did.

Just then, a barrage of exploding bombs shook the very foundation of our building. For a moment I thought we were hit. The lights flickered and then went out. The warden ordered, "No more talking and no candles or matches. We have to make our oxygen last as long as possible to keep from suffocating." What a horrifying prospect. There was another huge tremor and the building felt like it was collapsing, but it obviously didn't. We now had to lie flat on the floor, crowded together, but the closeness brought a sense of security. What I didn't know was that this very morning the U.S. Air Force had launched a one thousand bomber attack on the heart of Berlin and I got caught in it just one minute as the crow flies from the prime target area, the Reichs Chancery. It was the most devastating bombing I had ever experienced, a hell that seemed to have no ending.

It was noon when we finally heard the long, high tone of the all-clear signal. With shaking knees, we eventually emerged from the bunker, but what kind of world were we returning to out there? This part of the city was leveled to the ground and the only building left standing was the one we were in, now completely surrounded by only huge piles of rubble. The entire area looked like a gigantic stone quarry, a horror beyond description, with buildings smashed to the ground and people buried under piles of rubble. Fires were erupting everywhere around us, spreading intense heat. In utter terror, Dr. Hecht and I suddenly realized that we did not know which way to go because no familiar landmarks were left standing, and our suburb was fifteen miles away. We held hands for support and hastily started to stumble through the rubble in what we thought was the right direction, constantly fearing that we would get caught in the open in another air raid.

Survivors tried to dig others out of smoldering ruins. Our only thought was to get out of this inferno. At one point, we saw a kitchen stove literally hanging in the air from the skeleton of an apartment building. Wallpaper was flapping in the wind like a flag from what had been a living room on the fifth floor, but we saw no people who had lived there. They were probably all buried beneath us in the rubble, waiting for rescue, or were they dead already? No time to consider. Our desire to live was stronger since death was in pursuit. Were we walking over a giant cemetery? It was like crossing a huge ghost town.

We finally stumbled out of the man-made ravages unto a main road and recognized Potsdamer Strasse. Thank heaven it was still there. All we had to do now was walk straight ahead for many miles. We hardly recognized Potsdamer Platz. Once Berlin's equivalent of Times Square, it was now one chaotic rubble of stone. The S-Bahn and the station where I had arrived just a few hours earlier had both been blasted away. All of the surrounding buildings, the Columbus House, the department store Wertheim, were in flames looking like giant torches, including the famous and beloved Haus Vaterland with its many restaurants under one roof, where just a few years ago we had happily celebrated Papa's construction of his apartment house on Limastrasse. Dr. Hecht must have read my thoughts, looking around horrified, "No time for lingering in the past or self pity. Our only immediate goal is to get home alive."

Dead tired, we trudged on eagerly, and seemed to be the only people left alive in the world. Suddenly a German army truck came along and I waved frantically for it to stop. There was really no room for anyone else, but they picked us up, with me sitting on the lap of one of the soldiers in the cab and Mr. Hecht standing in the rear. We had to get off in Lichterfelde-West, about six miles from home, where the truck made a turn to go to the barracks. We again began walking toward Zehlendorf-West and finally arrived late that evening.

We had made it! How comforting to see that our homes, not far apart, were both still standing, and we parted with a last handshake. I rang the doorbell and Mutti immediately opened as if she had been waiting for it to ring. She was beside herself and looked at me as if she were seeing a ghost risen from the dead. We just fell into each others arms. Then Papa appeared on the scene, just as shaken, and with a sigh of relief, exclaimed, "There you are finally. NEVER DO THAT AGAIN!" If only I could remember today what was so urgent that I had to go downtown for in the first place.

We learned that Sieghardt's firm had been hit only moments after I had left it, and later burned to the ground. Luckily, his father and sister had been in the air raid shelter of a neighborhood newspaper and were now safe at home. Twenty-two thousand people perished around me that morning. There was one life, however, nobody cried about: Hitler's brutal executioner, Roland Freisler, the beast of Berlin. He was slain by stones in the collapsing Gestapo headquarters. Some of those he had sentenced to death survived, as they testified at the 1945 Nuremberg Trials. I had escaped that inferno unharmed, another incident of one of those guiding forces in my life. What would be next?

In cases of total destruction such as with the firm, Sieghardt was entitled to an emergency leave to close out the business, but it had been impossible to reach him by telephone. Someone had to go and tell him, and I was the logical one for the mission. His last address was still at Paretz near Potsdam and I had to wait until morning before I could leave to search for the military camp. I took the S-Bahn to Potsdam, but had no permission to use a train from beyond there, so I started off on foot, asking people for directions from time to time. After about five miles, an old forest ranger picked me up in his horse cart and gave me a ride part of the way to where he thought the unit was still located. I started out again on foot, and at one point, passed a group of about thirty POWs moving along slowly, guarded by two German soldiers, one in front and one in the rear of the group. I felt that they all could run away at any time, but where would they go? Some looked mean, some sad. So we shyly sized each other up, and I was relieved to finally have passed them, since I walked much quicker. It crossed my mind—was Günter perhaps walking around somewhere as a POW, too? I kept on walking and walking.

I finally reached Paretz that afternoon, a peaceful little town of brick houses surrounded by gardens and trees and no bomb damage. What a contrast to Berlin. I asked at one of the first houses where the military had its headquarters and a sergeant showed up and looked at me in a mean-spirited manner, as if I were an intruder. He listened rather grudgingly to my story and then picked up the phone and barked orders to someone on the other end to have Sieghardt here within ten minutes. So he was still there; what a relief. While waiting, I asked the sergeant where I might find a room for the night and he bruskly answered, "We don't have any." About that time, Sieghardt arrived and seeing me, feared for the worst. I quickly told him, "Nobody is dead, only property is lost." At that he seemed very relieved, but not so much when he heard that the entire firm was destroyed. He took me along to his commanding officer and after a brief conversation, was given an eight-day emergency leave effective the next morning, February 5.

Now, we scouted around looking for a place for me to stay that night, and it seemed impossible, so we finally ended up where we started in the same house where the sergeant lived. The owner took pity on me and had an old bed stored in the attic with a mattress and blanket, but no linens. At least, this gave me a roof over my head and no air raid alarms to disturb my sleep. Sieghardt had to return to his quarters, so in order to avoid that mean-spirited sergeant, I wandered through the village admiring the serene houses. The first snow drops were blooming in the gardens. I ended up in front of a large manor with all of the doors wide open, which was very unusual in Germany. I walked in and found myself in a large kitchen where the lady of the house was sitting, who was not even surprised to see me because hungry refugees often passed this way from the East. We had a short conversation about my venturing around here and she fixed me a rich sandwich without asking for food stamps, and that served as my evening meal. I could not help thinking about what might happen to her and this lovely place when the soviets invaded—and they did only a few weeks later.

Camping in my attic quarters for the night, I heard the sergeant snoring on the other side of the wall. Sieghardt returned early the next morning. My freshening up had to be improvised with a little bowl of water brought up to the attic for me. But I got some breakfast without food stamps. A jeep took us to Potsdam where we rode the S-Bahn back to Zehlendorf-West. With both of us arriving at home, there could hardly have been a more joyful return, although every day that passed, we lived in quiet desperation about our uncertain future. The men were busy closing the firm and the nights were spent mostly in the air raid shelters.

Meanwhile all the tenants on Limastrasse were busy preparing to live in the basement because of the continual air raids and approaching Allied forces. So Sieghardt helped me drag down a sleep sofa to use day and night when the artillery shelling came closer to Berlin. In front of the large shelter was a smaller, long one, called a "gas corridor." Here everyone was to leave their clothing before entering the main air raid shelter after a gas attack, which we luckily never experienced. Sieghardt designated the front cellar as Vita's and mine, and set up the sleep sofa along the long wall, and at right angles, against the short wall, he put the baby's bed. Beneath it, in the roomy storage space for the bedding, we stockpiled all kinds of canned food, especially for the baby, like some pasteurized milk in old beer bottles. All other tenants also brought down food and something to sleep on, mostly beach chairs. Soon more people would camp here because old Mrs. Zschimmer was anxiously awaiting the arrival of her daughter and four grandchildren from Dresden who would come to live with her. We assured her that it would be no problem because we all would help her.

Sieghardt's leave was rapidly coming to an end, but to his great joy, Vita was now calling him *Pappi* (daddy). It was a heart breaking goodbye so well known by families around the world in wartime, and as a military man, Sieghardt could return to his unit by train. Shortly after his departure, the next horror message came through—the senseless and horrible destruction of the historic city of Dresden, the capital of Saxony, and for ages a cultural center of music, art and architecture, known as the "Florence on the Elbe." It had no military or industrial significance, not even anti-aircraft artillery. On February 13 and 14, the Allied bombing destroyed 85 percent of the city and the British phosphorous bombs had transformed Dresden into a living hell, melting the asphalt streets and turning people into human torches. We had anxiously been awaiting the arrival of Mrs. Zschimmer's family, and when we didn't hear from them after the attack on Dresden, we became alarmed. Finally, a friend of her family who had been an eyewitness to the attack from outside Dresden, came to see her and he hid his shock at finding her alone.

He told us that the helpless population had been bombed for fifteen hours without being able to defend themselves. Several hundred thousand civilians were killed in the city, including more than twenty thousand Allied prisoners of war and two hundred Americans. The Allies had killed their own people. The entire city was in flames with the raging fire sucking the oxygen from the air, and people were suffocated or burned alive. During the attack, the streets were jammed with over a million refugees from the East who had sought refuge there. Low flying American fighter planes fired on the crowds of people in trucks and on foot in the congested streets. Battered survivors who escaped and huddled next to the Elbe River were also mowed down by the deadly fire from the low flying aircraft.

The British and the Americans aimed their bombing solely at populated areas, and our eyewitness said the sole purpose of the attack was the deliberate annihilation of the civilian population—an Allied war crime, military-wise pointless. The airport Klotsche was not even hit once, nor were any of the Elbe bridges. Dresden burned for five days and six nights. Distressed, he tried to look for his own friends, but it was impossible to identify anybody. Horribly burned and mutilated human remains were everywhere, literally glued to melting pavements.

The gentleman knew that Mrs. Zschimmer's family had tried to catch a night train to Berlin, but they were never seen or heard from again. Three trains parked outside the station that were loaded with refugee children from the East were destroyed and left no survivors. Railroad personnel stacked the little corpses in large piles, saturated them with gasoline, and then burned them because there was no time to bury the dead. The trains were already running again. When he left, the entire city was saturated with the unmistakable foul odor of decaying flesh.

We were beyond shock. Obviously Mrs. Zschimmer's entire family was wiped out. Stiff with grief beyond description she was weeping bitterly, not knowing how to endure such a tragic blow. Afterwards it was estimated that under the detonation of three thousand bombs, more people perished in one night in Dresden than in all of the German attacks on England combined, and even more people died than those that perished through the future atom bomb attack on Hiroshima. International controversial criticisms stated that Sir Arthur "Bomber" Harris, commander of the R.A.F. strategic bomber offensive, was responsible for the indiscriminate destruction of Dresden. The true number of victims could never be determined.

In Berlin, we were experiencing incessant day and night bombings, and we thought: better an end with terror, than terror without end. We were ready to give up. But frightening news leaked out concerning a Yalta conference between Roosevelt, Churchill and Stalin about our unconditional surrender, followed by the partitioning of Germany among them. Papa called it "gobbling us up like a portion of caviar." They would also determine the future boundaries of our country. We were faced with an uncertain future as to how we would be governed and by whom. What a horrible thought! But where was Yalta anyway? We soon learned that it was in the southern part of the Soviet Union, a Crimean health resort. In such a remote area, our fate was to be sealed even before the end of the war. What else could Germany do but continue fighting? We would only exchange a present terror with another, unknown and certainly bigger.

*S*hattered Dreams

*S*pring arrived early in 1945. March had always been our birthday month. Günter's came first on the eighth, and mine and Mutti's followed shortly thereafter. However, this year there was little to celebrate; happy birthday wishes for a long life, or maybe a painless death together? We hadn't heard from Günter since the previous autumn, and we were feeling the ever increasing woes of war at home. The Red Army was less than one hundred miles from Berlin and the Allies had already crossed the Rhine River. Our food rations had been further curtailed to make the existing supplies last longer, and gas and electric outages had been extended. We had to cook during air raids to take advantage of the power being on. Lucky were those who still had the old coal-fired stoves, while others were cooking over hot bricks in their back yards. Warm water was a luxury.

The month of March began with a very intensive air raid by American bombers and these attacks continued every evening at precisely the same time until April 24. The intent of these incessant air attacks was to create havoc within the civilian population, but it brought us closer together. We were ordered to start digging entrenchments and to learn how to use anti-tank and hand grenades, which was pointless since there were not enough grenades to go around. Hitler was still shouting his war-cry, "Berliners, the army of General Wenk is approaching. Rescue is coming. Hold out!" We all knew that this legendary army had long since been destroyed and only existed in Hitler's imagination. He refused to face the facts that we merely had a half million soldiers, which included youngsters and the elderly of the Volkssturm, to defend Berlin against 3 million rapidly advancing Soviets. A final battle for our survival was the last thing on our minds and the first reality we had to deal with. Everybody knew these were the final days of a lost war, but no one said anything out of fear for risking the death penalty.

Long ago, Sieghardt and I had taken our oil paintings off their frames and stored them with Gerda's parents in Domjüch. Now, with the Soviets nearing, Gerda and I decided to bring them back home. She could travel by train on her special worker's permit, but I had none. So, I sneaked into the train with her. Once inside, there were no inspections. This was Saturday, March 24, and on weekends, the train only went to the little town of Gransee, which was near Strelitz. Luckily several German army trucks were going to Strelitz and one of them gave us a ride. From there, we were picked up by horse and carriage that had been sent from Domjüch by Gerda's mother. It was a very pleasant overnight stay with no air raid alarms. I packed up the paintings and was also supplied with food from their pantry and fields. Next morning, on Sunday, we were fortunate again to find a ride in an army truck, and this time, all the way back to Berlin.

Since our adventure to Domjüch had gone so well, Mutti thought that we should make one more attempt to see our farmer friend in Beelitz to get extra provisions for an ominous future. We left Vita with Grandma Schwanenflügel and set off with our knapsacks and a sturdy bag in each hand, plus tobacco rations to ensure a friendly welcome. We rode the S-Bahn to Potsdam and then walked briskly for several hours to the home of our farmer friend. We found the family extremely busy in their big kitchen with an enormous bowl of freshly fried hamburgers on the table. They urged us to eat all we could straight from the bowl with our fingers, which we did, and the more we enjoyed this unexpected meal, the more the farmers were laughing. Finally, they told us that several wounded army horses had been shot on the highway and that everyone had gone out with butcher knives to obtain free, extra provisions. We were eating horse meat! To kill the slightly sweet taste, they had added big portions of onions, pepper and salt. There was a large tub filled with that meat and they offered to sell us as much as we wanted and advised us to prepare it in the same manner as they had. Of course we wanted it. Although we had never eaten horse meat before, we gladly bought as much as we could carry, plus some farm products and fresh milk for Vita, which they filled into an empty beer bottle.

While we were talking, we heard a rumbling in the distance. "That is Soviet artillery," they explained. "It's getting closer every day." With that sobering news, we immediately cut our visit short and headed back to Berlin, just in time to run into a neighbor of theirs who was about to leave with his horse and wagon for Potsdam. In exchange for cigarettes, he gave us a ride to the S-Bahn, which we took back to Zehlendorf-West. On the way home, Mutti and I debated how to break the news to Papa that he was eating horse meat. In the good old days, he had always stressed quality when it came to his food, but he had to be less choosy under present conditions. We decided it was best to say nothing for now.

Papa was glad to see us home safely and only glanced at the onions and vegetables spread out on the kitchen table as he left the kitchen. With him gone, we got out the meat grinder and began preparing our "special" hamburgers. There was not enough electricity to run the refrigerator, so we had to prepare all of the meat at once. In no time our kitchen looked like a version of today's McDonald's in action. We all enjoyed eating as much as we wanted, especially Papa. He only hesitated once or twice, but knowing that Mutti was a good cook, he asked no questions.

After he went to bed, Mutti decided we should make *sauerbraten* out of the remaining meat, and we spent half the night preparing, making individual portions, convinced the strong vinegar would kill the sweet horse meat taste. The next morning, Papa saw the efforts of our night's work and wanted to know where this abundance of meat had come from. Now the secret was out about what he had eaten yesterday, and he was torn between being repelled at the thought or being thankful that we had food on the table. He decided on the latter and we three worked together as a team to preserve the *sauerbraten* in glass jars which Papa buried in the back yard for use in a future time of siege.

It was fortunate that we made our trip to the country when we did because the Soviets were closing in on Berlin and it would soon be impossible to venture outside of the city. Gerda had suddenly been transferred from the factory to a prisoner of war camp in Wittenau where she was to serve as a business assistant because of her language skills. The prisoners were Russians, Poles and Frenchmen, and some had previously been her co-workers at the factory. Now, many of them were hospitalized. The office was heated much better and the work less messy, but she encountered another problem—fleas! She was bitten all over every day. Her duties as an interpreter were made a whole lot easier when she discovered that the educated Russians spoke French, because Russian was her weakest foreign language.

Now in March, the final news on the radio promised that additional troops for Berlin were on the way. But all we actually got was Goebbels' flimflam: "Soviets, the Mongolic storm of the twentieth century! Protect our women and children from the Red Hordes!" We didn't listen to him and hoped that the Americans would get here first to free us from both the Nazis and the Soviets.

The Americans entered the Ruhr district near the end of March and we began hoping that they would reach us before the Soviets did. Mr. Huber kept us better informed than Goebbels' official communique and we never questioned him as to the source of his vital information. The Americans would have an unobstructed path into Berlin because there was no German army division to prevent their entry. Why should we learn how to use grenades when no one wanted to fight the Western Allies? Just the opposite, we wanted to be liberated by them from the Nazi's brown tyranny and to bring peace.

On April 2, the Americans were getting close to Zerbst and Papa received a frantic call from Aunt Grete. "The Americans are coming. What shall we do? Shall we come to you?" Impulsively, Papa burst out, "You lucky ones. Stay where you are!" What an answer! Mutti was so afraid that Papa's shady remark would be overheard as treason.

Sieghardt's unit had been moved to Döberitz, near Potsdam. Immediately, his mother decided that since Sieghardt was nearby, Vita should see her father. Daytime air attacks were now less frequent, so on April 4, the three of us were on our way with the baby stroller, traveling first by S-Bahn to Potsdam, then walking the remaining distance to Döberitz. Vita watched as we greeted Sieghardt, and when her father picked her up, she shyly called him "uncle" as if she wasn't sure who this strange man was in the green uniform. In my letters I had always sent many kisses from her to daddy. Now, when I saw how disappointed he looked, I wondered if it would have been best not to come, but there might never be another chance to meet again. We kept our visit short so we could be back home in the late afternoon before the first evening air attack, which increased in intensity every day.

A week later, I received two postcards. One was hastily scribbled information from Sieghardt to let me know that on April 10, his unit had moved to the Harz mountains. What a relief because he would be safe now from the grip of the Soviets. The other card was from a Mrs. Döblitz, whom I didn't know, and the content was a complete mystery to me. It said, "I am bombed out again. Soon you will need me. This is my new address..." Although I did not know this person, the message seemed important, as if someone wanted to return a favor. Puzzled, I called Linda, Sieghardt's sister, and she immediately recognized the sender as a long-time faithful employee of their firm, Stempelkaiser. She was one of the Jewish-related employees whom Sieghardt had helped at his own risk when he was still with the firm, and Linda urged me to keep the postcard.

The Red Army was sweeping through Eastern Europe and had just taken Vienna. Who would be the first to reach Berlin? We were hoping it would be the Americans, who had already reached Hannover on April 11. On April 12, 1945, we received word that President Roosevelt had died after twelve years in office and Goebbels was jubilant in his radio announcement: "The Allies are near breakdown. Our Führer will overcome the crisis. We will defeat the enemy. Germans hold out!" For what? We wanted the Nazis no more than the Soviets.

Right now we were holding out in long lines in front of grocery stores, quickly taking cover when we saw or heard an enemy airplane. The air raid sirens were no longer working which meant we would be attacked without warning, but we couldn't worry about that. Sudden death had become a way of life and we had to be outside daily to get food. Our rations were now distributed on a daily basis and differed from day to day and store to store, according to availability. The Wilhelm Fürtwängler Philharmonic Orchestra performed its last concert. The musicians were ordered to play, even without an audience.

On April 16, 1945, the final battle for Berlin began. The Soviets gradually cut off the last escape route and we sat in a death trap from which survival would be a matter of luck. We could already hear the Soviet heavy artillery as we huddled together in the seclusion of our cellars, trembling for our lives and praying that the Americans would get here in time to liberate Berlin. We knew they were only sixty miles away. Why did it take them so long? There was no German army blocking their way. But our hope was in vain because General Eisenhower, the Supreme Commander of the Allied forces, had stopped the American troops the day before, April 15, to give the Soviets the sole honor of capturing Berlin. We were left like prey to the Red Army. Eisenhower played the siege of Berlin to the galleries of the world. Churchill issued a strong warning that Berlin should not be left in Soviet hands, as the capital was the key to Germany. And, he was proven correct because General Eisenhower's questionable decision started a power struggle between the Soviets and Western Allies, which created a world crisis for decades.

For us, the war dictated its last bloody chapter. Berlin's population had shrunk from over 4.5 million to about 2 million, mostly women, children and the elderly, such as my own family. Hitler's latest order was for everyone to assist in the war effort by helping to build new lines of fortifications from the rubble that was everywhere. There was no planned evacuation for the population before the city was encircled by the Soviets. We expected the worst and were to be subjected now to day and night air attacks by the Allies from the East and the West. One English air raid resulted in the total annihilation of the baroque center of the historic town of Potsdam, which was only ten miles from us. The Americans were approaching Leipzig.

Friday, April 20, was Hitler's fifty-sixth birthday, and the Soviets sent him a birthday present in the form of an artillery barrage right into the heart of the city, while the Western Allies joined in with a massive air raid. The radio announced that Hitler had come out of his safe bomb-proof bunker to talk with the fourteen to sixteen year old boys who had "volunteered" for the "honor" to be accepted into the SS and to die for their Führer in the defense of Berlin. What a cruel lie! These boys did not volunteer, but had no choice, because boys who were found hiding were hanged as traitors by the SS as a warning that, "he who was not brave enough to fight had to die." When trees were not available, people were strung up on lamp posts. They were hanging everywhere, military and civilian, men and women, ordinary citizens who had been executed by a small group of fanatics. It appeared that the Nazis did not want the people to survive because a lost war, by their rationale, was obviously the fault of all of us. We had not sacrificed enough and therefore, we had forfeited our right to live, as only the government was without guilt. The Volkssturm was called up again, and this time, all boys age thirteen and up, had to report as our army was reduced now to little more than children filling the ranks as soldiers.

In honor of Hitler's birthday, we received an eight-day ration allowance, plus one tiny can of vegetables, a few ounces of sugar and a half-ounce of real coffee. No one could afford to miss rations of this type and we stood in long lines at the grocery store patiently waiting to receive them. While standing there, we noticed a sad looking young boy across the street standing behind some bushes in a self-dug shallow trench. I went over to him and found a mere child in a uniform many sizes too large for him, with an anti-tank grenade lying beside him. Tears were running down his face, and he was obviously very frightened of everyone. I very softly asked him what he was doing there. He lost his distrust and told me that he had been ordered to lie in wait here, and when a Soviet tank approached he was to run under it and explode the grenade. I asked how that would work, but he didn't know. In fact, this frail child didn't even look capable of carrying such a grenade. It looked to me like a useless suicide assignment because the Soviets would shoot him on sight before he ever reached the tank.

By now, he was sobbing and muttering something, probably calling for his mother in despair, and there was nothing that I could do to help him. He was a picture of distress, created by our inhuman government. If I encouraged him to run away, he would be caught and hung by the SS, and if I gave him refuge in my home, everyone in the house would be shot by the SS. So, all we could do was to give him something to eat and drink from our rations. When I looked for him early next morning he was gone and so was the grenade. Hopefully, his mother found him and would keep him in hiding during these last days of a lost war.

On April 21, the Red Army reached the outskirts of Berlin with an artillery attack on the northern and eastern parts of the city. Their main objective was the Chancery, Hitler's underground bunker headquarters in the heart of the city. The next day, scared relatives of the old Scharnow couple suddenly appeared at our house. The daughter, grandchildren and great-grandchildren had escaped the carnage on foot since all transportation was destroyed in the abandoned areas. Totally exhausted, they told us how Soviet troops with tanks and heavy artillery had made their way into the eastern suburbs through heavy house-to-house fighting, looting on the way and leaving behind total destruction and utter panic. The German soldiers did their best, but for what? We were now eleven families cooking on one wood burning stove in the basement, trying to remain calm and preserve order as best as we could, with a growing understanding of others' misfortune.

A hectic secret activity suddenly seized our house. We were all possessed by the same idea to destroy all Nazi literature that had piled up over the past twelve years, before the Soviets arrived. Every household had received some Nazi books either as rewards at work instead of the customary gold watch, or as school books, such as Hitler's *Mein Kampf.* Mine derived from my school days.

We all rushed to our apartments during the short spells between air raids and brought all dubious materials back to the basement that would have made the Soviets believe that we were hard-core Nazi party members. But how does one dispose of Nazi material without attracting attention? To burn it would be the fastest way, but where? No one wanted to be seen in the garden destroying government printings and risk being caught and shot by the SS, even though Hitler's days were numbered. More and more people were hanged everywhere, even men in uniform wearing the Iron Cross, with signs around their necks: "I am a coward and not worthy to live." I saw one strung up close by the Argentinische Allee, a gruesome sight I will never forget.

Fortunately, we had a coal-fired, central heating system located in a common boiler room that served both apartment buildings and was accessible from both sides by metal doors. This proved to be a convenient place for some inconspicuous burning, hopefully without being seen by other people. Lately there were so many new refugees living with us in the basement, that we did not know whom we could trust. Since all of us suddenly had the same bright idea of burning the unwanted books, this created a congestion of residents of both buildings who all were desperately trying to dispose of the damaging evidence. No one wanted to admit why they were in the furnace room, and this resulted in some comic collisions. No one wanted to be caught.

The unusually warm spring weather which required no heat also presented another problem because our amateur burning was a very noticeable smokey and smelly affair. I happened to appear with my Hitler book as other volumes were still smoldering in the furnace. I could easily read the titles. *Mein Kampf* was a slow burner, and I had no time to rip out the pages to make it ignite faster. Now we had arranged our own book burning in the building. This time we destroyed Hitler's books as "Un-German literature," which was contrary to his book burning in 1933. In retrospect, what we did was a foolish mistake because just a few months later American soldiers were gladly paying top dollars for any Nazi items, just to take some home as souvenirs.

Since everybody eventually knew what everybody else was doing, there was no need for precautions any longer, so we decided that we should work as a team. Our first joint decision was to comb through all of the deserted apartments without regard to personal property rights, focusing only on our own survival, and dispose of anything that could get us in trouble. We went into the apartment above me that had been abandoned by the Birkholz family who had helped us build our bunker in the back yard. He was a member of the *Organization Todt*. His apartment was unlocked in case of fire, and it contained a gold mine of forbidden items, including a framed picture of Birkholz and Fritz Todt wearing their wide swastika arm bands, numerous books and even a brown uniform left in the closet. All this had to go.

In fear of additional surprises, we inspected the empty apartment of our former porter who was now at the front and whose wife and child had fled to the West. There, hidden under rags in the broom closet, was a complete Soviet uniform and rifle which the porter must have brought back from the Russian front as a war trophy. We were thunderstruck. Soviet tanks were already within the city limits and street fighting was going on day and night. If the Soviets would have found this, they would have accused us of killing their comrade and shot all of us on the spot. We had to make these Russian trophies disappear immediately, but we couldn't burn a rifle in a furnace. So we wrapped it all up and our brave team of men, consisting of Huber and Weissbach, carried it across the street that night and buried it in the rubble of a house that had been completely demolished in a recent air raid, unnoticed by the porter in the house next door who was believed to be a Communist. We assumed that the Russians would not bother rummaging through ruins when better houses nearby could be looted.

My parents were much better off with no Nazi literature or pictures in their home, only Hindenburg's portrait, and that remained on the wall. However, their dangerous Nazi neighbor, Mr. Reichelt, with his large supply of Nazi literature in the waiting room of his dental office, had to be in big trouble. Well, he wasn't, as we later learned. He had been amply provided with literature from Marx to Engels, well prepared to sail with the Communist wind. And, to disguise where the Nazi dentist lived, his wrecked dental chair was dumped one night into the bomb crater in front of my parents' house, to make it look as if he lived there.

While Mutti and Papa were debating what to do about this fatal object, the doorbell rang and there stood Mr. Reichelt. "Hello, Mr. Schmidt," he started in a very friendly manner, too friendly for Papa. Mr. Reichelt continued jovially, "We have to expect hard times on this street...ah ...we all should stick together." Papa looked at him reserved, remembering the incident two years ago over a trash pile dispute when the dentist had written a threatening letter using the power of his Nazi friends against him. Papa cut him off with, "What is the real reason for this confrontation?" Unperturbed Mr. Reichelt went on, "You know I never really meant any harm, and with all we've been through, let's forget our differences. Ah, by the way," and now he finally came to the point of his visit, "do you still have the letter I once wrote to you in anger?" "Yes," said Papa quietly. "I do."

Mr. Reichelt could barely conceal his shock. "Oh, I never meant to harm or upset you in any way," and in obvious fear he now asked if he could have his letter back. He knew that this incriminating evidence would seal his fate with the Soviets. But, Papa informed him that he had no intention of parting with it. Our neighbor, now obviously at the end of his wits, humbly asked what he intended to do with it. "Right now, nothing, as long as you behave," Papa replied and reminded him of that dental chair which had to be removed off his property. Mr. Reichelt regretted that he had no help to move such a heavy object. "Well, I don't either," Papa told him calmly, "and whoever put it there will have to take it away again within twenty-four hours," and he closed the door. The next morning, the dental chair was gone just as mysteriously as it had appeared.

Our next urgent task was to withdraw money from the bank so we would have plenty of cash on hand. Our tenants on Limastrasse followed our example. Fortunately, each apartment had a wall safe in one of the bedrooms, and I kept mine concealed by hanging a picture over it. We also had to hide our valuables and destroy any items which might raise suspicion, as the dreaded Red Army was coming closer every day. For instance, I had a beautiful dress which our dressmaker had made from scraps. On each grey sleeve she had attached a fancy appliqué of a large black eagle with its wings spread out. (I'm wearing this dress in the picture on page 287.) Would the Soviets think that this represented something military? I wasn't going to take any chances, so I took the dress to my parents' home where Papa and Mr. Thiemer were busy sealing the entrance to the coal bin by building a false wall using bricks from other ruins. The space was half empty, and there was plenty of room to hide suitcases and knapsacks filled with precious items, including my eagle dress. I felt very relieved afterwards.

The radio announced that the Führer would stay in Berlin to oversee the defense of the capital, but this would be done from the safe distance of his luxurious bunker a hundred feet underground, while we were condemned to sit helplessly in our cellars and wait for death. The Soviets had fought their way right into the heart of the city and the sound of their artillery became louder and louder. No one left the shelter except for food, and it became more and more perilous to stand in line outside with the constant Soviet gunfire attacks from the sky. Often I didn't know where to quickly take cover, but I had to be out to get the daily milk ration for infants. For emergency, I had already pasteurized some milk in beer bottles and stored them under Vita's bed.

On the night of April 23, we collected all of the alcohol in the house and drank wine, cognac, beer, one right after the other, so that it would not fall into the hands of the Soviets. Drunken Soviets were far worse than sober ones. To just pour it down the drain would have been throwing valuable calories away, and besides, it filled us up. We had a good night's sleep even though there was machine gun and rifle fire throughout the night in our suburb as the Soviets eliminated pockets of resistance. How many people were killed needlessly?

The next day at exactly 5:20 p.m., our house was rocked by a barrage of Russian bombs and we in the basement were shaken so violently that we feared we would be buried alive like animals in their holes. A deep crater yawned in the street, roof tiles were flung all over the garden, windows were shattered and cracks appeared in the front brick wall. Shortly thereafter, we heard the chatter of heavy machine gun fire across from the S-Bahn embankment which meant that the Soviets had fought their way into the area where Mutti and Papa lived. Were they still alive?

The Soviets battled the German soldiers and drafted civilians street by street until we could hear explosions and rifle fire right in our immediate vicinity. As the noise got closer, we could even hear the horrible guttural screaming of the Soviet soldiers which sounded to us like enraged animals. Shots shattered our windows and shells exploded in our garden, and suddenly the Soviets were on our street. Shaken by the battle around us and numb with fear, we watched from behind the small cellar windows facing the street as the tanks and an endless convoy of troops rolled by, heading for the restaurant *Alte Fischerhütte* on the lake Schlachtensee at the end of our street.

It was a terrifying sight as they sat high upon their tanks with their rifles cocked, aiming at houses as they passed. The screaming, gun-wielding women were the worst. Half of the troops had only rags and tatters around their feet while others wore SS boots that had been looted from a conquered SS barrack in Lichterfelde. Several fleeing people had told us earlier that they kept watching different boots pass by their cellar windows. At night, the Germans in *our* army boots recaptured the street that the Soviets in the SS boots had taken during the day. The boots and the voices told them who was who. Now we saw them with our own eyes, and they belonged to the wild cohorts of the advancing Soviet troops.

Facing reality was ten times worse than just hearing about it. Throughout the night, we huddled together in mortal fear, not knowing what the morning might bring. Nevertheless, we noiselessly did sneak upstairs to double check that our heavy wooden window shutters were still intact and that all outside doors were barricaded. But as I peaked out, what did I see! The porter couple in the apartment house next to ours was standing in their front yard waving to the Soviets. So our suspicion that they were Communists had been right all along, but they must have been out of their minds to openly proclaim their brotherhood like that.

As could be expected, that night a horde of Soviet soldiers returned and stormed into their apartment house. Then we heard what sounded like a terrible orgy with women screaming for help, many shrieking at the same time. The racket gave me goosebumps. Some of the Soviets trampled through our garden and banged their rifle butts on our doors in an attempt to break in. Thank goodness our sturdy wooden doors withstood their efforts. Gripped in fear, we sat in stunned silence, hoping to give the impression that this was a vacant house, but hopelessly delivered into the clutches of the long-feared Red Army. Our nerves were in shreds.

Mrs. Weissbach, from the adjoining apartment unit, sneaked over into our basement to reveal her sudden brainstorm. She was a registered nurse and suggested that we set up a temporary Red Cross station in our porter's empty basement apartment. What an ingenious plan to give us more security. Luckily, I still had my Red Cross uniform, extra arm bands and an emergency kit upstairs in my apartment and crept up very quietly to get them. I passed out the Red Cross arm bands immediately. One group took mattresses from deserted apartments and spread them on the floor to serve as beds. Another group converted a table into a professional looking arrangement, complete with bandages, cotton in empty jam glasses, and face cream jars labeled as salves and ointments. We even sacrificed a piece of our rare soap, as well as some towels, to complete the picture of a realistic looking first aid station. Even a bathroom was close by to lend an air of sanitation to the scene. Meanwhile a third group made a small Red Cross flag and attached it to a broom stick which was fastened through a small, grilled window next to the door on the side of the house. Our flag could be seen from the street, but not so well that it would attract unwanted attention.

We finished our Red Cross project around midnight and we felt very proud that we had accomplished so much with so little, and also somehow felt more protected. Shortly thereafter, there was a faint knocking at our cellar window. We carefully peeked out and saw a frightened old woman, who we quickly let in. I recognized her as young Marga Saal from next door wearing a disguise. She collapsed, totally exhausted, and eventually was able to tell us what had happened at her house. The Communist porter had stupidly greeted the Soviets who felt invited, and later returned for a rampage through the apartments. Every woman, regardless of age, was raped repeatedly because there were so many soldiers, and if they tried to resist, they were beaten or threatened to be shot. Marga had fled into the garden and hid in a remote corner, waiting until the Soviets were drunk and tired so she could escape over the wire fence to seek refuge in our house, which looked so quiet and untouched.

I knew Marga very well because our kitchen windows faced each other and we used to wave to one another. For years, she had lived next door with her widowed father who was a high ranking marine officer. At the moment, she was all alone because her father was downtown in the Department of the Navy, and she was in great despair because she had not heard from him. I offered to share my couch with her, and sleeping fully dressed, it would be a very crowded arrangement, but she would be safe. Nobody wanted more people in our cramped basement, but we decided she could stay on one condition, that she never go back to her apartment next door. Tearfully she agreed with everything. We wanted that our building looked empty and we did not want any relationship with the people next door. She would also eat with us although she had nothing to contribute. This was a gift of life with such a shortage of supplies. We lived off what we had. Nothing could be replaced. Meanwhile the Soviets made further advances in the Berlin battle. The tragedy seemed to be in its final stage—but the worst was yet to come.

The next morning, we women proceeded to make ourselves look as unattractive as possible to the Soviets by smearing our faces with coal dust and covering our heads with old rags, our make-up for the Ivan. We huddled together in the central part of the basement, shaking with fear, while some peeked through the low basement windows to see what was happening on the Soviet-controlled street. We felt paralyzed by the sight of these husky Mongolians, looking wild and frightening. At the ruin across the street from us the first Soviet orders were posted, including a curfew.

Suddenly there was a shattering noise outside. Horrified, we watched the Soviets demolish the corner grocery store and throw its contents, shelving and furniture out into the street. Urgently needed bags of flour, sugar and rice were split open and spilled their contents on the bare pavement, while Soviet soldiers stood guard with their rifles so that no one would dare to pick up any of the urgently needed food. This was just unbelievable. At night, a few desperate people tried to salvage some of the spilled food from the gutter. Hunger now became a major concern because our ration cards were worthless with no hope of any supplies.

Shortly thereafter, there was another commotion outside, even worse than before, and we rushed to our lookout to see that the Soviets had broken into the bank and were looting it. They came out yelling gleefully with their hands full of German bank notes and jewelry from safe deposit boxes that had been pried open. Thank God we had withdrawn money already and had it at home.

Luckily we had the foresight to protect our silver items from rampages like these. Long ago, we had wrapped them all in oil paper and then looked for a suitable hiding place. The steep rock garden that surrounded our terrace seemed to be the answer. We proceeded to remove some of the big rocks and then dug deep holes underneath. There we buried our precious possessions quite inconspicuously. After we were done, we carefully replaced the rocks to their original position and also planted greenery around so it would look just like before. No one was the wiser—we hoped. We were quite proud and pleased with our work, because it was known that the Soviets checked the lawns with metal sticks in order to detect hidden objects.

When Sieghardt had been home on leave, we had moved a long table from our Florida room to the central area of the basement where we now all ate together. Everyone contributed what modest supplies they had to be shared with everybody else. Even our combined contributions were not much and as we discussed our desperate situation, I suddenly remembered the emergency provisions stored in the garage of Mr. Birkholtz, who had since disappeared. We hoped that he had left behind his food supply and were eager to check it out. I got the garage key from his deserted apartment, and as soon as it was dark, several of us sneaked outside to his garage in the far corner of our backyard— curfew or no curfew—while the others watched for patrolling Soviets from our basement door. Those in the garage seemed very busy and they finally showed up heavily loaded with their arms full of canned goods and other food.

The trip to the garage was repeated several times until all the emergency stock had been relocated into our basement. We stacked everything on the table and it looked like a treasure to us. There were cans of milk, meat, sausage and sardines, plus fruits, vegetables and shortening, as well as chocolates, candy and other emergency items. Our survival was now assured for a while, and I even had canned milk for Vita. "Communism" could never have worked better than now among us "Capitalists." Otherwise we had nothing in common with the Communists, especially with those Germans who returned now with the Red Army from exile in the Soviet Union. They stormed through the streets demonstrating their new importance.

We did not dare return to our apartments for fear that the Soviets would notice some sign of life and break in through the ground level windows and doors. From the outside, the building appeared to be totally deserted with shuttered windows and locked doors. I still had no word about my family who was located on the other side of the S-Bahn, five minutes away. How desperately I missed them all! No one would have dared to be seen on the streets because the Soviets raped everyone, young girls, old women, nurses and nuns. Rapes took place wherever a woman was found, whether inside a building or outside in public. (Anyone who wants further details about the plundering of Berlin and how the Soviets treated even children can find very accurate accounts on the book market.)

The following night, we heard a soft tapping against the window with the Red Cross flag. It was repeated several times. We figured that a Soviet soldier would not be so gentle so the Weissbachs carefully peeked out and saw a blood-stained German who was completely exhausted. We quickly let him in and took him to our first aid station where our nurse, Heidi Weissbach, discovered that he had been shot in the lungs. We stopped the bleeding and sealed the wound air-tight with the waterproof padding off Vita's bed and then made him as comfortable as possible on one of the mattresses, hoping he was going to live. After some food and drink, he felt a little better and told us his story.

He was a journalist who happened to be in the restaurant *Alte Fischerhütte* by the lake Schlachtensee at the end of our street. The three-story house was filled to capacity with the owner's friends and relatives who were refugees from the East. The Soviets stormed in and ordered everybody outside and lined them up in the garden. With their rifles

The restaurant Alte Fischerhütte at lake Schlachtensee

cocked, they went down the line asking each person if they were a Nazi and as they would answer "no," they were shot on the spot. This procedure continued until they came to him, standing near the end of the long line. He felt the shot in his chest so he dropped to the ground and, although feeling great pain as blood soaked his clothing, he remained motionless. When the killing of all men, women and children was over, the Soviet soldiers roared in triumph and stormed back into the house.

After lying quietly for a while, he dragged himself from among the dead bodies and hid in some bushes. At night, while pressing his hands to his bleeding chest, he slowly trudged along our street until he saw our Red Cross flag. Now we understood why we heard so much shooting that afternoon coming from the direction of the Schlachtensee. (The word *Schlacht* means battle or slaughter, and the lake's name dates back to an ancient victorious battle of Christians over the heathen tribe of Wenden. Now it was the killing of Christians by the ungodly Soviets.)

Our patient told us another horror story about a nearby hospital that had been overcrowded with our severely wounded soldiers, many of them amputees who had just returned from the front. The Soviets stormed in and brutally threw everyone out in the street—patients, doctors and nurses. The wounded and young amputees without arms or legs were lying helplessly in the gutter and when neighbors came out of their homes to rescue them, the Soviet soldiers drove them back with their rifle butts. The Soviets' slaughter house was in operation according to Stalin's order. Living in our sheltered basement, we could not believe that such horrible events were taking place on the outside. How lucky we were to have our quiet cellar community. As I crawled onto the couch with Marga, I found Vita fast asleep in her own dream world, a picture of total peace.

The next morning, some Soviet soldiers banged on our Red Cross window. Our hearts pounded with fear, but much to our relief they only asked for a drink of water, which we gladly gave them. The next group just barged in for the purpose of looting, demanding *Urri, Urri* which was their pronunciation for the German word *Uhr* (pronounced "oor"), meaning watch or clock. Their arms were already adorned with watches they had grabbed while plundering homes, and it appeared that wrist watches were unknown to them and they wanted all they could get to take back to Russia.

While wildly searching for more booty, they discovered our patient and screamed in broken German, "Soldier! You hide soldier!" We were afraid they were going to kill him and us on the spot, but "nurse Heidi" calmed them down with, "No soldier, only old man." Everybody looked old and haggard at that time, even though our patient was only in his thirties. Still suspicious, they rudely turned him over with their boots and looked under the mattress, searching for a uniform. When they found only civilian clothes lying openly on a chair, they gave up and stumbled out. Apparently, a Red Cross aid station did not look promising enough to waste any more time in looting.

Some hours later, the Soviets stormed in on my side of the building through a door that someone had forgotten to lock, and three soldiers trampled down the basement stairs right into the midst of a dozen people, mostly women. First they started their cry of *Urri, Urri,* and when they found we had none left, they gesticulated wildly with their guns, hollering in Russian and pushed us against the wall, shoulder to shoulder. Within only a few feet distance, they pointed their rifles straight at us and performed a mock execution. It happened so quickly that all I could think of was little Vita who was peacefully playing behind the iron door in the air raid shelter.

Then shots rang out and I felt the draft of a bullet passing by my right ear. Mrs. Conrad next to me screamed. The shots were deafening in such a confined space, leaving me with a shrill high pitched ringing in my ears. Then there was only dead silence and a thick white fog settling around me, and with my eyes wide open, I thought, "So that's what it's like to be dead." Then the fog, which was caused by the rifle shots between our heads into the plaster of the wall behind us, gradually dissipated. I looked again. The three Soviets were still standing there, smirking with satisfaction, or had I perhaps lost my mind? No. There they were in front of me grinning, ready for more shooting.

Just then, the connecting door between our adjoining basements flung open and all of the people from the other house rushed in. Alarmed by the shooting, they wanted to know what was going on. The three Soviets felt cornered, suddenly surrounded by a crowd of Germans, and began to slowly back up as they kept their weapons aimed at us, and then they disappeared up the stairs to the outside. The sudden appearance of the people from the adjoining basement had undoubtedly saved our lives. The Soviets never liked to be outnumbered by too many Germans.

The experience with the three Soviet soldiers left us in a state of utter terror of the senseless brutality that could be our fate, and with no hope for the future, many of us thought of committing suicide. It was a part of every day life. If we had to die, why not now and in a manner of our own choosing, but how? Poison would provide the quickest and easiest method, but we had none. Hanging would mean that I would have to hang my own child first before I could hang myself, and this I could not do! Cutting the wrists with razor blades was not effective because we knew of several suicide survivors in the neighborhood who had tried that. The blood had coagulated and the bleeding stopped.

I felt very lonely and was terribly afraid. While desperately contemplating the various methods of suicide, I heard someone coming down the stairs, and there stood Mutti. Like a miracle, she appeared out of nowhere. "Mutti, you're alive!" My brave mother must have sensed my danger and desperation and showed up at the very moment when I needed her most. As we fell into each other's arms, she noticed the terror that prevailed among us. "What's going on here?" she asked, finding us all so terrified. With everyone trying to talk at the same time, we poured our hearts out, and even our thoughts of committing suicide. "You're all running around like chickens with their heads cut off," she exclaimed. "Don't give up so quickly. This won't go on forever." Then she turned to me. "You're out of your mind to even consider killing Vita. I left you on Limastrasse to be safer with all of these people close by rather than at our home where there are only a few neighbors around. Now I find all this panic."

With the inborn instinct of a loving mother, she had not even considered the risk of walking down a Soviet-controlled street, and refused to leave until she was sure I had come to my senses again. She told us that a barrier had been erected at the S-Bahn underpass to block the street, but when she mentioned *matka* (mother) in Polish to the Soviet guards, they somehow respected her and allowed her to pass. This way she arrived with only one thought in mind, to find us alive.

I finally learned that everyone had survived in their neighborhood, but the Soviets had arrived before Papa had a chance to complete the false wall in front of the coal bin behind which all of our valuables were hidden. The first group barged in the basement, threatening everyone with their rifles and ransacking whatever they could find. It was a maddening experience as they tore open the knapsacks and took Günter's gold watch and many other personal items. What one of them overlooked, the next one grabbed. They finally left to check out houses that looked more promising than our damaged one.

Sieghardt's family across the street fared much worse. The Soviets started to shoot wildly through the windows, then continued firing inside. The family and their old female cook escaped and ran over to Mutti's. "Now we were all together, a frightened bunch of eight," she said. Linda had been living in constant fear of being raped and spent hours hiding in a small crawl space under the roof in the attic which could only be reached by a ladder which she pulled up after herself. Although she was never discovered, she experienced moments of terror when Soviet soldiers stormed into the attic searching for young women to rape. It was unthinkable what would have happened if she suddenly had to cough or sneeze as she lay flat in her hiding place. The Soviets also poked sticks into the lawn to look for buried valuables, but fortunately missed our glass jars of horse meat.

Now it was our turn to tell Mutti about the precautions we had taken before the Soviets had arrived, such as the book burnings and destroying all suspicious items we found in deserted apartments, especially the porter's Russian war trophies. Then she asked, "And what did you do with Sieghardt's Walther pistol?" Good heavens. I had completely forgotten about that ticking time bomb in my own apartment upstairs since I had never seen Sieghardt with it. In fact, I didn't even know where it was, and Mutti decided that we should sneak up there that very minute and start searching for it. All of my rooms were dimly lit because the heavy wooden shutters were closed and only a little daylight shone through some of the small slits. We quietly searched through his desk and there it was, in one of the drawers in its leather holster with a supply of ammunition. What a shock; but now what? This threat to our safety had to go and we quickly hid it under our clothing.

Before leaving, I could not resist a quick look at my back yard and quietly approached the darkened window in the dim light and peeked through a slit in the shade. Whoa! I found myself eye to eye with a Soviet soldier who had picked that very moment to peek into my apparently deserted apartment. I shrank back into the shadows as he began to rattle the shutters, but they were too strong to be broken that easily. Had he seen me? Since he was standing outside in the daylight and I was inside in the darkness, I was not sure. He began pounding on the door of the Florida room, as Mutti slowly pulled me further back into the darkness and then out into the hall. We rushed down to the basement. What a frightful incident that had been, facing a Soviet soldier while carrying a concealed weapon and ammunition. Downstairs I had to confess what we found upstairs. The weapon had to go, but how? Mr. Weissbach immediately took charge. He had gone through so many miseries that he would survive this one, too, he said. Recently he had been buried alive under a collapsed building downtown, and was not rescued until the following morning. This disaster had gravely affected his health and left his speech with a hoarse rattle in his throat. Nevertheless, he would take care of the pistol.

Meanwhile Mutti had seen the wounded man in our first aid station. "He needs a doctor," she reasoned. "Doctor Zimmermann lives right at the corner." We had already asked him to come over but he was too afraid to leave his house. This answer would not do for Mutti. Slipping one of the Red Cross arm bands over her sleeve, she ran out to the doctor's house next door. Quite a while passed, but finally she returned with the doctor in tow who was now wearing her Red Cross arm band. She told us later that it was not easy to convince him to come, but here he was and better equipped to provide medical help that we could not render. This saved our patient's life. Long after the war, he returned for a visit, took pictures, and wrote an article in a newspaper about his rescue.

By now the curfew was in effect at 6 p.m. Soviet time, actually 4 p.m. our time, because our watches were reset to their Moscow time, from where all decisions were made for Berlin. This also created a two-hour time differential between the Soviet-occupied parts of Berlin and those where fighting was still in process. Since most of our watches had become Soviet booty, the lone bell of the Paulus Church in Zehlendorf-Mitte, which was overlooked when all the others were melted down, rang to inform us when the curfew started in bright daylight, and when it was over in the dark morning hours. Mutti could not go home that afternoon, leaving Papa up in arms about her absence. It could be good-bye forever. That night we both nervously watched Mr. Weissbach risking his life by slipping out into the yard and using a soup spoon to bury the pistol and ammunition in the soft earth behind the garages. The next morning, April 28, while we heard shots ring out in the still of the night, Mutti returned home as early as possible and I prayed for her safe walk.

Shortly thereafter, Mr. Huber surprised us with the good news, "Our baker has bread for the first time in days!" Each person could buy one pound with a new stamp on our old food ration card, and that was sufficient incentive for all of us to come out of hiding. What a feeling to be outside again. The baker down the street opened at 6 a.m., which was only 4 a.m. actual Berlin time, and endless lines had already formed outside. We had to wait three hours to be served, so different family members took turns waiting in line. The unfortunate people at the end of the line waited in vain, because the demand exceeded the supply.

Patrolling Soviet soldiers marched up and down and after selecting a young female at random, would force her into the bakery and then lock the door. After a while, the door would open again and the girl would come out carrying several loaves of free bread, and everyone knew why she had been so nicely rewarded. For us, the regular selling of bread would continue between these arbitrary interruptions. The baker's wife was helpless because she had already been raped repeatedly herself. People whispered about the many arbitrary arrests and deportations to Russia. Some neighbors had even been shot for no reason. Suddenly, Mutti appeared again and stood in line for me, insisting that I go back to my safe basement with all of the others who were returning with their bread. That same day, the Soviets ordered that all streets be cleared of air raid rubble. But how? We had to shovel the debris into our own gardens, solving this problem the Soviet way! While the older people labored outside, we younger ones cooked and cleaned inside to escape any unwanted Soviet attention.

One evening, we heard heavy shooting again that came from the nearby *Onkel Tom's Hütte* district, a residential area named after Uncle Tom's cabin. It was crowded with refugees and had been captured by the Soviets about ten days earlier. Suddenly, for no known reason, the Soviets began a massacre by firing their *Stalinorgel* (Stalin organ), a five-barrel grenade launcher mounted on motor vehicles that fired non-stop. We were more terrified now to go outside no matter for what reason.

Nevertheless, our next Soviet order, delivered by door-to-door messengers with the usual threat of death penalty for not complying, was to surrender all radios. They were to be delivered to the lawn in front of the S-Bahn station, where the beautiful and expensive sets piled up in heaps all day long without any protection from the weather.

The Soviets laughed proudly as they watched the collection grow. "We take all to Russia and then have automatic music like here." Apparently they had no concept of electrical outlets and wiring, which was not usually available in the average home in Russia. We saw the radios left outside for many days until they were carelessly loaded onto open trucks like sacks of potatoes to be taken to the Soviet Union. Mutti and Papa had to give up their wonderful *Blaupunkt* set, but took the chance to keep the little radio that Günter had built as a school boy, which was still working.

In the captured suburbs, the Soviets immediately took over all administrative and political leadership, even while fighting was still going on in other parts of Berlin. On April 30, it was announced that a German Communist had been appointed in our area as the liaison officer to their Kommandatura, the later Soviet district administration. What a terrible month all of April had been. What could we expect in May?

The next day, May 1, was a dreaded day for us. All Germans stayed off the streets to escape the wild revelry of an important Soviet national holiday. Marauding and drunken soldiers roamed the streets, screaming, shooting and banging against house doors from early morning on, and later in the day, the racket even increased when looting soldiers found more alcohol in the basement of a delicatessen store which was directly behind our back yard. They drank it to the last drop and people suffered the consequences. We felt surrounded by wild animals. All day and all night, we cringed in our basement hideaway and Hitler's May 1 celebration ten years ago flashed through my mind, when I had left Berlin for Godesberg with my tennis racket in hand, carefully avoiding all Nazi demonstrations. I could not have imagined such a stroke of fate that some years later I would be avoiding Soviet demonstrations of this type in Berlin.

The next day, General Wilding, the commander of the German troops in Berlin, finally surrendered the entire city to the Soviet army. There was no radio or newspaper, so vans with loudspeakers drove through the streets ordering us to cease all resistance. Suddenly, the shooting and bombing stopped and the unreal silence meant that one ordeal was over for us and another was about to begin. Our nightmare had become a reality. The entire three hundred square miles of what was left of Berlin were now completely under control of the Red Army. The last days of savage house to house fighting and street battles had been a human slaughter, with no prisoners being taken on either side. These final days were hell. Our last remaining and exhausted troops, primarily children and old men, stumbled into imprisonment. We were a city in ruins; almost no house remained intact. The son of the Weissbach's, Eberhard, a young officer, had been in combat around the Zoo bunker in the downtown area, and we anxiously awaited word from him. We hoped for good news because their other son had been killed earlier at the Eastern Front.

So, we were the lucky ones who had survived, but what did we have to survive for, and why just us? The Red flag was hoisted on the Brandenburg Gate. Where were the Americans? Some days earlier, Goebbels had shouted his last proclamation: "If one should force us to exit from this political stage, we will slam the door so hard that the whole world will shiver!" We had been shivering for years and finally outlived the Nazis' brutal dictatorship, now being left stranded in the ghastly graveyard of their fanatical dreams. It had been reported that Hitler had committed suicide two days earlier in his private, elaborate bunker under the Reichs Chancery along with Eva Braun. Who was she? We had never heard of her, nor of her relationship with Hitler. He, a man who had come from nowhere had vanished into nowhere, a man who had promised everything and delivered nothing, a tyrant drunk with power. His Nazism, a movement borne in Versailles, under his power had grown into a destructive monster, leaving a world plunged into chaos, and Germany poorer than ever. We in Berlin were bombed to shambles.

Goebbels also committed suicide after forcing his wife to poison their six children and then herself. It had been common knowledge that his wife had wanted a divorce for years so she could go with her children to Switzerland, but Hitler would not permit it, because it would have been a disgrace to the Party. It was said that Goebbels in his last cynical statement blamed the German people for having failed. The Nazis had always looked for a scapegoat, and found their first one in the Communists, then in the Jews, next in all enemies of the Party, and finally, every German. Since we were not victorious, we provoked our downfall ourselves and should perish, too. According to Hitler's statements, the great victories were due to his leadership and the defeats and failures were the fault of others!

After twelve agonizing years, the sun had finally set over the brown era. It left as its legacy a wasteland of ruins reaching into the sky, which formed the heart of our city. Berlin looked like a latter day Carthage, buried under 75 million tons of rubble with its ghost-like survivors roaming amongst the debris. Our streets were littered with wrecked vehicles and dead bodies. Temporary shallow graves had been dug in many gardens. Eighty thousand Berliners had lost their lives.

We hardly dared to emerge from our cellars with the wild Soviet soldiers screaming outside, "Germanski *kaputt*, Berlin *kaputt.*" Ivan's cry of "*Frau komm!*" (Woman come) could be heard all over. We lived like prisoners in our own homes, and nothing seemed to be left after prevailing over so many disasters in the past. Any form of normal life seemed impossible ever again. We had arrived at *Stunde Null,* the zero hour, a total vacuum.

The battle for Berlin had resulted in a complete breakdown of all public utilities and transportation. There was no electricity, no gas or running water except for a few outlying suburbs. Miraculously, we were among the fortunate ones because we still had slow running water in the basement and two toilets that were working on a limited basis, though this had to serve over fifty people living together. The shortage of water forbade the luxury of flushing after every use. Down the street, people had to bail their water out of lake Schlachtensee. Who cared how pure it was? For many, there was no water for days.

We began to understand the phrase, "enjoy the war, peace will be worse," because we had only exchanged Hitler's tyranny for a new international one. Instead of SS boots resounding on the streets and children in uniform, it now echoed with Soviet army trucks and the shouts of Russian commands. We realized that the term "peace" was a very empty word. We were enslaved by a brutal Communistic regime exactly like Nazism, or worse. We had no law or jurisdiction to protect us, not a single body to represent us, and all of our rights had been taken from us. Germany had been carved up into Allied occupation zones. Papa called it an international competition to slice up Germany, a heap of rubble about which the four Allies would quarrel now. We in Berlin were being treated as a separate territory, located geographically in the East, and isolated deep in the Soviet zone. We were a capital city without a country, a hundred miles from the American and British-controlled West Germany, and with no idea of how we could exist as such an enclave. Our future was one nightmare.

On May 4, Mr. Saal appeared. It was a heartbreaking reunion between father and daughter, to find her safe and sound with us. Without much ado, we added him to our basement community until his house next door was safe to return to. He was most grateful, having arrived empty-handed, yet being fed and sheltered. Since there was no radio or newspapers, we had depended on rumors of what had happened in the downtown area. Now, Mr. Saal provided us with an eye-witness account of those final days of fighting.

Hitler had ordered the German soldiers, mainly young boys and old men, to fight to the last man. What for? We were appalled. How many lives were needlessly sacrificed? Those fighting around the Zoo bunker had been decimated by Soviet sharpshooters and there had been few survivors. Upon hearing this, we were shattered and did not dare to look at the Weissbachs, because their last son had not yet returned from that area. A terrible worry; fear was in the air. Mr. Saal told us how units of the Berlin police, who had tired of useless fighting, surrendered under white flags. However, SS squads tried to stop them with gunfire, and people not only had to dodge the enemy bullets but also those of the SS. The ones who had taken shelter in the subway stations also had suffered heavy losses, and those who survived stumbled out into the streets when they learned of the capture of the Reichs Chancery. Once outside, thousands of homeless wandered around aimlessly in the rubble, first heading toward the suburbs, and then back again, searching for food and shelter.

Mr. Saal arrived just in time to register with us for our new ration cards, the first of many such registrations. Our grocer at the corner had crudely restored his wrecked store and had some fresh vegetables for the first time in weeks. Again, we stood in long lines to get our small amount of either potatoes or carrots, whichever was available for a stamp on our old ration cards. Later, we all stood in long lines again for the first time that minuscule amounts of butter or margarine were available, less than one or two ounces per person. The allowance was not much, but was better than nothing. Again we stood on the street in fear of the patrolling Soviet soldiers. Older women spared the younger ones from such exposure as Mutti did for me. Every aspect of our life was being dictated; endurance became our aim in life.

On May 6, we received an order to scrub the street in front of our homes on our hands and knees with a hand brush, beginning at 6 a.m. Moscow time, 4 a.m. our time. The primary purpose of this exercise was for the Soviets to find out who lived in each house. Again, the older women labored outside like slaves while we younger women worked inside, safe from the eyes of patrolling Soviets. As a result of so many rapes by the Soviets soldiers, venereal disease had flared up to such an alarming degree that hospitals offered free treatment. It was common knowledge that every doctor performed abortions, even though they were illegal.

On May 7, 1945, Admiral Dönitz, as Hitler's successor, ordered the signing of the German capitulation in Reims, France, finally ending World War II in Europe after five and a half years. On May 8, Field Marshal Keitel signed a second surrender in Berlin-Karlshorst, the Soviet headquarters. Germany was in ruins and Berlin was leveled under fifty thousand tons of bombs that had been dropped on the city. Millions were dead on battlefields, millions more were on the road fleeing from East to West and millions of others like us were looking for their scattered family members. We did not know where Sieghardt or Günter were, nor what had happened to Elsa and her relatives. We knew that Aunt Frieda had arrived safely in Hannover with her family and was existing in a bombed-out house that had been declared uninhabitable. They had sealed up the broken windows with pieces of wood and covered the holes burned in the floor with cardboard. Aunt Frieda was lucky to be alive and in West Germany, but she had no word of Uncle Conny or Cousin Hans. Aunt Grete and her family were still in Zerbst, which was now in Soviet- occupied East Germany.

Thank God, Hitler's short-lived millennium had ceased to exist, but was that the end of one nightmare, or just the beginning of another one? It was a day of great paradoxes for us. Finally freed of Nazi tyranny, we were newly imprisoned by the "liberators" via a rigorous occupation regime. Peace brought no relief.

The Aftermath

Following the surrender of Germany, Berlin was ruled by Moscow. The Soviets moved more troops into the city. The entire Goethestrasse, a street with large old villas, was confiscated and within minutes, all residents were ejected from their homes and not permitted to take anything with them.

Shortly thereafter, an old lady tottered into our first aid station, totally confused and staring at us in blank terror. She blurted out that all of her children had been killed in the war and that she and her husband wanted to be reunited with them in death. So, they planned to commit suicide. They lay down together in their bed and she took an overdose of sleeping pills. When her husband would see that she was dead, he would shoot himself. However, she didn't die, but woke up this morning to find her husband next to her, dead, in a pool of blood. At that very moment, the Soviets stormed into the bedroom and seeing her dead husband, screamed at her in broken German, "Only very bad people are afraid and kill themselves." They grabbed her and threw her out into the street with nothing but the clothes on her back. Fleeing from her home she ended up with us. We were shocked by her story and offered to include her in our basement family, but she only wanted to die, though she didn't know how. To take pills once more might just leave her paralyzed this time. After a short rest, she just wandered off into the streets, hoping to get shot by some Soviet soldier. Still drugged, we watched as she staggered down the street like a sleep walker, directly into the midst of some Russians. She never returned to us. Who would bury her dead husband? Some were just covered with dirt in the garden.

There were more and more requirements that forced us to be out on the streets, such as various registrations or searches for food. We could no longer keep the Soviets out of our house. When everyone was ordered to work outside cleaning the streets, they would take this opportunity to go into the homes. Only Marga Saal and I stayed inside.

One day when I was busy with Vita in my back cellar, I heard Marga shriek and it sounded like she was calling my name. I dropped everything and rushed out to her with my usual brisk steps, but stopped dead in my tracks. Someone was blocking my way, a massive dark figure against the light of the glass door upstairs. It had something like a stick on its back. No, that wasn't a stick; it was a rifle. Good grief! I had almost collided with a Soviet soldier! Marga was crouching in terror in a corner and I instinctively blurted out in my poor Russian, "I nurse, this hospital, Kommandanta forbidden (meaning raping). Out, Out!"

The effect was phenomenal. The soldier retreated a step, gave me a puzzled look and stated in poorly pronounced German, "I understand," and then withdrew backwards step by step, up the staircase and out of the house. I could not believe the instantaneous result of my new Russian sentences. Marga stammered, "My God, you just shouted at a Soviet soldier. You have courage!" Little did she know. It was not courage at all. I was in such a state of shock myself that I wasn't even aware of how I had reacted and called his bluff. But, I learned a good lesson in how to deal with the Soviets. Copy their tactics of being firm, loud-mouthed and commanding.

The Red Army showed little discipline engaging in looting, rape and often random murder. There was now a rumor that the newly arrived Soviet troops had orders to act well-behaved like the "great, victorious, civilized Russian army," whatever that meant. Berlin would be the show window of the world. We now even dared to sneak upstairs to our apartments for brief periods during the day, making us feel like human beings again instead of animals living in a cave. But we constantly had to be on guard. We still were without electricity and had to cook in the basement, and for protection, stayed together in groups, especially during the night.

One day, Vita began to cry constantly, awake or asleep, and no matter what we tried, we could not calm her down. We were unable to find any logical cause for her bitter crying, and were afraid the noise would attract unwanted attention to our building. Brave Mutti, who stopped by on one of her frequent visits, immediately took us to see our nearby pediatrician since I would not dare to venture out on the street alone, not even for the five-minute walk to the doctor's office. Together we arrived safely. I had just begun my tragic tale when the doctor took one quick look at Vita and then leaned back in his chair and laughed, "This is no tragedy. Your child is not sick at all, but the victim of the most popular byproduct of the Soviet occupation—lice!" And before I had a chance to contest this as being impossible, he showed me the living proof, digging a louse out of Vita's hair while she cried out in protest. Then to my further horror, he continued, "And you have them, too!" Without much further ado, he fished a louse egg out of my hair. By tending to Vita and hugging her, I had shared her misery without even noticing it.

Then the doctor told us an amusing example of the Soviets' idea of sanitation in the world-famous hospital Charité in downtown Berlin which was now occupied by them. Their instruction on hygiene was to cover all the writing desks with sheets for cleanliness, even though there were scarcely enough linens for the hospital beds, because "in a hospital, one does not work at dirty desks." Of course, these sheets were never changed and soon became a filthy playground for all kind of germs and lice. We were speechless.

He handed me an oily ointment to put on our scalps with the warning that it would burn terribly when applied and Vita would probably cry more than ever, but, it would get rid of the lice for good. It did both. I first tried it out on myself in the privacy of our upstairs bathroom and it burned excruciatingly. I had to bite my lip for the ten minutes that it was necessary to keep it on. Then I put it on Vita and it was heartbreaking to hear the poor child scream, "Mommy, mommy, no, ouch!" I obviously was the cause of her terrible pain. How do you explain all this to a child not even two years old? She was still sobbing in my arms even after everything had been washed out of her hair. An oily film persistently remained and now I understood why so many basement dwellers had such terrible greasy looking hair. We had become full-fledged members of a club that nobody talked about out of pure embarrassment. I discussed the situation with Mrs. Weissbach and she brought the "shameful secret" out in the open. Because the Soviets had frequented the basement, our close community was now infected with lice but everyone had been too ashamed to mention it. The only way to rid ourselves of this plague was for everyone to undergo the prescribed cure, and it worked.

Since we had no public transportation, our old bicycles became very useful for those of us who had to venture out. The Soviets watched us with total amazement as we easily rode them. One day, a young boy was accosted in front of our house by a Soviet soldier who pushed him off his bike and mounted it himself. He promptly collapsed with it. Furiously, he struggled to his feet and jumped on the boy screaming, "You bad boy. You bewitched bike to carry you, but not me." He beat him fiercely and left in great anger. This was so unreal, you had to see it to believe it. Didn't the Soviets know anything? However, they soon learned that riding a bicycle was more comfortable than walking and began looting our homes to steal bikes. I quickly hid Sieghardt's in the attic, but first I dismantled some of the parts, knowing that even if the Soviets found it they would not want a *kaputt* bike.

Bicycles were just one of the many problems the Soviets had in understanding our western civilization. Water faucets were a complete mystery to them, and they referred to them as "where water comes out of wall." They shrank back from wash bowls, and instead of using them, Russian women would kneel on the floor and wash their hair in the toilet bowl, which they found to be "very practical." At a neighbor's house, some Soviet soldiers had put some fish into the toilet bowl to wash them, then accidently pressed the flush button. When all of the fish vanished in front of their eyes, they screamed, "*Frau*, you stole fish. Bring back fish or we shoot you." Naturally, *Frau* could not bring back the flushed fish, so they shot her and her distraught family buried her in the back yard. Soldiers collected water faucets which they proudly displayed, holding them up against the wall and saying, "We take back to Russia and then water come out of wall there, too." They obviously had no idea about plumbing and pipes.

On May 5, 1945, the first Soviet-edited German newspaper was published and this way we learned that the blackout had been canceled. This was rather meaningless because without any electricity, we only had candlelight. There were extensive firework displays in the evening to celebrate the Soviet victory, and these usually turned into rowdy affairs with lots of drinking. We felt we had fallen into the hands of maniacs and barricaded ourselves in the basement. The next day, since "peace had broken out" and our situation was rapidly worsening, we rolled up our sleeves to help ourselves, and tried to put our house back in shape again. The roof still had a gaping hole from the last bombing of April 24, which had scattered many roof tiles all over the garden.

We started by gathering up all of the unbroken ones and carried them up to the fourth floor. I never realized how heavy they were, and could only carry two or three in a bucket on each trip. Mrs. Kage was in charge of fastening the tiles to the roof, dangling outside primitively, secured by a clothes line wound around her body to keep her from falling off. We handed the tiles up to her one at a time, and she knew amazingly well how to put them in place again. The remaining opening we patched with some wooden boards from old bookcases and then returned downstairs with a great sense of accomplishment.

Next morning, we learned that our long-time tenant, Mrs. Scharnow, had died peacefully in her sleep, surrounded by her loving family. Suddenly, several shouting Soviet soldiers who were drinking pure alcohol came trampling in. Upon seeing the corpse of the old lady in bed, the effect was stunning. Though drunk, they were obviously touched by the majesty of death and immediately quieted down and motioned for us to be silent also. Facing a person who had peacefully died at home had stopped them in their tracks, and, deeply affected, they tiptoed from the house. A strange reaction from those who had indiscriminately killed so many themselves. There it was again, the inscrutable Russian soul, this time with a human side. Mrs. Weissbach attended to the last rites, and we then had the difficulty of arranging a burial. There were no caskets available, and we had to pay a steep price to have a crude one made from some old doors, which took two days. We then had to transport her casket to our cemetery in Schlachtensee, a strenuous one-hour walk.

Watching Mrs. Weissbach help others, we were worried why her son Eberhard had not returned from the last severe fighting near the Zoo bunker. There were reports that Soviet snipers had killed many of our soldiers, and civilians later hastily buried them in shallow mass graves. Family members of missing persons had gone to the area in an attempt to identify loved ones by uniform insignia, items found in pockets or dental work. The bodies had begun to decay. Mr. Weissbach also attempted such a heartbreaking search and found the remains of his last son. He wrapped him in a canvas and brought him home, and we buried him the same way as Mrs. Scharnow, sharing in the agony of the Weissbachs.

A new way of life slowly began to emerge, and we dared to leave our basement sanctuary and return to our upstairs apartments to create a livable world. Marga Saal and her father moved back to their apartment building next door and so did others who had sought shelter with us since April. The Conrad couple moved in with me on the first floor instead of their own apartment above me so that I would not be alone with Vita. However, since we still had no electricity, we all continued to cook our meals on the iron stove in the basement.

Shortly thereafter, I had to venture over to my parents' home which was just a five-minute walk away. I don't remember what was so urgent but Maria came to pick me up. We had no problem as we pushed Vita's stroller through the new barrier at the S-Bahn station and walked along Lindenthaler Allee until we reached the corner of my parents' side street. There were three Soviet soldiers with rifles posted across the street and when they saw us, they shouted, "*Frau, komm*," and immediately started toward us. Using my best Russian, I reacted in a loud, firm voice, "Forbidden by Kommandanta." One of them said, "I Kommandanta," which I knew was not true, and then he asked to see my "document." I had my Red Cross pass with me which contained my photo in uniform, and they all admired it and passed it around. "Ahh, you doctor," at which point Maria slapped my shoulder. "She good doctor." The Russians smiled, but then wanted to touch Vita in the stroller. Frantic, I was ready to jump at them, which Maria hindered. She began laughing, gesticulating and speaking loudly in French, which temporarily confused the Soviet soldiers, and then in a joking manner, said to me, "Run, now!"

By this time the Soviets were so confused as to what she was talking about, understanding neither German nor French, that they laughed along with Maria as I took off pushing the stroller as fast as I could walk. Maria followed behind more slowly, all the while laughing and waving to the Soviets. With shaking knees we made it safely to my parents' house. They had watched the entire incident from behind a front window, but were powerless to help because if they had intervened, we would have all been shot. We had learned that the worst thing one could do when facing the Soviets was to show fear because that would make you easy prey.

My parents also told me that several Soviet officers had arrived in a car at the dentist's house next door and demanded some urgent dental work. While one was being treated upstairs, the others ransacked the downstairs and destroyed everything that they could not take with them. It was obvious that the Soviets were aware of the dentist's Nazi affiliation because they did not bother any other house on the street. Everyone watched the plundering with great satisfaction as compensation for the threats we endured before. Shortly thereafter, the dentist fled to the West where his background was not known. He still knew how to save himself.

Another time, a group of Soviet soldiers started roaming through the neighborhood and noisily forced themselves into my parents' house. One picked up Papa's typewriter and others started rolling up a Persian rug and were just going to tear the telephone out of the wall when Maria rushed upon the scene. "No, no, no," she screamed. "Not Germanski. All mine, Belgium property," and immediately snatched back the typewriter. The startled Soviets stopped their looting as Maria continued to rattle off long statements in French, interjecting with, "You capisco, not Germanski, all French, French," as she stood on the carpet that they had started to roll up. Suddenly, one of them called out something in Russian and they immediately dropped everything and departed emptyhanded. Courageous little Maria had saved the house from being looted and my parents could not find enough words to thank her. But, she merely replied, "This is my thanks to you. You gave me a home and were good to me right from the start."

The Red Army looted everything that was transportable, regardless of its size or weight, from pots and pans to carpets and furniture. Many of the Soviet soldiers had arrived with horses and wagons which they had stolen from German farmers. These were piled high with their loot, often covered with a Persian rug to protect against bad weather as they began their long journey back to the Soviet Union. Stalin's army stripped Germany of everything moveable and what could not be moved easily was dismantled, such as over 380 factories from Berlin alone. Even railroad tracks were torn up for transport back to the Soviet Union, and we could hear them hammering day and night to remove all but one track. German workers who were forced to do the dismantling told us that even our S-Bahn cars were hauled away for future use on the Moscow subway. Ironically, tons and tons of machinery stayed behind to rust because with just one single track left, only one train could leave daily for the East.

Life was unpredictable and ruled by fear of constant, new onslaughts and unwarranted arrests. Heinrich George, a world famous heroic character actor, lived near us in Zehlendorf-West with his beloved wife, the famous actress Berta Drews and their two sons Jan and Götz, both school boys. (The latter is also a well-known actor today.) One morning in June 1944, he was called away from the breakfast table by the Soviets for what they called a short interrogation, and never returned. Why? He was famous for his classic roles, not Nazi propaganda. He wasn't even a member of the Nazi Party.

We learned much later that he had been imprisoned in the Soviet concentration camp Hohenschönhausen, Soviet camp number 7, where hunger, torture and beatings had reduced his 220-pound physique to a mere skeleton of ninety pounds. He, an idol who had been world famous for his Gottfried von Berlichingen in Goethe's Urgötz, spent his last year performing to amuse brutal Soviet and German Communist guards until, enfeebled and sick, he succumbed at age fifty-three on September 25, 1946. Why this long, unjust and inhuman treatment? The war had never ended in Berlin. (Heinrich George was remembered and honored by a German commemorative stamp in 1993 as Germany's greatest actor of tragedies.)

A new kind of German self-government under Soviet military administration was announced on May 14, 1945, of course filled with Communists. We heard the name of Walter Ulbricht who had returned from exile in Russia as a Russian citizen to re-establish the Communist Party in Berlin, which was subservient to Moscow. It was also publicized that we would be issued new ration cards with classifications of one through five, depending on your age and ability to work. Class one would be given to hard labor workers, scientists, doctors and leading officials, and this would allow them the most generous portion of the future meager rations. Class two was for regular workers and employees, and they would receive twenty percent less than class one. Class three included all other employees who would receive about half of a class one allowance. Class four was for children of all ages and their ration would be less than class three. At the bottom was class five which included all the useless old and sick people, the unemployed as well as mothers and housewives because their work didn't count.

Our daily rations were to be measured in grams, and no classification would receive enough to maintain good health. The fifth class, which was the most inadequate of all, was what my family would receive. Daily rations would consist of 20 grams of meat (7/10th of an ounce), 7 grams of fat and 15 grams of sugar, all difficult to express in fractions of an ounce. These rations were soon called *Friedhofskarte*, or cemetery ticket—too much to die on and too little to live on. Of course this was only the paper plan for food rationing. With stores lacking groceries to sell, the actual availability of food was another matter. It was seldom adequate to meet the ration card allowances. Now, in so-called peace-time, we were experiencing hunger worse than during the last days of the war, trying to exist on less than one thousand calories a day. Old people who lived alone often didn't make it and were found in their beds, starved to death. They had survived the war but not the peace. The calorie level sank and raping and looting went up.

New twelve-hour work schedules were ordered on May 20, Pentecost, based on a Moscow schedule, from 6 a.m. to 12:30 p.m. and then from 2:30 p.m. to 8 p.m. In spite of our two most religious holidays, Sunday and Monday, all stores were ordered to stay open all day, even though they had no merchandise to sell. Although the stores were open, the banks were closed and our money was frozen, so we couldn't buy anything anyway. The weather was unusually warm and pleasant, and we dared to venture out into the garden for a few short moments to enjoy the afternoon sunshine.

At this same time, Soviet soldiers swarmed around again, peeked into my parents' empty garage, and forced their way into the house for looting. This time, Maria was not there to help and what happened that day can best be illustrated by Papa's letter three days later to the Soviet Kommandatura, submitted in a Russian translation:

Russian Military Commander   May 23, 1945
Berlin, Zehlendorf-West
Sven-Hedin Strasse 11

Herewith I take the liberty to immediately notify you of the following:

On the morning of May 20, in front of the house of my neighbor, a motor vehicle appeared with four Soviet soldiers and one civilian who, after a quick look into my empty garage, entered my house and started to ransack everything, demanding radios and cameras. They rummaged through several drawers. As they did not find anything, the leader, a Soldier with a blue cap, said that he had to take along the big carpet and my typewriter. Finally, he left without the big carpet, but in spite of my protest he took my typewriter (model Erika M) although it was, according to orders, registered at the Kommandatura. One of the soldiers spoke some German so he had understood my protest. Because I have registered the typewriter according to orders, I feel obliged to report that it is no longer in my possession. The typewriter, however, is urgently needed for my business, so I would be very much obliged if it would be returned.

With greatest respect,
Arthur Schmidt

Papa must have recovered his typewriter, because two months later some U.S. soldiers also tried to take it away, but before they could get it, I sneaked out with it through the back door.

The same day that Papa wrote his letter to the Soviet Berlin Kommandatura, Admiral Dönitz, Hitler's successor, was dismissed as the head of state by the Allies who took over the entire power to govern the smoking ruins of Germany. There was now no German government remaining, and Papa called this a very drastic solution because we were now deprived of any German representation and had no rights within our own country. Our people in uniform were prisoners in their homeland. For us, this was just a continuance of the war in peacetime, only with different means.

Also, on May 23, we received our first small distribution of potatoes and everyone started running for them. This again caused long lines at the stores, with people arriving as early as 6 a.m. in the hope of getting some of the available food. And, as usual, armed Soviet soldiers patrolled along the lines of the patiently waiting Germans. We had to bring our own containers, and luckily, we had a little basket that was big enough for the small amount that we obtained for a stamp on our old Nazi ration cards. The next day, we repeated the same procedure, but this time for a fraction of an ounce of meat per person, but it was better than nothing. All we could think of was food, and to feed a family was a full-time job, which is why Vita and I ate at my parents' house.

We couldn't keep the Soviet soldiers out of our house, and there was a constant problem with their ignorance of our Western ways. One of them roamed through my kitchen and picked up my meat grinder which aroused his curiosity. Full of expectation, he turned the handle again and again, finally throwing it on the floor and exclaiming, "Nix music? No good. *Kaputt!*" Next, he began searching through my kitchen cabinet for alcohol and found a bottle of vinegar from which he immediately took a big drink, only to spit it out and throwing the bottle on the floor, too. He left in disgust, cursing at the stuff Germans drink which Russians wouldn't even touch. As I picked everything up, I couldn't help wondering how primitive they must live at home. If these were the elite troops, it was difficult to imagine how the common troops fared.

Another time in our basement a Soviet soldier proudly showed off the treasures he had collected in a suitcase, which he laid open on our large table. Electric wires were dangling out on all sides because he had packed it so tightly. Looking closer I recognized an assortment of light switches torn out of walls of other houses and also several loose bulbs. Now he began to demonstrate: "This here," pointing with a switch to the wall, "and this here," holding a bulb to the ceiling, and with a big proud smile he exclaimed, "Ahhh, light!" We pretended to admire his great idea for his native village, which had no electricity.

Another amusing incident concerned the multitude of wrist watches that the Soviets had plundered from us. Since battery operated ones had not yet been invented, they all had to be wound up every few days. Wrist watches were a new status symbol for the Soviet soldiers and it was not unusual to see them wearing five to ten on one arm. So, they were confused when their watches stopped ticking and rushed to a watchmaker near us. "Watch is *kaputt*. You fix watch," they demanded in broken German. Keeping a serious face, the watchmaker promised immediate help and told them he would have to take the watches into the back room to fix them, where he merely rewound them. He returned to the front of the store and handed them back. Surprise, surprise! They were now ticking again. The Soviets were so impressed with such good service that they paid him well with money they had stolen from our bank across the street. A few days later, they came back because the watches were *kaputt* again, not ticking, and demanded he fix them. "Uh, oh," exclaimed the watchmaker. "You must be more careful with these watches." So, he took them into the back room and "repaired" them all again, but kept his method a secret. Fortunately, Soviet soldiers were frequently rotated and replaced by new ones whose watches also needed repair work. This way the watchmaker escaped being punished for repair work that didn't last.

A more dramatic incident occurred when some Soviet soldiers first came in contact with an alarm clock in our basement. Like children, they played with all of the moveable parts until suddenly the alarm went off with a loud shrill tone. In shock, they flung it away as if they had a time bomb in their hands. We had a hard time to convince them that this was just a special kind of *Urri Urri*, and that no one was trying to kill them. It had scared them so much that this was one item they actually didn't want to take with them.

But they did collect telephones. They tore them out of the wall and carried them around under their arms. Again and again they would try to talk to somebody and wondered why it would only work for Germans. They figured that this must be another case of witchcraft. Fascinated, they kept carrying them around, hoping someday to get an answer to their frequent "Hellos."

On May 25 at exactly 1 p.m., we were surprised with the return of electricity. Our long-time cooking on the basement stove was finally over and we felt like we had returned to some semblance of civilization. Since the current would only be on sporadically during unpredictable hours, I immediately got out my vacuum cleaner to dust off my neglected home. But, the motor only gave an unfriendly "Brrr" and then lapsed into silence. What a calamity with no mechanic available, but didn't Gerda have to do all kinds of mechanical work without any proper training? So there was no reason why I could not at least try to fix the vacuum. With my trusty screwdriver, I took the motor apart and could not find anything wrong. Small wonder since I didn't even know what to look for. Feeling rather foolish, I reassembled everything, and luckily nothing was left over at the end. Without much hope of success, I made another attempt to start the motor and to my surprise, it gave a lusty roar and then settled down to its normal tune. What a clever mechanic I was! Only I had no idea what I did to fix it, but it worked perfectly ever after. This taught me never to give up hope too soon.

Although the war was over, we heard stories of the cruel Soviet terror that had just started in the extermination of ethnic Germans in East

Germany. One evening, a tall, emaciated man who was stooped over knocked at my parents' door and we hardly recognized him. It was cousin Heinz's father, Mr. Seybold, who had fled from his home in East Prussia. As he sat exhausted in a chair, he told us how ordinary people, ethnic Germans, were driven from their East Prussia homeland. He had to flee from his old family estate overnight to escape either being slain or deported to a labor camp in Russia. We were stunned. He had traveled primarily on foot and his condition was evidence of his ordeal. According to him, in every train station, with no trains running, a vast number of people were lying everywhere on the floor, the exhausted next to the sick and dying. And, they continued to lie there while hunger and typhus raged because no official organization claimed responsibility for them. No institution of governmental authority existed in Germany to protect them. All he asked for was some water to drink, the opportunity to wash up, and a bed to sleep in that night, all a long-missed luxury. How lucky we were to be at home, even in a damaged house. We were unable to give him any information about Hans, Günter, Sieghardt or Uncle Conny. We would just have to wait and hope for the best.

With the arrival of Mr. Seybold, there was one more mouth to feed. This mobilized us into action and we held a family conference on how to get some additional food. As a result, Mrs. Vogel and Maria took off early the next morning to hunt for some egg-laying chickens, hopefully through some old business connections, while we prepared a home in one of the cellars to house our feathered newcomers. A long wooden plank served as a passageway through the cellar window into our garden. Since our fence had been partly taken down, we hoped the chickens would behave and stay with us. How much better off we were than people with quacking ducks on their balconies. They could only eat them, but we would have eggs first.

Mrs. Vogel and Maria returned in the early afternoon, with a pulsating sack of six healthy chickens and a bag of chicken feed to get started. What a stroke of luck! Our chickens loved being set free again and it did not take long for them to feel completely at home. They practically ruined our garden on the first afternoon with their constant scratching, pecking and digging holes in the flower beds to lie in. We hadn't counted on that, and it was clear we would have to sacrifice some of our garden for them and fence off a separate area so that we could plant vegetables in the other part. During the night, they all roosted very quietly in the cellar, each in their favorite spot. Next morning, Mrs. Vogel and Maria took off again and this time, like magic, returned with some wire fencing which the men used to enclose the part of the garden in front of the chicken cellar.

We now waited anxiously for our hens to start laying eggs, though at first they only produced one among all of them. They brought a lot of color into our grey, trivial every day existence and we became very attached to them, giving each one a name that matched their personality. "Stormy" tried to fly over the fence, tame "Susi" pecked food out of Vita's hand to her great joy, and she thought it was her doll. "Picky" and "Slowpoke" were slow egg layers, while "Blondy" and "Brownie" were the busy ones; sometimes we would find several eggs a day. They became more like pets than an egg-laying chicken unit, and they would even come running when we called them by name.

Some days later there was a cry of desperation: "Everyone off the streets. The Mongols are coming!" An alarming threat, the Mongolian syndrome, an apocalyptic vision was approaching, another onslaught on the German population. Immediately we looked like a dead town. We stayed in hiding until the signal was given that these feared troops had only passed close to us, to return to Russia over the nearby *Avus*, Berlin's almost six-mile long auto race track which also served as an expressway through and out of Berlin. This time we escaped the horror with only a shock. What would be next?

After a while we no longer lived happily ever after with our pet chickens; we discovered quite a drawback to them. In spite of our untiring efforts, feeding became a problem as soon as Mrs. Vogel's chicken feed was almost used up. Also their droppings were all over, inside and out, and had to be cleaned off constantly. Perhaps live chickens, after all, were not the right solution for our food problem, even though they produced some eggs.

So we held another family conference and came to the painful decision that the chickens had to go. But how should we dispose of them? The only solution was to eat them one by one, and each would provide a nutritious meal for all of us. Who should kill the first one? Maria volunteered. "Which one do you want first?" she asked Mutti. Mutti, irritated, looked aside, "Just anyone." So Maria went downstairs and called the hens. They came running and she grabbed the first one that appeared in the window while the others recoiled in alarm. Then followed an awful shrill squawk, and we all felt like cannibals ready to eat their friend. After a while Maria returned to the kitchen with an already plucked chicken in her hands. Which one was it? We all had our own pet. It was up to Mutti to prepare the meal and we stayed out of the kitchen.

Then it was dinner time. Mutti was a good cook and the chicken looked delicious, served carved with some potatoes around it. She set it on the lazy susan in the center of the table so everybody could help himself. "We are so lucky to have meat" she said. "Please, take some." As hungry as we were, nobody wanted to be first, and the lazy susan just kept spinning round and round. "Papa, why don't you help yourself? Men are the most hungry." Papa acknowledged that it was a real good meal for us and hesitatingly took a piece. Finally so did everyone else. But we could not enjoy our meal. Susi was the missing one, we knew it by now. But why Susi, Vita's doll? It felt like a meal after someone's execution.

After this dinner disaster, we had another family conference. We could not go through such a meal a second time, let alone five more, so we decided that Mutti and I would go to Mrs. Sauer's bakery on nearby Beerenstrasse. She was widowed during the First World War and had gone through many trials and tribulations during her life. She also had lovingly surprised us with bread and salt as a customary token of good luck when we had moved into our new home ten years ago and we had been her customer ever since. Mutti discussed our chicken dilemma with her and Mrs. Sauer offered to add our chickens to her flock in the garden behind the bakery. In return, she would provide us with bread and flour for a while, naturally without food stamps. Both parties were content. That evening, Mrs. Sauer arrived with the first two loaves of bread and a big sack to pick up our five remaining chickens. What a relief. Mutti and I looked at each other—no we would not make good farmers, and no more edible pets around the house.

Since our life-saving attempt with our own chicken coop had resulted in a big flop, we had to come up with a better anti-starving solution. One cannot exist on dry bread alone, especially when the ration for one entire day was eaten up already by lunchtime. There was never enough. So what now? The food situation had rapidly deteriorated and our nutritional level had reached the lowest point ever and fell far below the minimum number of calories needed each day. Child mortality and malnutrition increased and the sarcastic saying, "enjoy the war, peace will be worse" had become the bitter truth. The real hunger came now, after the war. There was a shortage of everything, and this brought about a black market which seemed to spring up overnight and flourished for three lean years, until 1948. Even though trading was strictly forbidden, people headed for the black market with anything that could be sold or exchanged for something else that was urgently needed. And this was practically everything since we were without the barest necessities of life. All our clothing, and especially shoes, had long since seen their better days, and food prices were hugely inflated with all of our funds frozen in the closed banks. With the complete breakdown of the supply system for Berlin, we were on the verge of famine.

Living from hand to mouth, we could not wait any longer for things to get better. The last resort for us Berliners was to head for the farmers in the country, soon designated as "farm crawling." All kinds of things were bartered, and many family treasures were diverted through the stomach at excessive prices. For us, food meant potatoes, carrots, cabbage and sometimes, as a rarity, onions. Forget about milk, butter, eggs, bacon or meat. However, the farmers lived far from Berlin and there was no transportation of any kind operational. To tackle that problem, we decided that our best choice would be Fahrland, a little farming community beyond Potsdam, which was about sixteen miles away on foot. I knew several farmers there from the days when Sieghardt and I went by boat to get food without ration cards. The real problem was that the round trip would have to be completed between the curfew-free hours of 6 a.m. to 6 p.m. But the men could not risk going out into the country because they would most likely never return. The arbitrary arrests, shootings and killings had never ceased in and around Berlin. So, Mutti, Maria and I decided to make the trip, equipped with bags and knapsacks. Hunger created greater willingness to take more risks, even those of running into the Soviets. Maria cut a ribbon of Belgium national colors into three pieces and we each attached one to our clothing to appear as Belgium nationals. Mutti quickly learned a few basic words in French such as *bon jour* and *au revoir*, besides *oui* and *non*, to make it look like we all spoke the language.

We realized that our shoes would never withstand a rapid thirty-two mile walk so we got out our hiking boots which we had not worn in years. They were as stiff as boards and the men did their best in trying to soften them for us. Our trio took off early in the morning of the last day of May and my heart was pounding with fear of the uncertain and dangerous hiking excursion that lay before us. Mutti and Maria may not have felt differently, but they did a good job of hiding it as they acted like fearless travelers. "Are you afraid?" Maria asked me. "No," I lied, and would have to trust my guardian angel from now on. Since there is safety in numbers, we took the busier Potsdamer Chaussee that runs from Berlin to Potsdam, and we were in the consoling company of many fellow travelers who were all out on the same kind of mission. The three of us were good walkers, and our boots were not too uncomfortable—at first.

After several hours, we ran into a large group of Soviet soldiers, and as we passed them, Maria chattered loudly in French, pointing to our Belgium colors. The soldiers just smiled and waved us on by, and we did not dare to look back to see how the other travelers had fared behind us. More hungry Berliners came from all areas to join our barter trek into the country. We soon reached the *Glienicker Brücke*, the Wannsee suspension bridge, but it no longer spanned the water. It was totally destroyed and lay in a mass of debris and twisted steel down below. The only way to get to Potsdam was over this bridge, but how?

While we were contemplating how we would get to the other side, some men appeared and, without asking, helped us descend down to the destroyed bridge and then cross the churning waters by balancing from one twisted beam to another, a frightening test of balance, physical and mental. Reaching the other side, we climbed up the bank and were now on the route straight to Potsdam. Mutti and I knew this way very well from our frequent car trips before the war, but it now seemed so much longer on foot. We were constantly on the alert for Soviet soldiers who were everywhere, lurking in the woods. Our nerves were on edge as we passed them from time to time, and we always tried to stay with a group of other people on the road until our routes forked off near Potsdam into different directions. By now it was about 10 a.m. and we felt the strain in all our bones, but we marched on resolutely.

Being familiar with the area, we soon passed by the once gorgeous gardens of Potsdam, now overgrown with weeds, and arrived at the rear of the rococo palace *Sans Souci* (Without Worry). We were amazed to see the magnificent summer residence of Frederick the Great, the most beloved Prussian king, was unharmed. Although much of Potsdam was destroyed. Seeing it again reminded me of the time when Elsa and I had frequently visited the picture gallery here with its priceless masterpieces by Rubens, Van Dyck and others. (These art treasures were hauled to Russia as war tributes. Since the 1990s, a strenuous dispute started about finally returning them.) As we passed by, we saw several delicate palace chairs that had been thrown down the garden slope and ended up broken in the street we were traveling. High up, outside the palace, sat two husky Soviet soldiers roaring with laughter as they got ready to throw more pieces down. I wondered why the dainty chairs didn't collapse under their massive weight. Mutti whispered, "Don't look up there. Act disinterested." It was a sight that I will never forget.

By then we had to leave the main highway and take a country road that forked off to the left that would lead us directly to the farms in the rural area. On the right side, behind some trees, we saw large German barracks that were still intact and now occupied by Soviet soldiers. We could not believe our eyes when we saw several of them with their buttocks hanging out of the upper story windows and relieving themselves down over the side of the building. By the looks of the walls, this was a frequent occurrence. Again Mutti warned me not to stare in that direction and to act disinterested, and, above all, to show no panic if we had any encounter with the Soviets.

The closer we got to Fahrland, the more shallow graves we saw along the side of road, one hilly sand pile after another marked with plain wooden crosses. We stopped and began to read names and ages. They were all twelve and thirteen-year old boys from the area who had been hastily buried where they had been killed. We were shocked at the sight of so many graves of children. They had been drafted into the Volkssturm during the last days of Hitler's senseless resistance and were cruelly sacrificed by an inhuman government when confronted by Soviet tanks. They would remain here as a grim memorial until they could be afforded a proper burial by their families, if they had survived.

We eventually reached Fahrland which had been badly damaged from the fighting that took place there. Our farmer was located on the other side of the village and the farmer's wife remembered me from my previous visits. Her husband had not yet returned from the war and her life had become frightful. We shared our own experiences of the war's end. On our first visit we did not have anything to barter, but she accepted our money and sold us vegetables anyway, including a lot of potatoes because we planned to plant some in our own garden, and she taught us how to do it properly. We were very generous in our payment, having in mind to return again and being remembered favorably.

There was no time to rest very long because of the curfew. We heaved our heavy knapsacks bursting with potatoes onto our backs, and with each hand grabbed a bag filled with carrots and cabbage. Looking like a parade of backpackers we started the jog-trek back. We needed every last breath for the long route home. I never knew that you can feel every single potato on your back. When we reached the main highway we dared to rest for a short while on a green embankment, realizing by now that we had also acquired sore feet.

After hiking for endless hours, we finally reached the destroyed Wannsee bridge again. That sorry sight gave me shivers. Yet, with mutual support of fellow sufferers, and trembling with fear, we made it safely across without losing our balance or any of our precious cargo. By now the heavy knapsacks had drained every ounce of strength from our feeble bodies. Totally exhausted, we just collapsed right on the curb of the Potsdamer Chaussee, all three of us close to tears. Our legs ached and I swore that I couldn't go any further and would die right here. I dropped everything and groaning, rested my head in my hands. Finally Mutti said, "We can't wait here to die. It takes too long. We have to be home before the 6 p.m. curfew." How true! We laughed, even though it was not funny at all. Adding to the torture, our old boots were killing us. With desperate determination we began trudging along the seemingly endless road, finally making it home just in time. Our family was in despair since we returned so late. So much could have happened to us. Finally we could afford to really collapse and remove the tormenting boots from our swollen and blistered feet. We swore that we would never make that trip again. But, of course, we did—we had to. Our life was a struggle for survival.

The following morning, June 1, we received orders from the Soviets to make flags in the colors of each of the Allies which were to be displayed for the first meeting of the Supreme Allied Control Panel that was supposed to take place in Berlin on June 5. We thought they must be out of their minds. How could we make a British or American flag? We were even supposed to provide the materials. All German down beds had red ticking, and the Soviets threatened to tear it off them if we did not immediately produce red flags. We had a better idea, and got out the old red Nazi flags and ripped off the white circle from the center which contained the black swastika. Presto, instant red flags! Although when we displayed them the faint outline of the swastika was still recognizable because that area had been discolored less. To our great amusement, this did not seem to bother the Soviets who were so impressed in seeing so much red that they forgot about all the other Allied flags.

There was obviously some truth to the rumor that there were new Soviet orders for greater Red Army discipline because, to our relief, the soldiers had been more confined to their barracks than in the past. One of their camps was the nearby former SS barracks in Lichterfelde where the huge square in front had been secured by a high wire fence. We had heard that Berliners were dealing with Soviets through the mesh of the fence since the soldiers were still after many "items of cultura." We badly needed money and the Soviet soldiers had plenty of it, which they had looted from German banks. A group on Limastrasse wanted to venture out there to try to make the same deal and I definitely wanted to be part of this.

So I searched through Sieghardt's desk and found a large quantity of fountain pens and mechanical pencils with the firm's name on them, all former advertisements. Grabbing a handful of them, I joined my neighbors for the two-hour walk to the Soviet barracks. When we arrived, I couldn't help laughing at the scene. It looked like a human zoo, only this time with people clinging on both sides of the fence—inside the Soviets and outside the Berliners. Hands reached through the meshes to make a deal, and we joined the crowd.

My pens and pencils were in great demand, but I wanted the money first before I would pass one through the wire. Though the Soviets protested, I eventually got my way. The deal went tit for tat. They had no idea of value of the German money, nor could they read the numbers on the bills. I sold each pen by pointing out which bill I wanted from the bundle in their hands with a one hundred, five hundred, or thousand on it, my private black market. We were warned not to take any of their bottles offered as cooking oil because the content was usually extended with urine. All these transactions were forbidden, like almost everything in our present life. So we concluded our deal quickly and left before being caught by the police. I returned home with an unexpected precious bundle of German money for the family.

By the end of the week, the results of our country pilgrimage were dwindling without any means of replenishment in sight. Mutti and I were painfully aware that we had to repeat the trip to the farm, this time without Maria. With our feet healed again, the boots softer, and our hearts pounding in fear, we departed at 6 a.m. Tuesday morning. We followed the same route as on our previous march with grim determination and soon passed the new Soviet monument in Nikolassee that everyone was talking about. It was a nine-foot high massive stone pedestal with a soviet tank sitting on top, aiming its gun at the passing traffic. It had been hastily erected in the middle of a green that separated a four-lane divided highway. Why here in the future American sector? The Soviets obviously wanted this monument to represent their sole conquest of Berlin. It was their city. They got here first, even though we all knew that the Americans had held back to allow the Soviets the honor of capturing Berlin. Now the Americans were only the late-comers moving temporarily into their sectors in July, tolerated as guests. A longstanding power struggle was pre-programmed.

However, some Berliners did not appreciate this Communist memorial in our western outskirts. After all, we were enthusiastically awaiting the Americans. The pedestal suddenly started to "inexplicably" begin to crumble. Every night, bit by bit it would be chipped away, since it was unguarded, and the Soviets had to be constantly repairing it during the day to keep the tank from crashing down. Finally, tired of the endless repairs, the Soviets surrounded the eroding base with a high wire fence. The Berliners, highly amused, joked that all the Soviets should be put behind there as well. But the fence did not stop the "deterioration" of the base. As we passed it, we were disgusted about such an eyesore in our area, but had to smile at the mysterious continual chipping away of the pedestal base. There would even be a postlude with the Americans later in July.

With a throbbing heart we arrived at the destroyed Wannsee bridge and fully expected another treacherous crossing. But, what a pleasant surprise; a clever Berliner had started a private ferry service with his own boat across the deep bay part of the Havel River. He could easily take twenty to thirty people at a time for a small fee. We boarded immediately and in less than a half-hour, would land on the opposite shore, which was to become the future British sector. This would shorten our hike by a few miles. The other passengers were very friendly and talkative, and exchanged their experiences with the Soviets. One nice young lady advised, "If you are in serious danger of being raped, the only way to prevent it is to act real calm. If you don't resist, and follow the Soviet willingly, he will be less likely to take you very far into the woods. Soon he can't wait any longer and when he drops his trousers, that is your chance to run away. He is in no position to give chase with his pants dangling around his ankles, and before he can catch you, you are back on the main street and lost in the crowds." She laughed, "Believe me, it works!"

When we disembarked, everyone forked off in another direction to their secret vital food source, so we resumed our hiking alone on the opposite shore. After several hours we finally reached our country road where we passed close to the Russian barracks, but what had happened here? Large sections of the tile roof had been blasted off and the floor under it was destroyed. It looked like bomb damage, though it was peace time. We walked by as if nothing unusual had happened. Later, farmers told us that some of the Soviet soldiers were just having fun and fired a cannon from the inside up through the roof and partially destroyed the building. As we approached Fahrland, we noticed that all of the crosses had been removed from the hilly roadside graves. We learned that there had been a Soviet order to remove them because only dead Soviets were to be remembered. But the real reason for it was that the Soviets did not want it to be so evident that the mighty Red Army had conquered Berlin over a defending force of school boys, leaving behind so many children's corpses.

When we reached our farm, we found that the husband had returned from the war, and the people seemed less friendly, having been spoiled by the many Berliners who were outbidding each other for their produce. We bought our vegetables as before, but at much higher prices this time, and immediately set out for our long walk home. The country road was very isolated and suddenly two Soviet soldiers jumped out of a ditch behind us and started to follow us. Even though we tried to speed up our walking, which was difficult with our heavy loads, the soldiers kept gaining on us.

All of a sudden, two more Soviet soldiers appeared a short distance in front of us. Our heart stopped, and Mutti calmly said, "We are in a trap. As soon as the four reach us, you run!" "No," I countered, "we stay together and put up a brave front." To our surprise, the two soldiers behind us stopped when they saw the two soldiers in front of us, and those two kept walking toward us, but acted irritated when they spotted the two soldiers behind us. As they passed, the one nearest me raised his fist as if to punch me in the face, and when I just looked straight ahead, he bluffed and I only felt his blow passing lightly by my left ear. Terrified, we kept on walking, always briskly onwards.

What had saved us? We knew that, officially, rape was forbidden. However, this did not prevent it from happening, and probably both groups had the same mischief in mind when they saw us, but had not counted on the presence of the other two. They had no way of knowing if they were all of one accord, or if the other two would turn them in. The four met behind us and entered into a heated discussion, but before they had reached a common agreement, we were out on the main road and mingling with all of the other travelers. This had been a close call and we decided not to mention anything about it at home because they were already worried enough about us being out on the road all day. We again crossed the lake by ferry and approaching the Wannsee bridge, we noticed that a large group of workers was already busy restoring it. After we landed, we plodded along for a few more hours, reaching home safely but worn out. We proudly displayed our treasures of potatoes, carrots, turnips, and, as a highlight, a head of cauliflower.

The next morning, a stranger knocked at my door on Limastrasse to inform me that nobody had to pay rent anymore because capitalistic house owners were dethroned. Naturally, I was shocked since in this case, the owners were my parents. I tried to find out more information, but the man knew nothing except that his message was a new Soviet rule for Berlin. While he was making the rounds in our apartment building to spread the good news, I rushed over to Mutti and Papa to tell them what had happened. They could not believe that it was true, but it was, although only for one month until it was overruled again. In our life, uncertainty was the only certainty of the day.

In the meantime, we kept our private Red Cross shelter open to take care of the many emergencies, but Mrs. Weissbach and I moved it from the basement into a room in her apartment. She had extra space, unfortunately. Her husband had never overcome the aftermath of being buried alive in an air raid in the city, and upon his recent death, she was now the sole survivor of a formerly happy family of four, losing a husband and both sons.

Lately people were also asking us for assistance in finding missing persons, and in desperation, offered us money to help us speed up our work. They were very disappointed when we would not accept their payment because it was much too early for any investigations. Instead, we prepared long lists of names and addresses of who looked for whom and where. I had not heard from Sieghardt since his unit was moved to the West in April, and my family had no word from Günter.

One day, we got a call from an old lady living next to my parents who asked for assistance in getting her nephew to a hospital. He was a soldier who had returned on foot from the Soviet Union in terrible condition. Feeble and famished, he pushed himself to make it home to her and collapsed upon arrival. There was no ambulance available, but Mrs. Weissbach miraculously managed to obtain a wheelchair and to get permission from the Soviets to transport a sick person to the nearby Martin Luther Hospital. They even provided a Soviet soldier, whom I recognized from passing his guard post near the house, to provide a safe escort for the thirty-minute walk along Beerenstrasse. Wearing our Red Cross uniforms, we picked up what appeared to be a haggard-faced old man, even though he was still in his early thirties. He was nothing but skin and bones and when we lifted him into the wheelchair, he felt as weightless as a doll. Our young Soviet escort was civilized and spoke some German, and was very helpful in getting the wheelchair around obstructions as we pushed on toward the hospital. He told us he was only nineteen and homesick for his family back in Russia. His sister had been drafted into the army two years ago and had never been heard from since.

While talking, we passed a driveway where several Soviet soldiers were milling around, and as soon as they saw us they began to yell, "*Frau komm.*" We tried to pass by quickly and they started to pursue us. Our young escort pushed us forward. "Run away as quickly as you can. These are bad soldiers. I will hold them back." We speeded up as much as possible while pushing a wheelchair over bumpy pavement. Our patient understood only too well our frantic speed and had been trembling all over ever since the yelling Soviets had approached us. Our escort eventually caught up with us, and we made it safely to the hospital where our patient finally received professional help. I never saw anyone so grateful for a clean bed and a kind word as he was. He smiled, squeezed our hands and didn't want to let go because he was finally not alone anymore. He looked younger already and we promised to come back soon for a visit—a promise we were unable to keep. Shortly thereafter, he died in his sleep from exhaustion, but smiling that he had made it home. We walked safely back to our house with our escort, and two days later he was no longer at his post. Perhaps he had been removed for being too friendly to us.

All banks remained closed but periodically the post office was open for several days and then closed again for no apparent reason. Somehow Papa had managed to get some dirndl-like dress material for Mutti and me from some old business friends in the West. It was a beautiful dark-colored print of a sturdy fabric that would be perfect for our country trips. Our home-made new dresses turned out beautifully, with two pockets on the outside and one inside for hiding money. They were our first new dresses in years, but I should never have worn mine.

On our next weekly trip to the country, as soon as the shrewd farmer's wife saw it, she loudly lamented that my dress was exactly what she had wanted for a long time. There was a tremendous difference in our size and even a blind person could see that the dress on my slim figure would never fit her or her plump daughter. I tried to tactfully point this out to her, but to no avail as she just kept insisting on having my new dress. After leaving with our usual cargo of produce for which we paid the expected high prices, Mutti said, "I'm so sorry, but it is very clear that we have to bring her your new dress on our next trip, of course as a gift, if we hope to get any food there in the future." We couldn't risk that, and there went my new dress that I had worn only once—surrendered to keep the farmer's wife happy.

This was a time when Berliners were giving all of their possession to farmers in the country, even furniture, just to get food. Their produce was no longer available for just money alone. As usual, the Berliners' dry wit found the funny side of even the most unpleasant situations with jokes like this:

> A farmer comes in from the field and sees his two daughters playing a four-handed duet together on the same piano. He exclaims, "Enough of that poor cramped nonsense on only one piano. Tomorrow, we'll get a second one."

It was understood the Berliners would be bringing it, as before furs and jewelry. But, the farmers' prosperity did not last too long either because they were soon compelled to live under Soviet jurisdiction which abolished private ownership. This meant that they lost their farms and were forced into a collective farming association with all land owned by the state.

At our boat crossing a man always sat next to us and talked about horoscopes. We should not be afraid, the next wars would be far away from Germany. By the end of the century the last "ismus" would be destroyed. Mutti urged me not to say anything. Right now Communism ruled us with an iron hand. (How could we foresee how right he was during the next fifty years, with wars never imagined outside as well as inside Europe. The dissolution of the Soviet Union occurred on December 25, 1991.)

Money was a constant problem because we could not withdraw from the closed banks or write checks. Prices rose every day, and it took cash or exchange transactions to exist. I ask myself today what did we all live on in 1945? Since we had to live from hand to mouth, we started to plant potatoes and other vegetables in our own garden. On Limastrasse every tenant had received a private plot of the large shared back yard to raise something edible. Besides vegetables, I had already planted twenty tomato seedlings with future barter in mind. However, nothing grows overnight, so month after month we had to make that dangerous weekly trip into the country every Tuesday.

At the end of June we heard a rumor about the forming of a new German party called CDU (Christian Democratic Union) with guidelines for a Christian and democratic policy for all of Germany, and a man named Konrad Adenauer was mentioned. Even though this took place one hundred miles away in West Germany, it still was a new ray of hope for all of us in isolated Berlin where we were being treated as a separate territory.

$\mathcal{D}$ancing With the Russian Bear

$\mathcal{T}$he Wannsee bridge was restored again, and traffic was surprisingly heavy between Berlin and Potsdam. Early in July, when Mutti and I made our weekly trip into the country, we took the baby carriage along to Fahrland. The buggy eased the burden of lugging our country goods home. As we approached the bridge early that morning, we noticed that the Soviet soldiers seemed to be acting silly, as some came toward us with outstretched hands with fingers spread wide apart to show us their new white gloves. They had never worn any gloves before, let alone white ones, and they waved their hands in front of our face, much too close for comfort, to make sure we noticed this new sign of culture. We smiled with pretended admiration and were greatly relieved to pass by without any further hassle. Why the strange and childish behavior? The answer would come later on our return trip.

We followed our usual route to Fahrland. This time the farmhouse smelled deliciously of fresh baked bread. Being very hungry from our long hike, I made the mistake of spontaneously asking the farmer's wife if we could try just one slice, but she started squirming like a worm. She claimed there was only enough for themselves and they could not part with any of it. Obviously I had forgotten to first offer a precious reward. Why had I humiliated Mutti and myself for a measly slice of bread? When would these frugal times finally end and the Americans arrive? We quickly concluded our usual business and packed our cargo of field products in the baby carriage. It was so much easier to push the buggy than to carry the produce in bags and knapsacks on that long walk back home.

We approached the Wannsee bridge in the afternoon, tired from the constant walking since early morning, and hoped to be home in a few more hours. Just the opposite happened. We were stopped abruptly by shouting Soviet soldiers who pushed us off the highway onto a small country road which headed in the wrong direction for home. We could not understand this rude treatment after the joyous welcome this morning, but we were not about to argue with a bunch of angry Soviets and hastily steered our buggy down this deserted road, not having the faintest idea where it would lead us or how to find our way back to our suburb.

We trotted along a wide, deep canal which we had to somehow cross to get back on our highway from Potsdam to Berlin. Every bridge we passed was hopelessly destroyed until we finally spotted something in the distance that looked like a newly built temporary bridge. But when we arrived, our hopes were dashed. This one was of the most primitive construction of small old planks with no handrails, just a rope on either side strung between poles on opposite ends. It was so narrow that you had to cross it in single file. How were we to manage our baby carriage with a load of fifty pounds? I had always been afraid of heights, and this shaky contraption was high above the water between two steep concrete walls.

As we stood there surveying the bridge, we saw two men appearing out of nowhere who began crossing from the opposite side. With each of their careful steps the planks swayed not only from side to side, but also up and down. But, they made it safely across and began to walk past us as they headed for the nearby woods. On impulse, I stopped them and begged them to help us cross the bridge with our buggy. They hesitated when they looked at our load, but finally agreed to escort us one at a time. Mutti wanted to go last and I didn't want to be first, so they started with the baby carriage, even though it would stand unguarded on the opposite bank, easily to be stolen.

All too soon it was my turn, one man in front of me and one behind. I squeezed their hands so tightly that they decided to support me under my arms instead. "Don't look down," Mutti called out to me. We started the crossing step by step. My swinging on this dangling contraption of hell seemed to last forever. I was afraid to look down but couldn't close my eyes, anxious not to miss a step. Shaking all over, I reached the other bank and very relieved stood on solid ground again. The men returned. Now I watched fearfully as they brought Mutti over. Safely across, she was shaking as much as I was. After three round trips our escorts were ready for their last crossing into the Soviet country zone. We asked them why, because men were kidnapped and disappeared without a trace almost daily. But they wanted to search for missing relatives. We wished them luck and they disappeared into the unknown. That incident was so typical of our time. The greater the misery, the more people felt bound together in mutual assistance with few words. No names were asked, and most likely we would never meet again.

But where were we now? This was a God-forsaken area. On our right was an enormous sandy embankment and we could hear traffic and voices at the top, so we assumed there must be a street above us. So we needed to be up there, too. With me pulling the carriage and Mutti pushing it, we used a running take-off to scale the steep bank, and made it half way up. There we got stuck in the sand. No matter how hard we pushed and pulled, we could not make any headway, and gradually sank deeper down in the sand. Apparently our voices had been heard at the top because several heads peered over the edge, curious about all the commotion. When they spotted our predicament, several men immediately formed a human chain and grabbed hold of the baby carriage. With one final jerk, with us hanging on, they pulled it loose from its sand trap and up over the edge of the bank. Here, we found ourselves on the street that was heading in the direction of home. What a relief!

But why was our carriage now lopsided? Oh no, it couldn't be true. The left front wheel was missing, still stuck somewhere in that sandy embankment. It was useless to search for it, so using a sturdy rope that we always carried for emergencies, we knotted it around the bare axle and I placed the other end over my shoulder so I could pull and Mutti could push. What a great solution. But the potatoes would not cooperate. Like lead, they grew heavier with every step. The rope began to chafe my shoulder and I kept shifting it from one place to the other with little relief. Finally, after about a mile, we had to leave the paved street to cross through some woods to reach the Potsdamer Chaussee which would take us home to Zehlendorf-West. The chafing rope was now much worse on the uneven terrain.

Suddenly there was another glimmer of hope. Not too far away, we spotted two young men through the trees who were obviously not Soviets and I called out to them. They looked in our direction and I waved both arms, motioning for them to come over to us. They hesitated, and after whispering to each other, finally came closer. It was then that we discovered they were American soldiers. Hurrah! The eagerly awaited

Americans must have just arrived. So that's why the Soviets had been dressed in white gloves, to look civilized when greeting the Americans, and that's why they refused to let us return on the main road. They didn't want the Americans to see us as examples of starved Berliners who had to haul their food from the country.

By now, the two young soldiers had reached us and saw our dilemma, which did not need my explanation in poor English. Without hesitation, they grabbed our heavy carriage and marched ahead so quickly that Mutti and I could hardly keep up with our tired feet. These nice young men were about Günter's age. Where might my brother be by now? We had no sign of life from him for ten months.

Soon we could hear heavy traffic that sounded like a military convoy. "Oh, we must be close to the Potsdamer Chaussee," Mutti and I rejoiced. Suddenly, our two helpers disappeared without giving us a chance to thank them. Why so abruptly? We would learn the solution to that puzzle the next day. So, we picked up the crippled carriage ourselves again and made it to the main highway in about ten minutes. As the long convoys slowly rolled by us, with the vehicles and troops looking so orderly and clean, we already felt protected from the mistreatment that we had endured these past terrible months from the Soviets. Thank God, the arrival of the long awaited Americans would end our misery and now we would receive so much more support and understanding from these people who were of the same breed and culture.

We plodded along without further help, but this time on an asphalt street, and reached our suburb in about two hours where Papa was looking for us at the intersection. He had been worried sick about our late arrival from the country. Horror stories were told about Oranienburg, a town near Berlin where women were abducted from the streets and confined like prisoners in Soviet barracks. Here, they were forced to bear children fathered by the Soviet soldiers, and the babies were to be "exported" to the Soviet Union. Russia wanted the German blood as a gift to the future. Women who did not survive were no problem. The dead ones were replaced by new, live ones to take their place. Nothing was normal anymore besides constant fear.

Deeply relieved, Papa grabbed our lame baby carriage and pushed it the last short distance home. Oh, how our sore feet hurt and how exhausted we were. All we could think of was that with the arrival of the Americans, our food problems would be solved and we would never have to make any more dangerous and tiring barter trips into the country. Our journey today may have been the last one.

The Western Allies were enthusiastically received by the Berlin population, the British even with flowers. The American sector of occupation included our west-end residential districts with woodlands and lakes. Papa told us that the Soviets had withdrawn, leaving their deserted barricades for the Americans to clear away. "We are able to freely move around the streets again," he said with a sigh of relief, "but the departing Soviets have totally destroyed the Tempelhof Airport so that the Americans cannot use it. They even burned down buildings." That deliberate vandalism was just a forerunner of Stalin's incidents against his own Allies.

But, our joy over the arrival of the Americans was short-lived, dashed the very next morning with public announcements posted all over with strict orders from General Eisenhower that ended with: "There will be no fraternization with the German population. We came as occupiers, not liberators." But the war was over! We could not believe what we read. He apparently felt that all Germans were Nazis from cradle to the grave, all painted with the same "brown" brush based on prejudicial stereotyped cliché opinion distorted by a discriminating press. How wrong he was. We were shocked at this position taken by Eisenhower, who like 60 million other Americans, came from German roots. His first ancestor arrived in America as Hans Eisenhauer in 1741.

Obviously, the war was not over for us Berliners who had expected miracles on the part of the Americans after the long strain of the Nazi regime and the horror of the Soviet despotism we had endured. What a mistake to believe in a new start with normal life and order. We found neither. Instead the additional laws were not commensurate with justice, but a new dictatorship with confusion everywhere. Bad events cast their shadows in front of us. Life was just as oppressed as before. We now understood that the whispered conversation between the two American soldiers who helped us the previous afternoon probably concerned the risk of violating Eisenhower's strict no fraternization order, and this was why they disappeared so abruptly when we came in sight of the American convoys. We hadn't seen each other as enemies. None of us had wanted the war.

The American presence was manifested to us in two ways. First, the Stars and Stripes had flown over Berlin since July 4, and second, all of the inane orders given before in Russian were now heard in English. There went our hopes for improvement. From the beginning, the Western Allies blindly retained all the rules and regulations enforced by the Soviets for all of Berlin, which soon would backfire. They were even reinforced with additional American orders. Some were completely unrealistic, such as the new "knife law" which stated that under the penalty of death, no household could have a knife with a blade longer than five inches. Since most normal kitchen knives are much longer, every Berliner would have to be executed, but we all survived under this "soon-to-be-forgotten" law. (It didn't come to our attention again until July 8, 1988, when a German newspaper in Berlin, the *Morgenpost*, proclaimed that the American knife-law, which was still on the books, had now been officially repealed).

Regardless of our insufficient housing, hardly a building remained intact, and many were beyond repair. The Americans confiscated most of the remaining habitable homes in Berlin-Dahlem and soldiers were billeted in civilian houses in this exclusive residential area. The residents were given twenty-four hours notice to evacuate them, being allowed to take only their personal clothing. Upon hearing this, we feared that we in Zehlendorf-West might be faced with the same situation. It was obvious that the Americans wrongly equated all Germans with the Nazis, a hatred dictated by the negative media propaganda in its anti-German hysteria, without realizing that Hitler was an Austrian and not even a German, and that their knowledge of German history encompassed only the period of Hitler's rule from 1933 to 1945. However, this was merely a short, dark chapter in our over one thousand-year-old history.

For centuries, Germany had contributed important achievements to mankind in the form of technology, science, music, art, literature and philosophy. One has to take history with its good and bad aspects, and every nation has both, or as they say, there is a skeleton in every closet. Ours was the Nazi regime under the little Austrian corporal and the genocide of those people he considered unfit to live. The United States had its own genocide with the massacre, starvation and internment of the American Indian. The anti-German hate propaganda completely ignored that for more than three centuries, Germans had made significant contributions to all areas of American life, and that Germans are the largest ethnic group in America. It was a German, Prussian Baron von Steuben who organized and trained the Continental Army of George Washington into an effective fighting force against the British in the Revolutionary War. His Prussian drill manual, written in German, is still the fundamental manual for the U.S. Army. And, regiments of German settlers played a decisive role during the struggle for independence of the first thirteen colonies.

We Berliners were completely baffled by the hostile attitude of the Americans, who, like the Soviets, let us starve. Our food ration cards had turned into a lottery ticket with mostly blanks. Famine was upon us as before. We had heard about the Eisenhower order that prohibited American soldiers from giving any of their surplus food to the starving population and required that it be destroyed instead. Initially, we considered that this was just malicious gossip until I personally witnessed how wide-eyed, emaciated children stood on our street corner watching some American soldiers throwing their cocoa and cookies on the ground and then, grinding everything into the sand with their boots. I led the children away in shock.

We also heard stories in our Red Cross station about a hospital in the suburb Botanischer Garten, which had been taken over by the Americans. The hungry population hung outside on the fence and watched as inside rich, clean food from the kitchen was dumped into garbage cans right in front of their eyes. The Western Allies were so absorbed in their blind hatred that they did not notice Stalin's intention to swallow West Berlin as he had already swallowed East Europe, and that the world was presented already with a fait accompli.

Berlin was to be occupied jointly by the three powers, the United States, Great Britain and the Soviet Union. But, the Soviets were a step ahead of the Western Allies and had already grabbed almost half of the city, including the historical center, the heart of Berlin. With 46 percent under Soviet occupation, the United States and Great Britain shared the remaining 54 percent. This ratio horrified us Berliners. When in August the French also demanded a presence in Berlin, we were convinced that this would equalize the distribution by reducing the Soviet area to merely one quarter. But, Stalin again outwitted the Western Allies by agreeing only to the presence of the French, but not giving up any of his already oversized area of the city. Alas, the Soviets kept the lion's share. So, the Americans and British, not realizing the trap that Stalin had set for them, willingly squeezed closer together to make room for the new French sector. The Western Allies didn't see what was happening while it was happening, and this would soon backfire and inevitably become a bitter and incessant East-West power struggle.

The worst was yet to come when the Western Allies again made the horrendous error of giving Stalin complete control over the entire system of the S-Bahn. The repair plants were in East Berlin in the working class district, and the Soviets slyly offered to take care of the total system maintenance. We Berliners were shocked that the Western Allies would be so naive as to consent to the Soviets' clever expansion of their influence into the West, because in one slick move, all S-Bahn stations in West Berlin became Soviet-controlled. The S-Bahn was now exclusively operated by the Soviets throughout the entire city and provided an open door for the legal infiltration of spies to the West. It wasn't long before people were literally "stolen" from the streets of West Berlin, brutally kidnapped by East agents and dragged screaming into the Soviet controlled S-Bahn stations, as I witnessed myself. The American soldiers had to watch, powerless, as the victims cried for help, because the Soviet-controlled S-Bahn stations in the American sector soon became off-limits to all American military and their dependents. When it was too late, the Western Allies finally realized that the Soviets had outwitted them in every area of negotiation and thus began a long battle of clashing opinions and disputes. However, the disputes never resulted in any solution because the Soviets, with their constant veto, became world champions in saying "Nyet", or No! Frustrated, all sides finally agreed to disagree.

Unfortunately, the Western Allies had also adopted the Soviets' meager food ration card system of five classes. Famine was once more upon us, and we were again driven to search for other food sources. Fighting the peace was worse for us than fighting the war, and we had expected miracles from the Americans. With dashed hopes, Mutti and I were forced to go back to our weekly trips to the country, which had the ever present danger of being stranded in the Soviet zone. We would leave early every Tuesday morning and return late that evening, relieved to have escaped all dangers. Lugging our heavy loads, we were totally exhausted and swore that we would never make the trip again. That desperate oath lasted just one week when our food supply was again used up by Sunday night.

On Monday, Mutti would ask me to hold our big soup pot with remnants of potatoes and carrots under the faucet. I needed both of my hands to do it. Then she would open the spigot and let the water run into it until it looked like enough to fill all our soup bowls with something that reminded us of food, wondering what our next meal would be. We became experts in cooking meals where the main ingredient was water. That same evening Mutti would say to me, "I'll pick you up tomorrow morning at six." Despite our fears, despite all the dangers and pains involved, the empty pots gave us the necessary boost. Thus we took off again into the Soviet countryside to haul potatoes and carrots back into the American sector; we returned in the evening exhausted, swearing we would never again.... Our life had changed into eternal repetition. We had become robots.

On one of these hunger trips, the farmer's wife warned us that drunken Soviets were on a raping spree again. Girls who resisted were dragged into the fields and had burning cigarettes pushed into their private parts. Some didn't survive. As we were leaving the farm house, a group of drunken Soviets approached, and we frantically ran back inside and out the back door where we hid in some bushes. After a long fearful wait, the farmer's wife finally signaled to us, indicating the coast was clear. When the soldiers did not find anyone in the house, they merely asked for a drink of water and then left. Shaken by our close call, we loaded up our produce and started with utmost caution on our long walk home, which we made safely. We attempted to exist among the Soviets, the Americans, and our hunger sprees.

A middle-aged lady knocked on my door on July 14, 1945. "I am Mrs. Schnell," she said, "and I bring you good news from your husband." Sieghardt was alive! Overjoyed, I asked her in right away. I had waited for such a message after all of these months of not knowing where he was or if he was even alive. There was no mail or telephone service and she was acting like a door-to-door messenger. She had just come from West Germany, she said, where Sieghardt was now. On April 20, his military unit was discharged and the Commandant had given everyone the choice of either going into American captivity or trying to make it home on their own.

Sieghardt and his Berliner friend Helmut Berger had risked an escape together, on foot, into the rugged Harz mountain range of north central Germany. Exhausted from running and hiding from the Americans, and totally famished, they had begged for some bread at the head forest ranger's house *Haferfeld*, but they were rudely turned away and told to go to hell or into American captivity. Other people were more humane, and one woman even gave them some clothes belonging to her husband who had been killed at the Eastern Front. They now could shed their uniforms, but had to remain in hiding in the mountains until they heard about the surrender of Germany.

It was still too dangerous for them to advance to Berlin, so on May 10 they stopped in Gröna, a little town near Bernburg on the Saale River. Having no money, they were taken in by the restaurant *Schlehdorn* and earned their keep by chopping wood, doing roofing and other repairs. Sieghardt could handle horses so they both were recommended to the nearby farm of a Mrs. Gertrude Koch who was waiting for the return of her own husband from the war and she happily hired them as farm hands. Mrs. Schnell finished her story with, "and your husband is still there, waiting to hear from home. What message can I take back to him? Nothing written, please, that is too suspicious." She waited for my answer.

I was so excited that I couldn't think where to start. Most important was that we were still alive so far, and were very relieved to have heard from him. As she prepared to leave, I offered her some refreshment, but she refused as she could easily see we had less than she in Gröna, and she had many more messages to deliver before returning to West Germany. "I feel like a traveling mailman," she laughed. When I asked how she planned to get back, she said the worst part would be the Soviet zone where a few trains were running again, but with very undependable schedules. There was no way of knowing how long the journey would take, which before the war, would have been a car ride of just a few hours. And then she was gone just as suddenly as she had appeared, and I rushed off to tell the exciting news to the family.

Unexpectedly, Elsa's husband, Heinz, showed up at my parents' house and we survivors had a happy reunion. We heard now that the city of Oschatz, where Elsa had stayed, had been overrun by the Soviets in April. It resulted in massacres, looting and raping. Thrown into panic, mass

suicides of the terrified citizens and refugees followed. From Elsa's gradu-
ating class of eight, only two girls survived, she and a girlfriend. Heinz
had gotten rid of his uniform and, wearing ill fitting clothes, unwashed
and unshaven, arrived in Oschatz by bicycle in early May, where he found
his family surviving in their basement refuge. It was a heart-breaking
reunion.

The group now included two other women. In April, Elsa had seen
two walking skeletons in front of her garden and had taken them in.
They told her that they came from a concentration camp which was
being emptied and the prisoners to be driven into Soviet artillery fire to
be killed. Suddenly the female guards ran away and the victims were
left to stray aimlessly through Oschatz, not knowing where to turn. Here
Heinz paused in his story. "I was horrified as this was my first personal
meeting with living proof that the unbelievable rumors about these "killing" camps were true. I saw with my own eyes the five-digit numbers
tattooed into their arms. When we were made to believe that Jews and
opponents of the Nazi regime were harmlessly resettled in the East, in
reality, they had been murdered."

We were equally horror-stricken to hear what had really been going
on in these Nazi-created "hell on earth" concentration camps. Papa
blurted out, "Where are the ones who are responsible for these atrocities? They are probably well hidden in safety and not wandering the
streets like their poor victims. Unbelievable!" Yes, the concentration
camps were a masterpiece of Nazi secrecy, as admitted by General Alfred
Jodl in the Nuremberg Trials, and that most German citizens never
learned the truth about them until the war was over. According to Heinz,
one of the two new ladies was the wife of the prominent *Kammersänger*
Neumann from Berlin. (*Kammersänger* is an honorary title conferred
on a singer of outstanding merit.) The other lady was a sculptress from
Prague. Mrs. Neumann knew that her husband was in a concentration
camp for men and that they had agreed to meet at the home of a friend
in Leipzig if he ever got out again. Elsa cooked a watery gruel soup for
them each day since this was the only type of food they could hold down.

Strangely enough, there was plenty of food in the house because
the depots had been opened shortly before the Soviets arrived and people
had stormed them, taking more than they could carry. Elsa merely picked
up from the street what others had dropped, such as long salamis, big

pieces of bacon, cheese and cartons of rolled oats to make her gruel soup. In order to escape being raped every night, Elsa would constantly change hiding places, sometimes dangerously on top of roofs and other times in a huge trash can, where Heinz would check on her from time to time to make sure she was getting enough air under the lid and the trash.

Then, they heard a rumor that the border to the West was to be blocked and they would have to flee at once to escape deportation and the Soviet system of forced labor. Heinz traded his bicycle for a hand-drawn cart in which they piled their meager possessions, their little son sitting on top. Mrs. Neumann gave them the name and address of her friend in Leipzig to bring them news of her, since she was too weak to make such a strenuous journey on foot. She and her friend were also protected by their tatoo marks from the concentration camp, which identified them as Nazi enemies. So everything was settled and they were on their exodus out of town, aiming westward toward the Americans.

Except they did not get very far. It was late afternoon and close to the curfew when Elsa and Heinz were stopped and forced into the gymnasium of a school. It was crowded already with refugees from the East, primarily women and children, while drunken Soviet soldiers could be heard carousing upstairs. Everyone was horrified at the trap that they were in, and Heinz tried to hide Elsa by placing her in his sleeping bag face down and pulling his cap deep over her head to hide her hair.

The Soviet soldiers soon burst through the door into the dark gymnasium and ran their flashlights over everybody, looking for women to pick for an orgy. One man who tried to protect his wife was brutally knocked down and others were trampled bloody. In the darkness, shots were fired inside and outside. Children were crying and women were screaming for help. Heinz hid Elsa from view by partly laying over her and pretended to sleep, snoring. His desperate trick worked. The orgy went on for hours until the Soviets finally collapsed from intoxication, and they were still laying drunk all over when the people escaped that inferno in the early morning. Dead bodies were crudely covered with paper. They spent the day walking with a group of French prisoners of war who proudly carried their national colors, and stayed the night with them in an abandoned ruin in the company of mice and shared the food.

The next day, they arrived at the bridge over the little Mulde River.

On the opposite bank began Nirwana, the no-man's land that separated them from Leipzig. They were stopped by the Soviet barrier with the order "*STOJ!*" Stop! Crossing the bridge, for Germans *NYET*." Heinz left Elsa under the protection of a Frenchman. They saw the house of a railroad gatekeeper on the other side of the bridge and agreed to meet there after Heinz would somehow cross on his own. The Frenchman put his arm around Elsa and they crossed the bridge as a French family pushing the cart with their child on top. The Frenchman was "big comrade" for the Soviets. From a distance, Heinz watched their safe passage and then pretended to be an old man collecting firewood as he disappeared into the woods and waited for nightfall. At an isolated spot downstream, he tied his clothing to his head and swam naked across the ice cold river.

The next morning, to everybody's relief, he appeared at the agreed upon house of the railroad gatekeeper. They parted company with the Frenchman and headed on their own for Leipzig which was at the time occupied by the Americans. At first, the American sentry refused them entry. Before they couldn't get out, and here not in, being Germans in Germany, but their knowledge of English and the fact that they had a message for a former concentration camp prisoner helped them. They found Mr. Neumann and he was overjoyed to learn his wife was safe and it was arranged for a car to go bring her to Leipzig. (Years later they all met in Berlin.)

Next, Heinz and Elsa headed for Landshut in Bavaria to find Elsa's parents at the agreed upon railroad station. With jeeps, the Americans were tracking down German soldiers who desperately tried to hide in the woods, and those found were arrested and turned over to the Soviets (a war crime after the war, and against the Geneva Convention). Heinz was in civilian clothes and they were incessantly scrutinized. Instead of *STOJ*, they now heard STOP. The guards looked at the little cart with the child and let them pass, but not so at the last military post in Bavaria. So they sat down in a ditch next to the American jeep and began to eat their meager food. Soon, a tall black soldier came out of the jeep and gave them some chocolate, cheese and other delicacies, murmuring something about "underdogs like us." Finally, after about two hours, it got boring for the American soldiers and they whispered, "Beat it!"

They trudged on south for two more weeks, sleeping in barns, churches and ruins. Each evening Heinz kneaded their shoes to keep them soft and to prevent more blisters. When the rainy period started and their clothes got drenched, farmers would take them in, dry their clothes and give the child some milk. They walked on again, always fearing that one of them would get sick.

On a beautiful Sunday, they finally reached their goal, Landshut, but found the agreed upon railroad station in ruins. What had happened to their parents' train? Was everything gone? In panic, they looked for the registration office of those days, which was merely a huge primitive, wooden board where people pinned messages, the self-made "Inquiry Office" of the homeless. Lame with shock they forced themselves to run through line after line of endless paper scraps with short information, and suddenly, a miracle, the clear handwriting of Elsa's father: "New quarters in the village of Margarethen with farmer Obermeier." Thank heaven they had survived somehow, somewhere. So they had not come on foot over three hundred miles through half of Germany for nothing. Immediately they walked on, sleeping the last night of their vagabond existence impatiently on the roadside.

In the early morning hour they met a milk wagon. The driver called out to them, "Go back, the war is over!" Go back where? He gave them a ride anyway to Margarethen. At the crack of dawn they stood with their cart in front of Obermeier's small farmhouse. At that moment a window opened on an upper floor and the white-haired head of Elsa's father looked down and he could not believe his eyes. "The children are here!" he shouted, beside himself with joy. Both parents stormed out of the house and greeted them in a tearful embrace. In rising despair they had watched for them every day in vain. The Obermeiers, neighbors and refugees also rushed to the scene. What a warm welcome. There had been no mail or newspapers, so Heinz and Elsa were pressed for information on what was happening in the outside world and if more refugees could be expected since everyone was waiting for missing relatives and friends.

Now it was Elsa's father's turn to explain what had happened to them. Their overloaded train had been totally destroyed in a bomb attack as it sat at the railroad station after their arrival in Landshut—family members and friends all annihilated. Fortunately, they were in town at the time hunting down lodging, which had saved their lives, but they were now left desperately poor with nothing but the clothes they were wearing. By now the Obermeiers had a simple meal ready. What a feast!

It was the middle of June and the small village was already hopelessly overcrowded with stranded strangers. But, the next door neighbor, the shoemaker Mr. Meyer, made a room available for Heinz, Elsa and their three-year old son even though he had seven children of his own. They stuffed straw mattresses for them. Without any money or worldly possessions, survival was the name of the game but they were together again as a family.

They quickly adjusted to life in the country and they all helped with the farming. Their modest meals were eaten jointly with Elsa's parents at the Obermeiers whose philosophy was, "We don't have much, but as long as we don't go hungry, you won't either"—the golden rule of a simple farmer's family whose greatness was dignity and humanity. In addition, Elsa learned to spin on a primitive spinning wheel, glean the fields for leftover grain which was ground into flour, and collect pine cones in the woods to fuel the big iron stove. Every single item was unbelievably scarce after the war, and not only in the little village of Margarethen. They even had to use rhubarb leaves in their outhouse for lack of any paper.

Right now Heinz was anxious to get back to his family, but his immediate priority was to check out his bombed apartment and see if anything could be salvaged. He then would return to West Germany, the American zone. This was the moment to invite myself along to visit Sieghardt in Gröna. Of course, this brought on the usual family uproar about my foolhardy and impossible plan, but Heinz agreed to accompany me providing I could be ready to leave the next day. Vita was left with Mutti, and early on the morning of July 25, 1945, wearing my Red Cross uniform, I was waiting with Heinz in Wannsee for the train to the West, along with hundreds of other hopeful travelers.

When the train arrived, there was a mad rush by the huge mass of people and it was filled within minutes. Heinz made it through an open window and then pulled me through. A milling crowd hung outside and also tried to travel dangerously on top. Just as the train was about to leave, a Soviet soldier on the platform spotted my Red Cross uniform and came running up to our window, shouting, "Comrade sick, you help. You come right now!" I made no move to leave the train, sick comrade or not. "Sick people in here, too," I said in desperation, as though I was in charge of something. I never carried any medical supplies when I wore my Red Cross uniform, but for a moment it looked as if he might try to forcefully remove me from the train. So I quickly reached into my Red Cross emergency kit and took out two small packets of old-forgotten sugar and handed them out the window to him. "This good medicine for sick comrade." He understood, smiled and ran off. This incident had been truly frightening. Heinz could not have helped me. It was dangerous for any German to intervene. Just then, with an abrupt jerk, the train finally started and we were safe for the time being.

After several hours of stops and starts, the train arrived close to the American border and we all had to get out and walk to a nearby village along a river where a bridge crossed to the American zone. Soviet soldiers were everywhere and we were directed into a schoolhouse gymnasium to spend the night before crossing the bridge on foot the next morning. Heinz had expected to cross by train as before. Now he decided he was going to resort to his usual way of swimming naked with his clothes tied to his head during the night. He invited me to join him in the naked swim, but I was not the excellent swimmer that he was. With heavy hearts, we parted company; I would be on my own from this point on—something I hadn't counted on.

Inside the packed gymnasium, I found space on a crude bench along the wall which gave me the luxury of having something to lean against. What an extravagance compared to the crowding at my feet with no space to move in any direction. Night was falling outside with the eerie sounds of darkness, and no light inside. The electricity was off, which in one way was advantageous. We would not attract unwanted attention. It got hotter and stickier with every minute. There was no deodorant, and no one dared to undress to wash a little under a spigot outside in the hallway. People were sweating with fear. The odor became oppressive.

The night was dark, threatening and endless, especially with a curfew from 6 p.m. to 6 a.m., interrupted now and then with Soviet voices hollering outside. There we sat in desperate hope that they would stay outside. My bench was far away from the entrance I realized with satisfaction. However, if a fire should break out, the consequence would be beyond imagination. Looking around, I saw we were of all ages, refugees with small children and travelers like myself, most of us to an unknown destination.

Finally, after what seemed an eternity, dawn broke and we stepped outside, sniffing the fresh air. In order to reach the American zone, we had to cross the bridge which was barricaded on the Soviet side. It was announced we had to get new Kommandatura papers which would be issued from a nearby shack. From experience, I knew this could mean standing in long lines anywhere from a few minutes to several hours, if you were lucky, or never getting a clearance paper at all, depending on their mood. I had heard a rumor that the wife of a seriously wounded German soldier would be permitted to cross with her husband. What a silly rule. Since when does a soldier come home from war accompanied by his wife? Whatever. So I eagerly looked around for a possible spouse.

I soon spotted a helplessly limping man in uniform with only one crutch. I wound my way over to him and offered my assistance. He gratefully accepted and agreed to my scheme that he would adopt me as his wife to help him across the bridge. In that case, I might not need a new document. But the bridge did not open before 10 a.m. We had to stand around for several more hours in the morning sun, waiting, always hoping not to be molested, and with nothing to eat, nothing to drink, but appearing content and peaceful. We had no choice. I stuck to my soldier. We used the interim to find out each others' names. They could not have been more different. What would happen if the Soviet guards could read? Then we would pretend to be newlyweds who had not yet received their marriage license. But how would we have gotten married when he just came home? Well, it had been a marriage by proxy, we reasoned. Our plan had to be flawless and not suspicious. I wore my wedding ring.

It was mid-morning when they finally lifted the barrier at the wide bridge entrance. I helped my "husband" to the far side of the mass of people pushing and shoving towards the control table. We both were worried about our shady documents and sneaked past the shouting and gesturing Soviets who were too busy stamping masses of papers. In the confusion, we hobbled unto the bridge unnoticed and safely made our way to the middle which was the dividing line between East and West, leading us into the promised land. But no sneaking by here. The passage was too narrow. We hovered between fear and hope.

As we reached the second controller, he gave us a serious look, "Document?" "Yes," I said firmly. "Document all right," as if we had been checked before, but fearing he might demand to see our papers. What if he could read? My nerves were on edge. Whether it was my Red Cross uniform or my "husband's" pitiful condition, the unbelievable happened. The Soviet soldier, without even glancing at our documents, brusquely motioned us through. With the next step we finally set foot in the other Germany. We could not believe it. We had passed. With shaking knees we took our time to reach the other end of the bridge. Incredible. We were totally wrung out by the strain of the last hours. Behind us a loudly arguing crowd was fighting for its crossing. What we had needed most were three things: to quickly adjust to new situations, luck, and our guardian angels.

There were several trains lined up not far from the bridge and I helped my wounded soldier into his, although he was without a ticket. It would take him on his long ride home which was near the Rhine River. We departed with a warm handshake and I was off looking for my train to Bernberg and gratefully climbed on. Nothing could alarm me any more, even the fact that I didn't have a ticket, and I collapsed in an empty compartment. I could hardly believe that I would soon meet Sieghardt, and closed my eyes and wept. I don't know why, but it felt so good. It made me forget my hunger and the times.

After a slow ride with several stops, the train reached Bernburg, where I got off and inquired about directions to Gröna. I had just started walking along the main highway when a milkman in a horse-drawn wagon passed and asked where I was headed, and gladly gave me a ride. What a stroke of luck! This peaceful area stood in amazing contrast to the dangerous Soviet countryside. Soon we arrived, and he directed me to the well known farm of Gertrude Koch. "Several ex-soldiers work there," he told me.

It was late afternoon on July 26, 1945, when I stood in front of a large, well kept farmstead which was enclosed with a solid stone wall. Hesitatingly I entered through a wide open double gate and crossed a large courtyard with a tall barn to the right and an impressive three-story farm house to the left, with stables in between. But there was no one in sight, and I felt like an intruder and loudly called "hello" several times. Finally an attractive middle-aged woman appeared through one of the doors. When she found out who I was, she greeted me warmly with, "You are the first one to arrive here. All the ex-soldiers have hoped that their wives would show up some day. You will find your husband in the field out there," and she pointed through the open gate.

I didn't have to walk far. There he was, sitting up on a tractor, scrawny and in baggy, shabby clothing, his face so pale and small. But it was he! I didn't look so great myself, but right now, our outward appearances had never been less important. He couldn't believe his eyes as he saw me and leaped off the tractor. Oh, was he thin. We fell into each other's arms. What does one feel in such a moment—happiness, fear, new hope? All that mattered was that we had found each other alive after all. We both climbed on the tractor where we hugged each other, not knowing who should start talking first. It seemed a thousand years had passed since we last saw each other. Sieghardt's work shift was done for the day, so he gave me a quick overall picture of his present situation.

All of his co-workers were soldiers who had also escaped captivity and had been given a home by this warm-hearted farmer's wife. She was eagerly awaiting the return of her own husband from the war. Back at the farm, we washed up in a large laundry room, which was my first chance to clean up since leaving home. Gradually, everyone returned from the fields and got ready for dinner. Boy, was I hungry. My travel provisions had been just a few slices of dry bread. It had been a common joke in Berlin to ask each other, "What did you have for dinner?" The answer was, "Bread with *Stulle*." "Oh, that fancy?" *Stulle* was Berlin slang for a slice of bread. So it is like saying "wheat on rye" with nothing in between. It meant one had the luxury of two slices of bread instead of only one.

A friendly group of about a dozen people gathered around the long table laden with food. What a sight. There were several cans of home-made sausages in addition to butter, cheese, fresh country bread and plenty of fresh milk. I could not help comparing the big milk pitcher with Vita's meager ration at home, and was struck by the way the war seemed to have passed this rural area by, compared with Berlin. Obviously our kind hostess believed in a hearty meal after a hard day's work. Mrs. Koch said the blessing and then encouraged me to eat well, which was a mistake on my part. I started with only a sandwich, but was constantly urged to eat more, which I did, eating non-stop until I felt like a balloon. When we all had our fill, the large amount of food that was still left on the table was more than my entire family would get to eat in weeks. I couldn't help comparing again. After the meal, we gathered outside where everyone wanted to know about life in Berlin and in the Soviet zone. Alas, I had much to tell, straight from my own experiences with Soviet soldiers and our struggles to exist under both Russian and American occupation. My audience was baffled by a world they had never experienced for themselves.

Dead tired I went to bed, only to awake violently ill around midnight. Fortunately, there was a bucket in the room and, tragically, all of that wonderful food from last evening's meal came up again. After being starved for so long, my system was not able to accept so much rich food, and in the morning, just the sight of it nauseated me. Here I was living as if in a magic fairy land and could not touch a single bite. Instead, Mrs. Koch prepared a watery soup for me much like we had at home, knowing it was the only thing my stomach would tolerate at this time.

It took five days before I was strong enough to travel and I knew that Mutti must be frantic, worrying about what might have happened to me. Sieghardt and I used this time to make some plans for the vague future, but all of the factors were beyond our control. He was safe here in Gröna, miles from isolated Berlin, but this would not be the case in the Soviet zone where people were kidnapped from the streets at random and never heard from again. The Potsdam Conference was still in session and, at this time, Germany had no government of its own. We decided it would be best for Sieghardt to remain here for the time being and I would return to Berlin alone, though I had hoped for us to return together. Our wishes, as usual, had to take a back seat to the necessities.

Finally, on July 31, I was able to travel and Mrs. Koch packed some special food items that were just a dream in Berlin. In order to get this precious cargo safely back to my family, I hid it within my clothing while carrying some inconspicuous hand luggage. Looking slightly overweight, I gave Sieghardt one final kiss and was off on my return adventure, following a very different and easier route recommended by Mrs. Koch. Early that morning, I hitched a ride with the milkman to Bernburg for the first part of my journey. This time I had a train ticket home, which I was only able to obtain because I lived in Berlin. I boarded the first available train with many other passengers who were also heading for Berlin, and we shared our experiences as we slowly rolled through the countryside.

On the return trip there were fewer problems going from the American to the Soviet zone, and the train just rolled over the bridge into the East. Of course, there were the usual inspections and transfers which were time consuming, hazardous and frightening, an unenviable experience. My Red Cross identification proved helpful again. Finally, late that evening, we breathed a sigh of relief as we arrived in Wannsee back in West Berlin. We immediately felt a distinct difference between East and West.

What a joyous welcome I got at home. The lost child had returned! They had been worried sick about my long absence. Now they were amazed to see how their slightly overweight daughter began to reduce right in front of their eyes as various treasures began to appear from under my clothing. Papa was so dumfounded that he even shortened his usual speech about me not to ever again dare such a risky adventure. We enjoyed a luxurious midnight supper while excitedly exchanging all of our news, and nobody in the family went to bed hungry that night.

The Potsdam Conference ended on August 2 with the decision that Germany would be disarmed and demilitarized, with Nazism completely abolished. At least, we agreed with the last point since all of our previous attempts to get rid of the Nazi regime had failed. Germany would be divided into four zones of occupation, each administered by one of the Allies. The country would be reorganized on a democratic basis and was to remain one political and economic unit within its 1937 boundaries, which included East Prussia, territories east of the Oder-Neisse line and Silesia. These had been historical German lands and would be placed "only for the time being" under Soviet administration pending a final peace treaty, which never came. Berlin would be a four-power city with all of the Allies jointly governing with control concentrated in the Berlin Kommandatura.

Papa was certain that our old homeland of Silesia would remain German since it had belonged for centuries to us or to Austria, but never to Poland. The 1937 boundaries seemed fair to him and he trusted the Potsdam Conference and its decision that the provisional Soviet occupation of the pre-war German territories would not last forever. "Nothing is settled unless it is settled justly," he said. In the meantime, the Soviets were not the only ones who were stripping the conquered land. The other Allies were also busy with dismantling activities of industrial plants and work installations all over the country. Additionally, the British were heavily cutting down the forests and shipping the timber to England. But, we had no say in the matter and lived under a virtual Allied dictatorship with not even a skeletal German government to represent us.

Mutti did not agree with Papa's political trust in the Potsdam Conference because she feared that the newly established agreement over Germany would be greatly violated since we were not in charge of our own affairs. She believed the Russian bear would dance exclusively his way, and always to his own tune and rhythm, regardless of the Conference agreements. Unfortunately, future events proved her correct. Everything turned out to be Stalin's great stage instead of a foundation of lasting peace. Eastern Europe was hardly discussed and ignited the rapid extension of Soviet power and influence, even over North Korea. The Cold War was underway.

The Potsdam Conference of the Big Three did not require that Stalin give back the 75,000-square mile Polish territory that he had grabbed in 1939 as an accomplice of Hitler. (This was half of Poland's pre-war 150,000 square miles.) Just the opposite, with Allied approval, he swallowed his Polish war booty of half the country with no mention of ever having to return it when a peace treaty would be signed. The Allies seemed to forget that Great Britain went to war in 1939 because of the Polish land grab, and now after the war to appease Stalin, they decided highhandedly that the land Poland had lost to Stalin in the East would be regained by taking land from Germany in the West. Of course the local German people were expelled.

An historical injustice began. The new Polish western border was pushed two hundred miles further west into historic east German country without regard to the inhuman expulsion of 10 million Germans who were banished from their ancestral land east of the Oder-Neisse line. Suddenly that part of Germany no longer belonged to Germany. They also totally ignored the fact that this rich farming land was Germany's "bread basket" which was the vital source of food production for the entire country. And, it now placed Berlin just fifty miles from the new Polish border. The German urban population from this area was to be deported to the West "in an orderly and humane manner," but just the opposite occurred. Lawlessness began. An uncontrolled mass deportation resulted in injustice and slaughter, and in this horror of expulsion, a vast number of people died like flies.

The final Polish borders were to be established in the permanent peace treaty, which never came. Poland even annexed Silesia and extended its border to the Oder and West Neisse Rivers when the East Neisse River had been decided as Polish compensation. Horrible injustices even occurred in East Prussia where the Soviets and Poles jointly began to expel all ethnic Germans with fire and sword, and from 1945 to 1947 and beyond, 15 million Germans were banished in the East from their over seven hundred-year old ancestral lands. As a comparison, the U.S. is only two hundred years old. Three million people perished in what was one of the largest inhuman ethnic expulsions of a nation in peacetime in European history.

They began arriving as dispossessed millions, Germans expelled from their German homeland with no money, no hope and no future. Famine and infection were upon them. They were exhausted from their long forced trek west, their children and elderly on top of their meager possessions in their push carts. As they dragged along the last of their family possessions, still searching for missing family members, it was an immeasurable suffering for innocent rural people. They arrived at our Red Cross station ragged and emaciated and sobbing, pouring out their stories of the horror and pain of their forced exodus.

On the east side of the Oder-Neisse line, posters were put up ordering all Germans to prepare for their "voluntary" departure to the West within four days. Anyone who resisted faced either imprisonment or deportation to the labor camps. Some even told of being forced to leave within twenty-four hours with only what they could carry in one suitcase not to weigh more than forty pounds. Along the way, they were beaten, robbed and raped by the Soviets, Poles and Czechs and many had friends who were even murdered. All of this was later validated in a book by Alfred M. de Zayas entitled *A Terrible Revenge—The Ethnic Cleansing of the East European Germans, 1944–1950* available from St. Martin's Press, or, *Expulsion Crimes on Germans, The Inhumanity of The*

Years 1945-1947 by Heinz Nawratil which was first published in 1986 by Herbig in Munich.

There was a rumor going around that a draconian Roosevelt-Morgenthau plan to be implemented by General Eisenhower would transform Germany into an agricultural state with the massive production base of the Ruhr area, our life line, to be destroyed. We were to be turned into a generation of enforced poverty, as collective penalty for the entire German nation. Papa considered this dangerous gossip because no such plan would work in a densely populated country like Germany. The economy was based on export industry and our barely self-sustaining agriculture would scarcely feed the population, let alone support the economy. He forgot we were not supposed to live. Americans, with their huge land masses, can't imagine how crowded Germany is with a population of 80 million people in an area about half the size of the state of Texas.

The Morgenthau plan existed, but thanks to the strong rejection of Secretary of War Stimson and Secretary of State Hull, the Carthaginian proceeding of the Roosevelt-Morgenthau plan was never carried out. Just the opposite; past history had taught that hatred and a revengeful Versailles Treaty had only led to the rise of a man like Hitler and World War II. Instead, President Truman approved a European recovery program proposed by General George Marshall, to be known ever after as the Marshall Plan, which would provide aid to Germany without any strings attached. This was the greatest humanitarian relief action of the century by assisting Germany with constructive measures, not punitive ones, which assured future European stability.

The next surprising news was that in July 1945, the British had voted out Winston Churchill, their war-time Prime Minister, and Clement Attlee was elected. Papa could not understand this action, since it was Churchill who had the political foresight to demand the invasion of Germany through Greece instead of through France. But, he was overruled by President Roosevelt who gave Stalin a free hand to expand his uncontrolled power throughout Eastern Europe without any Western presence or opposition. (If Churchill's demand had succeeded, the Soviets would never have had the chance to create an Iron Curtain, an expression originated by him.)

We in Berlin were still facing a severe food crisis because there was no definite system of stock replenishment to the stores. And, the supplies that were received were inadequate to meet the demand of even the minimum allowance of the ration cards. We often received dried fish instead of meat, cottage cheese instead of butter and flour instead of bread. Flour to bake bread was rather useless with the severe rationing of gas and electricity per person. Fresh bread was forbidden to be sold because stale bread would quench the hunger pangs longer. We rarely got vegetables. Berlin's supply lines were paralyzed in the Soviet zones surrounding the city and survival was a day-to-day challenge.

My own backyard vegetable garden was doing great and the green shoots of my potatoes were much higher than those of the other tenants, who quietly pitied me for having an abundance of greenery above, but nothing in the soil underneath. I did not say anything about their comments because they were not aware of my secret fertilizer. Each day I collected all of my dishwater in a bucket and then added Vita's daily potty. I stirred this mixture thoroughly and would slip out at night and feed my ground. But, our hunger could not wait for my vegetable garden to produce so Mutti and I still had to make our weekly trip into the country. Our nutrition level had dropped to its lowest ebb, barely one thousand calories a day, primarily potatoes and bread. The hospitals were overcrowded with patients suffering from starvation, cholera, typhoid and other diseases, with old-age and infant mortality increasing.

Food was not the only thing in short supply. Money was another growing problem and people fell behind with their obligations. Only the black market was booming with sky high inflationary prices such as 150 marks for a pound of flour, 1000 marks for a pound of butter, "only" 600 marks for a pound of margarine, and 5 marks for a single egg. Considering that the exchange rate was 4.20 German marks to one dollar, the black market price of a pound of butter would have been approximately $238.00 in U.S. currency. The banks were still closed with all deposits frozen, and the postal money order service was open occasionally, with no defined schedule of operation. Papa received some money from business friends in West Germany and from the rent of one apartment building in Münster. The other one was completely destroyed by a direct hit during an air raid, killing all of the tenants.

While we were struggling in our postwar so-called peace, the war was still going on in the Pacific area. Then we heard the news of this new terrible weapon, the atom bomb, that had been dropped on two cities in Japan, first on Hiroshima and three days later on Nagasaki, where the enormous atomic blast had caused almost total devastation of each city. Papa was deeply shocked by such a process of destruction and could not understand the world anymore where a single bomb could kill hundreds of thousands of people, and injure a huge number more. "Has Hell started already on earth? How much destruction can humans bring unto humans?" he asked.

On August 14, five days after the second atomic bomb was dropped, Japan surrendered to the U.S. and the fierce Asiatic war was brought to a speedy end. (Years later we read in newspapers that the first atomic bomb was originally planned to obliterate Berlin. This plan was not carried out, only because an erased Berlin would have decisively altered the balance of power in Europe in favor of Stalin and delivered the entire continent to Communism.)

During that same late summer of 1945, our power supply was gradually restored, and the electrified S-Bahn was now in service to Potsdam, although there were only two or three trains a day since the Soviets had stripped all but one track. This required that the same train had to run back and forth. But, this would save us many miles of walking and we also could resume our business with our farm friends in Beelitz who provided us with so much horse meat just before the battle of Berlin began the previous April. In order to catch the only morning train, we had to be on the platform at the crack of dawn joining hundreds of early birds with the same goal of getting on that single train, which was obviously too short to accommodate all the waiting people. As soon as the S-Bahn arrived, the so far peaceful crowd changed into a wild mob to try and get aboard.

Mutti and I had worked out a system whereby she would stand in front of me and I would push her forcefully from behind right through the crowd to the nearest door. When people would yell, "stop pushing so hard," she would reply, "Sorry, I'm being pushed myself," which was true. With me pushing and with her hands behind her back pulling me, we would make it inside the train. Luckily our system worked every time. What a struggle, but we had no choice. At home there were hungry mouths to feed. Many people were left behind on the platform. The compartments were so overcrowded that the automatic doors could not close, and I often ended up hanging in the open door frame, secured by Mutti's firm grip and others holding on to me. No one complained anymore because it was far better than the other alternative of walking on a hot summer day.

Meanwhile our Red Cross station was still functioning and we often had returning German soldiers visit us who had made the long dangerous trek home only to find there was no official help for them. With their haggard faces and tattered clothes they looked like beggars. They all told us about the same puzzling experience. For miles and miles along the isolated railroad track in the vastness of Russia they saw huge piles of household goods that had been dumped on both sides of the tracks and left to the elements. We immediately solved their puzzle. The Soviets had been allowed to loot Germany to their heart's content but not to bring their booty back home, because the contrast between our western high standard of living and their primitive existence would have contradicted the glory of the Russian workers' paradise.

This policy was confirmed by our relatives fleeing Leipzig from which the Americans had withdrawn. They owned a paper mill in which the Soviets became very interested. My aunt had a Russian maid for years and as soon as the Soviets took over, the girl became petrified and pleaded with my aunt to hide her because she had experienced too much western culture. The Soviets would now confine her in one of the rehabilitation camps to be again converted to Communism, and more likely, she would be killed to prevent her from talking about the better life she had experienced in the West. My aunt loved her, but it was impossible to just make a Russian citizen vanish when everybody knew she had lived with them for years. The Soviets would have shot my aunt's entire family.

As was to be expected, the Soviets "liberated" the girl from her "captivity" and some days later she secretly returned to tell them she was now running the household of a high ranking Russian officer due to her learned skills and refinement. Shortly thereafter, she showed up again in tears, and in mortal fear she begged my aunt to hide her and take her along wherever they would go. She was going to be returned to the Soviet Union to be killed because people like her were proof of a better life. My aunt urged her to stay in touch with them because the Soviets had pressured them to move with their paper factory to the Soviet Union.

Now fleeing themselves to Berlin, there might have been a risky chance to take her along. "She was such a lovely young girl," my aunt said. "But she never returned nor did we hear of her true destiny." This poor young girl was living proof that the common Russian population and their inhuman government were two entirely different things as in all other dictatorial governments, just like we were under Nazism.

For us, months after the war, the battle of Berlin was still in full swing. This time we became victims of an internal conflict among the occupying Allies. The West had nothing in common with the Soviets and tension was slowly building into what would eventually become a complete breakdown of East-West relations. It seemed that the only thing they had in common was a hatred of anyone who wore a German military uniform and they were automatically stamped guilty and accused of being of poor moral character, which was completely contrary to western law in which a person is innocent until proven guilty. The Western Allies' blind hatred kept them from seeing through the Soviets' systematic domination of Eastern Europe and the rapid extension of Soviet influence over all of Berlin and Germany. This was proven by the next deal between the Americans and Soviets when the Americans agreed to withdraw from part of West Germany, a territory they had conquered in the war, in exchange for their sector in Berlin. That would mean that Gröna would be swallowed up by the expansion of the Soviet zone into the Harz mountain range, an area sixty miles long and twenty miles wide, which would split the range right down the middle between East and West.

Stalin again outsmarted the Western Allies because his half of the mountain range would include the vital area of Dornhausen. It was here that Hitler had constructed an enormous arms factory called Mittelberg for the construction of the V-2 rocket. A new V-rocket was still stored there along with other important construction materials, and, many of the rocket experts lived in the surrounding villages. The Americans initially had this in their grasp, but willingly let it slip away to the Soviets. Stalin did not waste any time in relocating the material and the scientists, including their families, to the Soviet Union. According to German newspaper reports published later, women and children were heard screaming throughout the night as they were mercilessly deported by trucks and trains. Fortunately, the Americans had made some effort to round up well known German rocket scientists, such as Wernher von Braun, but the Soviets got the majority of them. (Consequently on October 4, 1957, the *Sputnik* was the first satellite to circle the earth and the Soviets took the lead in building rockets, German-made behind the Ural mountains. It was the German rocket specialist Wernher von Braun who developed the Saturn rocket and enabled the U.S. to place the first man on the moon on July 20, 1969. America had reconquered its leadership in space.)

As soon as we heard the rumor that Gröna would be under Soviet control, we had to get word to Sieghardt to get out of there somehow and get back to West Berlin as quickly as possible. I was the logical messenger, and left early on the morning of August 25 for my second pilgrimage to him, again wearing my Red Cross uniform which had proven so valuable on prior trips. The current one was miserable as usual, but thanks to some newly discovered train connections, I arrived late that same day at Mrs. Koch's farm in Gröna. They were all happy to see me, but my news soon dampened their spirits since they knew nothing about the pending grave exchange of territory that would place them under Soviet control. Everybody was upset, but Mrs. Koch was the most affected because she had just received word her husband was alive and she was eagerly awaiting his return. But now, return to what? Under Soviet control, their farm would be "socialized," they would lose private ownership and be forcibly transferred into a public agriculture cooperative.

I convinced Sieghardt that he had to leave before it was too late, and that living with the Americans was still the lesser of two evils. I tried to prepare him for the fact that he would not recognize the Berlin he used to know because it was so ravaged and had been blasted to pieces. Everyone was living on a near starvation existence with no food, work, or hope, and we were overdue for a change from old Soviet laws. Families such as ours continued to be placed at the very bottom of the scanty class five food ration cards. But, it was women who were carrying the load of cleaning up the ravages of war. That was being done by the *Trümmerfrauen,* the legendary "rubble women" of Berlin who, due the shortage of men, were everywhere salvaging all useful material. With their bare hands, they picked up every stone and cleaned off the mortar so it could be used again to rebuild the city brick by brick. They bore the main burden of the reconstruction work, and an outsider cannot even imagine the enormous value of their work which let Berlin emerge from under 75 million tons of rubble. But we courageous Berliners were determined to make our shattered city habitable again. We had survived the Nazis and the Soviets. Now it was our turn with the Americans.

I left Gröna alone after three days, on September 3, laden with provisions from Mrs. Koch, and arrived home late the same day after the usual weary and dangerous trip. Sieghardt's train ticket to Berlin had been refused in Bernburg and was granted only to Potsdam in the Soviet zone. So, he had to return to Gröna because without a train ticket to Berlin, he would be denied food ration cards at home, which was another of the new regulations which we Germans just could not understand. Now, he had to follow a seemingly endless trail of red tape to get official authorization to be issued a train ticket to Berlin. As the city was overcrowded, he could only get a ticket because it was his home town. The paper chase was in full swing everywhere.

Finally, after about three weeks, on September 21, armed with many more important looking stamps, he boarded a train from Bernburg on his way to Berlin. The train left for Güsten-Magdeburg in East Germany where he spent a dangerous night hiding in a cold tunnel near the railroad station. The next morning, he caught a bus to Biederwitz, and at 2:30 p.m. a train to Berlin-Wannsee, and finally the only evening S-Bahn to Zehlendorf-West. After an adventure of two days and one night, during which he often thought he wouldn't make it, he was finally safe at home. We never understood why it had to be so complicated for a German who was allowed to travel home within Germany, but we were most happy that he had arrived safely after all. That was our life at the time. Each Allied power had supreme authority in his own zone in Germany, but with conflicting rules. Again, our only certainty of today was the uncertainty of tomorrow.

Heinz continued to make frequent trips to Berlin to salvage items from their bombed out apartment, and one time he even managed to transport their bulky zinc bathtub back to the family in Margarethen. How he did it was a miracle to everybody. Now it was set up in the cow barn where the family baths took place. Because warm water was so scarce, everyone bathed in the same water, starting with Kristian, then Elsa and finally Heinz. The bathtub, considered a tremendous luxury, was in great demand and even loaned to others in exchange for food. Each time Heinz would prepare for a venture trip to Berlin, the farmers would come with butter and eggs, begging him to carry letters to towns he would be passing through, East and West. His knapsack was filled with messages since there was no newspaper or mail service, and families were torn apart.

One time it happened that when he crossed a river, swimming naked, again with all his clothing piled up and secured on his head, he made a big faux pas. He forgot his shoes and had to swim back to retrieve them, a detour of half an hour, while risking his clothing being stolen on the other bank, a frightening prospect. Shoes were a valuable possession and almost impossible to come by. Elsa was agitated whenever he stayed away too long. Would he return this time? Would he be caught by the Soviets, or shot at the border crossing?

Meanwhile Elsa made virtue out of necessity. She created the most darling dolls out of straw and scraps of material with small means and a lot of imagination. Her first doll was for Kristian, as his only Christmas present in 1946. It was also his only toy and he loved it. After that, everyone who saw it wanted one, offering food in exchange for it. Elsa's fame as a doll maker spread and customers came from as far away as Munich. Even the Americans wanted them in exchange for cigarettes, but Elsa would accept only food or dollars. Soon, she could no longer meet the demand, so she enlisted the help of some neighbors, and in no time had created a very profitable business.

They lived at the farm for two years, until Heinz eventually found work in his old line, and in 1950, they built a house for the whole family in Hindelang, Bavaria, with my father's assistance. They chose this area near the German border so they could quickly escape to Switzerland if another war started. As I write this almost fifty years later, Elsa is a great-grandmother and a well known artist and poet. Her art work is in high demand as once her straw dolls were, with customers coming from throughout Germany and other countries.

On the Roller Coaster of Life

Sieghardt's return to Berlin was a bittersweet homecoming, since in his absence, Germany's capital city had been completely devastated by war-time bombings and had changed into a Four-Power city. It was now ruled by a joint Allied administration rather than by us. We had become a western island located deep within the Soviet occupied zone. He spent his first night at home in my parents' house so that his homecoming would be less obvious. Too many families had awaited the return of their loved ones in vain and with great bitterness.

When the war ended, many German soldiers had voluntarily surrendered into American captivity in order not to fall into the hands of the Soviets where they would have little chance of survival. They trusted they would be treated fairly under the Americans. After all, they had been called to perform legitimate military duty which had nothing to do with the goals of the Nazis. Now, months after the war was over, the Americans were delivering them by the hundreds of thousands from West Germany to East Germany, right into Stalin's hands. We couldn't believe our eyes when we saw trainloads of overcrowded cattle cars loaded with German soldiers slowly passing through Zehlendorf-West day and night on their way to the Soviets. We could see the mortal anguish in their eyes as they peered at us through the small slits in the sides of the rail cars and we stared back in sick disbelief. For them, as for millions of others, this mass deportation was just a continuation of the horrors of war long after it was over. The train loads of German POWs from West Germany disappeared into the USSR, and they began their march toward certain death as they vanished into labor camps as slave workers or were delivered for liquidation. These same Soviets who sat as judges at the Nuremberg Trials to avenge such crimes were themselves now guilty of mass murder of tens of thousands of German ex-soldiers and POWs.

The Soviets had already dissolved the Red Cross in their occupied zone and in East Berlin. For us a new tyranny was established over the old one, this time unleashed by the Allies in an abuse of power. At the same time, long after the war had ended, thousands of defenseless German ex-soldiers suffered and died from starvation in West German prison camps where they were kept behind barbed wire in open fields under catastrophic sanitary conditions. The Allies were guilty of a war crime for this scandalous treatment of POWs, and one of the most notorious was the POW Camp of the Rheinwiesen Lager which had an alarming death rate. This was caused by a recent law signed by General Eisenhower concerning soldiers in captivity after the war, renamed by him as "disarmed enemy forces" or DEFs. This law stipulated that this new class of prisoners arbitrarily created by Eisenhower did not have to be cared for after Germany surrendered, and food was withheld. About a hundred thousand German DEFs were deliberately starved to death in captivity after the war, which was a direct violation of the Geneva convention. The British refused to accept Eisenhower's new DEF policy, and those German soldiers in British captivity were eventually released in good shape, as were those who had been captured in Italy by American forces under General Mark Clark.

Eisenhower's brutal artificially twisted designation of POWs into DEFs had never existed before, nor since then. Relief agencies, including the Red Cross, and reporters were not permitted access to these U.S. prison camps, and mail was withheld. Camp personnel drove German citizens away who tried to hand food through the fences to the famished prisoners, and if prisoners were caught reaching for food through the fence, they were severely punished. We could not understand such cruelty and why our ex-soldiers were not set free to go home instead of being imprisoned endlessly in their own country in peace time and deliberately starved to death. Instead, about a million perished after the war in camps in Germany and France. These facts are verified in a book by Canadian author James Bacque entitled *Other Losses*, published by Stoddart Toronto in 1989. The German translation is *Der Geplante Tod* (The Planned Death), published by Verlag Ulstein GmbH, Frankfurt-Berlin and Zug/Switzerland.

Sieghardt spent his first morning visiting his parents in their home across the street, where he received another joyous welcome. On his way back, he spotted a hastily erected pole at the street corner with a crudely nailed wooden board on top that read SUDEWEG. Nobody had noticed that new street sign so far. The renaming of our street was overdue since the Nazis had changed our lovely Margarethenstrasse into Glagauzeile in honor of one of their insignificant authors named Glagau. Now, with their downfall, Mr. Glagau had to go.

Sieghardt thought Sudeweg was a terrible name for a street, sounding like something that pigs would roll in. Out of curiosity, he strolled through the neighborhood streets looking at all of the new names that had popped up. On a distant corner, he found a rather pleasant one, VERONIKASTEIG. He thought that Veronika was a nice sounding female name much like our original Margarethe, and got the idea to switch street signs. We both left the house that night equipped with hammer and nails and while I kept a watchful eye on the street, he ripped down the loosely fastened Sudeweg, which I then hid under my raincoat. Now we headed for the pole where the lovely Veronika rested. She came off easily, too and we tacked Sudeweg in her place with some hasty hammer blows—loud enough to wake the entire neighborhood. Then we took off like two thieves, with Veronika hidden under my coat. Back at our own bare pole, Sieghardt took his time to firmly nail our conquest into place so nobody would play musical chairs with the new street names as we did. Since nothing had been officially recorded yet, my parents' street was entered later in the records as Veronikasteig and has remained that ever since.

The next item on Sieghardt's agenda was to take care of his mandatory registration with the German police, public health department and the labor office, to change his status from a farm hand to an executive member of his family's firm. This would entitle him to food ration card number one, but the authorities classified him as only class three, downgrading him from his former position as a junior boss to a mere "pencil pusher." Such a decision was final. Even at this lowly rating, there wasn't much demand for his service because the factory had been totally destroyed, and the only thing remaining other than the firm's name was a small office maintained in his parents' house. The ruins of the factory were in East Berlin right at the border with West Berlin. As we stood on the American side of the street we couldn't believe that the Soviet sector was just across from us. (Later, the Berlin wall was erected on the family grounds where the factory had stood.)

We all had to submit to compulsory vaccinations because typhoid fever and other communicable diseases were rampant. This precaution was not so much for our protection, but rather to prevent us from infecting the Americans who had close working contact with the German people. To this day I still have my certificate dated September 27, 1945, printed on such poor quality paper that I wonder how it has endured for more than fifty years. It was signed by our family doctor, Dr. Martin, who was married to a Jew. This was the second marriage for both and each had children from their previous one, plus they had one child together. Under the Nazi regime, his wife took her children to safety in Switzerland, leaving behind their common son who was half Jewish. Dr. Martin kept him hidden from the Nazis in his big villa and when the first Soviets arrived in 1945, the boy stormed out into the street to greet his liberators. As he demonstrated his new freedom, he was shot on the spot. That night, Dr. Martin carried the corpse back inside and buried his son in his own back yard. He was a broken man from then on.

The detested Soviet monument on Potsdamer Chaussee now stood in the American sector. Since the Berliners had never stopped crumbling off the base in an effort to make the tank fall down, the Soviets demanded that the Americans protect their monument. But their reply was short—they were not in Berlin to protect monuments. That suited us perfectly. Since the chipping away at the base continued incessantly, the Soviets finally were forced to move the monument out of our sector and into theirs, to the road junction *Drei Linden*, the border crossing from West Berlin into the East Zone. (After Germany was reunited in 1989, the Soviet tank was removed from the top of the pedestal and a witty Berliner replaced it with an old, excavating machine painted bright green.)

Since there were still no newspapers in Berlin, and poverty continued, people were forced to use trees as a place to post scraps of paper to advertise sales or exchanges of items. Some swapped their tobacco ration for food coupons. I traded my homegrown fresh tomatoes for bread coupons. Our daily ration was usually gone by noontime. Dry bread with nothing on it is not very filling, especially for hard working men. A loaf of bread on the black market was 50 marks, or $12 U.S. money, an exorbitant price that was well out of reach for the average person. None of us could manage to get by with the meager allotment, and no one did, at least not if one wanted to survive.

Mutti and I had six mouths to feed which was a day to day drudgery to come up with the food. Now that Sieghardt was registered in Berlin, he could venture outside the city for food hunts because his round-trip train ticket assured his return home. So, on October 8, to ease Mutti's food problem, Sieghardt and I dared to go on our first barter trip together. Rail traffic to and from Berlin was restricted to four routes, so we selected the one to Aaken on the Elbe River because there were less hungry Berliners pestering the farmers. Upon arrival, we started to go door to door offering good prices for any food they were willing to sell, often with poor results. We soon learned to put our pride aside. We found that the farmers' wives were more shrewd than their husbands and occasionally a farmer would secretly sell me some eggs before his wife would see it. It was Sieghardt's job to charm the women. In this manner, we were able to get a variety of food in addition to our usual carrots and potatoes. Our food search took the entire day so we had to stay overnight in a crowded Salvation Army shelter. Luckily, we managed to get adjacent upper bunk beds and staying fully dressed, we secured our food between us. This way, no one could steal it if we should both fall asleep at the same time. Mutti was overjoyed at our success.

Three days later we heard through the grapevine that my parents' entire street would be confiscated by the Americans—frightening news with our insufficient housing. At that same time Mr. Seybold left us to venture to friends in the West. With the proof that he would have a place to stay, he was able to purchase a train ticket across the Soviet zone. Meanwhile Mutti inspected our food reserve, but even our last amount of produce did not last long. She suggested that we head for Aunt Grete's place in Zerbst on our next trip because she always kept her own small flock of chickens and a large garden with fruits and vegetables. Her family was also well acquainted with the local farmers because they were customers of their agricultural machinery business. At the time we didn't know if they were even alive, but decided to go anyway.

At the end of October, we took the train to Zerbst. Such a trip was no picnic. What used to be a two-hour car ride now took a half day. We found that our relatives had survived, but it was a sad reunion. Cousin Ilse's husband had been killed just at the end of the war, leaving her with two small boys. Aunt Grete told us about a Soviet couple who had been quartered at one time in their upstairs apartment. The wife instructed her on cleanliness, showing her how to scrub down the beautiful dark wooden furniture with soap and water until the finish was completely ruined. Fortunately the Soviet pair always preferred to use the two outhouses in the courtyard that had been for the men working in the workshop. They claimed "Germans are dirty" because they relieved themselves in the house. At home they would never do that and always go into the woods. Flushing toilets inside the house seemed to frighten them.

Aunt Grete was still able to keep some poultry and raise a few vegetables in her garden. She also had butter and bacon, all bartered with the farmers for spare parts for their farm equipment. What a promising prospect of food to take home with us! Our evening meal was a real treat. With amazement I saw they also had stacked up a huge amount of large rolls of *Bindegarn*, a very sturdy rope that farmers used to bundle up wheat in the fields. I watched in fascination as my aunt split the rope like cotton twist into thinner layers and then knit panties out of it. I watched her carefully with the ulterior motive of copying her because new panties were not available and these would last forever.

We were soon interrupted by a Russian officer who now lived above them in a separate apartment, replacing the Russian couple they previously had, and he decided to join us. He sat with us around the table and behaved rather pleasantly. During our conversation in broken German and Russian, punctuated with many hand signals, he got out his white linen handkerchief and proudly placed it on the table in front of him, showing off that he had "cultura." We admired it as was expected of us and it lay there all evening, with him sometimes using it discreetly. Evidently circumstances had calmed down here between the occupiers and the people, so long as one did not run into drunken soldiers. Later, Aunt Grete explained to me that eventually, all property owned by people living in West Germany or West Berlin, like Mutti and Papa, would be confiscated without any compensation. Obviously something had to be worked out between our families so that everything would not be lost one day. Since Aunt Grete's family had lived on the property here in Zerbst from the time Papa had bought it twenty-one years ago, and Uncle Bodo had been running the business ever since then, they would pretend to be the owners until it became clearer what the future might hold. This was important information to take home to Mutti and Papa.

We returned to Berlin on November 1, 1945, loaded down with all we could carry, including a duck for Mutti. But our happiness was short-lived because my parents received an eviction notice the next day. They had to be out by noon the following day, November 3. Their entire quiet street was confiscated. Theirs was just one of more than two thousand homes in the suburb that were being seized for military quarters. No one was allowed to remove anything other than personal clothing. American soldiers immediately swarmed through all the confiscated villas to take inventory while the occupants were trying to recover from the initial shock. Many still didn't know where they would go for shelter. For my parents there was a refuge on Limastrasse nearby. But first things first.

As soon as the soldiers had left, we decided to "steal" as much as possible of our own furnishings and other personal belongings before the military moved in. Since a soldier had been posted outside the front door, we carried everything we wanted to save out the back door and over the terrace into the back yard where our long-time neighbors, the Doneckers, were already waiting to store it in their house for later pick-up. There went Mutti's and Papa's beds, mattresses, tables and chairs in exchange for the Donecker's old pieces from their air raid shelter which kept the furniture count the same as on the American inventory sheet. There were just a few substitutes!

Papa was busy in the basement burning personal and business papers in the furnace when he suddenly remembered some urgently needed things. He stormed upstairs and began debating with the guard posted outside to let him take at least his typewriter, desk and a few other business-related things so he could continue to work. The debate was long and loud, and negative, frequently in two languages, and while this was going on, Sieghardt and I sneaked the desired items out the back door to safety. When we returned, Papa was still pleading desperately and the soldier was shouting "NO! NO! NO!" I quickly ran to the front door and tried to get Papa to come inside by tugging at his sleeve, but the more I pulled, the more he resisted. Finally I dared to whisper, "*Alles schon raus*" (everything out already), hoping that this American soldier could not understand German, since many of them did, but not this one. What a blessing. To him I said loud and clear in English, "We understand, we understand," and he turned away mumbling in anger.

Papa finally came inside and was puzzled by the empty space where his desk once stood. He now worried about the dispute he had started and how accurately the American soldier had jotted down each item on his inventory. We had no alternative but to take the risk and again visit our neighbor's air raid shelter and fill the empty space with one of their old chairs. By evening, the house was full again, partly refurnished with an unimaginable collection of items to replace those we "liberated," and we hoped for the best when the contents were checked against the inventory. Later, another soldier came to inspect the house again, and as he went through the bedrooms upstairs, he exclaimed, "You couldn't have possibly lived this way!" I looked at him with big eyes. "Can't you see the terrible bombing we went through? We could not replace a thing." The bomb damage to the house was very obvious, so he just shook his head and left. That was the end of that.

While the Doneckers were already busy with the gradual carting of our belongings over to Limastrasse, Papa worked on arrangements to accommodate as many of the evictees as possible in the vacant apartments of the tenants who had long since fled to West Germany. For him charity started at home. During wartime, two and three families were sometimes assigned to one apartment. Mutti and Papa could stay at my place during the day and sleep in one room of the half empty apartment above where Mrs. Vogel and Maria would move in. Papa assigned Sieghardt's family to a large apartment occupied only by a bombed out couple, and there was even enough room for the firm's small office. By nightfall, everyone had a roof over their heads again, even though we were packed in like sardines in a can.

As Papa and Sieghardt searched for more living space and checked the building from top to bottom, they found more than they bargained for in the attic. They couldn't believe their eyes. In front of them lay a five-foot long unexploded Russian bomb that had left a remarkably small hole when it pierced the roof during last April's attack. A fire must have broken out unnoticed because there were burn marks and several holes in the wooden floor. Papa immediately rushed out to find an American bomb disposal unit who took care of the sleeping monster, as I suddenly realized we had been living with a potential time bomb for the past six months. This would have been enough of a shock for one evening, but it was not.

Like the old adage, haste makes waste, in our rush to evacuate the house we had forgotten the most important thing. Our old family heirloom, a beautiful nineteenth century grandmother clock from Switzerland, was still ticking on the wall on Veronikasteig. It had been a wedding present from Omi to Mutti back in 1911. How could we live without that familiar tick-tock?

By now, the Americans had set up floodlights and blocked both ends of the street, so Sieghardt and I sneaked in through Donecker's place and over the terrace into the living room to retrieve our prized possession. When we took the clock down from the wall, it left a very noticeable mark on the wallpaper which now stared at us—and we stared back at it. How obvious that something had been removed here! But we had no time to worry about that. On second thought, maybe the Americans would think this was just more bomb damage. Hiding the clock under a blanket, we sneaked out through the back again and started down the main street looking as innocent as possible. So far so good, but the clock wouldn't cooperate. Just as we passed behind some soldiers who were busy with their spotlights, the clock began to chime with every step we took. Shocked as we were, we both started coughing and talking loudly to drown out its melodious cling-clang. We were really lucky it didn't start striking midnight on top of it, since it was close to that time. But fortunately the soldiers didn't pay any attention to what was going on behind their backs, or didn't want to notice.

The next morning, Papa suddenly remembered he had forgotten to remove his heavy gold pocket watch with chain from its hiding place under a piece of furniture in the dining room where it was protected from Soviet looting. Mad at himself for his forgetfulness, he immediately returned to the house and found it already full of American soldiers and all of the furnishings moved around. He finally found the piece of furniture he was looking for, but the watch was gone. Immediately, he got hold of the German-speaking sergeant on duty asking him what had happened to his watch with chain, but the man claimed no one had ever seen it. Papa didn't believe that for one minute and was certain that his precious watch, a family heirloom, was now undoubtedly the prize possession of some soldier. He came home very upset and deeply disillusioned about honesty in general and the Americans in particular, because they were apparently no better than the Soviets. What the Soviets had not hauled away during the war, the Americans were taking after the war.

The U.S. Army had started to hire servants, and Sieghardt immediately applied at the local military office for whatever position that might be available, regardless of how menial it may be. He was willing to do anything to get a better food ration card, and as a common laborer he would be eligible for the highest rating of number one. The employment application contained over one hundred questions and he was instructed to answer every one precisely. Any omissions, incomplete answers or false statements were considered to be offenses against the military government and subject to severe punishment.

One of the endless questions was, "Have you ever been a Nazi Party member?" Sieghardt truthfully answered "yes," but there was no place for him to explain that in the Nazi heyday, at least one member of a family-operated business had to be a member of the Party in order to be permitted to stay in charge of their own firm. He had been designated the Party member and consequently was now "persona non grata" with the Allied forces. The next question asked for the position held in the Party and he easily answered that with, "None!" When he turned in the completed and signed application, the person in charge looked it over very carefully without comment, and then told him he would be notified if needed. He was then dismissed.

I was anxious to try my skill at knitting panties as Aunt Grete had done from the sturdy *Bindegarn* because we urgently needed them. Mutti helped me split the material, a procedure too complicated for two hands alone, and I was ready to begin. The knitted product had to be sufficiently wide because the material did not stretch, and my first finished masterpiece turned out so shapeless and ugly that we called it *Marke Ehetod*, or, a brand that would kill a marriage. Every female in the family wanted a pair anyway for lack of something better. Today we wouldn't be caught dead in one of these creations.

Since our new underwear proved to be so indestructible, I got the idea of making a shopping bag out of the yarn. With nothing but tough times ahead one had to be creative. So I crocheted two round disks, connected with a straight piece and added two sturdy braided strings as handles. The bag was closed with a flap and a big decorative button, which I also had to crochet since there were none available on the market. My first effort was such a masterpiece that I decided to make money with my skills by making the bags in mass production. I then sold them to a nearby store which needed products to fill its empty shelves. Accidently I had created my own line of merchandise. I produced more bags non-stop and Sieghardt used to jokingly ask why I didn't take them to work on while I was in the bathroom. Years later, while riding a bus, a lady sat across from me who had one of my long-forgotten, home-made shopping bags on her lap. She probably wondered why I kept staring at it. So people really had bought them and still kept using them. No wonder. They were practically indestructible!

As the days grew shorter and colder, we feared the long, grim winter ahead. No central heating could be run and all we had for heat was an old iron stove in one room. Fuel was so scarce that people cut down the trees in the parks rather than freeze to death, and still, many did not make it. Sieghardt studied the trees in our garden and we picked out one to fell together. Who could afford to remember an old law that prohibited cutting down any tree in one's yard. Using a long saw from the basement, and to conserve as much of the valuable wood as possible, we began sawing the trunk too near to the ground, which we didn't notice until it was too late and we had worked ourselves to sheer exhaustion. Luckily the mailman happened to come by. Seeing us laboring on our knees, he dropped everything to replace me, stating, "that isn't work for a woman." I couldn't agree more, happily allowing the two men to finish the job. Shortly thereafter the tree dropped safely. The voluntary assistance of the mailman was so typical of the times, as everybody helped everybody else. This was also the only tree I ever tried to cut down myself. Sieghardt had no problem chopping it later into firewood since he had plenty of experience doing that when he worked in the friendly restaurant *Schlehdorn* in Gröna.

While we were outside the next day working with the firewood, our close friend, Inge Wünsch came across the lawn. She was so emaciated and run down that I hardly recognized her. Overjoyed, we received her with open arms, glad she had survived also. "I came straight from the Sudetenland, mostly on foot," she said in a low voice. Then she began to tell us how one day long after the war had ended, the Czech people, their militia and the so called Svoboda army suddenly attacked the ethnic German people who had lived there for centuries. Now in peace time, they stormed the German houses and looted or burned them with in-human violence. A great manhunt began. Men and boys were driven out into the streets with clubs or whips and tormented, with many be-ing hanged on the spot. She sighed deeply, "I saw Hans being beaten as they dragged him away and I was put in prison for no reason whatso-ever, with no knowledge of what happened to our two small children." She then continued. "When I was released after several terrible days, I asked for my husband and was told he had been killed and thrown in a mass grave, and if I didn't take off with my brats rather quickly, we would end up in there also. So here I am back in Berlin after traveling hun-dreds of miles on foot."

We were shocked by Inge's account because Sieghardt was an old school friend of her husband and also the godfather of their daughter, and only three years ago, both of their children had strewn flowers at our church wedding. When they were bombed out in Zehlendorf-West in an air raid that had killed Hans' brother, they were invited to live with close Czech business friends in the Sudetenland, and we had also sent a package of personal belongings to them for safekeeping in stor-age. "Suddenly our Czech family had a convenient lapse of memory and could not remember anything," Inge continued, "including that they had taken our money, jewelry and other personal possessions for safekeep-ing. All I have left are the clothes on my back. The children and I now live with my mother in Nikolassee." We were appalled by her experi-ences and immediately offered our help, but she did not want anything nor did she want to stay. She was just relieved to see us alive and walked away as quietly as she had appeared. The inhuman blood bath by the Czechs against the centuries-old ethnic Germans in the German-speak-ing Sudetenland area eventually resulted in the expulsion of more than 3 million defenseless rural Germans, and the murder of hundreds of thousands in the land of their ancestors. Why such an historical injus-tice?

On Sunday Gerda showed up on a bicycle, haggard and famished. She came to pour her heart out as we had not seen each other for a long time. She also had a horror tale to tell. All of the tenants in her apart-ment house had lived together for weeks in the basement just as we had, and one night they collected all the left over bread and made a bread soup so there would be something to eat for everyone. They were without any water since April 25 so they had to walk for ten minutes to a pump located in an area where there was shooting close by and bombs falling. They badly needed drinking water and had to carry some home. Two days later, the Soviets stormed into their basement with weapons drawn and claimed all of their watches. Then, a husky drunken Soviet returned after midnight, smelling like a walking whiskey bottle, and demanded a woman for peeling potatoes in the Kommandatura. Everyone was numb with fear and he fumed since no one made a move, pointing his loaded rifle dangerously around. Someone finally said, "Gerda can speak Russian." So far she was huddled in a dark corner, hoping not to be noticed, but now he selected her.

The rest of her story was typical of the savage treatment to women by the Soviets. She was pushed out into the street with his rifle butt, and into the next deserted apartment building. There, he threw her on the floor which was covered with debris from the last air raid, and pressed a knife to her throat. She had no choice but to submit. Even dead bodies got raped. Later, she slowly crept back into her basement and nobody said anything, but everybody knew what had happened. From then on, she and all of the other young girls would jump out of a back window whenever Soviet soldiers entered the house from the street. Necessity had made her quite inventive. In order to protect her jewelry, which was mostly family heirlooms, she saved it all by splitting open one of her sanitary pads, which were then made of cloth, and sewed the pieces inside.

She told us how right after the war, committees sprang up which were formed by German Communists who had returned from Russia, and they now acted as if they controlled everything. As a former member of the BDM, she was sentenced as punishment to hard labor as an underground construction worker, from June on. No special clothing was issued, so she wore her one pair of overalls from her war-time job in the factory. She and her co-workers, which included teachers, doctors and directors, were ordered around with whips like slaves, and if she stopped for a moment to rest on her shovel, she was screamed at and threatened with a beating. As a canal digger, she had to help clean up a flooded subway tunnel in which many people had drowned and were still buried in the mud down there. The canal above the tunnel had either been hit by a bomb or blown up intentionally by the SS, and the water flooded the tunnel below which was being used as an air raid shelter. One third of the subway was under water. This heavy labor took its toll on her, and she had developed severe back trouble. (She did not know that it would later lead to her being disabled early in life.)

Gerda had to cut her visit short because she had a long bicycle ride back to where she lived in the English sector, and we had no idea when we would meet again. Although we both lived in Berlin, she in the English and I in the American sector, we were worlds apart because the different military commanders issued their own rules and regulations which often conflicted with those in effect in other sectors. To move from one sector to another was virtually impossible in this divided city of clashing regulations.

With each passing day, our extra food provisions also vanished. Vita only got some milk if there happened to be any in the stores. Deliveries were always uncertain. So Sieghardt and I had to hit the barter road again. This time, we selected Gröna. From our last travel experience we knew we could make it in one day. Like everything else, the price of train tickets had gone up, something we had not counted on. We left early in the morning on November 23 and arrived safely in Gröna that night. We found that the scene had changed drastically. All of the ex-soldiers had left and Mr. Koch had returned from the war. Now, he and his wife were in fear of losing ownership of their farm under the Soviets, but they were as hospitable as ever. Sieghardt arranged to ship home two sacks of potatoes by rail freight, each weighing 100 pounds, even though there was a chance that they might never arrive. We left after two days, loaded down with all we could carry and returned home safely from another dangerous hoarding trip into the Soviet zone.

We had just come back at the right time. There was a job notification waiting for Sieghardt to work for the Americans. He had been hired as a gardener and boilerman for several houses, including the one belonging to his parents. He was to report for work the very next day. This type of job suited him because as a plain laborer, he would finally get the food ration card number one. However, I wondered how he really felt to be hired for the most menial work in the house where he had been born thirty-five years ago and had grown up with servants.

Early the next morning, on November 26, 1945, dressed in his oldest clothes, he left for the five-minute walk to his new job. By noon, he was already back carrying his old army tin can filled to the brim with thick American pea soup. He told us how at lunch time, all of the German workers stood in a long line to receive some soup, so he rushed to the front with his old tin and hastily gobbled it down while going back to join the end of the line. This way, he received a second helping and hurried home with it for us. Mutti quickly emptied the unexpected soup into a pot and added enough water to stretch it for a delicious meal for the three of us at home. Who cared that Sieghardt had eaten out of that container before? Food was the only magic word and we all agreed that the Americans made very good soup.

Another irony was that Sieghardt discovered he was in the very best of company. Even though everyone looked like the dregs of society, they greeted each other with, "*Guten Morgen Herr Doktor*," or "*Herr Professor*" or "*Herr Direktor*," thus acknowledging their true status in life. Now they were all in the same boat, struggling for existence and happy to be common laborers so they could qualify for the highest food ration card. That was the only chance to buy food legally in the German stores, for German money at normal prices. Otherwise our old *Reichsmark* no longer had any true value. We had a new floating exchange rate, which had shifted into the "hard currency" of cigarettes. One carton of Pall Malls was 1,000 marks (250 dollars) at that time. Lucky Strikes, being shorter, were "only" 600 marks (150 dollars). Groceries were priced according to the typical chaotic black market prices.

Sieghardt returned home late that first evening and had more specific details about his job. He would be servicing five houses seven days a week in which he had to tend coal-fired furnaces which supplied both heat and warm water. The only thing he hadn't been told was what his salary would be.

Mutti and I heard about a miraculous place in Potsdam where people illegally traded personal belongings for food products from the country, other than the usual carrots and potatoes. Carrying a supply of my home-made bags, we took off for the new promised land, this time with butter and eggs in mind. We traveled by the newly improved S-Bahn. Upon arrival in Potsdam, we were shocked to see the enormous destruction that had taken place. Then we came upon the ridiculous sight of robust Russian women proudly parading around on the streets wearing our chic nightgowns as if they were elegant dresses. I started to laugh, but Mutti stopped me immediately. "Admire them and just smile. Pretend your marveling at their outfits." But, it was too hilarious watching these husky Soviet women flaunting themselves on the street in delicate long and short nightgowns that they probably got from looting a lingerie store.

We continued on through the mass of rubble straight to the market place where a shabby looking crowd was already milling around, trying to conceal the various items they had brought for black market trading, operating out of briefcases and paper bags. Starving people were willing to part with their most cherished possessions in exchange for food. But, before we could find anyone with whom to make a deal, people suddenly whispered, "Police, police, run quickly," and they fled in all directions.

Puzzled, we suddenly found ourselves standing all alone in the middle of the market place. Realizing that black market dealings were illegal and being quick-witted, we stuffed all the bags into one and casually made our way over to the ring of policemen as if we were seeking refuge in the attack. Mutti innocently asked them what was going on here. We pretended we were just on our way to look up some old friends in town. The policemen eyed us skeptically while glancing at our bag and asked exactly where in town we had planned to go. Fortunately, we were well enough acquainted with Potsdam to accurately point out an area just beyond the market place. Apparently our flim-flam story about our "purely accidental" presence here sounded convincing enough to them because they allowed us to go on our way, with Mutti wishing them a friendly "Guten Tag."

People who had already bartered quickly threw away their purchases in order not to be fined or imprisoned, and later, the policemen would go around and pick up everything for free to keep for themselves. Maybe that was the true reason for their casual round-ups. For us the promised land had turned out to be hell. But now what? We could not go home empty-handed. Then, Mutti remembered a couple who owned a store in Potsdam that sold deer and poultry. They had come every weekend for years to our market place at home, even during the war, and we had become one of their regular and best customers, paying their prices for ration card-free deer meat without batting an eye lash. We found their house still intact and they did remember us, although they were not quite as friendly as in the good old war times. Things had changed for them just like it had for everybody else. But, the wife was very interested in obtaining my sturdy bags, and as if by magic, produced a long salami and even a chicken as exchange. That made our day, but they did not encourage us to return anytime soon.

It had become routine for Sieghardt to leave the house early every morning and return late after a twelve-hour workday, with no free weekends. One important advantage though was that he could wash every night with warm water in the bathtub in the basement of his parents' home which had been installed at one time for their servants' use. This was a great luxury because on Limastrasse we could not afford any warm water since we were rationed to a scanty allowance of metered electricity. When it was time for two-year old Vita to take a bath, at best once a week, we would heat water in advance in pots on the kitchen stove. Then we would pour it into a small tub which was placed in the big bathtub. After Vita's bath, we would all take turns washing in the same warm water, and after all had finished, the laundry then went into the precious soapy liquid in the little tub. We did not have electricity to run our washing machine and soap was also a scarce item.

Miraculously we all survived, often with the support of our notorious Berliner humor, something that didn't need ration cards! The possibility of germs was not even considered, except as a joke. We were in such a sorry physical condition that even the germs wouldn't be attracted to us. We couldn't afford to get sick or depressed if we wanted to survive in our "peace time." We were all a grey mass of famished looking laborers.

One day when Sieghardt entered the kitchen in his own home, he found an open, ten-pound army can of lard sitting on the kitchen table. Before he realized what he was doing, he had plunged his bare hand deep down into the can, an uncontrollable instinctive reflex of a constantly empty stomach at the sight of such abundance. Deeply embarrassed by his spontaneous action, he quickly withdrew his hand that was now thickly smeared with lard, wiped his fingers on his big linen handkerchief, and smoothed out all traces in the can. When he got home he was still upset about his compulsive action, but Mutti calmed him down and freed him from the handkerchief that still had lard sticking to it. Then, when she was alone, she carefully scraped it all off and into a pan to preserve this unexpected rich supply for our meager cooking. We had to face that food was the magic word and we had learned to adjust to the changing circumstances.

At about this same time, my potatoes were ready to be harvested from our back yard, and the other tenants were flabbergasted about how large mine were and so numerous compared with those they planted. Of course, they still were not aware of how they were grown organically with the help of Vita. But, the potatoes were my only success as a farmer because my carrots turned out to be nothing but useless strings. So I took comfort in my parsley and chives.

One day, we had a visit from an American major who turned out to be Byron Skillin. He was married to Sieghardt's cousin Adele von Schwanenflügel for many years. Sieghardt's mother had always stayed in contact with them at their home in Maine, so he had no trouble finding the house, though it had now been seized by the Americans. But he managed to find us anyway. While talking to us, he offered a piece of chocolate to little Vita, but she shook her head and hid her hands behind her back. Cousin Byron was disappointed and called her a spoiled child. What he didn't realize was that Vita had never seen chocolate in her entire life and since it was brown, it looked like dirt to her and she did not want to touch it. All she recognized as hand-held food was bread and the tiny wild strawberries that grew around our terraced garden, which Papa would collect every morning and put on her hot cereal as vitamins, sometimes as many as eight. Fruits in grocery stores were a legend. Cousin Byron also offered us some chocolate and Vita could not understand that we so eagerly ate that "dark stuff" because we had always warned her not to put dirt in her mouth.

Byron also told us that the Nuremberg Trials of Nazi leaders had started on November 20, 1945, and that it might be in session for a long time. Papa was upset that the Soviets had representatives sitting in judgement because Stalin had sided with Hitler and was his accomplice, and should be tried for the same, and other crimes. He pointed out that it was well known that the Soviets had been involved in brutal mass killings ever since the Bolshevik revolution of 1918, especially in their concentration camps that were located throughout Russia. In fact, Germany was now on trial for copying the tactics of the Soviets and was being judged by them for doing it. But, the crimes of the Soviets were not an issue at the Nuremberg Trials even though they were as guilty as the Nazis. Papa shook his head. "The world still has much to fear from Stalin." Then he asked, "at this new international tribunal, aren't the prosecutor and defender from the same party? Isn't this something unheard of before?" Byron agreed this would be the first such proceeding in history. Before leaving, he told us that on his next visit, he would bring some milk for Vita and have Adele send some clothing that their children had outgrown.

In 1945, we experienced our first peacetime Christmas since 1938. Our scanty food supply had not changed very much, and there was no prospect for extra holiday rations, not even for coal. Food was the only thing available in the stores, plus our monthly ration of cigarettes—not packages but individual ones, twelve for men and six for women. We desperately wanted to give Vita a Christmas present, but how? She had never seen a ball and we searched everywhere for one, but none could be found. But, the *Christkind* (Christ child) had to bring her something, so Mutti and I decided we would make her a present ourselves, a picture book. Neither of us were artistic, but this didn't stop us. First, we had to find cardboard for pages, which we obtained from old shoe boxes, and then concocted a homemade glue out of our scanty flour ration mixed with water, the only ingredients we had plenty of! Then we tested our limited drawing ability and filled the six by nine pages with flowers, butterflies, trees, houses and other things familiar to Vita. Our creative design possibilities seemed unlimited. On Holy Eve it was the only present she received, but it provided the emotional highlight of Christmas. She didn't miss other presents because she didn't know any better. She held the book in her little hands, completely fascinated by the pictures, and happily called out every object that she could recognize. To her, it was the most wonderful Christmas present and it kept her busy for hours in the days that followed.

Sieghardt had his own Christmas surprise. On December 22 he finally received his first pay check for the first fourteen days of work, even though he had already worked for a full month. It was 133.43 marks for 168 hours of work which is the equivalent of $31.77 in U.S. dollars. This was not only a real shock to find out he was working for about nineteen cents an hour, or 79 German pfennigs, but also a tremendous blow to his ego because none of his own workers in the family firm had ever been paid such low wages. But, at least he had the satisfaction of having a number one ration card for his family. We now understood why the American housewives who had followed their military husbands suddenly had a maid or housekeeper over here in Germany when they could not afford to have one at home. We were being hired to work long hours for slave wages. However, because of our very limited income, we soon learned little tricks to help ourselves to "Christmas presents" in the bitter cold winter months that arrived very early.

Coal snatching from the coal trains that passed through the American sector was a daily practice. As soon as the trains had passed Wannsee they would slow down for the station of Lichterfelde West, not far from our suburb. German boys ran along the coal hopper cars and yanked on the lever that would open the bottom chutes just a crack. Coal would begin falling out as the train moved along to be picked up by freezing Berliners. Sometimes, the boys would climb up on top of the loaded, open cars and throw off as much coal as they could. Since the coal was destined for the Americans, they called this stealing, but Berliners considered it German coal since it came from our German Ruhr mines. Every form of this type of self-support was somehow against the laws of the occupation force, but in conformance with our conscience.

We did receive an unexpected family surprise just after Christmas when the potatoes that Sieghardt had shipped by freight from Gröna the previous month actually arrived. We had already written them off as an unfortunate experience. Our railway administration was again partially in German hands and some honest people must have been left there. Suddenly we were the proud owners of two big sacks of potatoes for our households. And, the new year of 1946 brought a second pleasant surprise when a South African gold mine company in which Papa had made a long-forgotten investment informed him that they would repay all his shares in full, plus the interest accumulated over the years. This sounded like Utopia. What once had been a small side venture now turned into life-saving payments that were spread out over a period of time. I can't remember how it worked, as all the banks were closed since the end of the war. It must have been through the postal service which functioned off and on. The only thing that counted was that some money dropped unexpectedly into our hands.

Since the old adage is that everything comes in threes, our third good fortune concerned me. All of the large villas on nearby Goethestrasse had been confiscated by the Americans. Some of them were looking for someone to teach them German, and I was recommended at the suggestion of my neighbors. Although I had considerable schooling and a limited background in the English language, I had no teaching experience. But, this job offered the prospect of food, and I reasoned that it shouldn't be that difficult to teach something to someone who knew nothing. So with a throbbing heart and a book under my arm, I went to the villa where the classes were to be conducted and found a half dozen well educated young men waiting for me. They had already bought a book on the German language, but didn't know how to use it, so I simply started with lesson number one. It was a very friendly atmosphere with no pressure, and I found the students were more interested in hearing about Germany and German life than actually learning the language. We conversed in English and talked about their families and mine, and they asked me to please return on a regular basis. Also, they wanted to know what I would need for Vita besides payments in German money.

On my next visit, there were several cans of milk on the table, back then costing only a fraction of a dollar. Of course, I had no American money with me because the German people were not allowed to have any, although some had been left for us by Cousin Byron. With my limited school English, I fell right into a language trap by telling them, "I do not have my senses with me," thinking I was saying that I had no cents with me. They smiled and asked where I kept them. I replied, "I left them at home." Now, they broke out laughing, "How did you do that? You don't look like it!" Becoming more irritated by the minute with this strange conversation, I tried to explain that I did not know that I would need my "senses" (cents) today. Highly amused, my students gave me their first English lesson: "cents are commonly referred to as small change in the English language," something I have never forgotten. They always brought food for me and never wanted my cents or my dollars.

One day, I noticed a strange bulky heap on the chair next to mine that was covered with a blanket and from time to time, one of the men would reach under there to adjust something. Although I was slightly irritated by the situation, I didn't ask any questions. But, I got my answer on the next visit when I could hear myself talking inside before I even entered the house. I was greeted with laughter because they had played a joke on me and had taped the entire lesson from the previous visit and were now playing it back. After my initial shock, they asked if they could tape every lesson since they might be transferred soon and they could take the tapes with them. I had no objection and was rather pleased that they thought that I was that good of a teacher. Unfortunately they were transferred shortly thereafter and my wonderful easy source of food and pleasant diversion came to an end. But, it proved that not all Americans had communication difficulties with those "terrible" Germans.

By now the Americans decided that the bomb-damaged home of my parents was too unsafe for quartering their troops and they permitted them to move back in again. Life is not without humorous events. On February 13, 1946, we began carrying back in through the front door everything we had sneaked out through the back door not more than three months ago. However, the interior of the house was a surprise because some of our neighbor's furniture was there and some of ours was gone. Many things had completely vanished, probably as souvenirs of the departing Americans. A few of our neighbors had also been permitted to return to their bomb-damaged homes, and we started to exchange our belongings. But one thing that we could never understand was the large pile of household items in the garden that had been deliberately destroyed. Some were items that had been fetched from the attic where they had been stored, such as antique china wash basins with matching pitchers, a bust of a female we nicknamed *Resi*, which was left over from Papa's bachelor days, and other outdated things, which today would be collectors items. My beautiful Hungarian carnival costume was torn to pieces, and even our cuckoo clock was thrown on top and totally smashed. As children, Günter and I had brought it back from the Black Forest as a souvenir about twenty years earlier, and it had cuckooed happily ever since throughout our homes in Münster and Berlin, day and night. Now it was dead forever. Why would something like that hurt me so much, even more than other losses? There did not seem to be any logical answer for this other than pure vandalism.

The next day, Sieghardt discovered our large dining room table in a house at the end of the street that had been used as a canteen for soldiers, but now stood empty. We secretly carried our table out that night but were afraid to take it to my parents' house until we were sure that the Americans would not miss it. So, we hid it in the pergola of the adjacent garden of Dr. Hecht. Nobody would ever know how it had gotten there. But first we had to remove all American traces, like all the old chewing gum sticking under the table top. Since nothing happened for two days, we carried it back home, and it promised not to walk off on its own again. Mrs. Vogel and Maria also decided to go back to their bombed out house and try to create living quarters in the basement. With the assistance of Mrs. Vogel's son and two grandsons, they gave the basement a good cleaning and made some makeshift repairs, which created a temporary habitable living quarter. So Mutti and Papa got their old-time neighbors back again. The grandsons later emigrated to Australia.

Meanwhile starvation had killed more old people. Though our ration cards regularly said "tea" on them, we had gotten just a small amount twice the previous October, and it would have been so helpful in the cold winter months of 1945/46. The general food delivery to the stores was more regular now but the allotted Soviet quota was still unchanged and too skimpy. So Mutti and I, for nearly a year now, had to venture again and again into the Soviet Zone for additional food to alleviate the frustration of every day living. We were careful not to appear too often at the same place and divided our barter trips between Fahrland, Potsdam, and Beelitz.

The American occupation forces rotated and with that, Sieghardt's job ended on April 10, 1946. The new military unit asked him if he had filled out the required forms, to which he replied in the affirmative, and no more questions were asked. He was immediately assigned to his old job on April 16, but he knew this could end very suddenly if his previous employment application was reviewed and they saw that he had been a member of the Nazi Party. We hoped it would take a while. Sieghardt needed work desperately and we needed his number one ration card. To the Americans, even the lowest job with them was too good for a former Nazi Party member.

On May 22, my doorbell rang early in the morning. Outside stood a strange lady with a medium-size suitcase in her hand. She introduced herself as Mrs. Röhr and presented an official paper which authorized her to immediately move into our apartment and occupy one of our rooms. I thought I didn't hear right. With an imploring look at me, she pointed to her suitcase and said in a low voice, "This is all I still own. I was bombed out at the end of the war and have been living in an improvised public asylum on the edge of the city." I was completely flabbergasted. How was I supposed to react? I slowly opened the door a little wider and let her enter. There we stood in my entrance hall sizing each other up. She seemed rather pleasant and appeared to be older than I. Her assignment was legal with no other alternative for me but to accept it. The homeless now made up about one fifth of the population, and this was just one of the many emergency orders to prevent total chaos by taking them off the streets, even if it required accommodating them in private homes. Since entire streets were confiscated by the Americans, even countless house owners were now homeless, too, which added to the number of asylum seekers and stranded people. Mrs. Röhr was abandoned, the most traumatic fear of all people.

I asked her to put her suitcase down and she breathed an audible sigh of relief because this obviously meant she would now have a friendly roof over her head. The housing problem affected almost every person in town, and now us. As we talked, it was evident that she was very refined and a widow without any children. Her late husband had owned a music publishing firm which had also been completely bombed out. We were both thrown into an unexpected situation and were determined to make the best of it. Looking back, there was sort of an understanding in the air for another person's unexpected misfortunes, and a tremendous amount of good will. In order to give all of us the utmost privacy, I decided on the spot to give her the room that Papa had added for the baby three years ago by breaking through the wall of our entrance hall into Mrs. Kage's apartment. It took most of the day to rearrange the furniture and when Sieghardt came home that evening, he found a roomer in our former bedroom and the study now converted to our's and Vita's bedroom.

Our new roomer turned out to be very pleasant and down-to-earth. She immediately found a position as a waitress in an American mess which had been set up in one of the nearby big villas that had been confiscated, and urged me to do something similar since the struggle against starvation was constant and she was working with food. Sieghardt was already employed by the Americans, so he could keep his eyes open for an employment opportunity for me. But, no matter how hard we looked, no luck came our way. As a result, Mutti and I were doomed to our weekly barter trips into the country in fair and foul weather—for over one and a half years by now. And, each trip carried with it the possibility of physical attack from the Soviets. Sometimes we were fortunate enough to get a short ride in a farmer's open truck that ran by burning wood in a tall burner which created a gas that operated the vehicle, smoking like a chimney. You could hear the motor's heavy "tuck tuck" beat for miles.

On one trip to Fahrland, we were lucky enough to flag down a farmer with a horse and wagon to take us through the isolated country road that led to the village. All of a sudden, some Soviets stormed out of a garden shed screaming, "*Frau komm*," but the farmer spurred his horse on at breakneck speed and we escaped while Mutti and I crouched in fear. Reaching Fahrland safely, we made our purchases but were both scared of the return trip. But, to our relief, we found the same helpful farmer who was familiar with the assaults in that area already waiting for us with his horse and wagon, and he even had a large empty barrel in the back for me to crawl under. Mutti put an old rug over her head and sat up front, pretending to be the farmer's wife. We hadn't gone very far when we passed Soviets screaming for women, but again, the farmer ran his old horse as fast as it could go and we passed safely while I huddled under the barrel holding my breath. But, that barrel must have been used for herring at some time because I seemed to have picked up some of the leftover drippings. So I was safe but smelly. At home it was almost impossible to remove that distinct odor from my body. But, we had no time to worry about awkward experiences. All that mattered was that our trip was successful.

The eastern agriculture areas had been Germany's bread basket, but this source of food had been cut off from us since it had come under Soviet or Polish administration. Berlin was a city on the edge between two worlds and carrying food from those eastern areas into our American sector became more and more risky. The Soviets were tightening their grip on West Berlin, and the Western Allies were looked upon as only temporary and undesired guests. Our bare existence was felt as a provocation. There was a constant increase in procedural differences among the victors in the four occupation zones which made political and economic uniformity impossible. The Soviets pressed their objective of bringing the entire West under Communist control which resulted in a growing rift between the Western Powers and the Soviet Union. In September of 1946, the Americans, British and French merged their separate zones into a tri-zone to be administered as one single entity. We didn't know then that this act of unification was the political milestone that would only two years later, in 1948, be the initial step in establishing our Federal Republic of Germany.

In the East zone, the Soviets had already forcibly merged last April the moderate Socialist Party (SPD) within the Communist Party (KPD) to create the new Socialist Unity Party (SED). The Communists held all key positions in the SED in order to structure the society according to a Soviet model. The new SED was also admitted in West Berlin and in West Germany as a political party in addition to the SPD, KPD, Christian Democrats (CDU) and the Liberal Democrats (FDP). The new SED became the target of the Berliners sardonic sense of humor with this latest one:

"Who invented the SED, the Soviets or the scientists?" "Why, naturally, the Soviets," answered the new little SED member.

"The scientists would have first tried it out on living beings."

The first, and the last, free election was held in all of Berlin on October 20, 1946, to elect a city parliament to operate under the joint supervision of the Four Powers. Over 92 percent of the eligible voters flocked to the polls and gave the Soviets a serious setback when the East SED was rejected by 80 percent of Berliners.

Our forays into the country in search of food were lately being hampered by the newly installed East German border guards, the so-called "People's Police," who had a dog-like devotion to Moscow. They were the same type of nightmare figures we had experienced under Hitler, now willing to carry out any new Soviet pressure tactics. Their latest harassment was hunting down hungry West Berliners on their barter trips and, out of the blue, demanding to see approved documents for exporting food to West Berlin. We had none because they did not even exist. But, without this nonexistent document, they confiscated all your food as illegal exports, which they probably kept for themselves. No one knew when and where the People's Police would strike, so Mutti and I

frequently had to protect our hard-won provisions by taking dangerous chances to avoid them during a sudden raid. More than once, we
hastily got off a train on the wrong side, slid down the railway embankment and hid somewhere until the coast was clear, and then dragged
home on foot. This was not the easiest task when you are loaded with
produce like pack rats.

With rail service now operating sporadically, we could visit our
farmer friends in Beelitz more often. They would willingly sell us eggs,
which I carried in a linen bag separated into different compartments to
keep them from banging together and breaking. I fastened this bag
around my waist under my clothing so that the eggs were dangling between my thighs. In addition to the eggs, one time they even sold us a
skinned wild rabbit, which was going to present a problem to get home
safely. It was a long animal, so I tucked it into my corset and laced it
tightly with the head between my bosom and its body stretched down
between my legs. I looked grossly out of shape and overweight, but our
valuable cargo was out of reach of the East German border patrol. Walking was not too bad, but when it came time to enter the train, I had to
develop an awkward twisting motion in order to climb the steep steps
without bumping the eggs against any metal corners, because the rabbit was in my way. People watching my peculiar slow motions trying to
enter the train exclaimed, "Oh, that poor woman. She is pregnant. Let
her have a seat." But, sitting was one thing I could not do with that cargo
under my clothing.

The last S-Bahn had already departed by the time we reached
Wannsee, so Mutti and I had to spend the night on the stone staircase
close to the platform where American soldiers were still patrolling. I
wanted to get the rabbit out of my corset so I started downstairs to the
restrooms, but half way down I heard women screaming who were being raped by the Soviets. Horrified, I returned upstairs. But now what?
The rabbit tortured me. Resolutely Mutti held a coat over me while I set
the animal free again. We settled on the steps against the wall with our
cargo secured between us as we tried to sleep. We dozed off many times.
Finally the big clock showed 2 a.m. We dozed off again, and this time
when we awoke, the big clock still showed 2 a.m. How could that be?
Oh no, to add to our misfortune, this was the night we went back to
standard time and gained one hour. What a double misery for us when

others enjoyed an extra snooze at home in bed. We survived that, too. We had no choice, even though we didn't know who was stiffer, the dead rabbit or we, but we caught the first S-Bahn home to find frantic husbands because we hadn't returned home the previous day.

If only these weekly forages were not such a vital necessity for our survival. Since 1945 we were primarily on the bread-and-potato diet, by now looking like string beans ourselves. Did it have to be like that forever, West-Berlin a testing place between East and West? Even though we were used to crisis situations, we found it hard not to wallow in self-pity. We were almost ready to give up, but not to the Soviets. When would the West help us? If the supply trucks were delayed for no reasons in the Soviet zone until the food rotted, we had no food even with ration cards.

Just when Mutti and I thought we could no longer survive the day-to-day struggle to provide food for the family, a miracle happened. The military selected Sieghardt's parents' house on Veronikasteig for an Officers' Mess, which was ideal for this purpose with three entrances, a huge kitchen with pantry, two inside staircases, eleven rooms on different levels, a large garden and garage. Four officers had moved into the bedrooms on the upper floor and two other officers from outside would take their meals there. Everything was ready to go except there was no cook, and Mrs. Röhr urged me to apply for the position. "That's your chance!" I nearly choked. My only cooking experience over the past years had been in making watery soups. But her theory was: "Let them find out if they like your cooking, but at least you got your foot in the door. Remember how many of us had to become *Fräuleins* just to exist." I was well aware of the many women who had to submit to liaisons with well-supplied American men who willingly provided for them and their hungry children. Faced with starvation, mothers could not even afford to cling to a code of morals. She prompted me with, "how lucky you are to start as a cook where there is food every day. Grab the chance before somebody else snaps it up."

Although I felt hopelessly unqualified, I knew she was right, and was amazed when Sieghardt somehow managed to get me the job that very day. It was never clear to me how. I was to start in two days, which didn't leave me much time to prepare for my new position, but I was familiar with the house and Vita could stay right across the street with my parents. My big hope was that I would be able to last at least one month of the extreme cold winter of 1946/47 which would get me close to Christmas.

Right away Sieghardt and I moved into his parents' house and occupied the empty servants' quarters on the third floor. It was a large heated attic room with running hot and cold water. What a luxury! The housekeeper lived in the other attic room which was equipped like ours. We even had our own toilet up there. The servants' bathtub, now for our use, was in the basement. This was a more desirable arrangement than it might sound. After all, the entire house was warm. Since I could eat there and provide for Sieghardt, Mutti got our food ration cards.

I showed up for work early in the morning of November 18, 1946, rather inappropriately attired in a fancy dress and high heels, which was the only decent outfit I had. Back then, all of our clothes were ragged and we made skirts out of men's old trousers by cutting out the most worn parts. We also patched together the usable pieces of two dresses to create one new one. But shoes were our worst problem because they were virtually unobtainable, except on the black market where a simple pair cost 600-800 marks, the equivalent of 150-200 U.S. dollars, an exorbitant sum. Before, good leather shoes sold for 20 marks, about 5 U.S. dollars. So here I was serving my first breakfast in my completely unsuitable get-up, and thanks to Mrs. Röhr's coaching, it went quite well. She told me to serve water and coffee with every meal and when I asked her why, she replied, "Who knows? These are their eating habits so give them what they want and keep your mouth shut! Just remember, Germans have no rights."

Although I set to work in my mother-in-law's familiar kitchen, busting with energy, things did not go as planned. In the middle of preparing toast, the electricity went off due to rationing during certain hours. So, working by candlelight on a dark November morning, I tried to do the toast in a pan on the gas stove, in addition to the eggs, bacon, pancakes and everything else that had been ordered. I had not expected to have to prepare six entirely different breakfasts for the six men who showed up at the table at different times. The coffee percolator had also stopped working. The housekeeper served the meal in the large dining room and relayed all new orders to me. So far I had survived my first crucial test.

When the dirty dishes were returned to the kitchen, some slices of cold toast had been left on the plates. I looked at them and they looked at me. I was not allowed to take any food out of the house, but I didn't think that it would apply to leftovers. I couldn't resist the temptation and quickly buttered a few pieces and having no paper or plastic bags, slipped them unwrapped into my dress opening. Then, I ran across the street to my parents' house as fast as my feet would carry me. They had watched from their window and were worried something might have happened. I will never forget their big surprised eyes the moment I opened my dress and took out the cold toast. Without any ceremony, they devoured it to the last morsel while we were still standing in the front entrance hall. How thin and emaciated they looked, their faces small, deep lines telling of their hardships, looking much older than their true age. As a matter of fact, they looked older than they did thirty years later when they died in their nineties.

My in-laws' house, now used as an officers' mess.

An enormous problem arose with cooking my first dinner. There was a huge roast of several pounds that looked more hostile than friendly. What was I supposed to do with this monster? That kind of abundance was just a memory to me, and here it was going to serve just six men for one meal. My first objective was to get it into the oven before the gas went off, and hopefully the electricity would stay on so that I could see what I was doing. Close to dinner time, the electricity went off, but the gas stayed on, and I was running around the big kitchen with a candle in my hand like a busy witch. While checking the roast I spilled wax on it, and on everything else cooking on the stove, like vegetables and potatoes, working with only one hand while holding the candle in the other. How would I know if that monster piece of meat was going to be done in time? The housekeeper, whose name was Rosemarie Gall and who was as mean as her name sounded, looked on cynically without offering me any assistance. What I did not know then was that she had fallen in love with Sieghardt and I was now in the way.

The men began arriving for the evening meal, and suddenly the whole cooking situation looked unmanageable to me. Here I was in a dark kitchen, catapulted overnight from my modest food supply at home into Utopia, with these Americans who I thought to be spoiled. How could I survive? That's when I panicked, ran out the back door and across the street to my parents, telling Mutti in tears that I could never go back to that kitchen again. Level-headed Mutti just grabbed her coat and mumbled something that sounded like "dumb girl," and took me in tow right back, entering the kitchen through the back door. She checked the meat in the oven. "It's done," she proclaimed, then proceeded to prepare everything else with her usual skills, and the meal was served by the housekeeper. The after dinner comments were very complimentary, thanks to Mutti who legally wasn't even authorized to set foot in the house. But who had time to remember that in the face of disaster? In no time, Mutti turned my panic into a big success.

From then on, Mutti came over daily, and as always, we stuck together through thick or thin. The officers got used to seeing her around. This way the Americans learned to eat what we cooked together, until I learned to cook what they were used to eating. It was no big problem really, since except for one, they were all recently from Europe, as first-generation Americans. We would have lived happily ever after, if several disturbing incidents hadn't come up. One could always expect the unexpected.

*M*ostly Heaven or Hell?

*M*y daily duties as cook for the officers' mess in my in-laws' house started at the crack of dawn each day. There were four officers billeted in the upstairs bedrooms and two lived elsewhere and came just for their meals. They were a very diverse group, representing many different nationalities, although all were officers of the U.S. Army.

I usually began serving breakfast around dawn when Lieutenant Colonel Wilson came down around 6 a.m. We called him the only genuine American. As soon as he would finish, the Polish-American officer from the distant Nikolassee would appear. We wondered why he even belonged to our mess, and not to one in his own area. He always brought his chow-chow dog along who sat on a chair next to him at the table, sniffing and licking every dish that he could reach, and finally getting to steal the remains from his master's cereal dish. Master like dog had one thing in common, a very nasty disposition. When these two finally left, we had to set up the table again for the next four officers who were not aware of what had just taken place at the now spotless table. Telling them would have meant complaining about a member of the Allied forces, an incredible impudence. So we made sure that we kept some chipped china for us in the kitchen from which the dog had never eaten.

Captain Moutner, the Austrian-American, who lived alone in a confiscated villa just down the street, wanted everything ready for him as soon as he sat down at the table, whether the electricity was still on or not. He wanted his toast to be thick and freshly made, his pancakes thin and piping hot, with bacon on the side and an egg fried according to his preference. The German chauffeurs helped me with this hard-to-please officer by calling out, "Moutner on the way," when they saw him leave his villa, and if the electricity and gas were cooperative, I was ready for him when he arrived.

It seemed that every officer desired his toast to be of a different shade and thickness from the others. And what was an egg "sunny side up?" Oh, they meant what we called *Spiegelei* (mirror egg) because of its mirror-like reflection and it always faces the eater squarely in the face. The pancakes and bacon also had to be cooked to each individual preference and whatever was fried wrong would be returned to me in the kitchen. Of the six breakfasts that I prepared each morning, no two were ever alike, and then, all of the orders may be different the next morning. At first I thought I'd go mad with such picky eating habits. Two things that were never a problem were the cereal which was self-service from a side buffet and coffee, which I had brewed in huge amounts before the electricity could shut off. I thought it odd to be so fastidious about an ordinary American breakfast when they rarely complained about an extensive dinner.

Such a morning performance was usually over by nine o'clock and then an immense cleaning job waited for us. Once, in the beginning, one of the officers had come into the kitchen, and pointing at the piled-up dirty dishes, gave us generous advice about correct cleanliness. That struck us rather funny; to have a foreigner lecture Germans in Germany about sanitation, when we are known for an aggravating tidiness with that Teutonic work ethic. We seized that convenient moment to remind him to supply us with plenty of dishwashing liquid. Afraid of more wishes, he made a quick exit. Back then the commissary was not yet stocked with every item as in the U.S.

I gradually learned a little about each of the officers. Lieutenant Colonel Wilson, the American-American, was very nice and friendly. The English-American officer, Captain Gabelia, and the French-American, who had moved in on October 6, 1946, were both polite but rather restrained. Captain Beer, the German-American, was just the opposite. He lived in the house since July 18, when officers replaced the earlier military mixture on Veronikasteig. He made himself noticed by his loud commands to everyone around. He simply whistled for Sieghardt to pick up his riding boots for polishing, even though Sieghardt had nothing to do with personal service. "Please" and "thank you" were not part of Captain Beer's vocabulary. The chauffeurs told us that when he spoke on the phone in German to his Jewish mother in Switzerland he was so rude that they felt sorry for the old lady.

We wondered what might have brought these six so very different men together in this small and rather private mess. They were all associated with the American forces. Obviously they had only one thing in common, mastering foreign languages, and the peculiar fact that their daily activities caused the German chauffeurs to be continually exchanging the license plates on their cars. If this was done for a secret activity, it was performed rather openly in our garage entrance where everyone could see it from the street. The political climate of Berlin already reflected the East-West conflict and this was the peak period for the full gamut of espionage, infiltration and double agents. Although I suspected that the six officers were involved in some type of intelligence work, my activity and interests were confined to the kitchen, and their activity was none of my business.

In recognition of the serious food shortage in Berlin, the American occupation forces were supplied directly from the U.S. stateside subsistence distribution system of the U.S. Army Quartermaster General. The officers bought their personal supplies at the Army Commissary and had them delivered to me at the house by a young American soldier. I stored everything in an unlocked walk-in pantry and a refrigerator, and would prepare the meat that they wanted that day, together with three vegetables. At the sight of all of that food, the housekeeper, Mrs. Gall, demanded that I give her a can of evaporated milk every day that she claimed she needed for her health. "How can I do that?" I asked with foreboding. I badly needed Mrs. Röhr's advice again and she suggested, "give that Gall woman one can a week just to maintain peace," and she also enlightened me that the Americans consider potatoes a vegetable. That was news to me. Otherwise I had only canned vegetables such as corn, carrots, peas and string beans, and nothing fresh such as lettuce, tomatoes or cucumbers. So I pointed out, "But with the two vegetables besides potatoes, they eat just about the same thing every day; with only one there would be more variety." "That's what they want in my mess also," she said. "Every day the same, but never serve corn with potatoes." I had never known that corn was for human consumption. For us it had been only chicken feed. But I soon learned their corn was mighty tasty.

Mutti came over every morning with little Vita for a visit. I collected empty milk cans daily and lined them up on the window sill to be filled with the used coffee grounds from the percolator. Mutti always took a can home to add to the tasteless Nazi coffee substitute we still got on our ration cards and when you mixed it with the grounds from the American coffee, it actually awoke the remembrance of real coffee. The Americans drank an enormous amount of coffee every day, so we had a rich supply of coffee grounds even for the chauffeurs to take home to their families.

Papa, being a good business man, had suggested from the very start that I keep my own accurate bookkeeping of all of the incoming food delivered by an American soldier. He also warned me not to do any business with the black market dealers who would probably be contacting me to make a bargain for food. I followed his advice religiously and kept very accurate records of all food entrusted to my care. As he predicted, it didn't take long before some black market dealers showed up at my kitchen door. They eloquently promised me a lucrative business for coffee and any other kind of food I would be willing to provide them, but I rejected each offer with a stern order never to return again.

But, I had other problems right in my own household, such as in the evening when the six officers brought six German female dinner guests totally unannounced. I only had six pork chops in the kitchen, and in desperation, pounded them as flat as a pancake to extend their size and then cut them in half. The portions still looked very skimpy and it didn't take long for the angry men to show up in the kitchen to demand what I had done with "their" meat. With my poor English, I tried to explain to them that if they planned to have guests they should purchase additional food in advance. Of course, it never occurred to them that the food they bought was based on serving only six. They left the kitchen with puzzled expressions.

There apparently were some shortages of food that I was not aware of because the German chauffeurs, some of whom were ex-officers, pointed out to me that my mess sergeant suddenly was wearing an expensive gold wristwatch. Shortly thereafter, he was replaced by a woman soldier. She did the entire food shopping and brought all the items to me each morning. Being a former Polish Jew, she no doubt hated me on sight and didn't try to disguise it. When I told her that I had never been a member of the Nazi Party, she brushed this off with, "You are a liar," and called me terrible names. I had no recourse but to accept this verbal abuse because she was an American soldier and I was just a German with no rights. For her we all were either criminals or a stupid beer and bratwurst society.

In early December, I couldn't believe my ears when she lectured me that the Christmas tree was a Polish invention and she would teach me how to put one up and decorate it. I should have listened without comment, but that would have been against my nature. Even though this statement may appear to be an unimportant trifle, I was stupid enough to contradict her. "Martin Luther brought the first Christmas tree into the home and adorned it with candles in 1535. The green fir was a symbol of hope. He also wrote many beautiful songs such as..." I never got a chance to finish because she stopped me in mid-sentence. Boy, did she get mad! My unscheduled educational remark could win me absolutely no sympathy. Often things I said in English came out harsh. As a German, I had no right to an opinion, not even about a German Christmas tree, and was supposed to accept every stupid statement without argument—something I had not learned yet.

Her next order in her broken German was that the fat should be cut off from every piece of meat she bought and it should be *für die Hund* (for the dog). But, instead of throwing it out, it later went to Mutti across the street where it became the backbone of a more substantial cuisine. Also, she was always criticizing the appearance of my shoes as being unfit for work, and she happened to be right this once. I finally asked her if she could get me a more practical pair in the Post Exchange, and that I would pay for it, since shoes were virtually impossible to obtain in the German market. I wished I had never asked her. My request was endlessly amusing to her and she cynically replied, "Germans don't need shoes. They can go barefoot." In a way, I could understand her hostility when I thought how I would react if I were a former Polish Jew, but hatred is like a boomerang, and with her attitude, she should not have been assigned as an American soldier to Germany at this time. She repeatedly blamed me for everything since mankind, and I wondered why it was not also my fault that Eve reached for the apple in Paradise.

Shortly after the arrival of this new female mess sergeant, the officers once more noticed a mysterious shrinking of the food in my kitchen. This reflected directly on me because I was in charge of the supplies and I was determined to solve this puzzle without a confrontation with an American employee. I made Sieghardt a simple sandwich each day and Mrs. Gall and I ate very modestly. Bread and butter were always plentiful in the house so the shortage could not have resulted from what the hired help was eating.

The next morning the mess sergeant left her inventory book lying open on the kitchen table. I quickly stole a glance at her list to compare it with mine and was amazed to see a mistake. The day before I had received two one-pound packages of powdered sugar while her list showed she had delivered two ten-pound sacks of regular sugar. Here in one item was a discrepancy of eighteen pounds. She caught me looking at her list before I could check any further and became furious when I took issue with her, despite my non-status, and dared to point out the accounting differences. As she quickly picked up her inventory list, she shouted at me, "When food is missing here, it is your fault alone," to which Mrs. Gall added, "No wonder she is short when she lets me have so much all the time!"

That accusation went too far and I shot back, "There are limits Mrs. Gall! You with your never-ending and impossible demands are never satisfied. Now that it's finally out in the open, the pantry will be locked from this point on and there will be no more self-service." The mess sergeant obviously enjoyed the fight she caused over food between Mrs. Gall and me, and that was the last time she ever left her inventory list lying openly on the kitchen table. I was in a quandary because I could not tell the officers about the mismatched food lists since that would have pitted the American officers against the American mess sergeant, an unforgivable affront. The thief would invariably be a German—me. I could only hope and pray that some situation would arise which would give me the opportunity to defend myself without a confrontation.

While I was still struggling with the problem of the food shortage, Mrs. Gall dropped another bombshell when she challenged me with: "Who hired you in the first place?" I didn't know. Arrogantly, she continued that she had been hired by OMGUS. Who was that? I was afraid to ask and silently wondered why she suddenly was so inquisitive about my work status. At night Sieghardt told me that OMGUS was the Office of Military Government for Germany (U.S.), which was located in Dahlem since October 1945, an elegant suburb of Berlin. Their function was to check on the background of people applying to work for the Americans and to select only those considered worthy, a big privilege because where there were Americans there was food. Former Nazi Party members and their wives were excluded. "Don't worry," Sieghardt assured me, "at my request, the officers here in the house agreed right away that you would cook for them."

It was only a few days later that a lady in the uniform of that ominous OMGUS suddenly appeared at the house. Was that Mrs. Gall's doing? The lady wanted to know why I was already working here but was not on their list of employees. Their office did not have a properly completed questionnaire on file from me and to make up for that, I was directed to appear at their office. I promised everything, but had no intention of ever going there. After some quick thinking, I blurted out, "Oh, I was hired privately," remembering the deal that Sieghardt had made with the officers. I had no intention of filling out any questionnaire if there was any way I could avoid it, because that form was exactly what I was afraid of. If it inquired about my husband's former membership in the Nazi Party, not only would I be fired, but also Sieghardt. It would cost us both our jobs, which served to keep the entire family alive at present in our struggle to survive. When Sieghardt had filled out his first application admitting to being a Party member, the first military group had hired him anyway. When the present military group took over, his papers were either lost or not reviewed, and we wanted it to stay that way.

The lady made some notes on her forms and left, and I hoped that the crisis had blown over and I would not be missed on any list for another month or so, so we would be able to get through the rugged winter. Some days later, another lady in uniform appeared, this time from the office of privately hired personnel, and wanted to know why I wasn't on their list either, because they were missing a proper employment questionnaire filled out by me. Again, thinking quickly, I said, "Oh, I think I was hired by OMGUS," hoping that I could get rid of both of them this way, or at least confuse them enough that the delay would allow me to keep my position through the grim winter.

This had been one of the worst winters in years, when old people were often found frozen and starved to death in their beds in unheated old houses that had been partially destroyed by bombs. There was no coal, wood or oil to operate the central heating in Berliner households and people stood in long lines for a small allotment of twenty pounds of briquettes per household when they were available, which was seldom. The *Tiergarten*, a public park in the English sector, at one time a beautiful island of woods, lakes and monuments with wonderful old trees that had survived the bombing, were now released to be cut down as firewood and would disappear in the iron stoves of freezing Berliners. My parents had set up an old round iron stove in Vita's bedroom with a chimney pipe extending out through a broken window pane. Fired with wood from the tree cut down in our garden, it kept the room reasonably warm, and sometimes in the evening, we added one or two briquettes from the rich mess supply to sustain its glow overnight to keep the chill out.

Shortly after the upsetting visitors from OMGUS, the mess sergeant came in one morning with an enormous package which appeared to be so heavy that I wondered how she was able to carry it in from her car. She ordered me not to touch it, as it was her private property, and a friend of hers who did not speak any German would pick it up later. We were to speak English to him. Sieghardt and I both had an odd feeling about this bulky bundle and the announced friend. It was early afternoon, we were alone in the house, when we noticed a stranger standing at the garden gate. We immediately knew he was a man from the UNRRA (United Nations Relief and Rehabilitation Administration) barracks for displaced persons in nearby Düppel. (It was founded in November 1943 for non-German refugees.) We motioned him to come in and he shyly greeted us in perfect German with a slight Polish accent, and confirmed that he was from the UNRRA barracks and spoke very little English.

We led him into the kitchen, and upon seeing that unmanageable package, he asked if we would help him break it down into two smaller bundles that would be easier to carry because he had come on foot. Nothing could have pleased us more because we were dying to see what was in that mysterious monster package. We all crouched down on the kitchen floor and watched as he unpacked it. I was perplexed at the sight: beef, pork chops, bacon, coffee, butter, sugar and much more turned up. These were all the groceries I would have normally received in my kitchen. Dumbfounded, we helped him repackage everything into two bundles and he departed. If all of these items had been charged to the mess account, like the sugar had been previously, how was I going to account for all of these missing supplies! I had a sleepless night over this discovery.

The next morning all hell broke loose in the house as the mess sergeant came storming in right after breakfast and highly infuriated, screamed for me until she was heard throughout the whole building. When I showed up, she yelled that I would have dared to touch her private property when I had strict orders not to, and then continued to call me a variety of names. If looks were daggers, I would have been dead. I tried in vain to explain that the man yesterday had opened it himself, and the reason why, but she just shouted me down, ever increasing her volume. Then, she stomped out as briskly as she had come in, but not before vowing to get rid of me and to push me into the deepest levels of hell. I felt like I was there already.

What she didn't know was that one of the officers had not yet left, and he came downstairs into the kitchen to find out what the uproar was about. This was the quiet and polite French-American and since he waited for an answer, I gave him a run-down of the facts, just as they had occurred, without any personal comment on my part. He listened quietly, becoming more interested with each passing minute, and then left. I breathed a deep sigh of relief that the secrecy surrounding the shortage of kitchen supplies had been lifted without me having to accuse anyone. Again my guardian angel had not let me down. That was the last we saw of the female mess sergeant. From then on, the officers asked me for a shopping list, and they did their own food shopping as in the beginning.

Life around the house would have been calm and enjoyable if it had not been for the repeated requests from various American offices asking who had actually hired me since I did not seem to appear on anyone's list. I did not want to bother the officers with my problem because this might lead to them just hiring another cook with fewer troubles. So, my mysterious status kept hanging over me as an imminent calamity. I was always a nervous wreck as soon as a stranger entered the house through the front door, and quickly disappeared up the back staircase to hide in the attic. I was not to be found anywhere, and whoever came had to return some other time to solve their pending paper problem. With a throbbing heart I watched from my look-out as the exasperated official drove off again.

This cat and mouse game with OMGUS worked successfully for a while, but one day in mid-December, I was surprised by a visitor at the back door, and I was stuck. I received strict orders to appear at their OMGUS office. I dutifully promised to do so, although I had no intention of showing up in the near future. My immediate goal was to survive here in the warm house at least over Christmas where I could help keep food on the table for my family.

Mrs. Gall watched my desperation with growing interest as she sensed a problem with my working status. She was convinced that I was the one who was in trouble and not Sieghardt, though my presence had never discouraged her from flirting with him. I began to wonder if she was not the one behind all of these sudden investigations as a means of getting rid of me so she could have Sieghardt all to herself. Lately, she had been asking him to do all kinds of little favors for her around the house, and even in her room, such as fixing a drafty window or some other imagined defect. One night, she even knocked on our bedroom door around midnight claiming that she had lost her room key in the garden and wanted Sieghardt to come and help her look for it. Although we were already in bed, this did not stop her from pleading for his help. He finally got up and, suppressing a curse word, got dressed again, and went downstairs with her. He was back soon, murmuring, "This irksome Gall woman must not be quite right in the head." I never asked him why he said that or what really happened outside, but he did tell me that the key was lying openly right at the entrance to the garden.

Because I was not on anyone's employment list, I was not paid either, but I never raised the issue because the worthless German marks could not buy anything at the inflated prices. Black market prices were sky high, ruled by the American cigarette currency and coffee, worth thousands of marks. The struggle against starvation was still the immediate problem and everyone schemed and schemed to find ways to get enough food for their family's existence. I occasionally "paid" myself with a can of evaporated milk for Vita which Mutti diluted with water and then stretched it over several days and meals for her. Nobody could, and nobody did, live on the old starvation rations introduced by the Soviets and maintained under the Americans for three long years from 1945 to 1948. This is what fueled the black market.

With the brutally cold winter came the full force of the food crisis. Some additional American rations began to appear on the market very slowly, such as a 4-ounce chocolate bar for each member of the family once a month. When butter or other fat was unavailable in the stores, they substituted flour or sugar for our allotted quarter pound of butter for ten days. All food deliveries through the Soviet zone continued to be uncertain and people existed primarily on bread and potatoes. I was satisfied to be paid with modest meals for my sixteen hours of work each weekday and eight hours on Sundays.

The Polish-American officer, a suspicious and unsympathetic type, began to show up more and more between meals and would roam through the whole house, particularly upstairs where the other officers' private bedrooms were. Since he was not billeted there, we wondered why he would come around after all of the men had left the house. What was he after?

One day, the French-American officer asked me to take care of his little poodle while he was on a two-day business trip. The poodle ran around playfully both in the house and garden when I suddenly heard a terrified yelping from outside. I rushed to the scene and found the chow-chow attacking the shrieking poodle. I screamed for the Pole, who finally called his monster dog and I grabbed up the little poodle in my arms, who was still crying like a baby, and was relieved to find he had not been injured. The Pole pointed at his beast and said proudly in broken German, "*Gestern er hat gerissen eine Mann!*" (Yesterday he attacked a man.) It could have only been a German in the street. Torn clothing was irreplaceable, and to be wounded would be even worse.

I immediately took the poodle to my attic room for safety and when I returned, the Pole was sitting at the empty dining room table facing a large oil painting of my father-in-law on the opposite wall, making nasty cracks about it. Then, pounding his fist vehemently on the table, he was shouting, "Schwanenflügel, Schweinenflügel" (swan's wing, swine's wing). I was shocked and relieved that Sieghardt was not around to witness this vulgar scene in his own home because he had already gone through too much humiliation. His aristocratic family tree and coat of arms went back approximately eight hundred years, and during the Middle Ages, one of his forefathers had been the mayor of the town of Göttingen, where his home is still classified as a historical monument.

Mrs. Gall continued to take out her frustrations on me, but not for too much longer. She finally gave up chasing Sieghardt and asked OMGUS for another housekeeping position. She left shortly thereafter.

It was necessary to provide a valid reason for such a transfer, but we never found out what it was. It could have had fatal consequences for us. The new housekeeper assigned was Martha Malayka, a refugee from Upper Silesia, my homeland. She had fled the Soviets and was living with an elderly couple in Schlachtensee who had taken pity on her, but she now moved into the attic room vacated by Mrs. Gall. She was a sweet and quiet person, unmarried and in her late twenties. What a pleasant change from the hateful Mrs. Gall. I immediately became quite attached to her and we worked famously together. Since her last name was so melodious, we called her Malayka rather than Martha.

The Americans could now buy monthly rations for their German workers in the commissary, and our officers started to do this for Malayka and me. Each of us received a fairly large carton that contained items which were otherwise only available on the black market, such as flour, sugar, canned milk, shortening, powdered eggs and Spam. Although the Americans were sick of powdered eggs and Spam, they were a delicacy to us. There also was much more, including a small amount of real coffee, which was quite a treat, and a pack of chewing gum that I could have done without. Since we ate at work, my food ration from the *Amis*, the nickname for Americans, went to Mutti, and Malayka's went to the nice old couple who still kept a room for her, and were overjoyed at her thoughtfulness.

With the departure of Mrs. Gall and the arrival of Malayka, there was finally peace and tranquility in the house. Everything could have been simply wonderful if it wasn't for the constant nerve-wracking hide-and-seek game with OMGUS which was still going on with Christmas approaching. Finally, somebody in someone's office lost patience with my "forgetting" to show up as requested, and I received strict orders to appear on a specified day at their office in Dahlem. Again, I promised to do so with no intention of going. Shortly before the appointed date I called them up, and since the Christmas holidays were just around the corner, I politely requested a postponement until after Christmas with the excuse that I was too busy with all the Christmas preparations for the officers. To my surprise they agreed, perhaps only because of their own holiday plans, but at any rate, they gave me a final deadline date shortly after Christmas. As usual, I agreed and hoped that with their constantly changing personnel, my papers may get lost by then.

Holy Eve is a German tradition and our highest holiday in the entire year, but this time it would be a poor evening for my family without much food on the dinner plate. There were enough other worries. We had not heard from Günter since his last visit in the late autumn of 1944, and by now we feared the worst. What an eventful year and crazy life this had been so far, good weeks and bad weeks in rapid succession, but I wanted nothing more than to hold onto this uncertainty—the longer the better. To succeed, I had to live by the German proverb: *Der Himmel erhalte mir meine gesunden Ausreden.* Let heaven preserve my healthy excuses.

Christmas of 1946 arrived icy and cold. Each employee in the mess received several pieces of soap as a Christmas gift, which was a luxury because our German soap on ration cards was inadequate in both quantity and quality. The Americans followed the German tradition of the two days following Holy Eve, December 25 and 26, being holidays. There was not much time left to go see OMGUS. The officers had planned a New Year's Eve house party for over one hundred guests and I had to make all of the preparations, including baking all of the cakes and cookies. Mutti came to my assistance, and we worked through the hours when the rest of the world was sleeping. Standing there laboring over the kitchen stove I often thought of my dear grandmother who had bravely saved her family the same way, but about half a century ago. What a parallel.

At the very last moment, I nervously called OMGUS to let them know that I was responsible for this big New Year's party that American officers were giving for a hundred guests, and if the secretary insisted on my keeping the appointment, it would mean that the party preparations would have to cease. In my desperation I even had the audacity to suggest that she could call Colonel Wilson and discuss the urgency of their paperwork, hoping that a secretary would not dare to bother the Colonel about straightening out their records right now during the holidays just at the time he was preparing to give an important party. The secretary didn't know how to respond that quickly and I used her hesitation to hang up the phone. My hunch was correct, because no one ever called and I had temporarily escaped the bureau's control again since I didn't even get a new interview date for 1947. It was a new year with fresh hopes. This bitter cold winter couldn't last forever.

Now I concentrated on preparing for the big New Year's Eve party and I worked my tail off. For this major event I was permitted to hire Mutti as a kitchen help and Gerda as an extra waitress to assist Malayka. One of the chauffeurs took the message to her and she was happy to come, both to earn some money and to have a chance to visit with me. The chauffeurs were also most eager to volunteer to serve food trays, so, counting Sieghardt, we had a staff of nine people. With foresight I had asked official permission to feed all the hungry helpers before the party started, so we enjoyed a simple meal of soup and fried potatoes flavored with bacon and onions, the latest delicacy in Berlin, and we all ate well. By satisfying their hunger I hoped there would be less of a chance of food disappearing from my delectable platters between the kitchen and the dining room.

I had not seen Gerda for quite a while and during the meal we had a chance to catch up with the past. After her job as a construction laborer, she worked as a *Trümmerfrau* (rubble woman), one of those fifty thousand legendary women who salvaged bricks from the rubble and symbolized Berlin's revival. (In 1953, a rubble woman monument was unveiled in a public park in Berlin-Neukölln.) In April of 1946, the labor office agreed to let her attend a refresher course of several months as an interpreter at the international language school in Berlin-Wilmersdorf, where she passed all exams with flying colors in September. She finally received her denazification as a simple member of the BDM and was now allowed to do any kind of work again, although nothing was available at that time but construction work. So, she went back to heavy labor because she needed money to support herself.

She also updated us on life in downtown Berlin. On the Kurfürstendamm, where fancy restaurants once stood, there were now some isolated and expensive hot dog stands operating in the midst of the shells of buildings. The Kaiser Wilhelm Gedächtniskirche (Emperor William Memorial Church) which was constructed in the 1890s, now a ghostly ruin, still stood there as a reminder of the horrors of war. (Once it had been the high society church of the city.) The Soviets had already started to demolish the bomb-damaged Hohenzollern City Palace, their royal residence from 1441 to 1918. (It could have been salvaged, but the Soviets wanted to clear the way for their new Red Square, renamed Marx Engels Platz.) We were stunned and not aware of this distressing news since Mutti and I never went downtown.

The first guests started to arrive around 8 p.m. and I soon noticed that the chauffeurs detoured through the entrance hall to carry the trays from the kitchen to the party rooms. The furniture there had drawers and it didn't take me long to figure out that I was better off not knowing what "new" contents these drawers held as the chauffeurs were discreetly hoarding some food from the trays to be retrieved later to take home to their hungry families. Since these pilferages were very minimal, I pretended not to notice, being fully aware of the food crisis and the suffering from malnutrition. Mutti stood tirelessly at my side for endless hours. All in all, we were a dependable and successful team, working productively hand in hand through the entire night. The party was a smashing success and we were highly praised for our untiring efforts.

In the early hours of New Year's Day, one of the officers came to the kitchen with a carton of Lucky Strike cigarettes and gave each of us a pack as payment for our work in preparing and serving at the party, keeping the tenth pack for himself. Since a carton of cigarettes had a black market value of 600 marks ($150), he figured that each of our staff of nine had been paid 60 marks ($15). Mutti took both of our packages home to Papa who, like many men, started smoking a pipe during the hungry times. Before he used good cigars with a beautiful aroma, but now the pipe contained an incredible mixture of ingredients that bore no resemblance to tobacco. These undefinable fillings also had names in the colloquial language like "once across the Grunewald," (a popular forest), which meant that common dry leaves were used. Another term was "homesteaders' pride," a collection from different garden plants, not necessarily related to tobacco at all.

Poor, half starved Gerda did not survive the party too well. She made the same mistake that I did the first night of my visit to Sieghardt when he was living at Mrs. Koch's farm in Gröna. With hungry eyes, she had stuffed herself on the soup and fried potatoes before the party started, and then kept sampling all the other goodies afterwards and in between. Shortly after midnight her stomach went on strike and she became one very sick person. I saw to it that she was at least present in the kitchen long enough to receive her important pack of cigarettes, but she was far too sick to make the journey home. Although it was forbidden to provide shelter for strangers in the house, Gerda was not a stranger to me so I secretly took her upstairs to our attic room and let her sleep on the couch. Luckily our badly-needed private toilet was close by. For days, the only food she could tolerate was dry toast and black tea, and Malayka and I shared the task of looking after her until she was strong enough to return home.

Before she left I wanted to know what had happened to her family. I knew that her father, the chief psychiatrist at an institute for the mentally retarded in Domjüch, was suddenly transferred in 1944 to the little town of Hagenau-Land, West Mecklenburg, as a district medical officer. The Nazis had taken over the institution, "relocated" all the mental patients to an unknown destination (disabled Germans were expendable as a non-productive population), and changed the place into a sanitarium for lung disease. After the British had withdrawn, the Soviets took over the district of Mecklenburg. Her father, as a government official, had to become a Nazi Party member, which now made him an outcast, she said. "He was stripped of his salary and all rights to his pension.

So far, her parents had survived in two small rooms and her father had started again as a general practitioner, but a Communist who he had once refused to hire at Domjüch, reported him to Soviet authorities as a pro-Nazi and anti-Communist. Anybody could easily be accused of anything so long as it appealed to the Soviets. Her father's life was being threatened, and all because of an unjust accusation. So, rather than to involve his wife in the continued persecution, he committed suicide by taking poison. When Gerda's mother returned from an errand, she found his body with a heartbreaking letter he had left to her. But, even after the funeral, the Communists continued to persecute her by saying her husband was not dead but merely in hiding. I was shocked. Now, Gerda's problem was trying to get her mother out of the Soviet zone and I promised to help her find a way.

Although Germany was currently under a Four-Power status, the city of Berlin was treated as a separate area, or a fifth entity. It was not part of any other zone, least of all the Soviet zone surrounding us. We were sort of an "Island City" in the "Red Sea" and Moscow was ready to swallow us any day. We Berliners, already called "The Islanders," fought for our survival amid the growing tensions of the East-West conflicts. Radio Berlin, exclusively Soviet dominated, called itself "The Voice Of The Truth," and pounded on us non-stop in the German language with

Moscow propaganda. The Western Allies had no access to Radio Berlin, so to counteract this, they established their own German language radio station called RIAS (Radio In the American Sector). Its daily broadcast in the German language provided a powerful voice of truth and freedom around the clock to the Germans, particularly the 18 million in the East who lived under constant distorted Communist propaganda. The Soviets naturally tried to jam RIAS, which resulted in both sides continually raising their wattage. It was quite a battle. In this way, RIAS became one of the strongest stations in Europe at that time and by far the most popular station in Berlin, capturing 96 percent of the radio listeners, which included Mutti and Papa, who listened to it every day.

In mid-January of 1947, we had a house party for about thirty people. The French-American officer was out of town that day and the Polish-American officer, who was billeted in Nikolassee, had not been invited. So far we didn't have to fear his mean dog. The party was in full swing when Malayka whispered to me, "The Pole just tiptoed into the house and went upstairs into the bedroom of the absent Frenchman." That was very suspicious. What is he doing there now, we asked ourselves, and how do we handle such a snoop? We discussed the Pole's action with Sieghardt and he and a chauffeur came up with a joint plan. The four of us sneaked up the back staircase in the dark which ended not far from the French-American officer's bedroom. The door was closed, but we knew the Pole was in there, so we threw open the door and stepped inside. The Pole was kneeling on the floor in the dark, using a flashlight to go through papers in the Frenchman's desk drawers, now wide open, which had been safely locked before, like everything in the house here lately. We had wondered about that sudden change. Caught red-handed, he yelled, "What are you doing here? Out with you!" Flipping on the light, Malayka told him we had to check all of the upstairs windows to make sure they were closed because it may rain that night. "You can see that they are closed," he blurted out furiously, but in a greatly subdued voice, obviously avoiding people's attention from the party downstairs. We retreated, mission successfully accomplished in less than ten minutes.

Shortly thereafter, we watched the Pole pussyfooting out of the house again, being careful to avoid everyone at the party. This left us with the problem of what to do about the situation since no American had noticed what had been going on right under their noses. How would we let the French-American officer know about the Pole intruder in his bedroom since it was an unpardonable sin for a German to accuse one member of the American military against another?

Malayka and I were alone in the kitchen the next morning when the Frenchman stopped in late for breakfast. I mentioned rather casually, "last night the Polish gentleman was here to pick up the papers out of your desk drawer that you wanted him to have." "What?" he burst out, and then regaining his self-control, said, "Oh yes, the papers, now I remember." We knew better. Malayka added a lengthy apology for barging into his room because of the window check. The Frenchman listened very attentively to every detail and then left hurriedly, even forgetting about his breakfast. We never saw the Pole again, which was good riddance. I was always suspicious of him and felt sure that he must be some kind of a double agent. Our alert action had a lasting impact on the officers in the house and from then on, nothing was locked as it was in the beginning. We finally were free of any suspicion because the officers knew by now who their real friends were.

We Berliners were very aware of the clash of interests between the U.S. and the Soviet Union. Dubious people from eastern areas poured unchecked into our western sectors by way of the Soviet-controlled S-Bahn. Suspicion was the order of the day and for our own survival, we Berliners had to be on the alert to weed out those who had been planted here from the East. No one seemed to have an answer as to how many schooled agents slipped through each other's screening process here in their main battle field of counter espionage. Whether Germans and Americans loved or hated each other, they could not do without one another as the escalating rivalry between the U.S. and Soviet Union threatened to become a new political conflict. Seemingly the war had never ended for us in Berlin.

But I myself was without any friends when near the end of January 1947, OMGUS remembered me again. This time it was a threatening phone call to let me know that if I didn't show up the next day, they would send a car to take me to their office in Dahlem. They had finally nailed me down. I was at the end of my wits, and very frightened.

There is a similarity between my job status in my own country at that time, and an employed illegal alien in America today. At best, one remained unknown. There was also one fringe benefit. Since I was not officially employed, I escaped the obligatory monthly venereal disease examinations required of all women working for the U.S. forces. At least the grim winter was half over already. This time I definitely had to show up. Finished with the cat and mouse game, I had no Aladdin's magic lamp to grant my wishes for further survival. Tomorrow I had to go to the "woodshed" hoping for forgiveness.

Right after breakfast the next morning, I took off by bus to Dahlem to meet my deadline and arrived shortly thereafter at the ominous OMGUS office. With a throbbing heart I sat in the corridor in rivalry with many others who were unemployed and hungry, waiting to be called for interrogation to be accepted for any of the highly desirable jobs for the Americans. Would I still have my cooking job after this scary interview? I was scared to death when my name was finally called and I entered a large room that was full of desks with an American secretary sitting behind each one. Since I was obviously expected, they all looked up and stared at me as if I were someone from outer space. I was ordered in front of one of the desks that was cluttered with papers and files, and the secretary had my file right on top. She did not invite me to sit down, and as I stood there, she sized me up and down from head to toe, as if I were a captured criminal. She heaped accusations on me for obviously avoiding to show up many months ago as ordered. Numb with fear, I only half understood what she was saying, but it was obvious that she hated Germans, especially German women, because too many American men had already married them, the so-called American after-war-brides.

I was ordered to fill out a long questionnaire right in front of her so I started to answer the questions. Married? "Yes." There was no further question about the husband. That took a big load off my mind. Member of the Nazi Party? "NO." BDM? "NO." Women's League? "NO." Labor Service? "NO." She watched me suspiciously and pointed an accusing finger at all of my capital "NO's" as if I was supposed to correct a false statement. But I made no move to change anything and she snapped at me, "So, you have performed a miracle! Impossible! Others have told me already that everyone under your Hitler had to be in at least one of these organizations. How do you explain that you are the only exception?" I could have tried in my limited school English, given the chance, but she just kept talking and never gave me the opportunity, sarcastically asking, "How can your statements be true?" And she was lying in wait for my confession. The tension was high and with my good conscience I silently looked her straight in the eye, well aware that I had no chance to win an argument with her. Just the fact that I was a German made me untrustworthy. For her we all were Nazis from the cradle on.

Since I made no move to change any of my "NO's", she continued with a harsh laugh and said, "Do not deceive me by lying. All Germans are liars!" For years I had heard that, and all of the other secretaries, being all ears, nodded their heads. She wrote a long note on her paper as I stood there waiting and saying nothing, then indicated that our meeting was over, and ordered me to sit on a chair against the wall directly opposite her desk. I sat there on pins and needles expecting the worst to happen while she continually watched me out of the corner of her eye. I knew I had to hold out, no matter what. I was well aware of how desperate and precarious my situation was. My cooking was the sheet anchor the entire family was dependent on. Looking down at my hands folded in my lap, my eye caught my wedding ring and this was a new dilemma, because if I kept it on it might attract the attention of the judge who would ask me about my husband. That would definitely be the end. But, to take it off might be too suspicious because my file showed that I was married. Maybe I should best keep the ring on, and my hands under the table during the ultimate cross-examination.

While I was trying to decide what to do, a door opened at the far end of the hall and my name was called to enter for questioning. I began to slowly walk toward the open door while hastily whispering to my guardian angel for assistance, and having the uncomfortable feeling of being on trial. Upon entering the room, the door behind me was immediately closed. This is it, I thought and found myself facing an enormous desk with a stack of papers, and behind it sat a tall gentleman in a military uniform. What luck, a man, not another American female again. After a friendly "Hello" he offered me a seat across from his desk. Now I was finally confronted by my judge and I glanced up at him and found myself looking into the face of a polite and friendly gentleman, no monster at all. What a relief. He immediately started a casual conversation about how beautiful Germany was. This did not seem like it was going to be the strenuous interview that I had been dreading and my intuition told me that his pleasant attitude was not a trap. In no time, we were in a friendly discussion, with me even talking with my hands to underscore my poor English, forgetting all about my wedding ring.

Suddenly he asked, "How do you like Switzerland?" Oh, I did, and I enthusiastically told him how much I enjoyed my visit to Neuchâtel in 1933, and as I talked, he settled back comfortably in his chair and just smiled and smiled, becoming more amused each minute. Nothing seemed to be new to him. All of a sudden it struck me that my vis-a-vis already knew that I had been in Switzerland in a boarding school fourteen years ago and probably everything else about my life history as a result of a painstaking and intensive investigation. Therefore, he knew that I had nothing to hide other than the fact that I had been ignoring the ordered interviews with him for the past few months. Still smiling, he stood up and informed me that I had passed the interview and was now officially employed. Words couldn't express the relief I felt and I had a sudden impulse to hug him and give him a big kiss, but I knew better. Instead, he gave me a warm German handshake with a friendly and well pronounced *Auf Wiedersehen*, and then guided me out through a special door so I would not have to meet any secretary. What I had dreaded for so long had turned out very well, and I felt like a released prisoner as I stepped out on the street.

With a thrill of fulfillment, I felt like singing, despite my poor voice. "All is endured. I can return to my work!" This meant picking up my daily treadmill, working seven days a week from early morning to late at night (seventy to eighty hours a week), putting up with all kinds of people and their silly demands, with annoying gas and electricity shortages at unexpected times, struggling with the English language, and so far all this without any pay—but what a blessing. I could return to my cooking for my American mess in our own, but confiscated house, from which my in-laws were thrown out overnight in November 1945. This was now early 1947. Sieghardt was equally relieved when I gave him the good news about my legal employment status, and we now felt that our troubles were over. This was a new beginning. Wrong again!

I returned to my day-to-day chores, optimistic that nothing disturbing could happen anymore, but it turned out that this was just a false sense of security and the lull before the storm. Shortly after my interview at OMGUS, Captain Moutner placed a spirit stove on the kitchen table that worked with alcohol, and said, "This will be very useful for your work, especially when the gas and electricity are turned off." However, it turned out that his thoughtful gesture had an ulterior motive, because from then on I had to use his stove to supply him daily with extras for his private guests in the afternoon when the electricity was turned off. It wasn't long before the other members of the mess wondered again about their rapidly shrinking food supply, and I pointed out Captain Moutner's stove and the records I had kept of the food he requested, including the date, and the amount I had prepared for his private parties. The officers accepted my records and asked me from then on to hand in a record of any food used for private guests so that the individual could be charged for it. That quickly put an end to Captain Moutner's use of my kitchen supplies for his social life, but I was very relieved to see that he left the spirit-stove on the kitchen table.

One day the officers returned from a hunting trip and they threw a half dozen bloody wild rabbits on the kitchen floor, expressing disgust at eating them themselves. We could have their trophies! Splendid. This was ration-free meat and there was enough for everybody. Mutti got a whole rabbit with the fur still on, even though skinning a rabbit was going to be a new experience for her. The butcher would have kept half of the animal for his services. Malayka took her rabbit to the nice couple in Schlachtensee who were still keeping a room for her, and they were overjoyed at such an unexpected ration-free present. So far so good— but not for long.

I had noticed that the usually cheerful Malayka had seemed deeply disturbed lately, so one evening near the end of March I asked her if something was wrong. "Very wrong," she said, breaking into tears. "I am pregnant and have been deserted by the man who promised me heaven on earth and to take me to America. He has vanished without a trace. How can I raise a child alone as a refugee with no money, no home and no future? I fled the Soviets in Silesia for security here, and now this!" I was startled. What should I do? She was already at the end of her second month and an abortion in Germany in 1947 was a crime. I felt responsible to assist her because she had no one else except the old couple in Schlachtensee who was also heartbroken and tried to help. They had heard of a young doctor who was looking for business, but none of us had money and with the worthless German mark, currency existed of cigarettes and coffee. We had no cigarettes, but we did have coffee in the pantry. I asked her how much the young doctor demanded. "One whole pound," she said. That was an enormous amount with a price of 1500 *Reichsmark* on the black market. "I will swipe a tablespoon a day from our pantry stock until we have the quota together," I promised. "Will you do it, please?" and her lips quivered, even though she was deeply relieved.

We finally collected the necessary amount early in April and Malayka left to see this new young doctor that no one had ever heard of. He would perform the illegal abortion in the old couple's apartment, which did not sound very professional to me, but we had no choice. She was in good spirits when she left and it was agreed that she would return to our house after the procedure and lay in her bed upstairs, pretending to be sick, and I would take care of her.

I anxiously awaited her return, but became alarmed when a full day passed with no word until the frightened old couple showed up at the back door. They told me that everything had gone wrong. Too late I learned that the doctor turned out to be just a medical student who had attempted an abortion and then vanished leaving Malayka bleeding heavily. Out of the blue, the German police had showed up and demanded details and names, and in their desperation they lied that they knew nothing about the pregnancy. All they knew was that Malayka had left the house and then returned a few hours later, but they did not know what had happened in between. The police had not believed them, and they would come now to interrogate me, too. What a precarious situation. Because of me, the German police was going to be in a house confiscated by the Americans!

They arrived rather quickly, fortunately when none of the officers were home. I had to lie, too. "No, I didn't know that Malayka was pregnant." The police made no secret of the fact that they didn't believe me either. I did learn the good news that Malayka was now in the nearby hospital Waldfrieden under professional medical care, but was not doing so well. She had a high fever. I told the American officers that the housekeeper was ill in the hospital and that I was going to see her and find out what was wrong.

The hospital was within walking distance, and upon my arrival I could not find her in the regular patient rooms because this hospital, like all others, was overcrowded with cases of acute malnutrition and other diseases so typical of our public health situation. I was finally directed to an emergency bed that had been set up in a small office and thought that I was in the wrong room because, at first, I did not recognize Malayka. I was shocked how terrible she looked. The head of the bed was in front of a window, and against the light, her face looked very old and yellowish, with sweaty hair around it. But it was she. How much she must have suffered to look like this, and as I sat by her bedside holding her hand, she was so weak that she could barely speak. She just stared at me with a look that seemed to plead, "Help me!" A nurse pretended to be busy at a desk but really was all ears to pick up some information about whoever had butchered her so terribly. Her pregnancy had turned out to be an ectopic pregnancy which the medical student had not recognized, nor its complications. Had she sought professional help, she would have received a legal abortion for this type of pregnancy. I felt miserable and very guilty for my part in assisting her to have the illegal abortion which resulted in her present serious condition. I tried not to think about how much better she would have been off without my taking the coffee, as it is written: Thou shall not steal. Why, in our difficult times, did things never go well?

I was at a loss as to what to do next when I thought suddenly of the magic word, penicillin, the new wonder drug to treat infections. I turned to the nurse: "Does the hospital have any penicillin?" She shook her head, "No, not if you mean that new and expensive antibiotic that only the Americans use on a regular basis. It is not available to us Germans." I told Malayka that I would go home and talk to our officers about getting her some penicillin, and I will never forget her grateful look. Upon returning to the house, I told the officers that Malayka was seriously ill in the hospital and needed penicillin that only the Americans had. They all liked the quiet, lovable and polite Malayka, but penicillin was not something that you could get as easily as butter in the commissary. I urged them to try and help, but even with their friendly smiles, I knew there was not much hope.

In the midst of my concern about Malayka, another crisis caught up with us. Somehow the employment questionnaire Sieghardt had initially filled out suddenly popped up at OMGUS, revealing his former membership in the Nazi Party. We wondered if this might be the work of Mrs. Gall who sought revenge by having Sieghardt checked out again. As a result, on April 11, 1947, he promptly lost his privileged job that he had held with the Americans for over a year, which was the kind of punishment dealt out by the Americans for former Party members. I can't remember why he did not have to move out of our attic room immediately, but maybe it was because I was now legally employed as their cook and this had been Sieghardt's family home. We had brought our own furniture into the spacious quarters, such as a bed, mattress, couch and some smaller items. Now we ran the risk of punishment for taking them out again under the new OMGUS ruling that you are not allowed to remove anything from a confiscated house even though this was our own house and we owned everything in it. We decided to play it safe by "stealing" our furniture piece by piece and returning it to our apartment back on Limastrasse where it would be safe, without any foreboding that even this might be only a solution of brief duration. By now Mrs. Röhr had moved out again into a well-heated attic of the confiscated house of the officers' mess she was working for, and we stayed in close contact.

All in all, these were very hectic days trying to visit Malayka in the hospital while keeping up with my chores at the house and sneaking our belongings from the house back to the apartment. Also, Sieghardt had to appear at the unemployment office so that he could at least receive food ration cards, and was told that he was to work as a gardener in Zehlendorf-Mitte with the city park service for six months, starting May 12, 1947. Before that happened, I received a shocking phone call from the hospital. Malayka was not able to hold on any longer and had died. What a blow, although I had been afraid of that since my first visit to the hospital. What a tragic outcome. Was it my fault? Without my help she might have had a better chance. That guilty thought haunts me till today. Could my life ever be the way it had been before?

Viewings are not customary with Lutherans in Germany so the funeral was to be on April 20 at the cemetery in Nikolassee. Everybody was shocked and the chauffeurs had arranged for a beautiful wreath which they temporarily placed on the table in our entrance hall. Captain Beer returned from horseback riding and, taking a quick look at the wreath, asked me what it was for. Near tears, I told him that it was for Malayka who had died. He looked at me as if he couldn't remember who she was, and then uttered, "Oh, another German less, so what," and went whistling up the staircase to his bedroom. I felt like taking his head off for such a comment coming from someone who had been a German himself just a short time ago. All of the other officers were visibly moved and offered to let us go in their cars to the funeral. It was heartbreaking. I don't know who paid for the pastor, the coffin and the grave site (which one buys for twenty years in Berlin), or if it was ever paid for. Nobody had any money. Regardless, this was the last thing we could do for Malayka, and we saw to it that she was buried decently.

To add to our misery, on April 26, we received an eviction notice from our apartment on Limastrasse because of Sieghardt's membership in the former Nazi Party. Even though my parents owned the apartment building, we had to vacate to make room for a Polish family who did not want to return to Poland. We were given three days to leave and were ordered to remove nothing except our personal clothing. So, we got busy again and secretly moved some of our furniture into the garage of my parents' home again (back to Veronikasteig!), and we replaced some of it with old items to furnish our apartment. But where should we go ourselves? The Berlin Senate had already lodged a mother and her five-year old son in my parents' home, but Papa worked on another plan.

There were still two empty attic rooms on the other side of the apartment duplex on Limastrasse, number 3, that had a half bath between them, but they were not in the best of shape. So Papa asked our architect friend, Paul Thiemer, to get ahold of Mr. Falkenberg, who by now was retired, to have him close the open entrance in front of the two attic rooms with a door, thereby making a little hall. Thus a two-room apartment was created, but there was no kitchen or bathtub. Sieghardt moved in on May 1, and one week later, the Polish couple with two small children moved into our former apartment in building 3a. Although Polish, they had the German name of Rottenberg, and they turned out to be rotten. Without authorization, they took another Polish family in who also had two small children. Wet diapers were hanging everywhere to dry, and much later when they finally moved out again, the walls were covered with mildew from the constant dampness. In addition, they stole everything that they could pack, including the baking sheets and pans for the electric stove. We were still outlawed and powerless.

My officers' mess underwent changes, too. They had never hired a new housekeeper to replace Malayka and suddenly, the wife of one of the officers arrived from the States. That created several comical moments because the officers were afraid of what I might reveal if she would ask about their private lives here at the house. As expected, the wife was naturally interested in what had been going on because there were many stories of the American military and their German girlfriends. To everyone's relief, my English was obviously too "poor" to understand her discrete probing. The officers' marriages were not my problem because I had enough of my own, and I was glad we had endured here through that grim winter of 1946-47. Otherwise it would have been sheer hell. The American lady soon moved out with her husband to a confiscated villa on Limastrasse near the lake, and I had the sudden impulse to move out, too, since I could apply for another cooking job with OMGUS. So I left on May 10 with the last of our belongings and moved in with Sieghardt in our modest attic apartment. They hired a new cook who only lasted for a few days, I don't know why, and shortly thereafter, what remained of the mess was completely closed.

Sieghardt started his new job as a gardener with the city park service in Zehlendorf-Mitte. Vita stayed at Mutti's place where we all met for our meals. We had no other choice. But, with all of these hardships, we still pretended to be a contented family peacefully living our simple lives. One amazing fact of life is our constant human desire for a ray of hope. Around this time, while the dismantling of Germany was still in full swing, President Truman had lifted the embargo for mail and packages to Germany, so Papa received a letter from a distant relative in New York who wanted to know if we had survived and did we need help? Then came the news that we had been so anxiously awaiting for so long. Johanna, Günter's wife, received an old postcard from him that had been written in a prisoner of war camp in Larissa, Greece, which had been mailed by the Red Cross. It said:

"My Dear Johanna:

I am alive and healthy.

Best wishes for your birthday and Christmas.

Thousand kisses to you, Dagmar and Helke.

Your Günter

16 November 1944"

Where was Larissa, anyway, and why had it taken over two years for the postcard to arrive? We found it on the map, a city in Thessaly about thirty-two air miles south of Mount Olympus. After the first joy of receiving the news, Mutti spoke out loud what we all had been thinking and were afraid to mention: "Why haven't we heard from him since, or, why didn't he somehow get word to us?" That thought terrified us all, but we assured each other that there was hope for his late return. A shadow had fallen upon the good news. Günter and I had been very close all of our lives and I always remember his last visit in June of 1944 as if it were yesterday—the heartbreaking picture of how he waved his last good-bye before he quickly turned away. Could he have had a strange premonition then that it would be his turn one day? Why was our life so different from the good endings that always occur in fairy tales?

Mutti and Papa during the war.

Mutti (with Vita) during the hungry times after the war, just a few years later—much more gaunt looking.

After the War,
the Battle to Live

My new appointment with OMGUS was on May 16, 1947. With great expectations I sat on a staircase outside of the conference room together with other job seekers when a lady came to sit beside me. To my surprise, she was the wife of our pharmacist who had so generously provided me with "baby oil" back in 1943 which I used as ration-free cooking oil. Amused, I reminded her of my experience with her husband, but she just looked at me sadly and said, "You don't know?" I shook my head. "Know what?" She continued in a low voice, "My husband was called to the Volkssturm in March of 1945 and was killed practically in front of our pharmacy on April 1 by the Soviets during the last ditch defense of Berlin. I am now alone, trying to feed my six children with our starvation rations." So, in desperation, she was applying for a job just as I was.

I was shocked. At the exact moment when my pharmacy friend was killed outside, I had sat trembling in our basement. I shuddered. What a tragic ending for this warm and compassionate man. I was at a loss what to say, other than "I am sorry." Just then, my name was called for an interview, so I squeezed her hand and we promised to stay in touch.

To my relief, I found that the entire American clerical staff had been replaced by our own personnel and I was interviewed by a friendly German secretary who praised my excellent recommendations and promised to find me a similar position. However, she asked that I accept a temporary assignment for just one day with a nearby American family to help out with the cooking. Since working for an American family would be a new experience, I readily agreed. She called the lady of the house to let her know I was coming and then gave me the address.

Upon arriving at a luxurious residence which had been confiscated for the American family, the lady of the house coolly sized me up before even inviting me in, and then took me straight to the kitchen. From there, I could see a big tomcat in the garden chasing birds and a boy about six years old chasing the cat. She gave me strict instructions as to what she wanted for dinner which was to be served punctually at 6 p.m. when her husband would be home. I was not used to such a cool atmosphere, but it was only for one day, so I cheerfully began to prepare dinner in the unfamiliar kitchen under her watchful eye as she casually, but a little too often, passed through the kitchen. When it was time to set the dining room table, I took the place settings from the buffet drawer and noticed that there was a ten-cent chocolate bar partially hidden under the silverware. I immediately suspected that I was being tested, which became more evident as I found more chocolate, and even a dollar bill.

I did not fall into her trap and after the dinner was over, she praised my work and my manners, which was followed by an order that I was to move into their attic room the next day and be available to them at all times. The big tomcat would be locked in with me overnight. She did not seem to know that a cat has a strong will of its own and chooses his sleeping quarters himself, most likely not shut up with a stranger. She also had apparently forgotten that I was only a substitute for that day, and I carefully objected that I had a small child and husband at home. She brushed this off with, "Other husbands did not even come home from the war, but yours did, so now you have to sacrifice and be without him." Finito. To her, the matter was closed, and I was ordered to be there punctually at 8 a.m. the next day. I just smiled politely because I knew I would not be back. She did not want a cook, she wanted a servant who would take care of everything around the clock including the cooking, cleaning, house and garden, child and cat. I was in a hurry to get out of there, feeling that she must have never had a maid in the U.S. since she didn't seem to know what to reasonably expect from a servant as Mutti had taught me when we had our own maid for years, the wonderful Lotte.

Instead, early next morning I went back to OMGUS and related my experience of the previous day. I found that this was a common occurrence and no one had ever agreed to stay in that household more than one day. While we were talking, a call came from the lady of the previous day, furiously reporting that I had not shown up for work. She was informed that yesterday was just a one-day emergency fill-in, and these short temporary assignments would continue until the office could find a suitable cook to assign on a full-time basis.

The secretary gave me a new position in a household of three officers on Hüningerstrasse, in Berlin-Lichterfelde West, not too far from Zehlendorf. Since everything had gone so smoothly, I was dying to find out what kind of phony reason Rosemarie Gall had given last year when she quit her job so abruptly at our officers' mess on Veronikasteig. So, before leaving, I casually asked how Mrs. Gall was and where she was working now. At first, the secretary did not seem to remember her. "Gall?" But after I mentioned where and when we worked together, she reacted with, "Oh, that one. She was a little strange, but don't worry about her because she is no longer with us." I did not dare ask any further questions, especially why I should not worry about her, so I never did find out what false story she might have made up in her vengeful effort to hurt Sieghardt and me. Her actions could have cost both of us our jobs, and I couldn't wait to tell Sieghardt about it, particularly the "don't worry about her" part.

That same day, Saturday, May 17, 1947, I went directly from OMGUS to my new position which was in a townhouse. The housekeeper, Mrs. Doberke, let me in. She seemed much older than I, very friendly, and showed me to a well-stocked kitchen where I immediately started to prepare my first dinner. At 6 p.m., three young, polite and very hungry officers arrived for dinner and highly praised my cooking. Then the conversation turned to my bicycle which they had noticed outside, my only mode of transportation, rain or shine. They decided that I should have a pass for the free use of the frequently-running American buses which would facilitate my coming in the morning and going home in the evening. How thoughtful! I knew there was a bus stop right around the corner from my house. Already the next day I was given my new unlimited pass.

It did not take long before one of the officers made a remark about my shoes being most unsuitable for standing in the kitchen all day. I agreed with him and gave a lively picture of how the nasty mess sergeant would never buy any for me. He shook his head, half amused and half amazed that the Germans always take the word "no" literally, and blindly follow orders instead of standing up for their rights. Of course he didn't remember that we had none, according to the U.S. government. Instead of debating that, I gave him my shoe size.

The very next day, the officers presented me with a pair of women's black leather walking shoes, and to their delight, I put them on immediately—and they hurt like hell. The American women generally have narrower feet than we Germans, so the shoes were very tight. Of course I couldn't ask that they exchange them for a wider width. Impossible. Men hate such a chore. Instead, I pretended that they were just perfect and offered to pay for them, which was promptly rejected. This was a present to keep their cook on her feet. That night, Sieghardt worked to stretch my new shoes while I nursed my sore feet and first blisters. Hopefully one day the shoes would get used to me and I to them. Anyway, I was the proud owner of a new pair. Taking the American bus was a relief, too. The work and atmosphere were very pleasant.

On June 18, 1947, the mess unexpectedly moved to a big villa in Dahlem on Hirschsprung 22. Luckily, I moved with them, but not the nice Mrs. Doberke who had finally found a job in her old secretarial line. The new location would be no problem because my American bus pass would take me free of charge wherever the Americans were. But what would the new housekeeper be like? I met her the same day, a Mrs. Leue, and she was fortunately a warm and pleasant woman who was anxiously waiting for her husband to return from the war. In addition to our mess with three officers, there was a second one in this house that consisted of a colonel and his cook, Mrs. Caravias, who owned the villa next door. By working for a generous man, she was able to put food on the table for her teen-aged daughter and herself. She was a widow whose husband had been a bank owner, and she, Mrs. Leue and I formed a lovely trio.

One day at noon, the three of us went next door to her villa for coffee and a snack since none of our officers ever came home for lunch. There, to my great enjoyment, I met Erna Berger, the famous opera singer. Her home had been completely bombed out and she now was comfortably residing on the entire first floor of the villa. I had admired her in many operas and she was as lovely and attractive in person as on stage. In our unstable postwar time, the road to recovery was so slow that it seemed we would never return to those times we once knew, like attending the opera and having a private life.

An old gentleman softly knocked on our back door one evening, holding in his hands a big sterling silver tray with a matching three-piece coffee set. He was thin and consumed with grief, but even in his ragged clothing, I could tell he was a gentleman and obviously starving in his elegant old house. It was not uncommon for Germans to offer their sterling silverware and other treasures at the doors of American households in exchange for food. He told me that he and his wife lived close by and they did not know how to survive with both of them having the lowest ration card, everything lost, the banks being closed and their children not home from the war. He urgently begged me to ask the officers to give him food in exchange for his silver. I could identify with his situation because it was similar to what my own parents would be going through if I was not cooking at these officer messes with fringe benefits. It was a valuable silver set, probably a family heirloom, and I promised to do my utmost right away.

It was just after dinner and the officers were all in the living room, a fitting moment, when I displayed the silver service and told them about the gentleman at the back door. They all admired the set and recognized its value, but none wanted to take it away from the old gentleman. They were not black market dealers as were so many others, but they did want to provide him with some food. They offered the set to me, but I didn't want it either. I had a similar one at home, so we returned it to the old man and provided him with plenty of food. I will never forget his look of gratitude when I gave him back his beautiful possession, together with a big package of food, and even some coffee. He was close to tears as he was trying to carry it all home. That was our good deed for the day and we felt elated helping others, too, with what we were fortunate to have every day. But, good days were scarce, and it seemed that there was always some misfortune just around the corner.

One day, Mutti told me that she had a dream: she had a vision of Günter standing with his back to her on a large wooden raft floating on the water. Then, he turned around and it was not Günter at all. She was very upset and finally said, "Günter will never return. First my brother in World War I and now my only son." What could I say to comfort her? He was my only brother and I had a flashback of the moment of his last goodbye on Limastrasse as he turned back in the door with that sad face and waved one more time. "Oh, Mutti," I said quickly, "this is only a dream. Günter will still come back." She only shook her head, trying to hold back the tears. But how can one live without any hope?

I also had not given up hope for Sieghardt's future life. The Allies had established the so-called German *Spruchkammern,* or special tribunals, all over Berlin to provide a judicial hearing for minor denazification cases. According to the Allied denazification laws, offenders were classified into five groups, based on their position and rank in the Party hierarchy, and were subject to various penalties. These classifications were:

    I.   *Hauptschuldige* (major offenders)
    II. *Belastetete* (offenders)
    III. *Minderbelastete* (lesser offenders)
    IV. *Mitläufer* (followers)
    V. *Entlastete* (exonerated persons)

Sieghardt fell into the minor denazification category, and cases, names and dates of hearings were announced on a public billboard. He was scheduled for an oral trial in the town hall in Zehlendorf on November 13, 1947 between 9 a.m. and noon in conference room 172. Before the trial, all persons over age eighteen had to fill out an extensive questionnaire—that of the Americans was the most voluminous. In view of the hundreds of thousands of small cases, amnesty could be granted to have the defenders return to productive work as quickly as possible. However, there was a drastic variation in judgements among the courts because of conflicting local rules. This created inequalities in the sentences of the accused. Our American sector was especially severe compared to the English and French ones.

Sieghardt's case was supposed to be a public hearing, but when we arrived, the only people allowed to be present in the courtroom was the assigned public prosecutor, and a lawyer with his two assistants, all Germans. Even I was ordered to leave the room, but I insisted on staying since I was his wife. With a look that could kill the judge ordered me to sit on a bench in the rear of the room. But, the prosecutor threatened that if I opened my mouth just once, I would be evicted from the courtroom. This court already was notorious for its unfavorable and prejudicial judgment in many other denazification proceedings, so I had a sinking feeling that Sieghardt was in trouble. Here every German was guilty until proven innocent, just the reverse of normal law.

The hearing started with Sieghardt standing before the officials who were comfortably seated behind an enormous desk. Immediately, he was accused of being a bad pro-Nazi and linked to generalized accusations, although the judge provided no specifics to back them up. These were obviously trumped up charges because the questionnaire that lay in front of the judge showed that Sieghardt was a compulsory member of the National Socialist Cavalry Corps (NSKK), which was a most non-political establishment within the Nazi Party. He had qualified for membership in the NSKK only because of his civilian experience in horseback riding, and was assigned such a subordinate position with no special function or authority that the only things he ever commanded were horses. He should have been classified as a "follower" which was defined under Allied Control Council directive number 38, dated March 1946, as a person, "who was not more than a nominal participant in, or supporter of, the national socialistic tyranny…and did no more than pay membership fees, participate in meetings where attendance was obligatory…." But, Sieghardt was never given a chance to testify in his own defense.

The penalties for so-called Nazi crimes were determined by the individual tribunals with widely varying interpretations of the Allied denazification laws, and the sentence meted out to Sieghardt could not have been more unjust. He stood there silent and stunned as he heard the verdict relegate him to a second class-citizen status with no voting rights and allowed only to hold positions of menial labor for an indefinite period. He was also fined. Shaken and with disbelief, Sieghardt said, "I have no money."

This was countered by the judge with, "You are wearing a winter coat, aren't you? Well, sell it!"

"But this is my only coat," Sieghardt objected.

The judge cut him off in a cold impartial tone he had practiced in thousands of similar cases. "That's not the court's concern."

Suddenly, there was a commotion outside and the courtroom door was forced open before the attendant guarding it could prevent it. A lady stormed in, with the guard on her tail, and demanded to make a statement in this case. It was Mrs. Döblitz, the former employee of Stempelkaiser, who had written that mysterious postcard to us just before the end of the war. The judge, certain that she would be giving first-hand evidence against Sieghardt, encouraged her to speak up. However, when she began telling her story of how Sieghardt protected her and other Jewish-related employees against radical Nazi workers, the judge immediately interrupted her and bellowed, "Do you speak for or against the accused?"

"Naturally I speak for him because I have known him for many years, and as a matter of fact..."

She got no further because the judge yelled, "Out, out with you. Not one word more!"

"But I want to speak in his defense," she insisted, and upon that she was rudely shoved out of the courtroom. Sieghardt's guilty sentence had been decided before the hearing had begun and the judge did not want to hear any evidence to the contrary from an expert witness.

I could not believe what I had just seen. The trial was declared over— a true "kangaroo court." The verdict was final and not subject to review (as under Hitler). The court wasted no time in ordering us to leave, and we met Mrs. Döblitz and other former Stempelkaiser employees outside who were embittered and frustrated to be so powerless against our new "judicial system." Sieghardt was punished so unreasonably due to the court's immense power. Was our new legal system going to continue the same prejudice, discrimination and abuse of justice that we had experienced under Hitler? Was one tyranny replaced with another? Who was going to protect us now against ourselves and German judges like these?

However, about a year later, some of these judges finally came to their senses when it was noted that many high ranking Nazi officials had received very light or no sentence at all while the "Party nobodies" like Sieghardt received unjustified high penalties for things they were not even guilty of. As a result, Sieghardt's verdict was reviewed and he regained his citizen's right to vote, but still was restricted to employment involving only menial work for an indefinite period.

By now the Stempelkaiser firm was making efforts to reopen again and Sieghardt was badly needed there. What a lucky coincidence. Just when we thought we could breathe freely again, it turned out to be another delusion. He was even forbidden to work in his own family's firm. Where should he work now? Friends of ours owned a bookstore dealing primarily with medical books. After being bombed out in downtown Berlin, their business was re-established in their own spacious villa just around the corner from us. They offered Sieghardt employment as a messenger boy and packer because his denazification sentence prevented him from holding a position as a salesperson. Even though they willingly would have hired him in a more meaningful position, it was too dangerous because one of the other employees may have reported this violation of his sentence. So, he was relegated to pushing carts heavily loaded with book packages to the local post office every day and performing other menial tasks around the store. It was a tremendous disillusionment to now be the same type of ordinary worker that he used to hire when he was a junior executive of Stempelkaiser, his family's firm. Under Hitler he had protected Jewish-related employees against strong Nazi attacks. Now he was an outcast himself, but he accepted this humiliation with grace and dignity.

Nothing seemed to last too long in our endless unpredictable time, and now it was my turn to be faced with change. One of the officers in our mess suddenly left for the States and his replacement, Colonel Borno, decided to move the mess on December 1, 1947, to a villa on Grunewald Allee 10. Although this new location was closer to home, it meant that I had to say good-bye to my lovely cooking trio and hello to another housekeeper at the new location. This time it was a Mrs. Winkler, a widow from World War I who was still awaiting the return of her only son from World War II. She was level-headed and congenial, and we would make a great team.

The villa was huge with a very spacious kitchen in the basement that had two large windows above ground level and an exit to the garden. Next to it was a laundry room big enough for drying clothes, and a large coal cellar which was filled to capacity with solid briquettes. I couldn't believe what I was looking at, which was the dream of every freezing Berliner. Mrs. Winkler told me that she took one or two briquettes home every night and I realized that I would need more than that to keep my entire family just minimally warm. Right away I remembered my big, sturdy bag at home in which I could carry several briquettes easily. What a temptation.

I immediately talked to one of my officers about the treasure in the basement and my need. He said I could do as I pleased in the basement, but if I ever got caught, he would not be able to protect me due to the still valid Eisenhower order against assistance. That was a good and honest deal for me. I would start the next day with acquisitions from my new source of warmth. So, I brought my big sturdy bag from home, and since no one showed up for lunch, I was able to take some home at noon on the American bus and also at quitting time in the evening. This way my family could get a little support for a better life, and that was the only thing that mattered.

The officers' laundry turned out to be another great advantage. Mrs. Winkler was in charge of it and making any necessary minor repairs to their clothing. There was plenty of hot water and an abundance of good detergent for the washing machine, which I noted, not without envy, because we barely had warm water at home let alone soap. Soap was available only of poor quality and in meager amounts on a ration card. Mrs. Winkler was well aware of what we had to put up with and suggested that I bring Sieghardt's shirts and other laundry from home since she had to run the washing machine every day anyway. What a splendid offer and an enormous help. She also took care of the officers' shoe repairs, carrying them to and from the American shoemaker, so she asked if I also needed some repaired. What a question! Sieghardt's shoes consisted of more holes than soles. People tried to reinforce their shoe soles by improvising with layers of newspapers inside. Right away, I brought in a run-down pair which she placed on the kitchen staircase, with the gaping holes facing up. Soon, one of the officers came down, stopped, looked at them in disbelief and then exclaimed, "What on earth are those? These certainly are not MY shoes!" No, definitely not and the housekeeper quickly explained that they belonged to the cook's husband. Our need for just the bare necessities was common knowledge. He turned to Mrs. Winkler. "Put them on my repair bill."

After the shoe incident, the officer explained the real reason for coming down to the kitchen. He wanted to ask us if, instead of the usual monthly German ration of many little tidbits, we would prefer the kind of food we needed most for the same amount of money. What a generous offer. I immediately knew what I wanted and asked for a big Army can of powdered eggs for Mutti. This was granted, but since it didn't use up all of the money allowance, I was encouraged to add more items, which I gladly did: either some bacon, butter, sugar, flour or whatever was available. Mrs. Winkler asked for the same, and the officer made some notes and departed.

The next day, our kitchen looked like Christmas morning, even though it was weeks away. The table was loaded with all of our wishes, plus some additional items, including a little coffee. We couldn't believe our eyes. After serving breakfast and expressing our thanks, the officers told us that one of their German chauffeurs would deliver the food supplies to Mutti's and Mrs. Winkler's homes. They did not want us to leave the house carrying them since Germans with large bundles were occasionally stopped and searched, and officially, we were not allowed to carry home American food. We felt that we had never had it so good, and Mutti was overwhelmed by the treasures that were delivered; what a stockpile for future meals.

The holidays were approaching, my second Christmas with the Americans, but this year it was different. The officers were all Americans born in the United States who were of high rank and very generous and thoughtful. They were in a foreign country far away from their family and friends, so Mrs. Winkler and I decorated the house according to German Christmas tradition, trying to make it as cozy and homey as possible for them. The officers deeply appreciated our efforts and announced that they would have more guests than usual, but this posed no problem for the two of us, for we all understood that we were living under drastically changing circumstances. The day before Christmas Eve, they came down to the kitchen with their arms full of containers of chocolates, candy and all kinds of food that was still the most valued commodity for Christmas 1947. We were overwhelmed, and as I looked at that pile of goodies on the table, I suddenly realized that here were my presents for my family.

My dear mother-in-law had a sweet tooth. She recently had made a deal with an American soldier. In exchange for a large, valuable 15-inch sterling silver bowl, he brought a 10 pound Army sack of sugar. But she had felt cheated. These ten American pounds were only nine German pounds. (The American pound is only 454 German grams, and not 500!) In vain she argued with him about the discrepancy in weight. Secretly she ate the sugar with a teaspoon, mostly to kill the hunger pangs. With her sense of humor she gave me a logical explanation: "Inside of me lives a wild beast, and he wants sweets. To keep him peaceful, I give them to him." And she appreciatively sucked on another spoonful. The elderly still starved on the meager food ration card number five, because the Soviet hunger rations of two and a half years ago were still in force.

However, in January we had a disappointing surprise when we visited the coal cellar. The easily transportable briquettes had been replaced by small egg-shaped coals that were buried in soot. I waited until late afternoon, when the boilerman left to work in his other houses, before I ventured into the coal cellar to collect enough of these new eggs for Mrs. Winkler and myself while she kept watch at the kitchen window. I was picking up the eggs out of the coal dust and putting them in an old basket when she suddenly called out, "He's coming!" In panic, I dumped out my coals on top of the pile of soot where they were plainly visible, and rushed out of the coal cellar, leaving the basket behind. Oh, how close to having been caught. This time he seemed to spend an eternity in there before he finally left with his usual friendly, "so long," as he suppressed a laugh. I rushed back to the coal bin and found my basket filled with "eggs" and neatly placed on a tree stump with a big message written in coal on a newspaper: "Happy Easter." So he had known all along what we did in his district. The next day we silently thanked him by placing a plate of fried potatoes on the same tree stump, and this now became our secret spot for exchanging mutual favors. That evening, the filled coal basket had replaced the plate of fried potatoes.

One evening shortly thereafter, his wife stopped by with an infant in a stroller, and while waiting for him, casually mentioned how difficult it was for someone who could not afford the black market to get a cookie or even milk for the child. I could easily read between the lines because if it wasn't for my cooking here, I would be faced with the same situation for my child. So, from then on, our quiet exchange at the tree stump in the coal cellar was expanded to include items for children. There were no witnesses and no thanks, just a mutual understanding of needs while everyone pretended not to know what the other did. The officers' kitchen supplies were generous and for my unrestricted use, without any bookkeeping. Here in the house a harmonious understanding ruled, with mutual trust. (It was not until years later when we ran into each other on the street that we were able to laugh about our secret exchanges on the tree stump.)

February of 1948 brought better conditions to West Germany when, triggered by growing East-West hostilities, the U.S., Great Britain and France included Germany in the European Marshall Plan. This would provide assistance to put postwar Germany back on its feet with no strings attached, and defeat Stalin's plan to extend Soviet domination throughout all of Germany and perhaps even West Europe. In vehement reaction, a month later the Soviet delegation walked out of the Allied Control Council which created the final split between the East and West. What would be next?

Meanwhile, the asparagus season had set in and Mutti sprang into action to supplement the family's meager circumstances. She took off again for the country, this time without me, but regularly and even more arduously than ever before when both of us had gone. She returned with white asparagus which, like all fresh vegetables, was in short supply in the American commissary. So most of the asparagus ended up on the dinner table of the officers who in turn supplied Mutti generously with what she needed most urgently. It was a strenuous but opportune method to overcome my family's daily shortages of almost everything, starting with soap which was still in short supply in our ill-stocked market three years after the war. Mrs. Winkler and I would spend nice days looking out of the laundry room windows at the passersby on their Sunday family walks, and it gave us the urge to take off ourselves and be private persons again. What a foolish thought; the luxury of a leisurely springtime walk had to be discarded right away. So we returned to our duties, content not to be hungry as so many others still were.

The latest was a rumor that a fairy godmother would appear to magically change on day X our worthless German mark into…but no one knew exactly into what. Some people began to rush out to buy whatever they could get with their present money while others stockpiled every penny they had for that magic moment. A vague secret hung in the air. Suddenly lightening struck! Currency reform was the magic formula that was initiated by the Americans to restore the German economy. It became effective instantly in the three western zones of occupation because of the worsening East-West disagreements. On Sunday, June 20, 1948, a brand new *Deutsche Mark*, also called a *D-Mark*, suddenly appeared and replaced the old, worthless *Reichsmark*. But, this did not happen in West Berlin where all four powers had to reach agreements together. The brand new *D-Mark* resembled the American dollar. No wonder. They had been freshly printed in the U.S. the year before and shipped to Frankfurt and stored under top secret military supervision.

So it happened that overnight the riddle was solved and 50 million West Germans obtained their first brand new money. As a starter, long lines of hollow-cheeked and poorly dressed Germans formed outside the issuing offices to exchange forty grubby looking *Reichsmark* for forty crisp new *D-Mark*. For one moment everyone was now equally rich or equally poor. To everyone's amazement, all of the stores suddenly were stocked with an unheard of selection of previously unobtainable merchandise in unlimited quantities, and at normal prices. It was a black day for black market dealers as prices hit rock bottom. Cigarette currency also died a sudden death, One *Ami*, as a single cigarette was called, used to be 30 marks, which was equal to 7.50 dollars. People started a buying frenzy since the urge for food and eating one's fill ranked number one in everyone's mind after three years of famine.

The Soviets vehemently opposed the new *D-Mark*, and in retaliation, introduced their own currency reform with an *Ostmark* or Eastmark just three days after the *D-Mark* was issued. But, this still proved to be a fiasco because they couldn't print the new Soviet banknotes fast enough, so they just pasted stickers on the old *Reichsmark* bills to transform them into the new currency. These were soon nicknamed, "sticker-marks" or "wallpaper money" and were just as worthless as the old money. According to order number 111 of Marshal Dokolowsky, the Eastmark was declared the sole legal tender throughout all of Eastern Germany and in Berlin, including the West sectors, which financially incorporated the West sectors into the East zone as part of their East German territory. The *D-Mark* was banned throughout the entire Soviet-occupied Germany.

Thereupon the Western Powers reacted swiftly and on June 23, 1948, implemented the new *D-Mark* with a special "B" stamp in West Berlin. We called this new Westmark "bear-mark" since the bear is our symbol. Now we West Berliners also stood in long lines to receive our new money, the 40 Westmark, with the same procedure and same success. All of a sudden the shelves of our previously empty stores were loaded with long-missed treasures. Bread and butter, eggs and meat, our food supply returned to the stores overnight, but with this joy there was also bitterness among many city dwellers who had been forced to give their last valuable possessions to farmers just to barter enough food to keep from starving. We were told to turn in all of our old *Reichsmark* and to declare what we had in deposits, but this did not mean that we would keep what we once owned. The new currency reform would force everybody to practically start over from scratch, but it was still better to have honest money for honest work compared to how it was when cigarettes sold on the black market for more than a whole month's salary.

With such a significant turning point three years after the war, we felt a new epoch had begun. Now that currency, an abundance of food and merchandise were available, my family decided that it was time for me to quit my cooking job that had kept them from greater misery since November 1946. I gladly agreed to give up my position and return to my private life as "only" a housewife and mother. Although he regretted my leaving, Colonel Borno wrote me an excellent recommendation.

Overnight, we in West Berlin had both the new Eastmark and the new Westmark side by side, but with a significant difference in value and buying power. The true ratio of the solid Westmark against the weak Eastmark fluctuated from 1:2 up to 1:8, which immediately resulted in a widespread black market with the Westmark. Public exchange offices, the so-called *Wechselstuben*, sprang up everywhere in West Berlin and flourished for years. The Eastmark/Westmark situation created economic and political confusion and it was only a matter of time before we Berliners fell victim to a full scale clash among the four victorious powers in an East-West currency crisis. The gap between the Soviet Union and the Western powers deepened. Stalin took the new *D-Mark*, which had also been introduced in West Berlin, as a reason to challenge the Western Powers to finally accept Soviet authority over all of Berlin, and oust them for good. His method was to block all road, rail and water access routes from East Germany to West Berlin and force the surrender of West sectors to Soviet power by starvation. Stalin showed his true face to the world.

On June 24, 1948, our radio announced that the Soviets had totally blockaded West Berlin. That night, they had also shut off all of their water and power supply. The climax of the East-West power struggle was reached. Since we 2.5 million West Berliners were dependent upon the Soviet surrounding countryside, to endure, we were faced with mass starvation and darkness. The lights literally went out that night, which was a calamity for hospitals and industry, and we were suddenly living by candlelight with doubtful means of cooking. Completely isolated within the Soviet zone of occupation, we faced the nightmare of being starved into submission. Using the currency reform as a pretext, Soviet General Kotikow ordered that food from the East zone was to be delivered solely to East Berlin and would be available to West Berliners only if they came over to get it and sign a declaration of consent. But we rejected that as a dirty trick.

Berlin was divided into West and East. In a mass demonstration in front of the old Reichstag, Professor Ernst Reuter, our mayor of West Berlin, addressed the free world and assured the governor of the American Military Government in Germany and High Commissioner for Berlin, General Lucius D. Clay, that we were determined to stand up for our freedom and would endure hardship rather than succumb to Soviet power.

General Clay immediately came to our rescue with a plan to free West Berlin from the Soviet stranglehold of a total blockade. His first plan to have American supply convoys escorted under military protection over land access routes into West Berlin was rejected by the Pentagon, because they feared it could escalate into war. So, as a brilliant tactician, he developed the largest air supply operation in history to provide isolated West Berlin with the daily necessities of life. Two days later, on June 26, 1948, the first twenty-five American cargo planes landed at Tempelhof Airport loaded with four hundred tons of supplies. They also dropped leaflets which read, "We provide for you!" "Have courage!" "Hold Out!" "America guarantees a free Berlin!"

By July 1, a fleet of 350 cargo planes were mobilized for Berlin duty from American air bases throughout the world and were landing in the city at intervals of just a few minutes with one thousand tons delivered daily. By the end of July, the delivery had been increased to two thousand tons daily, and the British joined the airlift using their Gatow Airport in the north, and also with Sunderland sea planes that landed non-stop on the Havel River. The Soviets harassed incoming planes with fighter planes and by jamming all radio and telephone links and blinding the pilots with searchlights, but the airlift continued around the clock in fair and foul weather. The shipments became larger and larger and the Soviets withdrew in protest from the Kommandatura in Berlin and the Four Power administration ceased to exist.

Dry food was lighter and space saving, so we learned to live on dried milk, eggs, vegetables, fruit, powdered potatoes, onions and chips, a new experience for us. To relieve the congestion at the Tempelhof Airport, twenty thousand Berliners, mostly women, with American cooperation, hastily constructed in just eighty-five days the new Tegel Airport in the French sector. Their primary working equipment was a hand shovel, and they worked seven days a week around the clock in three eight-hour shifts. By November 8, 1948, a plane could land in Berlin about every three minutes, and in addition to food, they were bringing in huge amounts of coal, fuel oil for industry, gasoline for vehicles, medical supplies for hospitals, paper for newspapers (even though they only consisted of four pages) and supplies for the gas and power industries to keep our city functioning. Our power blackouts were endless and everything was rationed.

In November, another dramatic incident occurred when two thousand students and faculty from the old Humboldt University in East Berlin fled to West Berlin to escape Communist pressure, which interfered with academic studies. (All students were forced to take two years of classes in Marxism and Leninism as mandatory subjects before being allowed to begin their own selected courses.) With the generous support from the Henry Ford Foundation the "Free University of Berlin" was established in the American sector.

Supply from the air was a life or death issue for West Berlin and the Soviets doubted that it could be accomplished because geography was on their side, as Berlin was 100 miles inside the Soviet zone. But Stalin miscalculated and it was done with a steady parade of planes, often one thousand in twenty-four hours, coming in via two Allied air corridors from Frankfurt and Hamburg, and leaving again over a third one towards Hannover. This created a vital life line for us in an around-the-clock operation—and that for almost a year. The constant roaring thunder of aircraft was music to our ears, and the string of "sky trains" a familiar sight. Each plane had less than thirty minutes to land, unload and take off again, an extremely stressful situation for the pilots in their untiring missions. If one of them accidently missed his approach, he immediately had to return to his base with his load, in order not to break the flow, and get in line again for another trip. They could not allow anything to hold up the precision of the long line of landing planes that rolled as a continuous column to the unloading zone where jobless people helped with the unloading. Many firms had to stop operating because they lacked materials.

Despite all efforts, food and fuel remained scarce and far from basic needs in that harsh winter of 1948/49. West Berliners lived with severe cutbacks and once again started scavenging for firewood by cutting down trees for private fuel consumption, and hunger-starved people warmed up in the heated American libraries. Their weary faces showed more than words could tell. Nevertheless, many still died of starvation or froze to death in their bomb-damaged homes during those harsh winter months. Electricity was sharply rationed, but success depended on our will to hold out. But we didn't consider ourselves to be tragic figures. With all that inexhaustible western support, freedom was not a catch-word for propaganda; it was alive here.

By now the western world, which had looked upon Berlin as the capital of fascism, now focused with respect on our will to stand up against Soviet reprisals and to break Stalin's blockade. They knew so little about the real Berlin and that vast majority of Berliners who were never Nazis. It took time until the bitterness on both sides eased into a normal relationship. The inexhaustible western support through the gigantic airlift brought about a significant change in relationship between the western occupiers and we Berliners. As an unintentional by-product, the Western Allies had become our protectors, allied with us against the Soviets to retain our freedom in our defiance of them. As a result, we gained mutual respect and became friends.

Our greatest friend from the beginning was the twenty-seven year old Air Force pilot, Lieutenant Gail S. Halvorsen, with his private operation "Little Vittles." Out of compassion for the war-torn children he attached sweets to the corners of large handkerchiefs and dropped them from his plane shortly before landing. These miniature make-shift parachutes floated down to the waving children below who stood atop the rubble of Tempelhof airport every day looking up to the sky and waiting for him to arrive. Over time, seventy thousand little parachutes glided from his propeller-driven plane, which bore the inscription "Isle of Christmas." Other pilots followed his example and dropped over two hundred fifty thousand parachutes all together, which were provided by the generosity of private American people and the candy industry. The Berliners soon lovingly called these Skymaster transport planes

"Raisin Bombers" or "Candy Bombers," and to this day, the Americans are fondly remembered.

We stubborn Berliners stood by our word and held out, as living proof that the U.S. kept its promise. At the peak of the life-saving airlift in April of 1949, thirteen thousand tons of supplies were flown in every single day and the airlift could have gone on indefinitely. After eleven months, General Clay's airlift, the most spectacular ever attempted, had defeated Stalin's stranglehold to starve out West Berlin. Over two hundred fifty thousand flights had delivered approximately 2 million tons of life-saving supplies in the largest humanitarian airlift in history, and guaranteed our continued freedom from the oppression of Communism. We West Berliners proudly felt that we had made world history because the ultimate success greatly depended on us, too, and Europe would be decisively altered if we had been squeezed out of existence by a Communist takeover. But the Soviets capitulated and at midnight on May 12, 1949, the barriers of all checkpoints were lifted and the first supply trucks, decorated with flowers and garlands, began rolling along the Autobahn and were enthusiastically greeted upon arrival at daybreak by jubilant West Berliners. Also, the first supply trains were under way.

It cost our American and British friends an estimated 250 million dollars to break the Berlin blockade, and more dearly than the money was the tragic loss of thirty-one American and thirty-nine British pilots and crew members, plus eight German ground personnel. A 63-foot high concrete airlift memorial was erected soon in front of Tempelhof Airport on which is inscribed the names of those who gave their lives in support of the operation. The monument is in the shape of the beginning of a bridge with three long arches pointing westward to symbolize the three Allied airlift corridors. A complementary half of the air bridge stands at Frankfurt Airport to symbolize the connection of the two parts and the bond between America and Berlin. The notoriously quick-witted Berliners with their dry humor in no time nicknamed the new airlift memorial the "Hunger Claw" or "Hunger Rake" because it resembled a fork with only three prongs.

In October of 1950, in the presence of forty thousand West Berliners, General Clay presented a copy of the famous American Liberty Bell to the Berliners as a gift of the American people, and it has been hanging ever since in the tower of the Schöneberg City Hall, the seat of the

Senate, in the former American sector, and is rung every day at noon. The signatures of the 17 million Americans who contributed to its cost are kept in the document chamber. In 1962, General Lucius Clay was made an honorary citizen of Berlin, and the Grunewald Allee in the suburb of Dahlem, where the U.S. headquarters was located, was renamed Clay Allee to show our eternal gratitude to his commitment to preserve Berlin's freedom.

Even after the legendary Berlin airlift was won, General Clay continued to stockpile reserves in West Berlin for several months in case the Soviet-ruled East Germany tried to create another crisis. In an attempt to provoke such an incident, they had already briefly cut off electric power to the western sectors. But, Stalin's failed effort to take over West Berlin became counterproductive because of a chain reaction of events.

Under American influence, on May 23, 1949, only eleven days after the blockade, the Federal Republic of Germany was born. Because of Berlin's loss of the role as Germany's capital, the city of Bonn was chosen as the provisional capital with Dr. Conrad Adenauer elected as the first chancellor and Professor Theodor Heuss as president. Under strong leadership over the next fourteen years, the Adenauer era went down in history as a reconstruction of a devastated country and lasted longer than Hitler's thousand-year Reich, and exactly as long as the Weimar Republic. Germany became one of the most prosperous countries in Europe.

In the spring of 1949, Superintendent Hildebrand called all parents of school age children to a meeting at the church. Since Vita belonged to that group, Mutti and I attended and were told that at the alleged insistence of parents, the new school administration had canceled all religion classes. We had never been asked for our opinion, and we knew immediately that this was the work of the new school authority which was still staffed with many Communists who wanted to abolish religion. It was an old German tradition that the schools offered religious instruction twice a week as a regular part of the curriculum and we added our names to the long list of signatures which demanded that classes in religion be continued. The school administration responded that if we insisted on the classes being reinstated, the church had to provide the teachers and we had to pay their salaries, even though all teaching was tuition free in public schools. We agreed, and Mrs. Weissbach who had experience teaching Sunday School, became Vita's teacher in the *Riemeister Schule*, a grammar school, which was about a thirty-minute walk from home. Even though we paid punctually for the salaries, it took the school several months to finally give the teachers their first pay, and then, only a fraction of what we had contributed. Years later, I read in the newspaper where the Berlin Senate had denied ever having banned religious instruction in the schools, but I knew differently because we signed the petition and paid for the salaries until about 1956.

Here I am with our two girls.

Our second child was born on May 13, 1950, another little girl whom we named Sylvia. Even though the war had been over for five years, I found many of the same necessities still in short supply as when Vita was born seven years earlier during the war. West Berlin was a spirited, but still struggling city that depended greatly on funds from Bonn. East Berlin and East Germany had no freely elected government by the people, but rather, a one-party dictatorship ruled from Moscow as part of the Communist block. As a result, the powerless population sought freedom of choice by voting effectively with their feet, fleeing the Communistic state, and escaping to the free West.

Meanwhile West Germany's rapidly growing prosperity was very evident in the 1950s as a result of Dr. Ludwig Erhardt taking the daring step to apply the principles of free economy. The Volkswagen, the legendary "Beetle", was soon produced by the millions and became the most popular German export. Unemployment became unknown and more than a million workers were imported from other countries to relieve the labor shortage.

But our pleasure was short-lived. A "free market" economy, and the brand new currency hot off the press, initially created negative aftershocks for us. It just about wiped out all savings and monetary possessions because bank accounts and investments could be exchanged only to a limited extent, and then only at a ratio of ten to one. That meant we lost 90 percent of everything we still had, or thought we had. In addition, all investments beginning with the word Reich, which were Hitler's compulsory government loans for the railway, post office and freeway (similar to U.S. municipal bonds) were a 100 percent loss with the simple explanation, "There is no Third Reich any more." All old government debts owed to the people were erased with a single stroke of the pen, which was the quickest and most radical way to provide the new government a fresh start. Also, many other stocks and bonds had deteriorated to a fraction of their value or had become completely worthless. So, most people had little more than nothing, and I wonder to this day how the Americans would have reacted to such revolting restrictions and reductions to pay off their government debts.

Those who owned real estate were also not exempt from carrying the general burden of debt. As far as my family was concerned, the World War II bombing of Münster resulted in the total loss of an apartment building for which no compensation was ever given. Papa sold the ground and used the money to repair the bomb-damaged apartment houses on Limastrasse in Zehlendorf-West. Then, the Berlin Senate decided that real estate ownership was a new way to raise funds, so they placed a large mortgage on the Limastrasse property, which before had none. Such an arbitrary act was called "equalization of burdens," a new law since September 1952, to provide compensation for war victims. In other words, those with savings had to pass some on to those who had none. They disregarded the fact that due to Soviet appropriation, we probably had lost considerable property that we had owned in Zerbst, East Germany, since the 1920s.

With generous loans provided by the Marshall Plan aid to citizens of West Berlin, my parents had their bomb-damaged house on Veronikasteig repaired. Our case resembled that of many others since the majority of homes were either severely damaged or completely demolished. Years later, Papa paid back every penny of the loan. The Marshall Plan had turned war-ravaged Berlin into an important city again. As far as I can remember, Berlin was the only city with rent control on pre-war housing, and while maintenance costs and other expenses constantly increased, the rents remained controlled. This discrepancy between income and expenditures for apartment owners affected my parents for many years and resulted in long-time tenants doing their own minor repairs.

However, the Berlin Senate still looked for a source of revenue, and one day, Papa received a request from them for funds to help needy children. He felt he was the wrong person to approach. So he replied that he was already doing his share by caring for his own four grandchildren without government aid, especially for those of his son, since Günter hadn't returned from the war, and if the Senate were to take care of them, he would make donations to others. His letter was never answered, and was probably filed in a wastebasket.

But material setbacks lose all of their importance in comparison with personal losses. One day, a stranger showed up at my parents' house and introduced himself as Heinz Gerd Fengler, a former seaman on Günter's ship. He had come personally to report Günter's death. So Mutti's dream had become true. He told us that while they were stationed in the harbor of Saloniki, Greece, their ship picked up desperate SOS signals on the afternoon of October 19, 1944, and they immediately set out to sea to save the shipwrecked people. Just off shore of their rescue mission, they were attacked by sea and air by the British, which severely damaged the ship and killed many of the crew members. Those who survived were forced to return to the harbor and were taken prisoners by the British and turned over to the Communist Greek Elath troops. They ended up in a large prisoner of war camp in Larissa, Thessaly, in the northern part of Greece. There, every morning the guards would call out names of officers and put them on trucks to an unknown destination, and the trucks always returned empty at night.

On the morning of December 16, 1944, the name of Commander Günter Schmidt was called, along with Heinz Gerd Fengler and other officers and crew members of his ship. The truck took them to a distant river where they were ordered to clear some mines from under a bridge. The guards figured that the prisoners would blow themselves up in the attempt to diffuse the mines, but they were experienced in mine warfare and survived. At nightfall, on the way back to camp, the truck was stopped and the guards ordered everyone to build a fire and sit around it. As soon as they sat down, the guards circled behind them and started firing machine guns into their backs. Those who were not killed ran off for cover, but were caught and shot. Günter was only wounded and managed to escape into the underbrush, but he was spotted later and gunned down. Heinz Gerd Fengler was the only one who got away and he didn't even know if they buried the dead.

He was very sorry to bring us such sad news, and even though we had been expecting the worst, we were devastated to hear the actual details. My dear brother was only thirty-one years old and the father of two small children when he was murdered in a prisoner of war camp by Communist troops. They were delivered to them by the British, according to an agreement with Stalin to do as he did, to kill fifty thousand of the German intelligence, and then one could handle the rest later! Roosevelt agreed because of all of his concessions to Stalin. Mutti never got over that tragedy. In 1914, it was the loss of her only brother, in 1944 her only son—my only brother.

The last picture of Günter

Papa immediately made many inquiries to a number of organizations, but they remained unanswered. All he ever received was one brief document dated April 12, 1948, from an agency of the British government which stated that officer Günter Schmidt was dead, shot by Greek partisans in Larissa, Greece. The British could not put in writing that he was killed as a POW by arbitrarily being executed just before Christmas 1944 in violation of all international laws. My brother was one of the fifty thousand officers that Stalin had demanded be killed without any court proceedings or intervention from the Allies, according to a 1943 Teheran Allied concession. Anyone who is interested in historical documentation, occasionally written like a fascinating novel, can find it in a book entitled *So gewannen sie den Krieg—und verloren den Frieden* (This Way They Won the War And Lost the Peace) by Rudolph Schwartz and published by Verlag Frankfurter Bücher, Frankfurt, Germany. It has also been translated into other languages.

Nevertheless, life had to go on as it always did—and had to. We were trained in surviving and to feed the illusion of peace. After the failure of Stalin's blockade, the Soviets entered a new phase of harassments. West Berliners who owned gardens in the East territory were suddenly no longer allowed to visit their property unless they had obtained a brand new East-issued "garden-passing-permit," called a *Gartenpassierschein*. These passes had to be applied for in writing and were required to be carried during all visits. This same regulation was in effect for taking care of the thousands of family graves in cemeteries outside of West Berlin.

Another mode of harassment was the S-Bahn over which the Soviets unfortunately had complete control throughout all of Berlin, in accordance with the ill-fated West Allied agreement of 1945. West Berliners were warned to get off the S-Bahn at the next-to-the-last station in the West because the train would occasionally deliberately skip the last stop and pass straight through to the first stop in the East sector. The East police was waiting for those West passengers who arrived involuntarily in East Berlin and treated them like criminals. They were charged with illegally "smuggling" West German newspapers and money into the East which was immediately confiscated and a heavy fine imposed that had to be paid in Westmarks of course. Often, these innocent victims were even arrested and were lucky if they were able to ride back into West Berlin that same day.

At one point, we stubborn West Berliners reversed the harassment by refusing to ride the S-Bahn controlled by the East. The Soviets desperately wanted the S-Bahn fare from us in our solid Westmarks to pay their spies with, rather than in their own worthless Eastmarks. We became aware of this and started to boycott the S-Bahn, even though it was the cheapest and most convenient transportation. Daily, the working people made costly, time-consuming detours by bus, subway and streetcar just to avoid subsidizing the Communists. We soon noted with great satisfaction that our extended boycott had the S-Bahn running almost empty and suffering a financial deficit. Another annoyance by the East in the 1950s was cutting off all telephone connections with the West for short periods of time.

To cope with the growing unemployment in the East, workers

crossed over into West Berlin seeking jobs, while at the same time we had West Berliners who were working in East Berlin. Approximately one hundred thousand border-crossers commuted back and forth daily. There were two different currencies, the Eastmark and the Westmark, and workers were paid in the currency where they worked, which was not accepted as legal tender where they resided. To possess Westmarks in the East sector was prohibited, because only the Eastmark was acknowledged, so a great confusion arose and some sort of compromise was necessary. The situation did not really concern us, but if I remember correctly, residents of West Berlin who worked in the East sector received from the Berlin Senate an exchange of 60 percent of their East pay into West money and they kept 40 percent in East money. East Berliners who worked in West Berlin received 25 percent of pay in Westmarks and 75 percent in Eastmarks, but East authorities exchanged their highly desired Westmarks into Eastmarks at a ratio of 1:1, which was a profitable business for them to pay their agents, since the actual ratio fluctuated from 1:2 to 1:8.

I could never understand why Sieghardt, who lived in West Berlin and worked in the neighborhood book store, was paid partly in Eastmarks and partly in Westmarks. We could only use the Eastmarks to buy groceries in West Berlin as it was not accepted for anything else. No wonder many West Berliners flocked to theaters and concert halls in East Berlin to pay with the practically worthless Eastmarks. The East theaters enjoyed great prestige with excellent performances. When we tipped the woman at the coat check with a Westmark, she looked around nervously first and then quickly grabbed it with a grateful smile.

Ernst Legal, the famous superintendent of the East Berlin theatrical activities, resided in our apartment building on Limastrasse, occupying the spacious apartment previously occupied by Mr. Birkholtz, the member of the Nazi Todt organization, who vanished before the battle for Berlin had started. A chauffeur-driven black, East limousine would pick him up each morning and bring him back home at night. Naturally, the Communists put the pressure on him to move into the East sector where he would need no money because he could purchase anything he desired just by signing his name.

One morning, the black limousine waited for hours outside of our house in vain, because Mr. Legal refused to come out of his safe apartment. We neighbors gathered on the street in his support to prevent an attempt at kidnapping, and after a tense morning the limousine finally had to return empty. Brazen kidnapping continued in our American sector. Mr. Legal had decided against the wonderful promises in the East. If he would have left with the limousine that day, they would not have allowed him to come back home again. We loved to listen to his beautiful piano playing on balmy evenings when the windows were open. Vita, who was seven by now, also had her own personal reason for being interested in him. She often visited Sofie, his housekeeper, who cut off big slices of salami for her, and since Vita ate everything on the spot, I was never aware of why she was so anxious to visit.

While in the East the simplest items remained scarce, we West Berliners were eager to share in the growing West German prosperity and strived for a new normal life. "Fashion," which was a long- forgotten word, became a thrilling reality again. Our West Berlin store windows displayed modern and comfortable low heeled shoes with one and a quarter-inch thick crepe rubber soles that squeaked animatedly with every step. We all wanted such a pair and each of us got one. Long mid-calf length skirts were in fashion—an irony—they required extra material, at a time when everybody was broke. Naturally I managed to buy such an outfit, of course in blue, my favorite color. (I still have a picture of myself proudly wearing it.) There also were those new, expensive nylons from America with a fashionable seam in the back, and the inevitable runs. Special needles were sold to repair them by picking up the lost "stitches." Of course I bought such a gadget, which I still have. Generally we became experts in window shopping. People were very money-cautious. But who could worry about the future when we were abundantly busy with arranging the new present?

In contrast, economic conditions in the East were wretched, with stores having little to sell and food was available only on ration cards, while ours had been abolished a long time ago. In order to share our good fortune, we began sending packages to Aunt Grete in the East with things she lacked badly. Besides food and clothing, she needed needles, thread, thumb tacks, nails, pencils, elastic for underwear and many other simple daily necessities. However, the East authorities made the sending of packages as difficult as possible as they did not want us capitalists from the West to be flaunting our new wealth.

There were strict rules and regulations that had to be followed to the letter in mailing a package to the East or it was confiscated over there. This included restricted dimensions and weights, and even the address had to be written in a certain way. First, in bold letters, had to appear: *Geschenkspackung, keine Handelsware* (gift parcel, no merchandise), and then the country's name as "German Democratic Republic," not just East Germany. A list of contents had to be attached to the outside of the wrapping paper so it could be easily inspected by the Eastern post office officials. There was a long list of banned articles such as any kind of medicine, and those items allowed were subject to a specific size and quantity.

For example, we could send either butter, margarine or oil, and only one can of meat or fish. The number of parcels that could be sent to any one person was also limited, but we got around that by addressing them to different family members. Since badly needed medicine was banned, we repacked the pills and declared them to be candy. Band-aids passed without objection, but newspapers or any printed material from the West was strictly forbidden. When some of the contents weren't to the liking for whatever reason, the packages were opened in the East and everything was confiscated. Because so many of them were stolen, West Berlin negotiated a new package insurance which required that the value of the lost parcel be reimbursed. This put a quick halt to their disappearance, but did not prevent the loss of individual items, and it was not advisable to accuse East officials of stealing.

Arbitrarily, Aunt Grete would be asked to pay for the postage, even though we had already paid it in full, including the insurance and delivery to her home. She could have obtained food without ration cards at the HO stores (*Handels-Organisation*), the State-owned supermarkets and giant department stores with horrendous black market prices that were far beyond the means of the average person. One could even buy with Westmarks in these East HO stores, but if you did, you were arrested for having them in your possession.

The United States, Great Britain and France officially terminated the state of war with Germany in July of 1951, which the Soviets protested as usual, but still there was no peace treaty signed. In protest that German POWs were still held in the Soviet Union, we Berliners lit candles in our windows during the Christmas season of 1952 to plead for the return of our men who had not yet come home seven years after the war had ended, and continued this each Christmas thereafter.

The tension between the East and West steadily increased as the living conditions split further and further apart. In the so-called Communist "workers' paradise," the people suffered and stayed poor and their food shortages continued. Only the Communist leaders, living in luxurious villas in secluded parks, enjoyed the horn of plenty from Russian caviar to French wines.

One day, we West Berliners were no longer allowed into the surrounding East German countryside. Since we had relatives and owned property in Zerbst, East Germany, we needed an East permit to travel there. I went to the nearest permit office to request a train pass for the following week and waited patiently for hours in a long line of others seeking travel passes. This required several trips because the office would close when all the permits for that day had been given out. Finally I was able to reach the desk where the passes were issued and the cross examination went something like this:

"Reason for visit?"

"My uncle is very sick."

"Well, if he is that sick, he will probably die soon anyway and you will then want to go to the funeral. There is no need to go now. Twice is too much. Permit denied. Next!"

I must mention that my uncle did die four years later and we tried to go to his funeral, and I had to go through the same time-consuming procedure again. This time it went something like this:

"The death notice is already several days old and it will take you a few more days to get a train ticket. By that time, you will have already missed the funeral. There is no reason for the trip. Permit denied. Next!" So, we never had a chance to look after Aunt Grete or to check on our property there in East Germany.

We in Berlin constantly lived with clouds of uncertainty on the horizon. The anti-Communist attitude of the East German people became more pronounced as time went on. While we received economic and financial support from West Germany, East Germany did not get any comparable assistance from Moscow, but rather, just the opposite. The Soviets even opposed the Marshall Plan that had contributed greatly to the recovery of Europe since 1948. Finally, in May of 1953, the East Germans revolted when their government announced a drastic increase in food prices and production quota with a 40 percent reduction in wages. Encouraged by Stalin's death the previous March, thousands of workers demonstrated in front of the unpopular Soviet puppet government headquarters of Prime Minister Otto Grothewohl and SED Secretary Walter Ulbricht, demanding freedom, justice, bread and financial stability. When this protest march was not successful, the workers called for a general strike, and early on the morning of June 17, three to four thousand workers who were fed up with the Communist "workers' paradise" demonstrated openly in the streets.

Similar demonstrations of hundreds of thousands of workers took place spontaneously throughout the towns of East Germany. The demonstrations were risky because it was rumored that there were already seventy thousand fully trained and heavily armed East German police and military quartered in barracks in and around East Berlin, in violation of the Potsdam Agreement, and the people asked themselves: "Better 'red' than dead?"

The demonstrators pulled down the red flag from the top of the Brandenburg Gate and other flag poles, demanding the resignation of the government and free elections. Our West radio, RIAS, had reported the uprising early in the morning and we were stunned to hear that martial law had been declared as the Soviets moved into East Berlin with heavily armed troops and tanks. We rushed to the home of our mayor, Ernst Reuter, in our Zehlendorf-West suburb and urged him that he at least try to supply our fellow Germans at the border with food and drink. Quite upset, we rang his doorbell but did not find him at home, and as we reflected on the situation, we realized that he would have had no authority to interfere in actions in the Soviet sector under Moscow's rule.

In the meantime, the situation in East Berlin had become a day of slaughter as Soviet tanks plunged into the masses of unarmed people in the street, leaving behind a bloody mass of hundreds of dead bodies and many more injured, and dead silence. The attempted anti-Communist uprising had been crushed by nightfall by force of arms, and the three Western Powers could not intervene in the Soviet-occupied sector or even help those who lay mortally wounded within sight just over the border. Our own police had to protect the huge Russian war memorial that stood in the British sector from the furious West Berliners who tried to demolish it. People also threw stones at the Soviet cars during the changing of the guards at the monument there. In East Germany, military courts handed out death sentences with immediate executions, while thousands of others were given harsh prison terms, with over a thousand receiving life sentences. The actual number of victims of the uprising is not known.

Our church provided the names and addresses of needy families whose men had been imprisoned and, although they were complete strangers to us, we started sending packages to them. Even though it was forbidden to send money, I found a loophole. There were packages of cookies on the market which were wrapped in aluminum foil, and after carefully opening them and slipping in a large East bill between the two layers of big, flat cookies, the aluminum foil, once resealed, would not permit X-ray inspection. When I received a letter from a mother of two children which said that the cookies were "good for her health," I knew this was her code to let me know the cookies had arrived safely with the money inside. All of my friends sent these packages for years to support the more unfortunate ones in the East.

June 17 was observed thereafter as a national memorial day to commemorate those brave victims of the oppressed revolt against the Communist government in the Soviet-occupied territory. In West Berlin, we had a "Strasse des 17. Juni," the 17th of June Avenue, which is an almost two-mile long boulevard leading from the Brandenburg Gate to the Ernst Reuter Platz. The failed uprising resulted in an increased flow of refugees from the East, and as a counter measure, the Communist government intensified its control of the entire border with West Germany. It had been patrolled by guards with automatic weapons, but now, they created a three-mile deep "no-man's land" on their side of the seven hundred-mile border with West Germany, by removing the entire rural population from north to south and converting the land to a heavily-mined death trap secured by double barbed wired fences which triggered an alarm when it was touched. Hundreds of police watch towers were erected within short distances of each other, and the entire area was flooded with search lights to detect any movement, while the rest of the population was urged to save electricity. The East border guards regularly patrolled on foot with a pack of dogs and in military cars with orders to "shoot to kill," and even had their dogs check trains passing through to the West to find people who could have been hiding underneath the cars.

Because of all these measures, West Berlin became the last remaining open exit. There was still unrestricted movement throughout the city due to the Four-Power status, and East Germans streamed into the three West sectors by all modes of transportation and on foot. The first ones to arrive, which included specialists and young skilled workers, came with suitcases. Those arriving later were afraid of being caught trying to escape into West Berlin, so they came with just a bouquet of flowers in their hands to make it appear they were attending a birthday party. However, in order to salvage something, they were wearing three layers of their normal underwear. They arrived by the thousands every day, and stayed with friends and relatives or in refugee camps until they were safely flown to the West.

The Berlin headquarters of the *Freiheitliche Juristen*, the Lawyers for Freedom, was located at the end of Limastrasse. They were a group of German lawyers devoted to exposing terrorism in Soviet-controlled East Germany and assisting people who were suffering from Communist pressures. You could easily recognize those who came seeking advice by their shabby clothing and the nervous manner in which they looked around as they left our S-Bahn station and passed us on the street.

One day, the *Freiheitliche Juristen* asked us to temporarily take in a man who could not return to the East so we put him in a guest room facing the back yard. That night we heard noises on our porch and discovered large footprints the next morning on the outside window sill of our guest's bedroom, which plainly showed that someone was trying to look into the room through the small upper slits in the partially closed shutters. Our lodger was very cautious whenever he left the house and never went out at night, or alone. A short while later, his wife and small children managed to get to West Berlin and they were all flown to the West.

Another incident involved a refugee from the East and his wife who had established a small vegetable market in the garage of a bombed-out villa across the street from us. He was soon approached by a stranger and asked to work as an agent for the East, and when he refused, one of the black limousines that was used to kidnap people continued to appear from time to time. We watched as he and his wife would hide every time the limousine would show up, and after several such occurrences, they abandoned their new business and were flown to safety in the West.

The border between Berlin and the East zone often ran through the middle of lakes and the many rivers around Berlin. Our friends, the Bannerts, owned a sailboat and we would often go sailing with them on Lake Wannsee and the Havel River, but being ever so careful not to drift beyond the middle into the East territory. That would have been looked upon as spying. The East police concealed themselves on the opposite side and observed us with binoculars. They also prevented their own people from escaping over the water to the West with a "shoot to kill" order.

One day, the Bannerts had an American co-worker on board and were relaxing after a swim when they suddenly felt a crash. A steel hook had been thrown into their boat and they were being pulled by the East police to the East shore. The family members, including two children and the American friend, were imprisoned in separate cells and the husband was pressured to work as an East agent if he ever wanted to see his family again. It was obvious that the East police was very well informed about his employment in an American office. In the confusion, the East police had not realized that the other gentleman in bathing trunks was an American, and the atmosphere changed abruptly as soon as this became known. They were suddenly all free to leave, shaken but unharmed, though with no offer to have the boat repaired or even an apology for the damage they caused. The unexpected presence of an American friend had saved them, but the severe pressure on the Bannerts to act as an agent for the East never ceased. It finally became so threatening that the entire family secretly fled to the West. Our friends' fate was by no means an isolated occurrence, just one of the typical happenings in West Berlin that never made the papers.

The over 100-mile long Autobahn from Berlin to Helmstedt ran through East German territory and was controlled by East German and Soviet authorities at checkpoints at each end. Traveling on the Autobahn was done solely according to their rules and regulations and they could deny passage to anyone at any time for any reason. My passport was valid worldwide, but was not recognized by them as personal identification, and I was required to obtain a special Berlin *Kennkarte* which was an I.D. card with my photo.

When I traveled to West Germany with an American friend, I had to get out of her car at Checkpoint Berlin-Wannsee because a German could not ride as a guest in an American car through the East. From the checkpoint, I hitchhiked with German transportation, mostly with truck drivers, which was safe and gave me a pleasant view from high up in the cab next to the driver. Unfortunately, this view consisted only of miles of barren no-man's land. My time entering the Autobahn at checkpoint Berlin-Wannsee was carefully recorded and so was my time of arrival at the other end, after a two-hour drive. If we arrived at the border at checkpoint Helmstedt too early, we were punished for speeding and if we arrived too late, there were even worse accusations and aroused suspicions. If I had a coat on when I left Berlin-Wannsee, the East Germans checked at Helmstedt to make sure I still had it and had not given it to an East German somewhere along the way. (How? It was forbidden to leave the Autobahn. We never spotted a soul beyond that wide minefield, the barbed wire entanglement and other control measures of the inner German border.)

I was greeted in Helmstedt with giant "Ami Go Home" posters, blaring music and loudspeaker slogans about the Communist workers' paradise, an ear-splitting propaganda. My American friend quickly passed through a separate Soviet-operated checkpoint while I had to put up with a long wait at the control point manned by East German officials. I was often arbitrarily slowed down for no real reason, and sometimes I even had to enter a barrack and stand in line in front of a huge wooden wall with a little opening under a small glass window. A claustrophobic atmosphere reigned here. I was ordered by a voice from the inside to pass my I.D. card through the opening where the hand of an unseen person grabbed it. It always worried me that I might not get my I.D. back, and sometimes, with butterflies in my stomach, I had to wait so long that my American friend was about to declare me missing. When I finally set foot in the West it was like entering another world, with the freedom of movement, but then, we had to repeat the same procedures on our return trip to West Berlin.

A friend of mine from West Germany once planned to be with us in West Berlin for the Christmas holidays. At checkpoint Helmstedt, her train was stopped and all of the passengers were ordered outside. Then a second order was shouted, "Everyone wearing a fur coat, line up!" My friend was wearing a genuine Persian coat and dutifully got in the line, but an official yelled at her, "You with the *Krimmermantel* (fake fur), get out of line!" Fortunately for her, the East police could not recognize a real fur from a fake one, and she was the only one from the line who was permitted to get back on the train to continue to West Berlin-Wannsee. The next day we found out that the others were kept in barracks all night, just out of spite, and missed Christmas with their friends.

The interference with the movement of people and goods between East and West did not cease throughout the 1950s. Border officials slowed all land transit to and from Berlin with inspections and controls, and merchandise was often intentionally damaged or food allowed to spoil by delays at the checkpoints. Goods to Berlin needed high insurance to make up for the constantly demolished articles.

The girls with Sieghardt's parents.
(A more prosperous life in West Berlin.)

All's Well That Ends Well—Almost

I was awakened at daybreak on Sunday, August 13, 1961, by the frantic ringing of our doorbell. Looking out, I recognized a friend of Lotte's. Lotte had been our maid until she was recruited by Hitler for essential war service. At the end of the war she had returned to us as a porter on Limastrasse, by now being married. Since she was currently out of town, her friend had been temporarily replacing her.

The young woman appeared panic-stricken and begged me to tend the coal furnaces which provided hot water to our two apartment houses. Barely catching her breath she explained she had to rush home right away to Machnow, a nearby suburb only a half-hour walk away, but which was already in the East German zone. Excitedly she told me that RIAS, the West Berlin radio, had just announced that as of midnight the East German government had started sealing off any access into West Berlin and was building fences along the border. All traffic, both rail and highway, between East and West Berlin had been halted, local streets torn up, and streetcar tracks leading to the West sectors cut up. Thousands of East police and military, heavily armed and ready to shoot, closely patrolled the East/West crossing.

I immediately turned on our radio and could not believe what I was hearing. They were reporting dramatic events of people desperately trying to make it across the border to the West. Some made it while others were caught by the East German border guards and no one knew of their fate. My parents were still in bed when I called to tell them the incredible news and I also alerted all of our tenants who quickly gathered on the staircase, some still in their nightgowns. We tried to persuade Lotte's friend to stay here, but her family was in the nearby East zone and she hoped that if she reached them, they could all escape together. I never heard from her again.

Prime Minister Ulbricht, being subservient to Moscow, had paved the way for the Soviets to seal off the border to the West overnight and we wanted to personally witness these happenings. We took off for the Brandenburg Gate where thousands of West Berliners had already gathered. The pavement had been torn up in front of the monument and a deep trench dug on the East side of the fence at the border. West police kept the crowd back several hundred meters to prevent any incidents while an East German crew strung coils of barbed wire between wooden poles along the East-West Berlin border, abruptly separating families and friends. I tried to take photographs while walking back and forth along the police line, not believing what I was seeing. Tension was high. Would this bring on another blockade?

We anxiously waited to see what the American reaction would be

Monday, August 14, 1961

since this was a definite testing of power between the East and West. But, to our dismay, it was just a diplomatic protest. We West Berliners could not understand how the Western Powers would basically ignore the action that ripped the city apart. It was obvious that the East action was not to keep West Berliners out, but rather, to keep the East population in the East, and to scare them enough so they wouldn't leave. The Soviets had already felt the sting of people escaping from their zone since about 4 million, or nearly 20 percent of their population, had already fled to the West. West Berlin was the only open window to escape from the Communist East because of our Four-Power status and the East was losing their youngest and brightest citizens at an alarming rate. Thirty thousand had crossed over in July and during those tense first twelve days of August another forty-five thousand arrived in the western sector merely by riding the S-Bahn or the subway. The Soviets realized that if they did not take drastic action to stop this daily flow of people to West Berlin, East Germany would soon be deserted. As a solution, they sealed off the last escape route to the West, which also immediately cut off sixty thousand East workers from their jobs in West Berlin. There was a rumor that in their June meeting in Vienna, President John F. Kennedy and Nikita Krushev had reached a silent understanding to avoid any new conflict.

The barricades that blocked off access to the West sectors ran at random through the middle of streets, through private property, parks, lakes and cemeteries. In one instance, it ran through a church that belonged to a West Berlin parish which stood on the East side but had its entrance on the West side. The Soviets constructed a brick partition across the inside of the church, so anyone who entered through the West Berlin entrance ran into a wall. In other instances, a dividing fence ran along apartment buildings in which windows on one side faced the West. This created heart-rending scenes where East Germans started jumping from the roof and upper windows of these four and five-story buildings into the West sectors where firemen had spread pads to cushion their fall. Parents would throw out their children first and then jump themselves, sometimes with a baby clutched in their arms. Sadly, some missed the pads and jumped to their deaths. Our West German police also threw smoke bombs in an effort to conceal the escapees from the East border guards who would rather shoot and kill their own fleeing fellow citizens than allow them to escape to freedom. (Since 1948, the *Schusswaffengebrauch-Bestimmung* already existed, a directive for the use of firearms to shoot.)

The East immediately began to brick up entrances and windows in buildings that faced the western side to stop people from escaping to the West, and shortly thereafter, forced all of the inhabitants to vacate entire apartment blocks on the border. Desperate to reach freedom, East Germans even tried to swim through canals, but they were soon sealed off by erecting barbed wire barriers through the water. The East began to replace the initial temporary fence and barbed wire barricades by building a high concrete wall along the border, which became known worldwide as the infamous Berlin Wall and marked the end of people's freedom.

The Berlin Wall

Berlin was split into East and West for the next twenty-eight years, divided between the two super powers in what was to become known as the Cold War. The Wall had not only divided Berlin, but also Germany, and split Europe in two. During those years, West Berliners laid flowers at the Wall and erected crosses and memorials for those who were shot by the border patrol and perished as they were trying to reach freedom, the so-called "state border violators."

General Lucius Clay and Vice President Johnson arrived in Berlin on Saturday, August 19, one week after the initial blockade action, to ensure our security and were enthusiastically received by the West Berliners. We all watched as they rode down Potsdamer Chaussee in an open car, a highway very close to where we lived. I took many pictures, which I still own today. The next day, new American troops arrived and every spot along their parade route that afternoon was crowded with cheering West Berliners. Nevertheless, having to look each day at the ever extending brick and concrete barrier was a depressing, visible sign of the increasing crisis atmosphere that the Cold War was creating in this divided city.

We're greeting the Americans (Vita is on the right).

Although the East was faced with serious housing shortages, they began to tear down entire buildings that were close to the border to make room on their side for a second 18-foot high concrete wall behind the first one, thus creating a cleared "no-man's-land" between the two walls. This area was mined and patrolled around the clock by East police with vicious dogs. At night, the entire area was continually swept by searchlights, and it became a death-trap day or night for anyone still trying to escape. The East forbade us to go near the Wall and ordered us to stay 100 meters away on our side. (I wonder how they would have reacted if *we* would have told them how close they could come on their side?)

Soon, the Wall ran 30 miles right through the city along the western sectors, and 75 miles around the outside along the East zone borders, turning West Berlin into an island of anti-Communism surrounded by total Communism. The Wall demonstrated that force was the only hold the Communists had to keep people from defecting to the West. On August 30, one of our newspapers printed the names of people who tried to swim through the canals to the West. They were shot in the water and drowned. As the East continually kept reinforcing the Wall, with bleak prospects of a reunification, it also created a never ending pressure on West Berlin. It effectively cut us off from the East countryside which was our primary source of food and fuel. Erich Honnecker, the boss of the Communist party, proclaimed that the Wall will last for a hundred years. (Didn't that sound like the lifespan of Hitler's thousand-year Reich?)

The military forces of the Four Powers still moved freely about the city in their cars, passing through the Wall at designated crossing points without being controlled. But lately, the Soviets started to harass the military with haphazard challenges to the Americans with authorized free access to East Berlin. News leaked out that the Soviets had brought in more troops to the East sector and were going to come over to West Berlin and finally "liberate" us.

On October 26, 1961, we suddenly found Soviet tanks sitting dangerously close to Checkpoint Charlie facing ten American tanks on our side, which were ready to take a stand against any military threat from the Soviet Union. Both sides were ready to shoot. We held our breath as the political tension was on razor's edge. Were we on the brink of World War III and the conflict only a matter of minutes? But, as these tanks openly confronted each other, we West Berliners fearlessly gathered in a large crowd around the American tanks to demonstrate our unity with them. My family wanted to witness this living history, and we stood there with the huge throng of people looking over into East Berlin at the Soviet tanks. But, there was no one on the East side because the Soviets prevented their people from congregating near the border for fear they would try to escape to our side. It was a highly explosive time from one moment to the next. We were on the summit of the Cold War.

I do not remember how long the tanks faced each other without a shot being fired, but those of the Soviets finally disappeared one morning and the American tanks remained the rest of that day before they also slowly moved away. Here war was prevented, not risked. Stalin's latest attempt to drive the Western Powers out of Berlin had failed, but one cannot help wonder what the Americans, British and French would have done, and how history would have changed, if the Soviet tanks had attempted to cross into West Berlin. It would have been an absolute nightmare. The confrontation had served the purpose in establishing the Western Powers' legal presence in Berlin and we remained the outpost of freedom behind the Iron Curtain in the worldwide struggle between democracy and Communism. The October 1961 confrontation at Checkpoint Charlie became a worldwide focal point of Cold War tension, a crisis that could have escalated into a Hot War.

With Berlin divided by the Wall, the pain of many families in the East and West was very real, especially at Christmas time when the holidays could not be celebrated together with loved ones on the other side of the Wall. But, from that time on, West Berlin erected an enormous Christmas tree near the Wall each holiday season where its bright lights were clearly visible far into the East for all of our fellow Germans to see.

In 1971, after ten years of forced separation, West Berliners were finally allowed one-day visits to the East sector—not out of humanity, but for pure business reasons. East Berlin charged each visitor 5 Westmarks for the passport which was good until midnight, and another 25 Westmarks for the visit itself. This provided the Soviets with a new source of badly needed Westmarks to pay their spies with. For a couple with two children, it would cost them 120 Westmarks to visit grandma for just one day, and many could not afford that.

The passport was not an automatic pass through an official checkpoint in the Wall. An individual had to enter a long windowless, dimly lit corridor which was locked on either end, a claustrophobic atmosphere. A window in the wall would open and an official would question each person as to their destination, reason for visit, and many more details, and occasionally check for any non-allowed items. After an unpredictable length of time, a door would mysteriously open at the other end of the corridor and the visitor was allowed to enter East Berlin.

It was like setting foot into another world. The contrast was like night and day. Life on the street reflected the dreariness of the East. There were only a few people on the streets and an occasional car. If by chance you did meet some East Berliners, they tried to avoid you for fear you might be a spy. It was a very sterile atmosphere and there was no evidence of any progress. Store shelves were practically empty. Time seemed to stand still here and life looked slightly backwards. The return to West Berlin followed the same procedure. Conversely, East German citizens were not allowed to travel to the West and even telephone calls between East and West Berlin were prohibited for eleven years, until 1972. After that, the situation improved somewhat. Again, for purely economic reasons, elderly and sick people in the East were permitted access to the West for four weeks a year. The Soviet reasoning was that if they didn't return, no manpower had been lost and the East would be saving the expenses for their support.

Since visitors from the West became such a lucrative source of income, the Soviets later extended the passport privilege to several days, charging 25 Westmarks a person for each day of the visit. And eventually, they even permitted visitors to drive their cars, requiring a daily fee of 25 Westmarks for the car and an additional 25 Westmarks for each person in the car. A passport was restricted to one specific destination. If it was for visiting grandma in East Berlin, you could not also visit a cousin in a nearby village. That would require another visit with another passport. I remember my girlfriend telling me that when her mother wanted to attend the funeral of her sister in East Germany. They would not let her in because her passport was not valid for that particular city. She could not gain entry and had to return to West Germany.

Strangely enough, the Communist regime called the Wall, *Friedensmauer*, which translates to Wall of Peace, even though there was a death strip on their side of the Wall to keep their people from escaping. They even passed a law which made attempting to flee East Germany a crime punishable by three years in prison. At Checkpoint Charlie, they would shove mirrors under returning American sightseeing buses to check for anyone who was attempting to use this method of escaping to the West. The West Berliners used their side of the Wall to express their opinions through satirical phrases and pictures. Oddly enough, this way it became the largest painting in the world and a tourist attraction.

The only thing that the Wall did not divide was the supervision of the Allied military prison in Spandau, West Berlin, where the convicted war criminals were imprisoned. Each power took its turn until the prison was closed in October 1987 when the last prisoner, Rudolph Hess, died. This was one area in which Moscow was very willing to participate with the other allies because it gave them the opportunity to legally infiltrate their agents to the West. Another ironic curiosity was the Wannsee Bridge separating East Germany from West Berlin, which the Soviets renamed *Brücke der Einheit*, or Bridge of Unity. It happened to be the spot were spies were exchanged, like horse trading.

History has recorded what happened since the Wall was first erected in 1961 at the high point of the Cold War, and then torn down in 1989 as the Soviet's failed attempt of forcing Communism over all of Europe. Throughout these twenty-eight years, Germany had again served as the buffer against worldwide Communism, while never having signed a peace treaty after World War II. Germany had been divided into two countries, East and West, with even different postage stamps, which are collectors items today.

By now, dramatic changes swept throughout Eastern Europe. In the autumn of 1989, Hungary opened its East German borders which prompted an unstoppable mass exodus of tens of thousands of East Germans into Hungary and from there into the West. The German Communist government was powerless and demonstrations demanding reform occurred throughout the country. As a result, on November 9, 1989, the East authorities announced that the travel restrictions for all citizens had been permanently lifted which allowed freedom of movement for the first time since 1961.

That evening, fifty thousand East Berliners streamed into West Berlin and were welcomed on our side with joyful embraces as if they had just been released from prison, dancing and weeping together. Many climbed on top of the Wall to celebrate there. Suddenly and unexpectedly the Wall had tumbled to reunify the city, and the Cold War ended. Germany ceased to be a divided country—unfortunately too late for my dear parents to live to see it.

Every East German coming to West Berlin for the first time was entitled to a welcoming token of 100 Westmarks, even if it was only a one-day visit. However, the West German government had not anticipated that virtually the entire East population would show up for a quick hello in Berlin, as well as all the other cities at the East-West border, in order to get their present of 100 Westmarks. The Berlin banks ran out of cash and quickly had to borrow money from the stores where those from the East were immediately spending their Westmarks to buy urgently needed items such as food and shoes. Their needs were best demonstrated by a woman who had packed her bag with light bulbs. When asked why, she replied, "Who knows when we will ever be able to see them again."

Mutti and Papa on his 90th birthday

The Communist regime resigned on March 18, 1990. On October 3, 1990, the two German states became one again with Berlin as its capital, and this date is now celebrated as a German national holiday. Berlin was finally restored to its former status. Both the United States and the Soviet Union had helped to clear the way for a German reunification and the end of the Cold War. A European unity would be possible since Europe had become two continents after World War II, one Communist and the other anti-Communist. The Soviet Union agreed to withdraw all of its forces by the end of 1994. But the Western Powers were asked to stay until the Soviets had completely pulled out.

After the initial jubilation had died down, problems began, and much work had to be done in closing the deep gap between the two German halves to promote the economy. The East workers were used to job security. The Communist government had always proudly declared that their workers never had to pay into any unemployment fund. Under their regime, no employer, private or state, could dismiss any employee. But with the shortcoming of the Communist economy there was a continuous lack of material on the market. Consequently only some worked full-time while others just watched them or played cards to pass the time during the normal working hours. The attitude was to work as little as possible for the pay. The destiny of such an economic system was bankruptcy.

Since the outdated East factories produced what nobody wanted, many East workers now suddenly found themselves jobless for the first time. But, they received an unemployment benefit from West Germany, which was actually a present because they had never paid a penny into the unemployment fund. But, the jobless people in the East did not see it that way and expected the same affluent life style enjoyed by those in the West, even though they had never worked and earned the money to achieve it. They expected too much too soon and endless presents from the "rich brother" in the West. Since years now the people in West Germany have to pay an additional tax to help out with the enormous financial burden of the reunification. For fifty years, those in the East were taught to follow orders blindly, without any own initiative, and integrating the two systems was more difficult and costly than expected. The differences between the East and West were too grave to overcome overnight, and for some, it may take an entire generation.

Since the unification of Germany, I have made frequent trips to visit the long-lost property my parents owned in Zerbst, which involved travel in what had been Communist-controlled East Germany. It is a beautiful and historic country and there have been outstanding improvements in their standard of living since the Wall came down. Remarkable headway had been made with streets completely repaired, many homes being renovated or rebuilt, and stores which previously had limited products of inferior grade items were now stocked with ample quantities of quality merchandise. The Government permits, which limited what you could buy, when you could buy it, and how much you could buy, are gone. People can now get anything they want in any quantity, and items which are ordered will arrive promptly instead of waiting two or more years as in the days under Communism.

With all these new developments, I thought it would be easy to reclaim the property my parents used to own, which I inherited, especially since I had endless records to prove my ownership. However, it was a battle that took many years. (I know there are many people like me out there.) The former business of selling farming machinery had changed into a bicycle wholesale and repair shop. My relatives who used to run the business had died long ago, and East people had taken over. Although they finally bought the property from me in 1998 through the help of a lawyer in Berlin, I cannot begin to describe the years of letter writing and red tape I had to endure.

If, during the Communist regime, someone had built something on a person's land which had been disowned—it could have been just a little shack—the original owner in West Berlin immediately lost his rights to the property. This is currently happening to friends of mine, and they are still fighting over their legal claim, because the person who built that little shack continues to hold the property right for the next ninety-nine years. Under Communism in East Germany, the government as well as the people lost the sense of personal property. It was looked upon as an offense, after having lived on someone else's property for many years, for the original owner to show up and claim his rights. Even now, years after the unification of Germany, many problems still are unsolved.

Back in July 1945, I experienced the hatred of the American forces arriving in war-torn Berlin of Nazi Germany, and I watched on TV in 1994 the huge farewell celebration as they departed with their last tanks after nearly half a century, as friends and protectors from a rebuilt West Berlin with a thriving economy. Berlin was called the most pro-American city in the world. The Soviet request to be included in the same farewell was rejected as the population was relieved just to have them depart before the last American tank left. Unlike the Americans, the Soviets stripped their occupied houses of everything moveable and took it back to Russia. They removed all the furniture and light fixtures, the bathroom and kitchen equipment, and even windows and doors, leaving these houses as skeleton structures.

Throughout the world today, nations are fighting each other over religious and cultural differences, and others are torn by internal strife. Peace is a word that is unknown to millions, even today. But, life has many sides and it is up to us what we make out of ours. If one's time is not up, Heaven spares us, as it did me so often during those dark days of World War II and those hard years thereafter that were called peace.

I am very fortunate to have been given the gift of a constant positive attitude that permitted me to carry on, often happily, under the most trying circumstances. Looking back, my life has been very eventful and, in general, altogether good. My homeland Germany was part of my childhood, and Berlin was a large part of my early adult life. Actually, sometimes I still feel like a Berliner.

The chaotic postwar times did have an unfortunate effect on Sieghardt and me which eventually resulted in an amicable separation. When the Berlin Wall went up I took our two daughters to the safety of the United States while Sieghardt chose to stay in Berlin. I later remarried but we always remained friends. I made certain that my children remembered their father, and we always visited him during our frequent trips back to Germany. As fate would have it, while I was visiting Sieghardt in 1993, he became very ill and passed away within a few days. After all we had been through, we were together at the end. As death us do part.

The United States, truly a land of freedom and opportunity, is now my home. Here, I could finally fulfill my dreams. I earned my masters degree from Georgetown University in Washington, D.C. and have taught students at several universities, and military personnel. For recreation, I became an avid student of ballroom dancing, and then learned square and round dancing. I dance every week, and, God willing, will continue to do so beyond the year 2000.

I am always amazed at how people admire me for my enthusiasm and spirit, but if I had not had determination, spirit and spunk, I would not have survived. It must be something in our genes, because I have passed on to my daughters that same will to live and the determination to make a success of your life.

My daughters always tell me that I am one of the few remaining souls who remember the hell that I, as well as many Berliners, went through in Germany. But, the past is the past, and I thank God for every minute I share in the joy of freedom—something most Americans unfortunately take for granted.

Graduation from Georgetown
in 1968

On my way to go dancing

Inspire Your Family and Friends with a Gift of
Laughter Wasn't Rationed!

MAIL ORDER FORM

Books: I want _____ copies of *Laughter Wasn't Rationed* at $24.95 each

Sales Tax: Please add 4.5% sales tax per book ($1.12) for shipments to Virginia addresses

Shipping Per Book: United States = $4.00 Priority Mail
International = $9.50 global priority

My check or money order (U.S. funds only) for $_____ is enclosed.

Name _____

Address _____

City _____ State _____ Zip _____

Telephone _____

E-mail _____

Please make your check payable and return to:

Tricor Press
P.O. Box 4372
Alexandria, VA 22303-4372
Phone: 703-329-8328 / Fax: 703-329-1320
E-mail:info@tricorpress.com

We have reduced rates for bulk copies for reading clubs, associations and family groups. Call or e-mail us!